HANDBOOK ON GENDER AND WAR

INTERNATIONAL HANDBOOKS ON GENDER

Series Editor: Sylvia Chant, *FRSA, Professor of Development Geography, London School of Economics and Political Science, UK*

International Handbooks on Gender is an exciting new Handbook series under the general editorship and direction of Sylvia Chant. The series will produce high quality, original reference works offering comprehensive overviews of the latest research within key areas of contemporary gender studies. International and comparative in scope, the Handbooks are edited by leading scholars in their respective fields, and comprise specially commissioned contributions from a select cast of authors, bringing together established experts with up-and-coming scholars and researchers. Each volume offers a wide-ranging examination of current issues to produce prestigious and high quality works of lasting significance.

Individual volumes will serve as invaluable sources of reference for students and faculty in gender studies and associated fields, as well as for other actors such as NGOs and policymakers keen to engage with academic discussion on gender. Whether used as an information resource on key topics, a companion text or as a platform for further study, Elgar International Handbooks on Gender aim to provide a source of definitive scholarly reference.

Titles in the series include:

The International Handbook on Gender, Migration and Transnationalism
Global and Development Perspectives
Edited by Laura Oso and Natalia Ribas-Mateos

Handbook on Gender and Health
Edited by Jasmine Gideon

Handbook on Gender in World Politics
Edited by Jill Steans and Daniela Tepe-Belfrage

Handbook on Gender and War
Edited by Simona Sharoni, Julia Welland, Linda Steiner and Jennifer Pedersen

Handbook on Gender and War

Edited by

Simona Sharoni

Professor of Gender and Women's Studies, State University of New York, Plattsburgh, USA

Julia Welland

Lecturer, Department of Politics and International Studies, University of Warwick, UK

Linda Steiner

Professor, University of Maryland, USA

Jennifer Pedersen

Independent Scholar, Ottawa, Canada

INTERNATIONAL HANDBOOKS ON GENDER

Cheltenham, UK • Northampton, MA, USA

Published by
Edward Elgar Publishing Limited
The Lypiatts
15 Lansdown Road
Cheltenham
Glos GL50 2JA
UK

Edward Elgar Publishing, Inc.
William Pratt House
9 Dewey Court
Northampton
Massachusetts 01060
USA

A catalogue record for this book
is available from the British Library

Library of Congress Control Number: 2016931514

This book is available electronically in the **Elgar**online
Social and Political Science subject collection
DOI 10.4337/9781849808927

ISBN 978 1 84980 891 0 (cased)
ISBN 978 1 84980 892 7 (eBook)

Typeset by Columns Design XML Ltd, Reading
Printed and bound in Great Britain by TJ International Ltd, Padstow

Contents

List of contributors   viii
Acknowledgments   xiv

Introduction: revisiting the relationship between gender and war:
reflections on theory, research, activism and policy   1
Simona Sharoni and Julia Welland

PART I   GENDER AND THE CONDUCT OF WAR

Introduction   23
Julia Welland

  1 Gender and militaries: the importance of military masculinities
     for the conduct of state sanctioned violence   29
     Victoria M. Basham
  2 On the imagination of 'Woman' as killer in war   47
     Linda Åhäll
  3 The twilight war: gender and espionage, Britain, 1900–1950   66
     Juliette Pattinson
  4 Cat food and clients: gendering the politics of protection in the
     Private Militarized Securitized Company   86
     Paul Higate
  5 Not all soldiers: hegemonic masculinity and the problem of
     soldiers' agency in an age of technological intervention   105
     Mary Manjikian
  6 Gender and 'population-centric' counterinsurgency in Afghanistan 127
     Julia Welland
  7 Gender and terrorism   146
     Caron E. Gentry

PART II   GENDER AND THE IMPACT OF WAR

Introduction   169
Linda Steiner

  8 Gender-based violence in war   175
     Laura Sjoberg

 9 Risk and social transformation: gender and forced migration   194
    Tania Kaiser
10 Girls as weapons of war   213
    Mayesha Alam
11 Gender and the economic impacts of war   232
    Joyce P. Jacobsen
12 The war comes home: the toll of war and the shifting burden
    of care   249
    Alison Howell and Zoë H. Wool
13 The sexual economy of war: implications for the integration
    of women into the US armed forces   270
    Joane Nagel and Lindsey Feitz
14 From woman warrior to innocent child: telling gendered news
    stories of women terrorists   290
    Dan Berkowitz and Qi Ling
15 Gender under fire in war reporting   313
    Linda Steiner

PART III   GENDER AND OPPOSITION TO WAR

Introduction   337
Jennifer Pedersen

16 CODEPINK and pink soldiers: reading feminist antimilitarism
    anew   341
    Ilene R. Feinman
17 Iraq Veterans Against the War: 'that whole gender paradigm'   361
    Cami Rowe
18 Gender and resistance to political violence in Palestine and Israel   380
    Simona Sharoni
19 In the rain and in the sun: women's peace activism in Liberia   400
    Jennifer Pedersen
20 Gender and the Campaign for Nuclear Disarmament in the 1960s   419
    Jodi Burkett
21 Gendered dimensions of anti-war protest in Japan   438
    Jennifer Chan

PART IV   GENDER AND THE AFTERMATH OF WAR

Introduction   461
Simona Sharoni

22 Gender and peacebuilding   467
    Laura J. Shepherd and Caitlin Hamilton

23 Gender and post-conflict security   483
    Megan MacKenzie
24 Gender and transitional justice   504
    Catherine O'Rourke
25 Gender and demilitarization in Liberia   526
    Christopher Hills
26 Girl soldiers and the complexities of demobilization and
    reintegration   550
    Myriam Denov, Alexandra Ricard-Guay and Amber Green
27 The United Nations' Women, Peace and Security agenda   572
    Soumita Basu

Index   591

Contributors

Linda Åhäll is Lecturer in International Relations at Keele University, UK. Her research interests include feminist security studies, the politics of emotions, and popular culture and world politics. She is the author of *Sexing War/Policing Gender* (2015), co-editor of *Emotions, Politics and War* (2015) and *Gender, Agency and Political Violence* (2012) and has published articles in journals such as *Security Dialogue*, *International Feminist Journal of Politics* and *Critical Studies on Security*.

Mayesha Alam is Associate Director of the Georgetown Institute for Women, Peace and Security and teaches in the School of Foreign Service at Georgetown University. Alam is the author of *Women and Transitional Justice: Progress and Persistent Challenges* (2014). She is a Visiting Research Fellow at the University of Cambridge's Centre for Science and Policy and previously worked for The World Bank, the United Nations and several NGOs.

Victoria M. Basham is a Senior Lecturer in Politics at Cardiff University. She researches feminist approaches to militaries, militarism and militarization. She edits Critical Military Studies and is the author of *War, Identity and the Liberal State: Everyday Experiences of the Geopolitical in the Armed Forces* (2013).

Soumita Basu is Assistant Professor of International Relations at the South Asian University, New Delhi. Her primary research interests are the United Nations, feminist international relations and critical security studies. She is an Associate Editor of the *International Feminist Journal of Politics*.

Dan Berkowitz is a Professor in the School of Journalism and Mass Communication at the University of Iowa. Berkowitz earned his PhD in 1988 from Indiana University. His research interests are in social and cultural approaches to the study of news, including news of terrorism, collective memory, boundary work and mythical narrative. His publications include the edited volumes *Social Meanings of News* and *Cultural Meanings of News*.

Jodi Burkett is Principal Lecturer in History at the University of Portsmouth. Her research focuses on the cultural and social impacts of the end of the British Empire, in particular on changing perceptions of British national identity, as well as racism and anti-racism in British society and culture. She is the author of *Constructing Post-Imperial Britain: Britishness, 'Race' and the Radical Left in the 1960s* (2013). She has published in *European Review of History*, *The British Journal for the History of Science* and *Twentieth Century British History*.

Jennifer Chan holds a PhD in International Comparative Education from Stanford University. Her research interests include international human rights law and social movements, antiracism and multiculturalism, gender, global health governance, the global justice movement, comparative education, and Japanese society and culture. She is the author of *Politics in the Corridor of Dying: AIDS Activism and Global Health Governance* (2015) and *Gender and Human Rights Politics in Japan: Global Norms and Domestic Networks* (2004), as well as the editor of *Another Japan is Possible: New Social Movements and Global Citizenship Education* (2008).

Myriam Denov holds the Canada Research Chair in Youth, Gender and Armed Conflict at McGill University. Her research and teaching interests lie in the areas of children and youth in adversity, and international child protection, with an emphasis on war and political violence, children in armed conflict, and gender-based violence. She is the author of *Child Soldiers: Sierra Leone's Revolutionary United Front* (2010).

Ilene R. Feinman is Professor of Democratic Cultures and Dean of Arts, Humanities, and Social Sciences at CSU Monterey Bay. Her book, *Citizenship Rites: Feminist Soldiers and Feminist Antimilitarists* (2000) was noted in *The Chronicle of Higher Education* as groundbreaking work on women, the US military, and militarism in the context of international relations. She has also published in collections and has been interviewed by NPR, *The Washington Post* and Air America regarding Abu Ghraib.

Lindsey Feitz is an Assistant Teaching Professor in Gender and Women's Studies at the University of Denver. She received her PhD in American Studies from the University of Kansas where she studied the intersections of US consumer culture, globalization, and US militarism. She has published works on the beauty industry, gender-based violence, and war. Her current book project, *The Approachable Feminist*, outlines the basic tenets of feminism and its impact on celebrity culture, social media and contemporary social justice movements.

Caron E. Gentry is a Lecturer in the School of International Relations at the University of St Andrews. Her most recent publication is (with Laura

Sjoberg) *Beyond Mothers, Monsters, Whores: Thinking About Women's Violence in Global Politics* (2015).

Amber Green holds an MSW from McGill University where she conducted research on topics including critical perspectives on women's mental health as well as gendered violence and maternal wellbeing in the context of war. Currently, she is working on a research project led by Myriam Denov on children born of wartime sexual violence in northern Uganda, funded by the Trudeau Foundation.

Caitlin Hamilton is a doctoral researcher and a research assistant at UNSW Australia. She is the Managing Editor of the *Australian Journal of International Affairs*. Her primary areas of research are gender and peacebuilding, and the intersection of popular culture and world politics.

Paul Higate is Reader in Gender and Security at the School for Sociology, Politics and International Studies at the University of Bristol. He has written on the gendered culture of the military and militarization with a focus on masculinity in a number of contexts. His current project focuses on those who travel to fight for or against groups such as Islamic State in Syria and Iraq. He is a former Ministry of Defence and Economic Social Research Council Fellow.

Christopher Hills is a final year PhD candidate at the University of Sydney. He currently lectures on the Gendered Politics of War at Australian National University and on Gender, Security and Human Rights at Sydney University. For several years he worked for NGOs in East and West Africa. His research focus is the intersection of post-conflict peacebuilding and African feminism(s).

Alison Howell is Assistant Professor of Political Science at Rutgers University – Newark, where she is also an affiliate member of Women's and Gender Studies. She is a Founding Editor of *Critical Military Studies* and an editorial board member of Critical Studies on Security. Her research examines the international relations of medicine, health, security and warfare. She is the author of *Madness in International Relations: Psychology, Security and the Global Governance of Mental Health* (2011).

Joyce P. Jacobsen is Provost and Vice President for Academic Affairs and Andrews Professor of Economics at Wesleyan University. She has published mainly in the area of gender and labor economics, including articles on sex segregation, migration, and the effects of labor force intermittency on women's earnings. She is the author of *The Economics* *of Gender* (2007), co-author of *Labor Markets and Employment Relationships* (2004), and co-editor of *Queer Economics: A Reader* (2007).

Tania Kaiser is Senior Lecturer in Forced Migration Studies in the Department of Development Studies, University of London. Her research interests are in forced migration and refugee experiences, violence, conflict, gender and generation, and in culture, aesthetics and social change. She has published articles in journals including the *Journal of Refugee Studies*, *Mobilities* and the *Journal of East African Studies*. She holds a DPhil in anthropology from the University of Oxford.

Qi Ling is a doctoral student in the School of Journalism and Mass Communication at the University of Iowa. Her research focuses on feminist media studies, popular culture and television studies. Her dissertation deals with the television industry and the women-focused drama series in post-socialist China.

Megan MacKenzie is a leading expert on gender, post-conflict reconstruction, security and women in combat and the author of *Beyond the Band of Brothers: the US Military and the Myth that Women Can't Fight* (2015). Megan is Senior Lecturer of Government and International Relations at the University of Sydney, Australia and a former postdoctoral fellow with the Belfer Center for Science and International Affairs and the Women and Public Policy Program at Harvard University.

Mary Manjikian is Associate Dean at the Robertson School of Government at Regent University in Virginia Beach, Virginia. A former Fulbright scholar and former United States foreign service officer, she is the author of three books on national security. Her work has appeared in *International Feminist Journal of Politics*, *International Studies Quarterly*, *International Journal of Intelligence and Counterintelligence* and *Intelligence and National Security*.

Joane Nagel is the Paul Gibbons Roofe and Helen Waddle Roofe Professor of Sociology at the University of Kansas and author of *Gender and Climate Change: Impacts, Science, Policy* (2016). Other recent publications include 'Gender, conflict, and the militarization of climate change', *Peace Review* (2015); '*Plus ça change*: reflections on a century of militarizing women's sexuality', *European Journal of Women's Studies* (2014); 'Climate change, public opinion, and the military-security complex', *The Sociological Quarterly* (2011).

Catherine O'Rourke is Senior Lecturer in Human Rights and International Law and Gender Research Coordinator at the Transitional Justice Institute, Ulster University, Northern Ireland. She is author of

Gender Politics in Transitional Justice (2013) and has an ongoing role in gender and conflict research and policy-making for the United Nations, the British and Irish governments, and for a number of non-governmental organizations.

Juliette Pattinson is a Reader in History at the University of Kent. She is a socio-cultural historian with particular interests in gender, war and personal testimonies. She has published on special operations, the French Resistance, gendered experiences of warfare, cultural memory, Britishness and oral history methodology. She is currently completing a co-authored book with Arthur McIvor and Linsey Robb about civilian men on the home front, entitled *Men in Reserve*.

Jennifer Pedersen holds a PhD in International Politics from Aberystwyth University in Wales, where her work focused on women's peace movements. She has worked in gender, peacebuilding and international development in several countries, and has published in *International Feminist Journal of Politics*, *Gender and Development* and the *Journal for the Association of Research and Mothering*. She currently works in politics in Ottawa, Canada, with a focus on Canadian foreign policy.

Alexandra Ricard-Guay is Research Associate at the European University Institute. She holds a PhD in Social Work from McGill University. Her thesis examined sexual exploitation of adolescent girls. Her research areas include human trafficking, gender-based violence, gender and irregular migration, gender and war. She is currently the main researcher of the study on 'Trafficking in human beings in the domestic work sector', conducted in seven European countries (part of DemandAT).

Cami Rowe is a Lecturer in Theatre and Performance Theory at Goldsmiths, University of London. She has pioneered the application of theatre and performance studies to the discipline of International Relations. Her research focuses on the theatricality of international politics, with an emphasis on performative acts of resistance by marginalized actors. She is the author of *The Politics of Protest and US Foreign Policy: Performative Construction of the War on Terror* (2013).

Simona Sharoni is Professor of Gender and Women's Studies at the State University of New York in Plattsburgh. She is the author of *Gender and The Israeli–Palestinian Conflict: The Politics of Women's Resistance* and numerous other publications. Sharoni serves on the editorial board of the International Feminist Journal of Politics.

Laura J. Shepherd is Associate Professor of International Relations at UNSW Australia. She is author/editor of five books, including *Gender

Matters in Global Politics: A Feminist Introduction to International Relations, now in its second edition (2015). Shepherd's research focuses on gender, peace and security, with a particular interest in the UN's Women, Peace and Security agenda.

Laura Sjoberg is Associate Professor of Political Science at the University of Florida. Her work in gender and international security has been published in dozens of journals and books in international relations, gender studies, geography and law. She currently serves as the homebase Editor of the *International Feminist Journal of Politics*, co-editor of *International Studies Review* and Vice President of the International Studies Association.

Linda Steiner is a Professor in the College of Journalism at the University of Maryland. Her co-authored books include *Women and Journalism* (2004); her co-edited books include the *Routledge Companion to Media and Gender* (2013) and *Key Concepts in Critical-Cultural Studies* (2010). She is editor of *Journalism & Communication Monographs* and has published 100 book chapters and journal articles.

Julia Welland is based in the Politics and International Studies Department at the University of Warwick. Her PhD focused on the masculinity required for contemporary counterinsurgency campaigns in Iraq and Afghanistan, and she is in the process of completing a book on this same topic. She has work published in *Review of International Studies* and *International Feminist Journal of Politics* and continues to research on gender, militarism and violence.

Zoë H. Wool is Assistant Professor in the Department of Anthropology at Rice University and author of *After War: The Weight of Life at Walter Reed* (2015).

Acknowledgments

This *Handbook* was conceived by Jennifer Mathers, who is Reader and Head of Department of International Politics at Aberystwyth University. She created a table of contents and contacted many of the authors. We thank both Jennifer Mathers for initiating the project and Rachel Vaughan, also at Aberystwyth University, who provided administrative support in the early stages of the project.

When unforeseen circumstances prevented the original editor from bringing the project to fruition, the four of us stepped in. We had not worked together before and in fact did not know one another prior to this work. Although we have all juggled multiple responsibilities over the past year, the *Handbook* became a priority. Our collaborative process was fueled by a desire to complete the manuscript in a timely manner. We updated the table of Contents and asked authors for updated chapters that reflect contemporary scholarship and debates on gender and war as they related to their topic. We also added several authors in an effort to reflect diverse perspectives from different parts of the world.

We would not have been able to meet this objective without the patience, dedication and flexibility of the *Handbook* contributors. We thank those who have been involved with the project since its inception for their trust and support. Special thanks to the new authors we invited; they worked under very tight deadlines.

We are grateful to Alan Sturmer, Victoria Raven and Alex Pettifer of Edward Elgar Publishing for their commitment to the project and their ongoing assistance and support during the transition between editors. We hope that the *Handbook* will become a useful resource to those interested in the gendered aspect of war and its aftermath.

Introduction: revisiting the relationship between gender and war: reflections on theory, research, activism and policy

Simona Sharoni and Julia Welland

CONTEXT

Gender has always been central to the practice and representation of war as well as to efforts to oppose war and rebuild societies in its aftermath. Feminist theorizing about gender and war, however, has only gained visibility and legitimacy in both the academy and among policymakers in the past three decades. The result is an impressive body of inter-disciplinary literature that has gone far beyond its original home in disciplines such as International Relations. As the contributions to this *Handbook* underscore, feminist-informed scholarly debates on gender and war have expanded to include sociologists, anthropologists, histor-ians, economists, geographers, and communication and media scholars, as well as scholars based in interdisciplinary fields like gender and sexuality studies and ethnic studies. Furthermore, this growing field of study is informed not only by academic research but also by discussions among policymakers and activists. As such, the literature on gender and war, and this *Handbook* in particular, are designed both for students and faculty committed to understanding the gendered dimensions of war. All the chapters in the *Handbook* include information relevant to activists, advocates and policymakers who want to reflect on their experiences and explore best practices to address the gendered aspects of war and political violence.

The evolution of feminist thinking about war can be generally under-stood in terms of three distinct phases: first, making women visible in discussions of war; second, focusing on 'gender' rather than 'women' and challenging the automatic association of men with war and women with peace; and third, analysis of gender in relation to other identities and structured inequalities that shape and are shaped by war. The first phase of feminist theorizing on gender and war dates back to the 1980s and reflects efforts to make women visible in studies of war and its multiple effects. The literature that emerged during this period was primarily

1

influenced by the work of Jean Bethke Elshtain and Cynthia Enloe. In her seminal work *Women and War*, Elshtain (1987) demonstrated the significance of gender to the distinction between the 'protector' and the 'protected'. Grounding her theory in a historical analysis of war narratives, Elshtain argued that most accounts of war describe courageous men ('just warriors') taking up arms to defend vulnerable women ('beautiful souls'). Around the same time, Cynthia Enloe, who, like Elshtain, had a doctorate in Political Science, began to explore the effects of war and militarization on women's lives. Enloe's *Does Khaki Become You? The Militarization of Women's Lives (1983)* and *Bananas Beaches and Bases: Making Feminist Sense of International Politics* (1989) inspired scholarship on the relevance of gender to understanding not only war but also international politics more generally.

As Elshtain argued, traditionally, and in most societies, men are the ones who have been expected to fight wars, while women and children have been relegated to the homefront (Elshtain, 1987). Over the past three decades, however, literature about women's experiences of war has flourished, expanding to give accounts of the multiple roles and experiences women have in wartime. The result is a more nuanced body of work about women as victims and opponents of wars as well as active fighters and perpetrators of violence, including sexualized and gender-based violence (Cohen, 2013; Sjoberg and Gentry, 2007; MacKenzie, 2009).

Starting in the 1990s, inspired by postmodern sensibilities, feminist theorizing about war became more complex, to warn against the tendencies to conflate the term 'gender' with 'women' and to essentialize gender differences; viewing men as warriors and women as peacemakers, feminist scholars said, overlooked differences among both men and women (for example, see: Runyan and Peterson, 1993; Sylvester, 1994). Feminists today have moved beyond simply comparing and contrasting the experiences of men and women in war. Instead, current consensus is that because gender is pivotal to identity formation and transformation, and to divisions of power and labor across cultures and contexts, it contributes greatly to the understanding of war and its aftermath. Gendered analyses of war and its aftermath are no longer focused on demonstrating that gender matters, but are instead designed to reveal *when* and *how* gender impacts the politics and practices of war.

The contemporary feminist scholarship on gender and war reflected in this volume is both interdisciplinary and international in scope, including original theorizing, research and policy-relevant recommendations. The chapters are divided into four sections addressing the gendered aspects related to the conduct of war, its impacts, opposition to war, and war's aftermath. Contributors to this collection share the premise that gender is central to the understanding of war and its effects, albeit not in terms of conventional or simple-minded binaries. Building upon this claim, they draw on and contribute to, at least one, but often several, of the following bodies of literature:

- feminist theorizing about violence, power, peace, security and justice;
- feminist intersectional literature on gender and war;
- feminist scholarship on men, masculinities and militarism;
- feminist analyses of the relationship between political violence and sexualized, gender-based violence; and
- critical feminist scholarship on gender mainstreaming in relation to gender and war.

By approaching war as a key site for the materialization of gendered power relations, contributors to the *Handbook* underscore that gender not only shapes assumptions about who fights and who is fought for, but is also integral to the enactment and justification of militaristic campaigns as well as to opposition to war. As scholars continue to unearth and analyze gendered myths, practices and power relations that enable violence in the international arena, our understandings of war continue to deepen.

FEMINIST THEORIZING ABOUT VIOLENCE, POWER, PEACE, SECURITY AND JUSTICE

Feminists have long been engaged in rethinking violence, power, peace, security and justice in an effort to capture the gendered dimensions of the experiences and struggles of women and men in conflict zones around the world. Feminist rethinking of the concepts key to the understanding of war have emerged from research on the roles of women and men in conflicts, as well as in the processes designed to bring about their just and peaceful resolution. Feminist reformulations of these central concepts represent an important step toward feminist theorizing about gender during war and in its aftermath.

Violence

Early feminist theorizing on violence addressed mainly direct, physical violence, and associated violence with men and nonviolence with women

(Eisler, 1989; Kirk, 1989; Boulding, 1992). These conceptualizations became more complex as feminists began to articulate connections between violence against women and structural and cultural forms of violence including the war system (Sharoni, 1994; Agathangelou, 2004; Sachs et al., 2007; Shalhoub-Kevorkian, 2009). The shift in feminist thought to theorizing differences and articulating intersections resulted in more nuanced conceptualizations of violence. Feminist conceptualizations of violence tend to be context-specific, grounded in particular struggles. They address systemic violations of people's rights and dignity based on gender, race, ethnicity, class and sexual orientation, among other dimensions, and based on the intersections of these dimensions. The resulting definitions of violence offer scholars and policymakers conceptual tools to help look beyond the symptoms of violence to examine its root causes. In most cases, these include structured inequalities and/or asymmetrical power relations, which tend to propel and fuel violence.

Power

Feminist reconceptualizations of power are based on a critique of the paradigm of power politics that has dominated the field of international politics and diplomacy for almost a century. Feminists take issue with conventional conceptualizations of power grounded in competition, control, dominance and violence, which often result in zero-sum power struggles that escalate into large-scale wars (Hartsock, 1983; Eisler, 1989; Boulding, 1992).

The powerful feminist slogan 'the personal is political' has inspired many feminist attempts to redefine power as agency, manifesting itself in examples of women's activism in conflict areas. As a conflict transforms their lives, women feel empowered to shape its course and outcome (Sharoni, 2001). More recently, feminists influenced by Michel Foucault have joined other poststructuralist theorists in treating power as a discourse. According to this formulation, power is everywhere, producing and shaping the meaning of everything we do (Shepherd, 2008). If everything we can see is shaped by and in turn shapes power relations, then everything we see is gendered, raced and imbued with structured inequalities. This complex and multifaceted conceptualization of power has much to contribute to the analysis and resolution of conflicts.

Security

Feminist scholars and activists have long challenged the tendency to conflate security with national security, which takes for granted state power and the existing political status quo. They raised serious concerns with the overwhelming priority of states to invest funds and energies in the military and then rely upon the threat of using the army to 'protect' the collective citizenry (Harris and King, 1989; Ruddick, 1989). Feminist case studies from around the world support the argument that nation-states, far from providing security, as is often assumed, have become a primary source of insecurity, especially for women and other under-privileged groups (Harris and King, 1989; Sharoni, 1994; Agathangelou, 2004; Scuzzarello, 2008). Based on this evidence, feminists have con-cluded that the more preoccupied a government is with its military power as a means to provide what it calls 'national security', the more insecure are its vulnerable citizens (Enloe, 1989, 2007; Sharoni, 1994; Abdo and Lentin, 2002; Sachs et al., 2007). Feminist reexaminations of the dominant security discourses point out that 'security' now operates more as an instrument of mystifying rhetoric than a concept with any analytical precision. Furthermore, appeals to the need for security have often been used (by states) to justify highly violent military campaigns and terri-torial expansions. The post-September 11, 2001 era has not only provided ample evidence to support this proposition but has also inspired some brilliant, highly original feminist scholarship (Russo, 2006; Faludi, 2007; Jiwani, 2009; Riley et al., 2008). Feminist reconceptualizations of security suggest a shift from thinking about security in mutually exclu-sive, zero-sum ways (i.e., 'national security') to focusing instead on 'human security' or 'global security'.

Many feminist engagements go beyond the critique of 'national security' to question the very idea of 'security' as a totalizing patriarchal concept that cannot accept any disorder, incoherence or lack of control. In contrast, feminists suggest that security is always partial, elusive and mundane (Sylvester, 1989; Tickner, 1992). Feminist interpretations of security do not treat it as an absolute end or as a scarce resource that needs to be possessed, but rather as a complex process that needs to be negotiated and renegotiated as change occurs in different historical and sociopolitical circumstances (Tickner, 1992).

Feminist scholars are also challenging previous definitions of security from feminists and peace activists who saw it as an outcome that can be achieved rather than as a discourse. In these older formulations, the term 'security' is often used interchangeably with the term 'peace', and both assume the end of armed conflict (Jabri, 1996; Mackay, 2004; Shepherd,

2008). Today, feminist reconceptualizations of security seek to transcend what Laura Shepherd (2008, p. 127) refers to as the 'theoretical tautology of defining conflict as the absence of security and security as the absence of conflict'. Along these lines, feminists like Megan MacKenzie (2012) have argued that security should not be defined in a vacuum but rather in relation to other key concepts such as development and conflict transformation, which are crucial to igniting wars, negotiating peace agreements and rebuilding conflict-torn societies.

Peace

Early feminist theorizing on peace and conflict defined peace as more than the absence of physical violence, insisting that 'real' peace must involve the absence of all forms of violence, including structural and cultural violence, and the presence of justice and equality for all (Boulding, 1992; Reardon, 1993, Confortini, 2006). Cynthia Enloe suggested a more modest definition that emerges from 'the conditions of women's lives', and involves 'women's achievement of control over their lives' (1989, p. 538). Building on this definition and drawing on examples from the ongoing conflicts and political processes in Israel, Palestine and the North of Ireland, Sharoni argues, 'the transition from conflict to post-conflict realities is more complex and multi-faceted than a simple departure from a negative situation (i.e. conflict) to a positive one (i.e. peace)' (2001, p. 174). While these definitions are both subtle and more complex than conventional conceptualizations of peace, peace is still conceived as a tangible good that is preferable to war.

Contemporary feminists suggest that peace has no fixed meaning and should be viewed as a political discourse (Shepherd, 2008). The definition of 'peace', as with any other term, reflects the political position of the person or group who defines it, as well as the particular sociopolitical context within which it is constructed. Different definitions of peace often reveal different degrees of commitment to social and political change or compliance with the prevailing status quo of power relations, including the gendered divisions of power and labor in a particular society. This formulation urges feminist scholars not to assume but to probe whose lives the signing of a peace agreement is likely to improve, and what structures of inequality it is going to dismantle or even uphold.

Justice

Feminist efforts to theorize justice in the context of war and its aftermath are relatively new. Early feminist theorizing of justice was based on a redefinition of peace not simply as the end of political violence but also the eradication of inequality and the adoption of policies designed to achieve gender justice (Ackerly and Attanasi, 2009; Fraser, 2013). It has evolved out of the project of gendering human rights and recognizing women's rights as human rights. In recent years, feminist theorizing of justice has been central to the expansion of scholarship on transitional justice. As Catherine O'Rourke points out, 'feminist engagement with human rights and transitional justice has always worked on two fronts, seeking both the protection of the human rights framework for violations against women, while also seeking to challenge and redefine the narrow understandings of violations that fall within the human rights frame' (2013, p. 37). Feminists have insisted that a redefinition of justice must be informed by the lived experiences of women in conflict zones, paying close attention to gender-based harms and taking into legal consideration their severity and short- and long-term impacts (Bell, 2009; Bell and O'Rourke, 2007; Buckly-Zistel and Stanley, 2011).

In sum, feminists have long realized that the processes of refining and implementing feminist interpretations of central concepts in the field cannot be limited to the confines of the academy (Giles, 2008). Contemporary feminists now agree that research on conflict and peacemaking needs to be grounded in the highly diverse experiences of women and men in conflict zones. By insisting on redefining concepts such as violence, peace, security and justice in order to account for the daily lives and struggles of women around the world, feminists and other critical scholars have expanded traditional definitions of these concepts to include not only gender, race and class inequalities, abuses of human rights, and attacks on cultural and ethnic identities, but also questions of development, environmental degradation and ecology (Agathangelou, 2004; Agathangelou and Ling, 2004; Philipose, 2007; Lind, 2010). Most contributors to this collection draw on the new feminist definitions of violence, power, peace, security and justice; with chapters by Tania Kaiser, Caron Gentry, Laura Sjoberg, Laura Shepherd and Caitlin Hamilton, Megan MacKenzie and Catherine O'Rourke all critically engaging with the theoretical debates among feminists about the political implications of the new definitions of violence, power, peace, security and justice. Moreover, the section on Gender and Opposition to War relies heavily on the new feminist definitions of these key concepts. Through detailed case studies, focused on both historical and contemporary activism, Ilene Feinman, Cami Rowe, Simona Sharoni, Jennifer Pedersen, Jodi Burkett and Jennifer Chan examine the message, strategies and efficacy of anti-war movements and peace campaigns from Israel, Palestine, Japan, Liberia and the United States.

FEMINIST INTERSECTIONAL LITERATURE ON GENDER AND WAR

Feminists have long argued that gender identities and gender relations are socially constituted through complex interrelated processes. As a result, the meanings and practices associated with being a man or a woman and the rigidity of the categories themselves are highly variable across cultures, contexts and times. Understanding the existing linkages between different, usually interlocking, systems of domination and oppression and between different cartographies of struggle is central to the analysis of conflicts and the exploration of prospects for their resolution. Feminists have also called attention to the fact that sexism, racism, colonialism and homophobia are examples of interlinked systems of oppression that reinforce one another because they share a logic of domination, of *us* versus *them*, thus, legitimizing the power of one group over another and justifying the use of violence against 'the other'.

Feminist intersectional analysis emerged in the context of and in relation to social movements led by people of color, gays and lesbians, women and working-class people. By 'intersections', feminists referred to the interconnectedness of gendered identities, structures of domination, discrimination, oppression, exploitation and violence (Davis, 1983; Crenshaw, 1991; Mohanty, 2003). These theories grew out of the experiences of women who felt that their histories and struggles were not reflected in the agenda of the feminist movement in Europe and North America. Women of color, lesbians, working-class women and women in the Global South argued that their experiences as women need to be examined in relation to other experiences shaped by colonialism, their race, culture, ethnicity, class and sexual orientation, among other dimensions.

Women of color in the US insisted that they could only be part of a feminist movement if it incorporated the notion of difference and did not force them to choose between their struggle against sexism and their commitment to end racism (Moraga and Anzaldúa, 1983; Hooks, 1984, 1990; Collins, 1991; Anzaldúa and Keating, 2002). Further, women in the Global South who were involved in a dual struggle for national liberation and for women's liberation, began to explore and address the linkages between gender oppression and the broader political context within which it unfolds (Jayawardena, 1986; Mohanty, 1991).

Taking difference into account and applying feminist theories of intersections to the analysis of war involves paying attention to how gender intersects with other markers of identity in a particular locale.

Thus, feminist intersectional analysis can be used to uncover the distribution of power within systems and relationships, and especially to reveal how unequal distribution of power and privilege can sow the seeds for and fuel political violence and war.

Feminist intersectional analysis has clearly informed several chapters in this *Handbook*, including those authored by Tania Kaiser, Joyce Jacobsen, Joane Nagel and Lindsey Feitz, Christopher Hills, Simona Sharoni, Julia Welland, Caron Gentry and Jennifer Chan. These authors demonstrate skilfully how age, social class, race, sexual orientation and geographical location enhance the analysis of the gendered dimensions of war and its aftermath. Similarly, as the chapters authored by Dan Berkowitz and Qi Ling and by Linda Steiner illustrate, attention to other relevant identities greatly impacts the ways gender is portrayed in news media about war and political violence.

FEMINIST SCHOLARSHIP ON MEN, MASCULINITIES, AND MILITARISM

Over the years, feminists have written extensively about men and the effects of men's identities and behavior on women, society and international politics (Tickner, 1992; Runyan and Peterson, 1993; Sylvester, 1994, Zalewski and Parpart, 1998 and 2008; Hooper, 2001; Whitworth, 2004). Nevertheless, critical feminist scholarship on masculinity and especially on the experiences of men during war and its aftermath is relatively young. Early feminist engagement with the topic emphasized men and masculinity's innate or natural proclivity towards violence and thus to war (for example see Ruddick, 1983; Reardon, 1985; Hartstock 1989). As a result, men and masculinity were 'often inadvertently still treated as unproblematic, undifferentiated wholes' (Hooper, 2001, p. 42).

Contemporary feminist scholarship on men and masculinities, however, seeks to 'problematize masculinities, the hegemony of men, and the subject of man within the theories and practices of international relations' (Zalewski, 1998, p. 1) (see for example Zalewski and Parpart, 1998 and 2008; Hooper, 2001). Within this expanding body of literature, the relationship between men, militarism and particular conceptions of masculinity has received the most sustained attention from feminists.

Building on Elshtain and Enloe's recognition that particular constructions of masculinity and femininity are required for wars to be waged, a significant body of feminist work now focuses on the production, operation and effects of military and militarized masculinities across the globe (for example, see: Whitworth, 2004; Belkin, 2012; Eichler, 2011;

Duncanson, 2013; Welland, 2013). Much of this work draws on and challenges Raewyn Connell's (1995) understanding of hegemonic masculinity. Connell argued that masculinities and femininities should be understood as relational concepts and urged scholars to examine the relationships both between masculinity and femininity, *and* between dominant and subordinate masculinities: 'relations of alliance, dominance and subordination ... constructed through practices that exclude and include, that intimidate, [and] exploit' (Connell, 1995, p. 77). Drawing on the work of Antonio Gramsci, Connell coined the term 'hegemonic masculinity' to denote 'one form of masculinity rather than others that is culturally exalted' (Connell, 1995, p. 77). While hegemonic masculinity works to reinforce male power and advantage, it simultaneously subordinates, and even culturally stigmatizes, those masculinities that fall outside its proscribed boundaries. In the Global North, hegemonic masculinity is often associated with whiteness, heterosexuality, socioeconomic privilege and higher education.

Feminist scholarship on men and masculinities as they relate to militarization and war reveals how traits and characteristics such as strength, dominance, courage and aggression are promoted not only by the armed forces and insurgency groups that rely on soldiers, but also by the communities that often adopt traditional conceptions of masculinity and femininity during war (Cockburn and Zarkov, 2002). Feminists have used both the concepts of 'military masculinities' and 'militarized masculinities' to understand the processes and practices of turning men into soldiers. Military/militarized masculinities are understood as being central to the perpetuation of violence in international politics, with the valorization of militarized and masculinized traits and the concomitant denigration of people who fail to embody them contributing towards occurrences of wartime sexual violence (Baaz and Stern, 2009), torture (Richter-Montpetit, 2007) and ongoing sexual discrimination and harassment within national militaries (Woodward and Winter, 2007).

While most contributors to the *Handbook* reference scholarship on men, masculinities and war, Victoria Basham, Julia Welland, Paul Higate, Mary Manjikian and Caron Gentry offer in-depth analyses of the role of particular understandings of masculinities in specific contexts and situations. These authors suggest that the patterns underscoring the relationship between men and war have changed dramatically over time as a direct result of the shifts in the policies and execution of modern warfare. Megan MacKenzie, Catherine O'Rourke and Christopher Hills discuss the relevance of the masculinities and militarism literature in the aftermath of war, especially in the context of Disarmament, Demobilization and Reconstruction (DDR) and transitional justice programs.

FEMINIST ANALYSES OF THE RELATIONSHIP BETWEEN POLITICAL VIOLENCE AND SEXUALIZED, GENDER-BASED VIOLENCE

Feminist research has pointed to the ways that violence against women results from complex sociopolitical and cultural institutions that normalize the use of violence (Reardon, 1985). A careful examination of the proliferation of small arms and their role in intimate-partner violence revealed higher rates of violence against women in militarized societies, often during and in the aftermath of wars. Feminists have called attention to the fact that militaristic interpretations of 'national security' and a significant presence of armed military and police personnel paradoxically heighten the sense of insecurity of women and minority groups (Cockburn and Zarkov, 2002; Sharoni, 2008). Additionally, it also appears that societal levels of militarism and rates of sexual assault, rape and intimate-partner violence prior to the escalation of a political conflict impacts upon gender-based violence at the height of the conflict (Sharoni, 2016). Likewise, the prevalence of violence against women during conflict tends to impact on the life experiences and safety of women in post-conflict societies (Cockburn, 2012).

Although the extensive use of rape during wartimes attracted little scholarly or media attention until the early 1990s, there is ample historical evidence that the use of mass rape is not merely a modern phenomenon (Buss, 2009). Throughout history, militarism has enabled and normalized gender-based crimes perpetrated against women during fighting. While sexual assault and rape are present in many societies in peacetime, the prevalence and magnitude of sexual attacks on women increases dramatically in wartime, with some cases involving the deliberate and systematic rape of thousands of women. Accounts from Africa, Asia, the Americas, the Middle East and Europe reveal that large-scale sexual violence was present in at least 51 countries over the last 20 years (Bastick et al., 2007).

Detailed accounts by UN agencies and by international humanitarian and human rights non-governmental organizations, which focused on the impact of armed conflict on women, confirm the prevalence of multiple rapes of individual women in many conflict zones (Leatherman, 2011; Kirby, 2013). The systematic sexual violence was sometimes carried out by various groups of men, including gangs of boys and men, local and regional militias, and organized armed forces, including UN peace-keepers (Whitworth, 2004). Women were raped in their homes, in refugee camps and in prison. In some militias that included women, they were held in sexual servitude by the fighting men. In other cases, sexual slavery was institutionalized (Yoshimi, 2002). The prevalence of sexual assault in the military and the lack of accountability for perpetrators is now a noted area of concern in the United States (Hunter, 2007; Nagel, 2014).

Though rape and sexual violence have been prevalent aspects of war throughout history, the phrase 'rape as weapon of war' became widely used by researchers, policymakers and media analysts only during the 1990s, as evidence surfaced about widespread use of rape and sexual assault in Bosnia (Salzman, 1998). Attention to this issue revealed the prevalence of gender-based sexualized violence in other conflict zones including Liberia, Rwanda, the Democratic Republic of Congo (DRC) and Sierra Leone, among others (Bastick et al., 2007; Baaz and Stern, 2013; Cohen, 2013). The recognition by foreign policy establishments that rape and other forms of gender-based violence are in fact tactics of war led to the categorization of these crimes as war crimes. As a result, gender-based violence has been a prominent issue, in recent years, on the agenda of both the United Nations and numerous human rights organizations (Sharlach, 2000; Kirby, 2013 and 2015).

A small, but growing, scholarship is centered on men's experiences during war, particularly in relation to their exposure to sexualized violence as victims (for example Sivakumarian, 2007; Nagel and Feitz, 2008). Several contributors to the *Handbook*, including Laura Sjoberg, Mayesha Alam, Myriam Denov, Alexandra Ricard-Guay, Amber Green and Christopher Hills address the interplay between political violence and gender-based, sexualized violence. In doing so, these authors examine the prevalence of gender-based and sexualized violence during war as well as its lingering effects in the aftermath of war.

GENDER MAINSTREAMING AND WAR

Unlike anti-discrimination laws that seek to achieve *equality* between men and women, 'gender mainstreaming starts from the recognition that gender *differences* shape policy processes and outcomes' (True, 2003, p. 369, original emphasis). Adopted as a global strategy for achieving gender equality at the 1995 Fourth World Conference on Women in Beijing, gender mainstreaming has achieved widespread endorsement from individual governments, regional supra-state bodies such as the European Union and Nordic Council of Ministers, and global governance institutions such as the UN and the Organisation for Economic Co-operation and Development (Andersen, 1993; Razavi and Miller, 1995; United Nations, 1997; Council of Europe, 1998; True, 2003).

The impact of gender mainstreaming on matters of international security and war is most notably demonstrated in the passing in 2000 of the UN Security Council Resolution 1325 on 'Women, Peace and Security'. Approved unanimously at a special meeting of the UN Security Council (UNSC), it was the first time the UNSC had discussed women and gender in relation to peace and security (Cohn, 2008). The resolution

> ... seeks to mainstream an official sensitivity to gender within UN institutions, as well as the decision-making processes of all governments, with regard to conflict resolution, peacekeeping, and peacebuilding; to include more women in all institutions involved in the prevention, management, and resolution of conflict; and to protect the rights of women, particularly with regard to ending gender-based violence, in wartime. (Pratt, 2013, p. 773; see also UNSC, 2000)

Also in 2000, the Department of Peacekeeping published a report titled *Mainstreaming a Gender Perspective in Multidimensional Peace Operations* (United Nations, 2000), which reiterated 1325's basic argument that women's involvement in peacekeeping missions enhanced peace negotiations. In the years following 1325, a number of UNSC resolutions were passed aimed at reinforcing the goals of the resolution, increasing the role of women in peacebuilding, and further protecting women and girls from wartime sexual violence.[1]

Many feminists heralded UNSCR 1325 as a feminist success story. Not only did the resolution's explicit recognition of gendered power relations challenge realist conceptions of security at the highest levels, but its focus on women as active participants of the peace process and post-conflict reconstruction challenged conceptions of women as only the passive victims of violent international practices (Cohn et al., 2004; Hill et al., 2004). As Carol Cohn has written: 'It is amazing that the world's largest international security institution has now publicly declared that attention to gender is integral to "doing security"' (Cohn et al., 2004, p. 139).

The initial celebration of UNSCR 1325 notwithstanding, feminists have raised critical questions about both its implementation and long-term transformative potential.[2] Among the concerns raised is whether the resolution can achieve its goals if the UN itself remains structured in a way that prevents words from being efficiently turned into actions. Cohn, who has been involved with the movement that ushered in the resolution, has identified several barriers to 1325's implementation and the degree to which gender mainstreaming can be effectively initiated. She notes that structural and logistical barriers to the successful implementation of Resolution 1325 include a lack of commitment to enforce the resolution, a failure to allocate the necessary financial support to gender programs, and a basic inability to think critically about how to enact gender mainstreaming in different contexts (Cohn in Hill et al., 2004, pp. 9–10). Other feminist critics of UNSCR 1325, informed by intersectional and postcolonial feminist critiques, questioned its celebration as an accomplishment of the feminist movement globally (Harrington, 2011; Pratt, 2013). Nicola Pratt (2013) views the resolution not as a positive step towards the transformation of women's (and men's) lives in conflict, but as a re-inscription of racial-sexual boundaries along the lines of the political economy of imperialism. In Pratt's reading, 'advocates of 1325 have become "securitizing actors," in that their discourses help to construct the threat of "dangerous brown men" and (re)affirm the legitimacy of international intervention in order to "secure" women and girls in conflict zones' (2013, p. 779). Pratt concludes that while 1325 may be a strategic tool for women activists in conflict zones, it simultaneously contributes to the legitimacy and normalization of gendered, raced and sexualized hierarchies (2013, p. 780). While several contributors to this Handbook, including Laura Shepherd, Caitlin Hamilton, Megan MacKenzie and Christopher Hills have explicitly criticized gender mainstreaming policies and their implementations, others, like Soumita Basu, recognize the groundbreaking impact of gender mainstreaming and its contribution to public debates and policies designed to advance gender equality and justice during and in the aftermath of war.

CONCLUSION

This *Handbook* is not designed to offer a definitive account of existing knowledge on gender and war but rather to contribute to ongoing conversations on the topic. Taken together, the authors in the collection raise thought-provoking questions that broaden and deepen feminist engagement with the gendered dimensions of war and its aftermath. Building on the contributions of feminist scholars who first paid attention to the workings of gender in international affairs in the 1980s, the chapters in this collection span multiple disciplines and make use of a wide range of methodological approaches. There are three areas in particular to which the *Handbook* contributes.

First, the authors in this collection engage in original feminist research and theorizing. Working through a range of theoretical approaches and using a multitude of methods, including historical records, field interviews, popular culture and policy documents, authors reveal how gender shapes the conduct of war and its multiple impacts, as well as resistance and opposition to war and the challenges of rebuilding war-torn societies. Because feminist research often involves asking questions that may have previously been dismissed as unimportant or irrelevant, exploring sites that have been otherwise ignored, and being concerned with what is presumed to be the banal or mundane, it has frequently made use of methods or ways of knowing dismissed by the discipline the researcher works within. In this *Handbook* feminist insights have been leveled on the early twentieth century to the contemporary period; across Europe, North America, Africa and the Middle East; and on a range of activities including Hollywood films, familial relations and protest movements in numerous countries. The scope of the *Handbook* and the number of insights garnered serve to remind us to remain always vigilant to the operations of gender at the personal and international, micro and macro, levels.

Second, while theoretically rich and a clear contribution to the academic field of feminist research on/about war, the chapters in this *Handbook* have obvious important policy relevance. Traversing topics such as policy decisions regarding who can and cannot fight, the economic and familial effects of war, and the 'post-conflict' moment, research within this *Handbook* reveals the uneven and gendered effects of war. With national governments, supra-national bodies and international institutions and organizations increasingly recognizing the importance of gender to international affairs, there must be greater effort for dialogue between academics and activists/practitioners. A number of authors draw on their own experiences of negotiating and traversing the divide between academic and practitioner communities, reflecting on the ways in which their research impacts on their practice and vice versa.

Third, and perhaps most importantly, the *Handbook* opens up new avenues for research and questioning. While the chapters in this volume shine a light on and bring visibility to particular places, bodies and types of violence, there are simultaneous silences and erasures that need to be addressed. Feminism is at its strongest when it remains open to new voices and perspectives, and when it is responsive to those who have felt excluded from its project. Increasingly, this means listening to those who have historically been excluded from setting the parameters of the debate or who have seen their own concerns sidelined or ignored, including people in the Global South, members of Lesbian Gay Bisexual Transgender communities, and racial and ethnic minorities, immigrants and refugees.

As we celebrate the breadth and depth of existing scholarship on gender and war, we continue to be mindful of key challenges facing us. The production and dissemination of new knowledge about gender and war depends to a great extent on our willingness to recognize and address the tensions between the Global North and Global South and between academics, policymakers, relief workers, activists, and, most importantly, those whose lives have been shattered by war and political violence. By engaging critically with the new knowledge presented in this *Handbook* while paying attention to gaps, silences and unanswered questions, readers can shape not only the next volume of scholarship on this topic but also the future of policy, advocacy and activism on gender and war. Above all, this *Handbook* is an invitation to readers to join a vibrant, transnational, critical conversation about feminist theorizing and a gender-sensitive analysis of war.

NOTES

1. Subsequent UNSC resolutions are as follows: '1820 (passed in 2008), which recognizes sexual violence in conflict as a matter of international security; 1888 (of 2009), which provides for mechanisms to strengthen the implementation of UNSCR 1820; 1889 (of 2009), which addresses obstacles to women's participation in peace processes and peace building; and 1960 (of 2010), which further strengthens calls to implement 1888 and 1889' (Pratt, 2013, p. 772).
2. For a critical engagement with UNSCR 1325 see the 2011 special edition of *International Feminist Journal of Politics* (vol. 13, no. 4), edited by Nicola Pratt and Sophie Richter-Devroe.

REFERENCES

Abdo, Nahla Abdo and Ronit Lentin (2002), *Women and the Politics of Military Confrontation*, Indiana University Press.
Ackerly, Brooke and Katy Attanasi (2009), 'Global feminisms: theory and ethics for studying gendered injustice', *New Political Science*, **31** (4): 543–55.
Agathangelou, Anna M. (2004), *The Global Political Economy of Sex: Desire, Violence, and Insecurity in Mediterranean Nation States*, Palgrave Macmillan.
Agathangelou, Anna M. and Lily H.M. Ling (2004), 'Power, borders, security, wealth: lessons of violence and desire from September 11', *International Studies Quarterly*, **48**: 517–38.
Andersen, Mary (1993), 'The concept of mainstreaming: experience and change', in Mary Andersen (ed.), *Focusing on Women: UNIFEM's Experience of Mainstreaming*, UNIFEM, pp. 1–32.

Anzaldúa, Gloria E. and Analouise Keating (2002), *This Bridge We Call Home: Radical Visions for Transformations*, Routledge.

Baaz, Maria Eriksson and Maria Stern (2009), 'Why do soldiers rape? Masculinity, violence and sexuality in the armed forces in the Congo (DRC)', *International Studies Quarterly*, **53**: 495–518.

Baaz, Maria Eriksson and Maria Stern (2013), *Sexual Violence as a Weapon of War? Perceptions, Prescriptions, Problems in the Congo and Beyond*, Zed Books.

Bastick, Megan, Karin Grimm and Rachel Kunz (2007), *Sexual Violence in Armed Conflict: Global Overview and Implications for the Security Sector*, Centre for the Democratic Control of Armed Forces.

Belkin, Aaron (2012), *Bring Me Men: Military Masculinity and the Benign Façade of American Empire 1898–2001*, Hurst.

Bell, Christine (2009), 'Transitional justice, interdisciplinarity, and the state of the "field" or "non-field"', *International Journal of Transitional Justice*, **3** (1): 5–27.

Bell, Christine and Catherine O'Rourke (2007), 'Does feminism need a theory of transitional justice? An introductory essay', *International Journal of Transitional Justice*, **1** (1): 23–44.

Boulding, E. (1992), *The Underside of History: A View of Women Through Time* (2 vols), Sage.

Buckly-Zistel, Susanne and Ruth Stanley (2011), *Gender in Transitional Justice*, Palgrave Macmillan.

Buss, Doris (2009), 'Rethinking "rape as a weapon of war"', *Feminist Legal Studies*, **17**: 145–63.

Cockburn, Cynthia (2012), Antimilitarism: *Political and Gender Dynamics of Peace Movements*, Palgrave Macmillan.

Cockburn, Cynthia and Dubravka Zarkov (eds) (2002), *The Postwar Moment: Militaries, Masculinities and International Peacekeeping*, Lawrence and Wishart.

Cohen, Dara Kay (2013), 'Explaining rape during civil war: cross-national evidence (1980–2009)', *American Political Science Review*, **107** (3): 461–77.

Cohn, Carol (2008), 'Mainstreaming gender in UN security policy: a path to political transformation?', in Shirin Rai and Georgina Waylen (eds), *In Global Governance: Feminist Perspectives*, Palgrave Macmillan.

Cohn, Carol, Helen Kinsella and Sheri Gibbings (2004), 'Women, peace and security, Resolution 1325', *International Feminist Journal of Politics*, **6** (1): 130–40.

Collins, Patricia Hill (1991), *Black Feminist Thought: Knowledge, Consciousness, and the Politics of Empowerment*, Routledge.

Confortini, Catia (2006), 'Galtung, violence, and gender: the case for a peace studies/ feminism alliance', *Peace and Change*, **31** (3): 333–67.

Connell, Raewyn (1995), *Masculinities*, Polity.

Council of Europe (1998), *Gender Mainstreaming: Conceptual Framework, Methodology and Presentation of Good Practices*, Final report of activities of the group of specialists on mainstreaming (Rapporteur Group on the Equality Between Women and Men, GR-EG), Committee of Ministers, 26 March.

Crenshaw, Kimberlee (1991), 'Mapping the margins: intersectionality, identity politics, and violence against women of color', *Stanford Law Review*, (43): 1241–99.

Davis, Angela (1983), *Women, Race and Class*, Random House.

Duncanson, Claire (2013), *Forces for Good? Military Masculinities and Peacebuilding in Afghanistan and Iraq*, Palgrave Macmillan.

Eichler, Maya (2011), *Militarizing Men: Gender, Conscription, and War in Post-Soviet Russia*, Stanford University Press.

Eisler, Riane (1989), *The Chalice and the Blade: Our History, Our Future*, Harper and Row.

Elshtain, Jean Bethke (1987), *Women and War*, University of Chicago Press.

Enloe, Cynthia (1983), *Does Khaki Become You? The Militarization of Women's Lives*, University of California Press.

Enloe, Cynthia (1989), *Bananas Beaches and Bases: Making Feminist Sense of International Politics*, University of California Press.

Enloe, Cynthia (2007), *Globalization and Militarism: Feminists Make the Link*, Rowman & Littlefield.

Faludi, Susan (2007), *The Terror Dream: Myth and Misogyny in an Insecure America*, Picador.

Fraser, Nancy (2013), 'Reframing justice in a globalizing world', *Fortunes of Feminism: From State-Managed Capitalism to Neoliberal Crisis*, Verso, pp. 189–209.

Giles, Wenona (2008), 'Reflections on the women in conflict zones network: lessons from the past and forward-looking possibilities', *International Feminist Journal of Politics*, **10** (1): 102–12.

Harrington, Carol (2011), 'Resolution 1325 and post-cold war feminist politics', *International Feminist Journal of Politics*, **13** (4): 557–75.

Harris, Adrienne and Ynestra King (eds) (1989), *Rocking the Ship of State: Toward a Feminist Peace Politics*, Westview.

Hartsock, Nancy (1983), 'Money, sex, and power: a theory for women?', in Linda Nicholson (ed.), *Feminism/Postmodernism*, Routledge, pp. 157–75.

Hartstock, Nancy (1989), 'Masculinity, heroism and the making of war', in Adrienne Harris and Ynestra King (eds), *Rocking the Ship of the State: Towards a Feminist Peace Politics*, Westview.

Hill, Felicity, Carol Cohn and Cynthia Enloe (2004), *UN Security Council Resolution 1325 Three Years On: Gender, Security and Organizational Change*, Roundtable discussion at the Boston Consortium on Gender, Security and Human Rights, Boston MA, 20 January.

Hooks, Bell (1984), *Feminist Theory From Margin to Center*, Pluto.

Hooks, Bell (1990), *Yearning: Race, Gender and Cultural Politics*, Turnaround.

Hooper, Charlotte (2001), *Manly States: Masculinities, International Relations, and Gender Politics*, Columbia University Press.

Hunter, Mic (2007), *Honor Betrayed: Sexual Abuse in America's Military*, Barricade Books.

International Feminist Journal of Politics (2011), Special edition examining UNSCR 1325 on Women, Peace and Security, **13** (4), edited by Nicola Pratt and Sophie Richter-Devroe.

Jabri, Vivienne (1996), *Discourses on Violence: Conflict Analysis Reconsidered*, Manchester University Press.

Jayawardena, Kumari (1986), *Feminism and Nationalism in the Third World*, Zed Books.

Jiwani, Yasmin (2009), 'Helpless maidens and chivalrous knights: Afghan women in the Canadian press', *University of Toronto Quarterly*, **78** (2): 728–44.

Kirby, Paul (2013), 'How is rape a weapon of war? Feminist international relations, modes of critical explanation and the study of wartime sexual violence', *European Journal of International Relations*, **19** (4): 797–821.

Kirby, Paul (2015), 'Acting time; or, the abolitionist and the feminist', *International Feminist Journal of Politics*, **17** (3): 508–13.

Kirk, Gwen (1989), 'Our Greenham Common: not just a place but a movement', in Adrienne Harris and Yenestra King (eds), *Rocking the Ship of State: Toward a Feminist Peace Politics*, Westview.

Leatherman, Janie L. (2011), *Sexual Violence and Armed Conflict*, Polity.

Lind, Amy (2010), *Development, Sexual Rights and Global Governance*, Routledge.

Mackay, Angela (2004), 'Training the uniforms: gender and peacekeeping operations', in Afshar Haleh and Deborah Eade (eds), *Development, Women and War: Feminist Perspectives*, Oxfam GB, pp. 100–108.

MacKenzie, Megan H. (2009), 'Securitization and desecuritization: female soldiers and the reconstruction of women in post-conflict Sierra Leone', *Security Studies*, **2** (18): 241–61.

MacKenzie, Megan H. (2012), *Female Soldiers in Sierra Leone: Sex, Security, and Post-Conflict Development*, NYU Press.

Mohanty, Chandra Talpade (1991), 'Cartographies of struggle: third world women and the politics of feminism', in Chandra Talpade Mohanty et al. (eds), *Third World Women and the Politics of Feminism*, Indiana University Press.

Mohanty, Chandra Talpade (2003), *Feminism without Borders: Decolonizing Theory, Practicing Solidarity*, Duke University Press.

Moraga, Cherríe and Gloria Anzaldúa (1983), *This Bridge Called My Back: Writings by Radical Women of Color*, Kitchen Table.

Nagel, Joane (2014), 'Rape and war: fighting men and comfort women', in Mindy Stombler, Dawn Baunach, Wendy Simonds, Elroi Windsor and Elisabeth Burgess (eds), *Sex Matters: The Sexuality and Society Reader*, W.W. Norton, pp. 641–8.

Nagel, Joane and Lindsey Feitz (2008), 'The militarization of gender and sexuality in the Iraq war', in Helena Carreiras and Gerhard Kümmel (eds), *Women in the Military and in Armed Conflict*, VS Verlag für Sozialwissenschaften, pp. 201–25.

O'Rourke, Catherine (2013), *Gender Politics in Transitional Justice*, Routledge.

Philipose, Liz (2007), 'The politics of pain and the end of empire', *International Feminist Journal of Politics*, **9** (4): 607–16.

Pratt, Nicola (2013), 'Reconceptualizing gender, reinscribing racial-sexual boundaries in international security: the case of UN Security Council Resolution 1325 on "Women, Peace and Security"', *International Studies Quarterly*, **57**: 772–83.

Razavi, Shahar and Carol Miller (1995), 'Gender mainstreaming: a study of efforts by the UNDP, the World Bank and the ILO to institutionalize gender issues', United Nations Institute for Social Development Occasional Paper No 4.

Reardon, Betty (1985), *Sexism and the War System,* Teachers College.

Reardon, Betty (1993), *Women and Peace: Feminist Visions of Global Security*, State University of New York Press.

Richter-Montpetit, Melanie (2007), 'Empire, desire and violence: a queer transnational feminist reading of the prisoner "abuse" in Abu Ghraib and the question of "gender equality"', *International Feminist Journal of Politics*, **9** (1): 58–9.

Riley, Robin, Chandra Talpade Mohanty and Minnie Bruce Pratt (eds) (2008), *Feminism and War: Confronting US Imperialism*, Zed Books.

Ruddick, Sara (1983), 'Preservative love and military destruction: Reflections on mothering and peace', in Joyce Trebilcot (ed.), *Mothering: Essays on Mothering and Peace*, Littlefield Adams.

Ruddick, Sara (1989), *Maternal Thinking: Toward a Politics of Peace*, Beacon.

Runyan, Anne Sisson and V. Spike Peterson (1993), *Global Gender Issues*, Westview.

Russo, Ann (2006), 'The Feminist Majority Foundation's campaign to stop gender apartheid', *International Feminist Journal of Politics*, **8** (4): 557–80.

Sachs, Dalia, Amalia Sa'ar and Sarai Aharoni (2007), '"How can I feel for others when I myself am beaten?" The impact of the armed conflict on women in Israel', *Sex Roles*, **57** (7–8): 593–606.

Salzman, Todd A. (1998), 'Rape camps as a means of ethnic cleansing: religious, cultural, and ethical responses to rape victims in the former Yugoslavia', *Human Rights Quarterly*, **20** (2): 348–78.

Scuzzarello, Sarah (2008), 'National security versus moral responsibility: an analysis of integration programs in Malmo, Sweden', *Social Politics: International Studies in Gender, State and Society*, **15** (1): 5–31.

Shalhoub-Kevorkian, Nadera (2009), *Militarization and Violence against Women in Conflict Zones in the Middle East: A Palestinian Case-Study*, Cambridge University Press.

Sharlach, Lisa (2000), 'Rape as genocide: Bangladesh, the Former Yugoslavia, and Rwanda', *New Political Science*, **22** (1): 89–102.

Sharoni, Simona (1994), 'Homefront as battlefield: gender, military occupation and violence against women', in Tamar Mayer (ed.), *Women and the Israeli Occupation: The Politics of Change*, Routledge, pp. 121–37.

Sharoni, Simona (2001), 'Rethinking women's struggles in Israel-Palestine and in the North of Ireland', in Caroline Moser and Fiona Clark (eds), *Victims, Perpetrators or Actors? Gender, Armed Conflict and Political Violence*, Zed Books, pp. 85–98.

Sharoni, Simona (2008), 'De-militarizing masculinities in the age of empire', *The Austrian Political Science Journal* (special issue: 'Counter/Terror/Wars: Feminist Perspectives'), **37** (2): 147–64.

Sharoni, Simona (2016), 'Militarism and gender-based violence', in Nancy Naples, Maithree Wickramasinghe and Angela Wong Wai Ching (eds), *The Wiley-Blackwell Encyclopedia of Gender and Sexuality Studies*, Wiley Blackwell, pp. 1–9.

Shepherd, Laura J. (2008), Gender, *Violence and Security: Discourse as Practice*, Zed Books.

Sivakumarian, Sandesh (2007), 'Sexual violence against men in armed conflict', *European Journal of International Law*, **18** (2): 253–76.

Sjoberg, Laura and Caron E. Gentry (2007), *Mothers, Monsters, Whores: Women's Violence in Global Politics*, Zed Books.

Sylvester, Christine (1989), 'Patriarchy, peace, and women warriors', in Linda R. Forcey (ed.), *Peace: Meanings, Politics, Strategies*, Praeger.

Sylvester, Christine (1994), *Feminist Theory and International Relations in a Postmodern Era*, Cambridge University Press.

Tickner, J. Ann (1992), *Gender in International Relations: Feminist Perspectives on Achieving Global Security*, Columbia University Press.

True, Jacqui (2003), 'Mainstreaming gender in global public policy', *International Feminist Journal of Politics*, **5** (3): 368–96.

United Nations (1997), *Report of the Economic and Social Council for 1997*, A/52/3, 18 September.

United Nations (2000), *Mainstreaming a Gender Perspective in Multidimensional Peace Operations*, Lessons Learned Unit: Department of Peacekeeping Operations, July.

United Nations Security Council (2000), Resolution 1325, Adopted by the Security Council on its 4213th meeting on 31 October.

Welland, Julia (2013), 'Militarised violences, basic training, and the myths of asexuality and discipline', *Review of International Studies*, **39** (4): 881–902.

Whitworth, Sandra (2004), *Men, Militarism & UN Peacekeeping: A Gendered Analysis*, Lynne Rienner.

Woodward, Rachel and Trish Winter (2007), *Sexing the Soldier: The Politics of Gender in the Contemporary British Army*, Routledge.

Yoshimi, Yoshiaki (2002), *Comfort Women: Sexual Slavery in the Japanese Military During World War II*, Columbia University Press.

Zalewski, Marysia (1998), 'Introduction: from the "woman" question to the "man" question in international relations', in Marysia Zalewski and Jane Parpart (eds), *The 'Man' Question in International Relations*, Westview, pp. 1–13.

Zalewski, Marysia and Jane Parpart (eds) (1998), *The 'Man' Question in International Relations*, Westview.

Zalewski, Marysia and Jane Parpart (eds) (2008), *Rethinking the Man Question: Sex, Gender and Violence in International Relations*, Zed Books.

PART I

GENDER AND THE CONDUCT OF WAR

Part I Introduction: Gender and the conduct of war

Julia Welland

The conduct of war has typically been understood as the killing and injuring of combatants (and often civilian populations too), the destruction of infrastructure and cities, and the conquering of territories. War, however, is also a profoundly gendered experience. Gender has been used as an excuse and justification of wars, as motivation to persuade (mostly) young men to join national militaries and fight, and to inflict particular forms of violence. Thus, paying careful attention to gender is integral for a fuller understanding of the conduct of war. All the chapters in this part view gender as central to the conduct of war and authors address three interrelated themes: the enabling of war, the day-to-day operation of war and understanding the conduct of war. At the same time, and given the complexity of the issues and the expansive scholarship on the gendered aspects of war, no contribution deals solely or exclusively with a single topic.

ENABLING THE CONDUCT OF WAR

Feminists have long noted that in order for wars to be waged and for soldiers and civilians to be willing participants and supporters, particular ideas and beliefs about gender need to be harnessed and reinforced. Cynthia Enloe (1983, 1989, 1993, 2000, 2004) and Jean Bethke Elshtain (1995) have both pointed to the need for particular understandings of masculinity and femininity to be sustained in order for militaries to operate and wars to be waged. Now a well-rehearsed feminist narrative – what Stern and Zalewski (2009) have termed a 'familiar feminist fable' – men are told that by joining a military and going to war they will embody the masculine attributes of heroism, valor and strength, while women are required to remain in the private sphere maintaining the feminine values of passivity and virtue – the 'beautiful souls' for the masculine 'just warriors' (Elshtain, 1995) to protect and save.

A number of authors in this part have drawn on this insight of how gender has historically shaped and continues to shape who fights and dies in the conduct of war, and in defense of whom. Victoria Basham explores how state militaries continue to rely on gender constructs to motivate predominantly male soldiers to conduct acts of state sanctioned violence. She examines how, despite overwhelming evidence that demonstrates that the presence of women and sexual minorities has no discernible negative impact on military cohesion and performance, gendered norms continue to shape how militaries organize themselves and prepare for war. This is seen most clearly (in the British case) through the continued expulsion of women from the 'front line' of combat. Militaries therefore remain highly masculinized institutions not because it is necessary for soldiers to kill and be killed, but because they are vested with the attendant power and privilege, which its members can earn and have taken for granted. This is both how militaries desire to see themselves and how many of their male members desire to be seen.

Linda Åhäll further explores the assumption that the military is a masculinized space through an analysis of women's agency in war with a focus on women who actively participate in perpetrating acts of violence. Using what at first appear as two very different empirical examples, Åhäll analyses scenes from the Hollywood blockbuster *Zero Dark Thirty* and justifications for the maintaining of the British ban on women in combat roles in 2010, claiming that representations of women 'being a killer' (or, indeed, not being one) operate as a boundary-making practice that is constitutive of broader cultural understandings of gender. For Maya, the female lead in *Zero Dark Thirty*, 'being a killer' is essential for her representation as a heroine of war and her value as a CIA agent. Åhäll argues, however, that Maya is punished in the film for occupying this subject position. Her expressions of emotionality are used as an excuse to displace her as a 'real' fighter and force her to return to a 'proper' feminine place. Further, like Basham, Åhäll draws attention to the fact that the real-life continued exclusion of women from combat roles demonstrates a fundamental inability of political establishments and societies as a whole to imagine women as killers in war. Both chapters expose assumptions about the gendered division of power and labor during war, revealing the ways in which gender remains fundamental to enabling war and to its conduct and operations.

THE DAY-TO-DAY OPERATION OF WAR

While gender is integral to making war possible through the marking of some (masculine) bodies as fighters and other (feminine) bodies as those that are fought for, gender can also be rendered visible in the everyday operation of the conduct of war. For while, as the first two chapters demonstrate, the fighting of wars depends – in part – on the masculinized identity of the armed forces, wars have never 'just' been about violence. Rather, the day-to-day doing of war consists of far more banal and mundane activities – secretarial work, the gathering of intelligence and the close protection of non-military personnel. Further, the extent to which masculinized soldiering identities and the 'heroic warrior' myth can remain 'complete' on the battlefield is contested – soldiers cry, find themselves incapable of firing their weapons and are unable to perform the masculine role expected of them. Several chapters in this part consider gender in the day-to-day operation of war, probing the ways it operates away from the front-line combat but still remains vital to its conduct. These chapters also shed light on how the conduct of war itself can work to undo carefully constructed gendered identities.

Juliette Pattinson utilizes official records, personal testimonies, newspapers and film in order to examine the gendered nature of espionage and counter-espionage in Britain in the first half of the twentieth century. Focusing on the experiences and public perception of the men and women engaged in espionage, Pattinson notes that popular discourse centered on the scrupulously patriotic British gentleman spy and the duplicitous foreign 'mata-hariesque' female spy-courtesan. Such perceptions rendered almost invisible the many women in the various branches of intelligence organizations, who undertook mundane, low-status and low-paid work that was crucial to the development, expansion and professionalization of twentieth-century British espionage.

Returning to the contemporary era, Paul Higate turns his attention to a specific gendered binary. Taking Judith Hick Stiehm's (1982) influential essay 'The protected, the protector, the defender' as his starting point, Higate argues against a straightforward reading of the protector/protected binary as one in which one actor, viewed as 'the masculine' exercises power over another actor presented as 'the feminine'. Using ethnographic field research of everyday interactions between bodyguards and clients, Higate examines the complex relationships between them in a private security company in Kabul, Afghanistan. As he analyzes how perceptions of risk and danger were negotiated between the parties, Higate argues that gender and class worked to confer authority on those on the protected side of the binary – the woman client – thus upending traditional readings of the binary.

Mary Manjikian upends understandings of the 'heroic warrior' even further through her exploration of the effects of new technologies on the conduct of war. As physiological and cognitive enhancements to warfighters eliminate a soldier's ability to display agency and autonomy, the extent to which human soldiers can embody the 'hegemonic masculinity' required for war-fighting is challenged. Manjikian's chapter considers three new types of soldiers: the enhanced soldier, the hybrid soldier, and the drugged soldier. In all three newly emerging types of war fighting, soldiers' experience of war is mediated through technologies that affect how they participate in war, think about war, and deal morally and ethically with its aftermath. Such technologies affect not just the conduct of war, but also call into question the privileges associated with professional service in a first-world military, making soldiers everywhere look more alike than different.

UNDERSTANDING THE CONDUCT OF WAR

Gender is not only central to making the conduct of war possible and to the everyday practices of warfare, it is also a central framing device for the broader understanding of war and its legitimacy. Gender, particularly when it intersects with race, is integral to understanding how the conduct of war is presented and understood. The gendered and raced identities of both fighters and civilians shape how they are represented, recognized and legitimated. The final two chapters of this part therefore focus specifically on this intersection of gender and race, and how these two identity markers provide a framework for understanding conflicts, as well as the participants involved.

Julia Welland pays attention to the ways in which gender is rendered visible in the population-centric counterinsurgency environment of Afghanistan and how gender informs dominant representations and understandings of the conflict. She first points to the particular type of militarized masculinity required for the conducting of the 'hearts and minds' warfare of counterinsurgency: a 'softer' and 'gentler' soldier who is distinct both from its previous warrior incarnations, and from the insurgent masculinities it is pitted against and the masculinities of the Afghan security forces it fights alongside. Secondly, Welland reveals how the conduct of counterinsurgency war requires a greater visibility of femininity, both physically in the bodies of women soldiers through the use of so-called 'Female Engagement Teams', and conceptually through the need for military personnel to demonstrate the 'feminine' emotions of compassion and concern. This re-scripted militarized masculine identity and greater visibility of femininity are central to the claims that the long war in Afghanistan was one in which the population's needs came first.

In the final chapter of the part, Caron Gentry explains how gendered and raced notions embedded within the 'Westphalian narrative' inhibit understandings of terrorism and political violence. Gentry argues that how terrorism is perceived depends upon a gender hierarchy implicit in the Westphalian system. Claiming that the Westphalian narrative makes the (Western) state a masculine exemplar, embodying rationality, autonomy and legitimate violence, implies that non-state politically violent groups are understood as feminized, irrational and illegitimate. This gendered and raced binary of legitimate versus illegitimate violence filters further down in Terrorism Studies' discursive constructions of terrorist organizations, disrupting Terrorism Studies' claims that terrorists should be seen as rational actors, as well as impacting upon how individuals who employ political violence are perceived.

Taken together these chapters reveal a multitude of ways in which gender is central to understanding the conduct of war. Gender enables the conduct of war, shapes and makes possible its day-to-day operations, and is integral for its legitimation and justification. These chapters show that paying attention to the ways in which masculinities and femininities operate can reveal what Åhäll terms a 'hidden politics': a politics that defines what some (masculine) bodies can do and what other (feminine) bodies can't. Some of the ways these chapters have demonstrated this hidden politics are in 'real world' policy decisions such as the UK woman combat ban, in the roles and assumptions applied to the women and men soldiers who were deployed in Afghanistan, and in the repre-sentation of a woman CIA agent in a Hollywood film. These chapters also lay bare the slipperiness and fluidity of gender as a concept, the ways in which it can work in confusing and contradictory ways, and its instability and precariousness. For example, femininity when intersected with class privilege can infer authority over masculinity, even when positioned in the role of the protected, and gendered identities have the potential to be undone by technological and representational shifts. It is then an appeal to remain vigilant to gender's slipperiness and fluidity that this introduction ends with. New gendered insights continue to emerge with queer, trans and non-'First Worldism' critique and scholarship, and these should be listened to and taken seriously in order for feminism as a movement, political project and 'way of knowing' to be strengthened. Further, attention must also be paid to the ways in which gender can be appropriated, both prior to and during the conduct of war, and used as a vehicle for a renewed politics of exclusion and violence.

REFERENCES

Elshtain, Jean Bethke (1995), *Women and War*, University of Chicago Press.
Enloe, Cynthia (1983), *Does Khaki Become You? The Militarization of Women's Lives*, Pandora.
Enloe, Cynthia (1989), *Bananas, Beaches and Bases: Making Feminist Sense of International Politics*, University of California Press.
Enloe, Cynthia (1993), *The Morning After: Sexual Politics at the End of the Cold War*, University of California Press.
Enloe, Cynthia (2000), *Maneuvers: The International Politics of Militarizing Women's Lives*, University of California Press.
Enloe, Cynthia (2004), *The Curious Feminist: Searching for Women in a New Age of Empire*, University of California Press.
Stern, Maria and Marysia Zalewski (2009), 'Feminist fatigue(s): reflections on feminism and familiar fables of militarisation', *Review of International Studies*, **35** (3): 611–30.
Stiehm, Judith Hicks (1982), 'The protected, the protector, the defender', *Women's Studies International Forum*, **5** (4): 367–76.

1. Gender and militaries: the importance of military masculinities for the conduct of state sanctioned violence

Victoria M. Basham

INTRODUCTION

Western armed forces, as we would recognize them, emerged with the establishment of the modern state in the seventeenth century. Max Weber (1991, p. 78, emphasis in original) famously argued that the modern state is best thought of as 'a human community that (successfully) claims the *monopoly of the legitimate use of force* within a given territory'; as such, military violence might be considered 'the *raison d'être* of the state's existence' (Malešević, 2010, p. 26). Whilst Weber may have overlooked the significance of non-state actors in armed conflict (Kaldor, 1999), he recognized war and military violence as profoundly social; that war makes states, societies and individuals, as much as states make war (Malešević, 2010). Feminists have also long argued that gender plays an integral role in the formation and practice of political phenomena and social activities, and perhaps chief among these are associations between war and manhood (Tickner, 1992; Goldstein, 2001). Indeed, the relationship between armed force and masculinities is possibly the most salient and cross-culturally stable aspect of gendered politics; and nowhere is this notion of war as a man's game more entrenched than in state militaries. The preservation of the military as an exclusively male domain has only been challenged relatively recently and minimally by the widening of recruitment practices. Most state armed forces continue to marginalize women and sexual minorities in ways that foster particular ideas about manhood, machismo and military service. Gender continues to shape who fights, who dies and in defense of whom.

This chapter explores dominant, salient constructions of gender in militaries, focusing in particular on ways in which certain ideas about masculinity are fostered in military environments. The aim is to demonstrate how armed forces continue to rely on gender constructs to motivate predominantly male soldiers to conduct acts of violence sanctioned by the state. The chapter begins with an overview of some of the most prevalent ways in which associations between masculinity and military service have been established, before moving on to consider why it might be that militaries continue to foster these associations, despite growing demands for wider inclusion of all citizenry. The chapter concludes that, ultimately, the military remains the most 'prototypically masculine of all institutions' (Segal, 1995, p. 758) because this is how it sees itself and how most of its male members *want* to be seen. Gendered norms continue to shape the ways in which militaries organize themselves and prepare for war despite overwhelming evidence that the presence of women and sexual minorities has no discernible negative impact on military cohesion and performance and that soldiers do not need to bond socially in order to fight. The masculinized character of military culture and identity thus remains significant; it provides 'the means of action', even if it does not actually provide the 'ultimate ends' (Farrell, 1998, p. 410). It facilitates war, even if it does not actually enable soldiers to kill and be killed.

BODIES OF MEN

Militaries, often described as bodies of men, have and continue to be overwhelmingly comprised of men.[1] The image of the soldier hero is a robust and highly influential form of idealized masculinity, particularly in the contemporary Western world; it pervades popular culture (toys, comic books, films, TV series, museum exhibits and video games) and dictates the support of 'our boys' in real war situations. A 'popular masculine pleasure-culture of war' (Dawson, 1994, pp. 3–4) ensures that, whilst most men are not soldiers, many still aspire to militarized symbolism. Activities dominated by men such as contact sports, reckless driving, risk-taking in business and acts of violence and aggression, can all be thought of as 'ritualized combat' (Connell, 2000, p. 214).

Perpetrating acts of violence does not come naturally to men, however. As Connell (in Higate, 2003a, pp. 210–11) argues, whilst almost all soldiers are men, most men are not actually soldiers; likewise, 'though most killers are men, most men never kill or commit assault; [and] though an appalling number of men do rape, most men do not'. Thus, whilst in most societies men structurally and interpersonally dominate most spheres, it is important to try to understand how individuals can be simultaneously privileged and disadvantaged by coexisting hierarchies of gender, race, class, age and so on (Miller, 1997). Such hierarchies exist even among men who share certain ascriptive categories and occupy similar social positions. For example, refusing to engage in heavy drinking might lead to some men seeming 'less manly' in the eyes of other men of the same class and racial background. The ways in which various configurations of manhood sustain the dominance of men as a social group in militaries and in civilian society are therefore multiple and complex.

Connell (1987, 1995) is perhaps most associated with examining how different types of masculinity interrelate and intersect with other social categories. Central to her analysis is the notion of 'hegemonic masculinity', a gender practice that exemplifies currently accepted legitimations of unequal social relations sustained through corresponding cultural ideals and institutional expressions of power (Connell, 1995; Hooper, 1999). Hegemonic masculinity not only concerns cultural dominance more widely but also hierarchical social orders among men; for example, ethnic minority masculinities are often subordinated to ethnic majority ones (Connell, 1995), and it is normative – it represents an ideal – so the number of men achieving and practicing it will be small. Importantly, though, whilst hegemonic masculinity may be more aspirational than actual, many men will still gain from the circulation of hegemonic ideas about masculinity because it underpins male privilege (Farough, 2003; see also Connell, 1987). War and its technologies can confer a 'virile prestige' on those at the tail end of conflict situations as well as the rough and tough combat soldier (Kimmel, 2004, p. 274; see also Cohn, 1987, 1993; Enloe, 2004). All this points to the socially constructed and contingent nature of gender relations, to the notion that gender roles and war roles are inextricably linked (*inter alia* Elshtain, 1995; Goldstein, 2001). Typically, men have been encouraged into combat through the cultural equation of manhood with heroism in battle and women have been maneuvered to support war and the men who wage it, as witnesses, mothers, sweethearts and nurses (*inter alia* Enloe, 1988, 2000).

This separation of roles means that within many societies there is a salient belief that military service turns boys into men (*inter alia* Morgan, 1987; Hockey, 2003) but as young men are not 'natural-born warriors' they must *become* soldiers (Snyder, 2003, p. 191). Basic military training is a key site for such transformational relationships between men, their bodies and the military (Janowitz, 1974). Stripped of close ties to civilian life, recruits learn the value of appearance, respect for superiors and traditions, cleanliness, obedience, rules for displaying aggression – rituals, initiations and uniforms that all foster a 'cult of toughness' (Barrett, 2001; see also Hockey, 1986; Hale, 2008). Some activities, such as the maintenance of uniforms and the cleanliness of accommodations (which are sex segregated), are more commonly associated with femininity but become controlled masculine activities in masculinized spaces

(Woodward, 2003). They can be just as important to the 'reproduction of a military way of life' as learning to be physically and mentally ready to fight because they 'promote a homosociability that works to exclude those who do not, or cannot, also perform this warrior ideal' (Atherton, 2009, pp. 826, 834). As Green et al. (2010) argue, coping with the stresses of military life is often a significant way for recruits to prove their manliness, but it is also possible for caring forms of masculinity to coexist with hyper-masculine traits if, in caring for their fellow soldiers, individuals are contributing to a sense of camaraderie. Essentially, 'hegemonic masculinity in the military incorporates aggression, violence and macho behaviors on the one hand and a caring, sharing ethos based on strong inter-dependent bonds on the other' because both are seen as conducive to cohesion among military recruits and therefore military effectiveness (Green et al., 2010, p. 1485).

Other activities are aimed at making the bodies of male recruits both 'a site of suffering and a vital resource', a site for the exhibition of worth or failure as men (Higate, 1998, p. 180). Repetitive and physically grueling activities emphasize to each recruit that 'just getting dressed in uniform is not going to make you into a soldier' (Ministry of Defence, in Woodward, 1998); they provide recruits with a sense that they are being given a 'thrilling experience that cannot be had elsewhere' that offers 'appropriate recompense for their efforts to achieve bodily and emotional self-control' (Sasson-Levy, 2008, p. 314). In the midst of these masculinized rituals, recruits are often told that their physical inadequacies make them 'girly' or 'gay' (Hockey, 2003) or are stereotyped 'by gender, nationality or race regardless of zero-tolerance policies on discrimination, bullying and harassment' (Adult Learning Inspectorate, 2007, p. 27).

Some have suggested that masculinity 'is achieved by the constant process of warding off threats to it ... by the rejection of femininity and homosexuality' (Weeks in Gutterman, 2001, p. 61); that recruits become men by proving they are not women or effeminate (Harrison and Laliberté, 1997). Belkin's (2012, p. 5) insightful work on the US military suggests, however, that hegemonic military masculinity often involves the marginalization of women and sexual minorities *and* homoeroticism: an embrace of the masculine/unmasculine. Belkin (2012) suggests the resultant confusion of this duality disciplines soldiers and brings them into conformity with military aims. For Higate (2012), homoeroticism can also help soldiers overcome some of the brutality of military service through a sense of closeness to others. Alongside these analyses, and following Kaplan (2005, 2006), I want to suggest that desire also plays a central role in facilitating homoerotic rituals: both the desire *between* (heterosexual) men, and the desire *of* men to maintain their social and institutional dominance. In order to demonstrate this, it is necessary to examine further how women and sexual minorities have been character- ized in militaries. As I suggest below, these characterizations involve a simultaneous warding off and embrace of the unmasculine, and an ongoing reconfiguration of what it means to be a man, so that the desires of military men to engage in homosocial and homoerotic rituals can be fulfilled.

DISTRACTIONS AND DISRUPTIONS: WOMEN IN ARMED FORCES

One of the most salient aspects of warfare is the construction of 'men as warriors and of women as worriers' (Yuval-Davis, 1997, p. 94). Whilst all soldiers are implicated in violence by extension of enlisting, hegemonic masculine ideals obscure the fact that most servicemen, as well as servicewomen, do not serve in combat positions, do not kill anyone and may not even engage in violence (Higate, 2003a). The cultural purchase of the notion that men are natural born killers obscures this, however, and men and women often experience military service in very different ways as a result.

The general pattern of women's mobilization in the West has been inclusion in times of necessity and exclusion or limitation at all others (Noakes, 2006). Though servicewomen nursed the wounded in nineteenth-century wars, and nursed, catered, administrated, drove and maintained vehicles in the First and Second World Wars, it was only in the late 1980s that women in most Western forces began taking on more combat-related roles (see Woodward and Winter, 2007 for a comprehen- sive overview). Scholarly debates on women's mobilization, particularly in close combat, are rich, numerous, cross-cultural and well-rehearsed. They generally coalesce around 'two ostensibly distinct yet fundamen- tally related issues: women's *rights* to serve and their *capacity* to serve' (Kovitz, 2003, p. 2, emphasis in original). Conservative opponents tend to argue that masculine privilege is necessary to motivate men to fight and that the presence of women threatens this (*inter alia* Gat, 2000; Van Creveld, 2000a, 2000b; Frost, 2001; Holmes, 2003). Liberal and civic republican feminists have challenged this on the grounds that military service is a (pre)condition to full-citizenship and that women have a right, and even a duty, to enlist (*inter alia* Stiehm, 1982; Feinman, 1998; Kennedy-Pipe, 2000). Others have problematized women's service on the grounds that it militarizes them (Tiffany, 1981; Klein, 2002), normalizes masculine military culture (Sasson-Levy, 2003) or violates the peaceful nature of women (Ruddick, 1989). These perspectives have in turn been criticized for ignoring women's militarism and violence (*inter alia* Bourke, 1999; Sjoberg and Gentry, 2007), men's pacifism and conscientious objection (Bibbings, 2003; Conway, 2004) or male victimhood (Jones, 2006). Others have pointed to the ethnocentricism of many of these debates; the notion of choice all too often obscures how for some women, especially in the Global South, armed struggle may be a matter of survival rather than deliberation (*inter alia* Yuval-Davis, 1997).

A number of Western state armed forces, including Australia, Canada, France, Germany, Israel and, more recently, the United States, have removed longstanding bans on women serving in close combat roles, those where hand-to-hand fighting is most likely. Women's participation in close combat remains minimal and liminal in these militaries, however; and in the UK, women are (at the time of writing) still excluded from close combat due to concerns about the impact that their presence might have on male bonding and unit cohesion.[2] Essentially, women have been characterized as potentially *disruptive* to male bonding, by introducing sexual tensions and cultural otherness into all-male units, or as *distractive* to male soldiers, who, it is assumed, may react more emotionally to the injury or death of a woman soldier than that of a man (Woodward and Winter, 2004; Basham, 2009a).[3] Though the evidence overwhelmingly suggests that soldiers bond through a shared commitment to tasks and military commands and not interpersonal links (*inter alia* MacCoun et al., 2006; King, 2006; Basham, 2009a), and that women often contribute to rather than undermine cohesion (Harrell and Miller, 1997; Kier, 1998; Ministry of Defence UK, 2002), by virtue of 'being non-men' women are 'intrinsically' problematic for state militaries (Woodward and Winter, 2006, p. 57). Combat exclusions, whether historical or ongoing, mean that combat remains the primary measure of women's abilities (Kovitz, 2003). Women in more combat-focused roles or those opting for close combat are gender non-conformists and they often find themselves subject to harassment and discrimination as a result (Basham, 2013).

BOYS WILL BE BOYS

The exclusion of women from close combat in spite of the evidence on cohesion and social demands for equality demonstrates the power that armed forces exercise *vis-à-vis* their role in applying state-sanctioned violence (Dandeker and Mason, 1999; Basham, 2009a, 2009b). Indeed, such dispensations saturate military culture with a sense of entitlement, contributing to their, at times, rather anti-democratic yet dogged insistence that they have a need to be different from the society they serve.[4] This attitude is especially discernible in the ways that military authorities tolerate and indeed *encourage* certain types of misbehavior by servicemen. The US military suggested 'boys were simply being boys' when dozens of women aviators were sexually harassed and assaulted by servicemen during the 1991 Tailhook incident (Kasinsky, 1998); when a 12-year-old Okinawan girl was raped by three US military personnel in 1995, Commander of the Asia-Pacific Forces Admiral Richard Macke pronounced, 'What fools! ... for the price they paid to rent the car [used to abduct and rape their victim], they could have had a girl [prostitute]' (quoted in Takazato, 2000, p. 43). Following the 1994 rape and murder of Danish tour guide Louise Jensen in the holiday resort of Ayia Napa by British soldiers, military commanders insisted the problem was that the soldiers were cooped up, easily frustrated and bored (Enloe, 2000). The normalization of sexual abuse, or merely promiscuity, among military men, especially when contrasted to the idea of women soldiers as disruptive sexual objects, demonstrates the perceived importance of sex to motivating servicemen. Whereas other rule-breaking behavior such as stealing is not tolerated, the denigration of women, because of its perceived value in sustaining the hegemonically masculine culture of militaries, not only frequently goes unchecked, but is enabled.

It is not only following incidents of extreme (sexual) violence against women (and indeed men – see Whitworth, 2004) that this is the case. Everyday practices involving the denigration of women and the reinforcement of hyper-masculinity are also frequently overlooked or encouraged by military commanders, despite being officially banned. Military authorities facilitate or overlook the desires of soldiers for 'birds, booze and brawling' (Hockey, 1986) through measures such as sexually denigrating women through language in training, providing cheap alcohol in military messes[5] and overlooking altercations between soldiers and locals in garrison towns the world over. Western militaries also have longstanding relationships with prostitution; from the Cantonments Act of 1864, which structured the sex trade within British military garrisons in India as part of a broader plan to regulate commercial activities in military towns (Enloe, 2000), to ensuring that prostitutes were 'organized to service' British servicemen in Belize in the 1980s (Kane, 1993, p. 966), to ongoing visits by US Navy warships to Pattaya, Thailand for 'rest and relaxation' which have regularly recurred since the Vietnam War. Throughout history 'military authorities, with varying degrees of covertness' have not only overlooked the sexual appetites of servicemen but have actively sought 'to provide outlets for the sexual needs of their men ... highlighting the well-established gendered contrasts between active masculine animality and female passivity' (Morgan, 1994, pp. 166–7).

The creation and perpetuation of rumors about the sex lives of servicewomen by servicemen has also been identified as a significant form of gendered harassment in the US and UK militaries (Miller, 1997; Basham, 2013). Whereas sexual bragging and sex are deemed normal for any red-blooded male, women soldiers are promiscuous and deviant. While women's bodies fulfill a symbolic, and integral, role in male military bonding, their actual presence is a different matter. Women's bodies are also often regarded as weak, leaky and reproductively prob-lematic (*inter alia* Theweleit, 1987; Miller, 1997; Van Creveld, 2000a; Czerwinski et al., 2001; Höpfl, 2003; Taber, 2005), reinforcing the idea that women are not naturally suited to military service whereas men are (Basham, 2013). Servicemen often perceive militaries 'as being in essence "macho" and physically demanding' and women as 'not strong enough physically or emotionally to do the job to the required standards' (Rutherford et al., 2006, p. 9; see also Taber, 2005; Sasson-Levy, 2008).

Each of these mythologies reproduces state militaries as masculinized institutions. The capabilities of individual servicewomen are always secondary to upholding the self-identity of armed forces and in this sense, women's bodies not only reinforce the hegemony of men as a social grouping in the military, but also men's rightful place as society's warriors. Though the military is by no means the only site where all-male groups tell sexual jokes, stories of sexual conquest, share pornography and denigrate women (Higate, 2003b), these activities can make men of recruits in military environments (Morgan, 1987). Furthermore, when situated within wider, axiomatic narratives about the life and death stakes of military service they neutralize challenges to existing military prac-tices. These gendered practices enable war-making; they make hyper-masculine responses to global conflict that little bit more reasonable (Tickner, 2002). Militaries pander to the desires of military men not because they need to maintain fragile bonds between them, but because they need to maintain the military's institutional identity as a masculine domain in which real men are prepared to fight.

HETEROSEXUAL POTENCY

In December 2010, the US Senate repealed the US military's 'Don't Ask, Don't Tell, Don't Harass' policy,[6] which had been in effect since the early 1990s. The policy meant that any member of the US forces who did not self-identify as heterosexual could be discharged if their sexual orientation was disclosed. Not asking, telling or harassing someone about their sexual orientation was therefore imperative, although evidence suggests that harassment was common and often vicious (Frank, 2009). Up until 2000, the British armed forces also routinely excluded sexual minorities from its ranks. Homosexuality was 'considered incompatible with service in the Armed Forces'; it was thought to 'cause offence, polarise relationships, induce ill-discipline, and, as a consequence, damage morale and unit effectiveness' (Ministry of Defence UK, 1996, p. 7). It was only after a 1999 European Court of Human Rights ruling that the British military had contravened the right of sexual minorities 'to respect for private and family life' (Council of Europe, 1950)[7] that the policy was overturned. Right up until the day before the ruling, military commanders resisted (Belkin and Evans, 2000). This is perhaps unsurprising given that the British military characterized sexual minorities as 'threats' to operational effectiveness (Ministry of Defence UK, 1996) and national security (Skidmore, 1998); as 'ill' (Belkin and Evans, 2000); 'unnatural' (Muir, 1992; Heggie, 2003); and sexually predatory, especially towards younger recruits (Muir, 1992; Ministry of Defence UK, 1996; Belkin and Evans, 2000; Heggie, 2003).

Though the idea of uniform heterosexuality has always functioned more 'at the level of rhetoric rather than reality' in militaries (Higate, 2003a, p. 209; see also Simpson and Zeeland, 2000; Frank, 2009; Bulmer, 2013), and evidence suggests the inclusion of sexual minorities has had no impact on military effectiveness (*inter alia* Frank et al., 2010), militaries continue to be sites where a demand for heterosexual potency is evident. The private/public dichotomy, much critiqued by feminist scholars for relegating women to the private sphere as an apolitical site that makes 'possible the masculine space of public' (Masters, 2009, p. 33), is also 'perhaps the most fundamental spatiality of sexual citizenship' (Bell and Binnie, 2000, p. 4). As Braidotti (2002, p. 80) notes, 'the economic, cultural and symbolic importance that Western culture has attributed to sexuality' means that sexual difference has become a central, though hardly unique, site for the constitution of subjectivity. Indeed, Western thought and culture are structured and fractured by 'a chronic, now endemic crisis of homo/heterosexual definition, indicatively male, dating from the end of the nineteenth century' (Sedgwick, 2008, p. 1) when the 'homosexual became a personage' (Foucault, 1990, p. 43). Indeed, the principal way in which gender regulates people's daily lives is through the fiction of binary sexualities, the hetero and the homo. In excluding sexual minorities from their ranks, militaries have reinforced heteronormativity, 'a discursively produced pressure that requires everybody to position oneself' in relation to a salient and prevalent notion of what constitutes heterosexuality on a daily basis (Motschenbacher, 2010, p. 16). Heteronormativity constructs a 'presumptively heterosexual world' (Chamallas, 1998, p. 309) and thus has the potential to marginalize anyone who does not fit neatly with assumptions about the normalcy of heterosexuality.

The 'inscription of heterosexuality into all aspects of culture' in armed forces persists, even in those militaries where sexual minorities are admitted (Higate, 2003a, p. 209; Basham, 2013). From uniform regulations that 'satisfy a male definition of attractiveness', and only make sense 'within a heteronormative paradigm' (Skidmore, 2004, p. 234), to evidence that disclosing a minority sexual orientation is seen as 'ramming homosexuality down people's throats' (Heggie, 2003; Basham, 2013), the normalization of 'straightness' continues. As scholars of hegemonic masculinity have suggested, whilst it often benefits men through the control of women it affords, perhaps the 'crucial difference between hegemonic masculinity and other masculinities ... is the control of men' it facilitates (Donaldson, 1993, p. 655). This may explain why some gay men in hyper-masculine institutions engage in the same 'quest for accomplishing and proving their masculinity' as their heterosexual counterparts; why they perform hegemonic or aspirant masculinities in order to avoid being 'unmasked' (Kaplan and Ben-Ari, 2000, p. 428; Carver, 2006; Yeung et al., 2006).

Whilst heterosexuality may be the norm in state militaries, 'homoeroticism ... [has played] a long-standing part in the military bonding experience' (Snyder, 1999, p. 153; see also *inter alia* Zeeland, 1995; Wither, 2004; Whitworth, 2004). For example, various state navies participate in versions of the ceremony known as 'crossing the line', an officially prohibited but tolerated and commonly practiced ritual which has been conducted since at least the sixteenth century. Crossing the line takes place when naval vessels pass through the equator; it usually involves heavy drinking, nudity, the ritual humiliation of junior recruits and the simulation of sexual acts, particularly anilingus in which sailors retrieve objects from other sailors' anuses (Hersh, 2002; Bronner, 2006).

Others have argued that the significance of hazing and homoeroticism to 'fratriarchy', or 'the rule of brothers' in militaries and other macho, heteronormative enclaves warrants further consideration (Higate, 2012). Belkin (2012) demonstrates how the 'embrace of the unmasculine' is just as significant to the performance of heterosexual masculinity in armed forces as the marginalization of sexual minorities and women; and Bulmer (2013) has shown how the integration of sexual minorities can simultaneously reproduce and trouble military patriarchy rather than fully subverting or being subsumed by it. The policing of hetero/homo boundaries – what Eve Sedgwick (2008) famously refers to as the epistemology of the closet – therefore reveals much about the need to maintain the innocence of homosocial/homoerotic practices in militaries and the complexities involved in doing so. Following Sedgwick, Kaplan (2005, p. 573) has argued that male 'emotional and sexual expression is often suppressed in the interest of maintaining power', and one of the primary effects of the hetero/homo binary is to inculcate fears about the uncertainty and ambivalence that surrounds sexual orientation (Sedgwick, 1985),[8] so that the unmasculine must, rather than being rejected outright, necessarily be recovered as a masculine pursuit. For servicemen, rituals and practices with homoerotic overtones might be best thought of therefore as 'a semi-arbitrary form of communication, involving multiple markers of humor and aggression that serve to produce and validate closeness and affection', rather than being an indication of repressed homosexuality, for example, though the latter is of course possible (Kaplan, 2005, p. 591). Gestures and practices involving sexual simula-tions and nudity when represented by the male soldiers engaged in them as jokes can thus enable them to express closeness, friendship and a desire for one another, without fear they will be labeled gay. A primary reason for marginalizing or denying gay personnel is, therefore, 'to protect homoerotic military rituals' so boys can play with boys, 'and not get called queers, and not get called girls' (Zeeland, 1995, p. 6; see also Britton and Williams, 1995; Snyder, 1999). Acknowledging the presence of a gay man in an all-male unit could threaten 'the possibilities for love among heterosexual men' (Phelan, 2001, p. 61); and so where 'male bonding is prescribed, homosexuality is proscribed' (Tosh, 2005, p. 38).

Homoerotic rituals are not actually necessary to motivate soldiers to fight but they do form a significant part of the social activities that take place between men engaged in organized violence. Militaries are keen to accommodate these desires as a way for soldiers to 'let off steam' because of the salience of the notion that men make the best warriors, and the difficulties militaries face in motivating soldiers to fight. The desires of servicemen, who consider themselves heterosexual, to engage in homoerotic practices necessitates the denial or exclusion of those – gay men, and women of any sexual orientation – whose sexuality (whether real or imagined) would undermine the innocence of these acts. Whilst homoeroticism and homosociability may be supplementary to the actual application of violence, the thrill of toying with sexual boundaries can facilitate social capital for the male heterosexual majority and in doing so reinforce the military's heterosexual and masculine institutional identity. Therefore when in the military, masculinity, homophobia, desire and homoeroticism all 'work in tandem to create a climate in which violent and demeaning hazing practices are more likely to be tolerated and even considered beneficial for young men' (Allan, 2004, p. 282), this amalgamation of social practices can also work to the benefit of a wider assumed geopolitical system in which real men fight.

CONCLUSION

Since their emergence in the seventeenth century, state militaries have been sites where associations between men, masculinity, violence and power have been normalized and habitually reproduced. Though men involved in military and militarized activities are in no way homo-geneous, and a multitude of performed identities co-exist in armed forces, the historical, political, social and cultural association of men with war, their embodied status as men, and social discourses on gender continue to converge in ways that enable and privilege masculinized ways of being and ensure that hegemonic ideas about masculinity remain relevant to the conduct of war. This is particularly evident when considering the ways in which women and sexual minorities continue to be characterized as inimical to military effectiveness and culture. Militar-ies pander to the desires of military men not because of the need to maintain social bonds between male soldiers as such, but in order to maintain the military's institutional identity as a masculine domain in which real men are prepared to fight. This distinction is a rather subtle one: military readiness may not require gender and sexual uniformity but the desires of military men for a boys' club may function as a carrot of sorts that makes it easier for military institutions to motivate their predominantly male soldiers to engage in violence. The participation of women in combat remains contingent because women's bodies fulfill important symbolic roles in male bonding, even though their actual contributions to military service may be valuable and even valued by servicemen. Similarly, whilst the sexual orientation of a soldier has no discernible bearing on his or her capability to fight, the desire of heterosexual military men to avoid being labeled queer and to play with boys without the fear of being given this label means that heterosexuality remains integral to military culture and identity.

State militaries have been and still are often able to evade some societal norms regardless of social, political and legislative challenges to the exclusivity of the military as a masculine domain. This is because as *the* institution responsible for conducting wars at the behest of and on behalf of the state, military authorities often claim that interfering with military culture and organization is a matter of life and death. As such, the desires of (heterosexual) military men to wage war continue to be prioritized by militaries. Perhaps, therefore, the most important function of the reinforcement of longstanding military norms, in which heteronormativity and masculine domination are promoted, is to make the very existence of militaries possible by normalizing war as a manly pursuit.

NOTES

1. For example, among the four largest financial contributors to NATO, women account for just 14 percent of military strength in the United States, 8.8 percent in Germany, 9.7 percent in the UK and 15.2 percent in France (NATO, 2012).
2. The most recent review of this exclusion in the UK, which took place in 2010, concluded that although the research on the impact of introducing women into all-male combat units was inconclusive, the exclusion of women from close combat roles should continue as a 'precautionary' measure (Ministry of Defence UK, 2010, p. 4).
3. The notion that servicemen would react in an exceptionally emotional way if a woman was injured has long made the rounds in many state militaries (Gal, 1986; Adie, 2006). It flies in the face of popular culture and personal accounts of war that characterize infantrymen as bands of brothers who leave no man behind.
4. See Dandeker (2000) for a discussion of 'the need to be different' and also Forster (2006) for more recent challenges to this in the UK.
5. Excessive alcohol consumption is more prevalent in the British military than in the general population, particularly among young, single men of the lower ranks (Fear et al., 2007).
6. The policy was mandated by US federal law, hence the need for the US Senate to approve its repeal.
7. The Convention was incorporated into British law via the 1998 Human Rights Act.
8. Belkin (2012) argues that the US military's (now repealed) Don't Ask, Don't Tell, Don't Harass policy, and the confusion, uncertainty and ambivalence it fostered, is implicated in male-on-male rape and other forms of sexual abuse between men.

REFERENCES

Adie, Kate (2006), 'A woman's place is at the front', *Daily Telegraph*, online edition, 9 May 2006, accessed 4 January 2012 at: http://www.telegraph.co.uk/culture/books/3652235/A-womans-place-is-at-the-front.html.

Adult Learning Inspectorate (2007), *Better Training: Managing Risks to the Welfare of Recruits in the British Armed Services: Two Years of Progress*, Adult Learning Inspectorate.

Allan, Elizabeth J. (2004), 'Hazing and gender: analyzing the obvious', in Hank Nuwer (ed.), *The Hazing Reader*, Indiana University Press, pp. 275–94.

Atherton, Stephen (2009), 'Domesticating military masculinities: home, performance and the negotiation of identity', *Social & Cultural Geography*, **10** (8): 821–36.

Barrett, Frank J. (2001), 'The organizational construction of hegemonic masculinity: the case of the US Navy', in S.M. Whitehead and F.J. Barrett (eds), *The Masculinities Reader*, Polity, pp. 77–99.

Basham, Victoria M. (2009a), 'Effecting discrimination: operational effectiveness and harassment in the British armed forces', *Armed Forces and Society*, **35** (4): 728–44.

Basham, Victoria M. (2009b), 'Harnessing social diversity in the British armed forces: the limitations of "management" approaches', *Commonwealth & Comparative Politics*, **47** (4): 411–29.

Basham, Victoria M. (2013), *War, Identity and the Liberal State: Everyday Experiences of the Geopolitical in the Armed Forces*, Routledge.

Belkin, Aaron (2012), *Bring Me Men: Military Masculinity and the Benign Façade of American Empire, 1898–2001*, Hurst.

Belkin, Aaron and R.L. Evans (2000), *The Effects of Including Gay and Lesbian Soldiers in the British Armed Forces: Appraising the Evidence*, University of California at Santa Barbara.

Bell, David and Jon Binnie (2000), *The Sexual Citizen: Queer Politics and Beyond*, Polity.

Bibbings, Lois S. (2003), 'Images of manliness: the portrayal of soldiers and conscientious objectors in the Great War', *Social and Legal Studies*, **12** (3): 335–58.

Bourke, Joanna (1999), *An Intimate History of Killing: Face-to-Face Killing in Twentieth-Century Warfare*, Granta.

Braidotti, Rosa (2002), *Metamorphoses: Towards a Materialist Theory of Becoming*, Polity.

Britton, Dana M. and Christine L. Williams (1995), 'Don't ask, don't tell, don't pursue: military policy and the construction of heterosexual masculinity', *Journal of Homosexuality*, **30** (1): 1–21.

Bronner, Simon J. (2006), *Crossing the Line: Violence, Play, and Drama in Naval Equator Traditions*, Amsterdam University Press.

Bulmer, Sarah (2013), 'Patriarchal confusion? Making sense of gay and lesbian military identity', *International Feminist Journal of Politics*, **15** (2): 137–56.

Carver, Terrell (2006), 'Being a man', *Government and Opposition*, **41** (3): 477–95.

Chamallas, Martha (1998), 'The new gender panic: reflections on sex scandals and the military', *Minnesota Law Review*, **83** (2): 305–75.

Cohn, Carol (1987), 'Sex and death in the rational world of defense intellectuals', *Signs: Journal of Women in Culture and Society*, **12** (4): 687–718.

Cohn, Carol (1993), 'Wars, wimps, and women: talking gender and thinking war', in Miriam Cooke and Angela Woollacott (eds), *Gendering War Talk*, Princeton University Press, pp. 227–46.

Connell, Raewyn W. (1987), *Gender and Power: Society, the Person, and Sexual Politics*, Polity.

Connell, Raewyn W. (1995), *Masculinities*, Polity.

Connell, Raewyn W. (2000), *The Men and The Boys*, Polity.

Conway, Daniel (2004), 'Every coward's choice? Political objection to military service in Apartheid South Africa as sexual citizenship', *Citizenship Studies*, **8** (1): 25–45.

Council of Europe (1950), *European Convention for the Protection of Human Rights and Fundamental Freedoms*, Rome, 4.XI.

Czerwinski, B.S., D.W. Wardell, L.H. Yoder, L.M. Connelly, M. Ternus, K. Pitts and K. Kouzekanani (2001), 'Variations in feminine hygiene practices of women in deployed and non-combat environments', *Military Medicine*, **166** (2): 152–8.

Dandeker, Christopher (2000), 'On the need to be different: recent trends in military culture', in Hew Strachan (ed.), *The British Army, Manpower and Society into the Twenty-First Century*, Frank Cass, pp. 173–87.

Dandeker, Christopher and David Mason (1999), 'Diversity in the UK armed forces: the debate about the representation of women and minority ethnic groups', in Joseph Soeters and Jan van der Meulen (eds), *Managing Diversity in the Armed Forces: The Experience of Nine Countries*, Tilburg University Press, pp. 55–71.

Dawson, Graham (1994), *Soldier Heroes: British Adventure, Empire and the Imagining of Masculinities*, Routledge.

Donaldson, Mike (1993), 'What is hegemonic masculinity?', *Theory and Society*, **22** (5): 643–57.

Elshtain, Jean Bethke (1995), *Women and War*, 2nd edn, University of Chicago Press.

Enloe, Cynthia (1988), *Does Khaki Become You? The Militarization of Women's Lives*, Pandora.

Enloe, Cynthia (2000), *Manoeuvres: The International Politics of Militarizing Women's Lives*, University of California Press.

Enloe, Cynthia (2004), *The Curious Feminist: Searching for Women in a New Age of Empire*, University of California Press.

Farough, Steven (2003), 'Structural aporias and white masculinities: white men confront the white male privilege critique', *Race, Gender & Class*, **10** (4): 38–53.

Farrell, Theo (1998), 'Culture and military power', *Review of International Studies*, **24** (3): 407–16.

Fear, N.T., A. Iversen, H. Meltzer, L. Workman, L. Hull, N. Greenberg, C. Barker, T. Browne, M. Earnshaw, O. Horn, M. Jones, D. Murphy, R.J. Rona, M. Hotopf and S. Wessely (2007), 'Patterns of drinking in the UK Armed Forces', *Addiction*, **102**: 1749–59.

Feinman, Ilene R. (1998), 'Women warriors/women peacemakers: will the real feminists please stand up!', in Lois A. Lorentzen and Jennifer Turpin (eds), *The Women and War Reader*, New York University Press, pp. 132–9.

Forster, Anthony (2006), 'Breaking the covenant: governance of the British Army in the twenty-first century', *International Affairs*, **82** (6): 1101–15.

Foucault, Michel (1990), *The History of Sexuality Volume One: An Introduction*, trans. R. Hurley, Penguin.

Frank, Nathaniel (2009), *Unfriendly Fire: How the Gay Ban Undermines the Military and Weakens America*, Thomas Dunne and St Martin's.

Frank, Nathaniel with Victoria M. Basham, Geoffrey Bateman, Aaron Belkin, Margot Canaday, Alan Okros and Denise Scott (2010), *Gays in Foreign Militaries 2010: A Global Primer*, University of California at Santa Barbara.

Frost, Gerald (2001), 'How to destroy an army: the cultural subversion of Britain's Armed Forces', in Alex Alexandrou, Richard Bartle and Richard Holmes (eds), *New People Strategies for the British Armed Forces*, Frank Cass, pp. 37–48.

Gal, Reuven (1986), *A Portrait of the Israeli Soldier*, Greenwood.

Gat, Azar (2000), 'Female participation in war: bio-cultural interactions', *The Journal of Strategic Studies*, **23** (4): 21–31.

Goldstein, Joshua S. (2001), *War and Gender: How Gender Shapes the War System and Vice Versa*, Cambridge University Press.

Green, Gill, Carol Emslie, Dan O'Neill, Kate Hunt and Steven Walker (2010), 'Exploring the ambiguities of masculinity in accounts of emotional distress in the military among young ex-servicemen', *Social Science and Medicine*, **71**: 1480–88.

Gutterman, David S. (2001), 'Postmodernism and the interrogation of masculinity', in Stephen M. Whitehead and Frank J. Barrett (eds), *The Masculinities Reader*, Polity, pp. 56–71.

Hale, Hannah C. (2008), 'The development of British military masculinities through symbolic resources', *Culture & Psychology*, **14** (3): 305–32.

Harrell, Margaret C. and Laura L. Miller (1997), *New Opportunities for Military Women: Effects upon Readiness, Cohesion and Morale*, RAND.

Harrison, Deborah and Lucie Laliberté (1997), 'Gender, the military, and military family support', in Laurie Weinstein and Christie C. White (eds), *Wives and Warriors: Women and the Military in the United States and Canada*, Bergin and Garvey, pp. 35–53.

Heggie, Joan K.F. (2003), *Uniform Identity? Lesbians and the Negotiation of Gender & Sexuality in the British Army Since 1950*, unpublished PhD thesis, University of York.

Hersh, Carie L. (2002), 'Crossing the line: sex, power, justice, and the US Navy at the equator', *Duke Journal of Gender, Law & Policy*, 9: 277–324.

Higate, Paul R. (1998), 'The body resists: everyday clerking and unmilitary practice', in Sarah Nettleton and Jonathan Watson (eds), *The Body in Everyday Life*, Routledge, pp. 180–98.

Higate, Paul R. (2003a), 'Concluding thoughts: looking to the future', in Paul R. Higate (ed.), *Military Masculinities: Identity and the State*, Praeger, pp. 201–16.

Higate, Paul R. (2003b), '"Soft clerks" and "hard civvies": pluralizing military masculinities', in Paul R. Higate (ed.), *Military Masculinities: Identity and the State*, Praeger, pp. 27–42.

Higate, Paul R. (2012), 'Drinking vodka from the butt-crack', *International Feminist journal of Politics*, 14 (4): 450–69.

Hockey, John (1986), *Squaddies: Portrait of a Subculture*, Exeter University Publications.

Hockey, John (2003), 'No more heroes: masculinity in the infantry', in Paul R. Higate (ed.), *Military Masculinities: Identity and the State*, Praeger, pp. 15–25.

Holmes, Richard (2003), *Acts of War: The Behaviour of Men in Battle*, 2nd edn, Cassell.

Hooper, Charlotte (1999), 'Masculinities, IR and the "gender variable": a cost benefit analysis for (sympathetic) gender sceptics', *Review of International Studies*, 25 (3): 475–91.

Höpfl, Heather J. (2003), 'Becoming a (virile) member: women and the military body', *Body & Society*, 9 (4): 13–30.

Janowitz, Morris (1974), *Sociology and the Military Establishment*, 3rd edn, in collaboration with Roger W. Little, Sage.

Jones, Adam (2006), 'Straight as a rule: heteronormativity, gendercide, and the non-combatant male', *Men and Masculinities*, 8 (4): 451–69.

Kaldor, Mary (1999), *New and Old Wars: Organized Violence in a Global Era*, Polity.

Kane, Stephanie C. (1993), 'Prostitution and the military: planning AIDS intervention in Belize', *Social Science and Medicine*, 36 (7): 965–79.

Kaplan, Danny (2005), 'Public intimacy: dynamics of seduction in male homosocial interactions', *Symbolic Interaction*, 28 (4): 571–95.

Kaplan, Danny (2006), *The Men We Loved: Male Friendship and Nationalism in Israeli Culture*, Berghahn Books.

Kaplan, Danny and Eyal Ben-Ari (2000), 'Brothers and others in arms: managing gay identity in combat units of the Israeli Army', *Journal of Contemporary Ethnography*, 29 (4): 396–432.

Kasinsky, Renée G. (1998), 'Tailhook and the construction of sexual harassment in the media: "rowdy boys" and women who made a difference', *Violence Against Women*, 4 (1): 81–99.

Kennedy-Pipe, Caroline (2000), 'Women and the military', *The Journal of Strategic Studies*, 23 (4): 32–50.

Kier, Elizabeth (1998), 'Homosexuals in the U.S. military: open integration and combat effectiveness', *International Security*, 23 (2): 5–39.

Kimmel, Michael S. (2004), *The Gendered Society*, 2nd edn, Oxford University Press.

King, Anthony (2006), 'The word of command: communication and cohesion in the military', *Armed Forces & Society*, 32 (4): 493–512.

Klein, Uta (2002), 'The gender perspective of civil–military relations in Israeli society', *Current Sociology*, 50 (5): 669–86.

Kovitz, Marcia (2003), 'The roots of military masculinity', in Paul R. Higate (ed.), *Military Masculinities: Identity and the State*, Praeger, pp. 1–14.

MacCoun, Robert J., Elizabeth Kier and Aaron Belkin (2006), 'Does social cohesion determine motivation in combat? An old question with an old answer', *Armed Forces & Society*, **32** (4): 646–54.

Malešević, Sinisa (2010), *The Sociology of War and Violence*, Cambridge University Press.

Masters, Cristina (2009), 'Femina Sacra: The "war on/of terror", women and the Feminine', *Security Dialogue*, **40** (1): 29–49.

Miller, Laura L. (1997), 'Not just weapons of the weak: gender harassment as a form of protest by army men', *Social Psychology Quarterly*, **69** (1): 32–51.

Ministry of Defence UK (1996), *Report of the Homosexuality Policy Assessment Team*, Ministry of Defence.

Ministry of Defence UK (2002), *Employment of Women in the Armed Forces Steering Group Report on Women in the Armed Forces*, Ministry of Defence.

Ministry of Defence UK (2010), *Report on the Review of the Exclusion of Women from Ground Close-Combat Roles*, Ministry of Defence.

Morgan, David H.J. (1987), *"It Will Make a Man of You": Notes on National Service, Masculinity, and Autobiography*, Sociology Department, University of Manchester.

Morgan, David H.J. (1994), 'Theater of war: combat, the military, and masculinities', in Harry Brod and Michael Kaufman (eds), *Theorizing Masculinities*, Sage, pp. 165–82.

Motschenbacher, Heiko (2010), *Language, Gender and Sexual Identity: Poststructuralist Perspectives*, John Benjamins.

Muir, Kate (1992), *Arms and the Woman*, Sinclair-Stevenson.

NATO (2012), *NATO Committee on Gender Perspectives: National Reports 2012*, accessed 22 August 2012 at: http://www.nato.int/cps/en/natolive/topics_101371.htm.

Noakes, Lucy (2006), *Women and the British Army: War and the Gentle Sex 1907–1948*, Routledge.

Phelan, Shane (2001), *Sexual Strangers: Gays, Lesbians, and Dilemmas of Citizenship*, Temple University Press.

Ruddick, Sara (1989), *Maternal Thinking: Towards a Politics of Peace*, The Women's Press.

Rutherford, Sarah, Robin Schneider and Alexis Walmsley (2006), *Ministry of Defence/ Equal Opportunities Commission Agreement on Preventing & Dealing Effectively with Sexual Harassment: Quantitative & Qualitative Research into Sexual Harassment in the Armed Forces*, Schneider-Ross.

Sasson-Levy, Orna (2003), 'Feminism and military gender practices: Israeli women soldiers in "masculine" roles', *Sociological Inquiry*, **73** (3): 440–65.

Sasson-Levy, Orna (2008), 'Individual bodies, collective state interests: the case of Israeli combat soldiers', *Men and Masculinities*, **10** (3): 296–321.

Sedgwick, Eve K. (1985), *Between Men: English Literature and Male Homosocial Desire*, Columbia University Press.

Sedgwick, Eve K. (2008), *Epistemology of the Closet*, University of California Press.

Segal, Mady Wechsler (1995), 'Women's military roles cross-nationally: past, present and future', *Gender and Society*, **9** (6): 757–75.

Simpson, Mark and Steven Zeeland (2000), *The Queen is Dead: A Tale of Jarheads, Eggheads, Serial Killers & Bad Sex*, Arcadia.

Sjoberg, Laura and Gentry, Caron E. (2007), *Mothers, Monsters, Whores*, Zed Books.

Skidmore, Paul (1998), 'Sexuality and the UK armed forces: judicial review of the ban on homosexuality', in Terrell Carver and Veronique Mottier (eds), *Politics of Sexuality: Identity, Gender, Citizenship*, Routledge, pp. 46–57.

Skidmore, Paul (2004), 'A legal perspective on sexuality and organization: a lesbian and gay case study', *Gender, Work and Organization*, **11** (3): 229–53.

Snyder, Claire R. (1999), *Citizen Soldiers and Manly Warriors: Military Service and Gender in the Civic Republican Tradition*, Rowman & Littlefield.

Snyder, Claire R. (2003), 'The citizen-soldier tradition and gender integration of the U.S. military', *Armed Forces and Society*, **29** (2): 185–204.

Stiehm, Judith Hicks (1982), 'The protected, the protector, the defender', *Women's Studies International Forum*, **5** (3/4): 367–76.

Taber, Nancy (2005), 'Learning how to be a woman in the Canadian forces/unlearning it through feminism: an autoethnography of my learning journey', *Studies in Continuing Education*, **27** (3): 289–301.

Takazato, Suzuyo (2000), 'Report from Okinawa: long term US military presence and violence against women', *Canadian Woman Studies*, **19** (4): 42–7.

Theweleit, Klaus (1987), *Male Fantasies: Women, Floods, Bodies, History, Volume 1*, trans. Stephen Conway, Erica Carter and Chris Turner, Polity.

Tickner, J. Ann (1992), *Gender in International Relations*, Columbia University Press.

Tickner, J. Ann (2002), 'Feminist perspectives on 9/11', *International Studies Perspectives*, **3** (4): 333–50.

Tiffany, Jennifer (1981), 'Equal opportunity trap', in W. Chapkis (ed.), *Loaded Questions: Women in the Military*, Transnational Institute, pp. 36–9.

Tosh, John (2005), *Manliness and Masculinities in Nineteenth-Century Britain*, Pearson Longman.

Van Creveld, Martin (2000a), 'Less than we can be: men, women and the modern military', *The Journal of Strategic Studies*, **23** (4): 1–20.

Van Creveld, Martin (2000b), 'The great illusion: women in the military', *Millennium: Journal of International Studies*, **29** (2): 429–42.

Weber, Max (1991), 'Politics as a vocation', in Hans H. Gerth and C. Wright Mills (eds), *From Max Weber: Essays in Sociology*, Kegan Paul, pp. 77–128.

Whitworth, Sandra (2004), *Men, Militarism, and UN Peacekeeping: A Gendered Analysis*, Lynne Rienner.

Wither, James K. (2004), 'Dedovshchina and hazing abroad: battling bullying in the British Army 1987–2004', *The Journal of Power Institutions in Post-Soviet Societies*, vol.1, online journal, accessed 5 January 2012 at: http://pipss.revues.org/46?&id=46.

Woodward, Rachel (1998), 'It's a man's life! Soldiers, masculinity and the countryside', *Gender, Place and Culture*, **5** (3): 277–300.

Woodward, Rachel (2003), 'Locating military masculinities: space, place and the formation of gender in the British Army', in Paul R. Higate (ed.), *Military Masculinities: Identity and the State*, Praeger, pp. 43–55.

Woodward, Rachel and Trish Winter (2004), 'Discourses of gender in the contemporary British Army', *Armed Forces and Society*, **30** (2): 279–301.

Woodward, Rachel and Trish Winter (2006), 'Gender and the limits to diversity in the contemporary British Army', *Gender, Work and Organisation*, **13** (1): 45–67.

Woodward, Rachel and Trish Winter (2007), *Sexing the Soldier: The Politics of Gender and the Contemporary British Army*, Routledge.

Yeung, King-To, Mindy Stombler and Reneé Wharton (2006), 'Making men in gay fraternities: resisting and reproducing multiple dimensions of hegemonic masculinity', *Gender & Society*, **20** (1): 5–31.

Yuval-Davis, Nira (1997), *Gender & Nation*, Sage.

Zeeland, Steven (1995), *Sailors and Sexuality*, Haworth Press.

2. On the imagination of 'Woman' as killer in war

Linda Åhäll

> [T]he Americans and the British have been among the most reluctant to give up the male-only combat rule. Thus, it is they who have continued to invest the most political energy in defining and redefining exactly what constitutes 'combat'.
>
> (Enloe, 2007: 84)

The conduct of war may be purportedly about security and protection, justified in the name of self-defense or to uphold international legal norms, but it is ultimately also about death, destruction and the taking of lives. The taking of lives, however, is controversial if we move away from the idea that it is a male subject who kills. This is because in traditional, gendered stories of war, men make war and women keep the peace; men go to the front and women stay at home; men fight and women are fought for. Jean-Bethke Elshtain phrases these binary constructions of men and women's roles in war as the personae of 'Just Warriors' and 'Beautiful Souls' and the relationship as the 'myth of protection' (Elshtain, 1995: 4, see also Enloe, 2000; Young, 2003). In this way, ideas about heroism in war are typically intimately linked to men, masculinity and patriarchal values, and 'combat' is seen as the ultimate signifier of manliness.

In recent decades, however, women have become increasingly visible, not just as those passive victims in need of protection in war, but as active agents of warfare, as those offering protection as UN peacekeepers, soldiers in states' armed forces or as intelligence officers/spies, and also as perpetrators of political violence more broadly, including as rebels, 'terrorists' and suicide-bombers (see, for example, Alison, 2004; MacKenzie, 2009; Parashar, 2014). Despite the historical resistance, recently there have also been significant policy changes with regard to the roles of women and others in the Anglosphere armed forces. The January 2013 announcement by US Secretary of Defense Leon Panetta that the United States was to remove its ban on women in combat roles followed the 2011 repeal of the 'Don't Ask, Don't Tell' policy that prevented the openly gay and lesbians from serving in the US armed forces; the lifting of a ban on women in combat roles in Australia in 2011; and an announcement from the British Ministry of Defence (MoD) in 2011 that women were to be allowed to serve on submarines from 2013. Although the MoD's initial response to the 2013 change in policy in the United States was that there was no need to review the ban before the mandatory third review scheduled for 2018, in May 2014 UK Defence Secretary Philip Hammond announced an immediate review. These changes appear to communicate a shift in the imagination of which bodies can and cannot engage in violence.

In this chapter I explore the increased visibility of women's agency in warfare through the imagination of 'Woman' as killer in war. This is not uncontroversial, not least within feminist academic and activist circles that most often (and rightfully so) choose to emphasize women's agency in peacebuilding and resistance to war, violence and militarization. My aim, however, is to demonstrate how gender, embodied as the subject-position of 'Woman' as killer in war, is policing understandings about bodies and violence in war more broadly. To do this, I am using the capitalized, single form of 'Woman' to signal that it is about the subject of the female-identified body more generally, rather than about any particular female-identified body. Moreover, I explore gender as a discursive power relation, as a logic that informs and produces global politics and as a way of thinking about how bodies matter, rather than as a variable that can be quantified and measured, or a fixed identity category that individuals – usually by being defined (and self-identify) as either male or female, belong to. Importantly, while the concept of agency is traditionally understood as a capacity to act, I analyze agency as representations of agency in specific 'texts'.[1] This means that the focus of analysis is not how particular *individuals* act and whether this decision to act was taken on their own initiative, but about how *subjects* are positioned within particular discursive structures such as sentences, images, scenes. The difference between a focus on individuals and subjects is that an individual can have multiple subject positions, while several physical individuals can constitute a single subject. Therefore, rather than attempting to give a complete view of a particular character or individual woman, the chapter aims to make an argument about how women's bodies are culturally imagined – verbally, visually, emotionally – as the subject 'Woman as killer' in the context of war and violence.

I make sense of the cultural intelligibility of women as agents of political violence by thinking about borders: not material, geographical borders, but societal borders, such as what is deemed culturally appropriate for some bodies to do, or be, but not for others. I draw on scholars who, inspired by Julia Kristeva's theory of abjection,[2] explore subject formation through bordering practices of the political present. This can mean different things. While feminist film-theorist Barbara Creed, who analyzes how woman-as-monster is produced in horror-films, identifies 'the border' as that which separates those who take up their proper gender roles from those who do not; or between 'normal' and 'abnormal' sexual desire (Creed, 1999: 253), sociologist Imogen Tyler shows how the British state – through the design of citizenship and other neoliberal policies – relies on the production of internal, abject, others such as Gypsies and Travellers, failed asylum-seekers, anarchists and protest-movements to constitute itself and draw its borders (Tyler, 2013). The main point is that thinking about borders in this way, as fluid practices in our daily lives rather than something solid, puts focus on how the subject is continually made and undone.

In this chapter, the metaphor of a border is used as a way to highlight how gender as a logic functions as a 'border agent' policing understandings of bodies and violence in war. These culturally constituted bordering practices are both imaginary in the sense that they concern ideas about what certain bodies should or should not do, and real in the sense that these ideas have real-life implications for what certain bodies can or cannot do. Furthermore, as my analysis of representations of gender, agency and political violence focuses on cultural meanings of bodies, power and gender – which are by no means limited to written or verbal 'texts' – my discourse-theoretical analytical framework is inspired by scholars and thinkers who in different ways have engaged with visual, emotional and/or aesthetic representations of (global) politics (Barthes, 2000; Hall, 1997; Weber, 2005; Shapiro, 2013; Bleiker, 2001; Butler, 2011; Ahmed, 2004; Zalewski, 2013). What is more, as the increased visibility of women as agents of warfare is noticeable in policy decisions, in media news reporting as well as in fictional pop culture accounts, I have chosen to look into two, at first glance, very different empirical examples: a fictional Hollywood film and a British government policy. These might seem to have very little to do with one another; however, both offer insights into how gender, embodied as the image and imagination of 'Woman' as killer in war, is culturally made sense of.

I start by analyzing scenes from a recent example of the increased visibility of heroines of war: the Hollywood blockbuster *Zero Dark Thirty* (2012), which tells the fictional story of Maya, the female CIA agent at the center of the intelligence operation that leads to the killing of Osama Bin Laden in 2011. I show how the writing of Maya as a heroine of war above all takes place through an emphasis on her 'being a killer'. In the second part, I explore the subject-position of 'Woman as killer' in war further by turning my attention to the 2009/2010 review of the British ban on women in combat roles. Although this chapter shows how there is a discrepancy between the conclusions of the latest review of the British exclusion policy and the MoD's justification for keeping the ban, my argument is not primarily an intervention in the debate on whether or not women should be allowed in combat roles. The chapter takes an analysis of the political decision to keep the ban in 2010, rather than an analysis of the ban itself, as its starting point in order to problematize what this discrepancy might mean in relation to the imagination of 'Woman' as killer in war. The chapter concludes by calling on scholars of global politics to stay vigilant to how bodies reach, cross or transgress imagined cultural borders in the everyday as one way in which to make visible practices of global politics that would have otherwise remained hidden.

THE IMAGE OF A HEROINE OF WAR

Director Kathryn Bigelow and screenwriter Mark Boal were already working on a film on the topic of the failure of the hunt for Osama Bin Laden[3] when the announcement of his death was made. Thus, Boal 'went back to his sources in the intelligence community and started from scratch':

> After a few months, I heard through the grapevine that women played a big role in the CIA in general and in this team … I heard that a woman was there on the night of the raid as one of the CIA's liaison officers on the ground – and that was the start of it. (Boal, quoted in Hill, *Rolling Stone*, 2013)

According to Boal, Maya is 'based on a real person, but she also represents the work of a lot of other women' (Boal, quoted in Hill, *Rolling Stone*, 2013). Elsewhere, I have discussed how *Female Agents*, a (fictional) film about the women who served as secret agents when France was occupied by Nazi Germany in the Second World War, was promoted with the slogan 'In times of war heroism is not just for men' (see Åhäll, 2012a). Similarly, *Zero Dark Thirty* was advertised with the slogan 'For ten years one woman never stopped searching for the most wanted man in history' and as such it fits into recent attempts at making women's active contribution to warfare visible/known through a story of heroism.

Motherhood, Sex, Emotionality

In an article explaining how women's political violence is portrayed through narratives of sexual deviance that reduce the actors involved to 'bad sex', Laura Sjoberg and Caron Gentry argue there are two main themes. Either the violence is explained as caused by a woman's sexual obsession and uncontrollable need to have sex with men, or through the erotic dysfunction narrative in which women's violence is blamed on the fact that they are either unable or unwilling to please men. The story goes that women become emotionally disturbed and translate this emotional trouble into violence (Sjoberg and Gentry, 2008: 10). Although these two particular subject positions – hyper-sexual or asexual – are perhaps most common in stories about female 'terrorists' or murderesses, and as such about violence deemed illegitimate, these stories are also told about women serving in militaries as a way to explain away their defiance of traditional gender roles, as well as to present in recent fictional popular culture accounts of female spies as heroines of war. For example, the character Carrie, the brilliant CIA agent in the television series *Homeland*, would be an example of the first, whereas, as I will return to, the writing of Maya as a heroine in *Zero Dark Thirty* includes an erotic dysfunction narrative.

Discussing women's agency in (illegitimate) political violence, Sjoberg and Gentry show how the implication of the erotic dysfunction narrative is that women who commit violence are seen to do so because there is something wrong with them that stops them from fulfilling their (normal) biological destiny of becoming wives and mothers (Sjoberg and Gentry, 2008: 10). Drawing on Judith Butler, who explains that the maternal body is an effect of a discourse and performance that requires the 'female body ... to assume maternity as the essence of its self and the law of its desire' (Butler, 2006: 125), elsewhere I argue that the writing of heroines in war as subjects with agency ultimately depends on whether a tension between life-giving and life-taking can be overcome (Åhäll, 2012a, 2015). In this sense, female subjects whose agency in political violence is explained through stories of erotic dysfunction have failed their gendered 'essence'. Importantly, however, such stories of a 'removal' or 'lack' of actual motherhood often involve an alternative motherhood narrative, as the following conversation between Maya and Jessica shows:

Maya walks in with eyes fixed on her phone.

Jessica: 'Maya, we're socialising, be social.'

Maya sits down and sighs.

Jessica: 'Look, I know Abu Ahmed is your baby, but it's time to cut the umbilical cord.'

Then, we learn some more information about Maya's personal life. Jessica asks Maya if she and Dan (her superior) 'have hooked up yet'.

> Maya: 'Hello, I work with him. I'm *not the girl that fucks.*'
>
> Jessica: 'So? Fooling around wouldn't hurt you.'
>
> [Maya sighs]
>
> Jessica: 'So, no boyfriend?'

Maya mumbles 'No', whereupon Jessica asks: '*Have you got any friends at all?*' Maya fails to answer, seemingly uninterested in any type of close relationship. In fact, Maya is predominantly portrayed as a loner with no friends, a socially awkward outsider. This is also displayed in a later scene, where the CIA Director approaches Maya while she's having lunch, alone, in the canteen:

> CIA Director: 'How long have you been working for us?'
>
> Maya: 'I was recruited out of high school'
>
> CIA Director: 'And you know why we did that?'
>
> Maya: 'I don't think I can answer that question, Sir.'
>
> CIA Director: 'Alright, what else have you done for us, beside Bin Laden?'
>
> Maya: 'Nothing, I've done nothing else.' [Melancholic music in the background]

The writing of Maya as a loner is calling upon the audience to feel sorry for her, or at least to recognize that she is 'different'. Maya's unwillingness or lack of interest in having sex with men means that she also refuses to perform the (perceived) basic function in heteronormative life: to sleep with men, to marry men and to become a mother. At the same time, the story of Maya involves a motherhood narrative: her lead in the hunt for Bin Laden, Abu Ahmed, is 'her baby'. Thus, Maya's purpose in life is not to give life, to be a mother as 'normal' women are; instead, it is her work, the hunt for Bin Laden, that is her main priority in life. Above all though, similarly to how women's motivations for committing violence are often portrayed in personal narratives (see for example Brunner, 2005; Eager, 2008), the focus on Maya's relationships and the inclusion of an alternative motherhood narrative works to make 'a woman's political decision not about strategy or politics but about emotions and relationship' (Gentry, 2009: 247). On the one hand, Maya is portrayed as someone highly committed to, and passionate about, her job, as well as very confident in her own capability as an intelligence agent. For example, in a meeting at the CIA Headquarters, and this scene is also part of the official trailer of the film, the CIA Director asks whether or not Bin Laden is in the suspected compound. A CIA officer says: 'We don't deal with certainty, we deal with probability and there's a 60 per cent probability he's there.' The other men in the room concur that the chance is between 60 and 80 percent, but from her position in the back of the room, Maya confidently intervenes:

> Maya: 'It's a 100. [Pauses] Ok, 95 per cent. I know certainty freaks you guys out, but it's a hundred.'

In the first series of *Homeland*, Carrie – the other contemporary fictional female CIA agent – also is brilliant because she 'knows' that the male main character, Brody, has turned; though no one believes her (see Zalewski, 2015). In this way, both Maya and Carrie act intuitively but their conviction of what is correct intelligence is not necessarily shared by others. Maya is obsessed with the hunt for Bin Laden, something that is also portrayed through her frustration that seemingly very little happens even though a potential compound has been identified. Maya approaches her boss at the CIA Headquarters:

> Maya: 'Morning George, 21 days since we found the house, nothing has happened!'

Maya writes the number '21' with a red marker pen and circles it on the see-through partition wall to his office. Then, we see her erase '51' and rewrite '52'. Later we see her write '78', '98' and '100!!!', and in yet another scene, again we see Maya impatiently writing a new number in red on George's glass wall. She writes fast, aggressively, underlines the number and walks off purposefully. In the last scene, George is in the room with 'Wolf', a shadowy high-ranking US government official, who says: 'It's her against the world', whereupon George says: 'O'yeah' and nods. In these scenes, Maya's actions are not simply communicated through emotionality and stubbornness, but her emotional behavior is erratic, neurotic, close to hysterical. This is not just describing someone who is 'normally' passionate about their job. Still, while Carrie's erratic and excessive behavior in *Homeland* is categorized as a form of madness (she has bipolar disorder, is on medication and given electroconvulsive therapy towards the end of season one) (Zalewski, 2015: 37), Maya's obsession is not portrayed as mental instability but the depiction of her being upset associates her with feminized hyper-emotionality.

Perhaps most importantly for the writing of Maya as a (hyper-) emotional subject, however, are the very last scenes of the film where she is actually crying. After the successful mission, Maya goes to unzip the body bag that the team of Navy Seals have brought back. She is shown breathing heavily as she nods to confirm the identification of the corpse of Bin Laden. She walks outside, sits down and closes her eyes. While Maya's emotionality could be interpreted as feelings of relief that the mission was a success and that all the guys came back alive, it rather portrays a sense of personal closure or ending. When Maya, alone, is boarding a huge military aircraft, the pilot asks her where she wants to go. Maya doesn't respond. As the camera zooms in on her face, melancholic music is playing in the background and Maya starts to cry. She is lost. Everything she has worked for in her career, to find and kill Bin Laden, that which has defined who she is, is over. In effect, she also is dead.

While the various subject-positions discussed so far play into stereo-typical character traits for women in war according to the gendered war story – the hyper-emotional narrative associates her with femininity but the erotic dysfunction narrative ultimately writes her as different from heteronormative femininity associated with motherhood – it is primarily another subject-position/character trait that facilitates the writing of Maya as a heroine of war: Maya is 'a killer'.

'She's a Killer!'

Zero Dark Thirty starts with voice recordings of some of the actual emergency phone calls from the 9/11 terrorist attacks before showing fictionalized scenes of 'enhanced interrogation' at a CIA 'Black Site' two years later. Maya has just arrived from the US and is observing her superior, Dan, use a range of 'interrogation techniques' on a detainee. Afterwards, Dan takes Maya to the US Embassy in Islamabad. When Maya heads upstairs for a scheduled meeting, Dan asks Joe Bradley, the CIA station chief in Pakistan:

> Dan: 'You don't think she's a little young for the hard stuff?'
>
> Joe: 'Washington says *she's a killer.*'
>
> Dan: 'A children's crusade, eh?'
>
> Joe: 'We need to put the next generation in the field.'

In this scene, which is also how the official trailer advertising the film starts, Maya is likened to a child at the same time as her authority and value as a CIA agent is mentioned together with references to her 'being a killer'. Later, when Maya finds out that her investigative lead, a man believed to be Bin Laden's messenger, Abu Ahmed, might be alive after all, she rather aggressively asks Dan to 'Move heaven and earth and bring me this fucking Sayeed family's phone number' in order to be able to follow through her lead. Dan goes to 'Wolf' and requests a couple of hundred thousand dollars to break open Maya's lead and give them a phone number. Wolf is initially hesitant but Dan says:

Dan: *'She is your killer*, Wolf. You put her on the field.'

In addition, there is yet another layer to the writing of Maya as a killer: her own 'urge to kill' Bin Laden. For example, in an earlier scene when Maya finds out about a suicide attack at Base Chapman in Afghanistan in which Jessica and several other CIA agents are killed, she is visibly upset. The male colleague sharing the news also informs her that her lead, Abu Ahmed, according to Saudi intelligence is long dead.

Male colleague: 'Sorry Maya, I always believed in this lead. What are you gonna do?'

Maya: 'I'm gonna smoke everyone out in this op ... [looking very tired, her hair in a mess] and then *I'm gonna kill Bin Laden.*'

Colleague: 'Right ... Right.'

The writing of a female body's heroism in war through killing is controversial. As we are accustomed to killing in war being reserved for male bodies, the emphasis on Maya 'being a killer' opens up for a transgression of an imagined border of violence. However, Maya is an intelligence officer and it is not her task to kill anyone. In other words, Maya's authority and agency as a heroine of war is made in the name of being a killer, but she is only a killer by proxy; the audience knows that she is not an *actual* killer. Towards the end of the film when a team of Navy Seals are briefed on the planned operation that will eventually kill Bin Laden, Maya's role as a killer by proxy is emphasized. With her arms crossed, Maya speaks confidently:

Maya: 'Quite frankly, I didn't wanna use you guys, with your [inaudible] and your bullshit. *I wanted to drop a bomb* but people didn't believe in this lead enough to drop a bomb. So, they're using you guys as canaries. And the theory is, if Bin Laden isn't there you can sneak out and no one would be the wiser. But Bin Laden is there. And *you're gonna kill him for me.*'

The Navy Seal looks her in the eyes. He believes in her conviction. Still, even though Maya's urge to kill Bin Laden is repeated and promoted, the audience is not invited to imagine her as an actual killer in the war on terror. In the end, and throughout, it is male-identified bodies that are active agents in torture, fighting and killing. Maya is thus playing a familiar role along the gendered war story, that of a woman as an object, supporting, encouraging and, ultimately, facilitating the violence of men.

Thinking through how gender acts as a logic policing the interpretation of Maya along tropes familiar in the gendered war story shows how the film fails to convey the message of a powerful, strong new type of heroine or agent in war. While the erotic dysfunction narrative writes her as different from heteronormative femininity associated with mother-hood, which, I would argue, is essential for the writing of her as 'a killer', the last scene of the film can be seen as a way in which to effectively punish Maya for being an atypical woman and masculinized subject, for 'being a killer'. In her research about women murderesses, Morrissey argues that those women gain humanity under only one circumstance and this is when they can be represented as politically neutered victims (Morrissey, 2003: 17). In this way, the film's ending with Maya crying concludes the story by depicting the heroine of war as an emotional weak feminine subject ultimately at a loss with regard to who she is and where she is going. This, in turn, works to 'recuperate female protagonists through returning them to a "proper feminine place"' (Morrissey, 2003: 165).

While the writing of Maya as a heroine of war is made through the image and subject-position of 'being a killer', it can be seen as a 'safe' version precisely because *Zero Dark Thirty* is a fictional account (although inspired by real-life events). Next, I turn to a non-fictional example of how gender – as the imagination of 'Woman' as killer in war – acts as a border-agent.

THE IMAGINATION OF 'TO CLOSE WITH AND KILL THE ENEMY'

As a result of the 2014 'immediate review' mentioned above, in December 2014, Defence Secretary Michael Fallon announced 'his hope' that the UK exclusion policy on women in close-combat roles would be removed in 2016, subject to a research program that will investigate physiological factors. In this chapter, however, I take a step back and explore the resistance involved in the previous review process in 2009/ 2010, that is, before both Australia and the US announced their change in policy.

After having opened up more and more positions to women during the 1990s, the MoD published the first exclusion policy on women in combat roles in 2002. Legally, the exclusion policy is exempted from European Union (EU) sex discrimination legislation by referring to combat effectiveness: women can be excluded from those posts where the military judgment is that the employment of women would undermine and degrade combat effectiveness (MoD, 2010a: 1).[4] Crucially, the reason as to why women are excluded from close-combat roles is not because of their perceived physiological and/or psychological differences from men, such as physical strength or aggression, but because the presence of women's bodies is seen to constitute a potential risk to team *cohesion*. A lack of cohesion in turn is seen to impact negatively upon combat effectiveness. While others have convincingly critiqued the justification with regard to what cohesion might actually mean – Victoria Basham has for example discussed how the MoD ignores research on differences in social versus task cohesion (2009; see also Woodward and Winter, 2007) – I would like to draw attention to two aspects. First, that the actual ban is made in the name of 'killing': women are excluded from so-called ground close combat roles defined as 'roles that are primarily intended and designed with the purpose of requiring individuals on the ground *to close with and kill the enemy*' (MoD, 2010a: 5, emphasis added). Second, that Brig. Richard Nugee, who was leading the 2009/2010 review, said that any decision to remove the ban would be taken for *military reasons*: 'The real point is that we now have practical experience of women in combat in Afghanistan and Iraq and we want to see, genuinely want to see, what effect that will have on our military.' (Nugee, cited in BBC News, 24 May 2009).

After considering the 2009/2010 review reports, the MoD decided that the ban should remain unchanged:

> Their capability in almost all areas is not in doubt, they win the highest decorations for valour, and demonstrate that they are capable of acting independently and with great initiative. But these situations are not those typical of the small tactical teams in the combat arms which are required deliberately *to close with and kill the enemy*. The consequences of opening up these small tactical teams in close combat roles to women are *unknown*. (MoD, 2010a: 3, emphasis added)

Andrew Robathan, Minister for Defence Personnel, Welfare and Veterans, explained:

> We looked closely at the findings of this review but the *conclusions were inconclusive*. There was *no evidence* to show that a change in current policy would be *beneficial* or *risk-free*, and so a decision was made to take a precautionary approach and maintain the current position. (MoD 2010b, emphasis added)

In my reading, however, the conclusions of the three separate reports are clear, not 'inconclusive' as the MoD claims.[5] Thus, next I show how there is a discrepancy between the results of the 2009/2010 mandatory review of the exclusion policy and the political decision in 2010 to keep the British ban on women in combat roles.

First of all, the report on academic literature suggests that there is no direct evidence that women are likely to have a negative impact on combat effectiveness. Instead, 'research indicates that cohesion and bonding are not adversely affected in mixed-gender groups and that men and women can work together effectively, especially when women are not a novelty in a unit' (Cawkill et al., 2009: 37). The report suggests that '*leadership* was found to be a major factor in how well units perform – *not the presence or absence of women*' (Cawkill et al., 2009: 41, emphasis added). Similarly, the qualitative study that compared the impact of a mixed-gender team on cohesion failed to find a link between gender, cohesion and combat effectiveness:

> None of the interviewees gave the impression that cohesion was low specifically because of the presence of a woman per se. Instead, interviewees that rated cohesion of the unit as poor, which was a very low number of men (4), referred to a specific female leader's lack of capability/experience. (Berkshire Consultancy Ltd, 2009: 47)

> A small number of men did explicitly point out that gender is irrelevant when comparing cohesion: 'it's difficult to compare. The same person under rocket attack can be fine one day, then wetting themselves the next. It's nothing to do with gender'. (Berkshire Consultancy Ltd, 2009: 57)

In fact, the report concludes that the 'experience of the vast majority of interviewees was that cohesion worked well during these incidents' (Berkshire Consultancy, 2009: 1). Interestingly, the report found clear, strong themes around trust, time spent together/knowing each other and people doing their jobs:

> Women need to have the time and opportunity to prove themselves, particularly as some men's pre-existing attitudes and expectations of women are more pessimistic than optimistic about their capabilities, especially where they are unused to working with women. (Berkshire Consultancy Ltd, 2009: 63)

The report concluded:

> Cohesion in mixed gender teams during ground close combat incidents was consistently reported to be *high*. The overwhelming message from the interviews was that cohesion is fundamentally *about trust and confidence* in other team members to do their job and that this builds over *time*. (Berkshire Consultancy Ltd, 2009: 2, emphasis added)

The quantitative study (June 2010), which is based on responses to a questionnaire that was sent out to all British women who had been deployed to Iraq and Afghanistan since 2002 and an equivalent sample of men, found that the number of times the team had operated together and the number of women present were significant factors driving cohesion both for men and women, and these factors were therefore seen to be important determinants of cohesion for all (Berkshire Consultancy Ltd, 2010: 40). Finally, and this is crucial, the report concludes that the nature of women's roles and the fact that many of them were *attachments* and had to be attached to combat units ad hoc did have a *negative impact* on cohesion. In other words, as a direct result of the ban itself, women tended to have spent less time with the team/worked with them on fewer occasions and it is this that is identified as a key factor in developing cohesion.

To sum up, these findings suggest that the ban itself, rather than the presence of women per se, is causing problems with cohesion. The conclusions of the reports thus are not 'inconclusive' as the MoD claims, but clearly demonstrate that the ban itself might be counterproductive with regard to combat effectiveness. This, in turn, suggests that the decision to keep the ban was not made 'for military reasons' as initially promised but was a result of a more hidden politics.

There are three aspects to how the MoD manages to keep a ban, justified along the lines of gender, cohesion and combat effectiveness, despite the fact that such a link is dubious at best. First, I would suggest that the argument that the 'conclusions of the review were inconclusive' is made possible because the review was set up asking the wrong questions. The 2009/2010 review was tasked with trying to find 'evidence' for a link between gender, cohesion in small teams and combat effectiveness because this is the only way in which the current ban on women in combat roles can legally be justified. The 'failure' of the review to establish such a link is not a failure but a finding.

The second aspect that I would like to draw attention to is that, as mentioned above, the ban is justified because one, supposedly, cannot know what the impact upon cohesion and combat effectiveness might be:

'The consequences of opening up these small tactical teams in close combat roles to women are *unknown*', so the MoD claims (MoD, 2010a: 3, emphasis added). Despite having an increasing amount of experience with women in ground close-combat *situations*, the MoD argues, this is different from ground close-combat *roles* where individuals are engaging in such activities on a daily basis. Effectively, this means that the ban is justified by referring to itself. It is precisely because of the ban that there cannot be any evidence of the effectiveness of women in ground close combat roles; the research undertaken in the review cannot, by definition, include incidents where 'women have been closing with the enemy'.

Perhaps the most important clue, however, is found in the press statement released by the MoD in 2010. It states that the 'Service Chiefs' 'evaluated the evidence that the individual pieces of research provided but also considered *the relative weight* that needed to be accorded to each of the conclusions' (MoD 2010a: 2, emphasis added). Consequently, the decision to keep the exclusion policy in 2010 was based not so much on the findings from the review reports, that is on the real-life experiences of women and men serving in combat roles/situations or on the knowledge-sharing from other countries (most of which do not distinguish between men and women in combat roles). Instead, the decision seems to be based on the undisclosed opinions of the Service Chiefs. While this is serious, not least from a democratic accountability point of view, my main point is to highlight that there is something else going on, a hidden politics, with regard to the 2010 political decision to keep the British ban on women in combat roles.

Critiquing the 2002 exclusion policy (which at the time of writing effectively remains), Victoria Basham argues that the MoD wants to keep the ban because the British military wants to ensure that the heterosexual masculine culture of the forces is not disturbed (Basham, 2009: p. 739; see also Chapter 1 in this volume). As the inverse to this, my argument focuses on what is kept out rather than what is kept in: women's bodies closing with and killing the enemy.

Not only is the ban designed to prevent women's bodies from performing tasks where the 'primary role is to close with and kill the enemy' even though women in reality are already engaged in combat roles,[6] but the decision to keep the ban after the 2009/10 review seems to have been founded on the *idea* of 'Woman' as killer, rather than evidence of actual experiences and events, shared by both women and men. The unease about including women in roles with the task 'to close with and kill' briefly resurfaced immediately after the 2013 change in US policy. In a debate on whether or not the UK should follow suit and remove their ban as well, British columnist Charles Moore said the following on the BBC Radio 4 program *Any Questions?*:

> I think the emancipation of women has produced an understanding that women and men are not the same. I actually would be very sad if the way that *women stand for peace* and gentleness in our society were taken away and I think that *if women were killing people*, which is what we're talking about, that would be *an uncivilized and retrograde act*. It's not a matter of courage; it's a matter of difference. (BBC Radio 4, 2013)

In her book *When Women Kill*, legal theorist Morrissey argues that the narratives about when a woman murders can be read as displaying evidence of trauma:

> When women commit murder, their abjection is even more extreme than that of men who do the same. Legal and media narratives of murders committed by women indicate that these acts are also generally more traumatic for heteropatriarchal societies than those of men. For the fear of women, of their power to generate life and to take it away, runs deep in male dominated societies. (Morrissey, 2003: 2)

Charles Moore's viewpoint that women's killing in the name of state-sanctioned political violence represents 'the end of civilization' is a testament to the fact that the ban might be in place because *the idea* of legitimizing women's killing impacts upon, destabilizes and ultimately threatens broader ideas about what women and men should or should not be doing, irrespective of what women and men are actually already doing in war. What I am suggesting here is that the UK ban, and in particular the decision to keep the ban despite the fact that it might not be the best for military readiness and combat effectiveness, is best understood beyond the military context, in a broader social and cultural context. This is because it concerns an imagined border of violence, about which bodies can and cannot engage in violence during the conduct of war. This is how gender as a logic functions as a border agent policing understandings of bodies and violence in war.

MAKING FEMINIST SENSE OF IMAGINED BORDERS OF VIOLENCE IN WAR

In this chapter I have analyzed two examples of how an increased visibility of women's agency in war is represented and culturally made sense of. By thinking about gendered societal borders I have shown how both examples communicate imagined borders of violence through the image and imagination of 'Woman' as killer in war. First, I showed how in *Zero Dark Thirty* Maya is often represented as an object, facilitator and supporter in the story of male violence, and then how the image of 'being a killer' is essential for the writing of Maya as a heroine of war. By being 'a killer' (albeit by proxy), however, Maya is punished, both by being not woman enough – as 'different' from heteronormative conceptions of femininity associated with motherhood – and by being too much a woman when positioned as a hyper-emotional, close to hysterical, subject. In the second part, I analyzed the UK ban on women in combat roles, which constitutes an actual barrier in the sense that bodies identified as female are excluded, with potential real negative implications for those women who want to pursue a military career. I showed how the 2010 decision to keep the ban was not made for military reasons – as the ban itself risks being counterproductive in terms of combat effectiveness – which indicates that there is a hidden politics at play: the UK ban on women in combat is also about an imagined border, the imagination of 'Woman' as killer in war.

Without feminist curiosity, the repeated writing of Maya as fit for her job as a CIA agent through the subject-position of 'being a killer', as well as the efforts to keep women out of positions with the task 'to close with and kill' despite the risk of it being counterproductive for combat effectiveness, fail to make sense. However, as feminist scholars have shown, representations of women's agency in political violence often include a sense of shock or surprise, precisely because women are not supposed to be violent (see Sjoberg and Gentry, 2007; Sjoberg and Gentry, 2008; Gentry, 2009; Åhäll, 2012b). What happens in these stories about women and violence is that individuals are often being judged and valued on the basis of the shape of their bodies rather than their actual capabilities and actions. By seeming out of place, these bodies are seen to 'act against their femininity' and it is this unease or confusion that highlights an imagined cultural border politics. This emotional communication 'is a testament to that we have reached some form of societal border-crossing as *common sense is no longer making sense*' (Åhäll, 2015: 142, emphasis in original). Or, as Sara Ahmed eloquently puts it: 'When the arrival of some bodies is noticed, when an arrival is noticeable, it generates disorientation in how things are arranged' (Ahmed, 2007: 163). This might lead to a crisis and disruption to the cultural grammar with which 'the consensual community' understand gender and sex to begin with (Åhäll, 2015: 141).

By thinking about gender as a border agent policing understandings of violence and war, I have pointed out how similar ideas about women in war play out in different cultural contexts. The conclusion that my analysis draws me towards is that as scholars of global politics we need to remain feminist curious and think about gender as a deeper logic fundamental to how the conduct of war is understood, performed and ultimately made sense of in the everyday. A focus on how bodies reach, cross or transgress imagined cultural borders, whether communicated in policy documents or popular culture, offers one way in which to do so, and renders practices of global politics that would have otherwise remained hidden visible.

NOTES

1. My understanding of 'text' here is not limited to written text or speech, but about meaning-making through language more broadly, including sound, emotions and body-language.
2. Julia Kristeva's theory of abjection is developed in *Powers of Horror: An Essay on Abjection* (1982). Here, abjection is about borders and the abject is that which does not respect borders, positions, rules. However, writing within the parameters of psychoanalysis, to Kristeva the abject is part of ourselves, that which we reject, that which identifies what we are not.
3. As the leader of the terrorist network Al Qaeda, Osama Bin Laden was one of the 'brains' behind the attacks in the United States on 11 September, 2001. He was killed by US Special Forces in Pakistan in 2011.
4. According to EU regulations, the exclusion policy has to be reviewed every eight years.
5. The 2009/2010 review includes an evaluation of recent academic literature on the effectiveness of mixed-gender teams in a combat environment; of women's roles in recent operations; and of other states' experiences in employing women in ground close-combat roles. The Defence and Science and Technology Laboratory (DSTL), which is part of the MoD, was tasked to undertake the review of academic literature and the experience of other states while an independent consultant, Berkshire Consultancy Ltd, was appointed to assess women's roles in recent operations in Iraq and Afghanistan.
6. For example, one report suggests that 55 women were serving in so-called 'male only' roles in the Territorial Army in 2012 (The Week, 2013).

REFERENCES

Åhäll, Linda (2012a), 'The writing of heroines: motherhood and female agency in political violence', *Security Dialogue*, **43** (4): 287–303.
Åhäll, Linda (2012b), 'Confusion, fear, disgust: emotional communication in representations of female agency in political violence', in Linda Åhäll and Laura J. Shepherd (eds), *Gender, Agency and Political Violence*, Palgrave Macmillan, pp. 169–83.
Åhäll, Linda (2015), *Sexing War/Policing Gender: Motherhood, Myth and Women's Political Violence*, Routledge.
Ahmed, Sara (2004), *The Cultural Politics of Emotion*, Edinburgh University Press.
Ahmed, Sara (2007), *Queer Phenomenology: Orientations, Objects, Others*, Duke University Press.

Alison, Miranda (2004), 'Women as agents of political violence: gendering security', *Security Dialogue*, **35** (4): 447–63.

Barthes, Roland (2000), *Mythologies*, Vintage.

Basham, Victoria (2009), 'Effecting discrimination: operational effectiveness and harassment in the British Armed Forces', *Armed Forces & Society*, **35** (4): 728–44.

BBC News (2009), 'Women's frontline-role reviewed', 24 May, accessed 26 May 2009 at: http://news.bbc.co.uk/go/pr/fr/-/1/hi/uk/8065604.stm.

BBC Radio 4 (2013), *Any Questions?*, 25 January, available at: http://www.bbc.co.uk/news/uk-21201509.

Berkshire Consultancy Ltd (2009), 'Qualitative report for the study of women in combat', accessed 12 January 2012 at: https://www.gov.uk/government/uploads/system/uploads/attachment_data/file/27405/study_woman_combat_quali_data.pdf.

Berkshire Consultancy Ltd (2010), 'Study of women in combat – investigation of quantitative data', accessed 12 January 2012 at: https://www.gov.uk/government/uploads/system/uploads/attachment_data/file/27404/study_woman_combat_quant_data.pdf.

Bleiker, Roland (2001), 'The aesthetic turn in international political theory', *Millennium*, **30** (3): 509–34.

Brunner, Claudia (2005), 'Female suicide bombers–male suicide bombing? Looking for gender in reporting the suicide bombings of the Israeli–Palestinian conflict', *Global Society*, **19** (1): 29–48.

Butler, Judith (2006[1990]), *Gender Trouble*, Routledge.

Butler, Judith (2011[1993]), *Bodies That Matter: On the Discursive Limits of Sex*, Routledge.

Cawkill, Paul, Alison Rogers, Sarah Knight and Laura Spear (2009), 'Women in ground close combat roles: the experiences of other nations and a review of the academic literature', Defence Science and Technology Laboratory.

Creed, Barbara (1999), 'Horror and the monstrous-feminine: an imaginary abjection', in Sue Thornham (ed.), *Feminist Film Theory: A Reader*, Edinburgh University Press, pp. 251–66.

Eager, Paige Whaley (2008), *From Freedom Fighters to Terrorists: Women and Political Violence*, Ashgate.

Elshtain, Jean Bethke (1995), *Women and War*, University of Chicago Press.

Enloe, Cynthia (2000), *Maneuvers: The International Politics of Militarizing Women's Lives*, University of California Press.

Enloe, Cynthia (2007), *Globalization and Militarism: Feminists Make the Link*, Rowman & Littlefield.

Gentry, Caron (2009), 'Twisted maternalism', *International Feminist Journal of Politics*, **11** (2): 235–52.

Hall, Stuart (1997), *Representation: Cultural Representations and Signifying Practices*, SAGE.

Hill, Logan (2013), 'Secrets of Zero Dark Thirty', *Rolling Stone*, 17 January.

Kristeva, Julia (1982), *Powers of Horror: An Essay on Abjection*, Columbia University Press.

MacKenzie, Megan (2009), 'Securitization and de-securitization: female soldiers and the reconstruction of women in post-conflict Sierra Leone', *Security Studies*, **18** (2): 241–61.

Ministry of Defence (MoD) (2010a), 'Report on the review of the exclusion of women from ground close-combat roles', accessed 12 January 2012 at: http://www.mod.uk/NR/rdonlyres/B358460B-4B2A-4AB5-9A63-15B6196B5364/0/Report_review_excl_woman_combat.pdf.

Ministry of Defence (MoD) (2010b), 'MOD completes review into women in close combat roles', Defence Policy and Business News, 29 November, accessed 12 January 2012 at:

http://www.mod.uk/DefenceInternet/DefenceNews/DefencePolicyAndBusiness/Mod CompletesReviewIntoWomenInCloseCombatRoles.htm.

Morrissey, Belinda (2003), *When Women Kill: Questions of Agency and Subjectivity*, Routledge.

Parashar, Swati (2014), *Women and Militant Wars: The Politics of Injury*, Routledge.

Shapiro, Michael (2013), *Studies in Trans-Disciplinary Method: After the Aesthetic Turn*, Routledge.

Sjoberg, Laura and Caron E. Gentry (2007), *Mothers, Monsters, Whores: Women's Violence in Global Politics*, Zed Books.

Sjoberg, Laura and Caron E. Gentry (2008), 'Reduced to bad sex: narratives of violent women from the bible to the war on terror', *International Relations*, **22** (1): 5–23.

Tyler, Imogen (2013), *Revolting Subjects: Social Abjection and Resistance in Neoliberal Britain*, Zed Books.

Weber, Cynthia (2005), *International Relations Theory: A Critical Introduction*, Routledge.

The Week (2013), 'Will British Army allow women to serve in combat roles?', accessed 3 May 2015 at: http://www.theweek.co.uk/defence/51198/will-british-army-allow-women-serve-combat-roles.

Woodward, Rachel and Trish Winter (2007), *Sexing the Soldier: The Politics of Gender and the Contemporary British Army*, Routledge.

Young, Iris Marion (2003), 'The logic of masculinist protection: reflections on the current security state', *Signs: Journal of Women in Culture and Society*, **29** (1): 1–25.

Zalewski, Marysia (2013), *Feminist International Relations: Exquisite Corpse*, Routledge.

Zalewski, Marysia (2015), 'Stories of pain and longing', in Linda Åhäll and Thomas Gregory (eds), *Emotions, Politics and War*, Routledge, pp. 34–44.

Zero Dark Thirty (2012), Film, directed by Kathryn Bigelow.

3. The twilight war: gender and espionage, Britain, 1900–1950

Juliette Pattinson

INTRODUCTION

An explicitly gendered notion of intelligence prevails with a popular perception having emerged that espionage is a male-dominated profession and that the few women involved deploy sex as their 'most deadly weapon' (Hoehling, 1967, p. 8). It has long been considered that women's 'innate' charm and duplicity makes them ideal spies. Female espionage is often regarded as intrinsically linked to feminine sexuality: their bodies their greatest asset. Yet women have also been perceived to be inherently emotional and susceptible to falling in love with their targets, leading author Bernard Newman to assert that 'generally speaking, women make rotten spies' (1941, p. 125). Mata Hari, the Dutch-born exotic dancer and courtesan, epitomizes the alluring and dangerous *femme fatale* that has become a recurring motif in the spy genre, her name becoming shorthand for an attractive, sexually independent female spy. Despite the fact that she did not actually engage in intelligence-gathering, she has remained a potent cultural icon casting a long shadow over women's contributions to the intelligence community. The popular image of the vampish, 'mata-hariesque' female spy-courtesan has resulted in a misconception about the role of women in intelligence generally and has both overshadowed and led to the misinterpretation of the experiences of other female spies.

Despite the stereotype, few of the women that were involved in intelligence work during the first half of the twentieth century utilized 'sexpionage'. Maxwell Knight, the chief agent runner in the 1930s and 1940s of MI5 (Military Intelligence Section 5 tasked with British domestic security), asserted 'I am no believer in what may be described as Mata-Hari methods. I am convinced that more information has been obtained by women agents by keeping out of the arms of the man, than was ever obtained by sinking too willingly into them' (National Archives, KV 4/227). Indeed, most female spies gleaned their information in more mundane ways, usually through vigilant observation. Thus, in contrast to the popular myth of the *femme fatale*, most of the women who engaged in spying during the two world wars 'worked as soldiers not seductresses' (Proctor, 2003, p. 5), compiling information about troop movements and weaponry. Moreover, the vast majority of women in intelligence were not spies at all but were concentrated in office support roles undertaking traditional so-called female-appropriate tasks such as filing and answering the telephone. About six thousand women worked in both civilian and military intelligence roles for the British Government between 1909 and 1919 (Proctor, 2003, p. 1) and even greater numbers in the Second World War. Because of the protracted nature of the wars and the resulting need for (wo)manpower, women, who had begun to work in a wide range of occupations, increasingly became required to staff the various branches of intelligence organizations. During the First World War, women were employed in an administrative capacity in MI5 (domestic intelligence and security), MI6 (foreign intelligence and security), MI9 (Postal Censorship), the Translation Bureau, the Military Press Control, Passport Control offices and the British Mission in Paris. In the Second World War, women were once more recruited in large numbers to staff MI5 and MI6, as well as the newly formed MI9 (with a changed function, now responsible for escape and evasion), the Special Operations Executive (sabotage), the Political Warfare Executive (propaganda) and the Ministry of Economic Warfare. As we shall see, women played key roles as field agents, intelligence officers and clerical workers and made a vital contribution to the creation of professional, modern espionage and counter-espionage institutions in Britain, as well as undertaking important intelligence-gathering roles in occupied Europe.

There has been some scholarly research on certain aspects of female espionage, including Julie Wheelwright's book (1992) and article (1993) on gendered myths concerning female spies, Deborah Van Seters' (1992) article on autobiographical accounts of secret service work, Tammy Proctor's (2003) monograph on women in intelligence during the First World War and Kathryn Olmsted's (2004) article about the American media's reporting of four female Communist spies in the late 1940s and early 1950s. The experiences of women are rarely afforded much attention, however, in historical accounts of MI5 and MI6, although the two official histories (Andrew, 2009; Jeffery, 2010), enabled by the declassification of intelligence documents, have begun to remedy that. Similarly, the intelligence organizations are often omitted from gendered histories of the First and Second World Wars. This chapter seeks to address these lacunae by providing a gendered account of espionage and counter-espionage from 1900 to 1950.

The terms 'spying' and 'espionage' refer to the gathering of intelligence, usually of a military nature, that is not openly available. For the purposes of this chapter, I am taking a broad definition of espionage incorporating deception, sabotage, subversion and security as well as covert intelligence-gathering. In a time of crisis, the need for military intelligence is crucial and the deployment of spies flourishes. This overview of espionage in the first half of the twentieth century begins by examining pre-World War I British spy fiction and film which fueled cultural anxieties about Britain's preparedness for war and which contributed to the decision to set up the world's first intelligence agency. With the establishment of the Secret Service Bureau in 1909, which remains active today albeit in a modified form, Britain has the oldest continual intelligence-gathering agency in the world. The chapter also charts the expansion of British intelligence during the two total wars and examines both the roles played by men and women who staffed the intelligence organizations in Britain, as well as those who gathered information in occupied countries in order to analyze the gendering of espionage.

THE GENTLEMAN SPY IN THE POPULAR IMAGINATION

The roots of the world's first intelligence agency lay in anxieties about Britain's declining place in the world in the face of challenges to British hegemony from Germany and America, which in turn led to a spate of invasion scares and spy novels. Although the British Government resisted setting up a secret service, regarding it as underhand, ungentlemanly and unBritish, a Directorate of Military Intelligence was established in 1883. Concerns about the conflict-preparedness of Britain were compounded by the Anglo–Boer War (1899–1902) and a Directorate of Military Operations was created in 1904 with separate sections for foreign intelligence, strategy, special duties and topography. Women were marginal in this fledgling intelligence bureaucracy: this was a man's world, something made very apparent in the spy fiction that flourished in the Edwardian period.

The fictional spy was invariably characterized as male. Duckworth Drew in William Le Queux's *Secrets of the Foreign Office* (1903) was the prototype of the fictional gentlemanly spy which was followed by a multitude of similar scrupulously fair, patriotic, upper-class, public school and Oxbridge-educated characters which populated the fiction of John Buchan, Baroness Orczy and E. Phillips Oppenheim. While the foreign spy became invested with the negative connotations of espionage as duplicitous, underhand and treacherous, the British secret agent that emerged in popular fiction in the Edwardian period was an amateur who unwittingly became embroiled in the world of espionage and remained ever the gentleman, loyal to God, King, class and country. In his examination of pre-war spy novels, David Stafford asserts:

> It would be difficult to find a single British secret agent in the literature of these years who does not in some way appear as a gentleman cast in this mould, a man of the right social class and with the correct education carrying out his duty to his country regardless of cost or sacrifice. (Stafford, 1981, p. 503)

Popular spy fiction thus promoted a particular version of British masculinity. This distinction between the foreign spy and the British secret agent became firmly entrenched as a convention of this genre of literature. In Le Queux's *The Invasion of 1910*, serialized in the *Daily Mail* in 1906 and subsequently published in book form and which was translated into 27 languages and sold over a million copies, a secret army of German spies passing as barbers, bakers and waiters paved the way for the German invasion. Le Queux also included female spies in his fiction and consequently suspicions were cast on German nannies and governesses residing in Britain. There was also a spate of films about foreign spies intent on invading Britain. Le Queux's 1906 serialization inspired the film *The Invaders* (1909) in which foreign soldiers dressed as women entered Britain. A number of spy films featured strong female characters who thwarted enemy spies (*Dr Brian Pellie and the Secret Despatch*, 1912; *O.H.M.S.*, 1913; *The Anarchist's Doom*, 1913). Taken as fact, these fictional novels and films contributed to a highly contagious spy fever and claims that up to 100 000 German spies were operational in Britain. Newspapers incubated this fever. *The Weekly News*, for example, offered £10 to readers to provide information on German agents to its 'Spy Editor' and received hundreds of letters alleging German espionage activities (French, 1978).

Spy paranoia played a crucial part in convincing the authorities to consider establishing a state-funded professional intelligence service to replace the somewhat haphazard system of casual informants and amateur agents. A sub-committee of the Committee of Imperial Defence was set up by the Cabinet to investigate the alleged German spy threat. Following the discovery of plans of a suspected German invasion, it recommended to Prime Minister Asquith the formation of an intelligence agency to be financed from government coffers and staffed mainly by civilians. This led to the creation in August 1909 of the Secret Service

Bureau which had dual objectives: a 'Home Section' under Vernon Kell, subsequently called the Security Service or MI5, which countered foreign espionage in Britain and reported to the Home Office; and a 'Foreign Section' under George Mansfield Smith-Cumming, later called the Secret Intelligence Service (SIS) or MI6, a branch of the Foreign Office which ran an overseas network of British spies to gather intelligence abroad on Britain's potential enemies. The creation of the Secret Service modernized, professionalized and centralized intelligence which had until then been gathered somewhat haphazardly by the Foreign Office, the War Office and the Admiralty. The sub-committee also recommended that the Official Secrets Act of 1889 be replaced by a more severe Act that equated espionage with treason. This was passed in 1911 to counter espionage.

COUNTERING GERMAN ESPIONAGE DURING THE FIRST WORLD WAR

The popularity of this highly formulaic spy fiction continued during the First World War with the gentlemen heroes of Le Queux, Buchan and Oppenheim rescuing Britain from disaster. The relatively new medium of film was also utilized with titles such as *The German Spy Peril* (1914) and *The Kaiser's Spies* (1914). Like his counterpart in popular fiction and film, the British spy was usually a public school-educated gentleman. In the theater of war, intelligence was performed by male actors. Yet, as we shall see, behind the scenes, women undertook crucial, albeit mundane, roles to counter German espionage.

Most German espionage in Britain was directed from Antwerp by Gustav Steinhauer. A spy school established there, providing a systematic training, was run by Elsbeth Schragmuller. Known as the Lady Doktor as she had graduated from Freiburg University with a doctorate, Ian Fleming immortalized her as 'Rosa Klebb' in *From Russia, With Love* (1957). One of the school's students, Lizzie Wertheim, provided information about the Allies' new secret weapon, the tank. Yet German intelligence had only limited success. The number of spies in Britain was small. According to Thomas Boghardt, 22 German spies were active in Britain in early 1915; by the summer of that year, only six were operational (Boghardt, 2004, p. 149). The first German spy on British territory, as well as the first to be captured and executed, was Karl Lody, a German naval reserve officer, who was arrested on 2 October 1914 for having sent telegrams reporting on the British fleet (National Archives, HO 144/3324). In total, 31 German spies were tried and 12 were executed at the Tower of London (Hiley, 1986, p. 668). The last spy was shot on 11 April 1916. Britain, unlike Belgium, France and Germany, did not execute the (five) female spies it convicted. As a result of tightening censorship, the introduction of passports from 1915 and the implementation of the Defence of the Realm Act, passed in August 1914 to target spies and traitors and enabling civilians to be tried by court martial and sentenced to death for assisting the enemy, it became increasingly difficult for German agents to operate in Britain. They were compelled to rely on spies who were in the country for a short period masquerading as traveling salesmen to memorize information and return to report in person.

Although German espionage in Britain was largely a product of the British imagination rather than a force to be reckoned with, British intelligence did achieve some notable successes in counter espionage. As a result of the capture of all three of Germany's main naval codes, the British codebreakers of Room 40 at the Admiralty cracked about 20 000 messages sent by the German authorities to their embassies, consuls, Zeppelins, submarines, navy and merchant marine (Knightley, 1986, p. 45). Room 40 also achieved possibly the greatest intelligence feat of the First World War. On 16 January 1917, Arthur Zimmerman, the German Foreign Minister, sent a coded message to the German Ambassador in Washington warning him of the unrestricted submarine warfare that was about to be unleashed which would include the targeting of neutral American ships in the Atlantic. This message was to be forwarded to the German Ambassador in Mexico, who was to urge Mexico to attack America from the south. Room 40 intercepted and decoded the Zimmerman Telegram and informed the Americans of its contents. Public outrage at the telegram, made public in March 1917, was a crucial factor in the American declaration of war against Germany in April (Gannon, 2010).

With the expansion of Room 40, women were recruited from 1917 as secretaries and to assist the decoding under the supervision of Lady Hambro. Women were also employed by MI5 in large numbers as drivers, orderlies, cooks and switchboard operators in Britain and a few were stationed in small offices in neutral or Allied countries to type up reports that came in. MI5 Headquarters employed 291 female clerks, as well as 15 male clerks and 84 officers (Hiley, 1986, p. 666) and, from September 1915, a large number of Girl Guides who replaced Boy Scouts as couriers of files, and messages between offices (Proctor, 2003, pp. 58–9). Many women employed by MI5 were from upper and middle class backgrounds, had been educated at Cheltenham Ladies' College and the women's colleges at Oxbridge and possessed foreign language skills. At least two women had PhDs and were recruited to write reports despite being over the age limit of 30; this age restriction had been imposed in 1916, amending a 1915 decision not to recruit women over the age of 40 (National Archives, KV 1/49). In his official history of MI5, Christopher Andrew noted that, on average, the female staff were more highly educated and from higher up the social scale than their male colleagues (2009, p. 59). Women often took on the roles of male officers on a temporary basis and then replaced them when the men were recalled for other jobs. Miss A.W. Masterton, for example, who had been a secretary, took over the running of accounts and, according to a 1920 report, was 'the only example at this date of a woman managing the finances of a Government office' (National Archives, KV 1/50).

MI5's administrative branch ran a registry staffed entirely by women from November 1914. A cartoon by Hugh Gladstone entitled 'The Lost File' made reference to this feminization with an attractive young woman telling a male officer, 'We've looked everywhere but we can't find any BAULZ in the Registry' (Andrew, 2009, p. 55). The women handled an enormous amount of information. The agency's system of card indexes, which totaled about a million cards, recorded detailed information on 43 000 enemy alien men, 10 000 women, 12 000 British women married to enemy aliens, 34 500 British subjects who had blood ties with the enemy and thousands of individuals who were under suspicion as a result of their actions, such as the 5246 pacifists that were investigated from June 1916 (Hiley, 1986, p. 646). MI9, the Postal Censorship branch, employed over 3500 women alongside 1300 men to undertake clerical work, translate, test for invisible inks and monitor all non-military incoming, outgoing and transit mail en route elsewhere (National Archives, WO 32/10776). In 1917 alone, MI9's female postal censors prevented 356 000 letters from being delivered, suspecting the authors of providing the enemy with information (Hiley, 1986, p. 647).

As the threat of invasion receded and German espionage proved to be less effective than anticipated, the remit of MI5 changed considerably. It evolved from a small organization tasked with countering espionage by identifying and arresting German spies to a vast intelligence-gathering body that turned its attention to domestic subversion, spending huge amounts collecting information on dissenters. By the time of the Armistice, 13 500 individuals had been entered on a 'Black List' of suspects (Hiley, 1986, p. 640). The definition of counter espionage had thus broadened to include any action that aided the enemy more than it assisted the British government (Hiley, 1986, p. 657).

As the war became a protracted affair and with conscription being introduced in January 1916 making men of military age liable to call-up, women were increasingly relied upon to plug the staffing hole. As

Tammy Proctor notes, 'without the exploitation of cheaper female labor, the British government could not have created the vast networks of surveillance that yielded hundreds of thousands of pages detailing the activities of enemy aliens, domestic dissidents and suspected spies between 1914 and 1918' (2003, p. 2). And the women did indeed provide cheap labor. This was decades before equal pay legislation was passed, and the government was able to pay women who worked for MI5 £7–10 a month, a fraction of the average male pay of £33. Similarly, the female clerks recruited by MI9 were paid £5 a week (about £250 a year) in comparison to men who earned an annual salary of between £400 and £500 (Proctor, 2003, p. 63). And while the men who worked in Room 40 were paid between £350 and £500 annually, their highest paid female co-workers earned only £200 (National Archives, HW 3/6). Albeit poorly recompensed, these women's contribution to countering the perceived threat of German espionage was invaluable.

BRITISH ESPIONAGE DURING THE FIRST WORLD WAR

British intelligence was not solely reliant on countering espionage through signal decryption: human intelligence also contributed significantly to its espionage achievements. Under the leadership of Smith-Cumming, codenamed 'C', MI6 expanded during the First World War. By mid-1915, Head Office employed over thirty staff, which included seven officers, eight clerks and twelve female typists, some of whom were married. Reports seen by Keith Jeffery during the research for his official history of MI6 reveal that a few women were also deployed abroad, although their names have been erased in the files to protect their identities (2010, p. 57). Moreover, a key actor in Anglo-Arab relations was archaeologist and 'lady traveler' Gertrude Bell (Howell, 2006). During her travels in the Middle East, she had amassed a huge archive of photographs, maps and notes that were of immense importance to the topographical and statistical division. From 1916 she served alongside T.E. Lawrence in the embryonic Arab Bureau undertaking important work in Egypt, India and Iraq, thereby becoming the first woman employed as an officer by British military intelligence.

While MI6 was unable to establish a significant presence in Germany, it did control and finance a wide network of men and women across Europe who gathered information about troop movements. The most successful was the Belgian organization *La Dame Blanche* (The White Lady). All members, numbering about 800 in total, swore a military oath of allegiance, were organized along military lines into three battalions and wanted to be recognized as soldiers or agents, thereby emphasizing their military role as patriotic intelligence gatherers, rather than as spies motivated by financial gain – about 250 were women. As a counterpoint to the dominant image of the Belgian woman, that of victim brutalized by the metaphoric rape of her country, the women of *La Dame Blanche* undertook active intelligence-gathering against the occupiers. The organization's British contact, Captain Henry Landau, wrote in February 1919 that female agents 'ran exactly the same risks as the men' (Imperial War Museum, *La Dame Blanche*, box 2). In September 1917, they began noting the number of trains that passed through areas of strategic importance on the French–Belgian border in order to ascertain German troop movements. Reports were then smuggled inside the hollow handles of kitchen brooms and in the corsets of female couriers. Tammy Proctor's analysis of *La Dame Blanche* led her to conclude that the success of their contributions set a precedent for the cooperation between resistance groups and the British government during the Second World War (2003, p. 78).

Four women in particular who were involved in espionage have been immortalized in print, film and stone, undoubtedly as a result of their gender as well as their deaths while in enemy hands. British nurse Edith Cavell, who smuggled over 200 allied soldiers and Belgians of military age out of German-occupied Belgium, and Margaretha Geertruida Zeller, the infamous Mata Hari, have together been the subject of over sixty biographies and several films. The legacy of Cavell, whose monument stands just off Trafalgar Square in London, is, however, somewhat ambiguous: according to Foot and Langley, her execution 'prejudiced MI9 against using women as intelligence agents in any manner' (1979, p. 56). Also celebrated in their native countries are Frenchwoman Louise de Bettignies, who passed on information to the British about troop movements and who is the subject of at least four biographies and a memorial in Lille, and the Belgian national heroine Gabrielle Petit, who provided information to the British about troop movements in the vicinity of Tournai, and has been the subject of two biographies and a memorial in Brussels (De Schaepdrijver, 2015). The intelligence work undertaken by Cavell, de Bettignies and Petit bears little resemblance to the popular notion of female spies as seductive temptresses.

BRITISH INTELLIGENCE IN THE INTER-WAR PERIOD

While still in its infancy, British intelligence during the First World War became increasingly bureaucratized and professionalized but, despite some successes, the government was skeptical about the need for a peacetime intelligence agency. The Treasury considered it absurd that almost four years after the Armistice Britain retained an intelligence organization operating on wartime levels. Resources were substantially reduced, with funding cut by a third to £200 000 per annum (Twigge et al., 2009). Women, who were only ever regarded as dilutees to be employed for the duration, were demobilized en masse. After substantially outnumbering their male colleagues during the war, the number of women in intelligence in the inter-war period plummeted. MI5 Headquarters shrank from a wartime peak of employing 844 staff to only a dozen in 1929 (Andrew, n.d.a) and at the end of 1938 still only employed 30 officers and 103 secretaries and registry staff (Andrew, n.d.b). While the establishment of the Joint Intelligence Committee (JIC) in 1936 increased the synchronization of the various intelligence branches, British intelligence remained under-funded, under-staffed and ill-prepared. On the eve of war it was in 'a state of crisis', not knowing who its enemies were at home or abroad (Grant, 2009, p. 501).

The British government's priorities had shifted in the inter-war period. Bolshevism was now perceived as the greater security threat to Britain and both MI5 and MI6 were preoccupied with attempting to combat the danger posed by the Comintern, the Communist International established by the Soviets in March 1919 as a tool for fomenting and coordinating communist activity abroad. While MI6 kept an eye on international communism, MI5 kept track of British communist groups that it suspected of having links with Soviet espionage. Nineteen-year-old Olga Gray, agent M-12, was recruited in 1931 by MI5 to penetrate the Communist Party of Great Britain and to get close to its National Organiser Percy Glading. In 1934 Glading entrusted her with a mission, which enabled her to confirm the long-suspected association between the British Communist Party and Soviet espionage. She identified the specific book on which their cipher system was based, enabling the Government Code and Cypher School, a cryptographic unit established in 1919 with staff from Room 40, to read the traffic, codenamed MASK, between Moscow and various Comintern representatives abroad (West, 2005). For seven years she reported on the activities of communists and in 1938 the entire spy ring was arrested and prosecuted under the Official Secrets Act, with Glading receiving six years hard labor. The judge summed up by saying 'I think that this young woman is possessed of extraordinary courage, and I think she has done a great service to her country' (National Archives, HO 45/25520).

In addition to monitoring communist spies, MI5 also targeted those with sympathies for Germany in the late 1930s. The *Abwehr*, the German military intelligence service under the leadership of Admiral Wilhelm Canaris, ran spies in Britain, most of whom had British nationality, but they were highly ineffective and unprofessional. Dundee-based Jessie Jordan, for example, acted as a postbox for the *Abwehr*, receiving letters from Nazi agents in America and then forwarding them to German addresses. She was arrested and given a four-year prison sentence in 1938 (Knightley, 1986, p. 99). Following the outbreak of the Second World War, MI5 stepped up its surveillance as Germany once more became the primary threat to Britain.

COUNTER ESPIONAGE DURING THE SECOND WORLD WAR

Reports of spies, Fifth Columnists and invasion scares flourished in the wake of the Dunkirk evacuation and the fall of France. Dennis Wheatley's spy novel *The Scarlet Imposter* (1940), the short film *Miss Grant goes to the Door* (1940) and feature-length films such as *Went the Day Well?* (1942) reminded the British public to be continually vigilant and on their guard against Fifth Columnists willing to assist an invasion and German spies posing as British soldiers. Female spies were once more a source of anxiety. Duplicitous women were depicted in posters, such as 'Beware of Female Spies' and 'Keep mum, she's not so dumb', in fiction, including Wheatley's *The Black Baroness* (1940) and Helen MacInnes's novel *Assignment in Brittany* (1942) and in films, such as *The Spy in Black* (1939), *Q Planes* (1939) and *Contraband* (1940). Lord Haw-Haw's radio broadcasts helped propagate the myth of a network of Fifth Columnists and a spy panic gripped Britain once more as individuals with foreign accents were suspected of being German spies. This widespread anxiety found expression in Defence Regulation 18B (1939, extended in 1940) which gave Home Security the authority to intern enemy aliens indefinitely, without trial, as well as those considered enemies of the state, such as the 920 members of the British Union of Fascists who were detained (Grant, 2009, p. 506). One of the groups MI5 monitored was the anti-Semitic and anti-communist Right Club which produced inflammatory leaflets about the 'Jews' war'. The investigations of three MI5 female infiltrators led to the arrest of Anna Wolkoff in

November 1940. When Wolkoff was sentenced to ten years in prison, she swore to kill one of the MI5 agents who had successfully penetrated the group (Miller, 1986).

While a few women were deployed undercover in Britain, the majority were employed in an administrative capacity. The Registry was an entirely female domain as it had been in the First World War, with the number of staff increasing from 133 in July 1939 to 939 in January 1943 (Andrew, 2009, p. 220). MI5 only ever employed one female officer – Jane Archer (née Sissmore), their main Soviet expert at the outbreak of war. Archer's interrogation of Russian defector Walter Krivitsky in early 1940 was the first professional debriefing of a Soviet intelligence officer and was regarded as 'a model of its kind' (Andrew, 2009, p. 220). She was sacked when she declared the head of MI5 to be incompetent and a regulation introduced in 1941 then made it impossible for a woman to be promoted to officer rank. Fifty-nine women were performing officers' roles in May 1945 but they did so without the pay or status that went with the title when it was held by a man (Andrew, 2009, p. 327).

As in the First World War, MI5 was tasked with capturing German spies as well as monitoring domestic threats. Between September and November 1940, over 25 German agents were infiltrated into Britain (National Archives, KV 3/76). Poorly-trained and ill-equipped to pass as British nationals, they were quickly picked up by MI5 who succeeded in 'turning' many so that they worked as double agents, reporting both to the Germans and to the British. Wulf Schmidt, for example, parachuted into Cambridgeshire on 19 September 1940 and was arrested by the Home Guard the following morning. The 26-year-old Dane agreed to become a double agent and was in continual wireless communication with Germany from October 1940 until May 1945 (Andrew, 1985, p. 671). The *Abwehr* infiltrated six female agents into Britain, four of whom were 'turned' into double agents. After the war, German intelligence files revealed that all of the 115 German agents sent to Britain had been caught. There were 14 treason trials in Britain during the Second World War resulting in 17 convictions, mostly of foreigners, who were sentenced to death.

Juan Maria Pujol, codenamed Garbo, was possibly the most successful double agent of the war. From 1941 when he walked into the German embassy in Madrid, he fed German military intelligence with false information about a network of 27 fictional agents. Garbo and his MI5 controller Tomás Harris wrote 315 letters, each about two thousand words long, to be passed onto German intelligence. One letter contained information supposedly derived from a Glasgow-based agent about a convoy of troopships leaving the Clyde with distinctive Mediterranean camouflage. The letter, dated before the landings, was deliberately intended to arrive too late to be of any military use. Nevertheless, it enhanced his reputation. It was his role in Operation Fortitude, however, that was crucial. Between January 1944 and D-Day, over 500 radio messages were transmitted between Garbo and the *Abwehr* via Madrid. At 1 am on 6 June he alerted the *Abwehr* to the fact that Allied troops had set off for Normandy. Despite being of no use to the German war effort as the message arrived too late to mobilize forces, the message cemented Garbo's standing with German intelligence. Consequently, his message of 9 June which stated that Normandy was 'diversionary in character' was accepted unquestioningly: the crack First SS Panzer Division en route to Normandy was diverted to the Pas-de-Calais where the main assault was expected to take place (National Archives, KV 2/40-2).

MI5 knew early on that Garbo's intelligence was being taken seriously because of the German wireless communications it had intercepted and deciphered at Bletchley Park, the country house that accommodated the headquarters of the Government Code and Cypher School. Bletchley only became well-known in 1974 with the publication of F.W. Winterbotham's *The Ultra Secret*. Shortly after the First World War, a German engineer invented an encryption machine, patented as Enigma. The German navy bought it in 1926, the German army two years later and the Poles in the early 1930s, who gave the machine and instructions on how it worked to both British and French intelligence. In 1937, as the likelihood of war with Germany increased, the Treasury approved the expansion of the Government Code and Cypher School and directives were issued for the earmarking of the 'right type' of personnel who would, on the outbreak of war, be recruited: 'Fifty six seniors, men or women, with the right background and training (salary £600 a year) and thirty girls with a graduate's knowledge of at least two of the languages required (£3 a week)' (Andrew, 1985, p. 632). It expanded greatly during the war under the Executive Head Commander, Alistair Denniston, from 100 personnel in 1939 to over 10 000 men and women in 1945, the majority of whom were between 25 and 30 years of age, middle-class, well-educated and interested in mathematics, computing, chess and crosswords (Knightley, 1986, p. 158). Two-thirds of staff were military personnel, including over three thousand members of the WRNS (Women's Royal Naval Service, popularly known as Wrens) who operated the machines 24 hours a day. Of the third of staff who were civilians, three-quarters were women employed as cryptanalysts, interpreters, linguists, cipher clerks, telephonists and teleprinter operators (Hill, 2004). Bletchley was, however, 'always uncomfortable with the prospect of hiring women into senior positions' and all section heads were men (Smith, 2015, p. 50). The deciphered Enigma codes were first used in the Norway campaign of spring 1940. Bletchley codebreakers succeeded in breaking the cipher used by the German air force on 22 May 1940, enabling them to read German traffic during the battle for France and from December 1940 *Abwehr* communications could be decrypted. About three thousand messages were decoded daily by the Government Code and Cypher School, which was renamed Government Communications Headquarters (GCHQ) in 1942, leading to a mass of intelligence codenamed Ultra (West, 1986).

While Bletchley is a byword for intelligence during the Second World War, another branch of the intelligence network has remained clouded in secrecy. The Y Service intercepted enemy air voice transmissions and was of particular use during the Battle of Britain. German-speaking WAAFs (Women's Auxiliary Air Force) such as Aileen Clayton, the highest-ranking female intelligence officer of the Second World War, were able to listen in and translate Luftwaffe communications, providing valuable tactical information about the location and altitude of planes outside the range of radar (Clayton, 1980). In addition to intercepting and deciphering radio communications, intelligence also took the form of scrutiny of aerial reconnaissance photographs taken by the Royal Air Force flying missions over Germany. On occasion, this provided invaluable information: in May 1943 WAAF officer Constance Babbington-Smith spotted what she thought was a launching ramp and a small aircraft in a photograph taken over Peenemünde the previous day. An enlargement was made confirming her supposition. Peenemünde, an island in the Baltic, was the testing site for the V1 and V2 flying bombs and was subsequently targeted by Bomber Command. Her discovery, which could so easily have been overlooked, delayed the first flying bomb attack by at least six months and without doubt saved thousands of civilian lives.

Intelligence operations during the Second World War also provided false information to the enemy. We have already seen how Garbo and his handler misled the Germans for several years. Another success was MI5's 'Operation Mincemeat', which misinformed the Germans in 1942 and 1943 about the location of the Allied invasion. The corpse of a man of military age who had died recently of pneumonia was deliberately washed ashore on the Spanish coast, looking as if he had drowned, with documents pertaining to the planned invasion of Southern France (National Archives, CAB 154/67). It convinced the Germans that the Balkans was the key area and thus when Allied troops landed in Sicily in summer 1943 they faced only two German divisions: the bulk of the German forces were stationed in Greece.

British counter espionage, which took myriad forms including infiltrating domestic dissident groups, capturing German spies, running double agents, monitoring German radio traffic, interpreting aerial photographs and deliberately misinforming the enemy, was of enormous significance during the Second World War. Britain also actively ran its own espionage operations in occupied Europe.

BRITISH ESPIONAGE DURING THE SECOND WORLD WAR

The Second World War witnessed a new breed of professional: trained allied agents who were sent into the field to wage ungentlemanly warfare against an enemy that was perceived to be not playing by the rules. Some of these British agents were women. The Special Operations Executive (SOE), established in July 1940, recruited men and women, trained them in armed and unarmed combat and infiltrated them into Nazi-occupied Europe to work with the local resistance in order to undertake acts of sabotage and subversion (Pattinson, 2007). Kenneth Mackenzie, who was one of the 480 British agents working undercover in France, noted 'I never consider myself a spy. I was just helping the Allies. I was an agent, yes, but for Britain, which makes all the difference' (Imperial War Museum, Mackenzie, 1996). Despite the fact that SOE agents did not view themselves as spies engaging in espionage, during the course of their work they inevitably stumbled across intelligence. Ben Cowburn, another British national who was sent by SOE to France, for example, supplied information about oil storage depots in his reports, which were invaluable to the RAF (Cowburn, 1960), while Jos Mulder Gemmeke, who was recruited by SOE's Dutch section, crossed enemy lines in 1944 with microfilm containing important information about the location of German divisions and the sites of the V1 and V2 factories. She recalled that she put the microfilm 'behind the glass in my powder compact and … in my shoulder pads from my coat' (Imperial War Museum, Mulder Gemmeke, 1996). Female agents frequently exploited the trappings of femininity to conceal clandestine materials. Many also record in their testimonies that they flirted with German soldiers on guard at checkpoints in an attempt to avoid their baggage, which may have concealed weapons or radios, from being searched. Consequently, women were often deployed as couriers in order to capitalize on German soldiers' failure to recognize that young women were actively involved in the resistance (Pattinson, 2007). Of the 39 female agents infiltrated by the British-run F(rench) Section, 12 died in concentration camps. Vera Atkins, one of the senior headquarters staff, traveled to Germany in 1945 to talk to captured officers to enquire about their fate (Helm, 2006). Additionally, a further 11 female agents were deployed to France by the French-run branch (RF Section), three to Holland and two to Belgium and over three thousand women, most of them members of the First Aid Nursing Yeomanry, served with SOE as coders, wireless operators, secretaries, keyboard operators and teleprinters at the base stations in Britain, North Africa, Italy, the Middle East and the Far East.

A highly gendered form of resistance, which might be regarded as humanitarian work rather than espionage, involved staffing the escape lines. Couriers and safe-housekeepers, on whom the lines depended, were virtually all women and several were run by women, including the Marie-Claire line led by Mary Lindell (Wynne, 1980). A branch of military intelligence, MI9, was assigned to oversee escape and evasion and it financed a number of large escape lines in Belgium and France, resulting in thousands of allied airmen returning to Britain, some of whom brought important information back with them (Foot and Langley, 1979).

While sabotage and escape lines might be stretching the definition of espionage, there were cells specifically devoted to collecting intelligence. MI6 ran a network of intelligence organizations, financing its operations as it had in the First World War. One of its principal French groups was Alliance. Following the arrest of its leader Georges Loustaunau-Lacau, Marie-Madeleine Fourcade led the three thousand-strong group. It provided reports on the location of the Luftwaffe's decoy airfields, on the Kriegsmarine submarine bases and the site of the V1 and V2 rockets at Peenemünde and assisted thousands of allied airmen out of France (Fourcade, 1973).

The number of British women employed by MI6 headquarters increased dramatically during the Second World War but, as in MI5, women were concentrated in subordinate roles providing clerical support. Claude Dansey, the assistant chief of MI6, was opposed to female intelligence agents, believing them to be untrustworthy. The Bland Report written in October 1944, which made suggestions for the future organization of the unit, noted that it had been 'backward in employing women' and it also rejected the inter-war practice of enlisting men of independent means in order to economize[1] (Jeffery, 2010, p. 598). In the wake of the Bland Report, regional controllers in May 1946 were required to consider where women might be employed as officers, both in Britain and overseas. Until then, posts in the diplomatic and consular services were filled by men only (McCarthy, 2009). There were a number of female officers who possessed the requisite qualifications and experience and were available for posting. The Director of Production, who noted that 'it was accepted policy that they should be employed in these appointments', ruled that women 'should be recruited on the same level as male officers, i.e. they should be able to be sent abroad to foreign situations'. Yet although 'there was no reason why a woman officer should not eventually become a representative ... this would be the exception rather than the rule'. Thus, in May 1946, the first woman to head an overseas station was posted, albeit to a minor one. When in April 1949 MI6 proposed sending a woman to head a sub-section in the new British legation at Tel Aviv, the Foreign Office refused and when MI6 suggested sending a female secretary to Amman in August 1949 the ambassador recommended that if it had to be a woman, 'she should be a person of a certain age and if possible of forbidding appearance, well able to take care of herself' (Jeffery, 2010, p. 696).

While it would be an exaggeration to claim that British intelligence won the Second World War, it certainly shortened it and saved many lives. Christopher Andrew asserts that reliable intelligence made possible three significant allied victories: Operation Torch (the invasion of North Africa in 1942); the North Atlantic naval war; and Operation Overlord (the invasion of the Normandy coast on D-Day, 6 June 1944). The latter, he noted, was 'perhaps the biggest intelligence success in the history of modern warfare' (1985, p. 679). The role of women in intelligence during the Second World War expanded greatly: women were recruited to executive posts by both MI5 and MI6, were used in large numbers to staff organizations and were in some instances deployed on operations overseas. There were, however, no women employed as station heads until after 1945 and a marriage bar was imposed on women employed by the Foreign Office until 1972. It was not until 1987 that the first married female ambassador was appointed (McCarthy, 2009, p. 320). Even in the late 1960s, new female recruits were told that 'women are happier in subordinate positions' (Andrew, 2009, p. 339). Stella Rimington, the first woman in the world to head an intelligence agency, who served as Director General of MI5 between 1992 and 1996, recollected that when she joined in 1969 'the nearest women got to the sharp end of things in those days was as support officers to the men who were running the agents', ensuring the safe houses were clean, tidy and supplied with refreshments (2002, pp. 102–3). Rimington was the first MI5 head whose identity was publicly known and, following the publication of unflattering photographs of her in the press, she was advised to wear make-up and have her hair styled. She was followed by Eliza Manningham-Buller who headed the organization between 2002 and 2007. There have been no female chiefs of MI6. By the 1990s, 50 percent of all MI5 staff were women, and yet the sensationalist myth of the *femme fatale* continues to overshadow women involved in espionage, as witnessed by the 2010 British press coverage of Anna Chapman, a Russian national with British citizenship living in the United States who was arrested for her involvement in an illegal Russian Federation spy ring. She was described as the 'real life Bond girl' (*The Telegraph*, 2010), 'the femme fatale spy' (Bates and Martin, 2010), the 'spy ring sex bomb' with 'a Licence to Thrill' (Crick, 2010).

CONCLUSION

Espionage, as with all aspects of warfare, is highly gendered, shaping the experiences of the men and women who engaged in it, as well as public perceptions of them. It has been considered an almost exclusively male profession and in the cultural imagination, the British male spy was very much the gentleman. By contrast, women have been regarded as marginal to formal intelligence-gathering organizations, their only contribution being to use their 'feminine wiles' to seduce their prey. Despite this perception, women's contributions were significant for the development of twentieth-century British espionage. Indeed, the expansion and professionalization of the British Secret Service would not have been possible without either the women who staffed the organizations in Britain, often undertaking mundane gendered tasks such as filing and report-writing, which have been valued far less than the work undertaken by men, or the women in occupied countries undertaking operational roles which were often also segregated along gender lines. Put simply, the crucial factor in expanding women's opportunities to participate in the intelligence communities were the two world wars.

NOTE

1. MI6 in the inter-war period used to employ men who did not require a salary (as they had family money) in order to save money. The Bland Report rejected this practice.

REFERENCES

National Archives, London

CAB 154/67 – War Cabinet: Plan Mincemeat. 1943–45.
HO 45/25520 – Home Office: Disturbances: Percy Glading. 1938–51.
HO 144/3324 – Home Office: Criminal Cases: Carl Lody. 1934.
HW 3/6 – Government Code and Cypher School and predecessors: Personal Papers, Unofficial Histories, Foreign Office X Files and Miscellaneous Records. 1914–19.
KV 1/49 – The Security Service: H Branch, Organisation and Administration. 1900–1919.
KV 1/50 – The Security Service: H Branch, Organisation and Administration 1920: first supplement on Women's Work.
KV 2/40-2 – The Security Service: Personal Files. World War Two. Double Agent Operations. Juan Pujol-Garcia. 1941–45.
KV 3/76 – The Security Service. German espionage from 1939. 1939–41.
KV 4/227 – The Security Service. The wartime history of M/S agents. 1945.
WO 32/10776 – War Office and Successors. History of Military Intelligence Directorate. 1920–21.

Imperial War Museum (Documents and Sound), London

La Dame Blanche Box 2.
Mackenzie, Kenneth (1996), SOE agent, interview 18154.
Mulder Gemmeke, Jos (1996), SOE agent, interview 18153.

Published Sources

Andrew, Christopher (n.d.a), 'MI5 in World War I', accessed 1 July 2013 at: https://www.mi5.gov.uk/home/mi5-history/mi5s-early-years/mi5-in-world-war-i.html.
Andrew, Christopher (n.d.b), 'The inter-war years', accessed 1 July 2013 at: https://www.mi5.gov.uk/home/mi5-history/mi5-between-the-wars/the-inter-war-years.html.
Andrew, Christopher (1985), *Secret Service: The Making of the British Intelligence Community*, Sceptre.
Andrew, Christopher (2009), *The Defence of the Realm: The Authorised History of MI5*, Allen Lane.
Bates, Daniel and Daniel Martin (2010), 'The great spy swap: bid to stop the femme fatale spy returning to Britain', *Daily Mail*, 13 July.
Boghardt, Thomas (2004), *Spies of the Kaiser: German Covert Operations during the First World War Era*, Palgrave.
Clayton, Aileen (1980), *The Enemy is Listening: The Story of the Y Service*, Hutchinson.
Cowburn, Ben (1960), *No Cloak, No Dagger*, Jarrolds.
Crick, Andy (2010), 'Licence to thrill', *The Sun*, accessed on 21 July 2015 at: http://www.thesun.co.uk/sol/homepage/news/3039578/Sexbomb-spy-Anna-Chapman-and-her-newlywed-Brit-hubby.html.
De Schaepdrijver, Sophie (2015), *Gabrielle Petit: The Death and Life of a Female Spy in the First World War*, Bloomsbury.
Foot, Michael and James Langley (1979), *MI9: Escape and Evasion: 1939–1945*, Book Club Associates.
Fourcade, Marie Madeleine (1973), *Noah's Ark*, Allen and Unwin.

French, David (1978), 'Spy fever in Britain, 1900–15', *The Historical Journal*, **21** (2): 355–70.

Gannon, Patrick (2010), *Inside Room 40: The Codebreakers of World War One*, Ian Allan Publishing.

Grant, Jennifer (2009), 'The Role of MI5 in the internment of British Fascists during the Second World War', *Intelligence and National Security*, **24** (4): 499–528.

Helm, Sarah (2006), *A Life in Secrets: The Story of Vera Atkins and the Lost Agents of SOE*, Abacus.

Hiley, Nicholas (1986), 'Counter-espionage and security in Great Britain during the First World War', *English Historical Review*, **101** (400): 635–70.

Hill, Marion (2004), *Bletchley Park People: Churchill's Geese that Never Cackled*, Sutton.

Hoehling, Adolph (1967), *Women Who Spied: True Stories of Feminine Espionage*, Dodd, Mead.

Howell, Georgina (2006), *Daughter of the Desert: The Remarkable Life of Gertrude Bell*, Pan Books.

Jeffery, Keith (2010), *MI6: The History of the S.I.S. 1909–1949*, Bloomsbury.

Knightley, Phillip (1986), *The Second Oldest Profession: The Spy as Bureaucrat, Patriot, Fantasist and Whore*, André Deutsch.

McCarthy, Helen (2009), 'Petticoat diplomacy: the admission of women to the British Foreign Service, c.1919–1946', *Twentieth Century British History*, **20** (3): 285–321.

Miller, Joan (1986), *One Girl's War: Personal Exploits in MI5's Most Secret Station*, Brandon.

Newman, Bernard (1941), *Secrets of German Espionage*, Withy Grove.

Olmsted, Kathryn S. (2004), 'Blond queens, red spiders, and neurotic old maids: gender and espionage in the early Cold War', *Intelligence and National Security*, **19** (1): 78–94.

Pattinson, Juliette (2007), *Behind Enemy Lines: Gender, Passing and the SOE in the Second World War*, Manchester University Press.

Proctor, Tammy M. (2003), *Female Intelligence: Women and Espionage in the First World War*, New York University Press.

Rimington, Stella (2002), *Open Secret: The Autobiography of the Former Director-General of MI5*, Arrow.

Smith, Christopher (2015), *The Hidden History of Bletchley Park: A Social and Organisational History, 1939–1945*, Palgrave Macmillan.

Stafford, David (1981), 'Spies and gentlemen: the birth of the British Spy novel, 1893–1914', *Victorian Studies*, **24** (4): 489–509.

The Telegraph (2010), 'Russian spy Anna Chapman poses for men's magazine', 19 October.

Twigge, Stephen, Edward Hampshire and Graham Macklin (2009), *British Intelligence: Secrets, Spies and Sources*, National Archives.

Van Seters, Deborah (1992), 'Hardly Hollywood's ideal: female autobiographies of secret service work, 1914-45', *Intelligence and National Security*, **7** (4): 403–24.

West, Nigel (1986), *GCHQ: The Secret Wireless War, 1900–86*, Weidenfeld and Nicolson.

West, Nigel (2005), *Mask: MI5's Penetration of the Communist Party of Great Britain*, Routledge.

Wheelwright, Julie (1992), *The Fatal Lover: Mata Hari and the Myth of Women in Espionage*, Collins and Brown.

Wheelwright, Julie (1993), 'Poisoned honey: the myth of women in espionage', *Queen's Quarterly*, **100** (2): 291–309.

Winterbotham, Frederick W. (1974), *The Ultra Secret*, Weidenfeld and Nicolson.

Wynne, Barry (1980), *The Story of Mary Lindell: 'Marie-Claire' of MI9 Wartime Secret Agent*, Robin Clark.

4. Cat food and clients: gendering the politics of protection in the Private Militarized[1] Securitized Company

Paul Higate

INTRODUCTION

Private Militarized Security Companies (PMSC) have assumed a significance not seen since the days of traditional mercenary armies prior to the emergence of national armed forces some three centuries ago. The privatization of security on a large scale, the controversial use of private security contractors[2] in Iraq and Afghanistan, and their almost exclusive reliance on male former soldiers deployed as the small proportion of armed employees working on the ground, represents an important transformation in the conditions under which violence is manifest in contemporary times.

While both regular military personnel and contractors have been implicated in human rights abuses, contractors are generally less accountable (Singer, 2008) and experience greater operational freedom than their regular-soldier peers.[3] It is therefore unsurprising that the ascendancy of private security has been seen by critical scholars of gender as an exemplary moment of (re)masculinization (Stachowitsch, 2013). Yet this claim requires careful scrutiny since there is a paucity of fine-grained, qualitative data with which to capture the diversity of those working as contractors. This empirical deficit is manifest through the continued misrepresentation of contractors in the media[4] as no more than clones of trigger-happy, pumped-up employees of the most notorious of companies, *Blackwater* – now renamed *Academi* – who have a reputation for creating insecurity amongst host populations.[5] There also exists a real lack of specificity in popular coverage of contractors' class, the kinds of security work they do and the contexts within which they work. With this in mind, I contribute towards the emerging interest in PMSC from a ground-up, gender perspective that also acknowledges the intersection of other identity markers, including that of class. In sum, it is argued that the abuses perpetrated by contractors – most notoriously the killing of 14 civilians in Nisour Square in Iraq by members of a Blackwater security team – co-exist with other more routine, less sensational, everyday practices that do not create havoc amongst local populations. I make this point through a focus on the gendered character of a particular community of contractors – Close Protection[6] (CP) officers – whose militarized and masculinized identities become most apparent when reflecting on interactions with their clients. Guided by Cynthia Enloe's (2004) keen sense of gender curiosity as applied to the everyday, this chapter shows that it is through the small details of occupational and masculine interaction that the threads of the gender order are woven into the social fabric of the PMSC industry.

The chapter is structured as follows. First it provides a brief overview of the PMSC literature and then moves on to discuss research on gender in private security. Judith Hicks Stiehm's (1982) influential essay 'The protected, the protector, the defender' provides an analytic framework for the qualitative data collected by the author during the summer of 2010 in a region deemed hostile. These findings are then considered in regard to Stiehm's protector/protected framework with which they appear to chime closely. Here, findings from my own field research suggest that CP officer/client relationships were played out along gender lines through clearly discernible, hierarchical power relations. These power relations signal a gender order marked by asymmetry whereby, following Stiehm, protectors exercise control over their clients in a fairly straightforward manner. However, as the research progressed, the sample of former British army CP officers were found to be *negotiating* rather than imposing narratives of risk and threat upon their female clients, an observation that invites analyses that go beyond Stiehm's protector/protected frame. Discussion then focuses on intersections of gender and class as they shape a particular gender order inflected with resistance and marked by competing definitions of security. Taken together, these findings represent an original contribution to the PMSC literature, focusing in substantive terms on the ways that security experts construct insecurity, resistance to these narratives and the militarized and masculinized roots to these 'expert' understandings.

CONTEXT: THE RISE OF THE PRIVATE MILITARIZED SECURITY COMPANY

Of all civilian occupational contexts, that of the PMSC industry resonates most strongly with soldierly occupational continuity where the demand for specialized skills has grown exponentially in this multi-billion dollar security enterprise (Singer, 2008; Higate, 2012a). A constellation of forces underpin the rapid growth of the PMSC sphere (Geraghty, 2007, pp. 22–31), facilitated by the dominance of post-cold war markets that have fueled a strong tendency to outsource traditional government functions and, consequently, spark debate around constitutional issues (Avant and Sigelman, 2009). Simultaneously, militaries have been downsized, providing a large number of men trained in the legitimate discharge of violence who are ripe for recruitment by PMSC (Cooling, 2010). An unknown yet significant number of these demobilized troops have gone on to become involved in conflicts in other states (Singer, 2008, p. 38). Subsumed under the generic label of security or military contractor, these (mainly) men are employed in a plethora of roles ranging from building infrastructure, feeding and housing troops, convoy security, close protection of dignitaries, kidnap and hostage work, static guarding of civilian and military installations, training of local personnel as part of security sector reform, and provision of logistical and support functions to military peacekeeping, combat operations and alleged support for an assassination program (Kinsey, 2007; Leander, 2009a, 2009b). Though PMSC have a global presence, a lengthy history and are involved in a diversity of tasks, the spotlight has fallen on contractors and companies working in Iraq and Afghanistan, areas of operation that provide for the employment of 207 600 contractors by the US Department of Defense alone (Schwartz and Swain, 2011).

Interest in PMSC has been dominated by scholars working in the mainstream of Political Science, International Relations (IR) and International Law. They have discussed such concerns as the state's eroding monopoly on violence (Mandel, 2002; Singer, 2008), the industry's overall legitimacy (Singer, 2002; Holmqvist, 2005), private security as a proxy for US foreign policy (Isenberg, 2008), international and historical norms governing the use of mercenaries (Percy, 2007), the place of security in contemporary politics and world order (Kinsey, 2007; Abrahamsen and Williams, 2010), different national attitudes to the privatization of security (Krahmann, 2010) and, framed in a more sociological sense, questions of professionalism along lines of national identity (Higate, 2012b). Concerns around the industry's legitimacy, how best to regulate private security and, ultimately, what might be done to rein in the violent excesses of a small number of contractors have generated discussion amongst academics and practitioners alike. Instigated in 2011 by stakeholders from across the industry, the self-regulatory International Code of Conduct for Private Security Providers[7] (ICoC) represents the culmination of much heated debate around company and employee accountability, and at the time of writing has been signed by over 700 companies.

Overall, the scholarly literature has turned on the big questions of states and their foreign policies, state sovereignty and, closely allied, the public/private divide in relation to the privatization of security. Explanations for the relative neglect of a gender perspective are therefore to be found in the dominant 'malestream' traditions informing these macro-level analyses that have tended – within IR and Political Science approaches at least – to have marginalized the everyday. Yet it is the gendered character of the everyday that shapes international politics, war and the performance of peace (Kronsell and Svedberg, 2011). With this in mind, one way to analyze gender relations as they play out on the ground in the PMSC context is to approach them from an interactional order perspective, an approach taken up below.

Emerging Literature: Gender and PMSC

Generated from within feminist and pro-feminist thought that conceives of gender as integral rather than epiphenomenal to the workings of international politics is an emerging scholarship focused on questions of power, identity and inter/intra-gender-relations in the culture of PMSC. An early, somewhat acritical contribution sought change from within the industry through gender mainstreaming, as argued in a report written for the Geneva Center for the Democratic Accountability of Armed Forces (DCAF) (Schultz and Yeung, 2005). The private security company Dyncorp's involvement in sex-trafficking and rape in the Balkans has been analyzed in more critical terms (Harrington, 2005; Sperling, 2011). Also focused on the Balkans are feminist analyses of the legal dimensions of PMSC with wider implications for operating in conflict and post-conflict contexts (Vrdoljak, 2011). More recently, women's participation in the industry has been placed under the critical spotlight in ways that highlight the complexities of PMSC gendered culture (Basu and Eichler, 2011). Informed by an explicit critical men's studies perspective, other contributions have foregrounded masculinity, and particularly militarized forms of masculinity, as crucial to understanding contractor identity (Chisholm, 2008; Via, 2010; Higate, 2011). The question of how far the industry can be said to rely on a benchmark masculinity that combines ethical warrior heroes and true professionals in PMSCs' representation of their contracting workforce has also been critically considered (Joachim and Schneiker, 2012). One of the first contributions of its kind focusing on identity and professionalism (albeit rather less attuned to critical men's studies) is Franke's survey of 223 US law enforcement officers working as contractors. In this study, masculinity was operationalized as one of a series of identity measures that revealed 'average levels of masculinity', high levels of patriotism and strong agreement with the importance of adhering to professional standards (Franke, 2009, pp. 26–7).[8] Intersections of race and masculinity have been examined in the case of contractors from the developing world (Barker, 2009), Ghurka contractors (Chisholm, 2011), Fijian contractors (Teaiwa, 2005; Maclellan, 2006; Bolatagici, 2011) and Latin American contractors (Higate, 2012c).

Finally, the concept of fratriarchy has been applied to the so-called Kabul Hazing in 2009 involving contractors of the US Embassy guard force in Kabul as one way to generate insights into the heteronormative and racialized character of bonding between men working for the private security company ArmorGroup (Higate, 2012d). While varied in their focus on the role that gender plays in PMSC, it is clear that critical scholars have only begun to scratch the surface of this field of study. Many opportunities for future research remain, including how to make sense of the links between militarized masculinities and accountability; what it means for local women and men to be regularly exposed to a high profile hypermasculine contractor presence, where weapons are on display and aggressive driving is employed; how different roles within the industry shape militarized and masculinized gender identities; and, finally, of particular importance to this chapter, what might be said about the ways that consumers of security negotiate, resist and challenge the narratives of risk and danger with which they are confronted by security experts. It is with this in mind that the chapter now focuses on the interplay of gender, identity, power and class as they are negotiated in one particular company. Judith Hick Stiehm's influential essay 'The protected, the protector, the defender' (Stiehm, 1982) provides an analytical point of departure for the particular gender order under scrutiny.

Stiehm's Contribution: 'The Protected, the Protector, the Defender'

The overall aim of Stiehm's essay was to highlight the gendered character of the protected and the protector in relation to state militaries. As she notes, 'only men are allowed to be protectors' (Stiehm, 1982, p. 367), and as such, are permitted to use violent force on behalf of those they protect. Though armed forces in the Global North have undergone far-reaching transformation in terms of female composition through increasing opportunities to serve as helicopter attack pilots on the front line, for example, the main tenets of Stiehm's argument stand. As noted above in regard to (re)masculinization, they may even be seen to have a renewed currency in the world of the security contractor where the armed CP role is overwhelmingly dominated by men. Chiming with Enloe's

(2002, pp. 23–4) identification of core militaristic values, Stiehm notes that protectors come to see violence as necessary, effective and appropriately exercised by men only (Stiehm, 1982, p. 367). Here, women tend to be placed in a subordinate role to protectors (military and militarized men) through their dependency upon them. Men and women are thus positioned in a power relationship leading, in some instances, to the abuse of the protected. 'Women are meant to be protected' by their protectors argues Stiehm, 'but frequently they are not' (Stiehm, 1982, p. 367). The respective status of the protector and the protected are then co-constitutive and mutually interdependent. He depends on her for his status as protector, and she on him for protection. Crucially, however, this relationship is *asymmetrical* since only one of the parties has access to the means (embodied skill-capital) and instruments (weapons) of force (Stiehm, 1982, p. 374). Framed in explicitly normative terms, Stiehm argues that it is important to move beyond the categories of protector and protected and its associated gender binary. Rather, a different status should be aspired to by all, whether male or female – that of the defender. Stiehm presents the defender status as mitigating women's dependency, low self-esteem and subordination (Stiehm, 1982, p. 374). Stiehm's insightful and provocative essay has an enduring heuristic relevance and is helpful in illuminating the gendered character of security in the international system.[9] It can be further developed through moving from the state to the micro-interactional order where we note an explicit narrative of protection as central to the occupational role of the contractors in question.

BACKGROUND: METHOD, CASE AND MASCULINITY

The fieldwork for this research was carried out with a private security company during the summer months of 2010 in Afghanistan. It involved 16 open-ended, semi-structured face-to-face interviews with male contractors lasting up to one and a half hours. It also used observation of two shifts of contractors (20 in total) working in the armed CP role whose job was to provide security to clients visiting the region. All participants were former members of the British army, of which two were female and one of these had served in a Commonwealth force. Ages ranged from mid-twenties to late forties. Many were married and had family in the UK. The majority had worked on the contract for a number of months and on the private security circuit (Shepherd, 2008) for a few years. During down-time in the crew room between jobs, participants chatted about life, home and work, and spent time on the internet while some of the younger members actively sought more lucrative contracts in riskier regions and roles. During discussion of 'getting out' (of the current contract), the younger men invariably referred to the relatively high wages to be generated elsewhere, together with an awareness of the greater risks that accompanied alternative armed convoy protection work.

Participants were billeted in a villa a few miles away from their place of work, and typically worked 12-hour shifts involving nine weeks on duty followed by two weeks of leave. Their main role was to provide security to visitors, which extended to around-the-clock deployment if required. Here, vehicle-bound CP officers would typically drive visitors to and from the airport, run them to the various ministries in town for meetings, ensure they returned safely to the secure compound from business/social functions, and also accompany them on private journeys to local markets and other leisure facilities.

All data was recorded in a fieldwork diary written up after each period of observation and interview(s), and occasionally noted in abbreviated form during time spent in the crew-room conversing with CP officers and observing intra-CP interaction. There was no opportunity to interview or meet with the clients/the protected, and the analysis in this chapter is based solely on observations and interviews generated from the CP officer/protector perspective. One of the primary aims of the research was to theorize the identity work of these individuals through the lens of gender, specifically the ways in which they framed security and insecurity within the particular gendered, interactional order in play.[10] As the research progressed, it was clear that participants' main concerns turned on their interactions with clients and was conveyed through masculine talk. Here, masculinity took the form of a shared understanding between men (Gough and Edwards, 1998, p. 414) that sustained morale during extended periods of inactivity in the crew-room. In terms of content, this masculine talk involved 'a complex of socially guided ... interactional, and micropolitical activities that cast particular pursuits as expressions of masculine and feminine "natures"' (Gough and Edwards, 1998, p. 415). Presented in its crudest sense, the gendered nature spoken of by CP officers invoked their rationality in opposition to the irrationality of the female clients in the face of risk. Taken together, both form and content of masculine talk registered during observation and interview 'conceived of gender as an emergent feature of [the] social situation ... as an outcome of, and a rationale for, various social arrangements' (West and Zimmerman, 1987, p. 126). In the current case the social arrangements clearly dominating the data concerned the ways in which participants had necessarily to negotiate with clients, an experience many of them found onerous, somewhat unexpected and a topic of central importance to the gender order as discussed further below.

Mapping the Gendered Terrain: Protector and Protected

Preliminary findings from the fieldwork appeared to validate Stiehm's protector/protected framework. First, it was almost exclusively men doing the protection,[11] and interestingly, though CP officers were frequently entrusted with the security of male clients, their invariable focus in interview and idle crew room banter was on the females they kept safe.

Second, the protector carried side-arms and was authorized to use deadly force, rules of engagement permitting. Though both parties were required to wear body armor, the protected were unarmed and therefore wholly dependent on the protector for security. Usually sitting in the rear of the vehicles in which they were transported, the protected had no control over the vehicle itself, the speed at which it might be driven, or how far and in what kinds of ways it might be maneuvered. This latter point is particularly important since aggressive driving by United Nations staff, national militaries and PMSC personnel in this and other conflict/ post-conflict contexts has been shown to exacerbate tensions amongst members of the host population, as well as drawing attention to the target status of the armored vehicle and its international occupants.[12]

Third, it was the CP officer who defined and categorized the threat faced by the protected through daily intelligence updates detailing 'specific' and 'non-specific' threats leading to the creation of threat assessments, which were then imparted to clients. This knowledge informed the protector's framing of danger against the backdrop of another broader, static narrative of threat concerning the region's overall hostile character. Despite the ambiguity of the threat with regard to (1) when it might come, (2) from whom it was likely to originate (i.e. generic references to terrorists, insurgents or simply bad guys) and (3) the particular form it would take (ambush, Improvised Explosive Device [IED], or kidnap leading to the wearing of a boiler-suit[13]), protectors distilled this wide range of possibilities into a tangible set of objective dangers. In rendering the unknown knowable (to some degree at least), a process that varied between individual CP officers, protectors derived their status from the knowledge–power nexus grounded in their ability to construct a compelling narrative of risk, danger and appropriate, professional response to any potential incident. As Stiehm (1982, p. 368) notes, 'the degree of danger posed by a particular threat is usually defined by the protector', though also with salience to the current work, she goes on to state that 'in real life ... the threat remains a brooding, ambiguous ...

presence' (Stiehm, 1982, p. 369). The narratives of risk and response appeared to sustain the CP officer's superior position in a hierarchy of knowledge and expertise influencing protector/protected interaction. Further, and in a more demonstrable sense, the attempted cultivation of fear and anxiety amongst clients was likely intended by CP officers as a disciplinary strategy to engender acquiescence and deference to the security expert. In no way were CP officers malicious in their intent to convey the risky nature of the environment, but rather it can be seen as a functional outcome of professional practice central to the protector/ protected relationship. Narratives of threat derived from good intention and occupational prerogative thus determined freedom of movement and, crucially, cemented the masculinized protector role rooted in control and authority. Or, so it seemed.

The Clients Resist: from 'Protected' to 'Wayward'

As the research evolved, it became clear that CP officers were preoccupied with their clients' *denial* of the hazardous hostile context within which the latter found themselves. It is at this point that Stiehm's static protector/protected framework can be usefully developed in ways that illuminate complexity, fluidity and contingency in the everyday setting of the particular interactional gender order under scrutiny.

For example, during a relatively quiet period in the crew room, a group of protectors relayed a story about the so-called 'cat food run' that had, by the time of telling, assumed a legendary status. It was also discussed extensively – with some consternation – by the second shift of CP officers. The compound housing the visiting clients provided an ad hoc home to a large number of malnourished stray cats that survived on rubbish and the odd scrap of food donated by caring staff. The 'cat food run' referred to the request by one of the (female) compound visitors to be driven to a local store in order to purchase a case of cat food so that the 'poor animals would not starve'. This required journeying through a threat-laden environment to a supermarket that was considered a target since it was frequented mainly by those who were easily identifiable as internationals. While CP officers are at liberty to refuse certain requests if they consider them to be too risky, in practice they generally defer to orders coming from the operations room and its senior personnel who authorize all such movements. In all likelihood, operations room staff would not know the exact products to be bought at the supermarket, nor would they really care, since they do not have time to engage in this level of detail. Perhaps more importantly, the staff of private companies are keenly aware that they are commercial operators providing a service to paying customers (albeit clients who do not pay directly pay for this security provision, but are beneficiaries on account of their protected status). Dutifully, the CP officer tasked with the 'cat food run' did as he was directed, despite clear concerns that tackling the roads of the city and parking in close proximity to a supermarket (one of which was bombed some months after) represented a wholesale disregard for his own security as well as that of his client. Subsequently, he and others deemed this a 'stupid and pointless job'. This story jostled with others, told with equal concern and zeal, about driving clients to a leisure and health facility to have pedicures, manicures and massages. CP officers talked of being 'glorified taxi drivers' or 'babysitters', who, despite developing a finely crafted occupational expertise in weapons use, driving skills, situational awareness, risk aversion and, in some cases, having 'seen the whites of the eyes of the enemy' during previous military service, were now mere adjuncts to the well-being of 'scrawny animals' and the beauty treatments of 'vain clients'. Protectors also complained at length about 'not being respected', of 'being talked down to' and as 'taken for granted'.

The visceral sense of frustration at being treated not as a professional replete with command of the situation, but rather as a subordinate whose role was to serve the interests of clients, was supported by a legitimating narrative about the risk to the protector himself. For example, when waiting for clients, CP officers had frequently to linger in areas vulnerable to attack by suicide bombers, IEDs and other armed opportunists. Hypothetically at least, hostile individuals were able to quickly identify the armored vehicle and its Western driver, and whilst attacks were few, anxieties were undoubtedly heightened. Though Standard Operating Procedures (SOPs) necessitated threat assessment where CP officers or colleagues would reconnoiter a villa or government ministry in advance of it being used for a meeting, they frequently found themselves parked in streets outside security compounds late into the night, particularly when clients were attending social functions.[14] To worsen matters, clients occasionally emerged intoxicated or 'pissed up' as one participant put it, thereby exacerbating the risk for themselves and the CP officer if there were to be an incident.[15]

There are numerous ways in which to read this data. One possibility, led by both its ubiquity and the strength of feeling with which it was expressed, concerned the contested definitions of risk played out between the two parties. Whereas CP officers had little or no desire to interact with the locals, numerous of the more 'troublesome female clients' expressed a stereotypically 'soft' desire to 'connect with local people', or 'get a feel for the city' and 'do the tourist thing', rather than adhere to a pre-planned, closely calculated vehicle move subject to threat assessment derived from a masculinized preoccupation with risk and danger. Despite the formal security protocols warning against non-vital movements and keeping the vehicle secure, a participant reported one client's insistence on lowering the vehicle window so that she could 'smell the air';[16] as Stiehm (1982, p. 372) notes with some insight, 'dependents can be draining' on their protectors. This perceived disregard for security and the client's rationale were anathema to CP officers who had little choice but to negotiate with clients. It was here that they spoke of a weakened masculine occupational identity since their superior position in the gendered interactional order was challenged. Failure to negotiate with clients could threaten their employability within the company as it brought into sharp relief their subordinate status as little more than service providers. What are we to make of CP officers/protectors' narratives turning on frustration with their clients' blasé approach to security? How far and in what ways do these stories speak to the salience of this particular gender order in the everyday, largely mundane gripes of this cohort of former military men working in the privatized context?

DISCUSSION

The Gender Order: Cats, Beauty and Disrespect?

Guided by the aims of the current project to examine the everyday gendered context of one particular element of this security company, and led by participant concerns, the tale of the 'cat food run' is revealing. But, why cats? In terms of gender, mention of cats is more than incidental to the data, but rather can be read as deeply symbolic. Unlike dogs, cats are not associated with being *man*'s best friend. Though cats can be explicitly gendered as male (the archetypal randy tom-cat), it is more typical to think of them as soft, cuddly creatures and as such at the polar extreme of the masculinized killer-dogs that have become de rigueur amongst gangs in the UK. Cats can also be coded as feminine in respect of their flighty and mercurial nature that, at one and the same time, also implies an unpredictable sense of neediness or dependence;[17] the sad and lonely 'spinster' doting on her cat further underscores this gendered trope. Caring for these creatures to the extent that one is willing to risk life and limb in a hostile environment may be counter-intuitive to a (male-security) occupational rationality that regards such compassion as an irrelevant diversion to the risky realities of the environment. Here, CP officers alluded to clients' 'hearts ruling the mind', with concern for animals being coded as feminine weakness. Beauty treatments are more obviously feminized, and the resonance of these anecdotes turns on the sense of decadence they invite in what many (not least security experts), would consider a war zone.[18] Much like men unable to fulfill the breadwinner role, these protectors articulated a sense of gendered redundancy where their militarized masculinity was regarded not as an asset in this context but rather, they thought, was considered excessively paternalistic by clients. At stake here was the protectors' *authority*, their ability to control, to direct and to lead. This challenge to authority spoke of disregard for many years' soldiering, facing danger and achieving a hard won militarized and masculinized status. Finely honed repertoires of risk-mastery suffused with an intuitive sixth sense of when things are likely to go awry generally failed to impress the female clients in question in the protector narrative.

Dealing with Hoity Toity Types: a Challenge for the Lads

Many of the female clients discussed by the CP officers were young, perceived as privileged and well educated; as such they were imbued with relatively high class and occupational status. In contrast, CP officers working the shift had fewer formal qualifications, were from lower socio-economic backgrounds, and traded on their physical rather than cultural capital in the market for force (Avant, 2001). Many of these men self-identified as squaddies, a term invoking practical skills developed hands-on in the testing crucible of military training and combat experience (Hockey, 1986). They embodied a blue-collar habitus with the barely perceptible subtleties of accent and deportment indicating their status, alongside the need for deference to their clients as a key part of their role as (security) service provider.

In this way, the order was derived from intersections of class and gender, where so-called uppity women[19] felt empowered to subvert the protector/protected hierarchy through asserting their status. In the protectors' view some, though by no means all, clients' reluctance to follow security protocol, to be attentive during pre-journey briefings, to wear body-armor when requested and, more generally, to defer to their bodyguard without question was derived from class relations, with young privileged females also referred to as 'hoity toity types'. To paraphrase Stiehm (1982, p. 368), and a position to which the troublesome clients subscribed, why should women consent to rules made by men ... that confine them to the category of the protected?[20]

The final section moves from the focus on everyday masculine talk, identity work and class in the particular company under scrutiny. Having examined the formation of those social arrangements underpinning a gender order characterized by resistance and negotiation, what might be said about the current contribution's potential to broaden and deepen the prevailing focus on the macro level in the PMSC literature?

Selling Risk: Accounting for the Consumers of Security

Many scholars working on the PMC debate have argued that 'privatization has altered the weight of different voices out of the public realm … into a restricted realm where [amongst other actors] PMCs can decide how [security] issues can be defined and handled' (Leander, 2006, p. 25).

Thus, set against the backdrop of the increasing commodification of security, and in their attempt to stimulate demand and grow market share, companies are constantly devising innovative ways in which to 'sell specific understandings of security and risk [to the extent that] … they become engaged in the *construction* and governance of insecurity and danger' (Berndtsson, 2011, p. 1; emphasis added). Clients seek, and in many cases are bound by the insurance industry, to garner solutions to (in)definable security problems in the form of what Leander (2006) has called the politics of protection. In order to succeed in the highly competitive marketplace for security services, then, companies have necessarily to convey a sense of authority in their ability to counter risk and danger. This they do through the use of '"security utterances" [which] help to make reality intelligible "in a particular way … *a security way"'* (Berndtsson, 2011, p. 5, citing Jef Huysmans; emphasis in original). Yet, if these security utterances in the form of imagery and vocabulary propagated through PMSC websites and individual security-experts (Berndtsson, 2011, p. 7) are to succeed, it is essential that they are seen to emanate from an authoritative source. Here, an important marker of authority is military background, where clients' concerns lay not with anxieties around using private services per se, but rather that they are hiring former soldiers who are often deemed as men of the right kind to conduct the business of security.[21] In addition, security experts' knowledge is militarized in so far as it deals with questions of 'military calculation [which] is portrayed as the epitome of rationality' (Stiehm, 1982, p. 375). These concerns turn on the salience of militarized masculinities[22] that are often received positively by consumers of private security. Here, consumers respond favorably to a particular 'set of beliefs, practices and attributes that can enable individuals – men and women – to claim *authority* on the basis of affirmative relationships with the military or military ideas' (Belkin, 2012, p. 4; emphasis added).

It will be recalled that Stiehm's essay and the PMSC literature sparked a line of enquiry that moved from institutional and state concerns to the everyday, gendered interactional level. In so doing, it became clear that those elements of the PMSC literature highlighting the ways that security experts construct insecurity, and the contributions of scholars arguing for the authority of militarized masculinities in the civilian sphere, could be further developed. Though some anecdotal evidence has pointed to understanding the ways in which clients consume private security, there has yet to be a sustained focus on this process at the micro level within the PMSC literature. Similarly, the authority of militarized masculinity in the civilian environment, while clear in many respects, is nevertheless far from straightforward since its audiences may actively negotiate the ideological messages central to these narratives. In this way, examinations of the everyday attempts by CP officers to establish a gender order derived from the authority of militarized masculinity and associated security expertise can be a precarious affair, and itself a metaphor for masculinity that has necessarily to be worked at, reproduced and (re)presented in order to be sustained (Connell, 1995). Thus, to extrapolate from the current study, evolution of security narratives is rarely without hindrance, as they encounter the frictions, resistance and intransigence of those who derive a different kind of authority from their class position, or simply subscribe to a contrasting notion of security, as noted in microcosm above. Though the character of international politics is made possible by a gendered architecture that runs from the everyday to the geopolitical in a seamless manner, by no means is the protector/ protected hierarchy a fait accompli, as we have shown here.

CONCLUSION

In seeking to contribute to the PMSC literature that lacks fine-grained, ethnographic insight, the chapter considered findings from fieldwork involving CP officers and their clients. Stiehm's influential essay provided the prime point of departure for analyzing the everyday context of the gender order in question, where the protector/protected binary was further developed through intersections of gender, class and competing definitions of risk. Framed in regard to the broader gender and war nexus, this chapter also revealed the importance of the everyday to understanding the interactional processes by which a small sample of security experts with military backgrounds attempted to establish a gender order based on the protector/protected hierarchy. It was further noted that, in this particular client-led context, as service providers, CP officers had necessarily to defer to the logic of the marketplace (the threat of unemployment), rather than to that of risk and safety through and by which their professional identities derived legitimacy. It is hoped that this small-scale study will be followed by others that further reveal the complexities of gendered interaction, and in turn the role that resistance can play in future challenges to the security realities with which we are routinely presented and the questioning of which can be seen as a political act.

NOTES

1. Debate continues about how best to categorize the industry and its particular companies that carry out a wide range of tasks. Rather than use Private Military and Security Company, I opt for Private Militarized Security Company in order to draw attention to its cultural, gendered and ideological dimensions.
2. Henceforth, contractors.
3. There is no consistency here in regard to effective mechanisms of accountability across the industry, unlike national militaries that tend to function with relatively uniform codes of justice of various kinds.
4. And by a range of commentators including the author in earlier work.
5. This observation is the starting point for much of the recent literature in the field.
6. CP officers are usually tasked to provide security to dignitaries and others of lesser status and are referred to colloquially as 'bodyguards'. Their skill sets vary but are likely to include proficiency in weaponry (especially small-arms), evasive driving techniques, threat assessment, surveillance, counter-surveillance and reconnaissance.
7. See: http://www.icoc-psp.org/ accessed 30 October 2012.
8. While a useful starting point for questions of identity, as Franke acknowledges, the study is limited by its survey approach that is unable to distinguish between what respondents say (or write on questionnaires) and what they do.
9. A much-discussed exemplar concerns one of the early justifications for intervention in Afghanistan – to protect the country's oppressed women.
10. Alongside participant reflection that tended to demean their female clients, as noted later in the chapter, were also moments of reflection and introspection where militarized and masculinized identity work was more nuanced, measured and empathetic. Social relations are a highly complex matter and gender-talk is frequently a prerequisite of group membership that may be in tension with sentiments expressed outside masculinized, norm bound interactions.
11. It was not possible to formally interview the two female contractors, though observations suggested that they interacted with their males peers as 'one of the boys'. There is no reason to think that their view of security would differ significantly from the rest of the male sample though of course it would have been interesting to establish the nature of their gendered interactions with female clients.
12. Aggressive driving by some contractors, legion in Iraq since 2003, has affected not only members of the host population but also fellow contractors. The latter continue to complain vociferously about such actions that exacerbate insecurity for all involved. It should be noted that members of the sample usually blamed the 'Americans' for 'driving like twats' (observation derived from author's fieldwork).

13. The boiler suit reference comes from the insurgent kidnap videos from Iraq and shown on the internet, where victims are clothed in such garments that, in turn, mimic the clothing worn by detainees at Guantanamo Bay.
14. Compounds might be full or too small to provide parking for all vehicles.
15. Security contractors have often commented on the irresponsibility of their clients in this respect. See memoirs by Bob Shepherd (2008) and John Geddes (2006), for example.
16. These observations resonate with the broad framing of security perception characterized by NGOs at one end of the spectrum through to militaries at the other.
17. An illustrative sense of the links between cats and femininity is recorded here from a 'Yahoo Answers' blog. In response to the question 'Why are cats considered feminine animals?', one blogger writes, 'I'd assume it's because cats are typically much more delicate; they're sleek and graceful, keep themselves clean, are picky and tend to be a little arrogant. This more-or-less makes them seem like some women. They're also more independent, so men that are used to being in control would be turned-off from them' (Yahoo! Answers, n.d.).
18. The question of decadence is also pertinent to the 'cat food run' narrative. Here, the wider context of grinding poverty, high levels of infant mortality and widespread malnutrition likely render cat food as not simply a luxury item, but rather a concept altogether alien to members of the host population. This point is underscored through the author's observation of the regular grazing of goats by local shepherds in open-air garbage sites containing all manner of waste, including rotting food and decomposing nappies [diapers].
19. CP officers' narratives of casting their (relatively young) female clients as 'uppity' may also have served a cognitive-dissonant role given that these women were sexually 'unobtainable' to CP officers as a consequence of class and status difference. These tensions may have been amplified within the context of the wider religious and hostile context where few women were encountered in private or work lives. This point was further supported by the frequent discussions of the 'best bars and hotels for picking up birds' located in the main flight hub – a neighboring country that served as a stop-off for team members going on leave.
20. Though of course it goes without saying that CP officers' primary aim was not control, but rather protection, which throws up questions of meaning in the gender order. On a personal level few, if any, CP officers derived much satisfaction from their work, rather they presented their (security) interactions in an altruistic sense, for the benefit of the client.
21. Berndtsson (2011) has discussed the authority of former military personnel in the protection of Swedish diplomats.
22. The (militarized) masculinities at play in the industry are also a matter of some complexity, with their legitimacy derived from a carefully crafted blend of both masculine and feminine attributes (Joachim and Schneiker, 2012: p. 167).

REFERENCES

Abrahamsen, Rita and Michael Williams (2010), *Security Beyond the State: Private Security in International Politics*, Cambridge University Press.

Avant, Deborah (2001), *The Market for Force: The Consequences of Privatizing Security*, Cambridge University Press.

Avant, Deborah and Lee Sigelman (2009), 'What does private security in Iraq mean for US democracy?', paper presented at Annual Convention of the International Studies Association, New York, 15–18 February.

Barker, Isabelle V. (2009), '(Re)producing American soldiers in an age of Empire', *Politics and Gender*, **5**: 211–35.

Basu, Soumita and Maya Eichler (2011), 'Women's participation in the military and security sphere: comparing the public and private sectors', paper presented at the International Studies Association Conference, Montreal, 16–19 March.

Belkin, Aaron (2012), *Bring Me Men. Military Masculinity and the Benign Façade of American Empire 1898–2001*, Hurst.

Berndtsson, Joakim (2011), 'Advertising danger, selling protection: private companies making sense and business of an (in)secure world', paper presented at Annual Conference of International Studies Association, Montreal, 16–19 March.

Bolatagici, Torika (2011), 'Representing Fijian bodies and the economy of war', *Asia Pacific Viewpoint*, **52** (1): 5–16.

Chisholm, Amanda (2008), *Warriors of Choice: The (Re)articulation of Militarised Masculinities in Private and Public Special Force*, MA Dissertation, Queen's University, Canada.

Chisholm, Amanda (2011), 'Marketing militarized masculinities: an ethnographic account of racial and gendered practices in private security contractors in Afghanistan', paper presented at Annual Conference of International Studies Association, Montreal, 16–19 March.

Connell, Raewyn (1995), *Masculinities*, Polity.

Cooling, Benjamin F. (2010), 'The military–industrial complex', in James C. Bradford (ed.), *A Companion to American Military History*, Wiley-Blackwell, pp. 996–89.

Enloe, Cynthia (2002), 'Demilitarising – or more of the same? Feminist questions to ask in the postwar moment', in Cynthia Cockburn and Dubravka Zarkov (eds), *The Postwar Moment. Militaries, Masculinities and International Peacekeeping*, Lawrence & Wishart, pp. 22–32.

Enloe, Cynthia (2004), *The Curious Feminist: Searching for Women in a New Age of Empire*, University of California Press.

Franke, Volke (2009), *Attitudes, Values and Professional Self-Conceptions of Private Security Contractors in Iraq: An Exploratory Study*, Bonn international Center for Conversion.

Geddes, John (2006), *Highway to Hell: An Ex SAS Soldier's Account of the Extraordinary Private Army Hired to Fight in Iraq*, Random House.

Geraghty, Tony (2007), *Guns for Hire. The Inside Story of Freelance Soldiering*, Piatkus.

Gough, Brendan and Gareth Edwards (1998), 'The beer talking: four lads, a carry out and the reproduction of masculinities', *The Sociological Review*, **46** (3): 409–55.

Harrington, Carol (2005), 'The politics of rescue: peacekeeping and anti-trafficking programmes in Bosnia-Herzegovina and Kosovo', *International Feminist Journal of Politics*, **7** (2): 175–206.

Higate, Paul (2011), 'Mavericks, mercenaries and masculinities: in the business of (in)security?', in Erika Svedberg and Annica Kronsell (eds), *Making Gender, Making War: Violence, Military and Peacekeeping Practices*, Routledge, pp. 182–96.

Higate, Paul (2012a), 'The private militarized and security contractor as geocorporeal actor', *International Political Sociology*, **6** (4): 355–72.

Higate, Paul (2012b), '"Cowboys and professionals": the politics of identity work in the private and military security company', *Millennium: Journal of International Studies*, **40** (2): 321–41.

Higate, Paul (2012c), 'Martial races and enforcement masculinities of the Global South: weaponizing Fijian, Chilean, and Salvadoran postcoloniality in the mercenary sector', *Globalizations*, **9** (1): 35–52.

Higate, Paul (2012d), '"Drinking vodka from the butt crack": men, masculinities and fratriarchy in the private militarized and security company', *International Journal of Feminist Politics*, **14** (4): 450–69.

Hockey, John (1986), *Squaddies: Portrait of a Subculture*, Exeter University Press.

Holmqvist, Carole (2005), *Private Security Companies: The Case for Regulation*, SIPRI Policy Paper No. 9, Stockholm.

Isenberg, David (2008), *Shadow Force: Private Security Contractors in Iraq*, Praeger Security International.

Joachim, Jutta and Andrea Schneiker (2012), '(Re)Masculinizing security? Gender and private military and security companies', in Linda Åhäll and Laura J. Shepherd (eds), *Gender, Agency and Political Violence*, Palgrave, pp. 164–91.

Kinsey, Chris (2007), *Corporate Soldiers and International Security: The Rise of Private Military Companies*, Routledge.

Krahmann, Elke (2010), *States, Citizens and the Privatisation of Security*, Cambridge University Press.

Kronsell, Annica and Erika Svedberg (eds) (2011), *The War Question for Feminism*, Routledge.

Leander, Anna (2006), 'Privatizing the politics of protection: military companies and the definition of security concerns', in Jef Huysmans, Andrew Dobson and Raia Prokhovnik (eds), *The Politics of Protection: Sites of Insecurity and Political Agency*, Routledge, pp. 19–33.

Leander, Anna (2009a), 'Security: a contested commodity', working paper organized for The Centre for Security Economics and Technology, the University of St Gallen and the Geneva Centre for the Democratic Control over Armed Forces.

Leander, Anna (2009b), 'Chimeras with obscure powers: hybrid states and the public–private distinction', paper presented at the Annual Conference of International Studies Association, New Orleans.

Maclellan, Neil (2006), 'From Fiji to Fallujah: the war in Iraq and the privatisation of Pacific Security', *Pacific Journalism Review*, 12 (2): 47–65.

Mandel, Robert (2002), *Armies Without States: the Privatization of Security*, Lynne Rienner.

Percy, Sarah (2007), *Mercenaries: The History of a Norm in International Relations*, Oxford University Press.

Schultz, Sabrina and Christina Yeung (2005), *Private Military Security Companies and Gender*, report prepared for Geneva Centre for the Democratic Control of Armed Forces.

Schwartz, Moshe and Joyprada Swain (2011), 'Department of Defense contractors in Iraq and Afghanistan: background and analysis', Congressional Research Service.

Shepherd, Bob (2008), *The Circuit*, Pocket Books.

Singer, Peter W. (2002), 'Corporate warriors: the rise of the privatized military industry and its ramifications for international security', *International Security*, 26 (3): 186–220.

Singer, Peter W. (2008), *Corporate Warriors. The Rise of the Privatized Military Industry*, Cornell University Press.

Sperling, Valerie (2011), 'Private military contractors, peacekeepers, and the sexual exploitation of women in conflict zones', paper presented at the International Studies Association Conference, Montreal, 16–19 March.

Stachowitsch, Saskia (2013), 'Military privatization and the remasculinization of the state: making the link between the outsourcing of military security and the gendered state transformation', *International Relations*, 27 (1): 74–94.

Stiehm, Judith Hicks (1982), 'The protected, the protector, the defender', *Women's Studies International Forum*, 5 (4): 367–76.

Teaiwa, Teresa (2005), 'Articulated cultures: militarism and masculinities in Fiji during the mid 1990s', *Fijian Studies*, 3 (2): 201–22.

Via, Sandra (2010), 'Gender, militarism, and globalization: soldiers for hire and hegemonic masculinity', in Laura Sjoberg and Sandra Via (eds), *Gender, War, and Militarism*, Praeger, pp. 42–53.

Vrdoljak, Ana F. (2011), 'Women and private military and security companies', in Francesco Francioni and Natalino Ronzitti (eds), *War by Contract: Human Rights, International Humanitarian Law and the Regulation of Private Military and Security Companies*, Oxford University Press, pp. 280–98.

West, Candace and Don H. Zimmerman (1987), 'Doing gender', *Politics and Gender*, **1** (2): 125–51.

Yahoo! Answers (n.d.), 'Why cats are considered "feminine" animals?', available at: http://answers.yahoo.com/question/index?qid=20110216093141AAriCZh, accessed 30 December 2011.

5. Not all soldiers: hegemonic masculinity and the problem of soldiers' agency in an age of technological intervention

Mary Manjikian

Feminist analysts have long been aware of the ways in which war is a gendered activity. In one of this argument's earliest incarnations, Jean Bethke Elshtain (1995 [1987]) drew our attention to the ways in which warfare has historically rested on a gendered dichotomy in which male warriors save and protect female 'beautiful souls'. Elshtain's argument relied on the notion of gender essentialism, in which analysts assumed that gender roles were fixed, dichotomous and attached to one's biological sex. It also highlighted the public/private distinction in which males were seen as performing public activities outside the home while females were seen as responsible for the private sphere and activities that took place within the home. This gender essentialism framework was later displaced by Butler's notion that gender was performative, and later, analysts interested in understanding the gendered nature of the military focused not so much on the activities of individuals differentiated by their biological sex, but instead on the ways in which gendered roles were performed within a particular militarized context. Within this context, Spike Peterson (1999) pointed out the ways in which the military as a whole is founded upon a culture of hegemonic masculinity, which serves to dictate and limit the gender roles of everyone who participates in it through presenting some roles as 'natural' and others as 'unnatural'. Hegemonic masculinity is a system in which individuals and institutions are privileged if they are seen to embody 'masculine' values – including (Donaldson, 1993, p. 645) 'courage, inner direction, certain forms of aggression, autonomy, mastery, technological skill, group solidarity, adventure and considerable amounts of toughness in mind and body.' As Peterson and others have pointed out, within the traditional military hierarchy, those roles and activities that are most associated with hegemonic masculinity are associated with higher status and value than those which are not.

Thus, as we begin to consider how emerging technologies affect the military and military activities in the future, it is logical to ask how emerging technologies will affect gender constructs and gender performances in this arena. Here, a number of concerns have emerged: First, analysts have begun to query the ways in which new technologies might subvert traditional understandings of hegemonic masculinity within the military. As Connell and Messerschmidt (2005, p. 832) have noted, hegemonic masculinity refers to a set of practices that set up a normative understanding of the 'most honored way of being a man'. In establishing an ideal of hegemonic masculinity and a 'right way' of being masculine within an organization, all other forms of masculinity are subordinated to the ideal. As Connell and Messerschmidt state, 'Hegemony did not mean violence, although it could be supported by force; it meant ascendancy achieved through culture, institutions and persuasion' (Connell and Messerschmidt, 2003, p. 829).

In considering new military technologies like drones, some analysts have therefore argued that such technologies will challenge the construct of hegemonic masculinity since drones would inhabit the masculine role through 'protecting' both men and women. Drones would thus also sever the heroic warrior/beautiful soul dichotomy described by Elshtain (Manjikian, 2013). Other analysts, in contrast, have suggested that the insertion of new players such as robots and autonomous drones into the arena of warfare might lead to a 'queering' of roles, as male warriors, female warriors and drone warriors come together to redefine new understandings of the roles one might take on in warfare (Daggett, 2015; see also, The Society Pages, 2013).

Finally, some analysts have begun to speculate about how technologies like physical and cognitive modifications of the warrior himself (or herself) might affect the gendered performance of military activities. Here, one can argue that the cyborg described by Harraway (1991) is now a reality. Others have been less optimistic, arguing that new technologies, including external exoskeletons, blue force linked fighting technologies (which allow warfighters to use technologies embedded in their helmets to communicate with each other and with their commanding units in real time through exchanging satellite data and messages) and other types of body modifications will not queer or end gender distinctions but will rather create them anew, with new hyper-masculine enhanced warriors exercising their new strengths and abilities over both females and 'regular' (non-enhanced) men, both in the developed and the developing world (Manjikian, 2013).

Thus far, however, analyses of technology's effect on gender issues in the military have relied heavily on the notions of performativity, gender roles and categories. We have asked whether new disruptive technologies might alter the gendered roles played by all warfighters. At the same time, we have asked how the inclusion of women soldiers in new sorts of units will affect the ways in which their biological sex continues to affect their ability to be seen as war-fighters (Sasson-Levy, 2008). However, in this work, I consider not so much the *roles* played by individuals engaged in warfare, but instead pause to consider certain *qualities* that have historically been associated with maleness in general and heroism in warfare in particular. Here I suggest that future technological developments are incompatible with the hegemonic masculinist figures of the heroic warrior and the heroic military leader because new technologies will not 'steal' the masculine role, but rather they will 'steal' the qualities of autonomy and agency away from soldiers through giving these qualities to the machinery itself.

THE HEROIC WARRIOR IN THE TWENTY-FIRST CENTURY

Here my argument departs from those who have argued in the manner of Edward Luttwak (1995; see also Baggiarini, 2015) that warfare in the twenty-first century has become largely 'post-heroic' due to the fact that the sacrifice of citizens as soldiers is no longer accepted in combat. Luttwak has argued that all warfare as conducted by Western partners is post-heroic in that all sides strive to reduce casualties through such methods as the use of drones and the increasing use of distance to remove troops from the battlefield.

My argument here is not that nations have altered the discourse they use in relation to warfare, but rather that new technologies (and the doctrines and practices which will arise as an accompaniment to these technologies) – including the creation of machine autonomy, man-machine interfaces and physical and cognitive implants within soldiers themselves – have created a situation in which traditional 'heroic' qualities can no longer be identified in or practiced by those individual soldiers who carry out warfare. In particular, I consider the twin notions of agency and autonomy – since both popular culture and military culture rely on a discourse in which the military hero is someone who acts autonomously and agentically, undertaking risks and engaging in actions that often endanger or risk their own life in order to protect a group.

In traditional military discourse, heroism is associated with initiative, the taking of risks and the carrying out of individual activity and a willingness to, if needed, engage in individual sacrifice. Those who have been labeled as heroes – through, for example, receiving a medal or other military honor – are those who have been intimately involved with killing and have had close personal contact with the enemy. Heroes are also constructed within military discourse as self-aware actors who are cognizant of the moral repercussions of their actions and who have consciously made decisions regarding the rightness or necessity of their actions – thus, as Shannon French (2004) points out, distinguishing themselves from 'mere killers', even in situations where the actions that are described as heroic may involve killing large numbers of people. The hero label, furthermore, describes not just a set of practices but also an identity. Those labeled and recognized as heroes often describe a situation in which they found their truest identity in battle, which provided the conditions for their own self-actualization.

Thus, while individual soldiers' actions are – most of the time – circumscribed within a hierarchical organization where individual decision-making and activity is not encouraged and often not allowed, both military and popular culture single out for praise individuals seen to engage in heroic activities demonstrating independent and autonomous decision-making and activity. That is, even within a masculinist organization like the military, there are still distinctions made between soldiers who carry out orders and those who give orders and take initiative. This is not, however, merely a distinction between officers and enlisted personnel. Rather, the discourse of heroism assumes that the conditions of battle provide an environment where anyone might find him or herself taking the initiative and acting heroically. Indeed, since the more intimate one's contact with one's enemies, the more likely one is to find a situation which calls for heroism, a hero may even be more likely to be found within the enlisted ranks.

This understanding that heroism rests on initiative and risk-taking, autonomy and agency, is illustrated in the criteria used to award medals for valor and heroism in combat. The official criteria used to decide which individuals will be awarded medals such as a Bronze Star (a US military decoration conferred upon those who are said to have engaged in heroic or meritorious achievement) or the Congressional Medal of Honor (the highest award for valor in action against an enemy force which an individual serving in the United States military can receive) make reference to individuals who engage in activities including: rescuing a comrade at risk to oneself; displaying extra aggressiveness (such as singlehandedly charging a target); grenade situations; engaging in rear defense (such as holding off the enemy in order to allow one's comrades to escape); continuing to fight while injured and refusing medical aid; and leadership (including spontaneously taking command) (Payne et al.,

2008). In each case the individual goes beyond their actual job description, displaying increased autonomy and in some cases breaking explicit rules or guidance in pursuit of a greater good, the rescue of their comrades.

Among those upon whom the military (and popular culture) have bestowed the label of hero, a pattern can be identified – in which heroes are those intimately involved in killing and who display agency in defying orders from superiors in order to get closer to the action. In the autobiographical memoir *American Sniper*, written by Chris Kyle, the author describes the ways in which he defied direct orders regarding the distance he was to remain from military actions in order to go in closer and protect his men (Kyle, 2012). A hero from 9/11, Marine Corporal Clifford Wooldridge, received a Navy Cross for his behavior in an incident that occurred in 2010. When faced with 15 Taliban attackers, Wooldridge used up all of his ammunition and when he ran out of ammunition proceeded to beat the final attacker to death with the butt of his machine gun, killing him with his bare hands. Here again, Wooldridge was rewarded for showing agency and autonomy through taking risks and 'going off script' in order to achieve a stated objective (Ingersoll, 2013).

In the military context, heroism, bravery and courage are thus linked with leadership. Future military officers at the US service academies are trained in the arts of decision-making, to include both practical issues and philosophical and moral training. Leadership studies manuals describe the best leaders as those who are self-actualized and who are able to realize their truest selves and identities in a situation where they are acting autonomously to make decisions (Allison and Goethals, 2013). This understanding is reproduced in press coverage related to Marine Corps Captain Douglas Zembiec, the so-called 'Lion of Fallujah' who died in battle in 2007. In a profile of Zembiec that appeared in the *Los Angeles Times*, the author describes him as follows (Perry, 2004):

> By his own definition Zembiec is a warrior, and a joyful one. He is neither bellicose nor apologetic: War means killing, and killing means winning. War and killing are not only necessary on occasion, they're also noble. 'From day one, I've told [my troops] that killing is not wrong if it's for a purpose, if it's to keep your nation free or to protect your buddy,' he said. 'One of the most noble things you can do is kill the enemy'.

Leadership is thus described as a set of practices and values that form the basis for one's identity as a military officer. That is, the most prized qualities within the hegemonic masculinity environment of the military are the ability to make decisions and the ability to act by oneself. An individual who fulfills the criteria for heroism thus occupies a higher rank in the highly hierarchical environment of the US military, regardless of gender. Thus, while most of those hailed as 'heroes' are male, not all are. For example, US representative Tammy Duckworth is a former Air Force helicopter pilot who lost both legs in combat while flying a helicopter (Weinstein, 2012). Here, she might be 'coded' as masculine because she is a hero, although her biological sex is recognized as female. Similarly, we can consider political candidate Kristin Beck, a former Navy Seal who has since come out as transgender (Larson, 2015).

In all of the cases examined here, the greatest threat to an individual embodying the construct of hegemonic masculinity posed by new technologies is the fact that many new technologies create situations in which decisions are made automatically, not by the warfighter (or leader) but by the technology itself. Indeed, new technologies may sharply circumscribe the amount of agency and autonomy granted to the individual warfighter in a variety of situations both on and off the battlefield.

I should note here that the ceding of decision-making authority and the ability to act to technological components such as robots, algorithms and code – and the shift away from imbuing individuals with these principles – is not an issue merely for the military in Western society. It is an issue which is occurring and which will continue to occur at all levels of society, both civilian and military. A few analysts have already begun to ask questions about these developments, often suggesting that the shift in autonomy and decision-making away from humans and towards machines will lead to a decrease in overall human freedom in many areas of life (Morozov, 2014). However, my specific goal here is to examine the ways in which changing notions of individual autonomy and agency as the result of technological developments will affect the construct of the hero as a facet of hegemonic masculinity within a military context.

UNITED STATES DEPARTMENT OF DEFENSE TECHNOLOGY PLANNING FOR THE TWENTY-FIRST CENTURY

Cannon fodder: noun: Soldiers regarded merely as material to be expended in war. (Oxford Dictionaries)

Pawn: noun: plural noun: pawns
A chess piece of the smallest size and value.
A person used by others for their own purposes.

Synonyms: puppet, dupe, hostage, tool, cat's paw, instrument
'a pawn in the battle for the throne'
(dictionary.com)

In recent years, a number of new technological developments have been introduced within the US military that will reduce the autonomy and agency of combatants. In the current environment of drawdown, the emphasis for planners has been on developing innovations that would help the military to become 'smaller and leaner' and yet still able to respond to the many contingencies which might arise in the international system (Department of Defense, cited in Williams and Shaffer, 2015, p. 40). In thinking about the military's future capabilities needs and how best to meet those needs in the future, planners have focused on several emerging knowledge areas that may have military uses. The list includes: nanotechnology; biotechnology; cognitive science; and human health and physical potential. Here, planners are particularly interested in developments such as gene-sequencing, brain imaging, human–machine interfaces, the creation of nanoelectric devices and wearable robotics, as well as the development of vaccines and performance enhancing pharmaceuticals (Williams and Shaffer, 2015, p. 41).

Thus, we can expect that in the future, the Department of Defense will divert resources away from projects that create large machines (like bombers) and towards the enhancement and refinement of the physical bodies of the warfighters themselves (Office of the Assistant Secretary of Defense, 2011). That is, the primary 'weapons' which will be developed going into the twenty-first century will be individual soldiers. Individual soldiers, including those in the infantry and other forward-deployed combat units, will thus not be autonomous actors who carry out actions to make war happen but rather inputs and raw materials who are then deployed by other more senior leaders in the creation of war activities.

These developments necessitate a radical reconfiguring of how we understand the gendered activity of warfare. For how can a soldier who is viewed as having little autonomy over their own physical body, their activities and their decisions be viewed as a heroic warrior or a leader? Instead, the notion of 'soldier as input' or 'expendable material' seems to be more in line with the construct of 'cannon fodder', a term used to connote a situation in which military members are essentially without agency, sent into situations where it may be known in advance that they are likely to lose their lives, and where what is required is mere 'mass' – large numbers of bodies, rather than a specific set of skills or abilities – in order to achieve a goal. This is not to say that military planners in the United States and elsewhere today do not consider the human costs of their decisions and the level of acceptable risk, nor is it to say that military deaths today are regarded as meaningless or unimportant either by those in the military or the general public. Rather, my point is that the current understanding of the soldier as a mere machine to be deployed at will by military planners suggests that, enhanced or not, the 'new soldier' is viewed in largely passive, rather than agentic, terms.

In the rest of this chapter, I consider three specific types of new soldier that could be created in the near future – the enhanced soldier, the hybrid soldier and the drugged soldier. The first label, the enhanced soldier, is used to describe a situation in which a soldier is no longer fully autonomous since s/he may be augmented in their activities by both hardware and software which s/he may not fully control him/herself. S/He is thus 'embedded' within a web of technology when s/he fights, using specialized equipment to view additional information about their environment, its challenges and the activities of their fellow warfighters and enemies. Nick Bostrom, the Oxford futurist, uses the term 'exo-self' to describe the notion that individuals in many situations today, including combat, can use technologies to have access to 'all their data' all the time. (For a combatant this might include reports, charts, images and other data that they have scanned into computer files prior to entering into battle, as well as additional data provided to them by fellow combatants and commanders.) Here, Bostrom and Sandberg (2009) suggest that one's identity is thus no longer merely internal, but is rather a function of external inputs as well. Within this context, it is difficult to see how traditional concepts of heroism and leadership will apply.

The next development that will affect the soldier is his or her inclusion within a hybrid fighting 'unit' which marries together humans and weapons. Military planners have already provided a glimpse of a future where a smart rifle will aim better than any human, responding to conditions such as wind speed to target an enemy with greater efficiency than even the most skilled warrior. In such a situation, the soldier might serve as an adjunct to the weapon itself, but the line might be quite blurred in terms of who is actually operating the weapon or making decisions regarding its operation. Such technologies affect the experience of war for the warfighter because they remove certain elements of agency and autonomy and also remove risks, often to the point that warfare is no longer properly understood as a process of 'reciprocal injuring', as Wilcox (2015, p. 135) has argued (see also Allenby, 2014).

Finally, and perhaps most interestingly, the development of cognitive enhancement measures, including pharmaceuticals, may serve in a very real sense to 'absent' soldiers from the conflict through alienating them from their own bodies and from their own human rational decision-making abilities. In this sense, they may become (in the words of Lin) 'biological weapons' or 'drones' (Lin, 2013, p. 8) – deployed in a conflict, but not behaving as we have traditionally thought of soldiers behaving – rationally, autonomously, participating in events because they believe in them and are motivated to take the actions that they do.

In each case, the new soldier who is created through the addition of new technologies can be understood as a sort of zero-sum figure in which new capabilities have been added at the expense of other elements including self-consciousness, autonomy, agency and independent moral reasoning. And each soldier in turn poses threats to the construct of hegemonic masculinity as it has traditionally been understood.

SCENARIO ONE: THE ENHANCED SOLDIER

In the Human Performance, Training, and BioSystems (HPT&B) Directorate (of the Office of the Secretary of Defense), we believe that DoD technologies are developed to extend the capabilities of the human, enhance the capabilities of the human, sustain the human, or repair the human. (Human Performance, Training and Biosystems Directorate, 2015)

Last year, the US Department of Defense's Human Performance Initiative budgeted over twenty million dollars towards the Human Performance Initiative program, aimed at enhancing force readiness, including physical, psychological and cognitive performance (House of Representatives, 2015). But what does it mean to enhance a force or to enhance a fighting body?

In considering what it means for a body to be enhanced I begin with the definition of enhancement, noting that enhancement refers to medical procedures that are applied and which are not truly medically necessary in the sense that there is no underlying disease or condition which is being treated. That is, traditional healing is aimed at restoring a body to its natural and healthy functioning by addressing an underlying illness or condition, while enhancing is about going beyond the natural state, conferring a new state which is arguably superior to the original state (Bostrom and Sandberg, 2009). Sandberg and Bostrom thus define enhancement as 'the amplification or extension of core capacities of the mind through improvement or augmentation of internal or external information processing systems' (Bostrom and Sandberg, 2009, p. 311). For those working in the field of human enhancement, these technologies are viewed as the 'next step' in a technological revolution in which engineers no longer seek to create better tools for humans to use in their daily activities, but rather seek to augment humans themselves, so that they too can serve as tools of warfare (Lin, 2013). In building a better warrior, then, engineers often strive to improve qualities that warfighters already have – including keen eyesight, better hearing or physical strength. Enhancements may also be put in place that would allow warfighters to overcome physical limitations (or human frailties) such as the need for sleep (Caldwell and Caldwell, 2005) or the need for food (Mehlman et al., 2013).

In such a scenario, it is easy for the feminist analyst to leap to the conclusion that these so-called 'super soldiers' represent merely a new application of the construct of hegemonic masculinity. If this were the case, then these new warriors would not upset existing gender paradigms in the military, but would rather reinforce these paradigms. The top warriors in the most elite combat units (most of which do not currently allow female members) could have their abilities in the areas of physical strength and mental prowess enhanced through the addition of physical and neurological inputs, and as a result warfare could become not less gendered, but more so.

However, when we begin to consider what such steps will mean for the agency and autonomy of soldiers, a new paradigm emerges. In writing about what a technologically enhanced human being will look like, Bostrom suggests that in the future an individual human might have an exoskeleton which could be applied to improve one's physical abilities (for example, enabling one to walk or run long distances or carry heavy objects). At the same time, an individual human might also have an exo-self, through having ubiquitous and real-time access to all sorts of files, websites and photos, so that he or she could easily call them up in the course of activities (for example, accessing a map during the fighting) (Bostrom and Sandberg, 2006). In such a situation, individuals will no longer be reliant only upon their own wits and resources as they attempt to understand and make sense of the battlespace, since they are instead embedded inside a web of data and technology, much of it created by others and which they may be being 'fed' by others who decide to do so on their behalf. In this way, no one individual can be seen to be acting individually as a warfighter nor would it be correct to speak about an individual warrior's experience of combat since that very experience is being in some ways mediated and controlled by others. One's experience of war might therefore be described as less authentic, and also less as one's own.

Arguably, the real 'skeleton' in this equation is the human whose physical body is mostly required as a hanger which can then be used to wear the new technologies, enabling them to function. The human soldier might thus be regarded as a host, much as an organism in the biological world can serve as a host for other parasitical organisms that take up residence within the parent organism. In this way, the soldiers of tomorrow might be viewed as interchangeable, rather than having their own personalities and skill sets. If the human behaves as merely the hanger for the technologies, then the humans could easily be substituted one for the other, as programmers and planners swap out or add enhancements to the 'raw material' of the recruit. The soldier is thus merely a type of fungible raw material – without individual agency or autonomy.

In addition, medical ethicists have already begun to raise issues related to the agency of soldiers who may not have a legal claim to refuse modifications within the confines of their employment. As Robbins (2013) has pointed out, military medical subjects have fewer legal protections than civilians do in regard to requirements that they participate in experimental medical procedures. She notes that soldiers may be court-martialed for refusing to obey an order and that commanding officers might in some circumstances order a soldier to ingest a substance (like an amphetamine which increases alertness) as part of preparing for or engaging in a specific mission.

If one subscribes to this viewpoint, then soldiers are seen less as the privileged recipients of enhancement technologies and more as the passive, weak victims of a military industrial complex which views soldiers predominantly as 'inputs' into a conflict and seeks to maximize their efficiency as products, even if it means imposing enhancements (many of which have not been rigorously or systemically vetted for safety) upon soldiers without their full knowledge and consent. Andrew Herr, a leading figure in the Department of Defense push for physical and cognitive enhancements, has spoken at length with *Wired* magazine about the ways in which new training technologies like transcranial stimulation could enable individual soldiers and units to learn new skills faster, so that soldiers could be trained 'just-in-time' for deployment to conflicts in the same way that a company might use 'just-in-time manufacturing' to produce goods in the run-up to holiday or other times of increased demand for consumer inputs (Herr, 2015; see also Fields, 2011). Herr in particular uses the language of efficiency in speaking about how soldiers could be used for longer periods of time, to perform at a higher level, so that they are maximized as inputs.

In considering this viewpoint on human enhancement, one can suggest that all soldiers in the future will be 'owned' by a military system, which treats them not as super-human, but rather as sub-human. Proposed enhancements aimed at 'overcoming human frailties' include the creation of substances that could be injected into soldiers' bodies which would enable them to work for days without sleep without succumbing to psychosis as well as the creation of substances that would alter soldier's physiology so that they do not feel pain or hunger. Other pharmaceutical enhancements could reduce soldiers' physiological response to stress through decreasing their heart palpitations, trembling or sweating (Shunk, 2015a). Still other proposed enhancements would allow individuals to act in oxygen-poor environments through relying on encapsulated oxygen stored in their blood or intestines (Patrey et al., 2009). Finally, additional new technologies would allow soldiers in a food shortage situation to gain nutrition from substances like cellulose or wood. Here one might argue that the new super soldier is not a superman but rather a type of sub-human creature who is not guaranteed or promised even such basic rights as food, shelter, rest or oxygen. As Grossman (2009) points out in his work, the notion that an individual would be the subject of medical experimentation, including being injected with substances that have not been approved for safety, would be considered a human rights violation outside a military setting.

For the feminist analyst, it is difficult to reconcile this vision of the enhanced soldier – as the subject of medical experimentation, as an input into an industrial complex and as an individual who is embedded in a technological matrix created by others – with the traditional symbols of hegemonic masculinity, including the warrior hero and the warrior leader. Indeed, the existence of such a creature seems to violate many of the assumptions upon which the construct of the warrior rests – since 'enhanced soldiers' cannot be said to act independently, fully cognizant of the risks inherent in their situation, and willingly to endure privations like pain and fear in order to engage in activities on behalf of their units. Instead, new technologies are likely to remove or nullify the ability of individual soldiers to act independently, to fully experience risk or to enter into a situation fully mentally or morally cognizant of the decisions that they are making and the possible ramifications of these decisions. Finally, debates about what enhancements soldiers would be allowed to keep if they return home suggest that enhancement is still regarded by many as unnatural. Ethicists have asked whether enhanced super soldiers would be able to be assimilated back into civilian life, or whether such enhancements should be removed prior to their retiring from the military. It is difficult to understand how an individual who was regarded as 'unnaturally enhanced' could simultaneously be viewed as a heroic warrior when many of the stories cited earlier about war heroes have stressed that these individuals succeeded by virtue of their own wit and strength, having engaged the enemy 'with their bare hands'. This new mode of warfare thus seems fundamentally incompatible with the construct of the heroic warrior, particularly when soldiers are increasingly viewed not as individual warfighters but rather as parts of a man–machine interface unit.

SCENARIO TWO: THE HYBRID SOLDIER

> Warfare has begun to leave 'human space' … The military systems (including weapons) now on the horizon will be too fast, too small, too numerous and will create an environment too complex for humans to direct. Furthermore, the proliferation of information-based systems will produce a data overload that will make it difficult or impossible for humans to directly intervene in decision-making. This is not a consideration for the remote science-fiction future. (Shunk, 2015a)

The next challenge to the construct of the hero soldier comes from the development of practices in the area of man–machine interface. In the past ten years, military planners and engineers have begun to speculate about the ways in which human soldiers and machines might work together for greater efficiency. In this scenario, it is not always clear whether the machine is meant to assist the human or whether the human is meant to assist the machine (Barnes and Jentsch, 2009). Instead, it appears likely that, as machines develop more autonomy in a particular situation, their human partners may have less autonomy in that particular situation. In time, it is even possible that humans may be left out of the loop altogether as they merely mind or service machines which will, in some situations, make decisions independently and only inform their human operators later.

Department of Defense planners have been engaged in ongoing debates about what it means morally, legally and ethically to create a machine that is autonomous and how such a scenario would affect the role of humans in combat. According to the Defense Science Board Task Force, machine autonomy is 'a capability or a set of capabilities that enables a particular action of a system to be automatic or within programmed boundaries, self-governing'. Autonomy is thus distinguished from automation since an automated process refers to the ability of a machine to carry out a series of discrete, repetitive tasks, while autonomy implies something more than this – the ability for a machine to 'think through' situations, respond appropriately and in this way act as a self-governing entity (Kendall and Winnefeld, n.d.).

In creating autonomous machines planners may specify that a machine needs to inform a human operator or even seek permission from a human operator, but in many cases this may merely be a formality which exists for legal reasons (in order to establish a chain of accountability in the event that the machine acts in error or malfunctions) rather than because it is truly necessary (Johnson and Noorman, 2014; see also Crootof, 2015). Further, new military doctrines like that of active defense in cyberwarfare will serve to authorize machines to act independently and automatically, responding to incursions without necessarily notifying a human or seeking authorization (Dewar, 2014). Active cyber defense measures include the taking of offensive steps to destroy the assets of an adversary who attacks a target, rather than simply taking passive steps to secure or protect one's own assets. One such active cyber defense measure therefore is a 'hack back' against an enemy target (Denning, 2013). Thus, it is now theoretically possible for a computer that is hacked by an adversary to automatically conduct a 'hack back' against the adversary without requiring authorization from a human operator. Finally, it is possible that machines that act according to the principles of artificial intelligence may 'learn' new strategies through carrying out activities without the knowledge or guidance of a human operator.

Here again, it is difficult to see how a soldier might be said to be engaged in leadership or acting heroically if in many ways s/he is now 'out of the loop' in a situation of conflict. Here new technologies like a man–machine interface will distance the warrior from combat both physically and emotionally, changing their experience of warfare and their experience of killing. This is not a new phenomenon, however, since the same could be said to be true of an Air Force pilot who drops a bomb on a city from a great height. They too could be said to be disengaged from the relationship with their adversary – and like the present-day example, one could argue that the conflict could be said to be taking place more properly between one's adversary and a machine, with the human merely standing by as an adjunct.

As noted earlier in this work, however, the construct of a 'war hero' rests on the existence of a relationship between the warrior and his adversary in which the hero makes a morally and psychologically cognizant decision to kill or injure the adversary, even as they understand the costs – including the costs to themselves – of doing so. Thus, any technology that reduces the risks to the warfighter, whether it is through using an airplane to conduct aerial bombardments or using a robot to deliver supplies to people in a post-plague or natural disaster situation (Metz, 2014), may be difficult to reconcile with the rhetoric of heroism.

Finally, Wolfendale suggests a scenario in which human assisted neural devices will be installed which will allow humans to control robots with their minds (Evans, 2013; see also Sparrow, 2007 and Killmister, 2008). However, the question remains as to whether the discourse of the heroic warrior could be modified sufficiently for a medal to be awarded to an individual who remotely assisted and protected others, using a device installed in his brain, or to an individual who acted in concert with a machine while not exposed to danger or risk himself, and not acting fully autonomously.

SCENARIO THREE: OUT OF THEIR MINDS

Thus far, we have considered the ways in which warfighters' actions and abilities might be enhanced through the addition of hardware or software inputs which make them faster and more efficient, as well as the ways in which they might be 'married' with technology such that the borders between the human and the machine fade, making it difficult to claim that an individual acted heroically through exercising autonomy and agency. The final scenario which we might consider as we think about how technological advances will change the character and nature of warfighting is the rapid progress being made in the area of neurochemical or pharmaceutical enhancement.

When one begins to comb the archives to understand the figure of the drugged soldier, it seems difficult to reconcile a figure of a Western, 'professional soldier' with that of a drugged soldier. For in considering those who belong to the military profession in nations like the United States, the assumption is that the individual is a member of a professional army which is professionally organized and regulated versus an ad hoc or militia type of organization. We also assume that absent of a draft, the individual has freely joined the military organization (leaving aside questions of structural inequities that might cause a person from a lower socioeconomic class to be more likely to 'choose' to join the military), and that the individual has legal rights as a military person resting on codified documents like the Uniform Code of Military Justice, such as the right to a speedy trial, legal representation and the opportunity to hear the charges that have been levied against him or her.

In contrast, when we think about individuals who are the subject of scientific experimentation, who are injected with untested substances, or who are sent to environments in which they have been first subjected to mind-altering substances which affect their ability to understand and respond to the environment naturally, we tend to apply labels like 'victim', since such activities connote not activity but passivity. Indeed, the few current examples which exist of situations in which 'soldiers' were drugged in order to improve their performance in combat seem to come largely from nations in the developing world where the individuals who were drugged were not members of professional armies but instead were those who were often drafted against their will into ad hoc, nonprofessional armies which emerged in situations such as a so-called 'failed state'. In such a situation, the 'soldier' is often a young child, a member of a marginalized group or someone who has little autonomy. And in this scenario, drugging a soldier is often presented as a human rights violation of the highest order.

A regime or group that resorts to drugging soldiers and forcing them into combat might thus be viewed by its opponents as weak and cowardly, rather than strong and resolute. This understanding is reproduced in a 2005 article about Mohammed Ali, a Saudi national, who described being given drugs by an Al Qaeda member who then attempted to induce him to participate in a suicide bombing. In the news story, an American military leader, Colonel Billy Buckner, describes the act as one of desperation by Al Qaeda (Fox News, 2005).

In this common understanding, drugs are often seen as a way to elicit compliance from a soldier who may not want to fight or who may not even understand the conflict. The soldier is thus robbed of their autonomy and coerced into fighting in a conflict which he or she (or the world at large) may regard as illegitimate. Since it is unlikely that in such a scenario an individual would choose to fight for this cause, drugs may be used to cause the subject to lose their rationality and to induce them to be violent. In retrospect, soldiers may describe themselves as 'numb' or 'divorced from the conflict'. They may describe a sort of dissociation occurring, in which they feel as though they are watching themselves inflict violence from a great distance but are not themselves actively present in the scenario when the violence is occurring.

This understanding of the drugged soldier is reproduced in an interview in a San Francisco newspaper with Ishmael Beah, who fought for the Army of Sierra Leone at 11 years old, after he was orphaned and captured. Beah describes being force-fed 'brown-brown', a mixture of cocaine and gunpowder, and forced into battle (Guthmann, 2007). A report on child soldiers published by Human Rights Watch (2008) quotes a 16-year-old who was forced to fight in Sierra Leone. She again describes the ways in which brown-brown was put in her food, and the fact that afterwards she was given a canister of kerosene and instructed to burn down a village. A 2005 article in *Der Spiegel* notes that 'drugged soldiers', high on stimulants and amphetamines, were also a feature of what is referred to as 'the Nazi death machine' (Ulrich, 2005).

However, in Western nations, one can identify an attempt by military physicians to distinguish between legal and illegal drugs, and legal versus illegal drug abuse among military personnel. That is, while one can find stories of atrocities committed during the Vietnam era by individuals and units high on illegal narcotics which were unofficially procured, one can also find stories of units of soldiers who might have been legally prescribed some form of stimulant to improve their cognition and alertness while engaged, for example, in an Air Force pilot exercise taking place at night. As Shunk (2015b) points out, the US military actually has a long history of prescribing performance-enhancing substances to improve performance during battle. It is likely that this trend will continue since – as noted earlier – planners who conceptualize soldiers as 'inputs' are interested in any substance which might improve the efficiency at which these inputs are trained and operated (Friedman, 2012).

For a feminist analyst, however, the question of the increased use of drugs by soldiers, both in and outside combat, is intriguing for three reasons: first, one can consider whether the individual soldier can be said to be truly autonomous in making a decision for or against cognitive enhancement drugs. Here, Lin (2012) argues that soldiers can be coerced into accepting such measures – even within a democratic society and a democratically organized and administered fighting force – if they are led to believe that those who decide to take such substances will be promoted faster or will be more successful in their professions. In this way, we may ask if soldiers really feel free to refuse such drugs (Russo, 2007). Thus, one can draw a line between 'drugged soldiers' who are force-fed unsafe pharmaceuticals in an unofficial army and individuals in a professional army who are encouraged for career reasons to subject themselves to untested vaccines and pharmaceuticals that do not yet have full FDA approval. In both situations, the soldier can be conceptualized as a victim rather than an independent agent.

Secondly, we may ask how the overall experience of warfare will change if individuals increasingly find that their experiences are mediated by pharmaceutical enhancements. In the future, a soldier might be able to fight without experiencing pain, fatigue and stress during combat (*Wired* magazine, 2012). As a result, their experience and calculation of risk would be fundamentally altered (Shunk, 2015b), as might their experiences of guilt, remorse and pity (Ashcroft, 2008, p. 48). Here again, it becomes clear that the warfighter's 'experience' of war is no longer their own, since, as Pool (2012) points out, it is possible that in the future a team of individuals might watch a warfighter's brain as they perform in conflict, intervening to 'dial down' their anxiety through manipulating their stress pathways. Here again, the question becomes, 'Who exactly is fighting? The warfighters themselves? The team that controls them?' It appears that the individual is participating in war but is no longer in complete control of their experience. Rather, they are semi-passive and semi-autonomous. Thus, it is difficult to see how one can speak of a 'hero' acting bravely in the face of danger and fear if those emotions are taken away from him or her. And if at the time when the soldier kills an enemy they are unable to experience human emotions like guilt or remorse, one might argue that they have not truly understood and internalized the costs of war, and that for him or her, at that time, it is not truly a process of reciprocal injuring. They cannot thus claim heroism as a result of having participated in combat.

Finally, it is worthwhile to consider the ways in which new pharmaceuticals will alter the ability of troops to form memories about the events in which they are taking part. While some analysts argue that troops will be less likely to suffer from post-traumatic stress disorder if they are unable to remember their war experiences and that such drugs are thus extremely humane, one again encounters the problem of agency. If a soldier cannot be said to have acted agentically in combat, then can one later claim agency or authority in speaking 'as a soldier' or 'based on one's experiences of combat'? In the current environment, individuals often make claims to certain types of civilian leadership positions (in corporations or in Congress or in the White House) based on having exercised leadership in conflict. Again, it is difficult to see how one can reconcile having been 'present but psychologically absent during conflict' with the claim to a leadership position in civilian life afterwards, or with the claim to authority as a military or political analyst based on one's own experience of conflict. In this way, those who participate in conflict while drugged can be seen as losing their autonomy as well as their voice or claim to authority later in life based on those experiences. Such a scenario may have large-scale implications for feminist analysts since it suggests that military experience will no longer create or elevate certain individuals to positions of authority based on participating in conflict, nor will it allow for the transfer of that authority gained while in the military into civilian life.

CONCLUSION

As this brief chapter has shown, new technologies that affect the bodies of soldiers have implications for our gendered understandings of war. In particular, new technologies will have impacts on the ways in which agency and autonomy are understood and practiced in war. In such a situation, the hegemonic masculinist organization of the military and the privilege accorded to some types of soldiers within that organization may be upended.

Here, it is worth noting that currently many analysts practice a type of gender essentialism in which they portray some categories of war-fighters – including child soldiers, women who have been put into service to support warfighters and those who have been drafted by authoritarian regimes – as largely without agency, fighting against their will on the orders of another (Hyndman, 2010; Murphy, 2003). These soldiers are often contrasted with the first world masculine warrior and portrayed instead as feminized, since they are not regarded as either fully autonomous or morally culpable for their actions and activities. Such individuals are thus involved in the business or work of war, but they are not regarded as warriors. New technological developments may now open up the possibility of making the same argument in regard to first world professional soldiers as well.

REFERENCES

Allenby, Braden (2014), 'Are new technologies undermining the laws of war?', *Bulletin of the Atomic Scientists*, **70** (1): 21–31.

Allison, Scott and George Goethals (2013), *Heroic Leadership: An Influence Taxonomy of 100 Exceptional Individuals*, Routledge.

Ashcroft, Richard (2008), 'Regulating biomedical enhancements in the military', *The American Journal of Bioethics*, **8** (2): 47–9.

Baggiarini, Bianca (2015), 'Drone warfare and the limits of sacrifice', *Journal of International Political Theory*, **11** (1): 128–44.

Barnes, Michael and Florian Jentsch (eds) (2009), *Human–Robot Interactions in Future Military Operations*, Ashgate.

Bostrom, Nick and Anders Sandberg (2006), 'Converging cognitive enhancements', *Annals of the New York Academy of Sciences*, **1093**: 210–27.

Bostrom, Nick and Anders Sandberg (2009), 'Cognitive enhancement: methods, ethics, regulatory challenges', *Science and Engineering Ethics*, **15**: 311–41.

Caldwell, John and J. Lynn Caldwell (2005), 'Fatigue in military aviation: an overview of US military approved pharmacological countermeasures', *Aviation, Space and Environmental Medicine*, **76** (7): 39–51.

Connell, Raewyn and James Messerschmidt (2005), 'Hegemonic masculinity: rethinking the concept', *Gender Society*, **19** (6): 829–59.

Crootof, Rebecca (2015), 'The killer robots are here: legal and policy implications', *Cardozo Law Review*, **36**, available at: http://papers.ssrn.com/sol3/papers.cfm?abstract_id=2534567.

Daggett, Cara (forthcoming, 2015), 'Killer drones: how "unmanned" technologies queer the experience of killing in war', *International Feminist Journal of Politics*.

Denning, Dorothy (2013), 'Framework and principles for active cyberdefense', unpublished manuscript, Monterey, CA: Naval Postgraduate School, accessed 18 August 2015 at: http://faculty.ndu.edu/dedennin/publications/Framework_and_Principles_for_Active_Cyber_Defense _-_11Dec2013.pdf.

Dewar, Robert (2014), 'The "triptych of cyber security": a classification of active cyber defense', *6th International Conference on Cyber Conflict*, Tallinn.

Donaldson, Mike (1993), 'What is hegemonic masculinity?', *Masculinities*, **22** (5): 643–57.

Elshtain, Jean Bethke (1995[1987]), *Women and War* (new edn), University of Chicago Press.

Evans, Nicholas (2013), 'A case study in neurowarfare', in Jessica Wolfendale and Paolo Tripodi (eds), *New Wars and New Soldiers: Military Ethics in the Contemporary World*, Ashgate: pp. 105–16.

Fields, R. Douglas (2011), 'Amping up brain function: transcranial stimulation shows promise in speeding up learning', accessed 24 July 2015 at: http://www.scientific american.com/author/r-douglas-fields/.

Fox News (2005), 'Failed suicide bomber: I was kidnapped, drugged', 19 September, accessed 24 July 2015 at: http://www.foxnews.com/story/2005/09/19/failed-suicide-bomber-was-kidnapped-drugged.html.

French, Shannon (2004), *The Code of the Warrior*, Rowman & Littlefield.

Friedman, Richard (2012), 'Why are we drugging our soldiers?', accessed 24 July at: http://www.nytimes.com/2012/04/22/opinion/sunday/why-are-we-drugging-our-soldiers.html?_r=0.

Grossman, David (2009), *On Killing: The Psychological Cost of Learning to Kill in War and Society*, Back Bay.

Guthmann, Edward (2007), 'Once a drugged child soldier, Beah reclaims his soul', accessed 24 July 2015 at: http://www.sfgate.com/entertainment/article/Once-a-drugged-child-soldier-Beah-reclaims-his-2645611.php.

Harraway, Donna (1991), *Simians, Cyborgs and Women: The Reinvention of Nature*, Routledge.

Herr, Andrew (2015), 'Will humans matter in the wars of 2030?', *Joint Forces Quarterly*, **77** (2): 76–83.

House of Representatives (2015), 'Department of Defense Appropriations Bill', accessed 11 August 2015 at: http://appropriations.house.gov/uploadedfiles/hrpt-113-hr-fy2015-defense.pdf.

Human Performance, Training and Biosystems Directorate (2015), 'Background, roles and responsibilities of the Human Performance, Training and Biosystems Directorate', accessed 24 July 2014 at: http://www.acq.osd.mil/rd/hptb/about/.

Human Rights Watch (2008), 'Coercion and intimidation of child soldiers to participate in violence', accessed 11 August 2015 at: https://www.hrw.org/news/2008/04/16/coercion-and-intimidation-child-soldiers-participate-violence.

Hyndman, Jennifer (2010), 'The question of "the political" in critical geopolitics: querying the "child soldier" in the "war on terror"', *Political Geography*, **29** (5): 247–55.

Ingersoll, Geoffrey (2013), 'The crazy story of a marine locked in hand-to-hand combat as the Taliban fighter reached for a grenade', accessed 11 August 2015 at: http://www.businessinsider.com/the-crazy-story-of-cpl-wooldridge-2013-12.

Johnson, Deborah and Merel Noorman (2014), 'Responsibility practices in robotic warfare', *Military Review*, May–June: pp. 12–21.

Kendall, Frank and James Winnefeld (n.d.), 'Unmanned systems integrated roadmap FY2011-2036', Department of Defense.

Killmister, Suzy (2008), 'Remote weaponry: the ethical implications', *Journal of Applied Philosophy*, **25** (2): 121–33.

Kyle, Chris with Jim DeFelice and Scott McEwen (2012), *American Sniper*, W. Morrow.

Larson, Kari (2015), 'Transgender veteran Kristin Beck on serving in the Navy and running for Congress at the Keystone Conference', accessed 24 July 2015 at: http://www.pennlive.com/midstate/index.ssf/2015/03/transgender_veteran_kristin_be.html.

Lin, Patrick (2012), 'More than human? The ethics of biologically enhanced soldiers', *The Atlantic*, accessed 11 August 2015 at: http://www.theatlantic.com/technology/archive/2012/02/more-than-human-the-ethics-of-biologically-enhancing-soldiers/253217/.

Lin, Patrick (2013), *Enhanced Warfighters: Risk, Ethics and Policy*, The Greenwall Foundation.

Luttwak, Edward (1995), 'Toward post-heroic warfare', *Foreign Affairs*, May/June.

Manjikian, Mary (2013), 'Becoming unmanned: the gendering of lethal autonomous warfare technology', *International Feminist Journal of Politics*, **16** (1): 48–65.

Mehlman, Maxwell, Patrick Lin and Keith Abney (2013), 'Enhanced warfighters: a policy framework', in Michael Gross and Don Carrick (eds), *Military Medical Ethics for the 21st Century*, Ashgate: pp. 113–26.

Metz, Steven (2014), 'The landpower robot revolution is coming', Strategic Studies Institute, USA.

Morozov, Evgeny (2014), 'The rise of data and the death of politics', accessed 24 July 2015 at: http://www.theguardian.com/technology/2014/jul/20/rise-of-data-death-of-politics-evgeny-morozov-algorithmic-regulation.

Murphy, William P. (2003), 'Military patrimonialism and child soldier clientalism in the Liberian and Sierra Leonean Civil Wars', *African Studies Review*, **46** (2): 61–87.

Office of the Assistant Secretary of Defense – Health Affairs (2011), 'Health system support concept of operations (CONOPS)', Department of Defense.

Patrey, James, Judith Lytle, William Sobotka, GeorgiAnna Sheppard and Susan Kayar (2009), 'Human performance enhancement for NATO military operations (science, technology and ethics)', RTO-MP-HFM-181, NATO Science and Technology Organization.

Payne, Collin, Koert van Ittersum and Brian Wansink (2008), 'Profiling the heroic leader: empirical lessons from combat-decorated veterans of World War II', *Leadership Quarterly*, available at: http://ssrn.com/abstract=1078914.

Perry, Tony (2004), 'The unapologetic warrior', accessed 24 July 2015 at: http://www.latimes.com/world/la-na-soldier-archive12may12-story.html#page=1.

Peterson, V. Spike (1999), 'Political identities/nationalism as heterosexism', *International Feminist Journal of Politics*, **1** (1): 34–65.

Pool, Sean (2012), 'Neurosecurity and the ethics of military cognitive enhancement', accessed 24 July 2015 at: http://scienceprogress.org/2012/05/neurosecurity-and-the-ethics-of-military-cognitive-enhancement/.

Robbins, Lauren (2013), 'Refusing to be all you can be: regulating against forced cognitive enhancement in the military', in Michael Gross and Don Carrick (eds), *Military Medical Ethics for the 21st Century*, Ashgate: pp. 127–38.

Russo, Michael (2007), 'Recommendations for the ethical use of pharmacologic fatigue countermeasures in the US military', *Aviation, Space and Environmental Medicine*, **78** (5): 119–27.

Sasson-Levy, Orna (2008), 'Individual bodies, collective state interests: the case of Israeli combat soldiers', *Men and Masculinities*, **10** (3): 296–321.

Shunk, Dave (2015a), 'Grail war 2050, last stand at battle site one', accessed 24 July 2015 at: http://cimsec.org/grail-war-2050-last-stand-battle-site-one/14135.

Shunk, Dave (2015b), 'Ethics and the enhanced soldier of the near future', *Military Review*, January–February: pp. 91–8.

Sparrow, Robert (2007), 'Killer robots', *Journal of Applied Philosophy*, **24** (1): 62–77.

The Society Pages (2013), 'Toward a drone sexuality, part II: boundary conditions', accessed 15 June 2015 at: http://thesocietypages.org/cyborgology/2013/12/19/toward-a-drone-sexuality-part-2-boundary-conditions/.

Ulrich, Andreas (2005), 'The Nazi death machine: Hitler's drugged soldiers', accessed 24 July 2015 at: http://www.spiegel.de/international/the-nazi-death-machine-hitler-s-drugged-soldiers-a-354606.html.

Weinstein, Adam (2012), 'Nobody puts Tammy Duckworth in a corner', accessed 24 July 2015 at: http://www.motherjones.com/politics/2012/08/tammy-duckworth-versus-joe-walsh-congress.

Wilcox, Lauren (2015), *Bodies of Violence: Theorizing Embodied Subjects in International Relations*, Oxford University Press.

Williams, Edie and Alan Shaffer (2015), 'Forum: the importance of capability prototyping', *Joint Forces Quarterly*, **77** (second quarter): pp. 34–43.

Wired magazine (2012), 'This scientist wants tomorrow's troops to be mutant-powered', 26 December, accessed 24 July 2015 at: http://www.wired.com/2012/12/andrew-herr/.

6. Gender and 'population-centric' counterinsurgency in Afghanistan

Julia Welland

The 'Long War' in Afghanistan (2001–14) challenged a number of traditional conceptions about what war is. Not only did the conflict deny a clear-cut victory for either the US-led invading forces or the Taliban, but it also provided the context for the revival of counterinsurgency doctrine and practice. Counterinsurgency – a term first coined by John F. Kennedy in 1960 – can be 'defined as asymmetrical warfare by a powerful military against irregular combatants supported by a civilian population'. While the term may have been coined in the mid-1900s, however, 'this particular method of fighting has long been the mainstay of colonial war-fighting and imperial policing' (Khalili, 2011, p. 1471), including British colonial fighting during the Malayan Emergency (1948–60) and against the 'Mau Mau' uprising in Kenya (1952–60), and US imperialistic missions in the Philippines (1899–1903) and against the communist threat in Vietnam (1965–73). Unlike 'conventional' warfare between states, counterinsurgency sees a 'regular' armed force deal with the threat of 'irregular combatants'. These 'unconventional forces' have been known 'through history as "insurgents", "rebels", "partisans", or "guerrillas" [and] are an armed segment of a population unwilling to submit themselves to a state authority, a particular regime or an ideology' (Dyvik, 2016 forthcoming).

Counterinsurgency utilizes not just a military response to these unconventional forces, but employs economic, social, political and psychological agendas in their effort to overcome them. As the conflict in Afghanistan merged from conventional war to occupation and back into war-fighting again, military strategists agreed that a shift from conventional 'search and destroy' tactics (Dixon, 2012, p. 29) was needed in order to secure a safe and stable Afghanistan for the future. In line with the majority of post-cold war counterinsurgencies, the approach taken in Afghanistan was that of 'population-centric' counterinsurgency, 'in which the civilian population is persuaded to defect to the counterinsurgent forces' (Khalili, 2011, p. 1472). In comparison to 'enemy-centric' counterinsurgency, which is predicated on the use of violence – 'kinetic force' – to deter civilians from cooperating with the insurgents, and thus has a greater degree of similarity with traditional Clausewitzian war and its annihilation of the enemy, population-centric counterinsurgency combines both 'kinetic' and 'non-kinetic' elements. It was this shift towards the non-kinetic and the centrality of the civilian population that was central to the specific counterinsurgency doctrine implemented in Afghanistan.

Population-centric counterinsurgency – or 'COIN' as it came to be shortened to – was implemented as the central military doctrine in Afghanistan in 2009. The doctrine drew heavily on *Field Manual (FM) 3-24*, written by the US General David Petraeus and a team of advisors, and had been previously implemented in Iraq in 2006. *FM 3-24* forwarded 'a strategy that stood in stark contrast to the "shock-and-awe" campaign that was successful in bringing down Saddam Hussein's regime but failed in the reconstruction phase' (Svet, 2012). In COIN, it was the civilian population, not the enemy's military that was located as the centre of gravity. *FM 3-24* states that civilian protection is not only part of the counterinsurgent mission, but is its *'most important part'* (US Army et al., 2007, p. xxv, my emphasis). Civilians are also included in the very *doing* of counterinsurgency. Civilian participation via political leadership is likely to be involved at every level of operations, as well as in 'nonkinetic activities' (US Army et al., 2007, p. xxx) such as the building of infrastructure, the provision of jobs and the creation of a functioning legal system, all of which acquire increasing importance given the primacy of political rather than military goals.

What does this 'new' population-centric form of counterinsurgency have to do with gender? Feminists have long argued that war (and peacekeeping) is both gendered and gendering (for example see: Elshtain, 1987; Enloe, 2000; Young, 2003). There has also been a sustained feminist engagement with the Afghanistan conflict; notably in relation to the ways in which women's rights were co-opted and instrumentalized in order to garner support for the 2001 invasion (for example see: Abu-Lughod, 2002; Hunt, 2002; Russo, 2006). Like all war-making, therefore, COIN requires specific constructions of masculinity and femininity in order 'to produce particular narratives, justifications and practices' (Dyvik, 2014, p. 411). This chapter explores how gender was integral to understanding the recent turn towards counterinsurgency and the implications of this for both the type of warfare enacted and the ways in which masculinities and femininities were rendered visible. First, the chapter details the particular type of militarized masculinity required for population-centric counterinsurgency, one that was reimagined as softer and gentler, and rendered distinct from the insurgent masculinities it fought and the masculinities of the Afghan security forces it fought alongside. The chapter then explores related ways in which COIN can be understood as a conduct of war that had a greater visibility of femininity – both physically and conceptually. While war has traditionally been assumed to be an almost exclusively masculine domain, COIN allowed for, even needed, women's bodies on the front line in the form of so-called 'Female Engagement Teams', as well as the 'feminine' attributes of compassion and concern. The chapter ends with some conclusions regarding the effects of this gendered and gendering counterinsurgency.

Throughout this chapter 'gender is understood as a concept that encompasses much more than a biologically grounded and predetermined understanding of physical bodies recognizable as "women" and "men"' (Dyvik, 2016, forthcoming). Use of the term 'masculine' does not simply refer to sexed bodies that (are presumed to) bear the physiological characteristics that distinguish a body as 'male'; likewise, 'feminine' does not simply refer to sexed bodies that (are presumed to) bear the physiological characteristics that distinguish a body as 'female'. Rather, drawing on Judith Butler (1999 [1990]), gender is understood as performative and fluid, with masculinity and femininity flowing between sexed bodies (with sex itself also constructed by the social conventions of gender), and its performances having real effects on the practices of counterinsurgency.

A SOFTER AND GENTLER FORM OF SOLDIERING

A burgeoning feminist and pro-feminist literature on gender and militaries reveals the ways in which militaries both produce and rely on particular gendered identities for their everyday workings and the enactment of force at home and abroad. One particular focus of this scholarship has been the specific type of masculinity required for war-fighting; a gendered subjectivity that has come to be termed as 'militarized masculinity' (for a selection of scholarship tracking this subjectivity see: Higate, 2003; Whitworth, 2004; Masters, 2005 and 2008; Duncanson, 2009 and 2013; Welland, 2013; Eichler, 2014). Following Maya Eichler (2014, p. 81), at its most basic level militarized masculinity can be understood as 'the assertion that traits stereotypically associated with masculinity can be acquired and proven through military service or action, and combat in particular', and that this gendered subjectivity 'is central to the perpetuation of violence within international relations'.

While the literature on militarized masculinities suggests a hetero-geneity of military personnel and a range of gendered characteristics, behaviors and traits that they encompass, assumptions about an 'ideal-ized' militarized masculine subjectivity – and the combat soldier in particular – have solidified around associations with 'toughness, violence, aggression, courage, control and domination' (Eichler, 2014, p. 82). After all, combat soldiers are expected and required to go into battle, close in on the enemy, kill and do everything possible to avoid being killed themselves. However, when war is not primarily concerned with the annihilation of the enemy, and when it is the 'hearts and minds' of the civilian population that are central to the mission, to what extent must a militarized masculine subjectivity also shift and change?

Laleh Khalili (2011) has argued that the counterinsurgency doctrines of Iraq and Afghanistan were gendered in the ways they were formulated, put into practice and experienced. Presented as the opposite of a 'hyper-masculine' and 'more mechanised, technologically advanced, higher-fire-power form of warfare', Khalili claimed (2011, p. 1473) that counterinsurgency was itself gendered feminine. Drawing attention to a 'new form of masculinity' (p. 1474) that she understands as emerging in the location where COIN policy and doctrine was produced, Khalili terms this new form of (militarized) masculinity 'the humanitarian soldier-scholar', whose 'softened' and 'sensitive' masculinity was 'authorised by ... neo-liberal feminism' that 'over-shadows the hyper-masculinity of warrior kings' (pp. 1474–5). Unlike the raw physical masculinity of a warrior, these soldier-scholars 'are not interested in chest-thumping gestures, [they] deploy the language of "hearts and minds" much more readily and see their wont as being the wielders of softer or smarter power' (p. 1487).

Building on Khalili's attention to counterinsurgency's production of new masculinities, but extending it from the location where COIN doctrine was produced to the everyday spaces in Afghanistan where it was enacted, a specific conceptualization of militarized masculinity can be traced. In the population-centric counterinsurgency context of Afghanistan, soldiers were expected to live, move and work amongst the local population, to talk with them, listen to them and earn their trust. As already noted, in Afghanistan the real battle was for 'civilian support for, or acquiescence to, the counterinsurgents and host nation government' (US Army et al., 2007, p. xxv). The priority therefore was for counter-insurgents to engage with the local community and create an environment where governance and development could flourish. Everyday counter-insurgency practices included holding *shuras*[1] with village elders, where senior military personnel would listen to concerns raised by locals and keep them updated with the security in their locality; ensuring the provision and safe passage of humanitarian relief such as medicines, food and winter supplies; and contributing towards the repairing or building of infrastructure projects. In this context, an effective and idealized militarized masculinity may better encompass compassion, restraint and cooperation, rather than aggression, toughness and domination.

Suggestions, however, that the militarized masculinity of a counterinsurgent was in some way feminized or less masculine than a 'conventional' combat soldier was strongly contested, both by those responsible for drafting the doctrine and the soldiers responsible for enacting it. During a speech to the US Government Counterinsurgency Conference, David Kilcullen (2006), an Australian counterinsurgency expert who helped design and monitor the Iraq war troop surge under General Petraeus, stated in relation to counterinsurgency tactics:

> If this [counterinsurgency] sounds soft, non-lethal and non-confrontational, it is not: this is life-and-death competition in which the loser is marginalized, starved of support and ultimately destroyed … . There is no known way of doing counterinsurgency without inflicting casualties on the enemy: there is always a lot of killing, one way or another.

Such a statement tallies with figures released by the UK Ministry of Defence in response to a Freedom of Information request from a British newspaper. These figures reveal that between 2006, when British forces deployed to Helmand, Southern Afghanistan, and their withdrawal in 2014, they fired 46 million rounds of ammunition at the Taliban. Up to two million rounds were fired from 9 mm handguns, suggesting such ammunition was used in fighting in close quarters with the enemy; around 10 000 bullets a day were fired from troops' SA-80 assault rifles and light machine guns; at least 80 000 105 mm shells were fired from light artillery guns used to attack targets two miles away; and 55 000 bullets were fired from the 30 mm cannons attached to Apache helicopters (Hughes, 2015). Afghanistan required not only counterinsurgents who could win the hearts and minds of the local population, but also highly masculinized combat soldiers.

Central to this (re)masculinization of the counterinsurgent was the continued emphasis on risk in relation to their duties and roles, and the threat of physical violence they were exposed to. *FM 3-24* explicitly states that counterinsurgency actually requires soldiers to assume *more* risk. Not only is the success of COIN premised on a reduction in the use of force, the manual also demands that soldiers interact with a local population infiltrated by the enemy. This, the manual states, 'is inherently dangerous' (US Army et al., 2007, p. xxvii). Dangerous because the insurgent exploits the civilian: 'Guerrillas dress in civilian clothes, hide behind women, use children as spotters, and store weapons in schools and hospitals' (p. xxvii). Speaking of the Taliban, Lieutenant Toby Glover says, 'One minute they will be walking down the street and have a woman and children surrounding them and the next the woman and children will disappear and he will be firing at you' (Gillan, 2006). The counterinsurgency soldier therefore faced danger, whether confronted by an insurgent or when engaging with the civilian population they were supposed to protect.

The counterinsurgency environment of Afghanistan detailed above required a counterinsurgent who was both war-fighter and nation-builder, one who was capable of deploying lethal force but knows when to hold it back, and who combined the 'hard' masculinity of combat and command with the 'soft' femininity of compassion and humanitarianism. While counterinsurgency soldiers were expected to be integral to the peace-building process, they were also expected to put themselves in harm's way and engage in combat and violence. It was not that force or kinetic power was no longer used, but that it was deployed differently and – according to COIN doctrine – more sparingly. Counterinsurgency there-fore provided the context for the emergence of a 'new' militarized masculinity. It suggested a softer and gentler approach to soldiering, while the warrior capabilities and technological superiority long associ-ated with Western militaries remained intact.

COLONIAL OTHER(ING)S

The so-called 'Orient' has long been considered a location of deviance, brutality and sexual excess. In *Orientalism*, Edward Said (1979) notes that since the late eighteenth century the region has been designated as a site of particular libidinous natures and eroticism. Today, stories told about the Middle East or Arabic culture reference 'medieval' forms of violence, the practice of men taking multiple wives and an assumed proclivity towards homosexuality. These colonial and orientalist under-standings of the region continue to inform and shape understandings and representations of those who live there. Thus, while the counter-insurgency environment provided the context for the emergence and production of a 'new' militarized masculinity, it also emerged in and through these long-standing orientalist discourses and in relation to other(ed) masculinities. In particular, NATO counterinsurgency soldiers were rendered visible in contrast to both duplicitous and violent insurgent fighters, and their lazy, disorganized and homosexualized counterparts in the Afghan security forces.

In line with COIN's positioning of the population, as opposed to the territory, as the battlefield, General Petraeus used his first tactical directive since assuming command of the international forces in Afghanistan in 2010 to double 'down on the orders imposed by his predecessor [General Stanley McChrystal] that put a premium on protecting civilians first' (Motlagh, 2010). Petraeus tightened the rules of engagement that had previously prohibited NATO forces from calling in air strikes on village compounds where the enemy might have been mixed in with civilians, by expanding it to a ban on air strikes and artillery fire on 'all types of building, tree-lined areas and hillsides where it is difficult to distinguish who is on the ground' (Motlagh, 2010). Further measures included a curb on small-arms fire that had yielded a steady stream of fatalities at checkpoints and in night-time raids on private residences. Echoing *FM 3-24*'s assertion that 'killing the civilian is no longer just collateral damage' (US Army et al., 2007, p. xxv), Petraeus stated: 'Every Afghan civilian death diminishes our cause' (Motlagh, 2010).

However, the insurgents who faced these counterinsurgency soldiers and their strict rules of engagement were represented as fighters who did not play by the same 'rules of the game'. *FM 3-24* observes that the 'rules' favor the insurgent and that '[t]he contest of internal war is not fair' (US Army et al., 2007, p. 4). While COIN doctrine was explicit about avoiding civilian casualties, insurgents 'kill civilians to show that the government can't protect its own citizens' (p. xxvii). Likewise, the rules of engagement that governed NATO forces' actions in battle with enemy combatants – what General McChrystal termed 'courageous restraint' – caused some soldiers to complain they were being forced to fight with 'one hand tied behind [their] backs' and blocked soldiers who were being shot at from shooting back (Harding, 2010). The insurgent, meanwhile, was understood as bound by no such conventions and engaged in violence that was cruel, barbaric and beyond the pale of 'ordinary' or 'conventional' warfare. Describing the rhetoric of the 'new wars' of the 'West' and 'East', Derek Gregory (2010, p. 170) writes that while 'our' new wars are represented as those fought by professional armies and high-precision weaponry, with an emphasis on international law and violence directed towards combatants, 'their' new wars are fought using improvised weapons, are outside international law and engage in indiscriminate killings.

In his study of military orientalism, Patrick Porter demonstrated that several military historians frame 'oriental' warfare as 'different and apart from European warfare', specifically with regard to its reliance on 'evasion, delay and indirectness' (Keegan cited in Porter, 2009, p. 11). Narratives such as these claim that whereas those in the West have 'historically preferred direct battle fought with guile to smash the enemy ... the "Islamic" way of war chose standoff weapons, deceit and attacking enemy cohesion' (Porter, 2009, p. 11). The tactics of the insurgents are represented as barbaric, sly and uncivilized. These characteristics are in turn remapped onto the bodies and masculinities of the insurgents themselves – supported and informed by a long history of colonial terms that encounters between the East and West have been portrayed and understood through. As the insurgents' masculinity – and the masculinities of Arab and Muslim men more widely – became associated and solidified around these characteristics, the counterinsurgent's militarized masculinity was associated and solidified in opposition to them.

However, insurgent masculinities were not the only masculinities that counterinsurgent subjectivities were produced in relation to. One of the key responsibilities of NATO forces in Afghanistan was training the local security forces in order to ensure security and stability once international forces left the country. American Embedded Training Teams and NATO Operational Mentor and Liaison Teams (OMLTs) were embedded in Afghan units as trainers and mentors, and tasked with facilitating the development of the Afghan National Army (ANA) (Younossi et al., 2009, pp. 34–5). OMLTs mentored ANA leaders on issues such as leadership; implementation of doctrine; operational procedures; tactics; and 'on the job training' during operations in the field. OMLTs also provided crucial combat enablers such as fire support; MEDEVAC; command and control; and close air support (Younossi et al., 2009, pp. 35–6). NATO troops who were a part of these OMLTs would eat, sleep, patrol and fight 'alongside soldiers of the ANA on a daily basis' (MoD, n.d.), with official rhetoric emphasizing the partnership and cooperation between the two sides. While relationships formed between NATO soldiers and their Afghan counterparts within OMLTs could disrupt the dominant colonial logics through which the conflict and its male population were predominantly understood, they could also work to remap and rearticulate divisions and distinctions between the white and civilized militarized masculinities of the counterinsurgents, and the non-white and primitive masculinities of the local population.

These distinctions were primarily mapped through two particular orientalist discourses: that of the feminization and homosexualization of Afghan men, and – somewhat paradoxically – Afghan men's hypermasculinization and uncontrollability.[2] Beginning with the former: in Western media reporting and Western soldier memoirs of the Afghanistan conflict there was a preoccupation with the bodies of Afghan soldiers – about what their bodies looked like and what their bodies did, particularly with regard to their sexuality. Frequent and repeated references were made with regard to Afghan soldiers' perceived more effeminate appearance: their hennaed hair, kohl-rimmed eyes and the flowers that adorned their weaponry and vehicles. Patrick Hennessey, a former officer in the British Army who served in Afghanistan, wrote that his first overwhelming impression of the ANA was that of 'sheer physical difference' (2012, p. 22). While Hennessey and his fellow British infantrymen literally embodied the archetypal militarized masculine figure ('all over 6 foot tall ... Giant, strapping, pink ... with similarly cropped hair' (Hennessey, 2012, p. 22)), the ANA were 'small', 'scruffy as hell' and likened to children (pp. 21–4). While feminists have long noted that the conflation of women with children is a way to infantilize women and femininity, this example shows its inversion: the infantilization of men to implicitly feminize them (Welland, 2015a, p. 295). Such feminization was compounded by the deployment of orientalist tropes of (homo)sexualization, sexual lasciviousness and deviance.

NATO troops who worked alongside Afghan soldiers reported unease with the behavior and attentions of their comrades. Afghan soldiers were affectionate with one another, held hands and sometimes wore make-up. According to one British newspaper, in order for Western troops to better understand the sexual behavior of Afghan men and security forces a report was commissioned as part of the Human Terrain Systems Project (Farmer, 2011). The American social scientist Maria Cardinalli's 2010 report concluded that a 'culturally-contrived homosexuality ... appears to affect a far greater population base then [sic] researchers would argue is attributable to natural inclination' (Cardinalli, 2010, p. 1). Not only does such a statement rearticulate orientalist assumptions that mark homosexuality as something 'Arab' men are culturally predisposed toward, but also that homosexuality affects more men than is 'natural', thus marking the Afghan soldiers as deviant in both their sexual preferences and their numbers (Manchanda, 2015, p. 136).

Given the intimate links between masculine gender, heterosexual competency and soldiering in Western militaries, it follows that the perceived effeminacy and homosexuality of the Afghan forces led to doubts over their combat ability by the NATO troops responsible for their training (Welland, 2015a, p. 298; see also Welland, 2013). Two seemingly opposed concerns were frequently mentioned. First, that ANA troops appeared to fear, or be unwilling to engage in, training or fighting. Soldier memoirs describe that when opportunities for training would arise 'a mysterious bell would ring, and the ANA would all disappear on cue – prayers, lunch, siesta, we never really knew to where' (Hennessey, 2012, p. 45), and that the ANA were 'not really interested in doing any serious training' (Docherty, 2007, p. 88). At an institutional level the ANA appeared to be written out of the Afghanistan mission; a 'quasi-official history' of one British regiment's tour failed to mention the ANA at all (Hennessey, 2012, p. 98). While in these representations Afghan soldiers were feminized through their separation from the combat zone, doubts about their fighting credentials also stemmed from their representation as hyper-masculinized and excessively violent.

Descriptions of ANA fighting often portray it as uninhibited, chaotic, unrestrained. Hennessey (2012, p. 88) uses the Afghan word *kharkus* to describe the ANA's fighting style, meaning a mixture of crazy and brave. These portrayals offer a mixture of envy and reservation. Envy in the abandonment of control, in the separation of fighting from instrumental purposes and complex battle plans. In contrast, discipline and control were central to the counterinsurgency militarized masculinity constructed and produced in these spaces and in relation to these other(ed) subjects. Their recourse to violence – of which they were more than capable – was underwritten with the assumption that it was legitimate, proportionate and controlled. Orientalism, 'a mixed bag of self-glorification and self-doubt' (Porter, 2009, p. 29), meant that the ANA and their actions were both desired and disparaged, both envied and denied (Welland, 2015a, pp. 299–300). Ultimately however, Afghan soldiers' lack of discipline, *kharkus* fighting and kohl-rimmed eyes signalled simultaneously a lack and an excess of masculinity, positioning their masculinity as always subordinate to that of the Western counterinsurgency soldier.

In the counterinsurgency environment an idealized militarized masculine subjectivity was produced not merely through COIN policy and doctrine, but also through soldiers' everyday *doing* of counterinsurgency and their relation with other bodies and masculinities that occupied the warscape. In the differences between the 'courageous restraint' of the counterinsurgency soldier and the unmediated violence of the insurgent, and in their carefully constructed and measured masculinity in comparison to the simultaneously effeminate and hyper-masculinized local fighting forces, a counterinsurgency soldier was shaped and molded. At the same time, this softer and gentler militarized masculinity rearticulated and reinforced the ultimate goals and mission of counterinsurgency as humanitarian, justified and legitimate.

RENDERING THE FEMININE VISIBLE

As militarized masculinity was reshaped and remolded in line with the needs and demands of counterinsurgency, the operation and practice of femininities also underwent a change. Notably, in the COIN environment of Afghanistan, femininity became increasingly visible, both physically in the bio-female bodies of women soldiers and conceptually in the need for more 'feminine' characteristics such as compassion for the effective doing of counterinsurgency.

War has traditionally been perceived as an almost exclusively male and masculine zone. When women did materialize and become visible in the warscape, they did so not as soldiers or warriors, but as 'camp followers' (Enloe, 2000) – as nurses, sex workers and the numerous other women responsible for ensuring male soldiers are 'combat-ready'. However, while women and femininity have always been integral to the fighting of wars, in Western militaries it wasn't until the end of the twentieth century that women began increasingly populating ranks more directly associated with combat and combat support. The 1991–92 Gulf War was considered a watershed moment, with 35 000 women deployed from the American armed forces, making up 7 percent of the total military personnel deployed.[3] It was the largest single deployment of women in history. Women served as aircraft pilots, logistical support and in supply and repair units. While women were not officially in combat, given the use of long-range artillery, lines between combat and non-combat were blurred and 11 US female army personnel lost their lives during the conflict (Skaine, 1999, pp. 64–5). This trend continued during the 2001 invasion of Afghanistan and the US and UK's second incursion into Iraq in 2003. Today, around 14 percent of the American armed forces are female and more than 280 000 women participated in a tour of duty in Iraq or Afghanistan, or contributed to the war effort in these countries from an overseas base (Harris, 2013). In the UK, the second largest troop-contributing country to the wars in Iraq and Afghanistan, 9.8 percent of the armed forces are female (MoD, 2013), with reports suggesting women made up around a fifth of the 8000 British service personnel deployed to Afghanistan (Bone, 2008).

Thus, while women have been deployed to warzones for years, what was distinctive about women's involvement in COIN was the instrumentalization of their feminine gender in very particular ways, specifically in the use of 'Female Engagement Teams' (FETs). In 2009 the few women US Marines in Afghanistan were haphazardly drawn together to form the first FETs. These all-women teams were attached to men-only units and tasked with meeting and speaking with Afghan women in order to find out what their concerns and needs might be. The following year, the Marine Corps began to formally train women members for duty on FETs, with 40 deploying to Southern Afghanistan (McBride and Wibben, 2012, p. 199). FETs visited Afghan women in their homes, distributed humanitarian supplies and, in cooperation with district governments, taught health classes (Pottinger et al., 2010). Crucially, what FETs made possible was interaction with a segment of the population that until that point, due to their gender, had been largely excluded from counterinsurgency efforts (Dyvik, 2014, p. 410).

It is not just that the gender of the FETs allowed them access to Afghan women, thus enabling a fuller enactment of the COIN doctrine, but that the 'feminine' qualities of both the women soldiers and the role of the FETs signaled towards the soft power of counterinsurgency. Given that women remained barred from serving in combat branches[4] during FET involvement in Afghanistan, the use of women soldiers in this way illustrated that this was not a conventional military deployment (McBride and Wibben, 2012, p. 209). As McBride and Wibben note in discussing FETs, women soldiers were allowed to be attached to frontline men-only units and carry out these tasks 'based upon gendered assumptions':

> Because of the ways in which tradition and religion condition Afghan women's lives, it is assumed that only women will have access to them – and that, because they are women, they are not 'real' (read: manly) soldiers; as such, they will be perceived as nonthreatening. These assumptions are shared by both U.S. males and Afghans. (p. 210)

A report by Matt Pottinger et al., the co-founders and trainers of the first FET in Afghanistan, quoted Afghan men saying, 'Your men come to fight, but we know the women are here to help' (Pottinger et al., 2010). The report noted that 'the presence of female Marines softened and facilitated the interaction with local men and children', with Pashtun men actually 'show[ing] a preference for interacting with them over U.S. men'.

Finally, like the other(ed) masculine subjectivities of the insurgents and local security forces, the femininity and visibility of the FETs did important work in the legitimation and justification of the military intervention and COIN doctrine. Like the softer and gentler counterinsurgency militarized masculinity, FETs helped frame the intervention as a benevolent and humanitarian mission. Furthermore, FETs justified the intervention by reinforcing the 'civilizational superiority' (McBride and Wibben, 2012, p. 210) of the Western nations to their publics back home. Just as the bodies of Afghan women were co-opted and became *the* signifier of the Taliban's monstrosity and incivility in the opening months of the invasion, in the closing years of the intervention the bodies of women counterinsurgents became the surface upon which the progressiveness of the mission and the civility of troop-contributing nations were written.

It is not, however, just the bodies of feminine soldiers that increased in visibility in the counterinsurgency context: 'feminine' characteristics such as compassion and empathy also emerged as central to COIN. Both scholars studying the military and soldiers themselves have long noted that military training has conventionally been structured so as to obliterate the feminine traits of passivity, weakness and emotionality within recruits. Not only does basic training continue to privilege the assumed masculine attributes of strength, aggression and physical and mental endurance, but recruits also face a variety of gendered, raced and sexualized insults crafted to play upon their specific feminine or masculine anxieties. Insults include: 'whore', 'faggot', 'sissy', 'cunt', 'ladies', 'pussy', and sometimes simply 'you woman' (Whitworth, 2008, p. 112). For Sandra Whitworth, the aggressively gendered terms that military training is organized and enacted through come as little surprise due to the intimate connections between military organizations and hegemonic representations of masculinity. Whitworth states that the inculcation of the 'myths of manhood' in a soldier during basic training relies upon a recruit denying all that is soft and feminine within himself (Whitworth, 2008, p. 114). A soldier emerging from basic training will be 'both physically and emotionally tough, portraying little emotion, with the possible exceptions of anger and aggression' (Whitworth, 2008, p. 114). Whitworth quotes the American conservative, George Gilder: 'When you want to create a solidaristic group of male killers ... you kill the woman in them' (p. 114).

A straightforward expulsion of femininity within the military, however, was never entirely possible. Soldiering involves many traditionally feminine traits such as 'total obedience and submission to authority, the attention to dress detail, and the endless repetition of mundane tasks that enlisted men ... are expected to perform' (Hooper, 2001, p. 47). Nonetheless, in the figure of the softer and gentler militarized masculinity required for counterinsurgency, traits conventionally associated with femininity were not only not expelled, but were privileged. Given that gaining the trust and winning the hearts and minds of the civilian population was at the center of COIN, the feminized attributes of collaboration, communication and empathy were considered more appropriate and relevant to the needs and demands of counterinsurgency than the more traditional and masculinized soldiering qualities of violence, aggression and domination.

Compassion is one of the feminine emotions that assumed a central importance in the understanding and doing of counterinsurgency. It is an emotion that opens up the one who experiences it to another's suffering (Welland, 2015b), positioning the experiencer in direct relation with another and giving rise to a desire to alleviate that suffering, to engage in what Carol Gilligan (1982) called an 'ethic of care'. As a sentiment that entails a revelation of vulnerability, an opening up of subjectivity, and an engagement in empathetic relations, compassion has been understood as a distinctly feminine emotion and one that is assumed as outside the (masculine) soldiering experience. However, in counterinsurgency, the annihilation of the enemy was no longer a goal in its own right; soldiers needed to live amongst the host population, and listen and respond to their concerns and needs. Thus, soldiers were now expected to engage in empathetic and compassionate relations with those they had been sent to protect. Compassion therefore emerged as a central framing device for understanding and reasoning the long military involvement in Afghanistan (Welland, 2015b). In particular, compassionate relations were visible in soldiers' encounters with both civilians *and* enemy insurgents.

Although the Afghanistan conflict was framed, in part, through a national security discourse in both the US and UK, when soldiers themselves were asked about their personal reasons for joining a military embroiled in two active wars, responses tended – particularly as the intervention stretched on – to assume a more humanitarian explanation than the security of their home nation. UK Guardsman David Walton told a journalist: 'It's not often in life that you get a chance to help people and defend the country, and that's what I think we are doing here' (cited in Rayment, 2011, p. 108). Likewise, in his memoir of his time in Afghanistan, Sergeant Doug Beattie recalled that what kept him going during battle was the 'idea that you are doing what is right, that you are helping people' (2008, p. 180). Many soldiers appeared genuinely excited about getting involved with the local population, with doing something more than just war-fighting, and had an unselfconscious desire to 'do good'. Claire Duncanson (2013, p. 114) has written about soldiers' empathy with the local population: although some soldiers engaged in 'Radical Othering', they also described the local population 'using terms such as friendly, loyal, brave, proud and lovely, and report building genuine relationships and attachments'. Duncanson argued that a 'peacebuilding masculinity' could be constructed through interactions with Afghan civilians and security forces, and 'through relations of equality, empathy, care, respect and recognition of similarities and shared experiences' (pp. 148–9). For Duncanson, this masculinity does not just substitute one hierarchical binary for another – for example, a denigrated hyper-masculinized Muslim insurgent replacing the feminized peace-loving woman in relation to a celebrated white, Western and militarized man – but upends and dismantles the binary, thus having the potential to 'contribute to peace and security, even perhaps the undoing of Empire' (p. 149).

As noted above, while insurgents' masculinity was read as violent, cruel and brutal through the tactics they used and orientalist logics, this was not the only way in which the counterinsurgency soldiers of Western states related to them. For Duncanson, a 'peacebuilding masculinity' meant that enemy soldiers were not always simply dehumanized, noting that British soldiers who had penned memoirs often 'express admiration and respect for the insurgents they are fighting' (2013, p. 108). It is not, however, only admiration and respect that counterinsurgents showed enemy fighters; they showed compassion too. Lieutenant Colonel Stuart Tootal describes a Taliban fighter receiving medical care by British soldiers despite fighting them only moments earlier (Tootal, 2009, p. 74). Sergeant Beattie explains why he removes the plastic cuffs binding a captured and dying Taliban fighter: 'If he was going to die in a strange place, surrounded by the faces of his enemy, then at least he was going to have a degree of dignity' (Beattie, 2009, p. 142). While such demonstration of compassion reflects the etymological roots of the word – deriving from the Latin *com*, together, and *pati*, to suffer – suggesting an emotion felt on behalf of another who suffers (Garber, 2004, p. 20) and thus a relationality with them, it can also work to remap differentiations between the insurgent fighter and a counterinsurgency militarized masculinity.

In their relations both with the local civilian population and enemy insurgents, the feminine emotion of compassion was crucial to the doing of counterinsurgency and the discursive construction of the project and militarized masculinities as softened and humanitarian. Rather than traits and characteristics associated with the feminine being expelled or denigrated, they occupied a central and hypervisible location in which narratives and 'making sense' of the counterinsurgency project took place.

CONCLUSIONS: THE EFFECTS OF GENDERING COUNTERINSURGENCY

The counterinsurgency environment of Afghanistan and the shift to 'population-centric' warfare provided the context for the emergence of a softer and gentler militarized masculinity and the rendering visible of femininity, both physically and conceptually. As this chapter has shown, however, gendered subjectivities were not only constructed in and through the practice and doing of counterinsurgency, but were themselves constitutive of understandings, justifications and legitimations of the long military intervention. The counterinsurgency militarized masculinity – particularly when positioned in relation to the violence of the insurgent, or the effeminacy or hyper-masculinity of the local security forces – was central for understanding the mission in a humanitarian framework. Likewise, the visibility of the (white, Western) feminine body in the use of FETs not only reiterated the benevolence of the military intervention, but also signaled towards the civilizational superiority of the interveners. As Dyvik has noted, counterinsurgency 'appropriated women's bodies and lives in order to function' (Dyvik, 2014, p. 422). Finally, 'feminine' traits such as compassion and concern for others, which would have previously been expelled from the masculine soldiering subject, were privileged and even prioritized over and above more traditional masculinized characteristics, reflecting and emphasizing the claims that this was a campaign where the civilian was at its center.

While gender is therefore central to understanding the operation of COIN in Afghanistan and how it was practiced, I want to gesture towards two specific effects of the gendered and gendering of counterinsurgency. First, as this chapter demonstrated, counterinsurgency has engendered a feminizing of the conflict zone; war was represented as softer, gentler and more concerned with civilians and humanitarianism. This re-gendered understanding of conflict allowed for a more intimate form of warfare – a type of engagement where it was no longer just the battlefield that was subject to soldiering presence and warfare was no longer purely concerned with the military defeat of the enemy. Instead, counterinsurgency permeated into spaces, places and people previously understood as outside the concern of the military. The use of FETs meant that Afghan women became the 'target' (Dyvik, 2014) of counter-insurgency operations, and the private sphere of Afghan homes became a public space of military engagement. The everyday practices, lives and doings of the Afghan population were no longer simply background to the military intervention, but their observation and regulation became integral for its success. The second and related effect of gendered/ gendering counterinsurgency is that this less masculinized form of soldiering and war has led to a renewed seduction of militarism. The softer and gentler militarized masculinity and 'feminized' operations of counterinsurgency worked very effectively at disconnecting their prac-tices from the simultaneous violence that continued throughout the military intervention. Indeed, although practices such as engaging with Afghan women and going on soft-hatted patrols were often integral for gathering information for later airstrikes or other kinetic operations, these latter actions remained radically separated from the humanitarian discourses and narratives that framed counterinsurgency. Gender was thus shaped and (re)produced by counterinsurgency, provided a framework for its understanding and justification, and was integral to its concealments and seductions.

NOTES

1. *Shura* is the Afghan word for 'consultation'.
2. The following section draws on previously published work on the British 'partnering and advising' of the ANA. For a fuller account see Welland (2015a).
3. Other allied nations also sent women: Canada sent 150 women, 3 percent of the total they deployed; France, 13 out of a total of 10 000; and Britain sent around 800, around 1.5 percent of their total (Skaine, 1999, p. 65).
4. In 2013 the US announced the lifting of the ban that excluded women from combat roles. In August 2012, the US Marine Corps ended its use of FETs in Afghanistan. The UK continues to exclude women from combat roles.

REFERENCES

Abu-Lughod, Lila (2002), 'Do Muslim women really need saving? Anthropological reflections on cultural relativism and its others', *American Anthropologist*, **104** (3): 783–90.

Beattie, Doug, with Philip Gomm (2009), *An Ordinary Soldier*, Pocket Books.

Bone, Victoria (2008), 'Women in the British Armed Forces', *BBC*, 19 June, accessed 23 June 2015 at: http://news.bbc.co.uk/1/hi/7463636.stm.

Butler, Judith (1999[1990]), *Gender Trouble: Feminism and the Subversion of Identity*, Routledge.

Cardinalli, AnnaMaria (2010), 'Pashtun sexuality', *Unclassified Human Terrain Team (HTT) AF-6: Research Update and Findings*, accessed 8 February 2013 at: http://www.scribd.com/doc/39111225/Pashtun-Sexuality.

Dixon, Paul (2012), 'The British approach to counterinsurgency: "hearts and minds" from Malaya to Afghanistan', in Paul Dixon (ed.), *The British Approach to Counterinsurgency: From Malaya and Northern Ireland to Iraq and Afghanistan*, Palgrave Macmillan, pp. 1–48.

Docherty, Leo (2007), *Desert of Death: A Soldier's Journey from Iraq to Afghanistan*, Faber and Faber.

Duncanson, Claire (2009), 'Forces for good? Narratives of military masculinity in peacekeeping operations', *International Feminist Journal of Politics*, **11** (1): 63–80.

Duncanson, Claire (2013), *Forces for Good? Military Masculinities and Peacebuilding in Afghanistan and Iraq*, Palgrave Macmillan.

Dyvik, Synne (2014), 'Women as "practitioners" and "targets": gender and counterinsurgency in Afghanistan', *International Feminist Journal of Politics*, **16** (3): 410–29.

Dyvik, Synne (forthcoming, 2016), 'Gender and counterinsurgency', in Claire Duncanson and Rachel Woodward (eds), *The Palgrave Handbook of Gender and the Military*, Palgrave Macmillan.

Eichler, Maya (2014), 'Militarized masculinities in international relations', *Brown Journal of World Affairs*, **21** (1): 81–93.

Elshtain, Jean Bethke (1987), *Women and War*, University of Chicago Press.

Enloe, Cynthia (2000), *Maneuvers: The International Politics of Militarizing Women's Lives*, University of California Press.

Farmer, Ben (2011), 'Paedophilia "culturally acceptable in South Afghanistan"', *The Telegraph*, 13 January.

Garber, Marjorie (2004), 'Compassion', in Lauren Berlant (ed.), *Compassion: The Culture and Politics of an Emotion*, Routledge, pp. 15–27.

Gillan, Audrey (2006), 'We made two mistakes. They punished us', *The Guardian*, 18 November.

Gilligan, Carol (1982), *In a Different Voice: Psychological Theory and Women's Development*, Harvard University Press.

Gregory, Derek (2010), 'War and peace', *Transactions of the Institute of British Geographers*, **35** (2): 154–86.

Harding, Thomas (2010), '"Courageous restraint" putting troops' lives at risk', *The Telegraph*, 6 July.

Harris, Paul (2013), 'Women in combat: US military officially lifts ban on female soldiers', *The Guardian*, 25 January.

Hennessey, Patrick (2012), *Kandak: Fighting with Afghans*, Allen Lane.

Higate, Paul (ed.) (2003), *Military Masculinities: Identity and the State*, Praeger.

Hooper, Charlotte (2001), *Manly States: Masculinities, International Relations, and Gender Politics*, Columbia University Press.

Hughes, Chris (2015), 'British army fired 46 million rounds at Taliban costing taxpayer £200m', *The Daily Mirror*, 7 April.

Hunt, Krista (2002), 'The strategic co-optation of women's rights: discourse in the "war on terrorism"', *International Feminist Journal of Politics*, **4** (1): 116–21.

Khalili, Laleh (2011), 'Gendered practices of counterinsurgency', *Review of International Studies*, **37**: 1471–91.

Kilcullen, David (2006), 'Three pillars of counterinsurgency', remarks delivered at the US Government Counterinsurgency Conference, Washington, DC, 28 September.

Manchanda, Nivi (2015), 'Queering the Pashtun: Afghan sexuality in the homo-nationalist imaginary', *Third World Quarterly*, **36** (1): 130–46.

Masters, Cristina (2005), 'Bodies of technology: cyborg soldiers and militarized masculinities', *International Feminist Journal of Politics*, **7** (1): 112–32.

Masters, Cristina (2008), 'Bodies of technology and the politics of the flesh', in Marysia Zalewski and Jane Parpart (eds), *Rethinking the Man Question: Sex, Gender and Violence in International Relations*, Zed Books, pp. 87–107.

McBride, Keally and Annick Wibben (2012), 'The gendering of counterinsurgency in Afghanistan', *Humanity: An International Journal of Human Rights, Humanitarianism and Development*, **3** (2): 199–215.

Ministry of Defence (MoD) (n.d.), 'Partnering and advising', accessed 28 August 2013 at: http://www.army.mod.uk/operations-deployments/22907.aspx.

Ministry of Defence (MoD) (2013), *UK Armed Forces Quarterly Personnel Report*, 1 October edn.

Motlagh, Jason (2010), 'Petraeus toughens Afghan rules of engagement', *Time Magazine*, 6 August.

Porter, Patrick (2009), *Military Orientalism: Eastern War Through Western Eyes*, C. Hurst.

Pottinger, Matt, Hali Jilani and Claire Russo (2010), 'Half-hearted: trying to win Afghanistan without Afghan women', *Small Wars Journal*, 18 February, accessed 23

June 2015 at: http://smallwarsjournal.com/jrnl/art/trying-to-win-afghanistan-without-afghan-women.

Rayment, Sean (2011), *Bomb Hunters: In Afghanistan with Britain's Elite Bomb Disposal Unit*, HarperCollins.

Russo, Ann (2006), 'The Feminist Majority Foundation's campaign to stop gender apartheid: the intersections of feminism and imperialism in the United States', *International Feminist Journal of Politics*, **8** (4): 557–80.

Said, Edward (1979), *Orientalism*, Vintage Books.

Skaine, Rosemarie (1999), *Women at War: Gender Issues of Americans in Combat*, MacFarland.

Svet, Oleg (2012), 'COIN's failure in Afghanistan', accessed 18 June 2015 at: http://nationalinterest.org/commentary/coins-failure-afghanistan-7409.

Tootal, Stuart (2009), *Danger Close: The True Story of Helmand from the Leader of 3 PARA*, John Murray.

US Army et al. (2007), *Counterinsurgency Field Manual*, University of Chicago Press.

Welland, Julia (2013), 'Militarised violences, basic training, and the myths of asexuality and discipline', *Review of International Studies*, **39** (4): 881–902.

Welland, Julia (2015a), 'Liberal warriors and the violent colonial logics of "partnering and advising"', *International Feminist Journal of Politics*, **17** (2): 289–307.

Welland, Julia (2015b), 'Compassionate soldiering and comfort', in Linda Åhäll and Thomas Gregory (eds), *Emotions, Politics and War*, Routledge, pp. 115–28.

Whitworth, Sandra (2004), *Men, Militarism and UN Peacekeeping: A Gendered Analysis*, Lynne Rienner.

Whitworth, Sandra (2008), 'Militarized masculinity and post-traumatic stress disorder', in Jane Parpart and Marysia Zalewski (eds), *Rethinking the Man Question: Sex, Gender and Violence in International Relations*, Zed Books, pp. 109–26.

Young, Iris Marion (2003), 'The logic of masculinist protection: reflections on the current security state', *Signs*, **29** (1): 1–25.

Younossi, Obaid, Peter Dahl Thruelsen, Jonathan Vaccaro, Jerry M. Sollinger and Brian Grady (2009), *The Long March: Building an Afghan National Army*, RAND National Defence Institute.

7. Gender and terrorism
Caron E. Gentry

INTRODUCTION

There is no doubt that the political violence labeled as terrorism is terribly, horrifically devastating. Yet 'terrorism', typically identified as violence done for political reasons by sub-state actors against civilian and non-civilian targets to create widespread fear (see Hoffman, 2006, pp. 3–27; Schmid and Jongman, 2005, pp. 4–25), is not the only devastating form of political violence. Violence carried out by the state, either against its own citizens, such as the *juntas* in South America in the 1970s and 1980s and currently in Myanmar/Burma, or against others, is arguably also terrorism. Such violence is not conceived of as terrorism, although controversy surrounds this (Jackson, 2008). This is an epistemic problem about how the monopoly on the legitimate use of violence is embedded in the identifiers of 'state' and 'statehood'. Therefore, this chapter argues that the 'Westphalian narrative' is a deeply gendered way of delegitimizing violence from particular actors as revealed by the intersections between statehood, racial, post-colonial and gender identifications.

As fields of study International Relations (IR) and the subfield of Terrorism Studies are interested in teaching, telling and producing scholarship that adheres to certain information, norms and ways of knowing. Thus, it creates an epistemic narrative, one that this chapter refers to as the 'Westphalian narrative', meaning the foundational idea in IR scholarship of the primacy and legitimacy of sovereign states. Information that coheres to this narrative maintains narrative fidelity and is privileged above any information that challenges it (Fisher, 1989, p. 47; see also Wibben 2011, p. 2). From this stems a power-wielding epistemic bias against non-state actors. In order to maintain the 'truth' of this narrative, anything that challenges the primacy of states, such as non-state violence, must be discounted. 'Terrorist organizations', 'terrorism' and 'terrorists' are labels that purposefully discount and discredit certain actors based upon a variety of identities – gender, race, religion, geographic location and, arguably, lack of statehood.

Gender is not the only tool for the maintenance of power; it often intersects with other identities that enable structural violence – for example, class, religion and race (Davis, 2008, p. 71). These factors are mutually constitutive and cannot be separated (Davis, 2008, p. 71; Yuval-Davis, 2006, p. 195). While one element may be more important at certain points in time (for example, gender may be more critical than race in a particular situation or time period), all elements are always present. Peterson and Runyan (2009, p. 7) provide a useful example, 'a white American working-class lesbian would be privileged by race and nationality but not by class, gender, and sexuality'. Yuval-Davis (2006, pp. 195, 201) argues it is important to see how all identity factors create marginalizing structural stratifications.

Scholarship on terrorism often reflects the intersection of gender with racial and religious biases to construct a particular image of those who engage in political violence. The label of terrorism is also reflective of the stratification caused by the primacy of the state within the Westphalian system. Thus, this chapter will examine how: (1) the construction of the state as the primary actor automatically removes legitimacy from non-state, politically-violent actors; (2) the geographic, racial and religious identities often associated with 'terrorists' delegitimize their struggle; and (3) the failure to account for the impact of gender on all people makes many scholars of terrorism blind to certain truths.

GENDER AND TERRORISM: THE INTERSECTING NARRATIVES BETWEEN WESTPHALIA AND NEO-ORIENTALISM

Intersectionality considers identifiers that are used to create and maintain power-over dynamics, a particular way of looking at how power is used to dominate and instill subordination from one actor to another. Intersectionality was introduced to examine how race, gender, sexuality and class intersect to impact African-American women in the United States (see Crenshaw, 1989). More recently, intersectionality has veered towards becoming an amorphous theoretical concept, where it has become a catch-all theory for identity politics. However, there is strength in the openness of this theory (Davis, 2008, p. 69). Using identifiers to classify people, whether economically, politically or socially, creates structural stratifications and binaries that help those in power maintain their position and keep those without power away from it.

In IR, feminist scholars have interrogated the ways that the social and interpersonal binary between masculinity and femininity has been abstracted to the Westphalian system, recreating a power-over at the structural level (Tickner, 1992; Sylvester, 2002). Thus the binaries of masculinity/femininity, and state/non-state actors always privilege one side, here masculinity and state actors. This problematic 'logocentrism' (where one word is discursively hierarchically positioned leading to the concept and associate actor being privileged) needs to be deconstructed: first by recognizing its existence, and then by moving beyond it. Feminism(s) through their focus on power production and reification as they pertain to gender intersected with other identifiers is poised to do the necessary, and difficult, deconstruction.

State primacy as established by Westphalia and further solidified over time is one such privilege. The state became not just a legal entity demarcated by territorial and governmental sovereignty, a population and the monopoly on the legitimate use of violence, but also a way of identifying which actors had the authority to act in international affairs. Authority is closely linked to the norms of Westphalia including sovereign equality (that is, all states are technically equal), non-aggression and non-interference. Yet Chris Brown, borrowing from Krasner, explores the 'organized hypocrisy' of the sovereignty system (2002, p. 127), a hypocrisy that privileges the actions not just of sovereign states over non-state actors, but of powerful states over weaker ones (Brown, 2002, p. 79). If weaker states break these norms, they are often labeled as 'pariah' or 'rogue' states. Yet stronger states can break the norms with little fear of censure or punishment. Westphalia has created a stratification not only among states, but also between states and non-states. For while weaker states are punished for contravening international law and norms, when non-state actors, particularly terrorist organizations, break these rules they are seen as even more illegitimate (see Gentry, 2014; Kochi, 2009; Held, 2008).

Further, Westphalia privileges Western imagery and identity over others. When Chris Brown examines humanitarian intervention in *Sovereignty, Rights and Justice* (2002, p. 141), he argues that this action was rarely undertaken until recently and that its purpose was to pursue the interests of the colonizing West in the non-West. He states this even more bluntly: the principle of non-intervention was only relevant within Europe, meaning if European colonizers wanted to intervene in other regions, they were free to do so (Brown, 2002, p. 141). Similarly, Tarik Kochi's criticism of Just War Theory (2009) is also a larger criticism of Westphalia and the Western sovereignty system. The West, he argues, does not often grant sub-state actors any legitimacy for their use of violence. If Westphalia previously established that states are the only ones that may be justified in their use of violence, then non-state actors that use violence in an attempt to change their state and possibly influence geo-politics will always be scripted as illegitimate. He argues that this is an evident epistemic bias, and one that fails to see the ethics of 'the other's war' (Kochi, 2009, p. 249). It is again a bias about identity – of statehood and of Western identity. Thus the narrative of state credibility and legitimacy is strongly linked to Western identity. This speaks to an ongoing pattern where Western regions have more access to legitimacy and credibility than the non-West, yet hold others to norms the West is free to break.

The privileging of states and their monopoly on power in turn delegitimizes other claims on power and violence, and gender is crucial for this simultaneous legitimation and delegitimation. As noted by Tickner (1992, p. 42), states are abstractions of masculine idealizations of privilege 'in terms of self-help, autonomy, and power seeking'. States in the construction and reification of what Brown and Kochi note above are therefore understood and legitimized as masculine actors. Building upon this and Connell's hegemonic masculinity (Connell, 2005[1995]), Sjoberg (2013) conceptualizes the international structure as not determined by anarchy but instead determined by gender hierarchy. War happens, she argues, because states and other actors engage in a competitive performance of masculinity. By extension this delegitimizes, or feminizes, politically violent sub-state actors, who are denied the right to use violence or to be rational actors. Paying attention to gender, as well as revealing its intersection with other identifiers, such as race, religion, geography and, yes, statehood, challenges the Westphalian narrative, which in turn uncovers the operation of power. Yet, reading power backwards and forwards in IR (Enloe, 2000, p. 196) requires a feminist to look below the macro-level of state politics and see how such a narrative affects marginalized people groups as it denies access to the form of power and violence available to states.

When reading power in scholarship on terrorism, neo-orientalism comes to mind. Orientalism, as introduced by Edward Said, is a particular perspective held by those in the West towards those in the Middle East or associated with Islam (making it neo-orientalism; see Tuastad, 2003). A condemning perspective, it portrays the people in question as uncivilized and uneducated, while also treating them as exotic, sexual objects (Said, 1978, p. 7; see also Nader, 1989; Yeğenoğlu, 1998; Akram, 2000). As neo-orientalism holds that such traits are immutable and natural, there is no reason to expect any changes or progress to be made. From a geo-political level to a personal level, the political violence under study is often attributed to race, religion and geographic location outside the Western ideal. Neo-orientalism implicitly corroborates the Westphalian narrative by furthering the illegitimacy of non-Western identities.

The gendered nature of neo-orientalism is obvious in the so-called 'war on terror' between the West, particularly the US, and radical Islamism (conflated with all of Islam). Within this contentious, Manichean construct, Western identity was conflated with white, rational, heternormative masculinity (see Nayak, 2006; Shepherd, 2006), whereas Muslim men were hypermasculinized as 'dehumanized and demonized' (Nayak, 2006, p. 50) and 'Irrational Barbarians' (Shepherd, 2006, p. 25). Thus, the racial elements of neo-orientalism intersect with gender and these problematic binaries suppose enormous differences between Western and non-Western identities. These are the lies that are perpetrated by the Westphalian narrative – that the now masculine (Western) state works against the raced and gendered (radical Islamist) non-state actor. The aim of this chapter is not to replicate these binaries but to understand why they exist in the first place and how they are harmful.

NARRATIVE FIDELITY: WESTPHALIA AND POLITICAL VIOLENCE

The most obvious, troubling binary in feminism is the divide between masculinity and femininity. Idealized masculine traits, such as autonomy, rationality, logic and power, are transposed upon the state, abstracting global politics to issues that exist between states and not individuals (Sylvester, 2002, pp. 160–61). Abstraction 'paints' security in broad terms and feeds the Westphalian narrative. Abstraction occurs when International Relations scholars and practitioners become wedded to generalizations used to explain various events as if they are discrete and solitary units, such as 'the state system', 'Westphalia', or 'the market' (see Sylvester, 1999, pp. 34–5). Such thinking translates to security through the use of 'hard power', or by focusing on the sovereignty of the state, rationality and capability. If one continues to regard this as a diametrically opposed binary (see Tickner, 1992) of the rational state versus non-state actors then legitimacy is granted to states and denied to non-state actors. This creates an epistemic problem – instead of thinking in terms of what *activities* or *causes* are legitimate, global politics practitioners think in terms of *who* has access to legitimacy (see Kochi, 2009; Held, 2008). States then are privileged insiders, and non-state actors, especially terrorist organizations, are outsiders (see Brown, 2002, p. 21).

All binaries privilege the behavior of the in-group and subordinate the activity and agency of the out-group. Terrorist organizations represent several affronts to the Westphalian system: they are non-state actors and they violate the monopoly on violence. Furthermore, the dominant paradigm in IR, neo-realism, values nothing more than rationality, the cost–benefit mode of making a decision based on capability, specifically the measurement of military power. Terrorist organizations continue to be described within rational actor models, even if reading 'between the lines' of these models reveals an opposing discourse. This creates a conundrum of sorts, where rationality is seemingly being 'granted' but then revoked through hidden subtexts related to intersecting identifiers, particularly related to gender and race.

Many definitions of terrorism include the term 'extranormative', which often refers to the 'breach[ing] of accepted rules' such as the targeting and murder of a large number of civilians and of violence outside declared war (Schmid and Jongman, 2005, p. 6). Implicit extranormativity is how terrorism challenges stability – both the stability of Westphalia and that of society. It challenges much of what lies at the heart of the Westphalian narrative: primacy, sovereignty, protection of populations and the monopoly on the legitimate use of violence. Yet, in all reality, terrorist violence is no more violent than the state violence that occurs in war or in peacetime against a state's own citizens (see Held, 2008). Further, not until the 1990s did terrorist attacks purposefully attempt to kill large numbers of people (see Hoffman, 2006, p. 19). The 'randomness' of attacks does contribute to a feeling of social instability, although the 9/11 attacks were not 'unanticipated' (Wibben, 2011, p. 108), nor should one assume that civilians are never viewed as acceptable 'collateral damage' in war. Therefore, one has to question what is meant by stability in different areas of the globe.

As Judith Butler explains, 'most Americans have probably experienced something like the loss of their First-Worldism as a result of September 11 and its aftermath' (Butler, 2004, p. 39 as quoted in Wibben, 2011, p. 107). One of the most apparent global structural violences is the stability afforded by power. If a state is already externally and internally stable, then the world is seemingly stable, although this stability arguably comes at a cost to its own population and to other populations (see Gentry, 2013). The US found the nearly 3000 dead from the 9/11 attacks destabilizing because it had experienced so little terrorism. In contrast, 47 000 people are assumed to be dead and another 70 000 are missing from the latest Kashmiri insurgency (1989–ongoing), as reported in 2009, and yet the world, and certainly the West, pays far greater attention to and places far more importance on the events of 9/11 (AFP, 2009).

Threats may exist, but if the states' leaders accept the assumptions and priorities of realism, then the state's capability affords it respite from external threats, or at least the threats that realist-leaning leaders care about. Arguably, this 'works' for the Western, developed world while leaving the rest of the globe to contend with economic and political instability (see also Wibben, 2011, pp. 107–8).[1]

One of the key debates in Terrorism Studies, how to define the term 'terrorism' itself, is located in this tension between the developed and developing world. Many different clichés pepper Terrorism Studies literature. One of the most prominent is 'one person's freedom fighter is another's terrorist'. In 1974, Dugard argued that the reason the United Nations (UN) could not settle on a definition stemmed from the division between former colonial powers and the newly-sovereign former colonies. The former colonizers, then the First World powers, wanted a stricter definition that did not recognize the post-colonial right to self-determination through revolutionary means (Dugard, 1974, pp. 72–3). This debate was taking place at the height of the Non-Aligned Movement and the G-77's power, both of which arguably presented a challenge to the Westphalian system (as did the UN) and the power of the West. The challenges created by this tension between the developed and developing world bring into focus the relationship between power and identity politics (see also Cronin, 2002).

Yet another cliché in the study of terrorism speaks to the question of rationality and capability. While scholars argue that rationality is inherent to terrorist choices and decisions, terrorist activity still defies IR's commitment to rationality and capability. It is often said that terrorism is the 'weapon of the weak', meaning that terrorist groups do not have access to the same amount of weaponry (capability) as states. Today this style of political violence is referred to as 'asymmetric warfare' (Thomas, 2001, p. 32). If one reads between the lines, terrorism is still regarded as irrational because it is the choice of the weak. Not only does the association of terrorism with irrationality and weakness allow for the preservation of the coherence of the Westphalian narrative, but the gendered character of the terms convey illegitimacy and lack of agency on those who engage in terrorism.

But terrorism troubles some of the most closely held beliefs about international relations, and scholars need to find a way of making sense of it in the face of the Westphalian narrative. Martha Crenshaw has for years argued that terrorist violence is rational and works within a Rational Actor Model (RAM) (Crenshaw, 1998; see also Crenshaw, 1995, pp. 17–18). Robert Pape cemented the RAM explanation in his 2005 book on suicide terrorism. In it he argues suicide campaigns are the product of rational decision-making. Pape (2005, p. 61) discovered that in states considered to be democracies (including tenuous democracies, such as Russia and Sri Lanka), suicide campaigns actually garnered concessions and led to favorable changes for the groups that used them. His conclusion was that suicide campaigns, rather than being chaotic and unplanned, are highly rational and very strategic (Pape, 2005, p. 61). Such reasoning and explanation manages to reconcile 'irrational' terrorist activity with the Westphalian narrative.

Nevertheless, problems emerge within the RAM's application to terrorist activity. Pape presents an account of terrorism that is supposedly neutral to facets of identity politics by claiming it as rational activity (2005, p. 39), as if identity is a facet of life that can be measured and calculated. RAM is a gendered proposition that fails to recognize that the rhetoric and construction of rationality is masculine in nature and that researchers have a tendency not to account for gender. For instance, both Pape and Mia Bloom (2005a, 2005b, 2011) argue that women who have been subjected to trauma, particularly sexual violence, are more prone to becoming suicide bombers. This removes trauma from the explanations for men's suicide bombings and political violence, and only attributes physical and emotional trauma to women's activities. Not only do men cite trauma as motivating factors for their involvement in terrorism (Saleh, 2005), but such a dichotomy is both deeply gendered and deeply problematic (see also Sjoberg and Gentry, 2008).

Scholarship has also dichotomized those who are involved in terrorism. So much attention has been paid to radical Islamist terrorism in recent years that it often appears to be the only form that terrorism takes. By setting a certain population aside as 'the' violent one, those who do the accusing can forget about their own violence or their complicity in the violence of others. This upholds the Westphalian narrative by believing that the violence is coming from outside the actors that it privileges.

IRRATIONALITY, IDENTITY AND POLITICAL VIOLENCE

Terrorism is a deeply-loaded term. Not only does it convey an illegitimate use of violence, but it is a term that carries with it assumptions about gender, race, religion and political credibility. The rhetoric that currently surrounds terrorism often uncritically revolves around Islam (see Richardson, 2004, pp. 22, 43, 79, 131; Jackson, 2007). One could argue that it all began with one of the most controversial lines in IR – 'Islam has bloody borders' (Huntington, 1993, p. 35) – but sadly blaming conflict on Islam is pervasive (see Tuastad, 2003; Kaplan, 2001). Political violence existed before and apart from Islam and is performed by many non-Islamic populations. Intersectionality reveals how the identity politics of gender, race, religion and non-Western statuses merge to create delegitimizing narratives within Terrorism Studies. For the most part this stays within a neo-orientalist narrative, where descriptions of Muslims (or those presumed to be Muslim) and absurdly monolithic accounts of Islamic culture create images of these populations as uncivilized, barbaric, violent and irrational. It is an overtly gendered dichotomy dependent upon the masculinized, rational Western state operating against the hypermasculinized, irrationally violent, non-Western terrorist other (see Nayak, 2006; Shepherd, 2006; Gentry, 2015).

Yuval-Davis argues that intersectionality helps researchers see how social stratifications 'tend to have certain parameters in common' in that they are 'naturalized', or 'seen as resulting from biological destiny linked to differential genetic pools of intelligence and personal characteristics' (2006, p. 199). When gender is intersected with orientalism and orientalism is extended to all Muslims irrespective of locale – becoming now neo-orientalism (see Akram, 2000, pp. 10–11, 15) – it calls out the assumptions that all men associated with Islam are controlling, abusive and violent, while the women are 'veiled' – controlled, submissive and abused (Moghadam, 1994, p. 2–3). Neo-orientalism shows up in the theories on culture and civilization as the newest cause of conflict and war (Huntington, 1993, 1997; Kaplan, 2001). It emerges in the descriptions of the cultures in which there is seen to be a high prevalence of political violence (see Tuastad, 2003). All of these ignore the high level of structural violence against these societies as well as the structural and physical violence that exists within Western cultures (Tuastad, 2003, pp. 595–6). This is finger-pointing and scapegoating at the highest level with some of the direst of consequences.

This was incredibly clear in the rhetoric of the Bush Administration in the period following the 9/11 attacks. Lee Jarvis (2009, pp. 98–9) analyzes how the Bush administration presented the attacks as 'the latest, most deadly, assault within a lengthy chronology of terrorist and non-terrorist attacks against the United States, and, indeed, others'. These rhetorical maneuverings uphold the Westphalian narrative and in turn enabled the Bush administration to cement support for the wars in Iraq and Afghanistan and for its counter-terrorist policies, such as the controversial PATRIOT Act. Gender was also employed; Annick Wibben highlights how First Lady Laura Bush's radio address on 17 November 2001 to support the war in Afghanistan manipulated imagery of what it meant to be a woman (and a man) in Afghanistan from a neo-orientalist perspective. Mrs Bush equated the insecurity of Afghan women as victims of domestic violence with the insecurity of the US in the 'war on terror' (Wibben, 2011, pp. 10–11). The rhetoric also fed into the supporting neo-orientalist narrative that the peoples who engage in political violence are 'evil' and 'uncivilized'.

'Barbaric' is nearly synonymous with 'irrational' and 'cruel' – all loaded, derogatory terms often used in descriptions of terrorist activity. Groups that resort to political violence are often seen as a product of society that has nothing left to gain or lose. In the first instance, it is a society that has never had anything (wealth, education, organized civilization) so that it does not know political violence is wrong (Tuastad, 2003, p. 592). In the second instance, it is a society that has fallen so far that it uses violence in order to regain any foothold. In both instances, ethnicities that employ political violence are often described as missing that intangible something that grounds its society in rational behavior – failing to recognize that these assumptions about what these societies are or have possessed are false. Gender is in operation in both instances: first, by feminizing societies as irrational and without access to Western progressive rationality, and second, by coding societies as hypermasculinized (which is not a virtue through its implications of frenetic action) and aggressive.

For example, Palestinian society has been described as having lost a moral compass, if it ever had one (Tuastad, 2003, p. 592). Much ado is made about the posters, television shows and music videos glorifying suicide bombers (see Bloom, 2005a, p. 156). This is often connected to the perceived control that radical Islam has over the Palestinian people (see Brunner, 2005). Such accounts fail to acknowledge the stagnant economic situation faced by many Palestinians or the violent retaliation from Israel within the Territories. It does not deal with the lack of opportunity and options, or the political frustrations the Palestinians feel after 60 years without sovereignty.

After winning one war and quasi-losing the second (as fighting continues), Chechens are often described as 'demonic', 'desperate' and having nothing left but a desire to fight (Russell, 2007, p. 54). Because of these two 'similarities' between Palestine and Chechnya, reporters now warn of the 'Palestinianization' of Chechnya (Gentry and Whitworth, 2011; Eke, 2003; Weir, 2003). For centuries, Russians have told stories to children and memorized poems such as Lermontov's 'Cossack Lullaby' that vividly portray Chechens as wolves, baby-snatchers and crazed killers (Russell, 2007, pp. 54–5). These images feed into the idea of a desperate Chechen society. One might assume the desperation is owed to Russia's actions in the region: the razing of Grozny, the pillaging of villages, the endemic gender-based violence or the ethnic cleansing. Most media accounts, however, attribute desperation to the 'rise' of Islam in Chechnya – ignoring that the majority of Chechens are historically of the Muslim faith (see Gentry and Whitworth, 2011). All of these othering narratives present the Chechens as violent without holding the Russian state responsible. Russia escapes relatively unscathed, even though it has one of the world's worst human rights records because of its actions in the Caucasus (Human Rights Watch, 2009).

Making sense of political violence while maintaining coherency with the Westphalian narrative is perhaps impossible. The Westphalian narrative is inherently flawed: the norms mean nothing in the face of power, while identity politics provide the mechanism through which power is constructed and maintained. Because identity politics are de-emphasized and rationality is overly revered, the notion that political violence could be a viable option makes no sense within this narrative. While the Westphalian narrative will linger, there is a possible solution offered by Terrorism Studies: process.

GENDER AND PROCESS: BEYOND IDEAL-TYPES

Up until this point, this chapter has examined how the Westphalian narrative affects scholarship on terrorism at the macro and meso levels, and how these levels are always already gendered. When one thinks initially about gender and terrorism, however, immediate thoughts may turn towards women who are involved with political violence. This section will delve into that tendency whilst also suggesting some paths forward for research on gender and terrorism at the micro level. It is incredibly important to understand how gender and identity politics impact the lives of people who chose political violence as a means of voicing their frustrations. Historically, IR has clung to gendered ideal-types of men and women, especially when it comes to violence and agency. A Western masculine ideal-type would expect a biologically-sexed man to be rational, calculating, physical, aggressive and un-emotional, and then expect the opposite traits – nurturing, patience, passivity and emotion – from biologically-sexed women in an ideal-type of femininity (Beckman and D'Amico, 1995 p. 4; see also Peterson and Runyan, 2009). Feminism(s) have laid bare the gendered dichotomies that haunt IR, starting with Cynthia Enloe's critique of how militarization reinforces men as perpetrators of violence and 'womenandchildren' as passive victims (Enloe, 1983, p. 166), to Jean Bethke Elshtain's de-construction of the Just Warrior and the Beautiful Soul (1995), and continuing with feminist investigations into women's agency in political violence and political violence more generally (Sjoberg and Gentry, 2007; Parashar, 2009 & 2011; Sylvester and Parashar, 2009; Brown, 2011; Parashar and Mackenzie, 2011). Despite (or in spite of) this, IR and Terrorism Studies have had a difficult time accounting for gender in motivations behind political violence.

Terrorism Studies tends to focus on why rather than how people become terrorists (Horgan, 2008). To ask 'why' leads the researcher down a complicated path: the question may never be answered concretely and it tends to be answered from an abnormal psychology perspective. In the first instance, it is hard to do a social scientific study without a control group, as West Germany discovered when it tried to understand the origins of left-wing radicalism from a psychological perspective in the 1960s and 1970s (Crenshaw, 2011, p. 382). Early research on terrorism suggested that certain mental health problems led to political violence. One leading scholar said that terrorists followed an inner 'psycho-logic', one that compelled the people to commit violence due to splitting and externalization of personality flaws that somehow remained both logical and political (Post, 1998, pp. 25, 27). Another (recanted) explanation linked suicide campaigns to Durkheimian anomic suicide (Merari, 1998, p. 206). These early arguments were contemporaneously disputed and are now considered defunct (see Victoroff, 2005).

Instead of asking why, scholars should be asking 'how': what elements in a person's life lead him/her to believe that political violence is a productive way to solve the problem (Horgan, 2008)? The leading psychological explanation for how people become involved in terrorism is 'process' theory. Max Taylor and John Horgan (2006) argue that there cannot be one profile of a terrorist and there cannot be one explanation for how people become involved in terrorism. Instead, involvement in political violence is the result of a series of choices, opportunities and socio-cultural factors that lead a person to a particular place. Yet process is too wedded to a linear model that does not account for people who have these 'radicalizing' elements in their lives but still do not turn to terrorism – or conversely, those without these elements in their lives and *do* turn to terrorism (see Githens-Mazer and Lambert, 2010). Process also significantly lacks an explanation for how gender operates in particular cultures and in the lives of particular people.

Similarly to intersectionality, process looks at the many different factors that impact people's lives – family, friends, social organizations, religion, culture, national politics, international politics and beyond.

Precisely because of these different variables, it is impossible to attempt to establish a singular profile of a terrorist. While process is helpful in speaking back to neo-orientalism and helps de-abstract the Westphalian narrative, it does not speak to all factors in a person's life. If a scholar is not specifically studying a 'woman terrorist', it is often assumed that 'terrorist' is either gender-neutral or a man. Knowing that gender-neutral studies are anything but that, as they typically rely upon masculinities to establish a baseline, a gender-blind study remains shallow in this regard (see Sjoberg and Gentry, 2008; Wibben 2011, p. 7). This is especially true when gender-blind studies, such as Pape (2005) and Bloom (2005a), then add in women. When women are added to the equation, they are often perceived to be engaging in political violence for vastly different reasons than the men.

Until recently, women's involvement in political violence has been treated as something of a novelty. Yet women have participated in political violence since at least the late nineteenth century, beginning with Russia's *Narodnaya Volya* (People's Will) and continuing through West Germany's Red Army Faction, the Popular Front for the Liberation of Palestine, Sri Lanka's Liberation Tigers of Tamil Eelam (LTTE) to the Hindu nationalist groups of India. Women have led and followed, planned acts of political violence, hijacked planes, planted bombs, committed suicide attacks and held hostages (see Sjoberg and Gentry, 2011, pp. 58–9). Women have done this for as long as the term 'terrorist' has existed in the common parlance,[2] and they engaged in political violence that occurred before the origin of the term (see Qazi, 2011). In short, women, like men, have the ability, onus and drive to use violence for political purposes. Treating 'women terrorists' as a new phenomenon is simply a reflection of the gendered reliance by academics, policy-makers and the media on ideal-types of gender.

Women's activities are presented through the use of particular narratives or stereotypes that conform to gendered ideal-types. Women are described either within the maternal constructions of feminine ideals or as deviating from them, thus casting them as sexualized or simply evil. Scholarship trying to deconstruct this and move IR past such assumptions has blown the field wide open (see Alison, 2004; Toles-Patkin, 2004; Brunner, 2005; Sjoberg and Gentry, 2007; Gentry, 2009; Parashar, 2009; Sylvester and Parashar, 2009; Gentry and Sjoberg, 2015). Now that the work has proliferated and continues to generate important and necessary scholarship, it is time to open new doors.

For all that has been written critiquing this bias in the past decade, getting mainstream scholars in IR and Terrorism Studies to recognize how gender operates has been difficult (for a similar account of resist-ance in Security Studies see Wibben, 2011, p. 5). For instance, Mia Bloom's 2011 book on female terrorists, *Bombshell*, relies upon process theory and acknowledges ideal-types of gender, but fails to account for how gender first operates as a tool for the maintenance of power, and second expects different behaviors and actions from men and women. It is wise to understand how cultures build ideal-types of masculinity and femininity. Different cultures are going to expect different gendered behaviors based on a person's sex. Bloom pays careful attention to process in *Bombshell*; the case studies are historically rooted, nuanced and empathetic to the circumstances that surround the women's lives. However, the book seems to accept gendered ideal-types as naturally immutable. So while it pays attention to gender, it does not do so in a way that recognizes men are *constructed* to accept the role of perpetrator and, vice versa, that women are *constructed* to be more passive as the victims of violence. Thus, *Bombshell* still needs to account for gender as one piece in the process for both actors.

Even more, it would behoove process theorists to account for gender in the lives of all people. Process needs to be able to answer how ideal-types are constructed and replicated within a particular culture. Do ideal-types contribute to the violence or do they stop it? Arguably it is a mixture of both. For example, Bloom essentially argues that ideal-types feed the violence. Without looking at the impact of gender on males, Bloom argues that female rape victims choose suicide bombings because they are dishonored, shamed and no longer have a place in their society (2005a, p. 143; 2005b; 2011, pp. 63–4, 153, 156, 224–5). This is a gendered problem with a gendered conclusion in need of deconstruction. Shame stemming from dishonor may indeed play a role, but so might an anger stemming from a personal awareness of political injustices. Gender is in both of these motivations – in the way some cultures intrinsically link honor with sexuality and in the roles gendered people are allowed to have in various societies.

Similarly, some women have used cultural significations of gender to make a political stance against violence. Women in Argentina, El Salvador and Mexico have taken advantage of their status as mothers in conservative societies to peacefully demonstrate against state terrorism (Agosin and Franzin, 1987; Berajano, 2002). These examples revolve around how gender is perceived by outsiders and/or claimed by the women themselves. While both these instances are examples of women, men's violence can be equally gendered. As Puar and Rai (2002) point out, reactions to the 9/11 hijackers discursively reconfigured these men as either hypermasculinized monsters or as homoeroticized ones. Older instances exist as well. Andreas Baader, one of the leaders of the first generation (late 1960s–early 1970s) of the West German Red Army Faction, was 'deaf to rational argument' (Aust, 1985, p. 280) and much was made of his fashion preference for tight, velvet trousers (Aust, 1985, pp. 89–91).

Looking at gender in political violence on the micro level needs both to recognize that gender is a lived and felt reality – it exists – but that it is also a social construction of power. It is a part of life that establishes power-over dynamics that are inherently harmful. Just as gender is used in the construction of a Western, masculinized and rational state's legitimacy and a non-Western, devalorized, irrational non-state actor's illegitimacy, so too is gender used in order to understand the actions of individuals who choose political violence.

CONCLUSION

Gender hierarchy, as inferred through rationality, power and autonomy, orders which actors we view as legitimate and credible in global politics. This is particularly obvious when looking at the discursive binary that differentiates between the legitimacy and credibility of the (Western) masculinized state and the illegitimacy of the (non-Western) feminized and devalorized non-state violent actor. This ordering takes place not just on the system level, but also appears in the identity politics of neo-orientalism and in the individual genderings of women's and men's involvement in political violence. It is problematic not just in the creation of power structures and hierarchies but because it decontextualizes the reasons behind people's decisions to become involved in political violence.

The Westphalian narrative and the supporting narrative of neo-orientalism not only impose legitimacy and illegitimacy upon certain actors based upon identity, the rigidity within the narratives inhibit creative ways of approaching the problem. In her book on feminist security studies and narrative, Annick Wibben argues that the '[r]igid framings' created by narratives 'inhibit more imaginative approaches to conflict and multifaceted forms of agency' (Wibben, 2011, p. 108). If the security community can only conceive of terrorism as completely illegit-imate violence committed by evil, barbaric people then there is no room to move forward and find a long-lasting and far-reaching solution. Rigid, uncompromising thinking has led to the actual wars that make up the more amorphous 'war on terror'. Rigid thinking also led to the genocide by the Sri Lankan government against the Tamils in the summer of 2009.

While Sri Lanka claimed to be ending the decades-long LTTE insurgency, the government's violence targeted all Tamils and included torture, gender-based violence and extrajudicial killings (United Nations, 2011).

Life is complicated and rarely affords the black and white clarity imposed by narratives. Therefore, researchers would benefit from accepting that the stickiness and intricacy of identity interrupts narratives. Interrupting narratives may seem like a threatening proposition because it removes an element of 'safety blanket' from scholarship; however, one cannot always rely upon the stories that have informed scholarship. The Westphalian narrative does not enable a full understanding of terrorist activity. First, it automatically denotes illegitimacy if any actor other than a state (and supra-state organizations given permission such as NATO) uses violence. So even if sub-state actors are using violence to separate from a state that has committed genocidal acts, this violence is seen as wrong, for example, in the case of the Chechens against the Russians. Second, it fails to see the 'ethic' of their war, to paraphrase from Tarik Kochi (2009).

All people have the capacity to be violent. When violence is associated with certain populations more than others, such as the Muslim community under a neo-orientalist gaze, this is damaging not just to the Muslim community (or any other stereotyped community) but also to the ones holding the gaze. Clearly not all the world's one billion Muslims are violent, either in their personal life or on a political level. To think so is ridiculous and racist. When violence happens that does not come from expected places, such as violence from the insider community or from outsiders not held within the gaze, it cannot be properly ordered, thus inhibiting prevention and an appropriate response. Scholars need to be thinking about how people possess agency and capacity to be violent, instead of creating fantasies that cloud judgment.

NOTES

1. Realists tend to argue that the incidence of war is declining and this is true if one only looks at interstate wars (Bova, 2009). However, the incidence of intrastate war has significantly increased in the Global South since the end of the Second World War.
2. It is commonly accepted that the use of 'terrorism' to describe this form of political violence emerged after the Reign of Terror in France (1793–94) (see Hoffman, 2006, p. 2).

REFERENCES

AFP (2009), 'Indian officials say 3,400 missing in held Kashmir', Dawn.com, 18 August, accessed 10 June 2013 at: http://archives.dawn.com/archives/100977.

Agosin, Majorie and Cola Franzin (1987), 'A visit to the Mothers of the Plaza de Mayo', *Human Rights Quarterly*, **9** (3): 426–35.

Akram, Susan M. (2000), 'Orientalism revisited in asylum and refugee claims', *International Journal of Refugee Law*, **12** (1): 7–40.

Alison, Miranda (2004), 'Women as agents of political violence: gendering security', *Security Dialogue*, **35** (4): 447–63.

Aust, Stefan (1985), *The Baader-Meinhof Group: The Inside Story of a Phenomenon*, The Bodley Head.

Beckman, Peter and Francine D'Amico (1995), *Women in World Politics: An Introduction*, Bergin and Garvey.

Berajano, Cynthia A. (2002), eLas super madres de Latino America: transforming motherhood by challenging violence in Mexico, Argentina and El Salvador', *Frontiers*, **23** (1): 126–50.

Bloom, Mia (2005a), *Dying to Kill*, Columbia University Press.

Bloom, Mia (2005b), lMother, daughter, sister, bomber', *Bulletin of the Atomic Scientists*, **61** (6): 55–62.

Bloom, Mia (2011), *Bombshell*, Viking.

Bova, Russell (2009), *How the World Works*, Pearson.

Brown, Christopher (2002), *Sovereignty, Rights and Justice*, Polity.

Brown, Katherine (2011), 'Blinded by the explosion? Security and resistance in Muslim women's suicide terrorism', in Laura Sjoberg and Caron E. Gentry (eds), *Women, Gender and Terrorism*, University of Georgia Press, pp. 194–226.

Brunner, Claudia (2005), 'Female suicide bombers – male suicide bombing? Looking for gender in reporting the suicide bombings of the Israeli–Palestinian conflict', *Global Society*, **19** (1): 29–48.

Butler, Judith (2004), *Precarious Life: The Power of Mourning and Violence*, Verso.

Connell, Raewyn W. (2005[1995]), *Masculinities* (2nd edn), Polity.

Crenshaw, Kimberlee (1989), 'Demarginalizing the intersection of race and sex: a black feminist critique of Antidiscrimination Doctrine, feminist theory and antiracist politics', *University of Chicago Legal Forum*, **140**: 138–167.

Crenshaw, Martha (1995), 'Thoughts on relating terrorism to historical contexts', in Martha Crenshaw (ed.), *Terrorism in Context*, Penn State, pp. 3–24.

Crenshaw, Martha (1998), 'The logic of terrorism: terrorist behavior as a product of strategic choice', in Walter Reich (ed.), *The Origins of Terrorism*, Woodrow Wilson Center, pp. 7–24.

Crenshaw, Martha (2011), 'The psychology of political terrorism', in Margaret G. Herman (ed.), *Political Psychology*, Jossey-Bass, pp. 379–413.

Cronin, Audrey K. (2002), 'Rethinking sovereignty: American strategy in the age of terrorism', *Survival*, **44** (2): 119–39.

Davis, Kathy (2008), 'Intersectionality as a buzzword: a sociology of science perspective on what makes a feminist theory successful', *Feminist Theory*, **9** (1): 67–85.

Dugard, John (1974), 'International terrorism: problems in defining', *International Affairs*, **50** (1): 67–81.

Eke, Steven (2003), 'Chechnya's female bombers', BBC.com, 7 July, accessed 6 August 2013 at: http://news.bbc.co.uk/1/hi/world/europe/3052934.stm.

Elshtain, Jean Bethke (1995), *Women and War*, University of Chicago Press.

Enloe, Cynthia (1983), *Does Khaki Become You? The Militarization of Women's Lives*, Pluto.

Enloe, Cynthia (2000), *Maneuvers: The International Politics of Militarizing Women's Lives*, University of California Press.

Fisher, Walter (1989), *Human Communication as Narration: Toward a Philosophy of Reason, Value and Action*, University of South Carolina Press.

Gentry, Caron E. (2009), 'Twisted maternalism', *International Feminist Journal of Politics*, **11** (2): 235–52.

Gentry, Caron E. (2013), *Offering Hospitality: Questioning Christian Approaches to War*, University of Notre Dame Press.

Gentry, Caron E. (2014), 'Epistemic bias', in Caron E. Gentry and Amy E. Eckert (eds), *The Future of Just War: New Critical Essays*, University of Georgia Press, pp. 17–29.

Gentry, Caron E. (forthcoming, 2015), 'Anxiety and the creation of the scapegoated other', *Critical Studies on Security*.

Gentry, Caron E. and Laura Sjoberg (2015), *Beyond Mothers, Monsters, Whores*, Zed Books.

Gentry, Caron E. and Kathryn Whitworth (2011), 'Desperate times? Neo-Orientalist framing of desperation in the Chechen struggle', *Critical Studies in Terrorism*, **4** (2): 145–62.

Githens-Mazer, Jonathan and Robert Lambert (2010), 'Why conventional wisdom on radicalization fails', *International Affairs*, **86** (4): 889–901.

Held, Virginia (2008), *How Terrorism is Wrong: Morality and Political Violence*, Oxford University Press.

Hoffman, Bruce (2006), *Inside Terrorism*, Columbia University Press.

Horgan, John (2008), oFrom profiles to pathways and roots to routes: perspectives from psychology on radicalization into terrorism', *The Annals of the American Academy of Political and Social Science*, **618** (1): 80–94.

Human Rights Watch (2009), *Who will Tell me what Happened to my Son? Russia's Implementation of European Court of Human Rights Judgments on Chechnya*, Human Rights Watch.

Huntington, Samuel (1993), 'The clash of civilizations', *Foreign Affairs*, **72** (3): 22–49.

Huntington, Samuel (1997), *The Clash of Civilizations*, Simon and Schuster.

Jackson, Richard (2007), 'Constructing enemies: "Islamic terrorism" in political and academic discourse', *Government and Opposition*, **42** (3): 394–426.

Jackson, Richard (2008), 'Ghosts of state terror: knowledge, politics and terrorism studies', *Critical Studies on Terrorism*, **1** (3): 377–92.

Jarvis, Lee (2009), *Times of Terror: Discourse, Temporality and the War on Terror*, Palgrave Macmillan.

Kaplan, Robert D. (2001), *The Coming Anarchy: Shattering the Dreams of the Post Cold War*, Vintage.

Kochi, Tarik (2009), *The Other's War: Recognition and the Violence of Ethics*, Birkbeck Law Press.

Merari, Ariel (1998), 'The readiness to kill and die: suicidal terrorism in the Middle East', in Walter Reich (ed.), *The Origins of Terrorism*, Woodrow Wilson Center Press, pp. 192–210.

Moghadam, Valerie (1994), 'Introduction and overview', in Valerie Moghadam (ed.), *Gender and National Identity: Women and Politics in Muslim Societies*, Zed Books, pp. 1–17.

Nader, Laura (1989), 'Orientalism, occidentalism, and the control of women', *Cultural Dynamics*, **2** (3): 323–55.

Nayak, Meghana (2006), 'Orientalism and "saving" US state identity after 9/11', *International Feminist Journal of Politics*, **8** (1): 42–61.

Pape, Robert (2005), *Dying to Win: The Strategic Logic of Suicide Terrorism*, University of Chicago Press.

Parashar, Swati (2009), 'Feminist international relations and women militants: case studies from Sri Lanka and Kashmir', *Cambridge Review of International Affairs*, **22** (2): 235–56.

Parashar, Swati (2011), '*Aatish-e-Chinar*: in Kashmir, where women keep resistance alive', in Laura Sjoberg and Caron E. Gentry (eds), *Women, Gender and Terrorism*, University of Georgia Press, pp. 96–119.

Parashar, Swati and Megan Mackenzie (2011), 'Making feminist sense of political violence', paper presented at International Studies Association Conference, March, Montreal.

Peterson, V. Spike and Anne Sisson Runyan (2009), *Global Gender Issues in the New Millennium*, Westview.

Post, Jerrold (1998), 'Terrorist psycho-logic: terrorist behavior as a product of psychological forces', in Walter Reich (ed.), *The Origins of Terrorism*, Woodrow Wilson Center, pp. 25–42.

Puar, Jasbir K. and Amit Rai (2002), 'Monster, terrorist, fag: the war on terrorism and the production of docile patriots', *Social Text*, **20** (3): 117–48.

Qazi, Farhana (2011), 'The *mujahidaat*: tracing the early female warriors of Islam', in Laura Sjoberg and Caron E. Gentry (eds), *Women, Gender, and Terrorism*, University of Georgia Press, pp. 29–56.

Richardson, John E. (2004), *(Mis)Representing Islam: The Racism and Rhetoric of British Broadsheet Newspapers*, John Benjamins.

Russell, John (2007), *Chechnya: Russia's War on Terror*, Routledge.

Said, Edward (1978), *Orientalism*, Penguin.

Saleh, Basel (2005), 'Palestinian suicide attacks revisited: a critique of current wisdom', *Peace and Conflict Monitor*, accessed 11 June 2013 at: http://www.monitor.upeace.org/pdf/suicide_attacks.pdf.

Schmid, Alex P. and A.J. Jongman (2005), *Political Terrorism*, Transaction.

Shepherd, Laura (2006), 'Veiled references: constructions of gender in the Bush administration discourse on the attacks on Afghanistan post-9/11', *International Feminist Journal of Politics*, **8** (1): 19–41.

Sjoberg, Laura (2013), *Gendering Global Conflict*, Columbia University Press.

Sjoberg, Laura and Caron E. Gentry (2007), *Mothers, Monsters, Whores: Women's Violence in Global Politics*, Zed Books.

Sjoberg, Laura and Caron E. Gentry (2008), 'Profiling terror: gendering the *Strategic Logic of Suicide Terror* and other narratives', *Austrian Journal of Political Science*, **37** (2): 1–16.

Sjoberg, Laura and Caron E. Gentry (eds) (2011), *Women, Gender and Terrorism*, University of Georgia Press.

Sylvester, Christine (1999), *Feminist Theory and International Relations in a Postmodern Era*, Cambridge University Press.

Sylvester, Christine (2002), *Feminist International Relations: An Unfinished Journey*, Cambridge University Press.

Sylvester, Christine and Swati Parashar (2009), 'The contemporary "Mahabarata" and the many "Druapadis": bringing gender to Critical Terrorism Studies', in Richard Jackson (ed.), *Critical Terrorism Studies: A New Research Agenda*, Taylor and Francis.

Taylor, Max and John Horgan (2006), 'A conceptual framework for addressing psychological process in the development of the terrorist', *Terrorism and Political Violence*, **18** (4): 585–601.

Thomas, Timothy L. (2001), 'Deciphering asymmetry's word game', *Military Review*, July/August, 32–37.

Tickner, J. Ann (1992), *Gender in International Relations: Feminist Perspectives on Achieving Global Security*, Columbia University Press.

Toles-Patkin, Terri (2004), 'Explosive baggage: female Palestinian suicide bombers and the rhetoric of emotion', *Women and Language*, **27** (2): 79–88.

Tuastad, Dag (2003), 'Neo-orientalism and the new Barbarism thesis: aspects of symbolic violence in the Middle East conflict(s)', *Third World Quarterly*, **24** (4): 591–9.

United Nations (2011), *Report of the Secretary-General's Panel of Experts on Accountability in Sri Lanka*, 31 March, accessed 19 May 2015 at: http://www.un.org/News/dh/infocus/Sri_Lanka/POE_Report_Full.pdf.

Victoroff, Jeff (2005), 'The mind of the terrorist', *Journal of Conflict Resolution*, **49** (1): 3–43.

Weir, Fred (2003), 'Chechen women join terror's ranks', *Christian Science Monitor*, 12 June.

Wibben, Annick (2011), *Feminist Security Studies: A Narrative Approach*, Routledge.

Yeğenoğlu, Meyda (1998), *Colonial Fantasies: Toward a Feminist Understanding of Orientalism*, Cambridge University Press.

Yuval-Davis, Nira (2006), 'Intersectionality and feminist politics', *European Journal of Women's Studies*, **13** (3): 193–209.

PART II

GENDER AND THE IMPACT
OF WAR

Part II Introduction: Gender and the impact of war

Linda Steiner

War affects employment, household income, access to health care and education, household stability and interpersonal relationships, besides the obvious impacts on the short- and long-term health of those who survive and of their families. The destruction of infrastructure and disruption of resources impact men and women (and boys and girls) unevenly; and people have access to different levels and kinds of services and resources. Unlike the conduct of war, the impacts are often not only difficult to see, but are actively hidden. But like other dimensions of war, the impacts are often gendered. This part highlights the gendered impacts of conflict and the ways that gender shapes people's experiences of war – as fighters, as families of fighters, as weapons of fighters, as well as refugees and survivors.

Gender is certainly not always more important than other dimensions of identity, nor are all impacts differentiated by sex/gender. So, gender should always be considered in relation to race, class and other relevant social categories. Just as militarization and the conduct of war reflect and respond to ongoing ideas about gender (and race and class), so do war's impacts. Meanwhile, the sex-differentiated social and economic impacts of war on civilians and refugees often reflect, for better or worse, other gendered divides. That said, these issues must be analyzed, as is the case throughout this book, not as independent but as interlinked systems.

Just as war's collateral damage is often invisible, so measuring its uneven and gendered outcomes is difficult. But every once in a while, the gendered consequences of war erupt into public attention. In August 2015, a *New York Times* foreign correspondent (Callimachi, 2015) reported that men fighting on behalf of the Islamic State were systematically raping and enslaving Yazidi women and girls; they used rape and sexual slavery of non-Muslim women to recruit new fighters. The coverage of the 300 Nigerian girls kidnapped by Boko Haram received much more ongoing front-page coverage and 'hashtag' activism than the enslavement of the 3200 Yazidi. That said, Callimachi's story drew 2572 comments in one day; hundreds of readers said the story was so horrifying and distressing that they had trouble continuing to read it.

Given the increasing amount of academic and media attention given to sexual violence in war, which in turn is forcing increased public attention, this part's focus on sexual violence is perhaps unsurprising. Noting that men regularly fight other men through their women, Laura Sjoberg revises [Clausewitz's famous description of war as 'politics by other means' to underscore how sexual violence in war is also gender politics by other means.] Women and girls may be subjected to sexual violence by enemy troops but also by men from their own community (and by women), including in 'required' sexual service, prostitution, sex trafficking, as well as domestic violence. Forced migration and the curtailing of refugee men's labor, and combat trauma may subject conventional perceptions of masculinity and dominance to pressures and tensions, ultimately leading to a cycle of negative consequences: substance abuse, mental illness and, thus, domestic violence.

In Chapter 8 Laura Sjoberg discusses gender-based violence. She cites data showing cases where household roles render women more vulnerable to the disruptions of wars. [So, women refugees may need to spend more time and effort than before on child-care, family feeding and household management. Such tasks are inevitably much more difficult than before; individual women may need to care for more people than before.] Meanwhile people commonly consider the availability of prostitutes in wartime as 'natural', voluntary and free when it may be abusive and coerced. Sometimes prostitutes are imported by occupiers to service what are regarded as the 'genuine and natural needs' of their soldiers. Moreover, the presence of international peacemakers in conflict zones can further spur black markets; many societies regard these as the acceptable cost of getting protection.

In Chapter 9, having adopted classic anthropological methods to her study of refugee camps, Tania Kaiser describes how civilian populations are increasingly bearing the brunt of war's chronic, protracted and unpredictable dynamics. The risks attendant on forced migration are also highly gendered. For example, the kinds of bureaucratic and legalistic systems (including gendered aspects of asylum law) confronting forced migrants are embedded in the gender relations of the states they leave, enter and/or pass through. Meanwhile women have an 'alarmingly ubiquitous' vulnerability to sexual violence. Moreover, the interventions offered to women are at best short-term; third country resettlement, for example, requires moving to unfamiliar and unknown communities. Women, however, are not always disadvantaged relative to men. In some cases, Kaiser found refugee camps may open up leadership and income-generating opportunities for women. Some women, previously restricted to domestic work, moved into leadership roles in the Christian churches that proliferated in Ugandan refugee camps she studied.

In Chapter 10, Mayesha Alam summarizes the distinct ways in which adolescent women and girls experience both war and post-conflict Disarmament, Demobilization and Reintegration. Alam emphasizes that wars often target females – as civilians, child soldiers and refugees – leaving them with profound sociocultural, economic, psychological and health burdens and thus distinct needs. Alam, who has worked for the United Nations and several NGOs, notes that for many refugee girls, even attending school necessitates serious safety risks, both when traveling long distances, as they often must, and also inside the classroom, where teachers may demand sexual favors. Parents may therefore keep their daughters at home, although this then compromises their career prospects. Meanwhile, girl soldiers – girls make up roughly 40 percent of child soldiers worldwide – are vulnerable to sexual abuse, torture and trauma. Although some girl soldiers serve in domestic or support roles, some are engaged directly in warfare, often used as human shields or to sweep minefields, because they are regarded as less valuable than boys. Alam argues that the international community has not efficiently tackled continued widespread rape of girls and women, despite many UN resolutions and 'lofty speeches' by world leaders. Indeed, UN peacekeepers have sexually abused girls. The UN peacekeepers' lack of accountability is symptomatic, she says, of an ill-equipped international justice and governance system.

In Chapter 11 Joyce Jacobsen focuses on a series of complex and intersecting economic impacts. On one hand, for example, men are more likely to participate in formal and informal education, including skills training, so disruptions of education can affect men disproportionately. Jacobsen points out that because women own fewer 'hard' assets (like land and buildings) than men and are less likely to engage in productive activities that utilize infrastructure, they are likely to suffer less from the depreciation and destruction of assets caused by war. Jacobson explains that because war causes higher rates of death and disability for men, women's participation in paid labor usually increases, including in sectors otherwise dominated by men. But the additional paid work that women may undertake as a result of war has its downsides. Women can earn money selling sexual services to soldiers, peacekeepers and aid workers that they cannot earn otherwise. But prostitutes are often victims of sexual violence; sex trafficking can result in unwanted pregnancies, physical injury, sexually transmitted diseases and emotional scars, all making postwar employment difficult.

In Chapter 12 Alison Howell and Zoë Wool document how the increasing pace of military operations necessitated by the US militarized response to 9/11 is taking an 'unacceptable' toll on both service members and their families. Returning service members often bring deep physical and emotional pain back with them, which complicates the difficulties of readjusting to the rules, expectations, and pace of life at home. Howell and Wool note that sexual offences committed by US soldiers have tripled since the 2003 invasion of Iraq. Many of these crimes were related to drug or alcohol abuse, suggesting that soldiers are trying to self-medicate; the military is likewise attempting to medicate troops in order to manage combat-induced anxiety, depression and pain. Moreover, Howell and Wool offer troubling evidence that resources have not increased for soldiers although military brass understand the 'unintended consequences' of involuntary enlistment extensions, extended rotations and reduced dwell time. Indeed, the military is attempting to shift the burden of treating problems from governmental and military institutions to soldiers themselves and their already over-burdened families.

Noting that the number of women in the US military has increased 15-fold since 1970, in Chapter 13 Joane Nagel and Lindsey Feitz analyze several outcomes of this integration of women. Playing on US President Dwight D. Eisenhower's famous 1961 speech warning about the military–industrial complex, they find a 'military–sexual complex'. Focusing on the 2003 US war in Iraq, they describe the role of sexuality in military recruiting and warfare, with women troops now conveniently around to perform as sexual partners to military colleagues. Women's sexuality was also deployed through the abuse and torture of Iraqi prisoners of war. Nagel and Feitz argue that servicewomen in Iraq were used to dramatize US troops' courage and Iraqi men's cowardice and depravity. They describe how the propaganda campaign launched to gain American support for the war featured pretty white 'damsels in distress' while marginalizing the bravery of Black and Native American women.

In Chapter 14 Dan Berkowitz and Qi Ling offer a close reading of dozens of accounts published by US and UK news organizations about suicide bombers. With an increase in the numbers and variety of roles within terror groups globally, women are increasingly acting as suicide bombers. In order to make sense of this otherwise strange phenomenon, journalists have deployed, adapted or invented four archetypes: the 'Woman Warrior', the 'Innocent Child', the 'Terrible Mother', and the 'Female Monster'. Berkowitz and Qi Ling show how news representations of women suicide bombers both reflect and perpetuate notions, often incorrect or exaggerated, about Muslim women, and their role in Muslim societies. The distorted reporting suggests how journalists lose their professional detachment and rely on ideological short-cuts. The four myths supported existing gender values and also reinforced the 'central-marginal' geopolitical order between West and non-West.

In Chapter 15 Linda Steiner analyzes the various ways that gender intersects with the war journalism, noting that women war reporters run a high risk of sexual harassment and rape, as well as threats of rape, by sources they are trying to interview and by troops and civilians taking advantage of the destabilized context of conflict. However, war correspondents who have been sexually attacked rarely tell anyone; they often fear that if they tell their editors they will be pulled off an assignment. Women's secrecy about being raped means their editors (usually men) remain unaware of the dangers and therefore do not try to increase women's security abroad or provide them with support when they return. Women reporters have received most of the credit for reporting about sexual violence in the context of war, although in recent years women have argued that this is an issue for any serious war reporter. Notably, regarding the report mentioned above, Callamachi told *The New York Times* that she had occasionally received threats from Islamic State fighters 'just as there are against any reporter who covers the subject', but also that these threats did not affect her reporting (Allen, 2015).

As Laura Sjoberg puts it, wartime violence is lived 'everyday'. Yet war's corollary impacts are not consistently or carefully studied, whether the issue is rape and prostitution, or the economic impacts. As a result, policymakers, practitioners and donors often misunderstand the risks, especially the ways that vulnerabilities are gendered. Thus, figuring out how experiences differ depending on context – and the policy implications of these differences – remains important. For example, women veterans (projected to comprise over 16 percent of US veterans by mid-century) are not getting the health care they need and are misdiagnosed by doctors accustomed to treating men (Thorpe, 2015). Changing policy requires research. No wonder that several authors in this part explicitly call for additional research.

REFERENCES

Allen, E. (2015), 'Kidnapping and sex slavery: covering ISIS' religious justification for rape', 14 August, accessed 17 August, 2015 at: http://www.nytimes.com/2015/08/14/insider/kidnapping-and-sex-slavery-covering-isiss-religious-justification-for-rape.html?_r=0.

Callimachi, R. (2015), 'ISIS enshrines a theology of rape', 14 August, accessed 17 August,
   2015   at: http://www.nytimes.com/2015/08/14/world/middleeast/isis-enshrines-a-
   theology-of-rape.html?_r=0.
Thorpe, H. (2015), *Soldier Girls: The Battles of Three Women at Home and at War*,
   Scribner.

8. Gender-based violence in war
Laura Sjoberg

INTRODUCTION

Mawazo Patience, a Congolese woman, was raped three times in a two-month period during the conflict in Congo. She explained: 'The third time I was raped, it was at the river when I had gone to the field to cultivate. After cultivating, I went to bathe in the river; as I was bathing, five people in uniform and arms jumped on me, held me, and made me fall down. Immediately, they opened my legs and ... .' (Theophile and Valérie, n.d.). Mawazo was too traumatized by what happened to finish her story, and remains scarred by both the violence committed towards her and the violence she witnessed.

Mawazo's experience of the conflict in the Democratic Republic of Congo (DRC) cannot be understood without reference to sex and gender. She was targeted on the basis of her sex, the abuse done to her was rife with gendered assumptions and gendered symbolisms, and the frequent invisibility of her experience of the war and conflict is a gendered silence. Women experience war and conflict in ways that are fundamentally (but not only) shaped by social structures of gender. These social structures include (but are not limited to) the assumption that there are two biological sexes and that membership in a biological sex category brings with it a host of social characteristics, constraints and meanings beyond the physical composition of the sexed body. These characteristics, constraints and meanings (positive and negative) are then mapped onto expectations about how people act, what jobs they will hold, what activities they can participate in, what resources they have access to and what roles they will play in war and conflict.

Gendered social structures are not generated with the beginning of any given war or conflict: before being raped in the DRC, Mawazo did not live in a world where gender was irrelevant. Instead, gendered social structures are born and manifested in much of daily life in many places around the world. This chapter opens with a brief discussion of gendered social structures and how they might be mapped onto war(s). The second section discusses the gendered structures and impacts of 'everyday' violence in the making and fighting of wars. I then discuss gender-based violence, sex-specific targeting and women's violence, and conclude by considering some of the implications of gender-based violence during war for the ways we think about both war and post-war justice.

GENDERED SOCIAL STRUCTURES

Feminists draw attention to many crucial places where [gendered social structures put women at risk even in times of 'peace'.] For example, many feminist political economists have pointed out places where women's household roles render them more vulnerable to the disruptions of wars. Studies have documented that women are often paid less in formal workplaces or relegated to informal economies (Gibson-Graham, 1996). In economic hard times, women are often the first to be laid off in the paid work sector and the last to eat in homes having trouble affording food (Peterson and Runyan, 2010). [The segregation of 'men's work' and 'women's work' often differentiates people on the basis of sex into different parts of economic and social life.]

The division of work into 'men's work' and 'women's work' in the economic structure of many societies translates into gendered distribution of risk, both generally and in conflict zones. If, for example, going to the market is 'women's work', then during a conflict, women who go to the market alone will experience an increased risk of rape, kidnapping and other crimes, since the responsibility to go to the market from home forces them to travel alone (Vickers, 1993). If women are responsible for caring for children and the elderly, fleeing a war zone quickly is more difficult for them. If gendered social structures make men the primary breadwinners and place women outside the formal labor force, women will have a difficult time providing for their households when their husbands go to war, especially in times of scarcity.

In these arrangements, it is not a limitation of a woman's body-as-female that is shaping her wartime experience, but gendered expectations of her. Exploring gender-based violence in war(s) needs to be done through these lenses. Instead of looking at men's and women's (assumed or biological) differences as if they result in some naturalized differences that, in turn, translate into sex-differentiated experiences, it is important to look at [how gendered stereotypes and expectations (that is, gendered social structures) impact the ways that people experience wartime violence] (e.g., Tickner, 2001). Gendered social structures influence experiences of war through the different ways that men and women are embodied (and thus their different vulnerabilities, see, for example,

Wilcox, 2009), the different things they symbolize both to their communities and to their opponents, the different roles they take up in their households and communities, and their different places in economic structures.

GENDERED SOCIAL STRUCTURES AND THE VIOLENT EXPERIENCES OF WAR

Every day, people die from violent conflict and war. Every day, the livelihood systems and communities of many others are damaged or destroyed. War and conflict damage communities directly and indirectly, through the destruction inflicted by guns and bombs and through secondary and tertiary impacts of refugee flows, infrastructural damage or destruction and disruptions to political stability and control. Wartime violence is lived, 'everyday' – in household income, access to health care, household stability, interpersonal relationships, domestic violence and the like (Cuomo, 1996).

Wartime violence is lived in gendered ways, including but not limited to experiences of unemployment and other economic changes, sex-specific threats to health, sex-specific risks to physical security, gendered experiences of destruction of community and increases in sexual violence. These gendered experiences of war are a form of gender-based violence that is often neglected in discussions of gender-based violence in war and conflict. One reason for this neglect may lie in the physical and sometimes temporal distance that often separates the wartime experiences of people identified as women (and especially women civilians) and those of men. In addition, many of the visible ways that women's daily lives are both impacted and changed by conflict are seen as natural and therefore become invisible. For example, when women need protection from war, it is almost a non-event, because women as women by definition need protection from war. When women become pregnant from war rape, it is often easy to ignore, because women as women become pregnant, and communities often prefer to keep silent about the shame of how those pregnancies began.

If we look at gendered social structures, however, it is possible to see how women's lives and wars are intrinsically interdependent (Cockburn, 2007). This is especially true at the subsistence level of community life, where the violence of war and conflict is often felt in ways that disproportionately impact women, especially at the household and personal levels. As discussed above, sex-differentiated divisions of labor often exist both inside and outside the household in a wide variety of different economic organizations. In agricultural economies, 'men's work' may include plowing, sowing and harvesting while women's work may include milking, maintenance labor and going to the market. In many economies, land ownership rights are sex-specific, and both owning land and inheriting property are the province of men. Sometimes, bank credit or state subsidies for agriculture are only extended to men as heads of households. These divisions of labor both regulate everyday life and form the foundation on which household units deal with war and crisis.

For example, in Europe during the Second World War, many women became the sole proprietors of farming households when their husbands were either away fighting in the conflict or became casualties of the conflict. Women who had recently become head of the household struggled to maintain their farms despite damage to their houses, their land and the infrastructure of their communities. Additional challenges were presented by the wartime breakdown of markets, the placement of landmines on farm property, and the death of livestock from wartime violence and diseases. Many households also struggled with changes to their composition – some losing family members but taking in orphaned children from other families. While some women can not only navigate but capitalize on the wartime challenges to farming economies, many others collapse under the gendered pressure of wartime structural violence.

This is because sex-divided tasks are often exacerbated by the circumstances of conflict. Families who are forced to split up in wars and conflicts then struggle to manage the duties previously provided by other parts of the family (see, for example, Vickers, 1993). Many women are forced to flee their homes in times of conflict without the male members of their households, or are bound by circumstance to remain at home while male members of their households flee. Either way, women in war-separated families usually lose their household's primary source of income. Many women who assume the role of primary income-earner face challenges that male heads of households do not. For example, women who run farms in wartime may not be able to access credit and may have trouble employing male labor for farm maintenance. In such circumstances, the sex-specified division of labor from everyday gendered social structures compounds women's struggles to survive in wartime. These struggles may also be compounded by wartime infrastructural damage to cities, towns and railways. While such damage seems victimless, it can make impossible women's tasks of getting to markets, attending to jobs, recruiting labor and selling crops.

The women who remain at home and try to head their households are not the only ones to experience the everyday consequences of war in sex-specific ways. Women who are forced to leave their homes in order to survive conflicts struggle to keep their families together at the same time that they deal with constant poverty, malnutrition and threats to their bodily security. Everyday tasks become gargantuan. For example, women often either cannot find food for their families or do not have access to simple cooking technologies. It may not be possible to meet specific nutritional needs of household members. In addition, women in refugee camps tend to experience higher rates of sexual violence, may lose their children to fighting forces and may not be able to find adequate health care or shelter (see Hynes and Cardozo, 2000).

In households that are not separated by war, domestic oppression often increases in wartime, when male heads of household are more attentive to restricting women's movements and activities. During war and conflict, levels of domestic violence increase significantly, as do levels of intimate-partner sexual violence (Adelman, 2003). While domestic violence rises in wartime, so does household participation in informal or illicit economies. Some illicit economies replace normal trade routes interrupted by conflict, but those illicit economies may be linked to trade in human beings and illegal drugs. Women who are unable to secure a place in formal economies or obtain a job working for wages may instead work for informal economies as household workers or even sex workers (see Mazurana et al., 2005). Women who become heads of household in war are particularly vulnerable to being forced into prostitution to earn a living. Not only does this radically change women's lives and their identities, it risks their health and their bodies. Women who turn to prostitution are at a heightened risk of getting HIV/AIDS or other sexually transmitted diseases, and are more likely to be the victims of sexual violence (Elbe, 2002).

The challenges of wartime upswings in prostitution (and in violence towards prostitutes) are made worse by the fact that people commonly consider the availability of prostitutes in wartime not only as natural but as an obligatory service. Soldiers, peacekeepers and humanitarian workers alike are often involved in either directly buying the services of prostitutes or indirectly making prostitution industries possible by patronizing the entertainment businesses that serve as the cover for prostitution rings (see Agathangelou and Ling, 2003). International presences in conflict zones make black markets (especially those for drugs and human trafficking) more vibrant, yet many societies consider these side-effects a natural and acceptable cost of the involvement of external organizations in peacemaking and protection (Mendelson, 2005).

One of the most frequent, and most obviously gendered, of these side-effects is the rise of prostitution. In many war zones, 'local' women turn to prostitution, and prostitutes are also brought in from the outside by occupying militaries. *The Daily Mail* reported that, in Kashmir, the Indian military employs both Kashmiri and imported Indian prostitutes to service the 'genuine and natural needs' of Indian soldiers, after analysts concluded that Indian soldiers deployed in the valley were committing suicide and killing colleagues out of acute sexual frustration and depression (Palmer, 2009). In this situation, women's engagement in prostitution is characterized as natural, necessary and beneficial for soldier health and behavior during conflicts (Bose, 2005). Such a characterization relies on the (mistaken) understanding of wartime prostitution as voluntary and free rather than abusive and coerced. If militaries recruit, supervise or control prostitutes for their soldiers (e.g., Moon, 1997; Bose, 2005), then wartime prostitution cannot be seen as outside of the central structures of war and conflict; it has to be recognized that this is a gendered structure of those wars and conflicts. In other words, not only does the Indian military see women's service as prostitutes as natural, it sees it as beneficial to the mental and physical health of the soldiers serving in the conflict zone (Bose, 2005). The Indian military recruited professional prostitutes *for soldiers*, counted them as members of the military, gave them basic military training and put them on a strict regimen of medical check-ups to make sure that they remained healthy (Bose, 2005). Understood in this way, wartime prostitution is not an anomaly or an effect of war but a crucial part of the political, economic and sexual production of conflict (Demleitner, 1994/5).

It is not only household income challenges presented by war that have gender-differential impacts. Other social structures are also impacted, and impact women's lives. For example, health care challenges are gendered. During war, health resources are redirected toward militaries, while civilian hospitals and clinics are destroyed. This means that access to health care – particularly preventive care such as pre-natal care – becomes difficult for civilians in conflict-ridden societies. The wartime inability to obtain health services has gendered impacts. In addition to the lack of availability of prenatal treatment, women are often more vulnerable to (usually treatable) infectious diseases (see, for example, Vickers, 1993). Again, rape and enforced prostitution put women at a higher risk of sexually-transmitted diseases and weak health care resources make those sexually-transmitted diseases more difficult to treat and easier to spread. Women are also more likely to allocate fewer food resources to themselves (or have fewer food resources allocated to them by a male head of household) in wartime, and therefore are more likely to suffer nutritional problems that would normally require medical care (see Mu and Zhang, 2008).

The civil war in Côte d'Ivoire in 2002–04 is a good example of these gender-differential impacts (see Raven-Roberts, 2012). Several nutritional and health side-effects of that conflict affected women and men differently. Catherine's story is an example (Amnesty International, 2007). Catherine was 14 when she was raped by a soldier fighting during the civil war. After she was raped, she was beaten, and lost consciousness. In addition to having to deal with being raped and beaten, Catherine had to cope with being discouraged from getting medical treatment because family members were embarrassed by what happened to her. When Catherine did make it to a hospital, the hospital personnel were unprepared to deal with rape victims and treated her as if her behavior had caused her rape. She was unable to find adequate health care, despite her willingness to speak out and her ability to pay for it. The weight of multiple gendered violence added up for Catherine.

The health problems that women experience in wars are exacerbated by increasing pregnancy rates – both within families and as a result of wartime sexual violence. During conflict women's wombs may come to be seen as tools to reproduce and ensure the continuity of the war-fighting group. In this context, women serve as 'biological reproducers of group members needed for defense, signifiers of group identities, agents in political identity struggles, and members of sexist and heterosexist national groups' (Sjoberg, 2006, citing Peterson, 1999). As a result, women impregnated by their husbands during wars are often pressured into caring for the resultant children to support their own nation, while women impregnated by enemy soldiers are shunned both during and after the war (see Carpenter, 2007).

SEX-SPECIFIC VIOLENCE IN ADDITION TO SEX-DIFFERENTIATED STRUCTURAL VIOLENCE

The few examples given in this chapter make clear that war and conflict can affect different women in many different ways. Feminist analysis suggests that militarization and gender-based violence are co-constitutive features of war (Enloe, 2010; Cuomo, 1996). In other words, gender-based violence is not something that can be weeded out of war, leaving war otherwise the same. It is a product of the masculinization of militarization, and, as such, a result of the ways that wars are currently practiced. During conflicts, gender-based violence often increases in both quantity and brutality. 'Gender-based violence' refers to the wartime targeting of people on the basis of (perceived) sex (Etienne, 1995). Gender-based violence in war targeted at women takes different forms.

Women are directly targeted by soldiers and other combatants in war. They are also kidnapped, forced into prostitution and/or sexual slavery, raped and forcibly impregnated. Women who are not the subject of gender-based violence by enemy troops are often victimized by men from their own community, either through domestic violence or in required sexual service.

Gender-based violence against women in war(s) is both physical and symbolic. Physically, damage is often done for damage's sake. Symbolically, particular acts of cruelty like amputation of body parts, rape with inanimate objects, and other degradations are meant to symbolize defeat, as discussed below (see also Sjoberg and Peet, 2011). One of the most common forms of physical and symbolic violence in war is wartime rape and sexual violence.

Given the proliferation of rape as a weapon of genocide in the 1990s, scholars have begun analyzing the relationship between rape and racial extermination (Card, 2003). This work, more often than not, defines genocidal rape as a crime where men are the perpetrators and women are the victims. 'The revolutionary changes that have taken place in this area of the law in large part reflect the growing mobilization and influence of non-governmental organizations articulating the importance of the rights of women' (Pilch, 2002, p. 4). Similarly, Todd Salzman (1998, p. 350) has characterized genocidal rape as 'an assault against the female gender, violating her body and its reproductive capabilities as a "weapon of war"'.

Since the end of the Cold War, international law has increasingly recognized rape and violence against women as war crimes (MacKinnon, 2001, p. 897). While previously wartime rape was inconsistently punished (MacKinnon, 2001), the 1990s saw jurisprudence classifying it as a war crime. Courts have also recently begun to recognize that *rape* and *genocidal rape* are different war crimes: rape is a crime against its victim and women generally, and genocidal rape is a crime used as a weapon against an ethnic or national group, attacking racial purity, national pride or both.

This distinction has been made in litigation concerning the Bosnian conflict, where genocidal rape was defined as rape 'with the specific intent of destroying ethnic-religious groups' (Kadic v. Karadzic, 70 F.3d 232 (2nd Cir 1995)). The International Criminal Tribunal for Rwanda also found that instances of rape can 'constitute genocide in the same way as any other [act] so long as they were committed with the specific intent to destroy, in whole or in part, a particular group, targeted as such' (Prosecutor v. Akayesu, Case No. ICTR 96 4 T (1998), 694). Accordingly, the court found that 'the rape of Tutsi women was systematic and was perpetrated against all Tutsi women and solely against them' (Akayesu, ICTR 96 4 T, 694, 731). Samantha Power (2002) estimated that approximately 250 000 women survived rape during the 100-day Rwandan genocide, and many more rape victims died during the conflict.

Such understandings of genocidal rape as a gendered tactic are important and accurate. Wartime rape is almost exclusively reserved for those persons biologically classifiable as female, and exclusively for those who are gendered female (and feminized) in political and social relations. Several feminist scholars have identified genocidal rape as a key threat to women's security (Hansen, 2001, p. 59). Judith Gardam explains that 'it is difficult to find any support for the view that non-combatant immunity at any time in its development has included [effective] protection from rape' (1993, p. 359). Gardam contends that this is a linchpin of gender subordination because 'nowhere is women's marginalization more evident than in the attitude of the law of armed conflict to rape, an experience limited to women' (1993, pp. 358–9). Therefore, she notes, 'in one sense, rape is never truly individual, but an integral part of the system ensuring the maintenance of the subordination of women' (Gardam, 1993, pp. 363–4).

Although analysis of and attention to wartime rape has increased recently, it has been a feature of war for as long as we have histories of warfare. In addition to narratives about war rape during the First and Second World Wars, the Bosnian wars and the Japanese invasion of China, ancient Greek and Roman stories of war also recount sexual exploitation of conquered women (Brownmiller, 1975). While recent uses of rape, particularly genocidal rape, have been condemned both politically and legally, the frequency and severity of the uses of sexual violence in war seemed to increase after the end of the Cold War. Gendered lenses must be used not only to think about the individual victims of wartime sexual violence and other gender-specific targeting, but also to consider the social processes and war-justifying logics that make gender-based violence in war one of the more consistent features in the history of the fighting of wars. I contend that this results from a link between some of the very logics that justify the making of wars and incentives to target women on the basis of sex.

SEX-SPECIFIC TARGETING AS GENDER-BASED VIOLENCE IN WAR(S)

As Judith Gardam (1993) noted, wartime sexual violence is never only singular or individual, but instead is part and parcel of the making and fighting of war(s). In addition to understanding the particular circumstances in the particular conflict that lead to the victimization of women on the basis of sex, wartime rape must be understood as co-constituted by gender relations and international relations. [It is an expression of the relationship between masculinities and femininities both *within* and *among* belligerents, and the extent to which they are socialized in warring communities and populations] All of these play into the seemingly contradictory set of circumstances we observe when we look for men and women in wars: men fight wars for women, but they also fight wars *through* and *against* women.

A key part of this story is that the practice of making and fighting wars has been largely (though not exclusively) reserved for people identified as men, and linked to standards of masculinity. Belligerents value masculinity (expressed as violence, aggressiveness, strength, toughness and courage) in fighters. Many militaries explicitly set up a relationship between masculinity and military service – where militaries make men from boys, and masculinity and virility are linked to soldiering, and soldiering to citizenship (Connell, 1995).

Yet the men who have historically fought wars, as Cynthia Enloe (2000) has repeatedly pointed out, depend on women's (often invisible) otherness, symbolically and practically. In practice, organized state militaries have relied on women in a variety of roles: nurses; entertainers; clerical workers; soldiers; logistical support; wives; mothers; food servers; and factory workers, to name a few positions. Non-state military actors have depended on women as messengers, porters, cooks, sex workers and smugglers, as well as in roles as fighters. Some might argue that, to the extent that women and men play different roles in war, those different roles are 'natural'. Those who take this view see men as more aggressive, and women as having a comparative advantage in peacefulness. This assumption of the naturalness of gender differences, however, ignores the way that gender roles and justifications for war-fighting are co-constituted. The practical reliance on using women as participants and differentiating their roles is juxtaposed with a symbolic reliance on women as wars' 'others'.

This is because gendered imagery constructs national identities as well as boundaries and inequalities between groups in a state (Wilcox, 2010). As such, 'nationalism is naturalized, or legitimated, through gender discourses that naturalized the domination of one group over another through the disparagement of the feminine, which draws on and reproduces discourses of naturalness of male dominance over women' (Wilcox, 2009). A large part of the link between discourses of domination and reproduction of gender inequality in war is the paradox identified above, where men fight wars to protect women, whom they hurt in those wars. The motivation of protection provides legitimacy, justification and sometimes even the possibility for making war (Young, 2003). This is because the existence of innocent, defenseless women *to fight for* motivates men to fight, even when they have no other motivation (Huston, 1982).

If symbolically protecting 'their' women is crucial to men fighting wars, then attacking the 'enemy's' women serves simultaneously to emasculate the 'enemy' and take away his reason for fighting (Sjoberg and Peet, 2011). If the *casus belli* for which male warriors fight is *their* women, it follows that one wins an absolute victory by exterminating women understood as 'belonging' to *the opponent* (Sjoberg and Peet, 2011).

Targeting women in war, then, would serve the function of taking away the opponent's *casus belli*. Feminist theorizing also points out another function that targeting women serves. Distinguishing hegemonic and subordinated masculinities (Connell, 1995) suggests that a belligerent will seek to validate its own masculinities. This validation is a zero-sum game, as masculinization of 'the good guys' is built on feminizing 'the bad guys' – a process based on exerting power and maintaining control (Sjoberg, 2007, p. 94; Huston, 1982; Peterson, 2010). One way a belligerent can do this is to render the opponents' men incapable of performing their own masculinity by targeting, killing and humiliating their women, thus rendering the opponent as feminine because it cannot protect them.

After all, it has been said that men fight other men through their women – a continuation of Clausewitz's famous phrase 'war as politics by other means'. Sexual violence in war is also gender politics by other means. Expressions of martial prowess and ruthlessness and brutality are in many cultures equated with masculinity. The deliberate violation of women is thus an attack on the masculinity of the opposing side by demonstrating that it cannot defend or protect its community. This is one of many ways that entrenched militarization sets up interlinked systems, reacting and responding to each other, which have sex-differential impacts on populations in war-torn societies. Separately, they often make individual women's lives difficult, and threaten their security in numerous, hybrid ways. Together, they tend to lead to a symbolic and actual reconstituting or reinforcement of the dominance of masculinity, combining the hypermasculinity of illicit economies, the chivalrous masculinity of protection and the aggressive masculinity of soldiering. Together, these mean that war renders many women not just absolutely worse off than they were 'before' the war or conflict, but relatively worse off compared to others experiencing the conflict in similar positions, all the while intensifying both attention to and devaluation of femininity.

The devaluation of femininity also helps to reinforce the requirements of masculinity that are necessary to get men to fight wars, and inspires gender-based violence done to men. For example, gender-based violence can be done to men in wars in service of employing and training soldiers, as extensive work shows (e.g., Goldstein, 2001). This makes war's masculinity an (intentional) social construction and makes it acceptable to inflict emotional and physical pain on men in preparation for fighting in wars. Also, as several scholars have noted, the association between men and soldiering often incentivizes indiscriminate violence towards men in wars on the grounds that they might be potential soldiers (e.g., Carpenter, 2005). In this way, gender norms and gender stereotypes (as they are embedded in nationalist narratives) shape gender-based violence against women *and* men.

WOMEN AS PERPETRATORS

Very few women are perpetrators of political violence, terrorism, war crimes, and sexual violence during conflict – but some women are. Most people assume, however, that if women are (largely, individually and collectively) the victims of wartime gender-based violence, men are exclusively the perpetrators. Women's perpetration, in some ways, interrupts the discourse of wartime rape as a crime that men commit against women. While that characterization is, as detailed above, largely accurate, women have participated in, encouraged and led gender-based violence in war(s). If it seems *unnatural* for women to perpetrate war violence and genocide (e.g., Sjoberg and Gentry, 2007), it seems even more unnatural for women to participate in, lead, encourage and plan gender-based violence (e.g., Sjoberg, forthcoming). If women have anything in common, some assume, it should be reluctance to participate in the very sexual violence that many consider the linchpin of gender subordination. If, as argued above, rape is a cornerstone of women's oppression, women's participation in rape is a perpetration of gendered oppression – *by the oppressed*.[1]

Perhaps the difficulty of conceptualizing the logic that would inspire such violence is what causes the conventional classification of women perpetrators of sexual violence in war as separate, different and often more violent than men who commit similar or the same crimes. Wight and Myers (1996, p. xii) explain that a violent woman's womanhood is 'the primary explanation or mitigating factor offered up in any attempt to understand her crime'.

For example, Biljana Plavsic was Acting President of the Republica Srpska in 1992 and again between 1996 and 1998 (Mundis and Gaynor, 2005). Throughout her academic (she was a biologist) and political careers, Plavsic had given many speeches advocating ethnic cleansing, sometimes even implying that rape was an appropriate method to achieve political goals. She 'used her knowledge of biology to convince people to share her ethnic hatred' and argued that 'Bosnian Muslims were "genetically deformed Serbs"' (Sjoberg and Gentry, 2007, p. 151; Fitzpatrick, 2000). After the conflict died down, the International Criminal Tribunal for the former Yugoslavia (ICTY) indicted her for genocide, crimes against humanity, and war crimes, given a series of crimes, including rape, committed by the Serbian military, political and government authorities under her command (Askin, 2003). Specifically, she was accused of masterminding and overseeing the Serbian genocidal rape strategy; she plea-bargained and served two-thirds of her sentence.

In 1997, the International Criminal Tribunal for Rwanda established 'an incredible precedent by being the first tribunal ever to charge a woman with genocide and rape' (Balthazar, 2001, p. 46; Harman, 2003). Pauline Nyiramasuhuko, who had held the cabinet position of Minister for the Family and Advancement of Women during the Rwandan genocide, was indicted for, among other things, two charges of rape: one as a crime against humanity and the other as a violation of the Geneva conventions on war crimes (Balthazar, 2001). Nyiramasuhuko 'had been open and frank at cabinet meetings, saying that she personally was in favor of getting rid of all Tutsi' (Melvern, 2004, p. 22). In 2011, she was convicted of seven charges and sentenced to life imprisonment.

Despite the existence of women like Plavsic and Nyiramasuhuko, those with a political interest in the gender order rarely hear or tell stories of women's participation in gender-based violence; instead, stories are produced and reproduced where women's agency in their violence is denied and violent women are characterized as singular and aberrant. Stories about women's violence 'become systems of signification which are productive (or reproductive) of their subject women' specifically and women more generally (Sjoberg and Gentry, 2007, p. 57). If violent women are seen as different from what *women as women* should be, then their existence can be explained away without interrogating the fundamental problems with stereotyped understandings of women as peaceful, virtuous, non-violent and so on. At the same time, stories of women as peaceful and non-violent not only ignore women's perpetration of gender-based violence, but reinforce the gender roles underpinning the logic described above of the victimization of civilians generally and women specifically.

PURSUING JUSTICE

The pursuit of justice for gender-based violence in war has been slow and uneven. Much of the early work on international actors involved in efforts to pursue justice in war-torn societies assumed that the impacts of war were sex-neutral and, therefore, that seeking justice for wartime violence could be accomplished without serious attention to sex. These analyses looked to prevent and prosecute crimes against humanity rather than crimes against women and crimes against men. For the most part, the laws and rules about how to treat people in war(s) remain sex-neutral, but an evolving jurisprudence on wartime rape enables consideration of the strengths and limitations of the processes of taking account of gender-based violence in war. The law has started to challenge conventional thinking about wartime rape and to document it as gender-based violence in war.

Wartime rape has been historically downplayed both in public understandings of wars' atrocities and in international law. For example, rape was excluded from the 'most egregious' crimes prosecuted in post-Second World War Germany. Initially, when wartime rape was prosecuted, it was considered a crime against men – their honor and property – rather than against the women who were raped. Although after the Second World War, the Geneva Convention officially classified rape as a crime against women instead of against the property of men, it maintained the notion that rape was a crime against honor instead of a crime of violence.

Growing attention to wartime rape as gender-based violence, however, brought not only the classification of wartime rape as a crime against humanity in international courts but also the classification of genocidal rape as a war crime. Amid legislation such as United Nations Security Council Resolutions 1325 and 1820 – both of which treat gender as an integral issue in international peace and security – policymakers and civil servants, especially, have begun to show a growing interest in the causes and effects of gender-based violence in war (e.g., Cohn, 2008).

At the same time, gender norms pose a continuing threat to post-war justice for gender-based violence, even when those processes are sensitive to the existence of gender-based violence. Megan MacKenzie's (2009) work demonstrates how 'gender-sensitive' Disarmament, Demobilization and Reintegration (DDR) processes had several sex-specific implications, including gender-based violence. In part, this is because limited funding and public opinion often stop the prosecution of wartime rape, as well as other sorts of gender-based violence. Mostly, however, the issue is that states, their citizens, and the international legal arena which often governs their interactions all still have a significant distance to go in order to understand the complex relationship between gender and justice in conflict zones, and the ways in which gender shapes both victimhood and discourses of victimhood. The assumed gender-neutrality of wartime violence marginalizes the victims of gender-based violence. Another key continuing problem is that courts and legal processes continue to be ignorant of the gendered reasons why gender norms make many victims reluctant to participate in public processes of justice (e.g., MacKenzie, 2009).

CONCLUSIONS

Any move towards a gender-conscious theory of gender-based violence in war needs at once to account for political and social motivations, gendered context and individuality. Including previously-hidden gender inequalities in the analysis of individual violence in global politics 'allows us to see how many of the insecurities affecting us all, women and men alike, are gendered in their historical origins, their conventional definitions, and their contemporary manifestations' (Tickner, 1992, p. 129). Finding women in the complicated matrix of victimhood and perpetration of gender-based violence is only a first step.

The problem will not be solved until both the people and values associated with femininity are 'more universally valued in public life' and 'women's agency in their decisions is as recognized as men's agency in theirs' (Tickner, 1992, p. 141). The beginning of this re-visioning is the recognition of human interdependence and relational autonomy, which shows that all decisions are contextual and contingent, not only women's, and all decisions are made, not only men's. Feminist theory provides a way forward for creating such an understanding of gender-based violence in war. Kathy Ferguson explains that 'praxis feminisms focus on affirmative intersubjective connections between persons rather than on autonomous or combative selves', which would cause them to suggest that individual violence be discussed in relational, rather than abstract, terms (1993, p. 69). This requires accounting for multiple layers of cultural, gender and international contexts as well as the agency of perpetrators.

Gender subordination must be understood as based on perceived membership in, and relationship with, rather than some sort of absolute and actual membership in, sex classes. There is not just one femininity and one masculinity. Instead, there are ideal-types of masculinity and femininity based on class, culture, religion, race, ethnicity and time – and other masculinities and femininities related to those ideal-types. Those multiple masculinities and femininities come together to set boundaries for what women should be and what men should be, situated in sociocultural contexts. These boundaries provide the content of perceived membership in sex classes, and constitute the underlying foundation for gender-based violence in wars. Understanding those deep foundations could allow for understanding the multiple military, social and political-economic dimensions of gender-based violence outlined above.

The beginnings of such an understanding could be operationalized in legal terms by a description of gender subordination as a socially-fluid but systematic form of discrimination on the basis of perceived membership in categories inscribed with gendered power, and an understanding that human perpetration and victimization exist in a world marked by both relational autonomy (incomplete independence) and unequal power (gender subordination). As such, women, individually and collectively, can be seen as victims of gender-based violence, while women, individually and collectively, are not robbed of agency by their classification as victims. Women's victimization in wartime gender-based violence could be seen in households, in hospitals, in workplaces, and in refugee camps as well as on battlefields and in jungles.

NOTE

1. Certainly, this has happened in the past (Jews who participated in the Holocaust, Tutsis who participated in the Rwandan genocide and so on). Still, the assumption seems to be that women would not rape women.

REFERENCES

Adelman, Madelaine (2003), 'The military, militarism, and the militarization of domestic violence', *Violence Against Women*, **9** (9): 1118–52.
Agathangelou, Anna and L.H.M. Ling (2003), 'Desire industries: sex trafficking, UN peacekeeping, and the neo-liberal world order', *Brown Journal of World Affairs*, **10**: 133–48.
Amnesty International (2007), 'Côte d'Ivoire – targeting women: the forgotten victims of the conflict', 15 March, AFR 31/001/2007, accessed 10 June 2013 at: http://www.unhcr.org/refworld/docid/45ffa4dd2.html.
Askin, Kelly D. (2003), 'The quest for post-conflict gender justice', *Columbia Journal of Transnational Law*, **41**.

Balthazar, S. (2001), 'Fulfilling the legacy: international justice 60 years after Nuremberg', *Gonzaga Journal of International Law*, **10**.

Bose, Sumantra (2005), *Kashmir: Roots of Conflict, Paths to Peace*, Harvard University Press.

Brownmiller, Susan (1975), *Against our Will – Men, Women, and Rape*, Simon and Schuster.

Card, Claudia (2003), 'Genocide and social death', *Hypatia*, **18** (1): 63–79.

Carpenter, R. Charli (2005), 'Women, children, and other vulnerable groups: gender, strategic frames, and the protection of civilians as a transnational issue', *International Studies Quarterly*, **49** (2): 295–334.

Carpenter, R. Charli (2007), *Born of War*, Kumarian.

Cockburn, Cynthia (2007), *From where we Stand: War, Women's Activism, and Feminist Analysis*, Zed Books.

Cohn, Carol (2008), 'Mainstreaming gender in UN security policy: a path to political transformation?', in Shirin Rai and Georgina Waylen (eds), *Global Governance: Feminist Perspectives*, Palgrave, pp. 185–207.

Connell, Raewyn W. (1995), *Masculinities*, Polity Press.

Cuomo, Chris (1996), 'War is not just an event: reflections on the significance of everyday violence', *Hypatia*, **11** (4): 30–45.

Demleitner, Nora (1994/5), 'Forced prostitution: naming an international offense', *Fordham International Law Journal*, **18**: 163–97.

Elbe, Stefan (2002), 'HIV/AIDS and the changing landscape of war in Africa', *International Security*, **27** (2): 159–77.

Enloe, Cynthia (2000), *Maneuvers: the International Politics of Militarizing Women's Lives*, University of California Press.

Enloe, Cynthia (2010), *Nimo's War, Emma's War: Making Feminist Sense of the Iraq War*, University of California Press.

Etienne, Margareth (1995), 'Addressing gender-based violence in an international context', *Harvard Women's Law Journal*, **18**: 139–70.

Ferguson, Kathy E. (1993), *The Man Question: Visions of Subjectivity in Feminist Theory*, University of California Press.

Fitzpatrick, P. (2000), 'It isn't easy being Biljana', *Central Europe Review*, **22** (2), accessed 9 August 2013 at: http://www.ce-review.org/00/22/fitzpatrick22.html.

Gardam, Judith G. (1993), 'Gender and non-combatant immunity', *Transnational Law and Contemporary Problems*, **3**: 345–70.

Gibson-Graham, J.K. (1996), *The End of Capitalism (as we knew it): A Feminist Critique of Political Economy*, University of Minnesota Press.

Goldstein, Joshua (2001), *War and Gender*, Cambridge University Press.

Hansen, Lene (2001), 'Gender, nation, rape: Bosnia and the construction of security', *International Feminist Journal of Politics*, **3** (1): 55–75.

Harman, D. (2003), 'A woman on trial for Rwanda's massacre', *Christian Science Monitor*, 7 March, accessed 10 June 2013 at: HTTP://www.csmonitor.com/2003/0307/p09s01-woaf.html.

Huston, Nancy (1982), 'Tales of war and tears of women', *Women's Studies International Forum*, **5** (3/4): 271–82.

Hynes, Michelle and Barbara Lopez Cardozo (2000), 'Observations from the CDC: sexual violence against refugee women', *Journal of Women's Health & Gender-Based Medicine*, **9** (8): 819–23.

MacKenzie, Megan (2009), 'Securitization and desecuritization: female soldiers and the reconstruction of women in post-conflict Sierra Leone', *Security Studies*, **18** (2): 241–61.

MacKinnon, Catherine (2001), *Sex Equality*, Thomson-West.

Mazurana, Dyan, Angela Raven-Roberts and Jane Parpart (2005), *Gender, Conflict, and Peacekeeping*, Rowman and Littlefield.

Melvern, L. (2004), *Conspiracy to Murder: Planning the Rwandan Genocide*, Verso Books.

Mendelson, Sarah Elizabeth (2005), *Barracks and Brothels: Peacekeepers and Human Trafficking in the Balkans*, Center for Strategic and International Studies.

Moon, Katherine (1997), *Sex Among Allies*, Columbia University Press.

Mu, Ren and Xiaobo Xhang (2008), *Gender Difference in the Long-Term Impact of Famine*, International Food Policy Research Institute.

Mundis, Daryl A. and Fergal Gaynor (2005), 'Current developments at the ad hoc international criminal tribunals', *Journal of International Criminal Justice*, **3** (5): 1134–60.

Palmer, Angela (2009), 'Indian army to deploy prostitutes as women battalion in Held Kashmir?', 8 September, accessed 14 July 2015 at: http://theasiandefence.blogspot.ca/2009/09/indian-army-to-deploy-prostitutes-as.html.

Peterson, V. Spike (1999), 'Sexing national identities/nationalism as heterosexism', *International Feminist Journal of Politics*, **1** (1): 34–65.

Peterson, V. Spike (2010), 'Gendered identities, ideologies, and practices in the context of war and militarism', in Laura Sjoberg and Sandra Via (eds), *Gender, War, and Militarism*, Praeger.

Peterson, V. Spike and Anne Sisson Runyan (2010), *Global Gender Issues in the New Millennium*, Westview.

Pilch, Frances (2002), 'Rape as genocide: the legal response to sexual violence', *Working Paper*, Center for Global Security and Democracy, Rutgers University, accessed 10 June 2013 at: http://www.ciaonet.org/wps/pif01/index.html.

Power, Samantha (2002), *A Problem from Hell: America and the Age of Genocide*, HarperCollins.

Raven-Roberts, Angela (2012), 'Women and the political economy of war', in Carol Cohn (ed.), *Women and Wars: Contested Histories, Uncertain Futures*, Polity.

Salzman, Todd (1998), 'Rape camps as a means of ethnic cleansing: religious, cultural, and ethical responses to rape victims in the Former Yugoslavia', *Human Rights Quarterly*, **20**: 348–78.

Sjoberg, Laura (2006), *Gender, Justice, and the Wars in Iraq*, Lexington.

Sjoberg, Laura (2007), 'Agency, militarized femininity and enemy others: observations from the war in Iraq', *International Feminist Journal of Politics*, **9** (1): 82–101.

Sjoberg, Laura (forthcoming), *Women as Rapists*, New York University Press.

Sjoberg, Laura and Caron Gentry (2007), *Mothers, Monsters, Whores: Women's Violence in Global Politics*, Zed Books.

Sjoberg, Laura and Jessica Peet (2011), 'A(nother) dark side of the protection racket: targeting women in wars', *International Feminist Journal of Politics*, **13** (2): 162–81.

Theophile, Mugisho and Bahati Valérie (n.d.), 'Up close: survivors of war rape in DR Congo', accessed 14 July 2015 at: http://www.asafeworldforwomen.org/fp-drc/cofapri/cofapri-blogs/403-stories-from-war-rape-victims-in-drcongo.html.

Tickner, J. Ann (1992), *Gender in International Relations: Feminist Perspectives on Achieving Global Security*, Columbia University Press.

Tickner, J. Ann (2001), *Gendering World Politics: Issues and Approaches in the Post-Cold War Era*, Columbia University Press.

Vickers, Jeanne (1993), *Women and War*, Zed Books.

Wight, Sarah and Alice Meyers (1996), 'Introduction', in Sarah Wight and Alice Meyers (eds), *No Angels: Women Who Commit Violence*, HarperCollins.

Wilcox, Lauren (2009), 'Gendering the cult of the offensive', *Security Studies*, **18** (2): 214–40.

Wilcox, Lauren (2010), 'Gendering the cult of the offensive', in Laura Sjoberg (ed.), *Gender and International Security: Feminist Perspectives*, Routledge, pp. 61–82.

Young, Iris Marion (2003), 'The logic of masculinist protection: reflections on the current security state', *Signs: Journal of Women in Culture and Society*, **29** (1): 1–25.

9. Risk and social transformation: gender and forced migration

Tania Kaiser

Forced migration is one of the most visible and disruptive consequences of armed conflict for civilian populations, regardless of gender. People flee their homes, often crossing international borders in order to escape specific instances or fear of persecution or of 'generalized violence' due to conflict and insecurity. As conflict has transformed in the decades since the end of the Cold War, front lines have been harder to fix, and civilian populations have borne the brunt of chronic, protracted and unpredictable conflict dynamics. The impacts are staggering in scale; the United Nations High Commissioner for Refugees announced in June 2015 that 59.5 million people were forcibly displaced worldwide at that time (UNHCR, 2015a).

No region of the world remains untouched by forced migration. Both Africa and Asia have been heavily affected by large-scale refugee movements over the last two decades, and South America has seen a vast Internally Displaced People (IDP) population in Colombia over many years. Numbers of refugees globally (just over 11 million at mid-2015; UNHCR, 2015b) are now considerably lower than those of IDPs (38 million in 2015; IDMC, 2015), for whom flight from danger does not necessarily lead to the crossing of an international border. In Asia, the largest refugee populations by far have for several decades been Afghans in Pakistan and Iran, and large numbers of Iraqis have also been displaced. More recently still, over 3 million refugees have fled Syria, with 6.5 million more displaced within its borders (European University Institute, 2015).

In Africa, several regional conflict complexes in the 1990s and 2000s brought forced migration, in West Africa, the Horn of Africa and Central Africa in particular. In the Democratic Republic of the Congo conflict has led to the deaths of nearly 4 million people and the continuing displacement of 2.3 million more (Coghlan et al., 2006; UNHCR, 2012). In Sudan, hundreds of thousands sought refuge in neighboring countries, while millions more were displaced within the country as a result of several linked conflicts. The secession of South Sudan and the creation of

Africa's newest nation in 2011 changed without resolving forced migration dynamics, since internal conflict within the new state has caused further displacement despite substantial repatriation in the last few years.

Despite the popular perception in the Global North, most forced migrants in the developing world remain in their regions of origin (UNHCR, 2015a). More men than women make the longer and often more dangerous inter-continental journey to claim asylum in developed countries. The numbers of men and women who flee their homes are roughly equal. Nevertheless, as detailed below, they may have different reasons for fleeing, as well as different experiences of flight and exile. Contemporary experiences of forced migration are so diverse, complex and contingent they cannot be generalized. Even for narrowly defined 'Convention refugees',[1] who have crossed an international border due to actual or feared persecution, the variety of their possible experiences and encounters is wide.

This chapter first indicates some of the ways that people are constituted as refugees and the ways in which their experiences may differ widely depending on context and positionality. In particular, I discuss how gender identity and subjectivities interact with the legal and practical exigencies of becoming a refugee or IDP. I then illustrate these issues with the case of South Sudanese refugees in Uganda, whom I studied. I make an argument about the significance of subjectivities in relation to the opportunities and risks afforded by forced migration by the South Sudanese through the lens of three analytical areas; namely, labor, social change and violence.

ENCOUNTERING FORCED MIGRATION

Refugee movements in the developing world are increasingly prompted by mixed motives. They may be heavily influenced by exposure to conflict in many forms, as well as being linked to economic triggers, and environmental and other factors. The dynamics and processes of contemporary conflict lead to massive pressure on livelihoods as well as on lives, and conditions of long-term insecurity and flux also undermine socio-cultural networks and the functioning of so-called local 'coping mechanisms'. In this context we need to understand diversity in each 'phase' of forced migration: during the pre-flight period, during a period of exile (however protracted) and in the context of any potential or actual durable solution. As an element of this, gender identity will construct and interact with the specific nature of an individual's encounter with conflict and forced migration.

For this and other reasons, there is no single 'refugee experience'. That said, some issues and dynamics can be identified as likely to impact the nature of forced migration experiences in diverse contexts, and especially in the developing world. Without endorsing simplistic circular notions of 'cycles' of forced migration, we can see patterns in the factors likely to be definitive in constructing experiences of forced migration: the kinds of environments from which people are obliged to flee and the choices available to them within these, the circumstances of their actual flight, the kind of reception offered to them in host states, the length of their exile and prospects for a satisfactory durable solution. Refugees exist, of course, within a specific political economy, and their reception and treatment is ever framed by the competing projects of interested actors, as well as by purer forms of solidarity and humanitarian response. Not surprisingly, therefore, the wider political and economic priorities and objectives of non-refugee actors and stakeholders assume considerable significance in the responses made to refugees in the developed and developing worlds. The recent difficulty faced by the European Union in trying to convince member states to offer resettlement places to Syrian refugees, despite their evident protection needs, is a case in point.

The kinds of bureaucratic, legalistic and disciplinary structures encountered by forced migrants are inevitably embedded in the gender relations of the states they leave, enter and pass through. The gendered aspects of asylum law, policy and practice, as well as the myriad other governance mechanisms against which refugees and IDPs come up, define responses and protection space available to them in ways that may be implicit rather than explicit.

In the developing world, as a consequence of the kinds of situations which force people to flee their homes, refugees and other forced migrants frequently move en masse, and are often recognized as refugees by host states on this basis. Instead of undergoing individual status determination procedures, therefore, they are given legal recognition initially as refugees as a group. Subsequent humanitarian responses to them are frequently conditional on them accepting a number of limitations, notably on their freedom of movement. Refugees who live in camps and settlements in sub-Saharan Africa and in many parts of Asia share many of the same challenges relating to the provision of adequate services, the availability of decent and sustainable livelihoods, and avenues for self-development more broadly. Increasingly, those who opt not to live in such institutional or bureaucratic contexts head instead for urban centers, where they mainly live unsupported by governments or aid actors, despite the paucity of options available to them in most cases. Most experiences of exile in the developing world last for a very long time, with millions of refugees having failed to find a durable solution after a decade or more (Crisp and Slaughter, 2009; Lindley and Haslie 2011).

To what extent can refugees in either rural or urban contexts integrate and build new lives for themselves in the context of protracted exile? Clearly, this is a legal as well as a socio-economic and political question, with as many answers as contexts. But an urgent question is how refugees can forge an acceptable life for themselves given the uncertainty, and often the poverty and marginality, of exile. Beyond this, refugees are usually assumed to aspire to a post-exilic life, or at least to the achievement of a durable solution which may imply settling permanently in the country of exile, again moving on, or returning 'home', among other more complex options. Each of these issues and questions is likely to point to differences between the way that women and men understand and respond to their experience of forced migration.

GENDER AND THE SIGNIFICANCE OF SUBJECTIVITIES

The diversity and variation in forced migration experiences implies the centrality of individual and group subjectivities in understanding how these have played out in specific contexts for particular people. The gender identity of refugees is one of a number of critical variables affecting how they construct and are exposed to danger, constitute and react to political and other threats, take decisions to flee, and engage with life in exile, including as objects of humanitarian aid. Age or generation, socioeconomic status, ethnicity, religious or other cultural identity may be equally significant in some contexts. As shown below, specific analyses should explore the ways in which each of these identities interact and motivate or facilitate response and action in situations of forced migration.

The analytical point of departure is the understanding of a mutually constitutive relationship whereby gender both affects the context and experience of forced migration, and is affected by it. Therefore, asking – as a kind of 'add-on' – how gender characterizes the experience of forced migration for men and women is insufficient and superficial. Rather, we need to understand how the very categories and classifications of forced migration discourse are constructed by the assumptions and practices associated with gender identities and relations, and vice versa. People do not necessarily experience even similar contexts of forced migration in the same way. Moreover, how gender identities are constructed, under-stood and interpreted, and how these processes relate to other aspects of their life and experience are also influential.

Analyses of the ways in which gender and refugees' experiences interact must be inclusive and extensive (Fiddian-Qasmiyeh, 2014). Thinking about gender and refugees means considering refugee experi-ences of flight, political identities, livelihoods and labor, intra-family dynamics, status, power and policy. All issues, including each of these, are constituted through constructed gender identities and relations, which are in turn affected by them. One important implication is that gender should not be used, as has often been the case, to refer exclusively to women, with the male category assumed as the neutral or default position (cf. Colson, in Indra, 1999). A gendered analysis of forced migration is expressly not only about women but about the multiple pressures and opportunities differentially available in the context of conflict and flight to men and women. A relational analysis is required that studies the mechanisms by which identities, activities and power are negotiated, contested and invested by forced migrants. An important recent body of literature assesses the ways that masculinity in particular finds itself under pressure in the context of forced migration, and what the conse-quences of this might be in socio-political and other terms. Achilli (2015), Dolan (2002), Hart (2008), Payne (1998) and Turner (2004), for example, highlight some of the ways in which men's status and product-ive activities can be undermined and stripped away in the context of forced migration, with negative consequences for self-esteem and devel-opmental opportunities, and with potentially linked impacts on drug and alcohol abuse, mental health and well-being, the prevalence of domestic violence in refugee settings, and indigenous political leadership systems and practices.

The principal refugee protection organization is the United Nations High Commissioner for Refugees, whose approach to identifying and responding to the gendered dimensions of forced migration has devel-oped considerably over the last two decades. The UN Refugee Conven-tion definition of a refugee cited above expressly does not refer to the applicant's gender or to any gender-specific forms of persecution. In its field-based protection and assistance activities, however, UNHCR has been obliged to address the specific challenges of flight, exile and the search for durable solutions for men and women forced migrants.[2] In policy terms it has come a long way from its 1991 'Guidelines on the Protection on Refugee Women' to its much more inclusive 'Age, Gender and Diversity Mainstreaming Forward Plan 2011–16' (UNHCR, 1991, 2011).

The experience of asylum-seeking women, perhaps particularly in the industrialized North, we now recognize, is likely informed by the difficulties of political and judicial institutions in understanding their experience and activities as political, rather than as domestic or 'cultural'. As Edwards (2010) points out, asylum determination systems are reluctant to view or interpret women's protection needs as 'political' (see also Crawley, 2001). Similar tensions are to be found in the Global South, where protection regimes still tend to focus on the kinds of activity and risk performed and experienced by men rather than women. The consequent threats to the security of women and children may be more difficult to prove. Women may be less likely to be treated as needing specific protection interventions *vis-à-vis* their political or public roles. Protection space has, however, been expanded with reference to 'newer' forms of persecution relating to women (for example, female genital mutilation), and to men and women in relation to their sexuality.

Perhaps starting with Harrell-Bond's seminal 1986 work *Imposing Aid*, a considerable body of literature addresses the causes and consequences of forced migration, and the ways in which populations of forced migrants are treated and managed. A minority of writers has addressed the gendered dimensions of forced migration in the developing world (Callemard, 1999; Camino and Krulfield, 1994; Daley, 1991; Hyndman, 2000; Indra, 1999; Martin, 2003). Some anthropologists in particular have included a gender perspective in their analyses of broader topics (Hammond, 2004; Grabska, 2010, 2014; Hart, 2008; Turner, 2010). Many of the themes which emerge as important both from the literature and from my own field research overlap and are entangled in the everyday business of living, working, having families and engaging in the public world. Contexts are critical, and I now briefly introduce the refugee groups I have studied in Uganda since 1996. The rest of the chapter will explore some of the gendered consequences of forced migration in sub-Saharan Africa predominantly through the lens of ethnographic material derived from research with this refugee group between 1996 and 2012.[3] I draw mainly on research with Sudanese refugees living in Uganda from 1992 to 2012. Early ethnographic research at the Kiryandongo Settlement in Masindi (then Kiryandongo) District was complemented by further research visits there as well as at Kyangwali, Ikafe, Rhino Camp and Achol-pi Settlements, and urban refugee locations in Arua, Masindi and Kampala. I adopted classic anthropological research methods including participant observation, formal, semi-formal and informal interviews with key informants, focus groups and collaborative research activities. The research is also informed by policy oriented research relating to forced migration with non-governmental organizations (NGOs) and UN organizations in West Africa and elsewhere.

Home to around 14 000 refugees for many years, the Kiryandongo settlement provided opportunities for families to develop agricultural as well as residential plots, and to establish numerous churches, schools and other public institutions. Public services were managed by a combination of government ministries, the United Nations High Commissioner for Refugees (UNHCR) and some of its implementing NGO partners, with a small number of refugee Community Based Organizations.

SUDANESE REFUGEES IN UGANDA

The Sudanese refugee population in Uganda includes a range of people, experiences and responses over an extended period. Uganda and Sudan have a long history of hosting each other's refugees, with Sudanese most recently present in Uganda from the late 1980s as a result of continued internal conflict in Sudan that ended with the signing of a comprehensive peace agreement in 2005. Many women among the refugee population in Uganda complained that they were entirely excluded from discussions prior to the signing of the agreement; this broadly reflects the difficulties some Sudanese women have long experienced in being heard in the public sphere.

Well over a quarter of a million Sudanese took refuge in Uganda during the conflict; their stay there was fraught in several ways. Although the government of Uganda presents itself as having been a generous and liberal host, any refugee hoping to benefit from humanitarian aid or UNHCR protection activities was required to register and remain in a refugee camp or settlement as defined by the state (Kaiser, 2006). This caused limitations in terms of access to and enjoyment of a whole range of rights, including social and economic rights. Refugees also suffered considerably from the insecurity associated with the long-term conflict between the government of Uganda and the Lord's Resistance Army in the refugee hosting area (Finnström, 2008).

The protracted nature of the refugees' stay in Uganda – most did not leave their camps and settlements to repatriate or pursue other durable solutions until after 2007 – brought challenges to them individually and collectively, including with respect to social change and transformation, livelihood and to physical security. Each of these is addressed briefly below.

SOCIAL CHANGE AND FORCED MIGRATION

Becoming a forced migrant can be characterized in several ways. One of the most important factors is that it is almost always a process of change; different actors manage this change in different ways with different outcomes. Very large numbers of refugees in Africa move from one rural area to another, and flight may well involve being established by host government or aid providers in a refugee camp or settlement, or similar setting. Recent years have also seen a massive increase in the number of so-called 'urban refugees'; some African countries have seen dense concentrations of refugees and asylum seekers in urban areas where they face many challenges. One of the main reasons why refugee men and women might travel to cities and towns is to try to find employment or income-generating activities there, often a difficult enterprise. The experiences of those remaining in rural areas may be defined by what kind of support they receive, how enabling their environment is, and the extent to which they can achieve reasonably sustainable livelihoods (Omata, 2011). Depending on which income-generating or employment opportunities are available in a given context, men and women may find themselves more or less able to access these in ways that are familiar from the 'home' context.

SOCIAL CHANGE: STATUS, ROLES AND ACTIVITIES

The social flux and opening up of usual social modes and practices can lead to new opportunities being made available to members of communities who had previously been limited. One frequent example of this in the context of forced migration is that women who have been used to being largely restricted to the domestic sphere may be encouraged or enabled to move out into the wider realm of public affairs and activity. This may be a matter of necessity: they need to pursue cash income in the absence of subsistence agricultural options. Or it may be due to a change in the way that local governance is enacted, with new, participatory governance committees or councils being invented in refugee settings. In these cases members are often elected according to sectoral specialism or technical expertise. In addition to posts concerned with 'security', 'education' and so on, councils often also include a secretary (or similar title) for 'women' and/or for 'youth'. Even if none of the other roles is taken on by women, in Ugandan camps the secretary for women has usually been a woman. Notably, refugee women are not always keen to commit themselves to committee work as they find they have little free time to spare, for reasons discussed below.

Opportunities may increase in exile, or they may decrease, as in the case of older men who find themselves relatively marginalized from leadership positions after having been used to them as if by right in the pre-flight period. Turner's work (2010) shows how individuals may suffer, for example, because they cannot speak the language (literally and metaphorically) of government staff and aid providers in refugee camps. But customary practices and leadership systems are also difficult to translate in mixed communities of people who may have quite different 'traditional' practices. In short, who you are in a community affects whether you are likely to gain or lose status and opportunities in the context of exile, and gender identity is highly influential in this respect.

In Kiryandongo and other Ugandan camps, one notable context in which women were able to play an increasingly prominent role, with the apparent support of their male peers, was in the increasingly dynamic world of church activity and management. Christian churches proliferated in the Ugandan refugee camps, and were a fertile ground for social, humanitarian and other activity for men and women.

In Uganda women have taken the opportunity to become involved over the years of protracted exile in a way that many say they would have found hard to do in Sudan, in business and money-making activities. Whether this relates to small-scale market selling or the production of food and drink, or relates to a higher level of trading activities, varies considerably. What is clear is that women who reported that they would have been dismissed for poor morality had they attempted such activity at home were increasingly free to pursue independent economic agendas. People's needs change too, of course, and the conflict which produced both men and women as refugees also had more single female-headed households; women who may previously have had few other choices open to them now had greater need to assert themselves economically.

What is clear is that power is not always easily shared, even when activities are diversified. For example, in order to support the 'empowerment' of refugee women in the late 1990s, the UN World Food Programme required that each food distribution team in Ugandan camps have a woman 'food basket monitor'. They presumably were not aware that unofficially men were trailing these officially appointed team members to sanction their decisions (or not) with the male authority that such decisions were locally supposed to require. Social change takes place slowly, and nothing ever guarantees that it will sustain as conditions change. This is something that needs to be ascertained on a case by case research basis.

LABOR AND ITS INTERCONNECTIONS

In general, one thing that is usually recognized and accepted by those working with refugees in rural areas is that the definition of the kind of labor that is culturally generally regarded as 'female' or women's work expands in the context of exile. This is partly because the reproductive tasks that women are usually burdened with increase in a context where networks have been disrupted, where the physical environment is not known, where relied-on natural resources may not be immediately available and so on. Women find themselves needing to spend more time and effort than they did before, carrying out the same child caring, family feeding, and household management tasks for which they always took responsibility. Importantly, households themselves may well have changed size and shape in the context of exile. Individual women may be struggling to feed and care for more people in exile than they did at home if they have taken over the care of orphaned or lost children, elderly people or others.

Paradoxically, as women's labor in rural refugee camp settings frequently increases for these reasons (see also Daley, 1991), men's labor and activities are often curtailed, with negative consequences for their ability to contribute to the household. If men cannot access the kinds of employment or productive activities in which they were engaged 'at home', their role and status as breadwinner and head of household may be compromised. It can be very difficult for refugee families in such circumstances to manage the changing labor patterns so that household requirements are met as much as possible, and so that personal identity and dignity are maintained. In Rhino Camp Settlement in northern Uganda, Sudanese women complained that they were burdened with heavy domestic work; moreover, the absence of employment opportunities for their husbands meant that they were forced into market work, selling baked or cooked goods to generate a cash income of sorts. The ultimate irony for them was that, having invested heavily in meeting family needs by doing arduous work, husbands who were unable to contribute at all vilified these wives for not being at home and producing food in a timely manner. Men may themselves feel emasculated or undermined by these scenarios, leading to 'negative coping' activities such as alcohol or substance abuse, or domestic violence (see also Payne, 1998). In Rhino Camp refugee women who participated in focus group discussions felt strongly that domestic violence had increased during exile, and that the frustration of refugee life for men was partly to blame for this.

The kinds of employment or training opportunities available to girls and women in the Sudanese camps in Uganda have changed marginally over the years, but have largely been framed by fairly conservative ideas about what were suitable activities for women. In Kiryandongo Settlement, young women struggled for a long time before a small number of them were finally accepted onto vocational training schemes for carpentry and other manual skills. More commonly, women were encouraged to engage in craft production, even in the absence of any market at all for such outputs. Professional training opportunities were very limited for men and women; of the relatively few who were able to qualify as teachers, for example, only a small minority were female.

The principal difficulties of refugee camp life for men and women in Uganda, when they live in places not affected by immediate physical insecurity, tend to revolve around the material challenges of achieving and sustaining an adequate livelihood. A wide range of economic activities are carried out, and contrasting pressures are felt by men and women whose responsibilities *vis-à-vis* the feeding and protection of their families are frequently hard to meet. Identifying those who are worst off in this sense is often a matter of looking at the quality of social networks and resources that individual refugees can call on for support. Poorly connected refugees are likely to face most problems. Feeding and educating children is exceptionally challenging for relatively impoverished single women with children (widowed or otherwise) who lack the effective support of brother, father or husband. While men may have more options in terms of gaining access to wage labor (even if they have to migrate for it, and it exposes them to other kinds of risk and exploitation), women may resort to entering into sexual or married relationships with partners they would not otherwise have chosen. Due to financial need, they may establish relationships on unfavorable terms, for example as a poorly treated second or third wife, in order to access some kind of domestic protection. A further difficulty in this context is that partners or husbands may not be willing to take on responsibility for a new wife's existing children.

RISK, PROTECTION AND VULNERABILITY TO VIOLENCE

As noted above, women's experiences of violence in the context of flight or exile are more likely to be analyzed as a domestic, cultural or interpersonal issue than those of their male counterparts. Men's experiences may be more likely to be assessed in terms of their political meaning and consequences.

Men and women refugees clearly experience risk and vulnerability in significantly different ways. This is partly because of the different ways that they are likely to be involved, directly or indirectly, in the conflicts that generate forced migration. Young men, as many sources show, are frequently considered to be, or actually are, more vulnerable to military conscription than young women of the same age. Girls and women may be pressed into military servitude or supportive labor (including sexual labor) as in the case of Ugandan and Sudanese women and girls abducted by the Lord's Resistance Army during the late 1990s and 2000s. Nevertheless, young men are more likely to be forced into fighting roles. In some cases, such as young Sudanese in Ethiopia in the 1990s, boys and young men are tricked into volunteering for what they have been told will be educational or training opportunities. Instead, they find that they have arrived at military training camps from which escape is very difficult. The avoidance of unwanted involvement in fighting for rebel or government forces is frequently cited as a reason for flight by young men who have chosen to try to pursue educational opportunities instead.

As Grabska's research (2011) in Kakuma Camp in Kenya shows, 80 percent of the 92 000 strong refugee population were under 30, and 59 percent were male. In the refugee camps and settlements of Uganda, many young men in particular reported having decided to flee Sudan when they realized that they risked conscription into the Sudanese People's Liberation Army (SPLA), or because they had no avenues for educational advancement at home. In some cases, for example among young men in the Ikafe and Rhino Camp Settlements in Arua District in the late 1990s and early 2000s, the two were directly linked: boys reported that SPLA commanders told the boys that they could go to school only when they had completed military service in Sudan, but not before. One of the consequences of conflict and forced migration from an educational perspective is that one finds 'pupils' much older than usual in classes intended for younger children. This can have consequences for classroom authority and dynamics, especially when students have experience fighting and are unused to school discipline. It also has implications in terms of what livelihood-generating activities young men can be involved in, if they are attempting simultaneously to acquire remedial education. So social life more broadly can be impacted by the gendered consequences of conflict and forced migration. A young man who is not making a living because he is still at school in a refugee camp has little chance of marrying and achieving adult status in many sub-Saharan

African refugee communities. Thus the social reproduction of society may also be disrupted in this way.

For women and girls, vulnerability to physical violence is alarmingly ubiquitous during forced migration. Not only is sexual violence frequent in conflict, which may itself be reason for flight, but risks of violence of this kind continue through the various experiences of forced migration in a depressingly wide number of contexts (Hyndman, 2000; Callemard, 1999; Grabska, 2010; Payne, 1998; Dolan, 2009). Women are frequently preyed upon by officials, soldiers and bureaucrats in the course of flight and asylum-seeking activities. In one refugee settlement in western Uganda in the early 2000s, the government representative responsible for issuing travel permits and other documentation was apparently recalled from his post at least partly because of repeated complaints from refugee women that he extorted sex from them when they went to apply for travel documents. Considerable evidence shows that sexual violence against women is also widespread in refugee camps in Kenya. In the notorious case of Dadaab camp, women leaving the relative protection of their domestic compounds to fetch firewood are at extreme risk of rape by perpetrators referred to mainly as '*shiftas*' or bandits. The strong implication is that many of these attacks are politically motivated and are carried out by people known to the women or their clan members. Yet efforts to prevent such attacks have been largely limited to practical and literal interventions such as the provision of fuel for cooking, rather than any deeper, more challenging response. It should also be noted that the kinds of supportive interventions offered to women who suffered sexual violence have also been said to attract fake complaints from women who hope to receive improved protection as a result.

In some cases, female refugees who have suffered from serious sexual violence including rape and/or severe domestic violence and who meet various other criteria have been offered third country resettlement as a protection solution. This is actively sought as a prize by some women and many men, but can be a mixed blessing. Third country resettlement inevitably means moving out of communities where women are known and, to some extent, supported. After resettlement women and their dependent children may find themselves in strange or unknown national environments where support networks are limited; the women must support children and make a new life in challenging social and physical environments. One woman in Kiryandongo who had suffered brutal and repeated attacks by her husband reported her desperation to leave the region in order to escape such beatings, but expressed serious reservations about a possible scenario whereby she could be resettled with her children to Denmark, where she knew virtually no one, did not speak the language and feared the climate. The government of Denmark was generously offering refuge to female victims of domestic violence from sub-Saharan Africa at that time, which women both appreciated and regarded with trepidation.

Proving causal links between gender violence and refugee settings is a highly problematic and fraught enterprise. However, relatively impoverished and marginal refugee camps and other refugee contexts clearly are likely to be high pressure environments giving rise to both multiple undesirable social activities and 'coping strategies' (Harrell-Bond, 1986; Kaiser, 2004). Anecdotal and observational evidence points to the likely correlation between the boredom and frustration of refugee life, especially where refugees are not provided with access to productive or income-generating activities, and increased alcohol and drug consumption (Martin, 2003; Dolan, 2009). In sub-Saharan Africa, for cultural reasons, it is usually considered women's responsibility or role to brew beer, distil alcohol and to sell these. Indeed, this is often one of the only available opportunities for generating small amounts of cash in refugee settings. Unfortunately, this trade can produce an alcohol-soaked social environment, especially during evenings, holidays or otherwise quieter periods like the dry season; this appears to lead to increased incidence of domestic abuse.

Refugee women in settlements in northern Uganda, notably Rhino Camp Settlement, linked alcohol consumption and increased 'wife beatings' in a casual and relatively uncomplaining way. They themselves pointed to the pain and frustration of life in refugee camps for men who are used to being active breadwinners and useful members of society. In this interpretation the fact that men feel useless is what leads them to drink and to beat their wives. These women went further and pointed to the skewing of aid interventions in Rhino Camp where, they argued, women (having been defined after research as 'reliable' and more likely to repay loans) were offered access to several income-generation schemes. The problem, in their analysis, was that their own workloads were very high. Finding time to participate actively in these opportunities was not always easy for them. Meanwhile, denied access to credit and loans, their frustrated husbands resented their activity and occupation as much as their actual opportunities and expressed their rage in the usual way. 'Do something for the men!' was the loud cry from these women.

Men and women of all ages have to take multiple and overlapping risks into account when making decisions. The signing of the peace agreement between warring parties in Sudan in 2005 put significant pressure on refugees to register for eventual voluntary repatriation to their home country from Uganda. While some young people in particular felt that their interests were best served by an early return, to demonstrate their willingness to invest in and contribute to the rebuilding of post-conflict Sudan, others were left with no means of support in Uganda when their families wanted to go 'home'. Very quickly, however, new risks for female secondary school students became apparent, as warnings circulated in schools in Uganda about the desire of SPLA commanders stationed in their home areas in Sudan to forcibly 'marry' returning students. Repatriates alerted those still in Uganda that refusal to marry was futile and could bring reprisals down on the heads of parents and family members. The self-help secondary school in the Kiryandongo settlement was not alone in hastily transforming a classroom into the most rudimentary of dormitories so that female students could remain in the relative safety of school in Uganda. Going 'home' was more dangerous for this particular category of refugee than remaining in Uganda, even without the protective presence of parents or other immediate family.

CONCLUSIONS: DIVERSITY, CHANGE AND RESPONSES

Forced migration inevitably brings changes. These changes are experienced differently by people for whom the only feature they have in common is their refugee-hood. Even within the same refugee group, individuals will experience flight, exile and the search for a solution to their problems in different ways. Social and political lives are complex and organic, and, as social scientists show, when a substantial shift takes place in one area of life, changes in other dimensions can be expected. This goes some way toward explaining the interrelatedness of many of the issues discussed here; certainly issues around social change, livelihood and protection were hard to disentangle for the Sudanese in Uganda during the 1990s and 2000s.

If one were to think of social change as a zero sum game, whereby power and opportunity are redistributed among a population as conditions change, one might argue that, overall, women refugees in Uganda have experienced a relative improvement in their standing and in the nature and extent of the opportunities open to them during their period in exile. Many of the activities in which they now engage enthusiastically – including, for women in Kiryandongo, 'digging' as well as weeding and harvesting, small trading activities and so on – were closed to them in Sudan on the grounds of their unsuitability for women. Similarly, among the Kiryandongo population, the number of educated women and of women professionals, businesspeople and public figures increased during their time in Uganda. Meanwhile, however, their domestic responsibilities are as onerous as ever, perhaps more so. The changes have inevitably been more evident for younger women than for the members of the older generation, whose roles and lives have arguably changed less. For the small minority of women who were able to buck the trend of early pregnancy in the settlement and progress to tertiary level education where sponsorship could be found, life chances in Uganda must be better than they were in pre-flight Sudan.

For men, the picture is different, but also mixed. As has been reported in other refugee settings, younger men in exile tend to assume the roles and associated positions of status formerly held by older men in the pre-flight period. The emphasis on the formal, public domain of decision making and governance has tended to give younger men an advantage over their fathers and grandfathers, since they are more likely than their older relatives to be multilingual and to have some familiarity with how local government and aid systems work. Older men seem to have lost power and authority in this interpretation, as the kinds of clan and ritual knowledge which were once emphasized and valued are less critical and relevant to refugee life in Uganda. This pattern has clear exceptions, however, so we should avoid thinking that new processes are firmly set and have replaced previous systems and priorities.

In 2002, for example, after an outbreak of communal violence in the settlement at Kiryandongo, members of all ethnic groups present asserted that elders played important roles in mediating between warring groups and hastening an end to the violence. It seems that the gravitas and quiet authority that elders brought to their intervention was welcomed compared to the more public, business-like interventions of the younger generation.

Avoiding the trap of ascribing all social and other kinds of change to the fact of forced migration is crucial. The Sudanese, for instance, moved from a much less to a much more developed socio-political environment. The fact that they did so as refugees was only one part of their story and their experience. Nevertheless, transformation in social process and relationships have been negotiated in interesting ways; the social categories and practices employed have been modified to allow change to take place while preserving valued features of socio-cultural life (see also Kaiser, 2008).

As the material discussed in this chapter shows, the differential opportunities and risks to which men and women are exposed in the course of forced migration are continuous in many ways with the patterns and priorities of their pre-flight lives. Changes observed should be read in this light, as should the variations in experience consequent to other social identifiers such as age, socio-economic status and so on. An important final point is that nothing guarantees that any social changes for good or ill will sustain in the next phase of refugees' experience, whether this is in the context of returning home, or some other solution. Change will continue; of this we can be certain.

If we turn briefly to the role of aid providers in refugee settings, on which I have deliberately not focused here, one finds an inevitable ethical dilemma. How can humanitarian and development agencies intervene in ways that support or oppose the agendas of specific sub-groups of the population? To consider a gender-related example, on what basis might an agency ethically set out, as many do, to improve women's situation in refugee camps, if this means not merely securing their physical safety and ensuring adequate livelihoods, but also 'empowering' them to assert claims for a greater say in decision making? In short, may agencies support the struggle for gender equality? Refugee settings frequently are intense places where competition over power and resources is evident, and where different groups will have different views about how best to proceed. In Kiryandongo as elsewhere, agencies have sometimes faced difficulties in trying to please everybody on gender and other issues. One international NGO that sought to support women in situations of domestic violence by providing safe houses was attacked for undermining local mediation and family dispute resolution mechanisms, and for attempting to impose 'Western' notions of equality and rights. Most importantly, the refugee population itself was divided as to whether the NGO had done the right thing, or even whether it even had the right to attempt to intervene.

The literature on 'refugee women' across the decades has emphasized that these women are not passive victims of circumstance, but active agents, even if the conditions within which they operate are difficult and limiting. Understanding gender as a relational category and seeking to understand the ways that men and women conceptualize and respond to the challenges of forced migration offers the best chance for recognizing the impressive and ingenious nature of their efforts to survive and transcend forced migration.

NOTES

1. Under the UN 1951 Refugee Convention, a refugee is someone who 'owing to well-founded fear of being persecuted for reasons of race, religion, nationality, membership of a particular social group or political opinion, is outside the country of his nationality and is unable or, owing to such fear, is unwilling to avail himself of the

protection of that country'. The Organization of African Unity expanded this definition in various ways in 1969 for refugees in Africa, and included 'generalized violence' as grounds for flight.

2. For UNHCR (2011), 'Gender refers to the socially constructed roles for women and men, which are often central to the way in which people define themselves and are defined by others. Gender roles are learned, changeable over time, and variable within and between cultures. Gender often defines the duties, responsibilities, constraints, opportunities and privileges of women and men in any context. Gender equality refers to the equal enjoyment of rights, responsibilities and opportunities of women, men, girls and boys. Gender equality implies that the interests, needs and priorities of each gender are respected'.

3. I thank the refugees and others who generously gave their time to participate in these research projects, to the Uganda National Council for Science and Technology for research permission, and to staff at the Ugandan Office of the Prime Minister for assisting with access. Staff at UNHCR and involved NGOs also contributed to the research. Finally, I would like to thank funders of the field research, including SOAS, the British Academy and the AHRC's Diasporas, Migration and Identities Programme. This chapter benefited from the expert editing and the constructive comments of the volume's section editor to whom I also give my thanks.

REFERENCES

Achilli, Luigi (2015), 'Becoming a Man in al-Wihdat: masculine performances in a Palestinian refugee camp in Jordan', *International Journal of Middle East Studies*, **47** (2): 263–80.

Callemard, Agnès (1999), 'Refugee women: a gendered and political analysis of the refugee experience', in Alistair Ager (ed.), *Refugees: Perspectives on the Experience of Forced Migration*, Pinter, pp. 196–214.

Camino, Linda A. and Ruth M. Krulfeld (eds) (1994), *Reconstructing Lives, Recapturing Meaning: Refugee Identity, Gender and Culture Change*, Gordon & Breach.

Coghlan, Benjamin, Richard J. Brennan, Pascal Ngoy, David Dofara, Brad Otto, Mark Clements and Tony Stewart (2006), 'Mortality in the Democratic Republic of the Congo: a nationwide survey', *The Lancet*, **367**: 44–51.

Crawley, Heaven (2001), *Refugees and Gender: Law and Process*, Jordan.

Crisp, Jeff and Slaughter, Amy (2009), 'A surrogate state? The role of UNHCR in protracted refugee situations', Working Paper No. 168, New Issues in Refugee Research, Geneva UNHCR.

Daley, Patricia (1991), 'Gender, displacement and social reproduction', *Journal of Refugee Studies*, **4** (3): 248–66.

Dolan, Chris (2002), 'Collapsing masculinities and weak states – a case study of Northern Uganda', in Frances Cleaver (ed.), *Masculinities Matter! Men, Gender and Development*, Zed Books, pp. 57–83.

Dolan, Chris (2009), *Social Torture: The Case of Northern Uganda, 1986–2006*, Berghahn Books.

Edwards, Alice (2010), 'Transitioning gender: feminist engagement with international refugee law and policy 1950–2010'; *Refugee Survey Quarterly*, **29** (2): 21–45.

European University Institute (2015), 'Syrian refugees', accessed 15 June 2015 at: http://syrianrefugees.eu/.

Fiddian-Qasmiyeh, Elena (2014), 'Gender and forced migration', in Elena Fiddian-Qasmiyeh, Gil Loescher, Katy Long and Nando Sigona (eds), *The Oxford Handbook of Refugee and Forced Migration Studies*, Oxford University Press, pp. 395–408.

Finnström, Sverker (2008), *Living with Bad Surroundings: War History and Everyday Moments in Northern Uganda*, Duke University Press.

Grabska, Katarzyna (2010), 'Lost boys, invisible girls: stories of Sudanese marriages across borders', *Gender, Place & Culture: A Journal of Feminist Geography*, **17**: 479–97.

Grabska, Katarzyna (2011), 'Constructing "modern gendered civilised" women and men: gender mainstreaming in refugee camps', *Gender and Development*, **19** (1): 81–93.

Grabska, Katarzyna (2014), *Gender, Home & Identity: Nuer Repatriation to Southern Sudan*, Boydell & Brewer.

Hammond, Laura (2004), *This Place will become Home: Refugee Repatriation to Ethiopia*, Cornell University Press.

Harrell-Bond, Barbara E. (1986), *Imposing Aid: Emergency Assistance to Refugees*, Oxford University Press.

Hart, Jason (2008), 'Dislocated masculinity: adolescence and the Palestinian nation-in-exile', *Journal of Refugee Studies*, **21** (1): 64–81.

Hyndman, Jennifer (2000), *Managing Displacement: Refugees and the Politics of Humanitarianism*, University of Minnesota Press.

IDMC (2015), *The Global Overview 2015: People Internally Displaced By Conflict And Violence*, available at: http://www.internal-displacement.org/publications/2015/global-overview-2015-people-internally-displaced-by-conflict-and-violence/.

Indra, Doreen (ed.) (1999), *Engendering Forced Migration: Theory & Practice*, Berghahn.

Kaiser, Tania (2004), 'Participation or consultation? Reflections on a "beneficiary based" evaluation of UNHCR's programme for Sierra Leonean and Liberian Refugees in Guinea, June–July 2000', *Journal of Refugee Studies*, **17** (2): 185–204.

Kaiser, Tania (2006), 'Between a camp and a hard place: rights, livelihood and experiences of the local settlement system for long-term refugees in Uganda', *Journal of Modern African Studies*, **44** (4): 597–621.

Kaiser, Tania (2008), 'Social and ritual activity in and out of place: the "negotiation of locality" in a Sudanese refugee settlement', *Mobilities* Special Issue: 'Migrant worlds, material cultures', **3** (3): 375–95.

Lindley, Anna and Anita Haslie (2011), 'Unlocking protracted displacement: Somali case study', RSC Working Paper No. 79, Refugee Studies Centre.

Martin, Susan (2003), *Refugee Women*, 2nd edn, Rowman & Littlefield.

Omata, Naohiko (2011), 'The livelihood strategies of Liberian refugees in Ghana', unpublished PhD thesis, School of Oriental and African Studies, University of London.

Payne, Lina (1998), 'Food shortages and gender relations in Ikafe settlement, Uganda', *Gender and Development*, **6** (1): 30–36.

Turner, Simon (2004), 'Angry young men in a Tanzanian refugee camp', in Philomena Essed, Georg Frerks and Joke Schrijvers (eds), *Refugees and the Transformation of Societies: Agency, Policies, Ethics and Politics*, Vol. 13, *Forced Migration*, Berghahn.

Turner, Simon (2010), *Politics of Innocence: Hutu Identity, Conflict and Camp Life*, Berghahn.

UNHCR (1991), 'Guidelines on the protection on refugee women', Geneva UNHCR.

UNHCR (2011), 'Age, gender and diversity mainstreaming forward plan 2011–16', Geneva UNHCR.

UNHCR (2012), '2015 UNHCR country operations profile – Democratic Republic of the Congo', accessed 14 June 2015 at: http://www.unhcr.org/pages/49e45c366.html.

UNHCR (2015a), '*World at War Global Trends Forced Displacement* in 2014', Geneva UNHCR, accessed 24 June 2015 at: http://unhcr.org/556725e69.html.

UNHCR (2015b), 'Global Appeal 2015 Update 2015', Geneva UNHCR, accessed 13 June 2015 at: http://www.unhcr.org/5461e5ec3c.html.

10. Girls as weapons of war
Mayesha Alam

In the twenty-first century, civilians are killed and injured far more frequently than combatants during armed conflicts; they bear a disproportionate burden as violence escalates (Lazar, 2014). Women and girls are no exception. While they are killed less frequently than male combatants, women and girls comprise the majority of forcibly displaced populations and are subjected to sexual violence and persistent human rights violations. Meanwhile, they are expected to project an air of normalcy within conflict-affected communities. Girls and adolescent women often go unnoticed as victims of war. Some are likely to become militants or support armed groups by non-violent means, whether voluntarily or through coercion, while others may engage in conflict mitigation to advance peace and stability. In other words, even in times of armed conflict and escalating tensions, girls and women have agency and are key stakeholders in any society, although historically they have been neglected.

The challenges facing women and girls are particularly acute during and after war; insecurity – both physical and economic – becomes a normal part of life. Girls and adolescent women have many insecurities in common with adult women but they also have distinct experiences during armed conflict. Policymakers, practitioners, donors and scholars, however, often misunderstand this exceptional vulnerability. The dearth of research, investigation and data related to the plight of girls in war and violent conflict significantly undermines the ability of policymakers and practitioners to address their needs effectively. Greater documentation, reporting, monitoring and evaluation about how girls and adolescent women experience conflict are critical to devising effective, sustainable and impactful interventions to alleviate suffering.

In the post-Cold War era, conflicts have changed significantly, making documentation and reporting on experiences during war and conflict all the more important. The majority of violent conflicts in the last twenty-five years have been intra-state, rather than inter-state, and a proliferating number of armed non-state actors have been aggressors in and aggravators of conflict. Civilian men, women and children – from South Sudan to Syria, from Ukraine to Myanmar – are not only caught in the crossfire but in many cases are the intended targets of violent attacks (Machel, 1996). The international community struggles to mitigate these aspects of conflict effectively, to the detriment of civilian populations. In 2015, there are more forcibly displaced people than at any other time in history since the Second World War and the average timespan of displacement is 17 years (UNHCR, 2015). The majority of refugees and internationally displaced persons do not live in camps managed by humanitarian organizations but rather are dispersed throughout urban communities in the host countries. Their informal and sometimes undetectable living arrangements make it all the more difficult to identify and address their needs. All of these issues have gendered dimensions that affect women and girls. According to the Women's Refugee Commission, over 140 million girls today live in conflict-affected and fragile settings (WRC, 2009). The severity and scale of this problem can be overwhelming, coupled with the paralysis of international policymakers.

In 2000, the UN Security Council adopted Resolution 1325, which recognizes the differential and severe impacts of war on women and girls as well as their necessary and important contributions to peace and security efforts. So 2015 marks the fifteenth anniversary of both that Resolution and of the adoption of the Millennium Development Goals, which include specific targets related to gender equality and the advancement of women's and girls' education, health and overall well-being. Additionally, twenty years have passed since the 1994 Fourth UN World Conference on Women, held in Beijing, where a comprehensive platform for action put forth a vision for change to advance the status of women and girls. Against this historical backdrop, we should reflect on progress that has been made but also recognize that much more needs to be done. This chapter provides in-depth analysis of the many ways in which girls and adolescent women experience conflict. The chapter also offers recommendations on how to ameliorate the plight of girls and adolescent women during armed conflict, including the recognition of their agency.

SOCIOECONOMIC IMPACTS OF ARMED CONFLICT ON GIRLS AND ADOLESCENT WOMEN

As direct victims of violent conflict, girls can be killed, injured, maimed, raped, tortured, forcibly impregnated, conscripted, recruited or kidnapped by combatants. It is important to note that disabled girls are doubly vulnerable as they may be marginalized further 'by a perceived lack of "worth" of the life of the child by the community and hence a consequent lack of care, attention and protection' (Delaney, 2006). Those who belong to religious, ethnic, tribal or linguistic minorities are also susceptible to targeted attacks, including sexual violence motivated by ethnic cleansing, as occurred en masse against Bosnians under the Milosevic regime, against Tutsi Rwandans by extremist Hutu militias, or against Yazidis by ISIS militants. Members of minority populations and those without any legal identity, or proof of identity, are especially likely to be trafficked during war (McKay and Mazurana, 2004). Legal scholars have noted that discrimination based on religion, social origin, class and race make minorities and the poor vulnerable to trafficking and sexual exploitation (Todres, 2009, p. 605).

Girls are not only primary victims during wartime, but also are secondary victims severely impacted in various ways by the violence inflicted upon their parents, grandparents, siblings, friends and other community members. Mazurana and Carlson (2006) note:

> As teachers are targeted and killed schools close down, as health care workers are killed or flee, clinics close their doors or provide only rudimentary services. Teachers and health care and social workers are a frontline of defense for protecting children from the ravages of armed conflict; when they are not there children are increasingly at risk. (p. 3)

In addition to the services lost when social workers are affected by conflict, children experience a devastating amount of trauma when their parents and other family members are injured or killed. Many such children are left without care or orphaned without shelter, and are left as prey for criminals to exploit.

Girls in certain cultures may be undervalued due to son-preference, seen as a burden to their families, or be unwanted by their families due to other sociocultural prejudices. This encourages early and forced marriage, which has 'been viewed as an unfortunate but inevitable social ill'; by 2030 more than 140 million girls will be married off before turning 18 (Lemmon, 2014, p. 19). Nine of the top ten countries with the highest child marriage prevalence rates are on the Organisation for Economic Co-operation and Development (OECD) list of fragile states (Lemmon, 2014). Lemmon argues, 'Child marriage does not cause fragile states, but it does reinforce poverty, limit girls' education, stymie economic progress, and as a result, contribute to regional instability' (p. 30).

Since the start of the Syrian civil war in 2011, the International Rescue Committee reported a spike in child marriage among refugee populations in countries bordering Syria. The increase in child marriages was seen as a means to protect the honor, purity, physical security and economic well-being of young girls (IRC, 2014). According to UN Women statistics, the rate of early marriage among Syrian girls caught up in the ongoing civil war was 51 percent (UN Women, 2013). However, many girls claimed that marriages were often arranged to much older men without their consent or their understanding of the reality they would encounter. Within the first year of the Syrian civil war, of Syrian girls who married between the ages of 15 and 17, slightly more than 16 percent of them married men who were 15 or more years older, compared to 6.3 percent for Palestinian girls and 7.0 percent of Jordanian girls who married early (IRC, 2014). This comparative analysis between three Arab states indicates the heightened risk of child marriage within protracted conflicts and crises. Similarly, in Rwanda before the 1994 genocide the average age for a girl to marry was between 20 and 25 years. In the refugee camps during and after the genocide, the average age for marriage was 15 years (UN Women, 2014). In Sri Lanka, parents forcibly married off their unmarried daughters to reduce the risk of abduction by the Liberation Tigers of Tamil Eelam (Wijeyesekera, 2011).

Early marriage has many short and long-term consequences. Early marriage increases with the rise of insecurity and poverty in conflict settings; it also worsens insecurity and poverty for girls and adolescent women. Many girls and adolescent women who are married early and without their consent are susceptible to physical and emotional abuse by their husbands or in-laws. Nonetheless, child marriage has failed to feature prominently in international guidelines and frameworks to address and prevent gender-based violence in emergencies (Save the Children, 2007). Consequently, humanitarian assistance providers are inadequately equipped with the knowledge, tools and resources to address child marriage in crisis and emergency settings. Child brides confront a myriad of obstacles that impact their mental and physical development after marriage. They may be completely unprepared both physiologically and mentally for sexual activity. They may also lack financial independence, leaving them without an exit strategy from unhappy, traumatic or unhealthy marriages. Marriages that are not officially registered are unlikely to be legal, so those wives often lack any rights. Children born out of such marriages may not qualify for citizenship or legal identity, especially in foreign countries. Early marriage also undercuts the ability of girls and young women to attain a formal education or receive vocational training; they may become confined to the home without any participation in public life.

Girls and young women are especially vulnerable during times of armed conflict and political upheaval because protections that exist in organized, functional societies break down. Even in countries where social protections and basic services are few and far between, the ravages of war bring extreme uncertainties and insecurities for civilians who are caught in the midst. A chaotic, new normal takes over. Daily life is entirely disrupted and family units are torn apart as violence escalates. The vulnerability of children drastically increases when they are separated from their parents because they become susceptible to recruitment as child soldiers, sex slaves, domestic servants and other forms of bonded labor. In other instances girls become the victims of intra-family femicide, otherwise known as honor killings. The Women's Refugee Commission explains, 'Honor killings are one means of handling daughters and sisters who have lost their "virtue", whether as a result of rape or through a consensual, but non-approved, relationship' (WRC, 2009, p. 10).

Worldwide, 20 million girls in conflict zones do not attend school (CARE, 2015). Not only are resources and efforts for providing education to girls in conflict-affected settings limited, but what little exists is predominantly focused on primary education. Neither donors nor relief agencies prioritize secondary schooling, which further buttresses the practice of early marriage and undervaluing girls, leaving them with little or no prospects for economic independence. In addition to literacy and numeracy skills, schools are where children and young adults get information critical to their survival regarding hygiene, clean water and energy supplies, safe sex, disease prevention and other issues. Schools also provide a routine for girls and boys that can offer a semblance of stability amidst the stark uncertainties of armed conflict. Yet in recent years schools have come under attack; this make it all the more difficult to encourage parents to send children to school.

When girls cannot attend school, as is the case for 40 percent of school-age girls in South Sudan, they miss out on what they may most need to know for their well-being. Building schools and requiring attendance for children in conflict-affected settings, however, also requires security risks to be assessed. For many refugee girls, attending school necessitates serious safety considerations, including sexual harassment or assault, especially when traveling, as they often must, long distances. Parents may prefer that their daughters stay at home in order to avoid these risks and keep their honor (i.e. virginity) intact to please potential suitors. In addition to the journey to and from school, girls are sometimes not safe within the classroom, where teachers have been reported to exchange grades and basic school supplies in return for sexual favors (WRC, 2009).

Ensuring access to education for girls despite war and displacement is effective in reducing and preventing early marriage. Yet access has many dimensions; getting to school is not sufficient. Schools and even makeshift community-based places of learning must be physically accessible at low cost and with low security risk. For students to focus, thrive and complete their course of study requires a holistic model of education. Teachers must be attentive, sympathetic and exemplary role models for their students. Gender-sensitive planning can help to ensure accessible toilets so that, during times of illness or menstruation, young women can practice proper hygiene. Lack of formal education or vocational training for girls and young women in conflict-affected settings has micro- and macroeconomic consequences. Their productive potential and purchasing power are reduced, as is their ability to participate in the formal economy and play a role in their country's labor force. At the same time, their ability to earn and retain resources – which they are most likely to invest in their children's nutrition, health and education – is also undercut. They are more likely to suffer from lack of self-confidence and become trapped in abusive marriages. The lack of education not only impacts the individual well-being and quality of life for young girls, but it also reverberates across community, national and global levels, and across generations: an educated girl will be better equipped to educate her own children.

Even after conflicts formally end, the transition to peace and stability is precarious and girls continue to deal with the emotional, physical and socioeconomic effects of war. For example, in Afghanistan in 2009, some 43 girls were reportedly injured as a result of land mines (Encyclopedia of Nations, 2009). Similarly, the UN Secretary General reported that the killing and maiming of children in Afghanistan resulting from improvised explosive devices increased 72 percent between 2012 and 2013 (UNSC, 2013). Worldwide, more than a hundred million land mines are thought to be active in some 60 countries (WRC, 2009, p. 3). Girls who are injured by land mines, bombs, shrapnel or other explosives may become unwanted or abandoned by their families. Such sociocultural prejudices need to be deconstructed, over time and through civic education. Alternative livelihoods and opportunities for self-improvement in post-conflict settings that are targeted to youth, including those who are disabled, also need to be provided so that they are not perceived as burdens.

SEXUAL ABUSE AGAINST GIRLS IN CONFLICT SETTINGS

Rape is used in times of conflict to terrorize communities, break social bonds, destroy families, and – in doing so – exerts power through fear, hatred and shame. While rape during times of conflict has existed since antiquity, it is not inevitable. It may be opportunistic or strategic but it is always an exercise of choice by the perpetrator. The International Criminal Court's Rome Statute regards rape as a war crime and a crime against humanity. The same applies to sexual slavery, enforced prostitution and forced pregnancy. Young women and girls – especially those forcibly displaced – are vulnerable to sexual exploitation and entrapment. The continued widespread rape of girls, and women, shows that this scourge of war has yet to be tackled efficiently or eradicated by the international community, despite many UN Security Council Resolutions and countless lofty speeches by world leaders. Yifat Susskind (2015) argues that no soldier will hold on to a weapon that does not work. What would be required to disarm rape as a weapon of war is a troubling question with which the international community continues to grapple (Buss, 2009).

Wartime rape of girls has acute consequences, in part because the power dynamics are particularly imbalanced, both physically and figuratively. Nordstrom (2004) argues that 'children are abused by those with more power and strength simply *because they can be*' (p. 32, italics in original). She adds: 'Many of the world's discourses on war, from Sun Yat Sen to Clauswitz, from The Seven Samurai to John Wayne, revolve around the notion of a moral contest between *equals*' (p. 32, italics in original). Children and adults are not equals and they cannot engage, in war or in peace, as equals in any interaction. Girls are particularly vulnerable, not only because they are less powerful but also because their suffering is less visible and voices are easily drowned out (Neer and O'Toole, 2014). As an instrument of war, rape is – simply put – an extremely effective means to an end.

The United Nations Security Council has stepped up its involvement in prioritizing children's issues during armed conflict. Among the important resolutions it has passed, SCR 1261 (1999) highlights protecting children from sexual abuse and including children in Disarmament, Demobilization and Reintegration (DDR). SCR 1314 (2000) emphasizes the protection of displaced and refugee populations and introduced child protection into UN peacekeeping mandates. SCR 1325 (2000) recognizes the human rights of girls and their right to protection, especially from gender-based and sexual violence, the special needs of girls in post-conflict situations, and the necessity of taking girls' rights and needs into account in designing peace agreements, camps for refugees and internally displaced persons and DDR programs. SCR 1379 (2001) calls for the naming of all countries in which abduction and forced recruitment of children is occurring.

Given weaknesses in sexual violence prevention and lack of teeth in its 2000 resolution, SCR 1820 (2008) recognizes sexual violence as a tactic of war, allowing the intervention of the Security Council; categorizes sexual violence as a war crime, crime against humanity and act of genocide, and excludes such crimes from amnesty provisions; and demands protection and prevention measures from parties in armed conflict. SCR 1820 also asked the Secretary-General for a report about the systematic use of sexual violence in conflict areas and proposals for strategies to minimize the prevalence of such acts. In 2009, the Council adopted Resolution 1888, which mandates peacekeeping missions to protect women and girls from sexual violence in armed conflict and reaffirms the commitments made in SCR 1325 and 1820. The Secretary-General's progress report, published in 2012, focused on the need to strengthen monitoring of abuses and enforce the recommendations and directives laid out in the resolutions. Noting cause-and-effect linkages between displacement and conflict-related sexual violence, the report explained that attacks can be opportunistic or strategic, including to 'extract information … during forced civilian disarmament' (pp. 4, 16–17). The report found that efforts for prevention were extremely rare, even in conflict contexts such as the Democratic Republic of the Congo, where rape was known to be rampant and used as a tactic of warfare. However, to deter perpetrators, the report emphasized the need for accountability and prosecution, including by providing extensive examples of individuals and groups known to be culpable. SCR 2106 (2013) adds more operational detail to prevent conflict-related sexual violence. The implementation of the principles and objectives in these resolutions, however, remains limited.

In 2008, the same year that the historic UN Security Council Resolution 1820 called rape a weapon of war, the UN Population Fund reported that 65 percent of victims out of some 16 000 new cases of sexual violence in the Democratic Republic of Congo (DRC) were under the age of 18 and at least 10 percent were less than ten years old (Human Rights Watch, 2009). According to the Women's Refugee Commission, 'the younger the victim, the greater the impact' (WRC, 2009, p. 5). Moreover, many rapes go unreported due to stigmas and lack of access to medical services or police protection. Gang rape is frequently committed by several groups, such as the Lord's Resistance Army in Northern Uganda, ISIS in Syria and Iraq, and M23 in the DRC. Sexual and gender-based violence, trafficking, and exploitation of girls and young women in conflict increase the spread of HIV/AIDS and other sexually transmitted diseases, and thus increase the risk of sexual infections as well as other medical conditions like fistulas. Girls and young women who are impregnated by enemy combatants often seek illegal and unsafe abortion procedures. Those who choose to keep their children are shrouded by societal stigma and marginalization. This causes even greater emotional distress to adolescent mothers; in Kosovo and Rwanda, for example, such mothers find it difficult to love and care for their children. The countless consequences of gender-based violence and rape make reintegration and reconciliation for mothers as well as the children resulting from these crimes virtually impossible.

ISIS has used mass rape as a combat strategy, a weapon to destroy its perceived enemy, as well as to motivate and reward fighters (Ahram, 2015). Girls as young as 9 years old have been abducted in groups and sold into sexual slavery (Ward and Marsh, 2006). The young women who are trapped in slave camps, sold at auction and held against their will are prisoners of war. Yazidis, an ancient religious minority found mainly in remote areas of Iraq, have been brutally targeted by ISIS because of their religious identity; more than 5000 Yazidi women and girls were abducted by 2014 (Brown, 2014). Herein, the strategy of mass rape and forced impregnation is multifold: it seeks to dehumanize and defile adolescent women and girls and is a form of ethnic cleansing. UN Special Representative on Sexual Violence in Conflict, Zainab Bangura, reported in 2015 that many girls were being sold for the equivalent of a cigarette pack (UN News Centre, 2015). Girls are not only weapons of war but they have also become tradable commodities. According to Bangura, young men, including foreign fighters, are recruited with this promise: 'we have women waiting for you, virgins that you can marry' (Agence France-Presse, 2015). Some families with the economic means have bought back their daughters from militants but most families are unable to afford the high cost.

Young women and girls are also made susceptible to rape and kidnapping due to societal roles and gender norms imposed by their communities. Around the world women and girls are responsible for collecting water and gathering firewood for their families. Women and children spend 140 million hours per day on these tasks (Water.org, 2014). In areas of armed conflict, this responsibility becomes simultaneously even more important and more dangerous. Given the risk of being killed, boys and men are not expected to venture away from shelter to collect firewood. But in undertaking this responsibility women and girls face what is perceived to be the 'lesser' threat of rape (WRC, 2009, p. 14). As displaced persons, girls and young women are vulnerable to attack in camp settings as well as urban dwellings. For instance, refugee camps are often poorly designed, without consideration for the security of girls and women; toilets sometimes are not adjacent to living quarters and they often lack locks and lights, which are essential to staving off attacks (Casey and Hawrylyshyn, 2014). Girls and young women also tend to lack the basic necessities for hygiene and sanitation, including for their menstrual cycles; this can add to the humiliation that comes with being a refugee. Traveling long distances through treacherous terrain heavily saturated with militias and armed combatants means that girls and young women become victims of opportunistic attacks. Intra-city refugees and displaced girls are also susceptible to rape, robbery, harassment and abuse, especially because they are perceived as illegal outsiders.

Abusers of girls and women are sometimes the very individuals meant to protect them in times of conflict: peacekeepers and humanitarian assistance providers. Extensive evidence, going back decades, documents sexual abuse committed by UN peacekeepers against women and girls. Save the Children's 2008 report stated that UN peacekeepers raped young girls in the Ivory Coast, South Sudan and Haiti (Csáky, 2008). Similar allegations were reported in Sudan and the Central African Republic (Lewis, 2014). Ndulo (2009) suggests that UN peacekeepers have fathered approximately 24 500 children in Cambodia and 6600 in Liberia. These crimes have destroyed local communities' trust in peace-keepers stationed in conflict zones and tarnished the reputation of certain peacekeeping operations.

The lack of accountability for UN peacekeepers who commit crimes against civilians they are meant to protect is symptomatic of an ill-equipped international justice and governance system. Given the norma-tive dimensions to this problem, such crimes are tolerated. Meanwhile, the practical dimensions include the nature of UN peacekeeping bureau-cracy, which gives responsibility for punishment to the countries that are contributing troops. UNICEF (1996) notes: 'Much of the tragedy befall-ing children is preventable ... . Brutality, violence, rape and torture – all would stop tomorrow if the will to stop them existed, or if the rest of us devised means to compel them to be stopped' (p. 6).

GIRLS AS TARGETS OF VIOLENT EXTREMISM

Violent extremism is not new but in the twenty-first century Islamic militants have dominated headlines for their multifaceted approach to achieving political ends. One key strand common to the strategies of the Taliban, ISIS and Boko Haram is the suppression of women and girls through violent and non-violent means. These groups have had devastat-ing impacts on all aspects of life for girls and young women. By severely restricting their mobility and in many cases prohibiting them from going out in public, young women and girls cannot attend school or access non-religious education. Their ability to make their own life decisions, seek employment or participate in political life is deemed unlawful. Meanwhile, violent extremist groups target girls to join their ranks through kidnapping and by luring young women from the West under false pretenses.

A young girl who is literate, capable of critical thinking, and conscious of her independent mind threatens violent extremists because she challenges their monopoly of power and oppressive ideology. Girls' schools enable entire communities to convene and access a variety of basic social services; this is essential to building resilience against violent extremism. Girls who remain uneducated under extremists' control are less capable of refusing their claim to power and much easier to convince and confine at home. Such girls are more likely to raise children who mimic the same brand of extremism. United Nations Population Fund (2012) suggests that girls without any formal schooling are three times more likely to become child brides compared to young women who have some secondary or higher education; those with primary education are twice as likely. Every year of schooling counts to deter early marriage. Young girls have been violently attacked to instill fear in others and dissuade them from pursuing education. The most famous case occurred in Pakistan when the Taliban shot Malala Yousafzai in the head on a school bus as a way to scare young girls away from the classroom. The Islamic militant group Al Shabab has attacked schools and universities in Kenya for similar reasons.

Boko Haram opposes knowledge and education: 'It is consistent with their ideology to take women and girls and deprive them of their right to education and use them as weapons of war' (GIWPS and WITW, 2015). In April 2014 the abduction of 276 schoolgirls from Chibok, Nigeria captured world headlines. The estimated total of women and girls abducted by Boko Haram in 2014 is around 2000. According to one former adolescent female girl taken captive, girls were killed en masse if they refused to follow the command of their captors to become militants, brides or slaves (Amnesty International, 2015).

The use of young women and girls as human shields or suicide bombers produces ripple effects in communities. Innocent girls become targets of mob action and vigilante justice, which furthers the agenda of extremist groups that seek to heighten insecurity and create perceived threats (Kaplan, 2015). Obiageli Ezekwesili argues that by failing to rescue and recover the Chibok girls and others like them, the world has said to every girl in troubled environments: 'You have to make a choice to either be educated or lose your life' (GIWPS and WITW, 2015). This, of course, is no choice.

Girls also may choose to become members of violent extremist groups, sometimes succumbing to local, national or international methods of recruitment. Online propaganda plays a key role in the recruitment of foreign fighters. ISIS recruiters have developed starkly different gender-specific appeals, successfully attracting young women from all over the world, including the United Kingdom[1], the Netherlands[2] and United States[3] to join their caliphate. A combination of thrill-seeking on the part of young women, false advertising by ISIS, and ideological brainwashing explains this (Bloom, 2015). Recruiters lure girls by painting a 'distorted view' of life inside the Islamic State, falsely advertising the 'joys of sisterhood' and living for a higher purpose; in reality, a 'woman's role is circumscribed for childbearing, marriage, cooking and cleaning, and they may not even be able to leave the house' (Binetti, 2015). Binetti argues that such recruiting under false pretenses could amount to human trafficking under international law.

Some women are coming together in innovative ways to prevent radicalization within their communities. Edit Schlaffer (2014) argues that galvanizing mothers is the key to preventing young boys and girls from becoming terrorists. Having surveyed more than 1000 women in six high-risk countries affected by extremism, she identifies key behavioral patterns indicating radicalization and the propensity for violent action. Equipping mothers with the know-how and listening skills to prevent or de-radicalize their children before they leave home is one of the most effective bottom-up approaches to fortifying societies against extremists (Schlaffer, 2014). As for those already radicalized, Schlaffer argues that these young women need to be recovered and rehabilitated instead of punished and isolated.

GIRLS AS CHILD SOLDIERS AND FORMER COMBATANTS

Reportedly, 40 percent of approximately 250 000 child soldiers from around the world are girls (War Child, 2015). The World Bank estimates that 12 500 girl child soldiers are in the DRC alone. They are a particularly difficult demographic to disarm, rehabilitate and reintegrate because they are less visible, and DDR programs often are not gender sensitive and tend to focus only on the needs and experiences of male combatants (Child Soldiers International, 2013).

Girls and adolescent women who voluntarily join armed groups may do so as a means to receive protection, shelter, wages, food and medical care. Their options may be so limited that becoming a soldier, wife, slave, cook, cleaner or other domestic support to armed groups is the only way to stay alive. At the same time, others are influenced by their circumstances and background to prescribe to the ideology of the armed group to which they belong. Reasons and motivations vary and can overlap but voluntarily becoming a child soldier remains a rarity because most who join are conscripted.

Both girls and boys are easy to brainwash; sex abuse can also be used as a tactic of coercion for children to commit violent acts. The Lord's Resistance Army in Northern Uganda not only conscripted girls and boys by abducting them but also required them to attack their families, friends and communities (WRC, 2009). Girls may also be coerced into committing crimes such as theft or drug trafficking and then are manipulated into a life of continued loyalty to criminal gangs and militias. Consequently, their captors not only expect girls and young women to engage in illicit activities but also consider them disposable and easily replaceable. Distinguishing here between sexual exploitation and transactional sex such as prostitution is crucial. Prostitution, as a business, requires consent. Girls and boys cannot offer consent. Delaney (2006) writes that whether a child appears to 'accept' or 'voluntarily' engages in such sexual activities is irrelevant. 'They may be tricked, deceived, or forced into it by situations beyond their control such as poverty, or as a result of societal conditions (including peer pressure) which can result in coercing a child in invisible ways' (p. 9).

In northeastern Nigeria speculation persists that some of the schoolgirls kidnapped by Boko Haram have been turned into suicide bombers (Obaji, 2015). According to UNICEF, Boko Haram has used girls as young as 10 years old as suicide bombers. As of May 2015, more than 20 such incidents were recorded (UNICEF, 2015). An investigation by Amnesty International revealed Boko Haram training camps where girls are forced to become child soldiers. One escapee reported that Boko Haram trained girls how to shoot guns, use bombs and attack a village. After three weeks of training they started sending girls on operations (Amnesty International, 2015). These girls have become instruments of insurgency manipulated by Boko Haram to carry out their violent agenda, but they are victims first and perpetrators second. In a separate report, escapees in early 2015 described instances of rampant sexual abuse and subjugation (Winsor, 2015). Sexual abuse, in other words, is also used to control girls and turn them into violent attackers.

Sister Rosemary Nyirumbe, who helps to rehabilitate girls and adolescent women previously held captive by the Lord's Resistance Army, argues that providing a purpose and livelihood to girls recovered from abductions is 'a way of mending broken lives' (Alam, 2015). When they become sex slaves and often bear multiple children from different abusers, they are deeply traumatized and emotionally distressed on multiple levels (Women in the World, 2015). Sister Nyirumbe explains that some of the girls abducted by rebels are so young that they do not recognize their captor as a criminal or abuser, but instead a potential father figure. She has developed an effective gender-sensitive, low-cost, locally grown approach to DDR that provides several resources including a new community and education. Former girl soldiers who were once trained to hold machine guns are trained to use sewing machines as a way to demonstrate how machines can not only destroy but also create (Alam, 2015).

DDR programming continues to suffer from two major challenges regarding the reintegration of women and girls: low formal registration and a lack of understanding of gendered needs and experiences (IAWG, 2012). As a result, most female combatants demobilize themselves, either with assistance from civil society groups or in some cases completely on their own, but without financial, psychosocial or medical support. This leaves women and girls, and their dependents, at heightened risk of becoming victims of human trafficking and exploitation. Gender sensitization of DDR programs and the proper resources to implement them are critical to increasing the participation of girls and adolescent women.

CONCLUSIONS AND RECOMMENDATIONS

Girls and adolescent women face heightened, sometimes unprecedented, vulnerabilities in war, bringing poverty, exploitation, homelessness and insecurity. The breakdown of social order and lawlessness that accompanies violent conflict or political upheaval can mean that customary laws and traditions, including those harmful to women and girls and perhaps contrary to existing actual laws, gain prominence amongst communities who return to what they know and trust without being held accountable to national laws. Nordstrom (1997) argues, 'The plight of war-victims, of girls sold into sexual or physical labor, of street children, and of girls harmed in their own homes and communities is qualitatively similar in many respects' (p. 1). Wartime conditions may exaggerate what they endure in the absence of violent conflict: 'What people tolerate in peace shapes what they will tolerate in war' (Nordstrom, 1997, p. 1).

Understanding the roles and experiences of girls and adolescent women in armed conflict is central to protecting them from suffering and ensuring their participation in conflict resolution. Informed intervention requires evidence, innovation and coordination. First and foremost, more research into the plight of girls and adolescent women in conflict-affected settings is critical, including for donors and humanitarian organizations. The research should include the collection of data disaggregated by sex and age in order to understand the separate needs and grievances of girls and adolescent women apart from other members of their communities. Furthermore, recording the narratives of girls in their own words is critical to developing programs that best address their needs.

Funding presents another important consideration, including, but not limited to, financial assistance to civil society and women's groups in order to address the needs and aspirations of girls and adolescent women within their own communities. Such groups are critical partners to large-scale humanitarian assistance organizations, yet often have a particularly difficult time securing funding, especially over long periods of time. Moreover, funding must be targeted in ways that increase resources for not only basic needs such as health, food and shelter but also psychosocial care, education (including secondary, post-secondary and vocational training), safe play spaces, rehabilitation and reintegration.

More effective communication and coordination between donors, humanitarian assistance providers, security professionals and development program implementers is essential. Stakeholders should leverage their respective areas of specialty in ways that complement, rather than duplicate, other actors on the ground. Gender-sensitive designs of camps for refugees and IDPs are critical to increasing the physical protection for girls and adolescent women and preventing the spread of illness or infection. Humanitarian workers should engage with and even lean on local elders and religious leaders, and appoint gender-sensitized child protection officers to protect girls from harmful cultural practices, including forced early marriage and honor killings.

The successful disarmament and reintegration of girls and adolescent women previously entangled with combatant or insurgent groups needs to prioritize access to livelihoods alongside mental health support. Programs should include accelerated learning, vocational training, financial literacy, awareness of rights, and childcare, to name but a few components that have the potential to transform lives of former female soldiers and sex slaves. Long-term social transformation and norm change that not only move past the immediate effects of war but also look towards building safer, more equitable societies require effective leadership, functional institutions and trust within and between communities. These ingredients are essential to fighting prejudices that undervalue girls and perpetuate cycles of victimization and marginalization. Rape and slavery, for example, must be recognized as criminal actions and not cultural phenomena such that accountability against perpetrators increases and stigma against survivors decreases.

Finally, non-violent means to counter violent extremism and prevent radicalization of youth deserve greater prioritization and support. Through arts, education, dialogue and public engagement, communities experiencing post-conflict reconstruction can counter violent extremism without picking up arms. A combination of these recommendations will improve the status of girls during and after violent conflict and in preventing the use of girls as weapons of war.

NOTES

1. See: 'UK "at edge of cliff" in fight to block Isis recruits, say MPs', *The Guardian*, online resource: http://www.theguardian.com/uk-news/2015/mar/26/uk-isis-recruits-advice-line-parents-mps.
2. See: 'Nations trying to stop their citizens from going to Middle East to fight for ISIS', *The New York Times*, online resource: http://www.nytimes.com/2014/09/13/world/middleeast/isis-recruits-prompt-laws-against-foreign-fighters.html.
3. See: 'Nations trying to stop their citizens from going to Middle East to fight for ISIS', *The New York Times*, online resource: http://www.nytimes.com/2014/09/13/world/middleeast/isis-recruits-prompt-laws-against-foreign-fighters.html.

REFERENCES

Agence France-Presse (2015), 'ISIS slave markets sell girls for "as little as a pack of cigarettes", UN envoy says', accessed 1 July 2015 at: http://www.theguardian.com/world/2015/jun/09/isis-slave-markets-sell-girls-for-as-little-as-a-pack-of-cigarettes-un-envoy-says.
Ahram, Ariel I. (2015), 'Sexual violence and the making of ISIS', *Survival: Global Politics and Strategy*, **57** (3): 57–78.
Alam, Mayesha (2015), 'Interview with Sister Rosemary Nyirumbe', accessed 8 August 2015 at: http://issuu.com/georgetownsfs/docs/interview_with_sister_rosemary_nyir.
Amnesty International (2015), 'Nigeria: abducted women and girls forced to join Boko Haram attacks', accessed 1 July 2015 at: https://www.amnesty.org/en/latest/news/2015/04/nigeria-abducted-women-and-girls-forced-to-join-boko-haram-attacks/.
Binetti, Ashley (2015), 'A new frontier: human trafficking and ISIS's recruitment of women from the West', *Georgetown Institute for Women, Peace, and Security*, accessed 3 July 2015 at: http://issuu.com/georgetownsfs/docs/i2a_-_isis_and_human_trafficking.
Bloom, Mia (2015), 'How ISIS is using marriage as a trap', accessed 5 July 2015 at: http://www.huffingtonpost.com/mia-bloom/isis-marriage-trap_b_6773576.html.
Brown, Katherine (2014), 'Analysis: why are Western women joining Islamic State?', accessed 7 July 2015 at: http://www.bbc.com/news/uk-29507410.
Buss, Doris (2009), 'Rethinking "rape as a weapon of war"', *Feminist Legal Studies*, **17**: 145–63.
CARE (2015), 'Women & children in emergencies', accessed 4 July 2015 at: http://www.care.org/emergencies/women.

Casey, Jean and Kelly Hawrylyshyn (2014), 'Adolescent girls in emergencies: a neglected priority', *Humanitarian Practice Network (HPN)*, accessed 1 July 2015 at: http://www.odihpn.org/humanitarian-exchange-magazine/issue-60/adolescent-girls-in-emergencies-a-neglected-priority.

Child Soldiers International (2013), 'Girl child soldiers face new battles in civilian life', *IRIN*, accessed 2 July 2015 at: http://www.child-soldiers.org/news_reader.php?id=630.

Csáky, Corinna (2008), 'No one to turn to: the under-reporting of child sexual exploitation and abuse by aid workers and peacekeepers', accessed 2 July 2015 at: http://news.bbc.co.uk/2/shared/bsp/hi/pdfs/27_05_08_savethechildren.pdf.

Delaney, Stephanie (2006), 'Protecting children from sexual exploitation & sexual violence in disaster & emergency situations', ECPAT International.

Encyclopedia of Nations (2009), 'Civilian girls injury – landmine and cluster munition monitor', from *The Landmine Contamination, Casualties and Clearance*, accessed 3 July 2015 at: http://www.nationsencyclopedia.com/WorldStats/LC3D-civilian-girls-injury.html.

Georgetown Institute for Women, Peace, and Security (GIWPS) and Women in the World (WITW) (2015), 'An interview with Obiageli Ezekwesili', accessed 1 July 2015 at: http://issuu.com/georgetownsfs/docs/an_interview_with_obiageli_ezekwesi.

Human Rights Watch (2009), 'Soldiers who rape, commanders who condone: sexual violence and military reform in the Democratic Republic of Congo', accessed 2 July 2015 at: http://www.hrw.org/reports/2009/07/16/soldiers-who-rape-commanders-who-condone.

Inter-Agency Working Group on DDR (IAWG) (2012), 'How-to guide: gender-responsive disarmament, demobilization and reintegration', accessed 30 June 2015 at: http://www.iddrtg.org/wp-content/uploads/2013/06/How-to-Guide-Gender-Responsive-DDR.pdf.

International Rescue Committee (IRC) (2014), 'Are we listening?: Acting on our commitments to women and girls affected by the Syrian conflict', September, International Rescue Committee.

Kaplan, Sarah (2015), 'Nigerian mob beats to death and burns teen girl they thought was a bomber – but likely wasn't', accessed 30 June 2015 at: http://www.washingtonpost.com/news/morning-mix/wp/2015/03/02/teenage-girl-thought-to-be-a-suicide-bomber-is-beaten-and-burned-to-death-in-nigeria/.

Lazar, Seth (2014), 'Necessity and non-combatant immunity', *Review of International Studies*, **40** (1): 53–76.

Lemmon, Gayle T. (2014), 'Child brides, global consequences', accessed 30 June 2015 at: http://www.cfr.org/children/child-brides-global-consequences/p33284.

Lewis, Felicity (2014), 'Human rights abuses in UN peacekeeping: providing redress and punishment while continuing peacekeeping missions for humanitarian progress', *Southern California Interdisciplinary Law Journal*, **23** (3): 595.

Machel, Grac'a (1996), 'Promotion and protection of the rights of children: impact of armed conflict on children', UNICEF, accessed 30 June 2015 at: http://www.unicef.org/graca/a51-306_en.pdf.

Mazurana, Dyan and Khristopher Carlson (2006), 'The girl child and armed conflict: recognizing and addressing grave violations of girls' human rights', United Nations: Division for the Advancement of Women (DAW).

McKay, Susan and Dyan Mazurana (2004), 'Where are the girls? Girls fighting forces in Northern Uganda, Sierra Leone and Mozambique: their lives during and after war', International Centre for Human Rights and Democratic Development.

Ndulo, Muna (2009), 'The United Nations responses to the sexual abuse and exploitation of women and girls by peacekeepers during peacekeeping missions', Cornell Law Faculty Publications, accessed 29 June 2015 at: http://scholarship.law.cornell.edu/cgi/viewcontent.cgi?article=1058&context=facpub.

Neer, Thomas and Mary Ellen O'Toole (2014), 'The violence of the Islamic State of Syria (ISIS): a behavioral perspective', *Violence and Gender*, **1** (4): 145–56.

Nordstrom, Carolyn (1997), *Girls and Warzones: Troubling Questions*, Life and Peace Institute.

Nordstrom, Carolyn (2004), *Shadows of War: Violence, Power, and International Profiteering in the Twenty-first Century*, University of California Press.

Obaji Jr, Philip (2015), 'The Nigerian girls who've become Boko Haram's best killers', *The Daily Beast*, accessed 3 July 2015 at: http://www.thedailybeast.com/articles/2015/05/25/the-nigerian-girls-who-ve-become-boko-haram-s-best-killers.html.

Save the Children (2007), 'Gender-based sexual violence against teenage girls in the Middle East', accessed 1 July 2015 at: http://www.essex.ac.uk/armedcon/story_id/000784.pdf.

Schlaffer, Edit (2014), 'Mobilizing civil society against IS', accessed 3 July 2015 at: http://www.huffingtonpost.com/edit-schlaffer/beyond-bombs-and-missiles_b_5937654.html.

Susskind, Yifat (2015), 'What will it take to stop ISIS using rape as a weapon of war?', accessed 5 July 2015 at: http://www.theguardian.com/global-development/2015/feb/17/disarm-isis-rape-weapon-war.

Todres, Jonathan (2009), 'Law, otherness, and human trafficking', *Santa Clara Law Review*, **49** (3): 605–72.

UN News Centre (2015), 'Feature: sold for a pack of cigarettes – UN envoy fights to help women suffering sexual violence in the Middle East', accessed 5 July 2015 at: http://www.un.org/apps/news/story.asp?NewsID=51196#.VYmfR1VViko.

UN Women (2013), 'Gender-based violence and child protection among Syrian refugees in Jordan, with a focus on early marriage', United Nations Entity for Gender Equality and Empowerment of Women, accessed 30 June 2015 at: http://www.unwomen.org/en/digital-library/publications/2013/7/syrian-refugees.

UN Women (2014), 'Facts and figures: peace and security', accessed 28 June 2015 at: http://www.unwomen.org/en/what-we-do/peace-and-security/facts-and-figures#notes2.

UNICEF (1996), 'The state of the world's children', accessed 28 June 2015 at: http://www.unicef.org/sowc96/intro.htm.

UNICEF (2015), 'Northeast Nigeria: alarming spike in suicide attacks involving women and girls', accessed 5 July 2015 at: http://www.unicef.org/media/media_82047.html.

United Nations General Assembly Security Council (2012), 'Conflict-related sexual violence', Report of the Secretary-General, accessed 30 June 2015 at: http://daccess-dds-ny.un.org/doc/UNDOC/GEN/N10/653/46/PDF/N1065346.pdf?OpenElement.

United Nations High Commissioner for Refugees (2015), 'Global trends: forced displacement in 2014', accessed 6 July 2015 at: http://unhcr.org/556725e69.html#_ga=1.225701913.2095888809.1417795315.

United Nations Population Fund (UNFPA) (2012), 'Marrying too young: end child marriage', accessed 5 July 2015 at: http://www.unfpa.org/sites/default/files/pub-pdf/MarryingTooYoung.pdf.

United Nations Security Council (UNSC) (2013), 'Report of the Secretary-General on the protection of civilians in armed conflict', accessed 28 June 2015 at: http://www.securitycouncilreport.org/atf/cf/%7B65BFCF9B-6D27-4E9C-8CD3-CF6E4FF96FF9%7D/s_2013_689.pdf.

War Child (2015), 'Child soldiers', accessed 4 July 2015 at: http://www.warchild.org.uk/issues/child-soldiers.

Ward, Jeanne and Mendy Marsh (2006), 'Sexual violence against women and girls in war and its aftermath: realities, responses, and required resources', United Nations Population Fund (UNFPA), Brussels.

Water.org (2014), 'Women', *Water Facts*, accessed 28 June 2015 at: http://water.org/water-crisis/water-facts/women/.

Wijeyesekera, Rose (2011), 'Assessing the validity of child marriages contracted during the war: a challenge in post-war Sri Lanka', Annual Research Symposium, University of Colombo.

Winsor, Morgan (2015), 'Boko Haram rescue: pregnant women, girls among those found in Sambisa Forest by Nigerian army', accessed 6 July 2015 at: http://www.ibtimes.com/boko-haram-rescue-pregnant-women-girls-among-those-found-sambisa-forest-nigerian-army-1906965.

Women in the World (2015), 'Sister Rosemary Nyirumbe: the woman who saved thousands from Joseph Kony', *YouTube*, accessed 10 June 2015 at: https://www.youtube.com/watch?v=t9daaB1Xkhk.

Women's Refugee Commission (WRC) (2009), 'Peril or protection: the link between livelihoods and gender-based violence in displacement settings', Women's Refugee Commission.

11. Gender and the economic impacts of war
Joyce P. Jacobsen

What are the possible economic impacts on humans of war, and why and how might they vary by gender? Neither economists nor other social scientists have given much attention to how war, which inevitably involves destruction of both human and physical assets, has lasting economic effects. A devastated society may need many years to return to its pre-war level of gross domestic product. However, war also often involves a wholesale reinvention of the affected society or societies. In this chapter I first consider the types of destruction that can occur and how they can affect women and men (and girls and boys) differently. I then examine historical cases whereby the reinvention of society following conflict has led to very different outcomes for women (generally considered relative to men) than they had experienced before hostilities began.

THE ECONOMIC EFFECTS OF WAR

War does not so much change a country's social or economic system as it involves destruction of assets and a temporary (albeit in some cases lengthy) increase in the level of violence in the country or society. What types of destruction occur, and how might they affect women and men differently?

War-related deaths, whether as a direct result of battle or as an indirect result of various systemic breakdowns during or following hostilities (including from higher levels of disease and inadequate treatment of chronic and acute illness), are the ultimate form of destruction. People who have died as a result of the conflict are no longer available to work (whether in the market or non-market sectors of the economy). War clearly can result in the deaths of both men and women. Nevertheless, men tend to bear the brunt of the death count, just as they do during 'normal' violence; fatality statistics show that men are significantly more likely to murder and be murdered (Jacobsen, 2002, p. 11). This tends to have significant effects, including, in some cases, on the postwar gender ratio. For example, many years after the Second World War the Soviet population still had a very low ratio of men to women; in 1999 it had only 31 men to every 100 women among those aged 65 and over (Jacobsen, 2002, Table 19).

For those lucky enough to survive, war-related disabilities can reduce their ability to participate in both paid and unpaid work. These can include both physical disabilities, such as loss of one or more limbs, and mental disabilities, including post-traumatic stress disorder. Again, men are more likely to suffer such disabilities from direct hostilities in the war because they are more likely to engage in combat. However, Ghobarah et al. (2003) find that women and children were disproportionately affected by death and disability attributable to the indirect and lingering after-effects of civil wars in the 1991–97 period, which increased specific diseases and medical conditions. As one example, the spread of HIV increases as a result of war, generally starting with mobilized males but eventually spreading to women and children. Untreated HIV, with its high rates of infection among working-age adults, is particularly destructive of productive capacity. More generally, war can lead to unanticipated but costly physical and mental changes for individuals that diminish their ability to participate fully in economic activity and to reach the pre-war levels of well-being after the war.

War also tends to depreciate other assets besides labor, because capital, land and other productive inputs – and the markets in which they are traded – are disrupted. While non-fixed capital tends to move out of disrupted countries, fixed capital (buildings and infrastructure such as roads, bridges and electrical and communications lines) cannot. For example, according to Hoeffler and Reynal-Querol (2003, p. 5), around forty percent of fixed capital in the agricultural, communications and administrative sectors of Mozambique was destroyed as a result of the 1977–92 civil war, and in the first Liberian civil war (1989–96) all major infrastructure was damaged. To the extent that women own fewer such assets than men and are less likely to engage in productive activities that utilize infrastructure, they may be less likely to suffer the direct effects of this depreciation. However, since women and men interact in families, women still suffer the indirect effects from depreciation of family assets. More research is needed on the relative effects by gender of the destruction of houses, factories, agricultural fertility and other productive assets.

Even if assets are not damaged or destroyed, when owners and users are separated from these assets they are then unable to make productive use of them during this period of separation. Moreover, the assets may require renovation and upkeep when the owners and users return. For example, farmers cannot tend their farms if they are displaced, and thus can easily miss whole crop cycles as well as suffering livestock losses. Persons displaced by conflict, whether refugees or internally displaced, appear to suffer disproportionate and substantial losses relative to the non-displaced. For example, in the case of civil conflict in Colombia, which has been ongoing since the 1960s, a 2000 survey finds that welfare losses from displacement are 37 percent of the net present value of rural lifetime aggregate consumption, with female-headed households slightly more likely to undergo displacement (Ibáñez and Vélez, 2008). Ibáñez and Moya (2010) find that labor income declines by 50 percent in the year after displacement. However, this is another area in which more research is needed to consider the relative effects by gender of displacement related to separation from productive assets.

Another aspect of war-related disruption is the disruption of skills acquisition (which can occur both for the displaced and the non-displaced). Both formal and informal education can be disrupted during wartime. Ironically, to the extent that men may have been more likely to participate in formal education, this disruption can then affect them disproportionately. For instance, the collapse of the education system during the 1975–79 Khmer Rouge regime in Cambodia (which can be thought of in part as a protracted period of civil war) meant that those who were of school age during that time had lower educational attainment than the preceding and subsequent cohorts; men were particularly affected, perhaps because they were more likely to attend school in general than were women (De Walque, 2006). Similarly, Justino et al. (2015) find some evidence of higher educational attainment in post-war Timor Leste by women who had been of school age during the earlier period of conflict; overall they find some evidence of increased female empowerment, but the indicators are mixed. Overall, it is hard to say whether boys or girls are affected more by schooling disruptions; one survey/symposium finds it depends significantly on the particular armed conflict context (Buvinić et al., 2014).

War may also lead to the development of 'bad', that is, destructive, skills in lieu of productive skills. For instance, training in military techniques (including extreme ones such as torture) does not have obvious productive uses, and may well make it much more difficult for such trainees to transit to civilian life. Again, while this seems like a more likely scenario for men (as the main participants in military training), more research is needed regarding the gendering of non-productive labor.

There is possibly some offset of depreciated and disrupted skills if productive skill development comes from maintaining a standing military, or if capital development for war has some peacetime value. There is also some potential offset if newer capital acquired as replacements after the war supplants less productive, older capital (particularly if outside funds are used to help rebuild, since countries affected by civil war or outside aggression would have less rather than more funds available for capital investment). Again, research is needed regarding gender differences in access to and realization of these offsets.

Wartime labor market phenomena appear to be the most studied impacts regarding the effects of war on women. These can be both direct effects on labor markets by which war affects the demand for and supply of female labor, but also indirect effects through demographic changes, that is, through the supply of and demand for marriage and children and changes in the structure of households. In particular, by causing relatively high rates of war-related death and disability for men, war tends to increase both the supply of and the demand for female labor and thus increases women's participation in paid labor. Exceptions to this tendency are cases where labor markets are so disrupted by war that the overall participation of the population in paid labor drops sharply.

The demand effect is that women are effectively regarded by employers as substitutes for men. When men are in short supply due to their increased level of military participation during wartime, employers increase their demand for women's labor. This demand effect is particularly likely in those occupations and industries that are normally male-dominated, including heavier forms of manufacturing. Thus, women's occupational distribution is predicted to change during wartime along with their increased participation in paid work, with many more women entering non-traditional occupations. This also means that the absolute earnings of women, in general, increase, although their earnings relative to those men remaining in paid civilian work need not rise. This is particularly so if the men who join the military are disproportionately drawn from the lower-paid men in the civilian labor force, which one might expect in voluntary rather than draft circumstances.

The supply effect comes from several sources. In wartime, married women will have less income available to their household from their husband or partner. This can be because the husband is dead or disabled or away fighting, or because the husband is less able to find productive work or utilize fully his productive assets during wartime. Thus women will be interested in engaging in paid work to compensate in part for this loss of household income. Women may also have reduced non-market work responsibilities during wartime when their husbands (and possibly other family members) are away. This frees up time for them to spend in paid work. Some women may, however, have increased non-market/household responsibilities if they have to care for more dependents in the absence of other able-bodied workers. This extra housework burden may be picked up partly by those women less likely to enter or re-enter the workforce, such as elderly women and young girls. Other women, due to postponed or preempted marriage as fewer marriageable men remain in their area, again have more freedom to work outside the home because they have fewer household work responsibilities while they stay single. The supply of female labor for paid work is also increased through reduced fertility rates, at least during wartime (since some may be postponed fertility rather than preempted fertility). This occurs both through the postponement or preemption of marriage and, for those women already married, the absence of the husband. Thus, again, women's non-market work responsibilities will generally be lightened with fewer children to care for, freeing up more of their time to take on paid work. Economic theory therefore tends to support the premise that women will participate in greater numbers in paid labor during wartime, subject to the caveat that there is sufficient labor demand (that is, functioning labor markets).

A final consideration regarding productive capacity that predominantly affects women is wartime rape and increased trafficking in sex. As the *Economist* (2011) documents, while rape is as old as war itself, the increased reporting of the crime has made its scale more apparent, as well as its associated damages. In addition to unwanted pregnancies, women experience physical and emotional scarring that can make engaging in productive work difficult. The fear of rape and the desire to avoid it can also lead to additional displacement of populations and thus indirectly further reduce productivity. A more complicated issue is increased incentives for prostitution during wartime; while compulsory prostitution and other forms of sexual slavery are clearly negative, the economics of prostitution are such that women often engage in it because they are unable to earn comparable money otherwise. Thus, while high rates of prostitution signal a lack of viable alternative options for women to earn money, they also provide some needed funds during times of social breakdown such as war. This is a difficult issue to analyze that again requires more research from a feminist perspective.

MEASURING THE ECONOMIC EFFECTS OF WAR

While the previous section listed inclusive categories of effects of war that can lead to societal costs, an ongoing research challenge is calculating the extent of these costs. Data limitations abound, particularly given the difficulty of carrying out systematic data collection during wartime in affected countries. The effects of war are generally going to be negative for most people involved, although some individuals may prosper as markets for their services expand during conflict, such as wartime racketeers and others who do relatively better in black markets and other less lawful situations. Still, the average economic effects of war can be measured for individuals, households and whole societies. These measurements are often of negative matters, such as income and earnings drops and casualties, but can also be neutral or mixed measures, such as changes in female labor force participation rates, and changes in occupational and industrial gender segregation.

While some economists have attempted to measure the overall costs of war on affected countries, these estimates have not been calculated separately for different demographic groups. Nonetheless, these estimates show that war results in substantial losses to the economy; for instance, in the case of civil war, the average costs are in the range of 1 to 3 percent lower growth in per capita real gross domestic product per annum (Ra and Singh, 2005; Hoeffler and Reynal-Querol, 2003; Imai and Weinstein, 2000; Collier, 1999).

Regarding gender differences in impact, more attention has been paid to the relatively neutral or mixed measures of women's labor force participation. While women have always participated in wartime mobilizations, this was either a relatively routine part of their activities in highly belligerent societies or ongoing periods of sustained warfare, or was more limited due to the smaller scale of war (or its confinement to the military rather than civilian population). The US Civil War, with its large scale, sustained length and high proportion of male population involvement, did see more significant changes in women's participation patterns, including women's entry into previously male-dominated occupations. During the First World War, women in Britain participated significantly in the wartime mobilization, working by the thousands in munitions factories and by the millions in many other paid and volunteer positions. However, formal agreements with the British trade unions required women to withdraw from many skilled positions after the war to return those positions to male veterans. In addition, many women worked as military nurses and in other support positions such as stenography and telephone operation. Most other countries' labor markets were less affected in these ways than Britain's so that women's formal work involvement was less noted in them.

The scale of the Second World War and the large degree of involvement for many countries led to a large shift in gendered employment patterns during that war. In the US, as men were conscripted and the production of war-related goods increased, women entered manufacturing in large numbers. War industries hired 1.3 million women of the 2.5 million who entered the labor force for the first time, as well as hiring about 700 000 out of other industries (Chafe, 1972, p. 142). Non-family child care became available for the first time on a widespread basis, because factories producing war-related products established round-the-clock child care centers so that women could work full time. Women's wages rose relative to male wages and occupational sex segregation diminished temporarily as women entered higher-paid manufacturing jobs and an increased number of military support positions (Milkman, 1987).

Many European countries involved in the Second World War experienced similar patterns of increased female labor force participation as well as female participation in the war effort. While the participation statistics for these countries are not as thorough as those available for the US, women's participation in military functions can be documented for many countries, including in front-line positions in the Soviet Union. German women served in the domestic defense corps, although German women were also urged to produce children for the Reich, so their labor force involvement was more limited than in the US.

On the demographic front, the Second World War caused a large drop in marriage and fertility rates during the war years, followed by a substantial rise in both directly following the war, as well as a sustained baby boom for the next decade and a half. Hence the indirect effects on female labor force participation through lowered marriage and fertility during the war did not appear to be sustained.

While the overall scale of recent civil wars in smaller countries is smaller than for a world war, the relative economic impact can be much larger on the particular country. In the case of a civil war, all effects are concentrated in one country, and a large proportion of the country's population can be directly affected. On the other hand, those fleeing from a civil war may find it easier to move to an unaffected area outside the country than those trying to escape the more widespread violence resulting from a world war. The circumstances of a civil war may therefore allow for some strategic migration and also potentially lead to different migration patterns by gender.

Again, most studies of the economic effects of post-1945 conflicts have not placed particular focus on their gender-differentiated effects. An important exception is Menon and Rodgers (2011), who studied in depth the effects of Nepal's 1996–2006 civil conflict (Maoist-led insurgency) on women's employment. They found that in 2001 and 2006, women were significantly more likely to be working, both in formal employment and self-employment, than at the beginning of the conflict period. This finding is consistent with the economic theory as outlined above whereby one would predict an increase in women's work participation, conditional on sufficient labor demand. Rena (2007) considers the 1961–91 war of independence in Eritrea. During this conflict women were increasingly likely to become the head of household and to participate in the economy, but they are still clustered in the lower-productivity and lower-status occupations. But reduction in the numbers of men caused fertility to decline substantially in Eritrea over the last few years of the twentieth century, although whether this will lead to a sustained drop in fertility is unclear (Blanc, 2004). De Walque (2006) found in the case of Cambodia that fertility and marriage rates recovered quickly from their very low levels during the Khmer Rouge era, in part because the age and education differences between partners declined to offset the shortage of eligible men.

Researchers have drawn attention to the pattern that more recent conflicts have been resulting in substantial numbers of displaced civilians and human trafficking. These displacements and trafficking disproportionately affect women and children (Akee et al., 2010). Regarding the civil war in Bosnia and Herzegovina during the early 1990s, where some 1.3 million people were displaced, Kondylis (2010) finds that displaced Bosnians are less likely to be working relative to their compatriots who stayed, and that, while displaced men have higher unemployment levels than non-displaced men, displaced women are more likely to leave the labor force altogether. On the other hand, Alix-Garcia and Bartlett (2015) find reduced unemployment rates for young women entering the labor market in one of the conflict cities in Sudan.

Overall, we know very little about the extent of economic impacts during wartime and the relative costs borne by women and girls relative to men and boys. One hopes more gender-disaggregated calculations of the costs of war will be generated (including for past conflicts that have not yet been studied).

ECONOMIC EFFECTS IN THE AFTERMATH OF WAR

The discussion above concentrates on economic effects that occur during the war itself, or in its immediate aftermath. But the more interesting research problem may be trying to estimate the longer-term effects of wars on affected countries and individuals. These would include a number of observables, including demographic effects as discussed above (marriage market changes, changes in fertility patterns) and permanent alterations in labor and other factor markets, including permanently-raised levels of female labor force participation (through either the direct effect of its increase during the war, or through the indirect effects on demographic variables). Postwar changes may be temporary or sustained, such as fertility drops that may either be largely offset by increased fertility after hostilities cease, or that signal a significant social shift downwards. For instance, an increased female labor supply might persist after the war ends for many of the same reasons that it increased during the war: fewer non-market responsibilities due to fewer men; fewer marriages; fewer children. For instance, in cases such as Russia, where the male population was decimated during the Second World War, one might predict that this would cause long-lasting changes in economic outcomes through both direct and indirect effects. The goal would be to calculate the long-term effects of war, for instance whether it alters economic growth rates for many years after the war ends, and, if so, by how much. Studying whether the economic balance between women and men becomes permanently altered following conflict would also be useful.

In addition to these continued direct and indirect effects that are comparable to the phenomena discussed above that occur during war, war can serve as the agency of change in gender relations in more systemic ways. First, either during war or in the aftermath of war, women and men (and children) may be exposed to new ideas that lead either to changes in preferences or changes in social norms. For example, as a result of their wartime work experience, women may discover that they both like and have the ability to do different types of work than they had traditionally performed. In addition, men may discover that women can do new types of work that they had not previously thought that women could do. Thus the very novelty of war and the changes that it forces can be an agent for change as women and men are pushed out of their usual roles into new unfamiliar roles, forcing involuntary 'learning by doing' and learning by observation as well. For example, the iconic 'Rosie the Riveter' image from the Second World War implies the very strength of women in taking on a traditionally male job and performing it well, thus providing positive reinforcement of a new, expanded view of women's capabilities for both women and men to see.

Second, war may lead to redistribution either towards or away from women. This can be as an outcome of changes in the political or social systems, but also as an indirect effect through changes in factor/input markets, particularly the labor market. For example, if women increase their labor force representation and move into higher-paying jobs and occupations as a consequence of having entered the labor force during the war, then they may end up with relatively better economic outcomes relative to men after the war. They may also de facto increase their representation due to the continued absence of men (due to casualties, migration or imprisonment) after the war. This appears to have happened in the Soviet Union after the Second World War. On the other hand, redistribution could easily turn against women as well. For instance, if women are more likely to be displaced than men, they may lose relatively more access to productive assets such as land and cattle and thus end up with an inferior economic status relative to men. Also, to the extent that women are highly dependent on male partners' incomes, the loss of these incomes during the war can be hard to replace and will tend to make them worse off. Of course, men are also worse off then. It therefore becomes a race to the bottom to see which group ends up being hurt more. This race to the bottom appears particularly likely in cases where large groups are displaced during wartime, such as in a number of recent African conflicts.

A third possibility is that, through the destruction of older structures and institutions in society, women will become in general either better or worse off. Improvements in women's situations might be particularly likely in cases where the older societal structure is patriarchal. Thus, a situation where no particular structure is being enforced at all can be preferable to the continuation of the prewar structure, because women might experience greater economic and social freedom. For instance, the mid-twentieth century in China was a period of political fragmentation before Mao took over, but women's position still probably improved relative to the older (pre-1912) dynastic regime. Alternatively, of course, if the social structure were relatively gender-equal, then women might be worse off if these structures are destroyed. The loss of rule of law may be particularly problematic for women, who may therefore be more likely to be victims of domestic violence and rape in the absence of legal retribution for their attackers. For instance, continuing unrest in Zimbabwe makes the enforcement of laws improving women's land rights very difficult to achieve.

Finally, the imposition of new structures and institutions in society may result in women becoming in general either better or worse off. Note that this can involve the replacement of a previous structure or the introduction of a new system into a void caused by war in which no particular social structure was enforced. Many would consider the 1979 revolution in Iran, leading to the deposition of the Shah and the installation of the current Islamic republic under Ayatollah Khomeini, as a major setback for women's political and economic status. The Afghan civil war provides a similar example. On the other hand, the subsequent removal of the Taliban government in Afghanistan resulted in an improvement in women's status (although not yet back to the levels experienced, at least by upper class, highly educated women, before the civil war).

So theoretically, as a consequence of war, gender equality could increase, decrease or display little or no change depending on whether the older or newer structure is more or less paternalistic, and on the overall direction of redistribution between the genders due to both direct and indirect effects on factor markets. Since theory provides no strong predictions regarding outcomes, examining the historical record to see what has happened following various wars and considering the factors that make it more or less likely that women will be positively affected is crucial.

Exactly which preconditions have more likely positive outcomes for women following conflict is not yet clear. Meintjes et al. (2002) argue that gender equality must be facilitated during conflict in order to lead to more favorable outcomes in the post-conflict phase. Also, is it unclear whether dynamics internal to a country are significantly affected by outside intervention during the modern era. Peksen (2011) argues that unilateral foreign military interventions may be prone 'to diminishing women's status by encouraging the persistence or creation of repressive regimes and contributing to political disorder' (p. 455). Actual empirical work appears to show that US interventions reduce women's political and economic status; non-US unilateral interventions appear to have little effect; and intergovernmental organization interventions are likely to have a positive effect on women's political rights. However, military interventions generally do not have a major impact on women's social rights.

ECONOMIC EFFECTS IN THE AFTERMATH OF WAR: MEASUREMENT

As with calculating the extent and distribution of costs during war, another research challenge is calculating the ongoing costs and potential benefits following a war's conclusion that can be attributed either to the war directly or to the regime change that it may have entailed. Similar measures of particular types of effects can be used, including changes in income and earnings, and changes in female labor force participation and work segregation. This too is a severely under-researched area in economics. A range of case study-based evidence is indicative of some outcomes for particular countries, but no overall calculation of when and why net effects are positive or negative on women relative to men is yet available.

Again, given data limitations, researchers often focus on phenomena that are more easily observed but do not yield an exact calculation of gains or losses. For instance, one observable phenomenon is the opening of new occupations to women, particularly if they were barred by law or hiring practice prior to wartime. For example, the US Civil War labor shortage led to the first hiring of female clerks as government employees (Davies, 1982). Among domestic workers, the substitution of African Americans, both male and female, for white workers also increased after the Civil War (Bertaux, 1991).

Due to the size and extent of the Second World War, the post-1945 period entailed a major adjustment in those countries that had been heavily involved in the war. In the US, the end of the war did lead to wholesale reduction of female industrial employment, both voluntary and involuntary, as men returned from their wartime roles, but in states with greater mobilization of men, women continued to work more after the war (Acemoglu et al., 2004). For example, the late 1940s and early 1950s marked an apparent return of women to the home, with a drop in age at first marriage and rise in fertility. Other trends that had been present before the war's onset continued and even accelerated, however, including the rises in divorce and married women's employment. While the majority of wartime entrants to the labor market exited between 1944 and 1950, half of all married women who were working in 1950 had also been working in 1940, and half of the married women who entered the labor force in the 1940s did so after the war (Goldin, 1991). Thus the view of this period as a watershed in gender relations (cf. Chafe, 1972, p. 195) has come into question, with other commentators contending that the rise in women's labor supply after the Second World War is due primarily to longer-term factors, including increases in opportunities for women in clerical employment and education (Goldin, 1991, p. 755). Indeed, the decade-to-decade trend in women's labor force participation shows no particular blip related to the Second World War but rather a steady increase from 1930 to 1960 (and beyond), with women's labor force participation at 22.0 percent in 1930, 25.4 percent in 1940, 30.9 percent in 1950, and 34.9 percent in 1960 (Jacobsen, 2007, Figure 14.1). Meanwhile the gender–wage ratio remained fairly constant at around .60 or lower over the mid-twentieth century, so relative demand for women's labor apparently did not outstrip supply. Overall indices of occupational gender segregation also remain fairly constant throughout this period. Apparently the increased demand for women's labor arose more in the growing areas of clerical and office work rather than in the manufacturing sector, so increased numbers of women workers did not increase the gender integration of the workforce.

An interesting contrast to the post-1945 US case of increased work participation for women is found in Germany (particularly the Western part). Germany was heavily bombed during the Second World War, with an estimated forty percent of the total housing stock destroyed nationwide. Since many of the men were gone (dead, wounded, or still returning from prison camps), it fell mainly to women to begin the reconstruction process, including the arduous task of removing the rubble. Mandatory work brigades were set up for able-bodied women to aid in the removal. Akbulut-Yuksel et al. (2011) explore the differences in city-level destruction in Germany and show that, in the longer run, this postwar mandatory employment actually reduced women's labor force participation and hours worked, although it also increased the female presence in mid-skill, female-intensive occupations. The authors hypothesize that the mental and physical exhaustion from working in such challenging conditions, as well as postwar increases in marriage and fertility rates, help to explain these phenomena.

Meanwhile several other countries experienced significant regime changes after 1945 as a direct result of the war and its immediate aftermath. In particular, the formation of the eastern European bloc under the mantle of socialism led to very different gender relations in a number of affected countries. The postwar leaders of Eastern European nations, China, and post-1959 Cuba all proclaimed the goals of complete equality of men and women before the law and women's economic independence through employment outside the home. This was a striking regime change to the prewar systems in these countries.

In Russia, which experienced a significant shortage of men (not only because of the Second World War but also the Stalinist purges of the 1930s, the First World War, the 1917 Russian Revolution, and the later Stalinist purges), women made major inroads into the crafts and professions. However, their earnings ratio still did not rise noticeably, nor was it higher than in Western Europe.

East Germany, however, which also operated under socialist rule, did notably better in terms of closing the gender gap. In contrast both with non-socialist West Germany and with socialist Russia, East Germany had higher labor force participation rates by women in the decades following the Second World War (up through the end of the socialist era in the early 1990s) and women were much less likely to work part-time than their Western European counterparts. Women attained high educational levels and their employment had a broad occupational and industrial distribution. These conditions appear to have been enabled to a large degree by the heavy use of state-provided child care and other support services that replaced women's traditional non-market activities. Preschools and nurseries were widely available, and many services, including laundry and hot meals, were available at workplaces. While women in East Germany worked long hours in the combined pursuits of paid work and non-market work, the East German system nonetheless managed to reconcile their dual pursuits more effectively than the other socialist nations (Jacobsen, 2007).

In socialist China, major social reorganization began after the 1949 revolution. While aspects of the reorganization, such as farm collectivization, were hard on everyone, it would be difficult to argue that women in China were worse off than before the Communist regime came into power. Again, the relatively widespread availability of child care, the establishment of paid maternity leave and improvements in health care and education for women, as well as a general doctrine of gender equality, were all innovations relative to the traditional patriarchal Chinese system.

Cuba is a final interesting case regarding the post-revolution socialist experience. Here, women's labor force participation rose substantially following the 1958–59 revolution. Fidel Castro spoke of freeing women from domestic slavery so that they could participate in production so as to benefit themselves and the country; he followed up on that with universal education, government provision of child care, and legislation regarding gender equality. Again, it is hard to argue that women in Cuba are worse off than before the regime change relative to men, even if Cuba's relatively low overall economic status has been an outcome of its socialist stance and the resulting US embargo.

More recent conflicts have provided more cases of potentially negative effects on women than in the immediate post-1945 era. Some wars have resulted in a clearly more paternalistic regime, such as in Afghanistan and Iran. The cases where this has been related to installation of a Muslim fundamentalist regime indicate a misreading of Islam, which is not inherently patriarchal. Cases such as Afghanistan perhaps indicate a reversion to an older tribal patriarchal structure, such as is found among the Pashtun, which was in abeyance until after the Soviet military intervention in Afghanistan in the 1980s. Afghanistan is a complicated case; because it has experienced a series of wars, attributing effects to any one conflict or action is difficult.

At any rate, these varying case studies indicate the impossibility of arguing that war, in its role in bringing on regime change, is necessarily either positive or negative for women in the long run. This holistic view of conflict also complicates efforts to calculate the overall net effect of war on either men's or women's well-being, since war is inherently multidimensional and redistributional along many dimensions. Nevertheless, narrowly viewing conflict as an isolated event which is unmistakably bad, rather than as an unfortunately sometimes necessary evil in bringing regime change, leads to a concomitantly narrow assessment of the gendered impacts of war.

CONCLUSION: MUCH REMAINS TO BE STUDIED

This taxonomy of possible effects and overview of partial evidence leads to the conclusion that much remains to be studied about the economic impacts of war and how these vary by gender. To the extent that research on this topic exists, it is fragmented across academic disciplines and published in various sources, so tracking down results is difficult.

On numerous related areas little to nothing has been written, leaving many important topics still virtually unconsidered. For instance, little is known regarding the effects of the rise of black markets during war and the gendered redistributional effects through this mechanism, as well as the potential increase in importance of non-market production and its potentially different effects on men and women. Both of these mechanisms may actually raise the economic importance of women relative to peacetime due to women's higher specialization in non-market production (which may be to a degree compatible with participation in black markets as well).

Third party attempts to mitigate negative changes from war have received little or no evaluation; for example, the gendered effects of spending time in refugee camps, or of being resettled (but see Kaiser's chapter, this volume, for a discussion of forced migration). While some recent literature criticizes humanitarian aid on several grounds (that it prolongs conflicts, promotes dependency, may help undeserving parties, is subject to waste and duplication of services), this literature does not focus on gender or women *qua* women, in their roles as either providers or recipients (Rieff, 2002; Terry, 2002; Polman, 2010).[1]

More broadly, the ongoing opportunity costs of militarization have received little current public debate: what is not funded because resources are dedicated to war and to maintaining standing armies? Militarization has certainly been a topic of important feminist research (cf. Enloe, 2000), but much of this discussion has not reached the general public. Nor have economists taken this topic to heart (although peace economics has been an ongoing subfield in economics since at least the mid-1950s). A variety of suppositions could be explored regarding what a demilitarized society might instead spend its resources upon, and whether such a society might be a more favorable place for women. Many women and men are likely to expect that it would be if, for instance, government funds were redirected to provision of other public or private goods.

Thus, the only real conclusion that can be drawn at this point is that war is a complex phenomenon whose gendered implications have been understudied. Perhaps the next generation of researchers will give more thought to developing a systematic framework for evaluation of the distributional effects of war across demographic groups, as well as working towards the lessening of war's ill effects on all persons through the process of attaining world peace.

NOTE

1. Rieff (2002) does mention in passing that some humanitarian groups did not want to support the Taliban in Afghanistan because the Taliban suppressed women's rights.

REFERENCES

Acemoglu, Daron, David H. Autor and David Lyle (2004), 'Women, war, and wages: the effect of female labor supply on the wage structure at midcentury', *Journal of Political Economy*, **112** (3): 497–551.

Akbulut-Yuksel, Mevlude, Melanie Khamis and Mutlu Yuksel (2011), 'Rubble women: the long-term effects of postwar reconstruction on female labor market outcomes', IZA Discussion Paper No. 6148.

Akee, Randall K.Q., Arnab K. Basu, Nancy H. Chau and Melanie Khamis (2010), 'Ethnic fragmentation, conflict, displaced persons and human trafficking: an empirical analysis', IZA Discussion Paper No. 5142.

Alix-Garcia, Jennifer and Anne Bartlett (2015), 'Occupations under fire: the labour market in a complex emergency', *Oxford Economic Papers*, **67** (3): 687–714.

Bertaux, Nancy E. (1991), 'The roots of today's "women's jobs" and "men's jobs": using the index of dissimilarity to measure occupational segregation by gender', *Explorations in Economic History*, **28** (4): 433–59.

Blanc, Ann (2004), 'The role of conflict in the rapid fertility decline in Eritrea and prospects for the future', *Studies in Family Planning*, **35** (4): 236–45.

Buvinić, Mayra, Monica Das Gupta and Olga N. Shemyakina (2014), 'Armed conflict, gender, and schooling', *World Bank Economic Review*, **28** (2): 311–19.

Chafe, William H. (1972), *The American Woman: Her Changing Political, Economic and Social Roles 1920–1970*, Oxford University Press.

Collier, Paul (1999), 'On the economic consequences of civil war', *Oxford Economic Papers*, **51** (1): 163–83.

Davies, Margery W. (1982), *Women's Place is at the Typewriter: Office Work and Office Workers 1870–1930*, Temple University Press.

De Walque, Damien (2006), 'The socio-demographic legacy of the Khmer Rouge period in Cambodia', *Population Studies*, **60** (2): 223–31.

The Economist (2011), 'Violence against women: war's overlooked victims; rape is horrifyingly widespread in conflicts all around the world', 13 January.

Enloe, Cynthia (2000), *Maneuvers: The International Politics of Militarizing Women's Lives*, University of California Press.

Ghobarah, Hazem Adam, Paul Huth and Bruce Russett (2003), 'Civil wars kill and maim people – long after the shooting stops', *American Political Science Review*, **97** (2):189–202.

Goldin, Claudia D. (1991), 'The role of World War II in the rise of women's employment', *American Economic Review*, **81** (4): 741–56.

Hoeffler, Anke and Marta Reynal-Querol (2003), 'Measuring the costs of conflict', Working Paper, Centre for the Study of African Economies, Oxford University.

Ibáñez, Ana María and Andres Moya (2010), 'Vulnerability of victims of civil conflicts: empirical evidence for the displaced population in Colombia', *World Development*, **38** (4): 647–63.

Ibáñez, Ana María and Carlos E. Vélez (2008), 'Civil conflict and forced migration: the micro determinants and welfare losses of displacement in Colombia', *World Development*, **36** (4): 659–76.

Imai, Kosuke and Jeremy Weinstein (2000), 'Measuring the economic impact of civil war', *CID Working Paper No. 51*, Center for International Development, Harvard University.

Jacobsen, Joyce P. (2002), 'What about us? Men's issues in development', Working Paper, World Bank.

Jacobsen, Joyce P. (2007), *The Economics of Gender*, 3rd edn, Blackwell.

Justino, Patricia, Marinella Leone and Paola Salardi (2015), 'Does war empower women? Evidence from Timor Leste', Evidence Paper No. 121, Institute of Development Studies, University of Sussex.

Kondylis, Florence (2010), 'Conflict displacement and labor market outcomes in post-war Bosnia and Herzegovina', *Journal of Development Economics*, **93** (2): 235–48.

Meintjes, Sheila, Anu Pillay and Meredeth Turshen (eds) (2002), *The Aftermath: Women in Post-Conflict Transformation*, Zed Books.

Menon, Nidhiya and Yana van der Meulen Rodgers (2011), 'War and women's work: evidence from the conflict in Nepal', Policy Research Working Paper No. 5745, World Bank.

Milkman, Ruth (1987), *Gender at Work: The Dynamics of Job Segregation by Sex During World War II*, University of Illinois Press.

Peksen, Dursun (2011), 'Foreign military intervention and women's rights', *Journal of Peace Research*, **48** (4): 455–68.

Polman, Linda (2010), *The Crisis Caravan*, Henry Holt.

Ra, Sungsup and Bipul Singh (2005), 'Measuring the economic costs of conflict', Asian Development Bank Working Paper Series No. 2.

Rena, Ravinder (2007), 'Women in Eritrea: reflections from pre- and post-independence period', *Indian Journal of Labour Economics*, **50** (2): 357–70.

Rieff, David (2002), *A Bed for the Night*, Simon & Schuster.

Terry, Fiona (2002), *Condemned to Repeat?* Cornell University Press.

12. The war comes home: the toll of war and the shifting burden of care[1]

Alison Howell and Zoë H. Wool

The difficulty of military deployments always extends beyond the battle-field; when units deploy, local consumer economies suffer, families must adjust to life without loved ones and with the knowledge of the danger those in the military may be facing. When service members return, they may bring physical and emotional pain back with them, exacerbated by the new daily rhythms their families have had to forge in their absence. The US military's post-9/11 engagements in Iraq and Afghanistan are taxing service members and their families like none before. One key reason for this is that, since the end of the draft in 1973, the military has increasingly drawn from portions of the US population disenfranchised by class, race and gender, including an increasing number of women. Over 200 000 women have served in the post-9/11 wars, compared to approximately 7000 during the Vietnam War and 41 000 during the 1991 Persian Gulf War (National Center for Veterans Analysis and Statistics, 2011: 1). Women now comprise about 15 percent of active duty forces (Office of the Deputy Assistant Secretary of Defense, 2013: 16). These marginalized groups are incentivized by the promise of stable work and the educational and health benefits that accrue from military service. All this means that veterans are now increasingly returning home to disenfranchised communities.

The nature of recent wars also registers on the homefront in a unique way. The deployments necessitated by America's militarized response to 9/11 are not only dangerous, but are also longer and more frequent than those of previous wars. The increasing pace of military operations necessitated by the US's militarized response to 9/11 – the operations tempo or what is euphemistically referred to as OPTEMPO – is taking an unacceptable toll at home on both service members and their families. As General Peter Chiarelli, the Army's Vice Chief of Staff, put it:

> We now must face the unintended consequences of leading an expeditionary Army that included involuntary enlistment extensions, accelerated promotions, extended deployment rotations, reduced dwell time and potentially

diverted focus from leading and caring for Soldiers in the post, camp and station environment. (Chiarelli, 2010: iii)

The summary of a Leadership Summit on Military Families noted consensus among participants that service members and their families are experiencing severe strain due to wartime deployments: 'The length and frequency of these deployments and lack of sufficient dwell time for recovery and reintegration has no parallel in the history of the modern all-volunteer force, or in the extent to which they tax Reserve component families' (Booth et al., 2009).

In addition to the more acute physical and emotional wounds, service members must upon their return manage with uneven access to services. They face the challenge of readjusting to the rules, expectations and pace of life at home and repositioning themselves in a social network that has shifted over the year or more they've spent in a war zone. Families who have struggled to persevere – scrambling for childcare, rearranging work schedules, trying to find social supports often in the absence of any family – must readjust to the presence of a loved one who may have been profoundly transformed by war and who may be unwilling or unable to explain that transformation. The honeymoon period that follows home-coming all too quickly gives way to frustration, fights and the fracturing of intimate relationships.

All these factors contribute to a potent home front mix of tense family relationships, physical and emotional pain, and, increasingly, drug and alcohol abuse and other risky behavior that imperils the safety at home for both service members and their families (Johnson et al., 2007). The consequence is to make military communities as a whole more precari-ous, meaning that both service members – especially soldiers and Marines who see the most combat – and civilian family members are subject to cycles of anxiety and trauma.

The effects of combat exposure, an increasingly common fact of life for service members in the post 9/11 era, are clear and lasting. Effects such as criminality, alcohol use, marital problems, mental illness and reduced life span are most pronounced in families that were already in precarious situations due to a wide array of socio-economic and health-related factors endemic to the largest, lowest ranking sectors of military communities (e.g., problems related to debt, financial illiteracy, alcohol and cigarette abuse, all of which are linked to military service and exacerbated by combat deployment) (Johnson et al., 2007; MacLean and Elder, 2007; Baker et al., 2009; Chiarelli, 2010; Bondurant and Wedge, 2009; Bray and Hourani, 2007; Pyle et al., 2007). In short, even when service members survive the immediate violence of combat, its lingering effects can be dangerous, even deadly, for them and their communities at home.

HOMICIDE AND VIOLENT CRIME

Concerns have long been expressed about the ways in which US service members who face the killing and dying of war might be broken by this and bring some form of it back with them, imperiling themselves and those around them at home.

The New York Times drew on this scenario in its 2008 series 'War torn', which described 121 murders committed by veterans of the wars in Iraq and Afghanistan (Alvarez and Sontag, 2008). Evidence shows that violence has increased in military communities (Chiarelli, 2010; Millikan et al., 2012; USACHPPM, 2009), especially in the Army, whose soldiers are most regularly exposed to protracted violence in the post 9/11 era, and among service members exposed to combat (including those without post-traumatic stress disorder (PTSD) diagnoses) (Jakupcak et al., 2007; Elbogen et al., 2010). Nonetheless, things are much more complicated than this image of the battle-broken veteran running amok would make it seem.

Since the invasion of Iraq in 2003, rates of violent crimes such as rape, murder, aggravated assault, and aggravated sexual assault have been increasing in the Army, with the steepest jump in 2007–2008 (Millikan et al., 2012). Sexual offences committed by active duty soldiers tripled after the 2003 invasion of Iraq (Chiarelli, 2010). Excluding incidents dealt with through the Army's internal informal investigation procedures,[2] 74 646 offences were recorded in FY 2009 (Chiarelli, 2010).

But this picture of criminality can too easily lend itself to a simplistic vilification of monstrous soldiers, ignoring the specific conditions of military life occasioned by the unsustainable pace and relentless violence of post-9/11 military engagements. To complicate the picture, consider: 16 997 of the FY 2009 sexual offences noted above were related to drug or alcohol abuse, which is connected both to soldiers' self-medicating with illegal drugs and alcohol and the military's attempts to medicate service members in order to manage their combat-induced anxiety, depression and pain. One third of all soldiers take a prescribed medication and 14 percent of them are taking heavy duty prescription painkillers (Chiarelli, 2010: 72). Rates of desertion (going AWOL, deserting, or missing movement) have more than doubled in the post-9/11 era, increasing by 234 percent since 2004 (Chiarelli, 2010).

Recent research with soldiers returning from Iraq and Afghanistan shows that soldiers exposed to violent combat, intense human trauma, or who kill another person are more likely to engage in a wide array of risky behaviors, including alcohol abuse and verbal and physical aggression, putting both themselves and those around them in danger (Killgore et al., 2008: 1119; Jakupcak et al., 2007). That is, the *violence of war* is precisely what puts civilians and returned service members at risk of violence at home. The 2009 case of Ft Carson is instructive, with its news of a horrifying cluster of brutal murders and acts of violence at Ft Carson (Philipps, 2009). Soldiers were killing and trying to kill strangers, girlfriends, each other and themselves. It was a perfect storm of military violence come home to roost: trained to kill, and repeatedly exposed to some of the bloodiest fighting in Iraq, soldiers came home to inadequate or negligent mental health services, a macho attitude that stigmatized help-seeking, and a command structure that turned a blind eye to how soldiers reproduced the intensity and violence of war at home, often fueled by drugs and alcohol. From 2005–2008, 14 soldiers at Ft Carson were involved in 11 homicides. One of them also killed himself (USACHPPM, 2009).

The news accounts sometimes were sensationalized, unintentionally implying that *all* soldiers have been subjected to a kind of moral deprogramming that makes them both deadly and pitiable. Such sensational accounts easily lost sight of the institutional facts, including that a third of all staff positions in the post's medical center behavioral-health unit were unfilled in 2007, when the base was experiencing an all-time high in PTSD cases (Smith, 2009). Meanwhile, the Army[3] made the issue *individual* background and behavior rather than the impact of military life and war experience; the Army primarily grounded the violence in 'individual predisposing factors, such as prior criminal behavior, drug or alcohol abuse'; 'environmental factors' such as combat were relegated to the background (Garamone, 2009).

What the original series of stories about the problems at Ft Carson was intended to show was that the exigencies of post-9/11 military life create a cascade of stress and trauma, subjecting the home front to the violence of war. The military repeatedly tries but fails to create new and better programs and techniques to deal with problems as they see them – everything from new sections of the Uniform Code of Military Justice to punish substance abusers more harshly and swiftly, to better record-keeping of incidents of sexual assault. But the record shows that these problems are a function of the militarized response to 9/11 in all its complexity: service members exposed to combat trauma and away from home too often and for too long; civilian spouses scrambling to hold families together in their absence; stresses and strains redoubled when deployments end and service members and the military look for quick fixes in drugs and alcohol.

The point is not that violent post-9/11 deployments do not contribute to violence and crime at home. Both research and common sense say they do. Rather, the point is to emphasize the various ways that the militarized response to 9/11 eats away at the lives of service members and their families. And none of these can be clearly comprehended in isolation.

VIOLENCE IN MILITARY FAMILIES

Domestic violence in military families has long been a concern, indeed, an increasing concern given the pace of post-9/11 deployments. Since 1999, Congress has been pushing the military to provide better resources and keep more reliable information about such violence.[4]

Nonetheless, a 2010 Government Accountability Office report complained that the military has been both unwilling and unable to do what needs to be done regarding domestic violence in the military. The Department of Defense (DoD) agreed only to three of seven GAO recommendations following a Congressionally mandated 2006 report on domestic violence in the military (US Government Accountability Office and Farnell, 2010: 4). One of the DoD's fundamental failures, as this GAO report pointed out, is its inability to keep consistent or reliable track of incidents of violence in its own service communities. This complicates attempts to track the specific impact of the militarized response to 9/11 on violence in military homes and between members of military families. But even the Army has noted that its rates of domestic abuse have skyrocketed, increasing 177 percent since 2003 (Chiarelli, 2010).

Research on the impact of deployment on military domestic violence rates in the pre-9/11 military showed that deployment need not necessarily lead to increased rates of domestic violence when service members return home (McCarroll et al., 2003). But the longer the deployment, the more likely is domestic violence (McCarroll et al., 2010). Transitions around deployment are especially difficult and cause spikes in spousal abuse rates, so the repeated deployments required by post-9/11 OPTEMPO exacerbate these dangerous patterns (Lutz, 2008). Again, the research indicates that longer, more frequent, and more dangerous deployments in the post-9/11 era are especially dangerous for military communities.

In Army families with previously substantiated cases of child abuse, the deployment of a parent led to increased rates of child maltreatment. The impacts were greatest when, after deployment of the father, civilian mothers were left to care for their children alone, after their fathers were deployed. Compared to when soldier fathers were home, this caused three times the rate of child maltreatment, four times the rate of child neglect, and nearly double the rates of physical abuse (Gibbs et al., 2007).

Service members exposed to combat may develop problems with substance and alcohol abuse as they seek to manage both the physical and emotional pain they continue to feel once they return. Because heavy drinkers in the Army are 66 percent more likely to abuse their partners (Bell et al., 2004), and alcohol abuse is a significant factor in suicides and dangerous high risk behavior, the increased exposure to war violence cannot be separated from the traumas in military families and communities. When service members exposed to the horrors of war attempt to manage their pain with alcohol or easily-accessed prescriptions, they imperil not only their own lives, but those of their family and community members.

BROADER IMPACTS ON CHILDREN

Beyond visible forms of violence and neglect in the homes of service member parents, the current shape of the military and the pace of deployments is having myriad negative effects on children. As of 2009, approximately 2 million children had one or more parents in the US military, and most of the children of active duty service members are 7 years of age or younger. In 2007 some 700 000 children had least one parent on deployment (APA, 2007: 4) and one year later more than 2 million American children had a parent who either was deployed or had been deployed in Iraq and Afghanistan (Chartrand et al., 2008). Many have lost a parent, or have had a parent return home wounded (National Center for Children in Poverty, 2010). These children are disproportionately from racialized communities, and as many as one in four may be depressed (Flake et al., 2009).

Among children of deployed service members, 32 percent were classified as at 'high risk', as compared to 18 percent in a peacetime survey of military families. A majority of parents surveyed reported that their children had trouble sleeping (Munsey, 2010) and many reported their children had problems at school, such as dropping grades, decreased interest and conflict with teachers (Flake et al., 2009). The problems these children experience at school are compounded by the frequent changes of school required by their parents' service: in 2009, the average military child could expect to need to change school systems between six and nine times between kindergarten and 12th grade (Military Child Education Commission, 2006). Few children of active duty service members attend Defense Department schools; the majority attend public schools (Department of Defense, 2010a).

The war has had a serious impact on the mental health of the children of service members. According to the *Marine Corps Times*, among children in military families, outpatient mental health visits doubled between 2003 and 2008, and psychiatric hospitalization for severe problems such as suicide attempts rose sharply (Hefling, 2009; Flake et al., 2009). In general, longer parental deployment was associated with higher rates of mental health problems in children. These problems are intensified among National Guard and Reserve service members who are called for duty, since they are less integrated into military social support networks. Moreover, military families cannot readily meet their childcare needs. In 2009 the military estimated that 37 000 military children needed but could not get childcare spaces (National Center for Children in Poverty, 2010).

SUICIDE

Suicide rates in the military have historically been lower than those in comparable segments of the civilian population, largely because the military recruitment process screens for the most significant forms of pre-existing psychological dysfunction including depression. America's militarized response to 9/11 changed that. Since 9/11 the suicide rate among civilians the same age and gender as the military population has remained steady at around 18 (suicide rates are calculated as deaths per 100 000 people in the population). In 2002 suicide rates across the Department of Defense began increasing from a previously steady rate of around 10. In 2003, when Iraq was invaded, suicides across the DoD accounted for more deaths than combat (Chiarelli, 2010: 15). Despite suicide awareness campaigns across the services, suicide outnumbered combat deaths again in 2008 (Chiarelli, 2010). By 2009, DoD-wide rates were approaching 20; in the Marines and Army, who face the worst and most direct combat in post 9/11 deployments, suicides are even greater. Based on 2004–2007 data, male veterans were twice as likely as their civilian counterparts to commit suicide (Kaplan et al., 2007). Female veterans under 35 were more than three times as likely to commit suicide as their civilian counterparts (McFarland et al., 2010).

The Department of Defense knows that deployments are bad for mental health, that repeated deployments make it worse, and that 'dwell time' between deployments is no solution. The 2010 Report of the Department of Defense Task Force on Suicide Prevention concluded that the number of forces is 'not sufficient to meet operational requirements *and* maintain the well-being of the force' (McFarland et al., 2010: 73). While the DoD regards this as an issue of 'supply and demand im-balance' (McFarland et al., 2010), if dwell time cannot solve the problem, neither will increasing 'supply', thereby exposing more Americans to the traumas of war. The only solution lies on the 'demand' side of this equation.

To soldiers, post-combat talk-therapy with counselors and therapists or chaplains who haven't been to war is often seen as futile: the gulf of understanding is too wide. Soldiers may resent how well-meaning counselors and therapists claim to understand what war is like. And research and policy recommendations consistently suggest that PTSD services are the most effective when provided within hours of traumatic events. The Army also knows that its lauded COIN (Counterinsurgency Operations) doctrine which, among other things, brings troops into the civilian population, makes providing adequate care harder. In 2008 the Army acknowledged that when soldiers were moved to smaller bases so that they could maintain closer contact with Iraqi civilians and security forces, they were farther from care providers at large bases (Harben, 2008).

To help manage this irresolvable problem of COIN operations, chap-lains, who are largely responsible for providing mental health services in the Army,[5] have been sent into combat zones with service members. This may give soldiers quicker access to counseling but imperils the lives of chaplains and can have unintended consequences. In 2010, Capt. Dale Goetz became the first chaplain killed in combat since Vietnam. A soldier who regarded Goetz as a friend and confidante cited his death as one factor that led to his depression and eventual mental breakdown; as a result, he shot and killed an Afghan prisoner he was supposed to be guarding (Perry, 2010). Moreover, the moral authority of chaplains can be a charismatic force, glossing over soldiers' moral and mental prob-lems. In 2003, profoundly disturbed after killing a civilian in Iraq, an Army Scout was apparently told by his chaplain to imagine 'I did it for God and Country ... . I'm a kind of tool of God' (Gutmann and Lutz, 2010: 132–3).

The alternative, and one increasingly supported by military and civilian researchers, is to ignore complexity and focus only on biological phenomena. This implies treating war trauma with drugs or attempting to 'prevent' it by means of everything from playing the video game Tetris (Laney, 2010) to monitoring biological markers of stress (Steinberg and Kornguth, 2009). Soldiers would be exposed to the same kinds of violence and trauma but their brains would not manifest the patterns researchers have identified as problematic. The patterns they *would* manifest are anyone's guess. This research, which focuses almost exclusively on PTSD – a diagnosis which is itself persistently hazy – suggests a bleak future if the post-9/11 military deployments continue: the 'solutions' and 'cures' such research provides suggest legions of American men and women sent into combat and treated as little more than collections of biometric markers, subjected to brain scans, medication and visual stimuli that keep their biochemical levels within predetermined ranges.[6] While this might eliminate PTSD, it is ethically indefensible.

While rates of disorders such as PTSD may be a canary in the coal mine regarding the lasting impacts of war at home, the almost exclusive focus on PTSD as the cause of suicide and other forms of violence in military communities is badly misplaced. Between 2005 and 2009, only 9 percent of soldiers who committed suicide had been diagnosed with PTSD and just over half had no behavioral health diagnosis at all (Berman et al., 2010: 17). And, as the 2010 Army report on suicide prevention rightly noted, assumptions about a single clear and easily fixable relationship between combat connected mental disorders and suicide grossly underestimate the problem's scale and complexity (Chiarelli, 2010). A 2009 study of the San Diego VA system found that when PTSD was (re)defined to include depression and clinical levels of substance and alcohol abuse, 64 percent of Iraq and Afghanistan veterans were suffering mental health problems (Baker et al., 2009) of the kind that increase suicide risk. The study also found that exposure to trauma and branch of service determined the likelihood of these diagnoses, rather than age, gender, race or rank (Baker et al., 2009). Perhaps most insidiously, failed and failing intimate relationships are the most consistent factor in military suicides, implicated in 65 percent of suicides across the forces (Berman et al., 2010). This pattern provides a damning link between suicide and the many family strains caused by the breakneck speed of post-9/11 OPTEMPO.

Reserve forces, on whom current deployments depend like never before, may feel the strains of combat more intensely than active duty components. For example, in the months after returning from Iraq, 42 percent of reservists needed mental health treatment, compared to 20 percent of active duty soldiers. Suicide rates among active duty troops across the forces are, however, more than double those in reserve components (Berman et al., 2010: 41).[7]

These patterns reflect the intensity and uneven social distribution of trauma as a consequence of America's militarized response to 9/11 as well as the failure of suicide prevention programs that have been in place for years. Moreover, researchers cannot pinpoint clear causes or predictors of suicide in the military, not because of poor research but because the complexity of the problem is not reducible to isolable causes or quick fixes.

DIVORCE

In 2005 many print and broadcast news stories reported the steady increase in the post-9/11 era in divorce rates among active duty military. The conventional wisdom was that military marriages were a casualty of increased deployments required by the military response to 9/11. In 2007, a RAND corporation meta-analysis substantially complicated the picture of deployments that destroy marriages, finding that longer deployments did not lead to higher divorce rates (Karney and Crown, 2007). Even so, divorce rates increased after 2001 for all active duty populations (except Navy men), with increases being especially large for women in the military.[8] The upshot of the RAND report was that deceptively straightforward metrics like divorce rates hide at least as much as they show.

For both enlisted and officers and across all branches of the military, the percentage of marriages that end in a given year has been steadily increasing in the military since 2000. For example, in 2000, 1.4 percent of officer marriages and 2.9 percent of enlisted marriages ended in divorce while in 2009, those numbers were 1.8 percent and 4.0 percent (Department of Defense, 2010a: 45). Rates among Naval reserve officers have skyrocketed in the post-9/11 era, reaching 6.5 percent in 2009 (Department of Defense, 2010a: 105). Among people married to active duty military members, 54.3 percent are 30 or younger and half of all military spouses are not employed, which means they are often dependent on their military spouses for both financial and social support (Department of Defense, 2010a: 56–7). Women service members are less likely to be married but many times more likely to get divorced than male service members (Department of Defense, 2010a). Enlisted personnel are more likely both to consider divorce and to actually get divorced than officers (Millikan et al., 2012; Karney et al., 2007; USACHPPM, 2009).

Explaining changes in divorce rates and finding their causes is much more complicated than counting them. Cautioning that absence of divorce is not necessarily proof of happy marriage, the 2007 RAND report indicated that exposure to *combat* (not just deployment), which is increasingly the case in the two post-9/11 counterinsurgency wars, does correlate with marital problems. And the post-9/11 increased deployment taxes segments of the service with new intensity, including the Reserves, National Guard and women service members. Because of this, *husbands* of service members and spouses of reserve component service members face new kinds of challenges and a lack of institutional resources to meet them.

What divorce rates hide are the manifold impacts of deployment on families. For example, a 2010 study (Lester et al., 2010) shows that while civilian spouses are themselves most distressed when their spouses are deployed, children of deployed parents show increased anxiety that continues after the parent returns. That is, the damage to families caused by deployment is cumulative, compounding, lasting. It is trackable in rates of anxiety: 24.7 percent of children of currently combat-deployed parents experienced anxiety, but the number was 31.9 percent for children whose parents had recently returned (Lester et al., 2010: 314–15).

Many service member spouses describe the dread that strikes them every time the phone rings, knowing that the voice on the other end could be bearing earth-shattering news. Service members do not often discuss the horrors of war with their family members, sparing them the full knowledge of the horrors of war, but also straining the intimacy that may once have existed. Such 'protective' silence may also contribute to service members' reluctance to seek help in dealing with war trauma. The alternative is not necessarily better: telling family members about combat can be traumatic for them and may add to their fear for their absent partner or parent. These strains are also felt by the deployed service members, and the longer the deployment, the more likely service members are to think about their marriages ending (USACHPPM, 2009). Even simple questions from loved ones – 'how are you' – put soldiers in ethical quicksand: tell the truth and burden your family, or lie about the things that weigh the heaviest on you to the people you love the most.

THE SHIFTING BURDEN OF CARE FOR 'INVISIBLE INJURIES'

Perhaps more insidious than endemic physical injuries and ailments that afflict returning service members, the burden of care associated with these mental health problems constitutes one of the central but invisible effects when the war 'comes home'. Accessing adequate, appropriate and timely mental health care remains difficult for many returning service members and veterans. In 2007, an American Psychological Association task force reported that, despite extensive study, they were 'not able to find any evidence of a well-coordinated or well disseminated approach to providing behavioral health care to service members and their families' (APA, 2007). Since then, several studies have shown that despite some improvements, fundamental gaps in the adequacy and quality of care as well as institutional barriers to access to care remain (Tanielian and Jaycox, 2008). Who bears the burden of care for armed services members experiencing difficulties as a result of their deployments? The answer: *Military policies and programs are increasingly working to offload the burden of care for the mental health of service members.* The burden of care has been shifted onto armed forces members themselves; their peers; and civilians and civilian organizations, including families, especially wives, children and, by extension, schools and communities. These groups are enlisted in doing unpaid work to take up the slack that results from the systemic inadequacy of care provided by the military and the VA.

MAKING ARMED FORCES MEMBERS RESPONSIBLE: INDIVIDUALIZING SYSTEMIC PROBLEMS

Members of the armed forces frequently are either denied appropriate mental health diagnoses, or misdiagnosed. This occurs often for the purposes of denying their claims to medical and disability benefits. The well-documented tendency to deny PTSD diagnosis in order to curb compensation claims became especially controversial with the release of the 'Perez email' in March 2008: A PTSD program coordinator sent an email stating: 'Given that we are having more and more compensation seeking veterans, I'd like to suggest that you refrain from giving a diagnosis of PTSD straight out'. Until recently, veterans were required to provide documentation showing that a particular event was at the root of their diagnosis before getting treatment. Whether recent policy changes designed to make getting the diagnosis (and therefore access to services) easier will have a positive impact remains to be seen (Martin, 2010).

Additionally, in many cases armed forces members have been diagnosed with pre-existing 'Personality Disorder' (PD): such diagnoses have been used to discharge soldiers without paying them disability or medical benefits. Since 2001 more than 22 600 soldiers have been discharged with PD (Vietnam Veterans of America, 2010). Armed forces members have been retroactively diagnosed with a purportedly pre-existing personality disorder, despite the standard psychological screening of enlistees. In these cases, because PD is deemed to be a pre-existing condition, the military is not deemed responsible for medical treatment; those diagnosed with the disorder are then also denied access to disability pay, and may be made responsible for paying back a part of their enlistment bonus, often thousands of dollars. This process has relied on a diagnostic sleight of hand designed to cut costs: although several veterans' organizations protest about this state of affairs (Kors, 2007), the diagnosis of PD had saved the military at least $12.5 billion by 2011 (Vietnam Veterans of America, 2010).

Both the misapplication of the diagnosis of PD and the frequent denial of the diagnosis of PTSD indicate a continuing serious systemic and persistent problem: it makes members of the armed forces who have experienced mental, and in some cases accompanying physical injuries, responsible for their own care.

THE TROUBLE WITH RESILIENCE AND PREVENTION

Military policies and programs have increasingly responded to pervasive mental health problems among members of the armed forces less by improving service provision than by turning to new models of resilience and mental fitness. The 2010 Army *Health Promotion, Risk Reduction, and Suicide Prevention* report (Chiarelli, 2010), for example, praises the new Army Comprehensive Soldier Fitness program. This program involves instructing soldiers in how to become resilient in the face of stressors. Members of the armed forces are inundated with messages about being responsible for their own stress reduction, mental fitness and ability to grow from the crucible of combat. In military terms, prevention is seen as 'proactive' and therefore better than a 'reactive' response.

Self-help and responsibility may carry positive meanings in neoliberal civilian contexts. In military contexts policy, however, shifts towards self-help, cognitive behavior therapy or positive psychology are problematic. When this kind of 'proactive' response is figured as an alternative to 'reactive' responses, medical, psychological and psychiatric care come to be treated as a negative outcome: treatment is reduced to being 'reactive', and necessary only when service personnel fail to be responsible for their own mental health.

MAKING SYSTEMIC PROBLEMS APPEAR INDIVIDUAL

Like the misdiagnosis of PD, and the failure in many cases to diagnose PTSD, preventive resilience and mental health programs work to make systemic problems appear individual. It is the individual soldier who is meant to be mentally fit and resilient. Yet this is not simply a matter of equipping soldiers to deal with problems, but an attempt to place the responsibility for mental and physical injuries on the service members themselves. Preventive models that exhort armed forces members to be resilient are simply cheaper than the costs associated with providing adequate care. This cost-effectiveness, however, shifts the burden of care onto service members themselves.

Notably, the military is a government employer. No other government or major civilian employer can expose their workers to severely unsafe work conditions and then demand employees to seek self-help and resilience training, rather than providing compensation for injuries sustained on the job. At a minimum, the military should be held to these standards.

MAKING PEERS RESPONSIBLE – 'SHOULDER TO SHOULDER' IN THE CONTEXT OF INADEQUATE SERVICES

In September 2010 the Army launched its Suicide Prevention Month with the theme of 'Shoulder to shoulder: I will never quit on life'. Colonel Deborah Grays described how the theme promotes the dual responsibilities of suicide prevention:

> Our pledge to be there for each other and our obligation to do everything we can to help ourselves ... . It's important to remember that while steps are being taken at all levels of the military to prevent suicides, the most effective level lies with individuals. It's imperative that we look out for each other. (Grays, 2010)

Her words reflect the wider military approach to mental health: the demand for soldiers to self-care, outlined above, is coupled with a demand for their peers to be vigilant about the mental states of their fellow service members. One US Army Medical Department Behavioral Health poster reads: 'Never let your buddy fight alone. Be willing to listen. Not all wounds are visible. Prevent suicide: It is your responsibility to get help for a fellow soldier'.

Getting help for a fellow soldier, however, is difficult in the context of inadequate service provision. Making peers responsible for suicide prevention displaces the burden of mental health care provision from trained professionals in the military to armed forces members themselves experiencing difficulties, and their peers.

MAKING FAMILIES AND COMMUNITIES RESPONSIBLE: THE UNBALANCED BURDEN ON WOMEN

In the absence of adequate support and care for service members experiencing mental distress, one of the major costs of the war is to their families, to communities, and to civilian agencies and non-governmental organizations. Military policy is increasingly asking military families to be responsible for the care of returning soldiers, in effect enlisting families, and especially spouses, as unpaid caregivers. Family members, in turn, pay with both their earning ability and their mental well-being.

This is a matter of intentional policy and programming. Therefore, for example, in 2009 the DoD began an extensive strategic planning process to enhance 'family readiness programs' (Department of Defense, 2010b). Families are systematically being called upon to do unpaid work in the name of supporting their loved ones, but for the express purpose of force multiplication: that is, rendering armed forces personnel fit for potential redeployment. The military expressed gratitude for the service provided by families and communities, but it does not pay for this service, and amplifies the highly gendered burden placed on families and communities by failing to provide adequate services. This voluntary, civilian and informal service therefore represents a significant and often unrecognized external cost of the wars in Afghanistan and Iraq in particular.

The cost is paid disproportionately by women. As of 2009, over 200 000 active duty service members were women, while over 1.2 million were men. More military men are married than military women. As a result, women comprise approximately 93 percent of spouses of active duty service members, and approximately 86 percent of spouses of reservists (Department of Defense, 2010a). The burden of the war for military spouses means a burden disproportionately borne by women. When the military discusses the importance of 'family support' for returning soldiers, it is primarily asking for unpaid care work from women. The work they do takes its toll, both emotionally and financially.

Women's status as military spouses, involving as it does significant unpaid labor as well as frequent involuntary relocations (approximately half of the spouses of active duty service members experienced a permanent relocation of their family as a result of their spouse's military commitments during 2007 and 2008 alone) has a significant impact on these wives' ability to earn a living. According to a recent comprehensive study, even though military wives are, on average, younger, better educated and more likely to live in a metropolitan area than their civilian counterparts, they are less likely to be employed and more likely to be seeking work than civilian wives; when they are employed, they are likely to be paid less than comparable civilian women (National Defense Research Institute, 2004).

The data regarding their mental health are even more dramatic. Data collected immediately following the onset of the wars in Afghanistan and Iraq (Mansfield et al., 2010) showed that 37 percent of women with deployed husbands had at least one mental health diagnosis. According to the National Institute of Mental Health, some 24 percent of wives of deployed husbands suffer depression, as compared to 9 percent among women nationally. Rates of disordered alcohol and drug use were nearly 50 percent higher among wives with husbands who had deployed, compared to those whose husbands had not. All of these problems were significantly greater among wives of junior enlisted service members (Mansfield et al., 2010).

Moreover, almost half of parents whose military spouses have deployed report 'clinically significant' parenting stress, and around a third report psychological problems in their children (Flake et al., 2009). This stress is one of the major factors in diffusing psychological problems into children of deployed service members. The 2009 DoD Quadrennials Quality of Life Review states that 'the Nation appreciates the sacrifices made by military members and their families' and 'acknowledges the heightened importance of families, *who also serve*, particularly during times of war and heavy deployments' (Department of Defense, 2009; emphasis added). Families serve, however, in ways that are most often unpaid, and when such help is figured as a resource in military policy, it becomes a cost of the war that is intentionally transferred onto families.

Military planning seeks not only to use the unpaid labor provided by spouses, who are most often women, but also by civilian communities, charities and non-governmental organizations. For example, the 2009 'Plans for the Department of Defense for the support of military family readiness' report identifies the needs of reservists and those living in civilian communities as particularly pressing, but identifies families and civilian resources as central assets to meet these needs. One of their recommendations is to 'harness community resources'. Among these are the 'Network of Care' program, which locates local civilian support and resources for service members, veterans and their families; and the 'Community Capacity Building' program that, according to the DoD, seeks to 'integrate existing resources provided by governmental and non-governmental entities into a comprehensive and sustainable system of support for military families living in civilian communities' (Department of Defense, 2010b).

The shifting of the burden of war onto civilians – whether families, communities, or the governmental, non-governmental and charitable sectors – is an express military policy. When the military seeks to enlist civilian services to provide the extra support necessitated by the war, it offloads its responsibility to service members, their families and their communities, and makes their support instrumental of broader military strategy. The costs of this support are made invisible in military budgets, making such support one of the hidden gendered costs of the heavily militarized response to 9/11.

NOTES

1. This chapter was originally published, with the same title, as part of the Costs of War project, and has been edited. The Costs of War project includes a series of ongoing reports detailing the costs of the United States' decision to respond to the 9/11 attacks with military force in Afghanistan, Iraq and Pakistan. The projects seeks to foster democratic discussion of these wars through full accounts of their human, economic and political costs, and to foster better informed public policies. Details are at: www.costsofwar.org.
2. These include investigations initiated under Army Regulation 15-6, which may or may not lead to formal charges and which need not include formal written complaints. The results of these investigations are only filed at the post where the investigation occurred and are not attached to soldiers' permanent records (unless they lead to formal charges or reprimand) or filed in any central database (Chiarelli, 2010: 47). If cases dealt with under AR 15-6 investigations were included, these numbers would undoubtedly be higher.
3. This response included a 2008 epidemiological consultation and subsequent 2009 report on the factors that led to the violence.
4. For example, in 1999, Congress mandated that the Secretary of Defense keep a database of domestic violence incidents involving members of the armed forces.
5. The use of chaplains is in tension with data from a 2010 Department of Defense survey finding that 25 percent of service members claimed no religious preference.

6.   See, for example, the 2009 special issue of *Military Psychology* on 'sustaining soldier high operations tempo performance' (Steinberg and Kornguth, 2009).
7.   In 2009 the suicide rate in active duty forces was estimated to be 20.3; for reservists it was 8.6 (Berman et al., 2010). The picture is different still when looking at the Army alone: active duty soldiers were overrepresented in Army suicides in 2009 (57 percent of suicides, but only 40 percent of the total Army) (Chiarelli, 2010: 18).
8.   This information came from comments made at the 2009 National Leadership Summit on Military Families made by Dr Rachael Mapes, Special Assistant for Policy, Planning, and Evaluation to the Deputy Under Secretary of Defense.

REFERENCES

Alvarez, Lizette and Deborah Sontag (2008), 'When strains on military families turn deadly', *New York Times*, 15 February, accessed 1 September 2015 at: http://topics. nytimes.com/top/news/us/series/war_torn/index.html.

APA (American Psychological Association) (2007), 'The psychological needs of US military service members and their families: a preliminary report', Presidential Task Force on Military Deployment Services for Youth, Families and Family Members, February, APA.

Baker, Dewleen G., Pia Heppner, Niloofar Afari, Sarah Nunnink, Michael Kilmer, Alan Simmons, Laura Harder and Brandon Bosse (2009), 'Trauma exposure, branch of service, and physical injury in relation to mental health among US veterans returning from Iraq and Afghanistan', *Military Medicine*, **174** (8): 773–8.

Bell, Nicole S., Thomas Harford, James E. Carroll and Laura Senier (2004), 'Drinking and spouse abuse among US Army soldiers', *Alcoholism: Clinical and Experimental Research*, **28** (12): 1890–97.

Berman, Alan, John Bradley, Bonnie Carroll et al. (2010), *The Challenge and the Promise: Strengthening the Force, Preventing Suicide and Saving Lives*, Department of Defense.

Bondurant, Stuart and Roberta Wedge (eds) (2009), *Combating Tobacco Use in Military and Veteran Populations*, Institute of Medicine of the National Academies, National Academies Press.

Booth, Bradford, Mady Wechsler Segal and Nick Place (2009), 'National leadership summit on military families final report', accessed 1 September 2015 at: http://down load.militaryonesource.mil/12038/MOS/Reports/Final%20Report%20-%20No%20 Appendices.pdf.

Bray, Robert M. and Laurel L. Hourani (2007), 'Substance use trends among active duty military personnel: findings from the United States Department of Defense Health Related Behavior Surveys, 1980–2005', *Addiction*, **102** (7): 1092–101.

Chartrand, Molinda M., Deborah A. Frank, Laura F. White and Timothy R. Shope (2008), 'Effect of parents' wartime deployment on the behavior of young children in military families', *Archives of Pediatric and Adolescent Medicine*, **162** (11): 1009–14.

Chiarelli, Peter W. (2010), *Health Promotion, Risk Reduction, Suicide Prevention Report*, Diane Publishing.

Department of Defense (2009), 'Report of the second quadrennial quality of life review', January, accessed 1 September 2015 at: http://cs.mhf.dod.mil/content/dav/mhf/QOL-Library/PDF/MHF/QOL%20Resources/Reports/Quadrennial%20Quality%20of%20Life %20Review%202009.pdf.

Department of Defense (2010a), 'Demographics 2009: a profile of the military community', accessed 1 September 2015 at: http://cs.mhf.dod.mil/content/dav/mhf/QOL-Library/PDF/MHF/QOL%20Resources/Reports/2009_Demographics_Report.pdf.

Department of Defense (2010b), 'Plans for the Department of Defense for the support of military family readiness', Report to the Congressional Defense Committees.

Elbogen, Eric B., H. Ryan Wagner, Sara R. Fuller, P.S. Calhoun and P.M. Kinneer (2010), 'Correlates of anger and hostility in Iraq and Afghanistan war veterans', *American Journal of Psychiatry*, **167** (9): 1051–58.

Flake, Eric M., Beth Ellen Davis, Patti L. Johnson and Laura S. Middleton (2009), 'The psychosocial effects of deployment on military children', *Journal of Developmental and Behavioral Pediatrics*, **30** (4): 271–8.

Garamone, Jim (2009), 'Officials unveil results of Fort Carson violent crime study', *American Forces Press Service*, 19 July, accessed 1 September 2015 at: http://www.army.mil/article/24546/officials-unveil-results-of-fort-carson-violent-crime-study/.

Gibbs, Deborah A., Sandra L. Martin, Lawrence L. Kupper and Ruby E. Johnson (2007), 'Child maltreatment in enlisted soldiers' families during combat-related deployments', *JAMA*, **298** (5): 528–35.

Grays, Deborah (2010), 'Shoulder to shoulder – I will never quit on life', Fort McPherson, GA, 15 September, accessed 1 September 2015 at: http://www.army.mil/-news/2010/09/15/45189-shoulder-to-shoulder—-i-will-never-quit-on-life/.

Gutmann, Matthew C. and Catherine Anne Lutz (2010), *Breaking Ranks: Iraq Veterans Speak Out Against the War*, University of California Press.

Harben, Jerry (2008), 'Army releases mental health advisory team V report', Press Release, US Army Medical Command, 6 March, accessed 1 September 2015 at: http://armymedicine.mil/Pages/Mental-Health-Advisory-Team-V-Findings-Released-.aspx.

Hefling, Kimberly (2009), 'More military children seeking mental care', *Marine Corps Times*, 7 July, accessed 1 September 2015 at: http://www.marinecorpstimes.com/news/2009/07/ap_children_mental_health_070709/.

Jakupcak, Matthew, Daniel Conybeare and Lori Phelps et al. (2007), 'Anger, hostility, and aggression among Iraq and Afghanistan war veterans reporting PTSD and subthreshold PTSD', *Journal of Traumatic Stress*, **20** (6): 945–54.

Johnson, Shannon J., Michelle D. Sherman, Jeanne S. Hoffman et al. (2007), 'The psychological needs of US military service members and their families: a preliminary report', American Psychological Association.

Kaplan, Mark S., Nathalie Huguet, Bentson H. McFarland and Jason T. Newsom (2007), 'Suicide among male veterans: a prospective population-based study', *Journal of Epidemiology and Community Health*, **61** (7): 619–24.

Karney, Benjamin R. and John S. Crown (2007), *Families Under Stress: An Assessment of Data, Theory, and Research on Marriage and Divorce in the Military*, Vol. 599, Rand.

Killgore, William D.S., Dave I. Cotting, Jeffrey L. Thomas et al. (2008), 'Post-combat invincibility: violent combat experiences are associated with increased risk-taking propensity following deployment', *Journal of Psychiatric Research*, **42** (13): 1112–21.

Kors, Joshua (2007), 'How specialist town lost his benefits', *The Nation*, 9 April, available at: http://www.thenation.com/article/how-specialist-town-lost-his-benefits.

Laney, Sam (2010), 'Tetris blocks PTSD symptoms', *Stars and Stripes*, 16 November.

Lester, P., K. Peterson, J. Reeves, L. Knauss, D. Glover, C. Mogil, N. Duan and W. Beardslee (2010), 'The long war and parental combat deployment: effects on military children and at-home spouses', *Journal of the American Academy of Child & Adolescent Psychiatry*, **49** (4): 310–20.

Lutz, Catherine (2008), 'Living room terrorists', in Barbara Sutton, Sandra Morgen and Julie Novkov (eds), *Security Disarmed: Critical Perspectives on Gender, Race, and Militarization*, Rutgers University Press, pp. 223–7.

MacLean, Alair and Glen H. Elder (2007), 'Military service in the life course', *Annual Review of Sociology*, **33**: 175–96.

Mansfield, Alyssa J., Jay S. Kaufman, Stephen W. Marshall et al. (2010), 'Deployment and the use of mental health services among US Army wives', *New England Journal of Medicine*, **362** (2): 101–109.

Martin, Rachel (2010), 'VA eases claims process for PTSD treatment', *All Things Considered*, NPR, 12 January, available at: http://www.npr.org/templates/story/story.php?storyId=128467680.

McCarroll, James E., Robert J. Ursano, John H. Newby et al. (2003), 'Domestic violence and deployment in US Army soldiers', *The Journal of Nervous and Mental Disease*, **191** (1): 3–9.

McCarroll, James E., Robert J. Ursano, Xian Liu et al. (2010), 'Deployment and the probability of spousal aggression by US Army soldiers', *Military Medicine*, **175** (5): 352–6.

McFarland, Bentson H., Mark S. Kaplan and Nathalie Huguet (2010), 'Datapoints: self-inflicted deaths among women with US military service: a hidden epidemic?', *Psychiatric Services*, **61** (12): 1177.

Military Child Education Commission (2006), *A Legislator's Guide to Military Children*, Military Child Education Commission, available at: http://www.k12.wa.us/operationmilitarykids/pubdocs/MCECLegislatorsGuide.pdf.

Millikan, Amy M., Michael R. Bell, M. Shayne Gallaway et al. (2012), 'An epidemiologic investigation of homicides at Fort Carson, Colorado: summary of findings', *Military Medicine*, **177** (4): 404–11.

Munsey, Christopher (2010), 'The kids aren't all right' (report of American Psychological Association, *Stress in America Survey 2009*), *Monitor on Psychology*, **41** (1): 22.

National Center for Children in Poverty (2010), 'Trauma faced by children of military families: what every policymaker should know', May, NCCP, available at: http://www.nccp.org/publications/pdf/text_938.pdf.

National Center for Veterans Analysis and Statistics (2011), 'America's women veterans: military service history and VA benefit utilization statistics', November, Department of Veterans Affairs.

National Defense Research Institute (2004), *Working Around the Military: Challenges of Military Spouse Employment*, Rand.

Office of the Deputy Assistant Secretary of Defense (Military Community and Family Policy) (2013), *2013 Demographics Profile of the Military Community*.

Perry, Tony (2010), 'Army private accused of murder in Afghan prisoner's death', *Los Angeles Times*, 29 November, available at: http://articles.latimes.com/2010/nov/29/nation/la-na-soldier-hearing-20101129.

Philipps, Dave (2009), 'Casualties of war', *Colorado Springs Gazette*, available at: http://gazette.com/casualties-of-war-part-i-the-hell-of-war-comes-home/article/59065.

Pyle, Sara A., Christopher K. Haddock, Walker S. Poston, Robert M. Bray and Jason Williams (2007), 'Tobacco use and perceived financial strain among junior enlisted in the US Military in 2002', *Preventive Medicine*, **45** (6): 460–63.

Smith, Christopher L. (2009), 'The Fort Carson murder spree', *Rolling Stone*, 12 November.

Steinberg, Rebecca and Steven E. Kornguth (2009), 'Sustaining performance under stress: Overview of this issue', *Military Psychology*, **21** (S1): S1.

Tanielian, Terri and Lisa H. Jaycox (2008), *Invisible Wounds of War*, Rand.

USACHPPM (2009), 'Investigation of homicides at Fort Carson, Colorado November 2008–May 2009', Aberdeen Proving Ground: Unites States Army Center for Health Promotion and Preventive Medicine.

US Government Accountability Office and B. Farnell (2010), 'Status of implementation of GAO's 2006 recommendations on DOD's domestic violence program', US Government Accountability Office.

Vietnam Veterans of America (VVA) (2010), 'Defense department wrongfully discharges nearly 26,000 veterans, refuses to release records', VVA, 15 December, available at: http://www.vva.org/PressReleases/2010/pr10-024.html.

13. The sexual economy of war: implications for the integration of women into the US armed forces

Joane Nagel and Lindsey Feitz

Sex and war have an intimate connection, from the intense camaraderie of men in arms, to survival sex in war zones, to mass rape and sexual enslavement in warfare, to the sexual service industry that encircles military bases and proliferates in troop 'rest and recreation' destinations (Johnson, 2000; Hohn, 2010). Depictions of both sides in conflicts are sexualized, from 'our' men who are brave, honorable, and virile, to 'their' men who are weak, perverted and rapacious; from 'our' women who are pure, virtuous and vulnerable, to 'their' women who are promiscuous, seductive and treacherous (Ducat, 2004; Cuordileone, 2005; Dippel, 2010; Garraio, 2013). And there is the phallic discourse of 'war talk': from weaponry (guns, missiles and bombs), to military campaigns (assaults, penetration, conquest and surrender) (Cohn, 1993; Cooke and Woollacott, 1993).

In 1961 former US President Dwight D. Eisenhower famously warned of a growing military-industrial complex in which a growing proportion of the economy was dedicated to weapons production and military preparedness. In the half-century since Eisenhower's admonition, US military 'preparedness' increasingly has translated into a global military 'preparedness' empire with bases and missions around the globe (Andreas, 2004; Bacevich, 2005). The steadily growing military-industrial complex has insinuated itself into the local economies of every state and generated broad-based, bipartisan political support for large-scale defense projects (Hartung, 2001; Ubaldi, 2015). The machinery of war depends on not only matériel, but also on the recruitment and retention of personnel. Congressional funding provides an incentive for military recruitment, but where life and limb are at risk, even to those with limited economic alternatives, military service can be unappealing. That is, until we consider the power of sex appeal.

Just as the military-industrial complex depends on war for profits and growth, war making depends on a military-sexual complex to recruit, motivate and retain military personnel. For instance, gender micro-cultures articulate well with the goals of military recruiters. The cultural components of many masculinities resonate with calls to military service and support for military undertakings. This is not to say that all men love war, make war or advocate war. It is to say that the intimate connection between war and manhood is longstanding and far-reaching. Attributes of hegemonic masculinities across time and space reference warrior traditions that emphasize bravery, toughness, daring, honor, strength, courage and virile manliness (Mosse, 1996; Tosh, 2004; Connell, 2005; Braudy, 2005). It is not only masculinity that provides a cultural infrastructure for militarism. Many femininities provide aid and succor to militarized masculinities. In their role as mothers, women play a critical role in gender projects to turn boys into men. As lovers and wives, heterosexual women are consumers of manliness and can succumb to the seduction of military power and prowess. Lesbian femininities that simulate qualities of militarized manliness and embody 'female masculinities' can mirror and lend legitimacy to hegemonic masculinity (Gershick, 2005; Halberstam, 1998).

Another aspect of the military-sexual complex that works to guarantee adequate personnel is provision of a multitude of sexual benefits for military men. Military bases in the US and abroad are surrounded by commercial districts that cater to armed service personnel. Among the many services these businesses provide are sexual services. Commercial sex business owners often work in cooperation with US military authorities to provide 'safe', healthy sexual rest and recreational opportunities for fighting men; they reap large profits from the sexual labor of local and imported women and men (Moon, 1997; Bishop and Robinson, 1998; Sturdevant and Stoltzfus, 1992; Miller and Jayasundera, 2002).

The military-sexual complex also provides sexual benefits to service personnel while on duty. The gender integration of the US military has generated on-base sexual opportunities for both servicemen and women to have sex with each other. This is not always consensual, however, and tends to be more a 'benefit' for men than for women, as reflected in the large and growing number of reports of sexual assault and harassment in the armed services made by women against men (US Department of Defense, 2015).

Finally, the military-sexual complex relies on marketing to recruit personnel. As promoters of other products have long noted, sex sells. One of the most durable means of marketing militarism – individual and collective – is to declare a threat to the homeland. No call to arms is more potent than the threatened 'rape' of one's land or one's women, and no argument for military intervention is more convincing than accusing the enemy of sexual threat. Appeals for protection against sexual violence and declarations of enemy sexual perversion are extremely durable weapons in the wars of words that accompany conflicts (see Stiehm, 1982; Goldstein, 2001).

In the next sections we briefly review the 'feminization' of the US military in recent history and then discuss transformations in the military-sexual complex as it has incorporated women and femininities, after considerable resistance, and the ways these transformations have shaped women's places in the armed forces and in conflicts such as the war in Iraq.

THE FEMINIZATION OF THE MILITARY AND THE MILITARIZATION OF FEMININITY

In the last half-century, the US armed forces adopted two policies that increased the recruitment of women: they eliminated a 2 percent cap on women's enlistment in the late 1960s and adopted gender-neutral recruiting policies in the 1990s.[1] The result has been a steady increase in the proportion of women serving in the US military. Table 13.1 shows the number and percentage of women in the US armed forces from 1970 to 2015.

Table 13.1   Women serving in the US armed forces, 1970–2015

Year	Number	Percent
US Army, Navy, Marines, Air Force active duty		
1970	27 948	1.1
1980	148 771	8.5
1990	188 913	10.9
2000	169 084	14.7
2015	201 383	15.3
US Army, Navy, Marine Corps, Coast Guard, Air Force Reserves		
2013	155 331	22.8

Source: Women in Military Service for America (2015).

As the table shows, 27 948 women served in the Army, Navy, Marines and Air Force in 1970; they comprised 1.1 percent of active duty personnel. In the two decades after the lifting of the 2 percent cap, but before gender-neutral recruiting was instituted, women's representation in the four branches of the armed forces grew five-fold, rising to 8.5 percent in 1980 and 10.9 percent in 1990. After the implementation of gender-neutral recruitment in the early 1990s, women's representation in the military increased again to 14.7 percent in 2000. In 2013 women comprised 22.8 of all reservists; in 2015, servicewomen comprised 15.3 percent of active duty personnel across the four branches of the US military (Women in Military Service for America, 2015). Women's duties and rank have expanded as their numbers have grown. Between 1973 and 2009 the number of women officers grew from 4.2 percent of the officers in the four branches of the military to 14.3 percent (Institute for Women's Leadership, 2009).

The 2003–11 Iraq war was the first major US combat operation that included large numbers of women. Women constituted 14 percent of the troops deployed in Iraq in 2003 compared to 7 percent of troops in the 1991 Gulf War and less than 1 percent in the Vietnam war (Quester and Gilroy, 2002; Curphey, 2003; Women in Military Service for America, 2015). Despite prohibitions against combat duty for women, most military observers reported that women were involved in military violence and combat situations on a daily basis during the war in Iraq (Williams and Staub, 2005; Zavis, 2013). This is partly because the Iraq conflict had no clear 'front line': urban warfare and guerrilla tactics defy conventional notions of battle zones. Moreover, women's expanded police and guard roles brought them into close contact with Iraqi combatants and prisoners, further blurring the line between combat and non-combat duty (see Jervis, 2005; Walters, 2005). Despite its insistence on women's official exclusion from combat, the US military was quick to capitalize on the presence of women soldiers in a variety of military settings in Iraq – as police and security workers searching Iraqi civilians, prison guards, supply clerks, cooks, pilots, and as wives and lovers of servicemen (Raddatz and Gorman, 2009), that is, in gender and sexual roles above and beyond the call of duty.[2]

The 'feminization' of the US military, in part, is the result of the ending of compulsory service in the 1970s. The end of the draft necessitated the often difficult recruitment of young Americans disaffected by the dangers of military service. In order to meet its staffing needs, the military has shown an elastic institutional capacity to stretch its boundaries to include women in a broad array of roles. Ironically, as women have penetrated more deeply and higher into the military's ranks, the patriarchal, gendered institutional character of the military as a male cultural and political space appears to remain intact.[3] Instead of being feminized by increased numbers of women, the military has developed new ways to take advantage of femininity and of women's symbolic and material presence. Below we examine three specific sites where women's sexuality and gender were militarized and deployed in the Iraq war, including the staged rescue of Jessica Lynch, whose sexual purity and female innocence was used by the military to garner domestic support for the war in its early days; the Abu Ghraib prison where white American female soldiers were used to legitimate and eroticize the torture of Muslim male prisoners; and the coercive sexual contact between US Marines, soldiers, sailors, flyers and Guardsmen.

DRAMATIZING THE RESCUE OF JESSICA LYNCH

On 23 March 2003, in the opening days of the US invasion of Iraq, a caravan of 18 vehicles and 33 soldiers from the US Army's 507th Maintenance Company, a support unit of clerks, repairmen and cooks, was attacked by Iraqi troops in southern Iraq. Eleven US soldiers were killed, seven were captured, and the rest escaped. The Iraqis took prisoner three women with the 507th: Jessica Lynch, Shoshana Johnson and Lori Piestewa (US Department of Defense, 2004a).

Private First Class Jessica Lynch of Palestine, West Virginia, was a 19-year-old supply clerk when the Humvee she was riding in crashed during the attack; she suffered lacerations, a broken arm, broken leg, and head and back injuries. She was taken by Iraqis to a hospital, treated, and rescued a week later by US forces. Her rescue was filmed by the US military and was widely circulated in the US media. Seven months later 500 000 copies of her biography, *I Am a Soldier, Too: The Jessica Lynch Story*, were released; during the next week she was interviewed by Diane Sawyer on ABC's '20-20', by Katie Couric on NBC, by David Letterman on CBS, and by Larry King on CNN. That August, Lynch received a medical honorable discharge from the Army and an 80 percent disability benefit (Bragg, 2004).

Army Specialist Shoshana Johnson of El Paso, Texas, was a 30-year-old cook who was captured during the attack; she was shot in the ankle and injured in both legs. She was held by the Iraqis for three weeks until she and six others were rescued by US forces. Johnson was the first African American woman POW. During the next few months Shoshana received awards and invitations to speak from a number of organizations including *Essence* magazine, the NAACP, the Rainbow Push Coalition, the Congressional Hispanic and Black Caucuses, and Fayetteville State University, a historically black institution. That December, Johnson retired from the Army with a temporary disability honorable discharge (Johnson, 2010). It's worth noting here the difference in how the US Army assesses injuries. Both Lynch and Johnson have lingering physical problems from the incident, including difficulty walking. But the Army classified Johnson as 30 percent disabled while, again, it said Lynch was 80 percent disabled. This is a difference worth several hundred dollars more a month for Lynch (see Grundy, 2003; Douglas, 2003; Wise, 2003).

Private First Class Lori Piestewa of Tuba City, Arizona, and member of the Hopi Nation, was a 23-year-old supply clerk who was driving the Humvee carrying Lynch when they were attacked by Iraqi forces. According to eye witness accounts (including from Lynch), Piestewa maneuvered the Humvee around firing Iraqi troops and debris, in an effort to give aid to her fellow soldiers until her vehicle was struck by a rocket-propelled grenade and crashed (Shaffer, 2003). She was wounded and died a few hours later in captivity. Piestewa was the first Native American woman to die in combat while serving with the US military. She was posthumously promoted to Specialist by the Army; the Arizona state government renamed a mountain 'Piestewa Peak'; the Grand Canyon Games organizers instituted annual Lori Piestewa National Native American Games; an Arizona freeway was named for her; and a plaque bearing her name is located at the White Sands Missile Range in New Mexico.

The story and image of Jessica Lynch has received much more attention than those of Shoshana Johnson or Lori Piestewa. Arguably, the bravery and actions of Johnson and Piestewa were more newsworthy than the passive role played by Lynch, who reported that she was knocked unconscious when her Humvee crashed. The fame and treatment of the three women constitute a kind of natural experiment for examining how race, class, gender and sexuality operate in the US military and in society at large: because all three women were from working class backgrounds and had similar rank, so gender and class are 'controlled for' in this experiment. Only race and sexuality are variables: Lynch was white, Johnson was black, Piestewa was Native American. Additionally, Shoshana Johnson and Lori Piestewa were single mothers. Jessica Lynch had no children, no marriages and no divorces. This absence made her attractive as a damsel in distress, one whose sexual purity and moral worth were easy to market. We argue that the racial differences and sexual histories of the three women were reflected in the circumstances of their rescue and, more importantly, in their treatment by the military and the media after their rescue.

Investigations after the women's release reveal that Jessica Lynch's rescue was dramatized, if not entirely staged, by the US military; it was filmed and promoted for media consumption. A BBC documentary, 'War Spin', challenged the authenticity of the US military's depiction of Jessica Lynch's rescue, referring to the story as 'one of the most stunning pieces of news management ever conceived', and questioned the entire 'rescue' – from the storming of the Iraqi hospital by US special forces to the filming of the operation on a night vision camera (Kampfner, 2003):

> Dr Anmar Uday [reported]: 'There were no [Iraqi] soldiers in the hospital ... . It was like a Hollywood film. They cried, "go, go, go", with guns ... without bullets ... and the sound of explosions. They made a show for the American attack on the hospital – action movies like Sylvester Stallone or Jackie Chan.'

In fact, a BBC correspondent, John Kampfner (2003) reported that two days before the snatch squad arrived, an Iraqi doctor had arranged to deliver Lynch to the Americans by ambulance. Referring to footage of the rescue, Kampfner quoted a US military spokesman as saying, 'Some brave souls put their lives on the line to make this happen, loyal to a creed that they know that they'll never leave a fallen comrade'.

In her testimony before Congress and concurrent interviews in 2007, Jessica Lynch confirmed Kampfner's skeptical account of her heroism in battle and rescue by the US military: 'I didn't even get a shot off. My weapon had jammed' (Scelfo, 2007). Ironically, she, too, said that when the Iraqi medical team tried to return her to the Americans, the ambulance was fired upon at a checkpoint, forcing the ambulance to turn around and return her to the hospital (Scelfo, 2007). Asked who was to blame for spreading misinformation about her rescue, she blamed the military and the media: 'The military for not setting the record straight and the media for spreading it, and not seeking the true facts. They just ran with it instead of waiting until the facts were straightened out' (Scelfo, 2007). Lynch expressed dismay over her official and media valorization: 'I'm still confused as to why they chose to lie and try to make me a legend' (US House of Representatives, 2007).

The discovery of Shoshana Johnson and her six co-POWs during a search of houses apparently was a much less made-for-prime time rescue story. In fact it was somewhat accidental; it was not filmed, nor was it the subject of made-for-TV movies, books or network talk show interviews. The names of her fellow male POWs are virtually unknown. Nor was the brave death of single-mom Lori Piestewa dramatized for film and television. Only the rescue of a pretty young white damsel in distress made it to the front pages of America's hearts and minds, in a media campaign designed to garner domestic support for the war in Iraq. The lesson here: not all gender is equally deployable or valuable in national political and media markets. Race matters and so does sexual purity.[4]

CASTING LYNNDIE ENGLAND AS AN EROTIC DOMINATRIX

Several months later another sexualized image of a female soldier captured the attention of the public, this time, however, imbedded in photographs of sexually demeaned, naked, male prisoners. The pictures of white women torturing Muslim men at Abu Ghraib provide another site in which to examine the militarization of female sexuality as an intimate – and strategic – technique of war-making.[5] Private First Class Lynndie England of Fort Ashby, West Virginia, was a 21-year-old US Army reservist serving in the 372nd Military Police Company at Abu Ghraib prison in 2003 when pictures were made public of her and other guards abusing prisoners. The most lurid photographs involved sexual positioning and posing of prisoners and guards, including England, Specialist Sabrina Harman, Specialist Megan Ambuhl, and Specialist Charles Graner.[6] England, Harman and Ambuhl also were pretty young white women, but their gender and sexuality was mobilized in a very different way – as dominatrixes in a bizarre chronicle of torture and abuse in a military prison. Social scientists have known for decades, based on the work of Stanley Milgrim, Philip Zimbardo, Robert Jay Lifton and Albert Bandura, among others, that people in hierarchical authority systems placed in charge of others defined as inferior or enemies are quite likely to uncritically follow orders, suspend moral judgment, and abuse those under their control (see Schlesinger, 2004). This is precisely what occurred at Abu Ghraib prison.

The prisoner abuse, however, was not simply a case of human nature in action. US military intelligence personnel and contract workers advising prison staff encouraged them to do so. In fact, similar programs of torture and humiliation had been underway for some time at the US prison in Guantanamo Bay, Cuba ('Gitmo'), where prisoners were made to put women's underwear on their heads, threatened with dogs, forced to appear nude in front of women, and sexually humiliated (White, 2005). The *New York Times* (2005) obtained a copy of a July 2005 Pentagon report which 'contained page after page of appalling descriptions of the use of women soldiers as sexual foils in interrogations'. The so-called 'Gitmoization' of operations at Abu Ghraib was facilitated by a Guantanamo prison commander who helped set up operations at Abu

Ghraib (Hersh, 2004).[7] The result, according to a *New York Times* (2005) editorial, was the 'exploitation and debasement of women serving in the United States military'.

Hersh (2004) argues that US military 'intelligence' and conservative 'intellectuals' had long been enamored of a theory of Arab masculinity based on two Orientalist texts written in the mid-1970s by Raphael Patai (1973) and Bernard Lewis (1974). Patai's *The Arab Mind* discusses the taboos associated with female sexuality and homosexuality. Hersh reported that the 1973 book became 'the bible of the neocons on Arab behavior' in the months before the invasion of Iraq, leading them to believe 'one, that Arabs only understand force and, two, that the biggest weakness of Arabs is shame and humiliation' (Hersh, 2004). Massad (2004) similarly argues that US government officials' view of Islamic culture stresses Arab sexuality and that the sexualized Othering of Arabs reflects a broad disdain for the people and the region that is part of an ongoing US imperial agenda of military, economic and political domination. Massad proposed that the photographs taken at Abu Ghraib were intended to blackmail prisoners who were told their families would see them, and were trophies for US soldiers.

Massad tends to depict the involvement of women soldiers in the Abu Ghraib torture as simply an extension of American masculinism – another way to feminize Arab men. But considerably more is going on. The women are not simply beating or manhandling the prisoners; they are positioned in very sexual ways – dragging a detainee on a leash, pointing at a hooded prisoner's genitals, posed with American men above them and Iraqi men below them. The apparent fun the Americans were having and the creative gusto with which they undertook their sport suggest that the scripts they were enacting were not only deeply racist, but also deeply familiar.

Indeed, the torture and sexual humiliation of prisoners of war and prisoners in general by mainly male guards is well documented. What was surprising to many who viewed the Abu Ghraib prison photos was the enlistment of women in these undertakings. This development probably shows something about guard demographics. We argue that the photographs from Abu Ghraib document how women's sexuality is a tool in an expanded military arsenal. This novel weapon capitalized on women's assumed unique sexual power to demean and humiliate enemy men, especially Arab men.

The gendered and sexualized nature of the torture raises important questions about the Orientalist gaze that the pictures represent, especially given that a specific brand of white, militarized, American female sexuality was central not only to the torture, but also in the photos that circulated around the world. Essentialized notions of Arab and Muslim gender and sexual norms were strategically exploited here by the assumed sexual power and prowess of white American female soldiers (Buruma and Margalit, 2004; Mamdani, 2004; Bilgrami, 2006). Increased military womanpower in Iraq not only provided a stable of women for men to protect and defend, as with Jessica Lynch, but also broadened the repertoire of weapons to subdue and emasculate the enemy, as with Abu Ghraib.

SERVICEWOMEN AS SEXUAL COMRADES IN ARMS

Women's increased presence in the ranks and on the battlefield also proved to be a valuable commodity to bolster servicemen's morale. The growing presence of women soldiers has become a portable R&R resource to the extent that servicewomen choose to be sexually available to their comrades or find themselves coerced into sexually entertaining the troops and servicing the servicemen. The sexual activity between American servicewomen and men is yet another site where the physical bodies of female soldiers became part of the military-sexual complex in Iraq.

Sexual abuse, exploitation and rape are perennial problems in the US military. The sexual mistreatment of women soldiers has resulted in recurrent scandals from the earliest days of gender integration in armed forces and military academies. For instance, in 1988, the US Department of Defense (DoD) conducted a survey of 38 000 military personnel from all branches of the armed services and found that 64 percent of women and 17 percent of men had reported at least one incident of sexual harassment during the previous year (Martindale, 1990). The 'modern era' of public military sex scandals began in 1991 when Navy and Marine pilots molested dozens of women at a Las Vegas Tailhook convention. In 1996 it became known that dozens of women recruits had been sexually assaulted at the Army Ordnance Center in Maryland. In 2003 some 142 women cadets alleged they were sexually assaulted at the Air Force Academy. The Pentagon dutifully but ineffectually launched studies and task forces after each of these and other revelations of sexual misconduct. In 2004, the Secretary of the Army released a five-year study of sexual assault in the Army that found 4.5 percent of servicewomen reported being assaulted (US Department of Defense, 2004b). In 2005, the DoD reported 2374 allegations of sexual assaults among armed forces personnel (US Department of Defense, 2005a). Rates of domestic violence were said to indicate a broad culture of violence against women in the US military (Rosenthal and McDonald, 2003). A 2013 DoD study reported 3553 sexual assault complaints in the previous 9 months – a nearly 50 percent increase over the same period a year earlier (Steinhauer, 2013.[8]

The apparent inability or unwillingness of the Pentagon to address the problem of sexual assaults against US servicewomen has become an impediment to both documenting and responding to military sexual abuse. Rates of rape and sexual assault are notoriously difficult to ascertain due to variations across time and place in defining, reporting and classifying data. During the decade before the Iraq war, Veterans Affairs researchers found close to one quarter of servicewomen surveyed reported being sexually assaulted (Herdy and Moffeit, 2004) and more than one third reported being sexually harassed (Murdoch and Nichol, 1995). Given the US military's poor record of responding to its (mainly) women members' sexual abuse, it is not surprising that during the early years of the Afghanistan and Iraq wars, the Department of Veterans Affairs found that nearly 75 percent of military women who said they had been assaulted did not tell their commanding officer (Martineau and Wiegand, 2005). This reluctance to report suggests that sexual harassment and rape rates are much higher than those reported by the Department of Defense.

Women soldiers in Iraq described a widespread atmosphere of sexual harassment and expectations for sexual availability. In a March 2005 article published in the *Sacramento Bee* newspaper, one of dozens of women soldiers interviewed stated: 'I think every female [soldier in Iraq] has been sexually harassed' (Martineau and Wiegand, 2005). Department of Defense estimates were much lower than 100 percent: between August 2002 to October 2004, 188 cases of sexual assault on military personnel were reported in Iraq, Kuwait and Afghanistan (US Department of Defense, 2004b). A 2012 Department of Veterans Affairs survey found that half of women deployed to Iraq or Afghanistan reported being sexually harassed and one quarter reported being sexually assaulted (Zoroya, 2012). But again, many cases go unreported.

In many ways, women soldiers being raped, molested or harassed is not surprising given the hypermasculine, patriarchal structure and tradition of the armed services and women's relatively low and controversial status within them. But sexuality enters into women's military service experience in other ways, too. The photographs from Abu Ghraib prison and the biographies of Charles Graner, Lynndie England, Sabrina Harman and Megan Ambuhl indicated that sex among the troops is part of the contemporary military service experience: Graner had sexual relationships with two, possibly all three women while in Iraq; England returned to the US pregnant with Graner's child; at about the same time England was giving birth, Graner married Megan Ambuhl.

Of course, many men and women enter into sexual relations willingly, even enthusiastically, and situations of danger and conflict can be powerful aphrodisiacs (see Williams and Staub, 2005). During the 1991 Gulf War, 'more than 1200 pregnant women (out of 40 579) were evacuated from the gulf region' (Monsen, 1997; see also Griffin, 1992). Since most sex does not result in pregnancy (even accounting for the fact that some women might have been pregnant prior to shipping out), a pregnancy rate of 3 percent suggests that rates of sexual relations were quite likely to have been considerably higher. We found no figures on pregnancy rates among women who served in Iraq, although an estimated 10.5 percent of active duty women aged 18 to 44 apparently reported an unplanned pregnancy in 2008 (James, 2012). Pregnancies notwithstanding, nothing suggests a diminution of sexual contact among the troops.

In situations where sexual harassment is potentially frequent, women may form sexual alliances, to 'hook up' with men (or women) in order to gain support and/or to place themselves off-limits to other service personnel. This is not to say that women are having sex in war zones and on military bases only out of intimidation or self-protection. Any consideration of sexuality in the US military, however, should reference the broader context within which soldiers enter into sexual liaisons. Is it fair to refer to women's sexual involvement with men in the military as 'servicing the servicemen?' Part of the answer to that question has to do with rank: are women's sexual partners of equal rank? It also involves the pressures 'to go along to get along' in an intense atmosphere in a hierarchical, male-dominated organization where most everyone is carrying a gun. We should not underestimate women's sexual agency, but we realize the limits of personal power when confronting a potent, exploitative and dangerous reality.

CONCLUSION

We have argued here that a military-sexual complex provides a critical libidinal infrastructure for war. Wars are sites of homosocial masculine solidarity, arenas of male sexual aggression, theaters of hypermasculine, heteronormative performance, and stages where class, race, gender and sexual scripts are enacted and reinforced. So what happens when women enter the masculinist spaces of the military and war zones? We find that the US military-sexual complex has incorporated and exploited women and femininity to achieve combat goals; despite much official rhetoric about the limitations of women in combat, the deployment of women as weapons of war has been integrated into the US military's structure and operations. Analyzing the Abu Ghraib photos, Zillah Eisenstein (2007) observed that the appearance of women dressed as men 'participating in the very sexual humiliation that their gender is usually victim to' was at first confusing until she realized that the US women of Abu Ghraib were 'gender decoys', serving as cover for sexual and racialized abuses, camouflaging gender and racial power relations. Eisenstein notes that such 'gender swapping and switching leaves masculinist/racialized gender in place [so that] just the sex has changed; the uniform remains the same' (p. 37).

In focusing on three troubling points at the intersection of gender, class, race and sexuality in the Iraq war, we found that women were deployed in a propaganda campaign to win the hearts and minds of the American people, as weapons of war in the Abu Ghraib prison scandal, and as intimate partners within the US armed forces. Although women are incorporated into military operations, they continue to occupy gendered spaces within the military. Not only are female sexuality and gender deployed and consumed by the military organization and its personnel, women are quite likely to be vilified, blamed and prosecuted when their exploitation becomes public. We could also compare the lack of disciplinary action against Major General Geoffrey Miller, who commanded the US detention facility at Guantanamo Bay and later helped set up US operations at Abu Ghraib (White, 2005), with the demotion of Brigadier General Janis Karpinski, who was put in charge of 15 military prisons in Iraq despite her lack of experience in corrections (BBC News, 2004, ABC News, 2005). Not only was Miller never disciplined, but also, after Karpinski was demoted, her command was given to him – the man who 'gitmo-ized' Abu Ghraib.[9] In April 2004, Miller was put in charge of all detainee operations in Iraq (Danner, 2004), and when he retired in 2006, Major General Miller received the US Army's Distinguished Service Medal. Former Brigadier General Janice Karpinski retired at the reduced rank of Colonel; she received no medals.

Women who choose military service are paying their dues and then some. Not only are they entering male domains, working at men's jobs, and facing serious injury and death like their male comrades, they also are serving a military 'second shift', deployed as gender decoys and sexual partners (Hochschild, 1989). We conclude that when women enter longstanding, entrenched masculinist spaces like military organizations, even when their numbers grow and they are promoted to positions of power and authority, they remain vulnerable to sexual exploitation and scapegoating and are limited in their ability to control the definition of the situation and their role in it. The case of servicewomen in Iraq illustrates the capacity of organizational social structure to sustain inequalities and particular patterns of power relations, even in the face of demographic changes in its personnel. The gendered imaginary of war, as illustrated by the experiences of women, is in fact very real. This reflects the gendered and sexed nature of battle that often is obscured in discussions of the economic and political spoils of war.

Policy changes in the US military more broadly defining sexual abuse, instituting expanded confidentiality rules, and revising guidelines for reporting and responding to service personnel reports of sexual assault have been presented as steps toward dismantling the military's longstanding 'don't tell, don't respond' strategy for *not* dealing with sexual harassment and assault (see US Department of Defense, 2005b; US Army, 2015). Recent investigations into ongoing problems of sexual harassment and sexual assault on US military bases constitute strong evidence that more fundamental and sweeping reforms are needed (Gillibrand, 2015). It remains to be seen whether these investigations and policy revisions can transform the military's gender and sexual culture and de-escalate the militarization of femininity.

NOTES

1. In 1967 Public-Law 90-130 lifted the 2 percent cap on women's active duty enlistment and in the 1990s the various services adopted gender-neutral recruitment policies; when the Navy later rescinded its gender-neutral policy because of constrained berthing policies on Navy vessels, the result was a drop in women's recruitment from 20 percent in 1995 to 14 percent in 1997, though that percentage of women recruited increased to between 17–20 percent after 1997 (Williams, 1998; Brown, 2012).
2. For a discussion of the ambiguities of women's role in combat zones, see Nantais and Lee (1999); Browder and Pflaeging (2010); Lemmon (2015).
3. For a discussion of gender assumptions about military service, see Mitchell (1989); Herbert (2000); Fenner and De Young (2001); Sjoberg (2014); Eden (2015).
4. Although *Glamour* magazine named both Jessica Lynch and Shoshana Johnson as its 2003 Women of the Year, critics point out disparities in the treatment, coverage and rewards given to the two women: Lynch became a poster girl for the US military and her rescue was re-enacted on network television as a dramatized spectacle of Special Forces derring-do; her story was sold to publishers and filmmakers. Johnson was neither a poster girl nor was her story sold broadly; there were no movie contracts or prime time interviews for Shoshana, though she published a memoir of her time as a prisoner of war and its aftermath (Johnson, 2010).
5. Not all detainees at Abu Ghraib are 'Muslim', 'Iraqi' or 'Arab', but we are unable to document the national or other identities of any of the detainees.
6. Charles Graner was found guilty on ten charges including aggravated assault, maltreatment and conspiracy and served 6.5 years of a 10-year sentence; Sabrina Harman was convicted of mistreating detainees and was sentenced to six months in

prison; Megan Ambuhl pleaded guilty to dereliction of duty and received a sentence with no jail time; Lynndie England pleaded guilty to conspiracy to mistreat prisoners and served 1.5 years of a 3-year prison sentence.

7. For a survey of official documents associated with the Abu Ghraib scandal, see Greenberg and Dratel (2005); Danner (2004); Strasser (2004).
8. Like all data on sexuality, exact rates of sexual harassment, assault or rape are notoriously difficult to determine. There are differences in legal definition, rates of reporting and rates of prosecution and conviction (US Commission on Civil Rights, 2013).
9. In 2005, military investigators proposed disciplining Miller for 'abusive and degrading treatment' of a prisoner at Guantanamo Bay prison in late 2002, but the recommendation was overruled and referred to the Army's inspector general (Mazzetti, 2005). Karpinski resisted being cast as a 'fall gal' for Abu Ghraib, and argued that the abuses there and elsewhere are part of a policy directed and implemented mainly by US military intelligence and its hired contract workers (Karpinski, 2006).

BIBLIOGRAPHY

ABC News (2005), 'Head of Abu Ghraib Prison speaks out', *ABC News Nightline*, 12 May, accessed 15 August 2015 at: http://abcnews.go.com/Nightline/IraqCoverage/story?id=751870&page=1.

Andreas, Joel (2004), *Addicted to War: Why the US Can't Kick Militarism*, AK Press.

Bacevich, Andrew (2005), *The New American Militarism: How Americans are Seduced by War*, Oxford University Press.

BBC News (2004), 'Iraq abuse ordered from the top', *BBC News*, 15 June, accessed 15 August 2015 at: http://news.bbc.co.uk/1/hi/world/americas/3806713.stm.

BBC News (2005), 'Abu Ghraib soldier gets prison term', *BBC News*, 18 May, accessed 15 August 2015 at: http://news.bbc.co.uk/1/hi/world/americas/4557613.stm.

Bilgrami, Akeel (2006), 'Occidentalism, the very idea: an essay on enlightenment and enchantment', *Critical Inquiry*, **32** (3): 381–411.

Bishop, Ryan and Lillian S. Robinson (1998), *Night Market: Sexual Cultures and the Thai Economic Miracle*, Routledge.

Bragg, Rick (2004), *I Am a Soldier, Too: The Jessica Lynch Story*, Vintage.

Braudy, Leo (2005), *From Chivalry to Terrorism: War and the Changing Nature of Masculinity*, Vintage.

Brockes, Emma (2009), 'What happens in war happens', *The Guardian*, 2 January, accessed 13 August 2015 at: http://www.theguardian.com/world/2009/jan/03/abu-ghraib-lynndie-england-interview.

Browder, Laura and Sascha Pflaeging (2010), *When Janey Comes Marching Home: Portraits of Women in Combat Veterans*, University of North Carolina Press.

Brown, Melissa (2012), *Enlisting Masculinity: The Construction of Gender in US Military Recruiting Advertising during the All-Volunteer Force*, Oxford University Press.

Buruma, Ian and Avishai Margalit (2004), *Occidentalism: The West in the Eyes of its Enemies*, Penguin.

CNN (2003), 'Lynch: military played up rescue too much', *CNN.com*, 7 November, accessed 15 August 2015 at: http://www.cnn.com/2003/US/11/07/lynch.interview/.

Cohn, Carol (1993), 'Wars, wimps, and women: talking gender and thinking war', in Miriam Cooke and Angela Woollacott (eds), *Gendering War Talk*, Princeton University Press, pp. 227–46.

Connell, Robert W. (2005), *Masculinities*, 2nd edn, University of California Press.

Cooke, Miriam and Angela Woollacott (eds) (1993), *Gendering War Talk*, Princeton University Press.

Cuordileone, K.A. (2005), *Manhood and American Political Culture in the Cold War*, Routledge.

Curphey, Shauna (2003), '1 in 7 US military personnel in Iraq is female', *Women's E-News*, accessed 15 August 2015 at: http://www.womensenews.org/article.cfm/dyn/aid/1265/context/cover/.

Danner, Mark (2004), *Torture and truth: America, Abu Ghraib, and the War on Terror*, New York Review Books.

De Atkine, Norvell B. (2004), 'The Arab mind revisited', *The Middle East Quarterly*, **11** (3): 47–55.

DeGroot, Gerard (2001), 'A few good women: gender stereotypes, the military and peacekeeping', *International Peacekeeping*, **8** (2): 23–38.

Dippel, John V.H. (2010), *War and Sex: A Brief History of Men's Urge for Battle*, Prometheus.

Douglas, William (2003), 'A case of race? One POW acclaimed, another ignored', *Seattle Times*, 9 November, accessed 15 August 2015 at: http://web.archive.org/web/20041206230652/http://seattletimes.nwsource.com/html/nationworld/2001786800_shoshana09.html.

Ducat, Stephen J. (2004), *The Wimp Factor: Gender Gaps, Holy Wars, and the Politics of Anxious Masculinity*, Beacon.

Eden, Jude (2015), 'Women in combat: the question of standards', *Military Review*, March–April, accessed 5 August 2015 at: http://usacac.army.mil/CAC2/MilitaryReview/Archives/English/MilitaryReview_20150430_art009.pdf.

Eisenstein, Zillah (2007), *Sexual Decoys: Gender, Race and the War in the Imperial Democracy*, Zed Books.

Fenner, Lorrie M. and Marie De Young (2001), *Women in Combat: Civic Duty or Military Liability?* Georgetown University Press.

Fuoco, Michael A. (2005), 'Abu Ghraib prisoner abuse trial set to begin Monday', 8 January, accessed 14 August 2015 at: http://www.post-gazette.com/news/nation/2005/01/08/Abu-Ghraib-prisoner-abuse-trial-set-to-begin-Monday/stories/200501080113.

Garraio, Julia (2013), 'Hordes of rapists: the instrumentalization of sexual violence in German Cold War anti-Communist discourses', *RCCS (Revista Crítica de Ciências Sociais)*, *Annual Review*, **5**, accessed 5 August 2015 at: http://rccsar.revues.org/476.

Gershick, Zsa Zsa (2005), *Secret Service: Untold Stories of Lesbians in the Military*, Alyson Books.

Giles, Wenona and Jennifer Hyndman (eds) (2004), *Sites of Violence: Gender and Conflict Zones*, University of California Press.

Gillibrand, Kirsten (2015), 'Snapshot review of sexual assault report files at the four largest US military bases in 2013', US Senate report, accessed 15 August 2014 at: http://www.gillibrand.senate.gov/imo/media/doc/Gillibrand_Sexual%20Assault%20Report.pdf.

Goldstein, Joshua (2001), *War and Gender: How Gender Shapes the War System and Vice Versa*, Cambridge University Press.

Greenberg, Karen J. and Joshua L. Dratel (2005), *The Torture Papers: The Road to Abu Ghraib*, Cambridge University Press.

Griffin, Rodman D. (1992), 'Women in the military: what role should women play in the shrinking military?', *CQ Researcher*, **2**, 25 September, 835–55, accessed 17 August 2015 at: http://library.cqpress.com/cqresearcher/document.php?id=cqresrre1992092500.

Grundy, Garry (2003), 'Three-fifths of a heroine', *The Record* (Harvard Law School), 6 November, accessed 13 August 2015 at: http://hlrecord.org/?p=11074.

Halberstam, Judith (1998), *Female Masculinity*, Duke University Press.

Hartung, William (2001), 'Eisenhower's warning: the military-industrial complex forty years later', *World Policy Journal*, **18** (1): 39–44.

Herbert, Melissa S. (2000), *Camouflage isn't only for Combat: Gender, Sexuality, and Women in the Military*, New York University Press.

Herdy, Amy and Miles Moffeit (2004), 'Betrayal in the ranks', *The Denver Post*, 16–18 November, Parts I, II, III accessed 15 August 2015 at: http://extras.denverpost.com/justice/tdp_betrayal.pdf.

Hersh, Seymour (2004), 'The gray zone: how a secret Pentagon program came to Abu Ghraib', *The New Yorker*, 24 May, 38–44, accessed 14 August 2015 at: http://www.newyorker.com/magazine/2004/05/24/the-gray-zone.

Hochschild, Arlie (1989), *The Second Shift: Working Parents and the Revolution at Home*, Viking Penguin.

Hohn, Maria (2010), *Over There: Living with the US Military Empire from World War Two to the Present*, Duke University Press.

Horgon, John (2013), 'How can we condemn Boston murders but excuse the US bombing of civilians?', *Scientific American*, 19 April, accessed 14 August 2015 at: http://blogs.scientificamerican.com/cross-check/how-can-we-condemn-boston-murders-but-excuse-u-s-bombing-of-civilians/.

Institute for Women's Leadership (2009), 'Women in the US military services', Rutgers University, accessed 6 August 2015 at: http://iwl.rutgers.edu/documents/njwomencount/Women%20in%20Military%202009%20Final.pdf.

James, Susan Donaldson (2012), 'Unplanned pregnancies hurt military women, mission readiness', *ABC News*, 25 January, accessed 15 August 2015 at: http://abcnews.go.com/Health/unintended-pregnancies-military-double-generation-population-study/story?id=18307178.

Jervis, Rick (2005), 'Despite rule, US women on front line in Iraq war', *USA Today.com*, 27 June, accessed 15 August 2015 at: http://usatoday30.usatoday.com/news/washington/2005-06-26-female-troops-face-front_x.htm.

Johnson, Chalmers (2000), *Blowback: The Costs and Consequences of American Empire*, Henry Holt.

Johnson, Eric (2011), 'Abu Ghraib abuse ringleader greener released from prison', *Reuters*, 6 August, accessed 13 August 2015 at: http://www.reuters.com/article/2011/08/06/us-prisoner-abughraib-idUSTRE7752GS20110806.

Johnson, Shoshana (2010), *I'm Still Standing: From Captive US Soldier to Free Citizen – My Journey Home*, Simon & Schuster (Touchstone).

Kampfner, John (2003), 'Saving Private Lynch story "flawed"', *BBC News*, 15 May, accessed 15 August 2015 at: http://news.bbc.co.uk/2/hi/programmes/correspondent/3028585.stm.

Karpinski, Janis (2006), *One Woman's Army: The Commanding General of Abu Ghraib Tells Her Story*, Miramax.

Lemmon, Gayle Tzemach (2015), *Ashley War: The Untold Story of a Team of Women Soldiers on the Special Ops Battlefield*, Harper.

Lewis, Bernard (1974), *Islam: From the Prophet Muhammad to the Capture of Constantinople*, Vols I and II, Harper and Row.

Mamdani, Mahmoud (2004), *Good Muslim, Bad Muslim: America, the Cold War and the Roots of Terror*, Pantheon.

Martindale, Melanie (1990), *Sexual Harassment in the Military, 1988*, Defense Manpower Data Center.

Martineau, Pamela and Steve Wiegand (2005), 'Women at war', *Sacramento Bee*, 7 March, accessed 17 August 2015 at: http://freedomarchives.org/pipermail/news_freedomarchives.org/2005-March/001042.html.

Massad, Joseph (2004), 'Imperial mementos', *Al-Ahram Weekly*, 20–26 May, No. 691, accessed 14 August 2015 at: http://weekly.ahram.org.eg/2004/691/op2.htm.

Mazzetti, Mark (2005), 'General rejects call to penalize ex-Guantanamo prison chief', *Los Angeles Times*, 13 July, accessed 15 August 2015 at: http://articles.latimes.com/2005/jul/13/nation/na-gitmo13.

Miller, Jody and Dheeshana Jayasundera (2002), 'Prostitution, the sex industry, and sex tourism', in Ronald M. Holmes and Stephen T. Holmes (eds), *Current Perspectives on Sex Crimes*, Sage, pp. 56–71.

Mitchell, Brian (1989), *Weak Link: The Feminization of the US Military*, Regnery Gateway.

Monsen, Maj. Kathleen P. (1997), 'Pregnancy in the US armed services and its impact on readiness', unpublished paper, Air Command and Staff College, Maxwell Air Force Base, Montgomery, Alabama.

Moon, Katharine H.S. (1997), *Sex among Allies: Military Prostitution in US–Korea Relations*, Columbia University Press.

Mosse, George L. (1996), *The Image of Man: The Creation of Modern Masculinity*, Oxford University Press.

Murdoch, Maureen and Kristin L. Nichol (1995), 'Women veterans' experiences with domestic violence and with sexual harassment while in the military', *Archives of Family Medicine*, **4** (5), accessed 17 August 2015 at: http://www.ncbi.nlm.nih.gov/pubmed/7742963.

Nantais, Cynthia and Martha F. Lee (1999), 'Women in the United States military: protectors or protected? The case of Prisoner of War Melissa Rathbun-Nealy', *Journal of Gender Studies*, **8** (2): 181–91.

New York Times (2005), 'The women of Gitmo', *Opinion Pages*, 15 July, accessed 15 August 2015 at: http://www.nytimes.com/2005/07/15/opinion/15fri1.html.

Patai, Raphael (1973), *The Arab Mind*, Charles Scribner's Sons.

Quester, Aline O. and Curtis L. Gilroy (2002), 'Women and minorities in America's volunteer military', *Contemporary Economic Policy*, **20** (2): 111–21, accessed 15 August 2015 at: http://www.dtic.mil/dacowits/research/Women_Minorities_in_Amer_Vol_Military.pdf.

Raddatz, Martha and Elizabeth Gorman (2009), 'Female warriors engaged in combat in Iraq, Afghanistan', *ABC News*, 25 October, accessed 15 August 2015 at: http://abcnews.go.com/WN/Politics/roles-question-females-warfare/story?id=8879944.

Rosenthal, Lynn and Susan McDonald (2003), 'Seeking justice: a review of the second report of the defense task force on domestic violence', *Violence against Women*, **9** (9): 1153–61.

Scelfo, Julie (2007), 'Jessica Lynch sets the record straight', *Newsweek*, 4 April, accessed 14 August 2015 at: http://www.newsweek.com/jessica-lynch-sets-record-straight-97863.

Schlesinger, James K. (2004), 'Final report of the independent panel to review DOD detention operations', reprinted in Mark Danner (ed.), *Torture and Truth: America, Abu Ghraib, and the War on Terror*, New York Review, pp. 329–408.

Shaffer, Mark (2003), 'Piestewa went to war for Lynch, book says', *Arizona Republic*, 12 November, accessed 15 August 2015 at: http://www.azcentral.com/news/specials/veterans/articles/piestewa-3.html.

Sjoberg, Laura (2014), *Gender, War, and Conflict*, Polity.

Steinhauer, Jennifer (2013), 'Reports of military sexual assault rise sharply', *New York Times*, 7 November, accessed 14 August 2015 at: http://www.nytimes.com/2013/11/07/us/reports-of-military-sexual-assault-rise-sharply.html?_r=0.

Stiehm, Judith H. (1982), 'The protected, the protector, and the defender', *Women's Studies International Forum*, **5** (3–4): 367–76.

Strasser, Steven (2004), *The Abu Ghraib Investigations: The Official Independent Panel and Pentagon Reports on the Shocking Prisoner Abuse in Iraq*, Public Affairs.

Sturdevant, Saundra Pollock and Brenda Stoltzfus (1992), *Let the Good Times Roll: Prostitution and the US Military in Asia*, The New Press.

Tessier, Marie (2003), 'Sexual assault pervasive in military, experts say', *Women's E-News*, 30 March, accessed 15 August 2015 at: http://womensenews.org/story/rape/030330/ sexual-assault-pervasive-military-experts-say.

Tosh, John (2004), 'Hegemonic masculinity and the history of gender', in Stefan Dudink, Karen Hagemann and John Tosh (eds), *Masculinities in Politics and War; Gendering Modern History*, Manchester University Press, pp. 41–58.

Ubaldi, John (2015), 'It's long past time for reforming the military industrial complex', *Homeland Security Today*, 4 March, accessed 5 August 2015 at: http://www.apus.edu/ news-events/media-coverage/2015/03-04-2015-its-long-past-time-for-reforming-the-military-industrial-complex.htm.

US Army (2015), *Army Sexual Harassment/Assault Response and Prevention*, accessed 15 August 2015 at: http://www.sexualassault.army.mil/.

US Commission on Civil Rights (2013), *Sexual Assault in the Military, Military Panel*, C-SPAN2, 11 January, accessed 14 August 2015 at: http://www.c-span.org/video/ ?310331-3/sexual-assault-military-military-panel.

US Department of Defense (2003), *Defense Task Force Report on Domestic Violence*, accessed 15 August 2015 at: http://www.ncdsv.org/images/Year3Report2003.pdf.

US Department of Defense (2004a), *US Army Official Report on 507th Maintenance Co.: An Nasiriyah, Iraq*, accessed 13 August 2015 at: https://www.metavr.com/casestudies/ aar507ambush.pdf .

US Department of Defense (2004b), *Task Force Report on Sexual Assault Policies*, 27 May, accessed 14 August 2015 at: http://www.ncdsv.org/images/Army_TaskForce ReportOnSexualAssaultPolicies_5-27-2004.pdf.

US Department of Defense (2005a), *Report of the Defense Task Force on Sexual Harassment and Violence at the Military Service Academies*, June, accessed 15 August 2015 at: http://www.sapr.mil/public/docs/research/high_gpo_rrc_tx.pdf.

US Department of Defense (2005b), *Confidentiality Policy for Victims of Sexual Assault*, accessed 15 August 2015 at: http://www.defense.gov/news/Mar2005/d20050318dsd.pdf.

US Department of Defense (2015), *Annual Report on Sexual Assault in the Military, Fiscal Year 2014*, accessed 6 August 2015 at: http://sapr.mil/public/docs/reports/FY14_Annual/ FY14_DoD_SAPRO_Annual_Report_on_Sexual_Assault.pdf.

US House of Representatives (2007), 'Hearing on Tillman, Lynch incidents: Jessica Lynch's opening statement', Committee on Oversight and Government Reform, accessed 14 August 2015 at: https://www.youtube.com/watch?v=l0OyihqYfF4.

US Senate (2014), *Committee Study of the Central Intelligence Agency's Detention and Interrogation Program*, Senate Select Committee on Intelligence, accessed 13 August 2015 at: https://web.archive.org/web/20141209165504/http://www.intelligence.senate. gov/study2014/sscistudy1.pdf.

Walters, Joanna (2005), 'As casualties soar, America's women face reality of front line', *The Guardian*, 30 April, accessed 15 August 2015 at: http://www.theguardian.com/ world/2005/may/01/usa.gender.

White, Josh (2005), 'Abu Ghraib tactics were first used at Guantanamo', *Washington Post*, 14 July, accessed 15 August 2015 at: http://www.washingtonpost.com/wp-dyn/content/ article/2005/07/13/AR2005071302380.html.

Williams, Kayla and Michael E. Staub (2005), *Love My Rifle More Than You: Young and Female in the US Army*, W.W. Norton.

Williams, Rudi (1998), 'Military women take 200-year trek toward respect, parity', *DoD News*, accessed 5 August 2015 at: http://www.defense.gov/news/newsarticle.aspx?id= 43226.

Wise, Brian S. (2003), 'On Shoshana Johnson, Jessica Lynch and disability', *In Dissent*, No. 140, 28 October, accessed 15 August 2015 at: http://www.intellectualconservative. com/article2798.html.

Women in Military Service for America (2015), 'Statistics on women in the military', accessed on 5 August 2015 at: http://www.womensmemorial.org/Press/stats.html.

Zavis, Alexandra (2013), 'New US combat policy affirms role women already play', *Los Angeles Times*, 18 February, accessed 5 August 2015 at: http://articles.latimes.com/2013/feb/18/world/la-fg-us-women-combat-20130219.

Zoroya, Gregg (2012), 'VA finds sexual assaults more common in war zones', *USA Today*, 26 December, accessed 14 August 2015 at: http://www.usatoday.com/story/news/nation/2012/12/26/va-finds-sexual-assaults-more-common-in-war-zones/1793253/.

14. From woman warrior to innocent child: telling gendered news stories of women terrorists

Dan Berkowitz and Qi Ling

During the twentieth century, women terrorists played prominent roles in leftist groups and secular organizations, mainly in Western Europe, Latin America and Western Asia (Bloom, 2014; Hudson and Majeska, 1999). Some research indicates that women constituted 30 percent of European terrorists (Hudson and Majeska, 1999). In the twenty-first century, with an increase of the numbers and variety of roles within terror groups across the globe, however, Islamic groups began to employ women as suicide bombers (Bloom, 2011, 2014). Women have served as suicide bombers, as perpetrators, recruiters, fund-raisers, and propagandists for terror, and as sexual brides. Key to this rise in women's activity in terrorism has been a shift in terrorism from attacking military targets to civilian targets. Women are especially useful in the latter respect since security checks are less invasive on women than on men (Bloom, 2014; Nossek et al., 2007). In addition, women as suicide terrorists conflict with societal images of women as relatively harmless and peace-loving; this brings an additionally damaging psychological element (Sofer and Addison, 2012).

In 2002, Palestinian women suicide bombers gained media attention as a novelty because of their gender. More recently, young girls and women of Western origin have participated in terrorism, garnering media attention in doing so. News coverage about this tends to emphasize women's novelty and serious commitment to a cause, producing greater impact and 'shock value' compared to men (Pounds, 2014; Sofer and Addison, 2012).

Western culture offers many culturally resonant gender-specific myths to help both journalists and audiences make sense of social life and maintain gender order. Myths provide patterns by which people make sense of a world that is otherwise too random, too unfamiliar, too complicated, or too inexplicable (Lule, 2001; Bird and Dardenne, 2009). For instance, the Good Mother archetype helps safeguard the ideal of self-sacrificing mothers (Lule, 2001); the Female Monster surfaces when a society is uncomfortable with women stepping into traditionally male-privileged realms such as politics and violence (Berrington and Honkatukia, 2002; Ritchie, 2013). While male suicide bombers have been cast as part-human, part-animal Tricksters who are driven by lust and physical appetites, journalists have deployed different archetypes to manage the surging occurrences of women terrorists (Berkowitz, 2005a).

To show how gendered archetypes are invoked in news about women terrorists, this chapter explores four cases, each representing a distinct type of women terrorist. After discussing news as mythical narrative we offer a qualitative textual analysis of relevant news stories from mainstream English-language news media.

NEWS AS MYTHICAL NARRATIVE

Professional journalists are expected to convey information objectively and impartially. But bits of reality are not converted to news articles randomly. To organize information from the real world effectively, journalists must present coherent and reasonable narratives within the constraints of their organization's timeframes and resources. One way to navigate between reality and story-telling is to draw from myths, which are marked by identifiable narrative structures that become formulaic through repeated application, complete with common central actors and predictable outcomes (Bird and Dardenne, 2009; Cawelti, 1984; Lule, 2001; Silverstone, 1988). By evoking taken-for-granted beliefs about a society, mythical narratives seem natural rather than ideological, thus reaffirming the existing social order (Bird and Dardenne, 2009; Slotkin, 1992).

To view news as myth is not to negate its accuracy in reflecting reality, but to explore how it interprets and represents the world via certain narrative patterns. Both parts of their culture and storytellers for that culture, journalists construct stories through narrative conventions that are culturally resonant for themselves and their audiences (Ettema, 2005). Journalists know how their stories are supposed to go and what they must do to produce them (Berkowitz, 1992; Kitch, 2002). Even when reporting unusual and unexpected events, news workers explain situations in ways that become relatively familiar and usual.

Nossek and Berkowitz (2006) note that a *professional narrative* follows from the intersection of journalism's professional norms with community rules. A professional narrative serves informational purposes and is presented as chronicle, a basic, direct record of society's goings-on, using details of an occurrence. When society's core values are threatened, however, such as during incidents of terrorism, *cultural narratives* are deployed to remind audiences of the dominant cultural order; here news is embedded within the long-standing, enduring values that shape a society. A cultural narrative is assembled in the form of story; incorporating an entertainment function, information is couched within something more akin to folklore (Bird and Dardenne, 1988; Nossek and Berkowitz, 2006). Further shaping the nature of cultural narratives is cultural and geographical proximity. When an event takes place geographically far away or reflects a different set of cultural meanings, cultural narratives normalize these little-understood occurrences and bring familiar meanings to audiences.

Bird and Dardenne (2009) differentiate between 'news as myth' and 'news as storytelling'. News as myth represents a relatively static portrayal in terms of the narrative's elements that are told; this perspective centers on universalities. News as storytelling, in contrast, moves away from universalities and considers news as a set of story narratives, not based so much on value-laden archetypes as on regularly telling stories in a way that appears natural and true (Berkowitz, 2005a, 2005b). Myth helps make news believable and coherent, while also helping the task of reporting get done one time and in an acceptable form. When news takes place outside a country's borders, myth helps create a narrative that turns news of others into yet more stories of ourselves (Berkowitz, 2005a).

In sum, a society's myths set up models of social life, define right and wrong, validate the shared culture, and reassure and familiarize shared community experiences. Myth is 'an important way that a society expresses its prevailing ideals, ideologies, values and beliefs' (Lule, 2001:15). Gendered news of terrorism, however, illustrates how news narratives are not rigidly fixed, but rather adapt to their cultural contexts while connecting to familiar stories about how things are supposed to go. And telling a news story in one way may exclude stories that could otherwise be told (Bird and Dardenne, 2009).

GENDERED ARCHETYPES IN MEDIA

Women terrorists have been portrayed in news media, documentaries and popular culture via the lens of normative femininity, although actual stories are more complicated than what gender boundaries have defined (Bloom, 2011; Talbot, 2000). Women terrorists are often framed in terms of their physical appearances or family connections, as driven by love or gender liberation/equality, and as either as tough as men (or tougher) or 'bored, naïve, out-of-touch-with-reality' (Nacos, 2005: 435–51). Most scholars agree that men's involvement in terrorism is taken for granted while women's involvement seems to require more explanation in terms of personality, psychological status and relationships (Friedman, 2008; Patkin, 2004; Struckman, 2006). For example, women terrorists are usually assumed to be 'more depressed, crazier, more suicidal, or more psychopathic than their male counterpart' (Bloom, 2011: 4). It's another example of how mass media are often oriented by and in turn perpetuate gender myths undergirded by sexual difference (Carter, 2005).

To examine news depictions of women terrorists, this study adopts the lens of archetype, with three archetypes having particularly relevant gender meanings. One archetype, which often surfaces in news coverage related to motherhood, is the Good Mother, or variations thereof, namely, the Patriotic Mother or the Flawed Mother (Barnett, 2006; Slattery and Garner, 2007). The Good Mother is characterized by her maternal nurturing qualities, goodness and self-sacrifice (Lule, 2001). For instance, in covering women who killed their children, journalists ignored complex societal causes and instead drew on the failure of the 'all-knowing, all-loving, and all-powerful mother' to explain infanticide (Barnett, 2006).

Another popular culture archetype is the Woman Warrior, whose antecedent can be traced back to Athena, the Greek goddess of war, peace and wisdom. Contemporary Woman Warriors – the 'daughters' of Athena – are cast as 'strong, intelligent, heroic warriors who defend the right as they see the right' (Wilcox, 2003). Although the balance of elements has varied over time and the archetype has evolved, Woman Warriors can be identified by an amalgam of toughness, smartness, beauty, sexuality and defiance (Inness, 1999). In the 1990s, a sense of justice – the 'Just Warrior' crusading to save society – was added into this blend (Early and Kennedy, 2003).

The Female Monster archetype reflects male anxiety about women, particularly women who demonstrate ability in areas that are typically reserved for men, such as politics, violence and artistry (Berrington and Honkatukia, 2002; Gubar, 1977; Ritchie, 2013; Sternadori, 2014). Such women are susceptible to being unfairly characterized as deviants who are abnormal, untamed and unlikely to fit in social norms (Lewis, 1998). These aberrant women could be psychologically problematic (Sternadori, 2014), have personal problems, or embody a blend of male and female, human and animal characteristics (Ritchie, 2013).

In recent years, a growing trend of teenage girls participating in terrorism has called for a new archetype. Popular culture associates teenage girls with several gendered attributes that both vary from and are in a continuum with women. Media culture has often reinforced the ideas that girls are cute and silly, primarily concerned with romance and prioritizing marriage as their ultimate goal (McRobbie, 1978; Douglas, 1995). More recent mediated messages usually associate adolescent girls with pop music, fashion, beauty, celebrity culture and boy-watching (Gill, 2007: 184–5). This would predict, for example, that news coverage of young women terrorists would resonate with prevailing assumptions about teenage girls.

In sum, terrorism is often regarded as both culturally and physically distant, so that journalists – and their audiences – cannot effectively relate to the narratives of localized meanings. Mythical narratives provide a plausible substitute that resonates with those detached audiences. When terrorists are women, that resonance becomes even more difficult to achieve because women are associated with non-violence, nurturing, materialism and femininity. Thus, news narratives of women terrorists tend to play out in opposition to the conventional vision of man-as-violent-terrorist. To make narratives of women terrorists plausible and 'terrorist appropriate', media portrayals turn to extreme renditions in terms of behaviors, motivations and overall presence.

This chapter moves forward with two large questions: How do media narratives of women terrorists draw on mythical elements? How are these narratives gendered in the characteristics they propagate?

METHOD

This study offers a qualitative thematic textual analysis (Brennen, 2012; Lindlof and Taylor, 2010) of four cases related to women terrorists that appeared in the US and UK news over the past 14 years, beginning with news coverage during 2002 of women Palestinian suicide bombers (Berkowitz, 2005a). We searched Google, Google News and LexisNexis using the terms 'woman terrorist', 'ISIS women', 'female suicide bombers' and 'Jihad brides' to identify relevant cases. (LexisNexis – like other news databases – can be uneven in terms of its search results, sometimes including little-known media sources while at other times omitting items because of the peculiarities of specific search terms.) Beyond the cases of the Palestinian women, most of the other cases occurred between 2010 and 2015. In all, we analyzed 122 news items related to four cases spanning a timeframe from 2002 to 2015. We noted central themes and compared notes to achieve a shared interpretation. Examples were then drawn from these notes and conversations to illustrate these themes, as described below.

THE WOMAN WARRIOR

US news (and more broadly, Western news) has long been portraying suicide bombers as crazed fanatics who revel in the destruction they will cause (Berkowitz, 2005a, 2005b).[1] They are often portrayed as young men who – on the surface – are shy and religious (Philips, 2001). The archetype of the Trickster applies here as well – an 'anti-hero' who has little control over his impulses but causing problems for society (Lule, 2001).

But when news surfaced in 2002 about Wafa Idris, the first Palestinian woman to carry out a suicide bombing, she was quickly called the 'new suicide bomber' (Bennet, 2002c). Idris was immediately contrasted with the men before her who had been suicide bombers: rather than appearing as another Trickster, she became the Woman Warrior. To accomplish this, journalists declared a *new phenomenon*, a radical young woman eager to seek martyrdom and clear a new path to inspire other young women (Beaumont, 2002). Archetypically, unlike the Trickster, the Woman Warrior is smart, tough and defiant, while committing an act 'virtually unheard of for a woman' in that culture (Bennet, 2002b). The Woman Warrior is simultaneously defined by beauty. Wafa Idris, for example, was described in news accounts as having 'chestnut hair curling past her shoulders' (Bennet, 2002a), with a 'pale complexion' (Matza, 2002) and wearing 'sleeveless dresses and make-up' (Walker, 2002). Other Palestinian women suicide bombers received similar news treatment. Heba Daraghmeh was described as 'well-dressed and wearing high heels' (Gozani and de Quetteville, 2003). Hanadi Jaradat was likened to a Middle-East folk singer, 'with her ruby-red lips and black headscarf' (Toolis, 2003).

Despite killing civilians, these Woman Warriors retained positive, noble attributes of *personality* and *character*. Wafa Idris was portrayed as 'confident and composed' (Bennet, 2002a), 'a model young woman ... a good friend, a loving daughter and a social activist' (Beaumont, 2002). Ayat Akhras was described as 'a quiet, diligent schoolgirl' (Hazboun, 2002) who was 'months away from graduation and then marriage' (Ripley, 2002). Hiba Daraghmeh was a 'devout ... forceful young woman who was in some ways the emotional rock of her family ... a young girl with a great future ahead' (Nessman, 2003). These kinds of archetypal characteristics stood in clear contrast to men as suicide bombers.

Without using the term 'Woman Warrior', much of the news coverage of these Palestinian suicide bombers sketched an image of a heroic warrior, striving to serve a just cause. One writer explained: 'But there are no women heroes, no Joans of Arc, in Islamic tradition. That is, until now. And that's the cultural revolution springing out of the West Bank today' (Leung, 2003).[2]

The *Jerusalem Post*, an Israeli newspaper read chiefly by Americans and expatriates, explained that the Palestinian Authority 'heaped praise on Palestinian women who carry out suicide attacks in Israel, describing them as heroes and symbols of the Palestinian national struggle' (Toameh, 2003).

Another characteristic of these Woman Warriors was seeking revenge for a *just cause*. Wafa Idris, for example, had a brother imprisoned for ten years, and she had worked as a medic rescuing wounded Palestinian men. Ayat Akhras decided to become a suicide bomber because, in her view, Palestinian men had not done their jobs effectively: 'I am going to fight, instead of the sleeping Arab armies who are watching Palestinian girls fighting alone' (Hazboun, 2002).

Another aspect cementing the archetype was the element of *celebration*. *Time* pointed out: 'These days Palestinians celebrate the suicides in newspaper announcements that read, perversely, like wedding invitations' (Ripley, 2002).

Likewise, the father of suicide bomber Hanadi Jaradat stated: 'I will accept only congratulations for what she did. This was a gift she gave me, the homeland and the Palestinian people. Therefore, I am not crying for her' (Levy-Barzilai, 2003).

The evidence of the Just Fight – and the larger image of the Woman Warrior – was thus clear. These women were presented not as violent murderers, but as cultural heroes who, in fighting the occupation of their land, undertook a quest to right what been wronged. Their Trickster-male counterparts had failed. Thus, in characteristics and in cause, the first six Palestinian women who became suicide bombers clearly emerged as Woman Warriors, an archetype that offered journalists a plausible presentation of the news.

The seventh woman, however, broke the mold. Like the first six women, Reem Raiyshi entered Israel with the intent of committing political violence. In appearance, though, she dressed according to cultural conventions. Personally, she was also quite different: a married mother of two, and an adulterer. Rather than fighting the Just Fight for the Palestinian people, Raiyshi's purpose was more personal. She wanted to redeem her family's honor. Having engaged in adultery, she was forced to wear a bomb vest provided by her lover; her husband then delivered her to her target site (*Washington Times*, 2004). Detonating a bomb that killed her and 11 others did not reflect a long-term commitment to a social cause; she had long suffered depression and had tried to commit suicide before (McGreal, 2004). Relatives said she was not particularly devout although her martyr video contained undertones of religious beliefs (Greenberg, 2004). Her act, at least as Western journalists presented it, represented an element of decay in her society. Her death did not reflect the key attributes of the Woman Warrior: beauty, sexuality, smartness, toughness and defiance. In fact, a positive archetype simply did not fit. Instead she was cast in the news as the Terrible Mother, the inverse of the Good Mother.

In all, the Palestinian women suicide bombers in 2002 required news media to shift their gendered approach to the narrative to tell the story in a cogent way. No longer a Fool or a Trickster, these women were noble warriors – at least until another woman's suicide bombing, under different circumstances, required yet another albeit still gendered, narrative shift. This archetype, the Terrible Mother, will be explored later. Over the following years as other women acted as terrorists, gendered mythical narratives continued to shift to make the news story resonant to US society.

THE INNOCENT CHILD

In 2014, journalists were apparently surprised to learn that teenage girls and young women living in the Western world would join a dangerous organization in the Middle East such as ISIS. These teenage girls mainly came from Britain, the United States, Canada, Australia and France. The most reported cases included three British girls – Amira Abase, 15, Shamima Begum, 15 and Kadiza Sultana, 16 – whose images were seen on a surveillance camera at Gatwick airport when they were leaving for Syria in February 2015. Another case involved the 'Terror Twins', Zahra and Salma Halane, 16-year-old girls from Manchester, England who disappeared in July 2014. Attention was also drawn to Aqsa Mahmood, who left her home in Glasgow, Scotland, in November 2013, and a 20-year-old high school graduate named Hoda,[3] who ran away from her Alabama home in November 2014. The media dubbed each girl who headed for Syria as a 'Jihadi bride', causing widespread anxiety in the West. Although the Jihadi Bride was not a long-standing news narrative, its repeated depiction across these three cases suggests it has become a new archetype.

In reporting on these young women, two relatively independent narrative dimensions helped shape the stories. One dimension considered their identity as teenagers, which is relatively gender-neutral, embodied in the aspects of youthful idealism and cultural tastes. The second dimension had an internal tension: it brought out girlish or womanly attributes shared by other girls, as well as a challenge to these traditional gendered narratives. Meanwhile, similar to their male counterparts, these girls were portrayed in news stories as religiously loyal and politically active. Further, they were often allowed to express their attitudes about the war, their ambition to change society, and their dedication to the cause they believed in – most of which was based on their interpretation of religious laws (Aly, 2015).

This kind of agency, however, was usually treated more as the fanatical worship typical of young people than as rational, deliberate choice. Their behavior was often connected to the girls' immaturity, which contributed to their dissatisfaction with current situations and their commitment to building a better society via radical actions (Khaleeli, 2014). These young girls were believed to be driven by righteous, humanitarian concerns, yet they were portrayed as unrealistic or even wrong in their ambition to help Syrians (e.g. Fantz and Shubert, 2015; Yan and Elbagir, 2015). Journalists described these teenagers as mistaking the terrorist organization ISIS for a 'utopian society', 'a paradise' and 'a safe place' (e.g. Shubert, 2015; Robinson, 2014), where they could escape their dissatisfactions with Western society.

To develop this narrative of the Innocent Child, journalists portrayed these teenage girls as normal or good students, enjoying adventures and enjoying the same popular culture elements as other young people. Sometimes they faced typical teenage problems such as lacking a sense of belonging or making stupid and dangerous mistakes. In short, their identity was partially defined by their youthfulness, which could be found in any typical youngster in Western societies, regardless of gender. For instance, a *CNN* segment titled *The Women of ISIS: Who Are They?* described the three British girls as typical London teenagers who care about 'which shoes to buy: Vans; her favorite football club: Chelsea; her most hated school subject: statistics' (Shubert, 2015). Likewise, the parents of Aqsa Mohammad described their 20-year-old daughter, apparently now in Syria recruiting other girls, as someone who 'listened to Coldplay, read Harry Potter novels and drank Irn Bru, a Scottish soft drink' (de Freytas-Tamura, 2015).

Being similar to young men, however, was not sufficient to complete the story of a teenage girl joining ISIS. To make the news of these young women more resonant and to facilitate US society's understanding of teenage girls in ISIS, a gendered narrative was drawn upon to distinguish them from teenage boys. In an effort to make sense of these teenage-girls-turned-terrorists, journalists referred to negative gender stereotypes (trivial, narcissistic and materialistic) but also positive, gender-specific terms (caring, loving and sweet). Mahmood, for example, was portrayed as a girl who 'loved Harry Potter books and bought lip gloss and giggled about boys' and who 'cared for her three younger siblings and her grandparents at her home' (Blum, 2014; de Freytas-Tamura, 2015). The Halane twins were described as typical teenagers 'pouting for selfies and shopping at Primark' (Tozer et al., 2014). The *Daily Mail* selected a tweet from Zahra Halane's Twitter page to begin its account: 'But schoolgirl Zahra Halane has revealed her biggest worry: the welfare of her cat … . The 16-year-old tweeted about her fears for her missing ginger kitten yesterday, saying it had "disappeared" after her "husband[4] threw [it] outside"' (Taylor and Narain, 2014).

Journalists from many news outlets critiqued ISIS strategies for recruiting young girls. These included promoting unimportant material goods, the ideal of marrying a man, and a warped sense of girl power. During a *CNN* interview with a college professor, news anchor Carol Costello claimed that ISIS lured women with kittens, Nutella and emojis. Other journalists, however, ridiculed this assertion. *New York* magazine mocked Costello: 'If you're a lady walking down the street and you come upon a kitten covered in Nutella posing next to a poster of the nail emoji, beware! ISIS operatives could be lurking nearby, ready to recruit you and make you their jihadi brides – at least according to *CNN*' (Roy, 2015).

The false image of heterosexual romance or marriage underpinned by the generic notion of 'strong men, weak women' was also claimed to be a key strategy exploited by ISIS. *The Guardian* asserted: 'They are going for adventure, just like the young men … . Many are also attracted to the idea of marrying a foreign fighter, seen as a heroic figure willing to sacrifice himself for a cause' (Khaleeli, 2014).

An *Express* article began: 'She was young, disaffected and impressionable. He was older, charismatic and he promised her the world. When he proposed he told her, "When you get here, you'll be treated like a princess"' (Pukas, 2015).

Somewhat challenging this narrative was the idea that girls could be attracted by a counter-feminist message. Journalists suggested that, instead of being drawn away by men or being attracted by cute icons, these young girls were inspired by the freedom to embrace conservative gender ideals, such as choosing to be a mother and covering their bodies to avoid objectification. The *Telegraph* quoted Melanie Smith, a co-writer of the report 'Til Martyrdom Do U Part': 'They're saying, "the West tells you to have a career and not have children. But we won't shame you for the decision to stay at home" … It's empowering in such a warped, pseudo-feminist way' (Sanghani, 2015).

In sum, young 'jihad brides' were portrayed as Innocent Children; once normal, typical teenagers, they were cheated by villains manipulating their girlish desires. Making reference to cultural narratives of all young people on the one hand, and of typical girls on the other hand, helped journalists to present a cohesive and resonant story of a modern Western girl.

THE TERRIBLE MOTHER

Besides Reem Raiyshi, the adulterous mother of two mentioned above who became a suicide bomber to redeem her family's honor, two other Terrible Mothers surfaced in 2012. This time, they were not suicide bombers but were actively engaged in recruiting and planning. Faduma Jama, known as Mama Shabab, grew up in Somalia and later lived in Canada. Eventually, she moved back to Somalia where she married a leader of the terror group, Al-Shabab, which had links to Al-Qaeda. This was the organization that masterminded an attack at the Westgate mall in Nairobi, Kenya in 2012. Jama soon took on a vital role as what the *Toronto Star* called a 'den mother', recruiting Westerners to Al-Shabab (Callahan, 2013; Shephard, 2012, 2013): 'But with their valuable passports and their seeming willingness to die fighting, the Western recruits have intelligence agencies worried – and they keep Mama Shabab on the radar.' '"She is very important, as everybody went to her safe house", one security official, who has collected reports on Jama for years, told the Star on the condition he not be identified.' 'At least nine of the Americans, including Jehad Mostafa, went through there.'

Likewise, news coverage emphasized the growing importance of women to the success of terrorist movements. A Canadian journalist explained this new role for women such as Jama:

> But a *Toronto Star* investigation based on interviews with security, intelligence and law enforcement officials, in addition to leaders in the Somali diaspora here and abroad, reveal a portrait of a female leader vital to the organization.
>
> Her role facilitating Western recruits exemplifies the increasing importance of women to the Shabab – although her position of authority is rare, as most females are recruited only as wives for the fighters or suicide bombers. (Shephard, 2012)

The *New York Post* quoted terrorism scholar Mia Bloom, emphasizing the strategic importance of women for the success of terrorist organizations like Al-Shabab:

If and when those first marriages fail – due to death, planned or otherwise – these women continue to marry within their terror networks, rising in esteem for their devotion to martyrs. In an otherwise rigidly patriarchal society, this is how women derive their power: raising money, acting as couriers, goading men into jihad by accusing them of being weaker than women. (Callahan, 2013)

In 2015, Jama gained further visibility when her daughter Amal Farah – who had been estranged from her mother for five years – learned from two people from an anti-terror unit who appeared at her door that her mother was an infamous terrorist. A *Mirror* headline read, 'My shock at discovering my mum is a jihadist terrorist linked to the White Widow'. The writer portrayed the daughter as 'a model, law-abiding British citizen' who was stunned by the information about her mother. Searching online once she got to her job, she learned more: 'As I read about what she'd done I felt so alone. I couldn't just turn to my colleagues and say, "Guess what? My mum's a wanted terrorist." I couldn't believe my own mother was involved. I cried non-stop for days after that' (Fox-Leonard, 2015).

Nonetheless, although she thought Mama Shabab was a 'horrible name', the daughter came to realize why her Terrible Mother received the moniker: 'She explained: "She could be very kind and charming. I can see how natural it would be for her to be that motherly figure ... She is utterly devoted to what she believes in and being a wife of a jihadist is a way she can help as a woman"' (Fox-Leonard, 2015).

But while playing up the positive attributes of her mother, Farah also commented on Mama Shabab's deviance:

But the image of her mother as Mama Shabab is a long way from the woman of Amal's earliest memories.

She said: 'When I was little my mum loved fashion. She had these fantastic hairstyles. Her brother lived in Geneva and she would visit him and bring back all these amazing clothes.'

'Mum was an independent, educated woman. She even divorced my dad because she wanted to travel.' (Fox-Leonard, 2015)

If Mama Shabab's mythical narrative appeared as fanatic and deviant, yet nurturing, journalists played up the strategic value of another woman's Terrible Mother attributes. Sally Jones, a British mother of two boys and Muslim convert, moved to Syria with her 10-year-old son to recruit young women for ISIS. A news item in the *Medway Messenger* (part of the UK's KM Media group) titled 'Happy mum turned to hate' described her transition from Good to Terrible:

A decade ago Chatham mum Sally Jones was in relaxed mood as she posed for the *Medway Messenger* with new born bundle of festive joy, baby Joe Dixon.

It was Christmas 2004; three thousand miles away Sunni militants had just claimed responsibility for bombing a US-base in the Iraqi city of Mosul, killing 22 people, but the troubles of the Middle East must have felt a world away from this scene of maternal and festive bliss.

Now Jones and her 10-year-old son, renamed Hamza, are in the midst of them, and the mother of two has spoken out about her mission to join Jihadist group Islamic State. (Hunter, 2014)

Highlighted in many of the news reports was Jones's past life. For example, a *Sunday Times* article titled 'My son and I love life with the beheaders' explained: 'Jones's transformation from a miniskirt-wearing guitarist in a rock band in the early 1990s to a jihadist bride who now believes that music is "haram", or forbidden, is the most startling tale of all the Britons who have travelled to Syria and Iraq' (Gadher, 2014).

Other news reports condemned Jones for other lifestyle choices:

Pals of the unemployed mum, who had her two sons with two different fathers, say she was so hard pressed for money she turned to prostitution before converting to Islam.

One neighbor said: 'She was a nightmare. She was always screaming and shouting and up all hours of the night'.

'Men would come and go – I'm pretty sure she was a prostitute. Everything about her was extreme. She had problems with debts so one minute she was there and the next she'd scarpered'. (Ward, 2014)

In summary, a mixture of deviance and fanaticism – coupled with an intense effort toward furthering terrorism – worked to depict Mama Shabab and Sally Jones as Terrible Mothers. They were evil scheming strategists who shirked their motherly duties while luring other women's children into a life of terrorism.

THE FEMALE MONSTER

The Female Monster mainly surfaced in news articles about women terrorists who are widows or divorcees. Like those adult women who were characterized as Terrible Mother, these 'monsters' also play active roles as recruiters, propagandists, trainers, fundraisers, attackers or even commanders within terror groups.

This archetype is exemplified in demonizing news coverage of three women terrorists. Hayat Boumeddiene, a 26-year-old Parisian, is suspected to be an accomplice of her husband Amedy Coulibaly, who killed four people in a kosher supermarket in Paris in 2015 before commandos killed him. Samantha Lewthwaite, a 32-year-old British woman, is the widow of Germaine Lindsay, one of the 7/7 London bombers. Allegedly linked to the Somali Al-Qaeda-allied terror group Al-Shabab, Lewthwaite is suspected of being connected to a 2013 assault in Nairobi. Both Boumeddiene and Lewthwaite are still on the run. Collen LaRose, a 52-year-old woman, known as Jihad Jane and Fatima LaRose, is an American who was caught by police and convicted of plotting to murder a Swedish cartoonist for his cartoons of the prophet Muhammad and of participation in other terrorist offenses. In 2009 she was sentenced to 10 years in jail.

English-language news media repeatedly described these women as 'very dangerous' or 'the most wanted women' on the watch list of multiple intelligence services (Pukas, 2012; Witte and Murphy, 2015). They rose to prominence as crucial to terrorist missions – in recruiting, financing, propagating and ordering, they sometimes surpassed male terrorists in rank. Although these women were portrayed as fighting for a cause they believed was just, the accounts of these figures were by no means heroic.

Samantha Lewthwaite, for example, was portrayed as capable but ruthless. Nicknamed the 'White Widow', she is believed to be an important high-status commander in Al-Shabab, which called her 'Mother of Holy War' because she could directly communicate with the leader Ahmad Umar (Odowa, 2015; *Banbridge Leader*, 2015). She trained women terrorists and allegedly served as the financier and explosives expert for an Al-Shabab cell (Brown, 2012). She was 'not just a small cog' (Carpenter, 2013), but 'the mastermind behind four atrocities' (Odowa, 2015). A news account of LaRose, however, countered that the negative characterization of her 'proved more farcical than frightful, more absurd than ominous' (Pilkington, 2012). *The Washington Post* made similar assertions about Boumeddiene's fear-inspiring persona:

> Authorities never previously believed she was a danger, though they now say she may have been the force behind her husband … . Now counterterrorism officials say they fear Boumeddiene's position as the wife of a martyr may make her a powerful figure within extremist ranks. Some even believe she may return to Europe to carry out more attacks. (Birnbaum and Mekhennet, 2015)

These women were described as having special – sometimes unfeminine – qualities that enabled them to accomplish their roles. Boumeddiene was described as 'armed and dangerous', 'cool and composed and always stayed calm when questioned' (Cook et al., 2015; Hurley, 2015). Lewthwaite was 'evil but clever', suspected of trying to separate herself from her husband's bombing in London by claiming that she had some conflicts with him before the bombings (Pukas, 2012). The elusiveness of Lewthwaite and Boumeddiene made them even more dangerous for the police. Lewthwaite 'has proved remarkably elusive and remains at large somewhere' and 'is rather good at wriggling away' (Pukas, 2012; Carpenter, 2013). Boumeddiene was referred to as a 'spook' who was difficult to capture (Collins, 2015).

Whereas coverage of male terrorists usually focused on their actions, journalists gave much more background information about the women terrorists' personality, persona, relationships and family history, all of which, for Monsters, turned out to be problematic. A childhood friend told the *Los Angeles Times* Boumeddiene was: '"impulsive", emotionally fragile, childlike, quick to cry, with little self-confidence, prone to sending religious text messages and venting about her growing sense of alienation as a Muslim' (Hennessy-Fiske, 2015).

Reuters quoted LaRose's attorney describing her as 'a lonely and vulnerable woman easily manipulated by others online' (Shiffman, 2014). *The Guardian* highlighted her eccentricity, quoting neighbors: '"She was the weird lady who lived across the hall. We always called her the crazy lady", said Eric Newell, but he never thought she was dangerous. His wife said LaRose used to talk to her cats' (Pilkington, 2010)

Moreover, LaRose was reported as having a dark, sordid past: she once worked in prostitution, later became a heavy drug user (McCormack, 2015; Shiffman, 2014), and had been arrested for writing bad checks and driving while intoxicated (Johnson, 2010). In addition, her traumatic childhood was often brought up: her mother did not try to stop her biological father from raping LaRose (McCormack, 2015; Shiffman, 2014). In contrast, little personal, relational, and familial information was given about LaRose's male co-conspirator, beyond that he was a criminal juvenile, as if his violent actions needed no explanation. Similar contradictions appeared with Boumeddiene, whose mother reportedly died when she was six years old; she was later put into foster care. In contrast, much less personal information was reported about her husband Coulibaly (Cook et al., 2015; Birnbaum and Mekhennet, 2015).

What reinforces these women terrorists' image as deviant is the description of them as transgressing the typical definition of femininity. Journalists relied on feminine attributes (and their opposites) when depicting women terrorists. News articles described these women as resembling a cheerleader (LaRose), or once favoring make-up and rambling phone calls with friends (Boumeddiene), or worshiping entertainment stars, loving fashions, dieting and being a typical caring young mother (Lewthwaite) (Birnbaum and Mekhennenet, 2015; Grier, 2010; Hardy, 2014). Nonetheless, they became life-threatening, ruthless terrorists disassociated with any Western feminine traits. The *Herald Sun* ran a photo showing Boumeddiene in a full veil, and suggested that she was 'once content to relax on a sunny beach in a bikini, [but] soon after meeting Coulibaly she was happier undertaking crossbow training in rugged woodland' (Hurley, 2015).

Their sexuality and personal relationships – issues often associated with women rather than men in coverage of terrorists (Nacos, 2005; Friedman, 2008; Patkin, 2004; Struckman, 2006) – were also represented as deviant. Lewthwaite and LaRose were both represented as having difficult experiences such as early marriage and pregnancy. Lewthwaite, according to *The Times*, was pregnant with her 19-year-old husband's second child when he blew himself up in London (O'Neill, 2013). LaRose was first married at 16, was divorced twice, and had several boyfriends (Connor and Siegel, 2015; Nunnally et al., 2010).

In sum, the archetype of the Female Monster was evoked to help organize accounts of Boumeddiene, LaRose and Lewthwaite, who were either widows of terrorist fighters or middle-aged divorcees and were stepping into male-dominated realms in terror organizations. While men's involvement in terrorism was taken for granted, these women terrorists were to a certain degree deviant in terms of psychological status, persona, relational well-being, and gender norms.

CONCLUSION

The four archetypes of women terrorists (the Woman Warrior, the Innocent Child, the Terrible Mother and the Female Monster) showed that journalists drew on gender-specific mythical narratives to tell the stories of unfamiliar women in a way that made sense to the journalists themselves and resonated with their audiences. Gender narratives familiar to Western society – empowered womanhood, good and terrible motherhood, appropriate and deviant femininity, youthfulness and girlishness – were invoked so that the stories could seem logical and plausible rather than random assemblages. Girls and adult women of cultural backgrounds (Western and non-Western), roles within terror groups (sexual brides, suicide bombers, commanders, supporters), and marital and family status (single, mother, widow, divorcee or youngster) called for different forms of storytelling. Not surprisingly, the mythical archetypes used for the 2002 news of Palestinian suicide bombers as well as the archetypes that appeared more recently remained gendered. Motherhood, girlishness, family relationships, physical appearance and sexuality are still key indices in making sense of women terrorists. The four cases studied here make clear how news narratives depended on gendered characteristics to create an archetype that both displayed norms and built a portrait of deviance from those norms. By doing so, news of women terrorists appeared novel and exceptional, thus suggesting that gender norms were safe.

As to how these narratives were gendered in opposition to the dominant narratives of men as terrorists, the case was clear for the Woman Warriors: everything they did was virtuous, in contrast with the men who became suicide bombers. For the Jihadi Brides, the young women's aspirations and traits were clearly antithetic to those for young men: news audiences would never believe that young Western men would travel so far to meet women from a restrictive culture. Likewise, the characteristics of the Terrible Mother would not be inappropriate for men in a society that does not expect men to be nurturing or caring. Finally, men would not be Monsters because it would not be abnormal for them to take active and leading roles in non-domestic spheres.

The Woman Warriors were portrayed in a positive light, whereas the Terrible Mothers and the Female Monsters were stigmatized or demonized; the Innocent Child lies somewhere between these two extremes. This could probably be accounted for by the geopolitics of gender between the West and non-Western societies. For Western journalists, characterizing Palestinian women suicide bombers as Woman Warriors offered a counterpoint to the conservative gender culture of the Middle East. Thus, this portrayal resonated with feminism and human rights discourses common in the West and made those women appear more like 'us'. Alternatively, journalists seemed uneasy with women terrorists from Western backgrounds who left for less-developed, gender-restrictive societies; they were cultural traitors. They could be irresponsible mothers, monstrous women, or innocent girls making mistakes.

What underlie such contradictions are the binary constructions opposing the relatively modern, democratic West to the cultural Other of the anti-modern, dangerous and patriarchal Muslim world. Such a premise is consistent with the Western ideological framework for the war on terror, of which emancipating the women of the cultural Other is a part (Eisenstein, 2010). The four mythical archetypes discussed here not only supported the existing gender values, but also reinforced the 'central-marginal' geopolitical order between the West and the non-West, confirming 'our' cultural identity. Thus, these myth-based news narratives reinforce gender order within Western societies and influence the cultural attitudes towards the Middle-East, Africa and other distanced societies where terrorism is active.

NOTES

1. This section has been adapted from Berkowitz (2005a).
2. Other sources suggest that this assertion is incorrect (see Victor, 2003; and Davis, 2003).
3. Her family requested that BuzzFeed News not use Hoda's last name, or the names of her mother or siblings, 'due to concerns about their safety' (Hall, 2015).
4. The husband referred to here is her new ISIS husband.

REFERENCES

Aly, Anne (2015), 'Jihadi brides aren't oppressed. They join Isis for the same reasons men do', *The Guardian*, 3 March, accessed 1 September 2015 at: http://www.theguardian.com/commentisfree/2015/mar/04/jihadi-brides-arent-oppressed-they-join-isis-for-the-same-reasons-men-do.

Banbridge Leader (2015), 'White Widow behind terror atrocities in Kenya – claim', *Banbridge Leader*, 29 May, accessed 1 September 2015 at: http://www.banbridgeleader.co.uk/news/local-news/white-widow-behind-terror-atrocities-in-kenya-claim-1-6763230.

Barnett, Barbara (2006), '*Medea* in the media: narrative and myth in newspaper coverage of women who kill their children', in Daniel Berkowitz (ed.), *Cultural Meanings of News*, Sage, pp. 285–300.

Beaumont, Peter (2002), 'From an angel of mercy to angel of death: her family recall a lively tomboy', *The Guardian*, 30 January, available at: http://www.theguardian.com/world/2002/jan/31/israel.

Bennet, James (2002a), 'Arab woman's path to unlikely "martyrdom"', *The New York Times*, 31 January, accessed 1 September 2015 at: http://www.nytimes.com/2002/01/31/world/arab-woman-s-path-to-unlikely-martyrdom.html.

Bennet, James (2002b), 'Arab press glorifies bomber as heroine', *The New York Times*, 11 February, p. A8.

Bennet, James (2002c), 'Mideast turmoil: the bombers: rash of new suicide bombers exhibit no patterns or ties', *The New York Times*, 21 June, p. A1.

Berkowitz, Daniel (1992), 'Non-routine news and newswork: exploring a what-a-story', *Journal of Communication*, 42: 82–94.

Berkowitz, Daniel (2005a), 'Suicide bombers as women warriors: making news through mythical archetypes', *Journalism & Mass Communication Quarterly*, 82 (3): 607–22.

Berkowitz, Daniel (2005b), 'Telling what-a-story news through myth and ritual: the Middle East as wild west', in Eric W. Rothenbuhler and Mihai Coman (eds), *Media Anthropology*, Sage, pp. 210–19.

Berrington, Eileen and Päivi Honkatukia (2002), 'An evil monster and a poor thing: female violence in the media', *Journal of Scandinavian Studies in Criminology and Crime Prevention*, **3** (1): 50–72.

Bird, S. Elizabeth and Robert W. Dardenne (1988), 'News as mythological narrative', in James Carey (ed.), *Media, Myths, and Narratives: Television and the Press*, Sage.

Bird, S. Elizabeth and Robert W. Dardenne (2009), 'Rethinking news and myth as storytelling', in Karin Wahl-Jorgensen and Thomas Hanitzsch (eds), *The Handbook of Journalism Studies*, Routledge, pp. 205–17.

Birnbaum, Michael and Souad Mekhennet (2015), 'Hayat Boumeddiene, wife of Paris attacker, becomes France's most-wanted woman', *The Washington Post*, 2 February, accessed 1 September 2015 at: https://www.washingtonpost.com/world/europe/wife-of-paris-attacker-now-frances-most-wanted-woman/2015/02/02/b03c6950-a7da-11e4-a162-121d06ca77f1_story.html.

Bloom, Mia (2011), 'Bombshells: women and terror', *Gender Issues*, **28** (1–2): 1–21.

Bloom, Mia (2014), 'Female suicide bombers are not a new phenomenon', *The Washington Post*, 6 August, accessed 1 September 2015 at: http://www.washingtonpost.com/blogs/monkey-cage/wp/2014/08/06/female-suicide-bombers-are-not-a-new-phenomenon/.

Blum, Ruthie (2014), 'British feminism, Jihadi-style', *The Algemeiner*, 9 September, accessed 1 September 2015 at: http://www.algemeiner.com/2014/09/09/british-feminism-jihadi-style/.

Brennen, Bonnie (2012), *Qualitative Research Methods for Media Studies*, Routledge.

Brown, David (2012), '"White Widow" will not escape, say Kenyan police', *The Times*, 6 March, p. 11.

Callahan, Maureen (2013), 'How an average, middle-class English girl became the jihadi terrorist White Widow', *The New York Post*, 29 September, accessed 1 September 2015 at: http://nypost.com/2013/09/29/how-an-average-english-girl-became-the-white-widow/.

Carpenter, Julie (2013), 'Where is the world's most wanted woman?', *Express*, 20 May, available at: http://www.express.co.uk/news/uk/400904/Where-is-the-world-s-most-wanted-woman.

Carter, Cynthia (2005), 'Gendered news?', *Journalism*, **6** (3): 259–63.

Cawelti, John (1984), *The Six-gun Mystique Sequel*, Bowling Green State.

Collins, David (2015), 'Did spooks know of the plot in advance?', *Daily Mirror*, 15 January, p. 12.

Connor, Tracy and Stephanie Siegel (2015), '"Jihad Jane" Colleen LaRose became a terrorist for love', *NBS News*, 14 January, accessed 1 September 2015 at: http://www.nbcnews.com/news/investigations/jihad-jane-colleen-larose-became-terrorist-love-n284636.

Cook, Fidelma et al. (2015), 'Deli gunman's "wife" is already in Syria', *Mail Online*, 9 January, available at: http://www.dailymail.co.uk/news/article-2903601/Wife-Kosher-supermarket-killer-armed-dangerous-run-police-warn.html.

Davis, Joyce M. (2003), *Martyrs: Innocence, Vengeance and Despair in the Middle East*, Palgrave Macmillan.

De Freytas-Tamura, Kimiko (2015), 'Teenage girl leaves for ISIS, and others follow', *The New York Times*, 24 February, available at: http://www.nytimes.com/2015/02/25/world/from-studious-teenager-to-isis-recruiter.html?_r=0.

Douglas, Susan (1995), *Where the Girls are: Growing up Female with the Mass Media*, Three Rivers.

Early, Frances and Kathleen Kennedy (eds) (2003), *Athena's Daughters: Television's New Women Warrior*, Syracuse University.

Eisenstein, Hester (2010), 'Feminism seduced', *Australian Feminist Studies*, **25** (66): 413–31.

Ettema, James S. (2005), 'Crafting cultural resonance: imaginative power in everyday journalism', *Journalism*, **6** (2): 131–52.

Fantz, Ashley and Atika Shubert (2015), 'From Scottish teen to ISIS bride and recruiter: the Aqsa Mahmood story', *CNN*, 24 February, available at: http://www.cnn.com/2015/02/23/world/scottish-teen-isis-recruiter/.

Fox-Leonard, B. (2015), 'My mum is a jihadist who helps suicide bombers and is known as Mama Shabab', *The People*, 29 March, pp. 26, 27.

Friedman, Boudicca (2008), 'Unlikely warriors: how four US news sources explained female suicide bombers', *Journalism & Mass Communication Quarterly*, **85** (4): 841–59.

Gadher, Dipesh (2014), 'My son and I love life with the beheaders', *The Sunday Times (London)*, 7 September, available at: http://www.thesundaytimes.co.uk/sto/news/uk_news/National/Terrorism/article1455900.ece.

Gill, Rosalind (2007), *Gender and the Media*, Polity.

Gozani, Ohad and Harry de Quetteville (2003), 'Fifth suicide bomber in 2 days strikes Israel', *Daily Telegraph*, 20 May, p. A1.

Greenberg, Joel (2004), 'Family irate relative used as bomber', *Chicago Tribune*, 16 January, available at: http://articles.chicagotribune.com/2004-01-16/news/0401160211_1_gaza-strip-four-israeli-security-personnel-al.

Grier, Peter (2010), '"Jihad Jane": how does Al Qaeda recruit US-born women?', *The Christian Science Monitor*, 10 March, accessed 1 September 2015 at: http://www.csmonitor.com/USA/2010/0310/Jihad-Jane-How-does-Al-Qaeda-recruit-US-born-women.

Gubar, Susan (1977), 'The female monster in Augustan satire', *Signs*, **3** (2): 380–94.

Hall, Ellie (2015), 'Gone girl: an interview with an American in ISIS', *BuzzFeed News*, 17 April, accessed 1 September 2015 at: http://www.buzzfeed.com/ellievhall/gone-girl-an-interview-with-an-american-in-isis#.gtAVXZzbd.

Hardy, Alex (2014), 'The girl who went from Aylesbury to al-Qaeda', *The Times* (London), 3 July, p. T2.

Hazboun, Ibrahim (2002), 'Schoolgirl launches strike: two Israelis die in "courageous act"', *Ottawa Citizen*, 30 March, p. A4.

Hennessy-Fiske, Molly (2015), 'Female terrorists finding their place in Islamic militants' ranks', *Los Angeles Times*, 25 January, accessed 1 September 2015 at: http://www.latimes.com/world/europe/la-fg-france-terror-women-20150125-story.html#page=1.

Hudson, Rex A. and Marilyn Majeska (1999), *The Sociology and Psychology of Terrorism: Who Becomes a Terrorist and Why?* Library of Congress.

Hunter, Chris (2014), 'Happy mum turned to hate', *Medway Messenger*, 12 September.

Hurley, David (2015), 'How Hayat Boumeddiene became France's most wanted woman', *Herald Sun*, 10 January, available at: http://www.heraldsun.com.au/news/how-hayat-boumeddiene-became-frances-most-wanted-woman/story-fni0fiyv-1227180888950.

Inness, Sherrie A. (1999), *Tough Girls: Women Warriors and Wonder Women in Popular Culture*, University of Pennsylvania.

Johnson, Carrie (2010), 'JihadJane, an American woman, faces terrorism charges', *Washington Post*, 10 March, available at: http://www.washingtonpost.com/wp-dyn/content/article/2010/03/09/AR2010030902670.html.

Khaleeli, Homa (2014), 'The British women married to Jihad', *The Guardian*, 6 September, accessed 1 September 2015 at: http://www.theguardian.com/world/2014/sep/06/british-women-married-to-jihad-isis-syria.

Kitch, Carolyn (2002), 'A death in the American family: myth, memory and national values in the media mourning of John F. Kennedy, Jr', *Journalism & Mass Communication Quarterly*, **79** (2): 294–309.

Leung, Rebecca (2003), 'Mind of the suicide bomber', *CBS News*, 23 May, accessed 1 September 2015 at: http://www.cbsnews.com/news/mind-of-the-suicide-bomber/.

Levy-Barzilai, Vered (2003), 'Ticking bomb', *Haaretz Daily*, 15 October, accessed 1 September 2015 at: http://www.haaretz.com/ticking-bomb-1.102712.

Lewis, Lillian Lohr (1998), *The Wild Woman Archetype: Myth, Magic, and the Feminine Personality* (unpublished dissertation), Pacifica Graduate Institute.

Lindlof, Thomas R. and Brian C. Taylor (2010), *Qualitative Communication Research Methods*, Sage.

Lule, Jack (2001), *Daily News, Eternal Stories: The Mythological Role of Journalism*, Guilford.

Matza, Michael (2002), 'The final hours of a female suicide bomber and "martyr"', *Daily Telegraph*, 1 February, p. 24.

McCormack, David (2015), 'I became a terrorist out of love', *Daily Mail*, 14 January, accessed 1 September 2015 at: http://www.dailymail.co.uk/news/article-2910373/I-terrorist-love-says-Jihad-Jane-U-S-housewife-converted-Islam-tried-kill-Swedish-cartoonist. html.

McGreal, Chris (2004), 'Palestinians shocked at use of suicide mother', *The Guardian*, 26 January, http://www.theguardian.com/world/2004/jan/27/israel.

McRobbie, Angela (1978), 'Jackie: an ideology of adolescent femininity', occasional paper (mimeo): *Women series*, 53, Centre for Contemporary Cultural Studies Birmingham.

Nacos, Brigitte L. (2005), 'The portrayal of female terrorists in the media: similar framing patterns in the news coverage of women in politics and in terrorism', *Studies in Conflict & Terrorism*, **28** (5): 435–51.

Nessman, Ravi (2003), 'Women's paths cross: a Palestinian and an Israeli, an English Literature student and a security guard', *Gazette*, 21 May, p. A22.

Nossek, Hillel and Daniel Berkowitz (2006), 'Telling "our" story through news of terrorism: mythical newswork as journalistic practice in crisis', *Journalism Studies*, **7** (5): 691–707.

Nossek, Hillel, Annabelle Sreberny and Prasun Sonwalkar (2007), *Media and Political Violence*, Hampton.

Nunnally, Derrick et al. (2010), '"JihadJane": A life story "like a country music song"', *Philly.com*, 11 March, accessed 1 September 2015 at: http://articles.philly.com/2010-03-11/news/25215936_1_federal-court-pennsburg-life-story.

O'Neill, Sean (2013), 'Worldwide terror hunt for the "White Widow"', *The Times* (London), 27 September, pp. 1, 2.

Odowa, Mohamed (2015), 'White Widow Samantha Lewthwaite now commands an army of 200', *Daily Mail*, 20 May, accessed 1 September 2015 at: http://www.dailymail. co.uk/news/article-3087939/White-Widow-Samantha-Lewthwaite-commands-army-200-jihadi-widow-spies-pretend-street-sellers-hotel-receptionists-call-Mother-Holy-War.html.

Patkin, Terri Toles (2004), 'Explosive baggage: female Palestinian suicide bombers and the rhetoric of emotion', *Women and Language*, **27** (2): 79.

Philips, Alan (2001), 'New assassins queue eagerly for martyrdom: when death came from the sky and terrorists gained their reward', *The Daily Telegraph*, 13 September, p. 7.

Pilkington, Ed (2010), 'Colleen LaRose: all-American neighbour or terrorist Jihad Jane?', *The Guardian*, 11 March, accessed 1 September 2015 at: http://www.theguardian.com/world/2010/mar/10/colleen-la-rose-jihad-jane-terrorism-arrest.

Pilkington, Ed (2012), '"Jihad Jane" explains her strange journey from victim to radical Muslim', *The Guardian*, 9 December, accessed 1 September 2015 at: http://www.the guardian.com/world/2012/dec/08/jihad-jane-journey-victim-radical.

Pounds, Keith (2014), 'Female suicide bombers', *The Prepper Journal*, 5 February, accessed 1 September 2015 at: http://www.theprepperjournal.com/2014/02/05/female-suicide-bombers/.

Pukas, Anna (2012), 'Hunt for the white widow', *Express*, 7 March, accessed 1 September 2015 at: http://www.express.co.uk/expressyourself/306587/Hunt-for-the-white-widow.

Pukas, Anna (2015), 'How to lure a Jihadi bride: New book reveals how young girls are seduced away from home', *Express*, 26 May, accessed 1 September 2015 at: http://www.express.co.uk/entertainment/books/579731/New-book-lure-Jihadi-bride.

Ripley, Amanda (2002), 'Suicide bombers: Why young Palestinians like Wafa Idris are willing to sacrifice their lives to kill Israelis', *Time*, 15 April, accessed 1 September 2015 at: http://content.time.com/time/covers/europe/0,16641,20020415,00.html; http://content.time.com/time/magazine/article/0,9171,1101020415-227546,00.html.

Ritchie, Jessica (2013), 'Creating a monster: online media constructions of Hillary Clinton during the Democratic Primary Campaign, 2007–8', *Feminist Media Studies*, **13** (1): 102–19.

Robinson, Martin (2014), 'I love the name of Terror Twin ... I sound scary', *Daily Mail*, 7 August, accessed 1 September 2015 at: http://www.dailymail.co.uk/news/article-2718746/I-love-Terror-Twin-I-sound-scary-What-schoolgirl-fled-Syria-married-Isis-fighter-said-hearing-nickname.html.

Roy, Jessica (2015), 'CNN uncovers ISIS's dastardly scheme to lure Western women with kittens and Nutella', *Daily Intelligencer*, 18 February, accessed 1 September 2015 at: http://nymag.com/daily/intelligencer/2015/02/cnn-isis-recruiting-western-women-using-kittens.html.

Sanghani, Radhika (2015), 'AK47s, heart emoji and feminism: how jihadi brides are luring British girls to join Isil', *The Telegraph*, 28 May, accessed 1 September 2015 at: http://www.telegraph.co.uk/women/womens-politics/11635643/How-Isil-jihadi-brides-lure-British-girls-AK47s-emoji-and-feminism.html.

Shephard, Michelle (2012), 'Canadian plays den mother to Somali militants', *The Toronto Star*, 12 July, p. A1.

Shephard, Michelle (2013), 'Al Qaeda blueprint followed to the letter', *The Toronto Star*, 23 September, p. A6.

Shiffman, John (2014), 'U.S. woman known as Jihad Jane sentenced to 10 years in plot', *Reuters*, 6 January, accessed 1 September 2015 at: http://www.reuters.com/article/2014/01/06/us-usa-jihadjane-idUSBREA050PC20140106.

Shubert, Atika (2015), 'The women of ISIS: Who are they?', *CNN*, 29 May, accessed 1 September 2015 at: http://www.cnn.com/2015/05/29/middleeast/who-are-the-women-of-isis/.

Silverstone, Roger (1988), 'Television, myth and culture', in James Carey (ed.), *Media, Myths and Narratives: Television and the Press*, Sage, pp. 20–47.

Slattery, Karen and Anna Garner (2007), 'Mothers of soldiers in wartime: a national news narrative', *Critical Studies in Media Communication*, **24** (5): 429–45.

Slotkin, Richard (1992), *Gunfighter Nation: The Myth of the Frontier in Twentieth-century America*, Atheneum.

Sofer, Ken and Jennifer Addison (2012), 'The unaddressed threat of female suicide bombers', Center for American Progress, 5 January, accessed 1 September 2015 at: https://www.americanprogress.org/issues/security/news/2012/01/05/10992/the-unaddressed-threat-of-female-suicide-bombers/.

Sternadori, Miglena (2014), 'The witch and the warrior: archetypal and framing analyses of the news coverage of two mass shootings', *Feminist Media Studies*, **14** (2): 301–17.

Struckman, Sara (2006), 'The veiled women and masked men of Chechnya documentaries, violent conflict, and gender', *Journal of Communication Inquiry*, **30** (4): 337–53.

Talbot, Rhiannon (2000), 'Myths in the representation of women terrorists', *Eire-Ireland*, **35** (3–4): 165–86.

Taylor, Rosie and Jaya Narain (2014), 'The British jihadi bride hell-bent on murder', *Daily Mail*, 9 September, accessed 1 September 2015 at: http://www.dailymail.co.uk/news/article-2749939/The-British-jihadi-bride-hell-bent-murder-whining-lost-cat-Terror-twin-tweets-fears-missing-kitten-posting-pictures-holding-AK47.html.

Toameh, Khaled Abu (2003), 'Palestinian authority newspaper lauds female suicide bombers', *Jerusalem Post*, 12 March, p. 3.

Toolis, Kevin (2003), 'How women suicide bombers make the seemingly impossible task of stopping attacks even more difficult', *The Mirror*, 6 October, p. 2.

Tozer, James et al. (2014), 'The jihad sisters', *Mail Online*, 9 July, accessed 1 September 2015 at: http://www.dailymail.co.uk/news/article-2686684/The-jihad-sisters-Bubbly-exceptionally-bright-twins-28-GCSEs-set-train-doctors-Now-theyre-Syria-training-killers.html.

Victor, Barbara (2003), *Army of Roses: Inside the World of Palestinian Women Suicide Bombers*, Rodale.

Walker, Christopher (2002), 'Sight of her people's blood fired bomber', *The Times*, 1 February, p. 7.

Ward, John (2014), 'Rock chick Jihadi who took son, 10, off to war', *Daily Star* (Sunday edition), 7 September, p. 7.

Washington Times news staff (2004), 'Atoning for adultery with "martyrdom"', *Washington Times*, 20 January, accessed 1 September 2015 at: *http://www.washingtontimes.com/news/2004/jan/20/20040120-121444-6737r/?page=all.*

Wilcox, Rhonda V. (2003), 'Foreword: out far or in deep', in Francis Early and Kathleen Kennedy (eds), *Athena's Daughters: Television's New Women Warriors*, Syracuse University, pp. ix–xii.

Witte, Griff and Brian Murphy (2015), 'Additional evidence that widow is in Syria?', *The Washington Post*, 13 February, p. A10.

Yan, Holly and Nima Elbagir (2015), 'Authorities scramble to find teen girls before they join ISIS', *CNN*, 23 February, accessed 1 September 2015 at: http://www.cnn.com/2015/02/23/europe/uk-syria-missing-girls/.

15. Gender under fire in war reporting
Linda Steiner

As journalism's highest status, most dangerous and most competitive beat, war reporting is widely regarded as a male domain. Nonetheless, war reporting has always attracted women. Ironically, *The* (Chicago) *Herald*'s Teresa Dean drew resentment for arriving in South Dakota in 1891 to cover the Sioux uprisings in part because her very presence undermined the air of dangerousness. In excluding Dean from a group photograph of the reporters, one man literally asked how it would look, after weeks of hair-raising accounts of the Wounded Knee Massacre, to be photographed in the company of a fashionably dressed woman (Jones, 1972). In fact, no war occurred at Wounded Knee, but Dean went on to cover the Spanish-American War, the Boxer Revolt and the Philippine Insurrection. Meanwhile, Suzette La Fleshe, an Omaha tribe member, was already reporting the conflict at Wounded Knee. Whether or not La Fleshe's husband, as editor of the *Omaha World-Herald*, sent her there to exploit the novelty of an Indian woman covering an Indian war, La Fleshe's reportage (and to some extent, Dean's) contradicted the sensationalized news that exaggerated or even fabricated stories about bloodthirsty Indians and stirred up anti-Indian sentiment (Reilly, 2010). A century later, Christina Lamb, who traveled with Mujahideen fighting Soviet occupiers in Afghanistan, said she always wanted to cover wars, revolutions and insurgencies as part of the 'camel corps': 'They were all men and to me they were like gods' (Lamb, 2008, p. 12).

A variety of reasons, some more spurious than others, have been cited for excluding women from war reporting, including the lack of ladies' bathrooms. May Craig (1889–1975) was eventually accredited by the US Navy to cover the Second World War and later Korea, but she once joked that she would always be remembered by the word 'facilities' because 'so often it has been used to prevent me from doing what men reporters could do' (Library of Congress, n.d.). Charlotte Ebener titled her 1955 memoir about providing 'the women's angle' on several wars, *No Facilities for Women*. Although women nowadays are no longer excluded from war reporting on grounds of 'facilities', toilets are now again relevant, albeit in a different way: for safety reasons, reporters must always be in full sight of soldiers, that is, clearly exposed to their subjects and sources. Meanwhile, war reporting remains journalism's most dangerous and most openly sexist domain.

Of 1600 reporters officially accredited as war correspondents during the Second World War, 127 were American women (Jenkins, 2003). In the 1950s, less than 4 percent of the US foreign correspondents in Europe were women (Kruglak, 1955). Given a major shift during the Vietnam war, by the mid-1980s, women accounted for 20 percent of foreign correspondents (Edwards, 1988). In the 1990s their numbers again increased, especially after 9/11, when, having cut back on foreign bureaux, many newspapers and broadcasters needed journalists in Afghanistan and Pakistan. At its peak, approximately 50 percent of the US press corps in Iraq were women (Amoruso, n.d.). The Pentagon invites women to its media boot camps. That said, this chapter will feature the stories of several other US and UK individuals to highlight the continuing debates and tensions regarding women's war reporting. Their presence continues to be controversial; several accusations persist about women reporters that would never be charged against men.

Moreover, women's bodies are quite literally exploited. Just as in the 1970s savvy television executives suddenly realized the commercial value of blonde women news anchors, they learned that pretty faces leavened the sight of body bags. In 2001 veteran war correspondent Kate Adie – who apparently, as a rookie, in the 1960s willingly wore mini-skirts and figure-hugging sweaters – criticized BBC management for softening news by hiring inexperienced women with 'cute faces, cute bottoms and nothing else in between' (Cohen, 2001). Hilary Andersson, who covered bombings in Afghanistan for the BBC, similarly attributed the vogue for assigning women to cover the second Gulf War to broadcast executives' belief that audiences want to see women cover wars; women's 'wow' value derived from the amazement that women could cover what was 'the epitome of everything male' (Andersson, 2003, p. 20). Andersson doubted women would continue once the novelty of women's presence wore off. But, women have long been used to attract audiences for war reporting. As early as the Spanish–American war, a Toronto daily newspaper sent its women's editor, famous for her pen name Kit Coleman, to Cuba solely as a stunt; and Teresa Dean may have been sent to Wounded Knee for the same reason.

So the growth in the number of women reporting from war zones does not necessarily reflect gender equity. In spite of the general feminization of journalism, women war reporters continue to face obstacles from all quarters. Men colleagues snidely imply that beautiful women, especially their reporting rivals, cannot be intelligent, or accuse women of flirting to obtain information from military sources, even from enemies. Male bosses threaten to ground women for fear that they might be assaulted in some foreign land. Audiences condemn women, especially mothers, for undertaking hazardous forms of journalism. Men almost never face similar obstacles.

EARLY WOMEN WAR REPORTERS

Nearly every modern war, it seems, has been covered by at least one woman. Margaret Fuller (1810–50) is widely regarded as the world's first woman foreign correspondent. In 1844 Horace Greeley hired Fuller, who had already co-edited a literary journal and published a major treatise on women's rights, as the *New York Tribune*'s literary critic. In 1846 she went Europe to cover the revolution in Italy. She became a passionate supporter of Italian independence, fell in love with an Italian revolutionary and gave birth to a son, whose existence she kept secret, presumably lest Greeley fire her (Von Mehren, 1994).

As a widow needing to support herself and her two children, Lillie Devereaux Blake (1833–1913) wrote short stories and novels but earned the most money as a Civil War correspondent for, among others, the *New York Evening Post, New York World, Philadelphia Press* and *Forney's War Press*. She could not cover battles, but wrote detailed accounts of War Department decision-making and she met with President Abraham Lincoln, Andrew Johnson and General Ulysses S. Grant. Three Southern women covered the Civil War for Confederate papers. All three wrote under pseudonyms; although the constraints on proper feminine behavior loosened slightly during the war, writing for the public was still regarded as unfeminine (McNeely et al., 2010). Two supplied correspondence about troop preparations and camp life without moving from their home towns. The third woman moved from her South Carolina home to a Virginia battle zone to be near her son in case he was wounded (he was not). *The Charleston Courier*'s front page showcased her 'Spartan Mother' stories, ranging from diatribes against immodest women to descriptions of soldiers' medical care.

In 1898–99 Anna Benjamin (1875–1902) photographed and wrote about the Spanish–American War for *Leslie's Illustrated Newspaper*, having reached Cuba on a ship transporting coal. After covering the Filipino insurrection for the New York *Tribune*, Benjamin also sent stories from China and Russia. Editors often labeled Benjamin's stories as offering a woman's angle, but this did not protect her from vicious attacks from rivals. Referring to Benjamin, the New York *Journal*'s James Creelman[1] wrote, 'But with the advent of woman came sorrow.

The swish of the journalistic petticoat on the edge of the military camp meant the hidden leaking of news ... . For a woman, when she cannot drag forth the secrets of an army by strength, will make a sly hole in some man's discretions' (Creelman, 1901, p. 336). Creelman described women reporters as eager to see slaughter and thus unnatural: 'Curiously enough, women seldom show any signs of timidity or shockability on the battlefield' (1901, p. 337).

Resistance from the US Army severely limited the number of US women able to cover the First World War. Nonetheless, the Newspaper Enterprise Association hired Mary Boyle O'Reilly (1873–1939) in 1913, sending her to Mexico, Russia and England. At the beginning of World War I, she entered Belgium disguised as a peasant; she was imprisoned with three other war correspondents, but returned to Belgium after her release. A mother, highly popular magazine fiction writer and trained nurse, Mary Roberts Rinehart (1876–1958) persuaded the *Saturday Evening Post* to send her to Europe as early as 1915, indeed, before many American men journalists reached the battlefields (Rinehart, 1948). The first woman to get official US accreditation as a war correspondent was Peggy Hull (1889–1967) who went to France in 1917 and Siberia in 1918 for the *El Paso Morning Times*. She also reported from the Pacific theater during the Second World War.

Several women journalists covered the 1917 Russian Revolution and its aftermath. Having first moved from the women's pages to covering labor and women's issues (she also edited the *Suffragist*), Rheta Childe Dorr (1866–1948) became famous for covering political unrest in Russia in 1906. After denouncing the Bolsheviks, Dorr experienced significant difficulties getting access to combatants during her 1917 trip to Russia, but she was able to cover the Western Front in Europe, where her son was serving (Dorr, 1924). Another suffragist, the radical feminist Louise Bryant (1885–1936), and her husband John Reed also covered the 1917 revolution in Russia. Bryant wrote for several outlets, including the Hearst newspaper chain, although Reed's arrest resulted in her losing work.

THE SECOND WORLD WAR: NEW OPPORTUNITIES

As journalism historians correctly emphasize, during the Second World War many women were hired to replace newsmen going off to fight; nearly as many lost their journalism jobs or were reassigned to women's pages when the men returned. Meanwhile, some women had long wanted to move from women's pages and fashion 'ghettoes' to high status 'hard news', including war reporting. Women who won overseas jobs by promising a distinctly 'woman's perspective' on war had to be competitive, hard-headed and creative. Scottish-born Evelyn Irons (1900–2000), women's editor at *The Evening Standard*, for example, was determined to report on the Second World War from the battlefield. Refused permission to travel with or cover British forces, Irons obtained accreditation to the Free French Army. Irons was (legally) armed when she helped the French capture a Bavarian village. In 1954 she broke a news embargo on the overthrow of Guatemala's president by hiring a mule to get into the country while other journalists, forbidden to cross the border, waited in Honduras (Wilkes, 2001).

Marguerite Higgins (1920–66) is arguably the canonical case of the tensions over gender roles confronting women war reporters. Despite an air and appearance of fragility, Higgins worked her way into foreign reporting for the *New York Herald Tribune*. Her prize-winning reporting on the end of the Second World War led to her being named to head the *Tribune*'s Berlin bureau at the age of 26. Higgins was initially banned by US military from covering the Korean War on the grounds that the front lacked facilities for ladies. General Douglas MacArthur reversed that order, advising Higgins to ignore what jealous men said about her (Higgins, 1955). Higgins's Korea work proved, as one male colleague said, that 'women are just as brave and sometimes braver than men' (Hoffman, 2008, p. 105). Higgins and five men shared a Pulitzer Prize for their Korean War reporting, but Higgins's achievements were challenged: both biographers and rivals (men and women) suggested that Higgins furthered her career by offering sexual favors to military sources. Higgins herself acknowledged that many men associated 'the combination of femininity and blonde hair with either dumbness or slyness, or both' (Higgins, 1955, p. 56). As a result, she particularly treasured evidence that men colleagues respected her, albeit as an exception, when they commented: 'The front line is no place for a woman, but it's all right for Maggie Higgins' (Higgins, 1955, p. 40).

Many women war correspondents shared the determination expressed by *Life* magazine photojournalist Margaret Bourke-White (1904–71) to be feminine and glamorous *and* professional, although this regularly disrupted romantic and marital relationships. Bourke-White (1944) expressed concern about leaving behind her husband, the novelist Erskine Caldwell, with whom she collaborated on three photo-documentaries, when she went dashing around the globe. The marriage did not last. Accredited to the US Army Air Force during the Second World War, Bourke-White witnessed combat in Russia, North Africa and Italy, and, later, the violence that erupted at the partition of India and Pakistan. She even flew on bombing raids, although she was initially refused air transport to Europe by authorities who claimed that flying was too dangerous for women.

Martha Gellhorn (1908–98), a well-known pacifist, literary journalist and fiction writer, was yet another talented and romantic figure who was married, however briefly, to a celebrity. In 1930, determined to become a foreign correspondent, Gellhorn worked for two years at the United Press bureau in Paris, while at the same time becoming active in the pacifist movement. In 1936, after a few years in the US, Europe and Mexico, writing for various newspapers, news agencies and high quality magazines, she joined Ernest Hemingway in covering the Spanish Civil War. Gellhorn eventually covered Russia's invasion of Finland, the Japanese invasion of China, the Second World War and wars in Indonesia and Israel. Contemporary (women) war correspondents regard her as a model. Obituaries of Gellborn, however, consistently highlighted her status as one of Ernest Hemingway's ex-wives.

Women journalists faced distinctive obstacles in getting executives in the new medium of radio to acknowledge their abilities, given the assumption that women's voices would not come across as authoritative, at least not to men. Betty Wason (1912–2001), for example, started reporting for CBS in 1938, when she was in Prague for a wire service. CBS had her cover fighting in Norway, Turkey and especially Greece. Yet she was ordered to find a man to broadcast her reports because she sounded young and feminine. Moreover, CBS said, women were not knowledgeable enough to handle serious subjects. After the war, CBS dismissed Wason as a 'mere' freelancer. The frustrated Wason remarked, 'The tough struggle to make it as a woman correspondent, ending with the cruel rebuff by CBS, cooled my desire for more overseas war reporting' (Davies, 2002).

So, the first century of women war reporters offers several patterns, beginning with highly gendered scrutiny and an unrelenting suspicion of their femininity. On one hand, women reporting on war needed to be just as brave and just as 'macho' as men. On the other hand, they were deemed unnatural for their bravery and professionalism. A prominent US senator bitterly denounced Jane McManus Storms (1807–78) for her 'masculine stomach for war and politics' (Reilly, 1981, p. 21) after writing about battles in 1847 between Mexican and American troops, as well as a civil war, for the *New York Sun* and other newspapers. What was said about women reporting the Second World War could have been said about women reporting all these wars. 'For theirs was a double war: the war against the enemy, and the war against the system. They had to fight red tape, condescension, disdain, outright hostility, and downright lewd-ness' (Jenkins, 2003).

REPORTING THE VIETNAM WAR

By the 1960s, news organizations had allowed few women opportunities to gain war reporting experience, and then refused to send those few veteran reporters to Vietnam. As it turns out, two of the exceptions both died in Vietnam. Dickey Chapelle (1919–65) was the first war corre-spondent killed in Vietnam. An award-winning photojournalist who had previously covered wars in Korea, Taiwan, Algeria, Hungary, the Middle East and Cuba, she was hit by shrapnel while on patrol with Marines. Marguerite Higgins, by then a mother of two, also went to Vietnam, where she contracted a fatal tropical disease. Nonetheless, despite the many obstacles and restrictions, a significant number of women filed from that conflict: ultimately some 467 women covered Vietnam (267 were American; most of the others were Vietnamese).

Part of the reason women managed to make such inroads in Vietnam was that guerrilla combat and the absence of distinct front lines meant fewer military restrictions on war correspondents. Freelancers could obtain press passes merely by showing that three news organizations were interested in their work. Because special permission to travel to Vietnam was not required, reporters could book their own commercial flights, and several women paid their own way. For example, when *Look* magazine refused to send Jurate Kazickas to Vietnam, she used money won in a television game show to get there, where she was wounded during a mortar attack while covering a siege (Bartimus et al., 2002).[2] Covering Vietnam did mean, however, remaining childless. 'Those trail-blazers often sought to outmacho the men, and giving birth wasn't compatible with their lifestyle' (Matloff, 2004, p. 10).

Just as Vietnam represented a new form of warfare, it also required new skills from the journalists who reported on it, such as the ability to improvise, make spot decisions and transition easily from covering dangerous jungle warfare to dressing up for embassy parties in order to network with politicians. UPI's Margaret Kilgore said a reporter in Vietnam 'must be a political reporter, an expert on tactics, more familiar than many soldiers with a vast assortment of weaponry, a linguist diplomat, administrator, daredevil and one of the most suspicious, cautious people on earth' (Hoffman, 2008, p. 7). Having mastered the required range of roles, however, after the fighting in Vietnam concluded, most women moved into other kinds of reporting or into different careers altogether.

Many women who reported on the Vietnam war ignored the women's movement, by then in full swing, or even made fun of 'women's libbers' (Bartimus et al., 2002, p. 88). Perhaps they thought identifying with the women's movement would be professionally injurious. On the other hand, a few women credited feminists with giving them confidence they could do anything they wanted and many women mentioned being inspired by individual women who had succeeded as war reporters. In any case, even women journalists who kept their distance from feminism did not have an easy time. Liz Trotta badgered NBC television management for six months for the Vietnam assignment (Trotta, 1991). Men demeaned women correspondents as 'donut dollies and do-gooders', 'as husband hunters, war groupies, or thrill seekers who created difficulty for "real" (male) journalists who had a job to do' (Hoffman, 2008, p. 9). Many news organizations forbade them from getting near combat, given the very real dangers. After UPI's Kate Webb (1943–2007) was captured by North Vietnamese troops and held as a prisoner of war in Cambodia for 23 days, the UPI wrongly thought she had been killed, so denied combat assignments to other women. (She went on to cover the Gulf War and Afghanistan.)

Military resistance to the presence of women war reporters was even stiffer. Having quit the women's pages to follow her reporter boyfriend (later husband) to Vietnam, Denby Fawcett recalled: 'The main difficulty for women journalists in the early days of the American military escalation was talking your way into combat zones. Military commanders did not like the idea of male reporters getting killed, and they were even more horrified at the thought of a woman reporter getting shot' (Bartimus et al., 2002, p. 7).

When Fawcett encountered General William Westmoreland at an army base, Westmoreland, a family friend, tried to ban women from the battlefield. Apparently not realizing that women were covering combat, he feared that women correspondents would either endanger soldiers who would rush to protect them during an attack, or 'collapse emotionally when faced with the horrors of combat' (Bartimus et al., 2002, p. 13). His proposed ban occasioned the only time women reporters in Vietnam united in solidarity: they successfully lobbied the Pentagon to retain their battlefield access. Otherwise, women war correspondents did not form close-knit sororities. According to Kazickas, 'The women were never really a group ... . There was fierce competition between women. The last thing I wanted to see was another woman on the battlefield' (Bartimus et al., 2002, p. 13).[3]

Moreover, the fact that the few US military women in Vietnam were either nurses or serving in other more traditionally female support roles made women reporters even more conspicuous. 'This is no place for a woman', a military officer told *New York Times* correspondent Gloria Emerson, a former fashion writer who continued to produce highly-regarded important work about Vietnam after the war. Some women reporters said their visibility meant they were noticed at press conferences and had their questions answered first; some said male soldiers liked talking to women, helped them. Adopting the persona of a sister, wife, mother or girl-next-door could encourage men who were deprived of female company to remove their macho masks and confide in them. Others claimed precisely the opposite and disliked the gendered attention paid to them.

The war in Vietnam also represented the first opportunity for black women to report on war for 'mainstream' media. During the Second World War, African-American newspapers sent correspondents to the front lines to report on the experiences of black soldiers. For example, *The Chicago Defender*, a prominent black newspaper, sent Ethel Payne (1911–91) to Vietnam to see how black troops were faring (Currie, 1987). It had hired her after publishing her notes about racial issues she witnessed while working for a Red Cross-type club in Japan; and in the late 1960s Payne and another African-American journalist, Lillian Wiggins, covered the civil war in Nigeria. Elizabeth Murphy Phillips (1917–98), who worked for her family's *The Afro-American* in Baltimore, was the first accredited black woman overseas war correspondent, although illness forced her early return to Baltimore. One of her sisters went to France as a member of the Women's Army Corps and reported on military prejudice and racism, while another sister taught journalism (Ingersoll, 1992).

Philippa Duke Schuyler, better known for her success as a child prodigy pianist and composer and for her unorthodox upbringing by her African-American father and her white mother, reported for US and European newspapers. Fluent in several languages, and disillusioned with the racial and gender prejudice she encountered, she abandoned music and followed her father into journalism. She was covering Vietnam in 1967, when the military helicopter in which she was a passenger crashed into the ocean and she drowned (Talalay, 1995). But the only pattern that can be associated with African-American women covering war is that there were very few of them. The forms and extent of gender differences in Vietnam reporting continue to foment debate. Some women and men reporters congratulated women for being more attuned to the 'human side' of the war and the Vietnamese point of view, while men zeroed in on the nuts and bolts of the US and military perspectives. Some women hated – or refused to do – 'women's stories', either because they felt demeaned to be assigned according to what they regarded as a sexist stereotype, or because these stories were more likely to be cut. Others, however, wanted to do stories about Vietnam children and nurses, because war is not about 'bang-bang' but about destruction. In all, men and women wrote substantially similar kinds of stories, including the so-called 'human interest' stories conventionally expected of women, as well as analyses of the complex politics leading to war (Elwood-Akers, 1988). Likewise, despite a common assumption that women are more anti-war than men, both men and women reporters ran the gamut of political views, from Marxist to anti-communist, from pacifist to hawk.

WOMEN'S WAR REPORTING IN THE TWENTY-FIRST CENTURY: DANGERS AND DEBATES

War reporting is clearly hazardous. During the Spanish Civil War, for example, Gerda Taro (1910–37; real name Gerta Pohorylle), regarded as the first woman war photographer, died while traveling with a car carrying wounded Republican soldiers. The German-born Jewish Taro, who had already been arrested for distributing anti-Nazi propaganda, and the photojournalist Andre Friedmann took news photographs which they jointly sold under the name Robert Capa. Frances Davis Cohen smuggled news stories written by senior correspondents into France. Davis was struck by shrapnel while reporting for the London *Daily Mail* and developed septicemia. Nonetheless, intentionally harming women journalists was long taboo (Hampton, 2009). Post-9/11 conflicts have changed this. Indeed, warring factions are targeting journalists, including women.[4] In 2001, Taliban leaders promised to reward the murder of Western journalists; two women were among the eight killed in the next seventeen days. The targeting of Western women journalists in particular has been described as a 'war zone trifecta' (Hampton, 2009, p. 145).

Nor are the dangers exclusive to Western women. Russian troops beat and threatened Anna Politkovskaya, an anti-war reporter who covered how the Russian military brutalized Chechens. Politkovskaya, who viewed her journalism an act of combat, was murdered in 2006. The same year Atwar Bahjat, an Iraqi woman journalist, was murdered while reporting conflict in Iraq for Al Arabiya television. Jila Baniyaghoob covered wars in Lebanon, Afghanistan, Palestine and Iraq before being imprisoned and then banned from working as a journalist for 30 years; in any case, Iranian authorities shut down every publication she worked for. Because her coverage of armed conflict, massacres and terrorism put her on a militant group's hit list, Salima Tlemcani writes under a pen name for a French-language daily in Algeria.

The dangers, pressures and strains of modern war reporting affect both men and women: war reporters apparently develop Post-Traumatic Stress Disorder (PTSD) at a rate five times higher than the general population. *The Sunday Times* reporter Marie Colvin (1956–2012), for example, suffered PTSD after covering conflicts in Chechnya, Kosovo, Sierra Leone, Zimbabwe, Sri Lanka (where she lost an eye) and East Timor, where she stayed with women and children at a UN compound to force their rescue (Colvin was killed while covering the siege of Homs in Syria). Alcohol is a common response to these stresses. A study of frontline journalists who worked in conflict zones, of whom 25 percent were women, found that women drink just as much, if not more, than the men – although men are generally much more likely than women to drink to excess (Feinstein and Sinyor, 2009).

But while some war reporting stresses are similar for women and men, interviews and autobiographies suggest that more women admit to quitting (or considering quitting) war reporting as a result of the dangers, fear or burn-out. Siobhan Darrow (2000) confessed to being wracked with fear during the 15 years she spent covering wars in Russia, Chechnya, Albania, the Balkans, Lebanon, Israel and Northern Ireland. This fear included the concern that she would never marry and have children, given the disruptions to relationships whenever CNN moved her to a new trouble spot. After marrying a *New York Times* correspondent, she quit.

Some women feel selfish and guilty about the worry they inflict on loved ones. Anne Garrels retired more than once from National Public Radio out of concern for her ever-worried husband, but repeatedly returned to war zones. Katherine Skiba asked her husband, a *USA Today* reporter, for forgiveness for risking danger while reporting in Iraq; she advised him to marry someone nice if she were killed (Skiba, 2005). A *Boston Globe* bureau chief who covered conflicts in Bosnia, Albania, Kosovo, Rwanda and Afghanistan, Elizabeth Neuffer (1956–2003), once observed that 'being a war correspondent is an act of violence against the people you love the most because they end up having to stay behind worrying about you' (Lee, 2002). In presenting an award to Neuffer, the International Women's Media Foundation recalled that she had been menaced by gun-toting rebels, subjected to death threats, abducted by soldiers, robbed and threatened with rape. In 2003, she was killed in a car accident in Iraq while on assignment. Christiane Amanpour, chief international correspondent for CNN until 2010, reported on Rwanda, Bosnia, two Gulf Wars and Afghanistan. Amanpour admitted the challenge of always living in 'fear of being shot ... of being kidnapped, of being raped by some lunatic who hates your stories or blames you for bringing NATO bombs down around them. We manage the fear, but the strain takes its toll' (Amanpour, 2000). Amanpour once said she never expected to marry or have children, although eventually she did both.

Female war reporters run a high risk of sexual harassment and rape. A 2005 survey of 29 women reporters found that more than half reported sexual harassment while on assignment. Many have been raped. But correspondents who have been sexually attacked – often in combat zones – rarely tell anyone, sometimes out of compulsion to be part of the macho club and much more likely, fear of being pulled off an assignment. South Asia bureau chief Kim Barker never admitted that she had been molested in Pakistan, lest the *Chicago Tribune* ground her (Barker, 2011). Judith Matloff, who covered civil wars across Africa for Reuters and *The Christian Science Monitor*, points out that women's secrecy about being raped means their editors (usually men) remain unaware of the dangers and therefore do not try to increase women's security abroad or provide them with support when they return. Matloff never told her editors about how a mob in India started tearing at her clothes while policemen silently watched (Matloff, 2007). As she later explained:

> I put myself out there equal to the boys. I didn't want to be seen in any way as weaker. Groping hands and lewd come-ons are stoically accepted as part of the job, especially in places where Western women are viewed as promiscuous. War zones in particular seem to invite unwanted advances, and sometimes the creeps can be the drivers, guards, and even the sources that one depends on to do the job. ... But female journalists tend to grit their teeth and keep on working, unless it gets worse. (Matloff, 2007)

The tension between career and family is not new to women war reporters, nor, of course, is it unique to them. The increasing number of women war correspondents who are parents and the increasing dangers and risks of war reporting, however, have made this especially controversial. A backlash erupted in 2001 when the Taliban arrested *Sunday Express* reporter Yvonne Ridley, who had disguised herself in a burqa in order to get from Pakistan to Afghanistan. Ridley spent her daughter's ninth birthday in jail. Many journalists argued that the success of BBC world affairs editor John Simpson, who had entered Afghanistan wrapped in a burqa, put pressure on other journalists, especially women, to follow suit. After Ridley's arrest, Christina Lamb (2001) recalled discussing with Ridley how editors were explicitly suggesting that if Simpson could do this, 'surely you as a real woman can easily slip in'. At the time, Lamb said she would not try this, because of her son. (Ironically, in 2003, Lamb did enter Basra, dressed as a local Iraqi woman.)

In any case, vociferous critics said Ridley had recklessly pandered to tabloid journalism values merely to glorify her career, endangered her interpreter and driver, and, especially as a single mother, immorally risked leaving her child motherless. Ridley told an interviewer, 'I thought this was an argument that was long, dead and buried and forgotten about. And here we are in the new millennium questioning my right to go out and do my job as a journalist because I'm a single mother' (Ridley, 2001).

Moreover, feature stories about women journalists as mothers tend to emphasize the significant problems they face in attempting to balance career and family responsibilities, including feeling guilty about leaving their children, struggles to remain connected with their children's daily lives while on the road, and difficulties in readjusting to 'normal' life after they return from dangerous assignments. Hannah Allam worked for McClatchy Newspapers in Iraq while pregnant, but once she started 'showing' military officials made dangerous activities off-limits for her. Allam said, 'Yes, it's dangerous, yes, I am responsible for another life, but I don't see how it's that much different than a man who comes here while his wife is pregnant at home. You are still putting a parent at risk, you are still putting your child's future at risk' (Amoruso, n.d.). Lamb explained to multiple interviewers why she resigned from *The Sunday Times* (a resignation she immediately rescinded): her son, seeing television news showing the explosion of a bus his mother was riding in Pakistan, had asked her journalist husband, 'Do you think Mummy survived?'

Some journalists argue that women and men have fundamentally different approaches to combining a dangerous career with a family. On one hand, Kristen Hampton argues that, unlike men, women 'tend to view international reporting as a zero-sum career, one that can be successful only if they give up any hope of family or personal life' (Hampton, 2009, p. 143). Hampton quit the *Chicago Tribune* after becoming romantically involved with an Army captain she met in Iraq. Other women, especially single mothers, continue to report but stop volunteering for hotspots. Facing her own 'excruciating' dilemma after 20 years in 'nasty places', Judith Matloff ultimately decided she could not risk leaving her son motherless (Matloff, 2004, p. 10). On the other hand, a few war reporters claim that mothering kept them sane or made them better reporters, with sharpened insights into suffering. Moreover, fathers are not accused of damaging their children by pursuing their journalism careers. Men are not asked analogous questions. If asked, however, men might also describe how parenting and families – or lack thereof – entered into their decision-making.

Both anecdotal and formal studies of combat journalists suggest that most men are married, while the majority of women are single (Feinstein and Sinyor, 2009). Of the *Chicago Tribune*'s foreign correspondents in 2006, one of four women but six of eight men were married (Hampton, 2009). The *Chicago Tribune*'s Liz Sly warned women considering a war assignment, always nomadic and unpredictable: 'If you have a boyfriend, you will lose him. If you don't have one, you won't find one' (Hampton, 2009, p. 148). In any case, the majority of the married women war reporters are married to other reporters. This is hardly unsurprising: if anyone will understand the demands of this life, it is another reporter. Many of the rest have married men they met in that intense and potentially life-altering arena of conflict, terror and loneliness. Describing reporters' methods for blocking out the war, Fawcett said in Vietnam 'sex was like breathing good air, a stamp of gratitude for being alive' (Bartimus et al., 2002, p. 19). Higgins and Hampton, among many others, married men involved directly or indirectly in the military; while other women took on war assignments only after getting divorced.[5]

Mothers or not, women journalists face restrictions that their male counterparts never encounter. For example, since women in Saudi Arabia are not permitted to travel alone, Western women reporters traveling alone need what they describe as 'I am not a whore' letters from their consulate, authenticating their business (Moore, 1993, p. 31). But many women journalists argue that, despite the gender-specific restrictions and problems, they enjoy some distinct advantages. Some women have admitted to using 'feminine' attributes to gain an edge over their male competitors, or at least exploiting how men who don't take women seriously, tell women things they wouldn't tell men. Hannah Allam confessed, 'I would much rather be known as a professional, no-nonsense reporter than someone who uses her "womanly wiles" to get information. That being said, however, I don't ignore the advantage I have in walking into a roomful of US troops who haven't seen a woman in months ...' (Amoruso, n.d.). EveAnn Prentice, who covered Balkan conflicts in the 1990s for *The* (UK) *Times*, said she could tell when 'old style' political leaders thought, '"Oh here comes a nice stupid woman, how wonderful." But that's great; I love it – because the stupider they think you are, the more they are likely to tell you. So especially, in my younger days I would shamelessly take advantage of this' (quoted in Playdon, 2002, p. 272).

According to many women journalists, getting through checkpoints without being treated with suspicion is easier for them than for men; women's very subordinate status sometimes helps them get away with subterfuges. Especially in places where women rarely hold prominent public positions, people assume women reporters are harmless. Allam admits to exploiting this:

> In Iraq and the rest of the Arab world, I have found that being a woman is a major advantage. Women tend to be underestimated all over the world, but especially here, so I find that clerical and political leaders are much more willing to chat when they think what you write doesn't have an impact. (Amoruso, n.d.)

French war correspondent Anne Nivat, who has covered Chechnya, Afghanistan and Iraq, said that in Afghanistan, women count for nothing and Afghanis regard the few women working as journalists there as 'worthless sluts' (Reporters, 2011, p. 6). Ironically, this made her work easier. Afghanis, she said, trusted her, at least when she dressed like local women in a burqa, more than they trusted men: 'You can see without being seen' (Reporters Without Borders, 2011, 9).

The notion that women take a human-interest and distinctively 'women's' approach to war has long persisted, but of all allegations, this is the most contested. Women themselves often agree that women and men work differently and bring different emphases to their interpretations of war. Many assert that women are drawn to political intrigue and human-interest stories, while men do 'bang-bang reporting'. Prentice matter-of-factly attributes the rarity of war stories featuring women's angle to (men's) news values: 'Newspapers are still run by men, mostly, and they do like their wars ... their blood and guts and thunder' (Playdon, 2002, p. 274).

Gender differences in war reporting may be every bit as socially constructed as the concept of gender itself. Women may gravitate to stories about the consequences of war because of their gender/sex, or their outsider and marginalized standing. Alternatively, this focus may continue to represent what they promise in order to get hired, what they are hired or assigned to do, or how their work is edited, placed and published. During the first Gulf War, *The Washington Post*'s Style section requested 'the women's story' from senior correspondent Molly Moore (1993), although she wanted to discuss US plans for defending Saudi Arabia and the impact of a harsh desert environment on troops. Sometimes sources themselves assume women reporters want women's stories and therefore steer them into domestic spaces. Meanwhile, gender inflection may be read into something simply because the author is a woman. Contrasting his own neutral, 'good old BBC stiff upper lip' approach, John Simpson once disdained the coverage of his colleague Kate Adie as 'horribly emotional'. Later, however, he conceded that Adie provided a real feeling of the awfulness: 'You felt how frightened she was, as indeed most of us were and I thought she gave a damn sight better account by seeing the aftermath than the real thing' (quoted in Sebba, 1994, p. 269).

Certainly by the time of Vietnam, stories that went beyond events and battles to offer analysis represented the best of what all reporters were trying to achieve. At the least, women's 'humanized' stories were not 'soft' in the conventional sense. The best writers, like Gellhorn and Emerson, depicted mangled bodies, grief, chaos and death. Moving away from an insistence that reporters must adopt an objective, detached position, and instead allowing for a personal, or at least openly subjective account, war reporting has become feminized. Whether because of men's departures from journalism, women's visibility or audience demands, more emotive 'journalism of attachment' has emerged, using a phrase coined by the BBC journalist Martin Bell. Finally, human-interest approaches to covering war also reflect current forms of warfare because now combatants fight on neighborhood streets, rather than on isolated battlefields.

CONCLUSION

This chapter illustrates that even as women have found some increasing acceptance as war reporters and certainly have achieved visibility, gender continues to be an important issue, albeit in often problematic ways, for reporters, news executives, military and political sources, and audiences. The impact of gender on war reporting has been fueled by sexism, which has disappeared from neither society at large nor journalism. The clothes, hair, jewelry, and literally the bodies of women continue to be objects of much attention and concern, including for war reporters. Even while reporting from conflict arenas, women are consistently judged by their appearance. They face a double bind: mocked for their careful grooming, but criticized for lack thereof. Speech and 'attitude' likewise pose a double bind. On one hand, war zones are famously sexualized domains requiring masculine toughness. On the other, a Navy commander complained that *Miami Herald* foreign correspondent Carol Rosenberg sexually harassed him and used abusive language (Franken, 2009). The *Herald*'s investigation ultimately cleared Rosenberg. Similarly 'rude' and 'offensive' language from men reporters would presumably have gone unremarked and unnoticed.

The gendered and sexual abuse of women reporters also continues, literally and overtly. Lynsey Addario described being one of four *New York Times* staffers kidnapped in Libya in 2011 (she was also kidnapped in Iraq in 2004): 'There was a lot of groping ... . Every man who came in contact with us basically felt every inch of my body short of what was under my clothes' (Shaddid et al., 2011). Indeed, every issue mentioned in this chapter came into focus when CBS chief foreign correspondent Lara Logan was sexually assaulted while covering protests in Egypt in February 2011; that assault was 'symptomatic of the risks that women run when they work as journalists' (Reporters Without Borders, 2011, p. 4). Even while she was recovering in a hospital, Logan, who has covered conflicts in Africa, Europe and Asia, was criticized for going to a dangerous place, demonized as an absent mother, mocked as an ex-swimsuit model, derided as naive for wearing pearls, and labeled a war junkie.

The success of women journalists covering war and political violence is uneven. According to one Al Arabiya staffer, Arab women war reporters came into prominence during the Israel–Lebanon conflict of 2006 (Tamimi, ND). Now half of al Arabiya's reporters are women. Despite their lack of preparation, these women 'proved to be daring, and professionally competitive compared with their male colleagues' (Tamimi, n.d.). On the other hand, when Al Jazeera expanded its Iraqi bureau, it had three women and 130 men; moreover, even experienced women were usually assigned women and children's issues, while less experienced men got the 'serious' assignments (Welsh, 2006).

Nonetheless, bearing the imprint of the women's movement, women are visible in war. In the US, women have increasing presence and authority as military officers, public information officers and combat soldiers; three women have served as Secretaries of State. These developments have directly helped women establish themselves in war reporting. Some women joke that Iraq reporting is becoming a women's job. With news organizations having trouble finding staffers willing to risk their lives (despite its continued career-making status), volunteers tend to be ambitious, young, single – and female (Hampton, 2009, p. 149). The dramatic demographic shift in war reporting also reflects economics. The increased use of women foreign correspondents as stringers and free-lancers points to a profit-driven shift to cheaper workers. Moreover, because market-driven executives are constantly seeking ways to boost dwindling news audiences, some women journalists may get war assignments merely to spice up the drama. Most observers credit women reporters with exposing the systematic rape of women as a weapon of war, although the story of the sexual harassment of women reporters themselves is only beginning to be told. But men have also campaigned against rape in conflict zones. In 2011 men attending a press conference in Libya tried to protect a woman who said she had been raped by paramilitaries. Men and women journalists seem either to suggest that everyone has, to varying degrees, both masculine and feminine values, or that gender makes no difference in war reporting. BBC foreign correspondent Lyse Doucet said: 'I know as many women who are interested in the bombs and bullets as I know men whose main concern is the human cost' (Wells, 2002).

Whether women are advantaged in reporting on conflict is more controversial. Many women journalists claim that they are advantaged as such, although their specific claims are often contradictory. Women argue both that they can interview Middle Eastern women when men cannot and that Middle Eastern men trust them, both that Muslim men treat Western women as 'freaks' and that they talk to women reporters openly. Most likely, being a woman may be both advantageous and disadvantageous. In the short term, women reporters may be able to exploit assumptions about femininity and gender to compensate for the downsides of sexism. In the long term, however, the emphasis on difference by sex or gender would not seem to serve women professionals or to reduce sexism.

NOTES

1. James Creelman was also the source of the now wholly-discounted tale that William Randolph Hearst told his photographer, 'You supply the pictures; I'll supply the war'.
2. Of the 18 women, primarily UK or US, who reported on the Spanish Civil War of 1936–39, Deacon (2009) found only two on the Nationalist side, which could be expected to have a more autocratic, inflexible and sexist stance toward journalists. In contrast, the 1982 Falklands War between Britain and Argentina was fought over islands 400 miles from the nearest land mass; correspondents could reach battle zones only via ships. UK military authorities selected no women reporters to accompany the military task force. The sole woman traveling with the British was the official war artist, Linda Kitson.
3. Likewise, then and now, given their foreign assignments and the attracting of war for loners, war reporters rarely join professional organizations or press clubs, including those specifically for women.
4. Between 2003 and 2011, some 230 journalists were killed in Iraq.
5. This, in turn, raises the otherwise unspoken and hidden problem for lesbians (who, statistically, are less likely to find partners easily).

REFERENCES

Amanpour, Christiane (2000), 'Speech to the Radio and Television News Directors Association', accessed 1 September 2015 at: http://gos.sbc.edu/a/amanpour.html.

Amoruso, Carol (n.d.), 'Women on war', accessed 1 September 2015 at: http://02e1137. netsolhost.com/Villages/Hispanic/latinas/women_war0401.asp.

Andersson, Hilary (2003), 'The wow factor', *British Journalism Review*, **14** (2): 20–24.

Barker, Kim (2011), 'Why we need women in war zones', *New York Times*, 19 February.

Bartimus, Tad et al. (2002), *War Torn: Stories of War from the Women Reporters Who Covered Vietnam*, Random House.

Bourke-White, Margaret (1944), *Purple Heart Valley: A Combat Chronicle of the War in Italy*, Simon and Schuster.

Cohen, Nadia (2001), 'Adie slams new news culture', *Daily Mail*, October, accessed 23 June 2013 at: http://www.dailymail.co.uk/tvshowbiz/article-80181/Adie-slams-new-news-culture.html.

Creelman, James (1901), *On the Great Highway: The Wanderings and Adventures of a Special Correspondent*, Lothrop.

Currie, Kathleen (1987), 'Ethel Payne interview', 25 August–17 November, Washington Press Club Foundation, accessed 23 June 2013 at: http://beta.wpcf.org/oralhistory/payn1.html.

Darrow, Siobhan (2000), *Flirting with Danger: Confessions of a Reluctant War Reporter*, Anchor.

Davies, Tom (2002), 'Betty Wason', accessed 28 March 2011 at: http://indiana journalismhof.org/2002/01/betty-wason/.

Deacon, David (2009), 'Going to Spain with the boys', in Michael Bailey (ed.), *Narrating Media History*, Routledge, pp. 66–78.

Dorr, Rheta Childe (1924), *A Woman of Fifty*, Funk and Wagnalls.

Ebener, Charlotte (1955), *No Facilities for Women*, Alfred Knopf.

Edwards, Julia (1988), *Women of the World: The Great Foreign Correspondents*, Houghton Mifflin.

Elwood-Akers, Virginia (1988), *Women War Correspondents in the Vietnam War 1961–1975*, Scarecrow.

Feinstein, Anthony and Mark Sinyor (2009), 'Women war correspondents: different in so many ways', *Neiman Reports*, Winter, accessed 1 September 2015 at: http://nieman reports.org/articles/women-war-correspondents-they-are-different-in-so-many-ways/.

Franken, Bob (2009), 'Miami Herald clears Carol Rosenberg of harassment allegations', *Politics Daily Blog*, 4 August, accessed 23 June 2015 at: http://www.politicsdaily.com/2009/08/04/miami-herald-clears-reporter-carol-rosenberg-of-harassment-alleg/print/.

Hampton, Kirsten Scharnberg (2009), 'Covering war through a woman's eyes', in June O. Nicholson, Pamela J. Creedon, Wanda S. Lloyd and Pamela J. Johnson (eds), *The Edge of Change: Women in the Twenty-first Century Press*, University of Illinois Press, pp. 143–54.

Higgins, Marguerite (1955), *News is a Singular Thing*, Doubleday.

Hoffman, Joyce (2008), *On Their Own: Women Journalists and the American Experience in Vietnam*, Da Capo.

Ingersoll, Fern (1992), Frances L. Murphy Interview, Washington Press Club Foundation Oral History Project, tapes #1–6, accessed 1 September 2015 at: http://beta.wpcf.org/oralhistory/murph1.html.

Jenkins, Mark (2003), '"Gal reporters": Breaking barriers in World War II', *National Geographic News*, 10 December, accessed 23 June 2013 at: http://news.national geographic.com/news/2003/12/1210_031210_warwomen.html.

Jones, Douglas C. (1972), 'Teresa Dean: lady correspondent among the Sioux Indians', *Journalism Quarterly*, **49** (4): 656–62.

Kruglak, Theodore E. (1955), *The Foreign Correspondents: A Study of the Men and Women Reporting for the American Information Media in Western Europe*, Librairie E. Droz.

Lamb, Christina (2001), 'Yvonne told me: "I miss Daisy, my daughter, so much"', *The Telegraph*, 30 September, accessed 1 September 2015 at: http://www.telegraph.co.uk/news/worldnews/asia/afghanistan/1358056/Yvonne-told-me-I-miss-Daisy-my-daughter-so-much.html.

Lamb, Christina (2008), *Small Wars Permitting: Dispatches from Foreign Lands*, Harper-Press.

Lee, Carol (2002), 'Foreign correspondent willing to return to danger zone', Women's eNews, 17 April, accessed 23 June 2013 at: http://www.womensenews.org/story/journalist-the-month/020417/foreign-correspondent-willing-return-danger-zone.

Library of Congress (n.d.) 'May Craig', accessed 1 September 2015 at: http://www.loc.gov/exhibits/wcf/wcf0014.html.

Matloff, Judy (2004), 'Mothers at war', *Columbia Journalism Review*, July/August, pp. 10–12.

Matloff, Judy (2007), 'Unspoken foreign correspondents and sexual abuse', *Columbia Journalism Review*, May/June, accessed 1 September 2015 at: http://www.cjr.org/on_the_job/unspoken.php.

McNeely, Patricia G., Debra Reddin van Tuyll and Henry H. Schulte (2010), *Knights of the Quill: Confederate Correspondents and their Civil War Reporting*, Purdue University Press.

Moore, Molly (1993), *A Woman at War: Storming Kuwait with the U.S. Marines*, Charles Scribner's Sons.

Playdon, Peter (2002), '"Under friendly fire": an interview with Eve-Ann Prentice', *Journalism Studies*, **3** (2): 267–75.

Reilly, Hugh J. (2010), *The Frontier Newspapers and the Coverage of the Plains Indian Wars*, Praeger.

Reilly, Tom (1981), 'Jane McManus storms: letters from the Mexican War, 1846–1848', *Southwestern Historical Quarterly*, **85** (1): 21–44.

Reporters Without Borders (2011), 'News media: a men's preserve that is dangerous for women', 8 March, accessed 22 June 2013 at: http://en.rsf.org/IMG/pdf/international_women_s_day_2011.pdf.

Ridley, Yvonne (2001), Interviewed by Michael Buerk, 30 October, for 'The Choice', BBC Radio 4.

Rinehart, Mary R. (1948), *My Story*, Rinehart.

Sebba, Anne (1994), *Battling for News: The Rise of the Woman Reporter*, Hodder and Stoughton.

Shadid, Anthony, Lynsey Addario, Stephen Farrell and Tyler Hicks (2011), '4 Times journalists held captive in Libya faced days of brutality', *New York Times*, 22 March, p. A1.

Skiba, Katherine M. (2005), *Sister in the Band of Brothers*, University Press of Kansas.

Talalay, Kathryn (1995), *Composition in Black and White: The Life of Philippa Schuyler*, Oxford University Press.

Tamimi, Iqbal (n.d.), 'Arab women war reporters: who cares about them?', *Daily Telegraph*, accessed 22 June 2013 at: http://www.newssafety.com/stories/insi/arabwomenjournalists.htm.

Trotta, Liz (1991), *Fighting for Air: In the Trenches with Television News*, Simon & Schuster.

Von Mehren, Joan (1994), *Minerva and the Muse: A Life of Margaret Fuller*, University of Massachusetts Press.

Wells, Matt (2002), 'Shooting star', *The Guardian* G2, 8 January, p. 3.
Welsh, May Ying (2006), 'R.I.P.', accessed 22 June 2013 at: http://www.global-sisterhood-network.org/content/view/780/59/.
Wilkes, Roger (2001), 'Inside story: a woman of no little importance', *The Telegraph*, 27 June, accessed 1 September 2015 at: http://www.telegraph.co.uk/property/property advice/propertymarket/3290232/Inside-story-a-woman-of-no-little-importance.html.

PART III

GENDER AND OPPOSITION TO WAR

Part III Introduction: Gender and opposition to war

Jennifer Pedersen

The literature on gender and opposition to war is vibrant and comprehensive. Many feminist scholars have keenly engaged with questions about 'women', 'motherhood', 'feminism' and 'peace' by exploring examples of women organizing against war, militarism and political violence globally. This research offers compelling evidence of how the relationship between women and peace is more complex than an essentialist position would propose: women are not inherently peaceful; women hold multiple identities in times of conflict, as victims, soldiers, instigators or activists for peace. Further, women who use their gendered identities in protest often embrace and challenge gender norms at the same time.

Adding to this growing body of work that reveals the complicated gendered nuances of opposition to war, militarism and political violence, the chapters in this part offer research on six particular contexts of feminist activism around the globe. Read together, these chapters provide a fascinating picture of how women articulate their claims for peace within different and challenging contexts. They highlight an important set of questions about feminist action against war from multiple perspectives, including those of military veterans, survivors of sexual violence, survivors of civil war and women living under occupation. They examine how individual feminist activist movements have changed over time, adapting to new realities of conflict and violence, while challenging gender norms and pushing for a feminist anti-militarist agenda that stretches beyond formal wartime. Importantly, the chapters in this part draw on women's direct experience with war or political violence in different contexts. As such, they start where women are and pay close attention to the lived experiences of women. These experiences are important to understanding why some women choose to engage in anti-war or anti-violence organizing.

In Chapter 16, Ilene Feinman explores feminist anti-militarists' articulations of, and actions towards, a gender-just peace, through their opposition to masculinist constructions of militarism, with particular focus on the activist groups CODEPINK, Women's International League for Peace and Freedom (WILPF), and Women in Black.

In Chapter 17, Cami Rowe examines the anti-war activism of Iraq Veterans Against the War (IVAW) in post-2001 United States, looking closely at gender hierarchies within the US military. The powerful myth of the 'Soldier' figure is central to Rowe's argument; IVAW's activism challenges stereotypes of the 'Soldier' by critiquing the underlying principles behind gendered military power. Rowe concludes by examining IVAW's support for WikiLeaks whistleblower Chelsea Manning and support for transgender veterans.

In Chapter 18, Simona Sharoni maps the history of gendered resistance to political violence in Palestine and Israel over nearly three decades. Beginning with the first intifada in 1987, through to December 2014, Sharoni traces the shift from joint initiatives, based on dialogue between Israeli-Jewish and Palestinian women, to parallel initiatives by each collectivity. She argues that many differences between the Israeli and Palestinian contexts have impacted resistance work by grassroots feminist activists in both communities, and shows how gendered and sexualized violence are linked to the many forms of violence inherent in occupation.

In Chapter 19, Jennifer Pedersen examines a women-only peace movement in Liberia led by Leymah Gbowee, who became a Nobel Peace Prize laureate in 2011. The Women in Peacebuilding Network mobilized thousands of women from all walks of life for peace in 2003 during the Second Liberian Civil War. This was largely a grassroots movement that both challenged the absence of women from decision-making processes, and made a concerted effort to unite 'women' under one banner in order to overcome entrenched class, religious and ethnic differences that were so prominent in the Liberian conflict.

In Chapter 20, Jodi Burkett explores the complicated and multi-dimensional dynamics of gender within the Campaign for Nuclear Disarmament (CND) anti-nuclear movement in the United Kingdom in the 1960s and later years. Burkett investigates how activities and actions of CND were informed by gendered attitudes and how the organization used traditional gender norms to appeal to the public. CND both reflected these traditional gender norms and challenged them, by creating space for women to become politically active in post-women's liberation-movement Britain.

Finally, in Chapter 21, Jennifer Chan examines post-Second World War anti-war movements in Japan from a gender perspective. Chan describes how diverse feminist movements in Japan and Korea have challenged dominant narratives on gender equality by incorporating issues of nation, colonialism, race, class and empire. She draws on two case studies to show the complexity of feminist anti-war activism, namely, war crime responsibility and opposition to American military bases on Japanese soil.

Together, the six chapters in this part explore the tensions between stereotypes about the feminine anti-war movement and masculine war-making, thus challenging binaries still common in some discussions of gender and opposition to war. For example, in Chapter 16, Feinman examines how feminist anti-militarists articulate their claims within a complicated context of female participation in militaries. Using the case study of the United States military, Feinman observes the relationship between gender and militarism from both the perspective of inclusion of women in militaries, and from the perspectives of feminist critiques of militarism. In Chapter 17, Rowe illustrates how disaffected veterans returning from American missions abroad challenge both gender norms and military power through social performance. In Chapter 19, Pedersen describes how the women-only peace movement in Liberia both embraced and manipulated stereotypes of 'peaceful' women in order to gain public support and play a role in the 2003 peace process. In Chapter 20, Burkett notes CND's reliance on traditional gender norms in the early years of activism and how these norms were challenged in later years.

This collection of chapters also illustrates the importance of approaching gender analysis from an intersectional perspective, adding new insight into how gender interacts with different forms of oppression. For example, Chan's chapter engages with the effects of colonialism, empire and race on feminist organizing in Japan. Rowe engages with the important issue of oppression of transgendered soldiers. Pedersen shows how entrenched class, religion and race differences were explicitly challenged through women-only organizing for peace in Liberia. Sharoni illustrates the asymmetrical nature of the Israeli–Palestinian conflict – between occupier and occupied – via a feminist examination of power and structural inequalities between Palestinian and Israeli women. Sharoni argues that recognizing the conflict as asymmetrical, not as a war between equal parties, is essential to understanding how gendered resistance to political violence is intimately linked to the structure and politics of Israeli occupation.

Many of the findings in these chapters will be of interest to students of social movements and non-violence as well as feminist international relations. Several of the chapters in this section draw attention to the importance of public non-violent acts of resistance and specific gendered tactics of protest used by feminist organizing against war. For example, Rowe explores the performative activism of Iraq Veterans Against the War – veterans engaging with the role assigned to them by society and the media – who challenge both the soldier stereotype and cultural gender norms. Pedersen shows how women in the Liberian movement used culturally-specific gendered tactics of protest, such as sex strikes, public stripping and women-only fasting, to gain support for their movement. Feinman offers new insight into CODEPINK's gendered tactics of protest.

Finally, each of this part's chapters illustrates potential new directions for feminist organizing against war. In Chapter 16, Feinman's analysis leads to a crucial question: how does the increasing inclusion of females in militaries, diplomacy and governance challenge meanings of gender and war – and how will feminist critiques of militarism adapt to this changing context? In Chapter 17, Rowe concludes her chapter with important questions about the future of gender activism and the anti-war movement, including new avenues of protest and solidarity among different progressive and transnational movements. Like Rowe, who discussed IVAW's support for transgender veterans in the US military, Sharoni explores in Chapter 18 how the Boycott, Divestment and Sanctions movement's support for the global queer movement offers new avenues for feminist activism and anti-war protest. In Chapter 19 Pedersen shows how the Liberian women's peace movement had to redefine itself in the post-conflict period in order to continue to push for women's participation in formal decision-making processes. In Chapter 20, Burkett explores the opportunities for women activists within the Campaign for Nuclear Disarmament to 'awaken their activist spirit', leading to the transformation of gender norms in later years. Finally, Chan's Chapter 21 shows how alternative gender narratives coming out of feminist anti-war activism, including those coming from indigenous and minority perspectives, offer new insight into understandings of war and gender in Japan, and thus enable the rewriting of history and international law concerning women's wartime experiences.

We are left with a number of important questions for further research, for example: can feminist activism and increasing inclusion of women in decision-making challenge perceived essential characteristics of war? How can an intersectional approach to gender, including better understanding of ethnic, class and colonial oppression, lead to more insightful conclusions about war and peace? Finally, what is the future of opposition to war, especially with regard to building relationships with other progressive social movements?

16. CODEPINK and pink soldiers: reading feminist antimilitarism anew
Ilene R. Feinman

INTRODUCTION

> We call on women around the world to rise up and oppose the war in Iraq.
> We call on mothers, grandmothers, sisters and daughters, on workers,
> students, teachers, healers, artists, writers, singers, poets, and every ordinary
> outraged woman to be willing to be outrageous for peace. Women have
> been the guardians of life – not because we are better or purer or more
> innately nurturing than males, but because the men have busied
> themselves making war. (Starhawk, CODEPINK, 2002)

If feminist antimilitarism is to have salience in twenty-first century discussions of gender and war, it must address the ways that females[1] appear both as warriors and peacemakers. By now we should understand that females also war. How are questions about the efficacy of analyzing war from a feminist perspective modified by the inclusion of some females as soldiers, the racialized organization of those inclusions and exclusions, by the international scope of the War on Terror, and by the evolution of antiwar activism itself? How do females for peace articulate their claims in this context?

By looking closely at the continued paradigmatic racially gendered constructions of militarism, we observe the trace of masculinist racist militarism. The evidence is international: rape is still a systemic practice in war; males are still mobilized predominantly as warriors; ethnic and racialized hierarchies organize war geopolitically, economically and otherwise; and we continue to accept and even expect the intertwining of warring and manhood globally. Race and class operate cross-culturally and cross geopolitical boundaries to shape who joins the military to enact the bidding of militarism.

These issues and contexts demonstrate the importance of continuing to examine the relationship between gender and militaries from the perspectives of both feminist arguments for females' inclusion in militaries and feminist critiques of militarism. Placing these two agendas side by side encourages us to think broadly about the ways that gender can be deployed and reiterates gender as a driving force in militarization processes. Gender continues to organize military cultures of belonging, and in feminist antimilitarism there is explicit organizing around female experiences of war.

I situate my analysis in regard to the US military because it remains a dominant institution in geopolitical and military projects worldwide. In particular, because of the global reach of the United States, the War on Terror is augmented by the global spread of US military bases and access. The reach of the US military is exemplified by the number of places in which we fight, or assist with the machinery of war for others to fight, and the number of bases we have around the world from which to assess and access sites of existing or potential conflict. US military bases worldwide are widely cited as numbering at 737 (US Department of Defense, 2014). The US Department of Defense organizes the world by command zones, known as the Unified Combatant Commands (UCC). These UCCs cover the entire globe.

It is hard to overstate the influence of US military machinations around the globe and yet dangerous also to analyze from 'here' given the easy slippage to reification of the US perspective. For instance, we should not assume that other militaries are coping with: the inclusion of females in general, as well as gays and lesbians; the predominance of females in danger in war zones; and especially the assumption that females' experiences are the same from one geopolitical location to another and within any given zone. A long and rich history of transnational feminist work teaches us to be mindful of these nuances. Nevertheless, the United States performs a dominant role, and in this chapter I make use of that knowledge to analyze what this means for peacemaking.

In this chapter I begin by reviewing the US military in relation to its females. I look at the ways feminist activists are engaging in antiwar work in relation to the effects of war on females, to share a broad view of females in peace movements that are currently constituted in the United States but doing their envisioning in relation to the rest of the world, and finally to consider some ways we might increase the efficacy of global/local work for peace. I consider whether the feminist question is answered in the military; whether or not the feminist question is answered, or relevant, in peace activism; and the ways that feminist inquiry may have reshaped inquiry about war and militarism.

THE WOMAN IN THE MILITARY

'To tell you the truth, I didn't even think about that issue,' said her platoon commander ... First Lt Riannon Blaisdell-Black of Virginia Beach. 'Out here we don't see gender, we don't see race.'

Specialist Snyder was ... from a military family; her father had been in the Navy and her sister is, while a brother is in the Army. She enlisted straight after graduation, choosing the military police, because, as one of her platoon mates put it, 'We had the best and biggest guns.'

... Specialist Snyder expressed interest in becoming a deception analyst in what is known as the military's psychological operations. Her physical fitness scores often exceeded the Army's perfect 300, and she was determined to become a sergeant – an honor awarded to her now posthumously.

At the same time, on deployment she carried a hot pink pocketknife and pink duct tape, and at her unit's base in Fort Richardson, Alaska, she kept an off-road vehicle, also painted pink. 'She definitely had her feminine side,' said Lieutenant Blaisdell-Black. 'Even her tattoos were all flowers and girly things.' (Nordland, 2011)

This excerpt from an interview regarding US Army Sergeant Snyder demonstrates the complex gender tropes at play for female soldiers. The conditions of work and life for females within militaries, and the ways females express their own gendered agency within military culture, lead in two directions: one is a world where 'we don't see gender, we don't see race'; and the other is a world in which sexual harassment and assault, as well as racism, are still the tools for social control in a slowly shifting environment.

In 2000, before the advent of the 'War on Terror', I argued that we needed 'to create a dialog about women in the military that simultaneously acknowledges the horrors of militarism and the achievements, interests, and longings of women soldiers' (Feinman, 2000, p. 2). Now females ably assume increasing access to billets and the War on Terror is the first US war where females are officially in combat billets. The question remains, however, how to resolve the tension of a feminist antimilitarism that chooses not to engage the fact of females fully deployed in the military.

Feminist readings of the conditions of work and life for females within the military, especially in the US, are an important way to understand how gender within the military shapes military culture. Here, I compare this cultural discourse with the ways that US female peace activists articulate their claims in order to draw out the tension between females' desire, choice and agency to soldier and females' desire, choice and agency as peace activists. This comparison illuminates what is at stake in articulations of peace activism, and its need to fully engage the variety of feminisms in the US and much beyond. Feminist readings provide a more nuanced understanding of actual and potential changes in the exercise of power within the military and help answer the earlier queries about whether the full inclusion of females would disrupt the masculinist militarism of the military.

As of 2015, females comprise approximately 14.5 percent of the armed forces in the United States. In 2009 the Military Leadership Diversity Commission, through the National Defense Authorization Act for Fiscal Year 2009, Section 596, Public Law 110-417, argued that it is no longer viable for females to be excluded from Military Occupational Specialties (MOSs) for which they are qualified. The Commission suggested that the arguments used to exclude females from these MOSs, such as unit cohesion and females' capacity, are no less suspect than arguments once used to exclude males of color, or most recently, lesbian and gay soldiers. The Commission stated that current policies are 'fundamentally discriminatory because they stipulate that assignment decisions should be based solely on gender, without regard to capability or qualifications' (Military Leadership Diversity Commission, 2011, p. 75).

The 2010 legislative directive to rescind the 'Don't Ask, Don't Tell' (DADT) policy[2] might lead to a sea change in military culture. The secreting and punishing of queer soldiers had the added 'benefit' of policing the behavioral possibilities for all soldiers. While formally females are included in most MOSs, this study and policy shift marks the continued practice of diminishing females' work in the forces and constraining the possible expressions of females' expertise as inappropriate and unacceptable. This policy shift coupled with the rescinding of Don't Ask Don't Tell promise the possibility of soldiers serving in their highest capacity. Precisely because these sexual orientations are now legal in military code, there would be no viable threat against females acting their genders in ways they see fit. In other words, the heretofore powerful accusation of being lesbian or gay in response to one's workplace performance or sexual availability would cease to have purchase. This transformation in the gender performance rules of military culture has the potential to radically transform the US military.

Currently, even in the worst examples of soldiering culture, females appear in proportional numbers to their demographic in the military at large. The revelations of the Abu Ghraib prisoner abuses signaled widespread prisoner abuse and changed the public sense of female soldiers' innocence in relation to torture and other forms of war outside the Geneva Convention. This led to extended discussions over whether female soldiers are as capable and culpable as male soldiers when it comes to deploying violence and the use of sexual trope for humiliation and domination (e.g., Feinman, 2007; Taguba, 2004; Schlesinger, 2004). We have advanced the broader discussion of female roles in the military such that their presence is a given in its positive and negative connotations. There is stark evidence that females and males of varied sexualities, racial and ethnic origins can be trained to dehumanize the 'enemy' and act in ways derogatorily called masculinist – exercising power over others, sexual and otherwise. As the gender performance codes change, these 'shared' behaviors may also shift.

Annual reports from the US Department of Defense Sexual Assault Prevention and Response Office (SAPRO) document the ongoing phenomenon of sexual assault in the forces. SAPRO was initiated as a task force in 2004 in response to the requirement by that fiscal year's Defense Appropriations Act that the Department of Defense bring a sexual assault policy forward by 2005 and report annually on sexual assault rates in the forces and the academies.

The 2014 report (published on 1 May 2015) indicated that females continued to be abused at the hands of their fellow soldiers. The frequency of sexual abuse that is tracked each year is 15 percent of military females reporting sexual assault and 56 percent of females reporting sexual harassment (US Department of Defense SAPRO, 2014). According to the American Civil Liberties Union, one out of every three females in the military reported sexual harassment; a rate nearly twice that of their civilian counterparts (Park, 2010). Reports of sexual assault have increased over the decade that they have been collected, which may be due to more stringent reporting and training guidelines. Nevertheless, most of the recent data tell us that females, as a class, still experience a disproportionate level of sexual assault. This reporting lags behind the recent changes, so we may have to wait several years to see how radically the culture can shift with an increased openness to sexual orientation and an increased access to combat billets.

Given the formal inclusion of females in many nation states' militaries – indeed several led the way with females in combat before the United States – we must now answer a different question: what to do with a military that includes females in its ranks yet does not treat them formally or informally with the same respect as males are afforded. In part, this question is being answered by the transformation of formal structure, such as the task force recommendation to open all MOSs and the vote in Congress to rescind DADT, and annual reporting on sexual assault and harassment. The broader cultural problem of a dominating masculinism has yet to be resolved. Feminists interested in militaries still have a lot to say here, but the terms are indeed changing.

MILITARISM AND MASCULINISM

In order to think about contemporary militarism it is necessary to consider the ways that militaries and their exigencies have evolved. Mary Kaldor (2006) guides us with her insights about the revolutions that have taken place in the social relations of war, in the context of globalization and with the changed nature of political authority. Kaldor's analysis suggests 'the new wars involve a blurring of distinctions between war ... organized crime ... and large scale violations of human rights' (Kaldor, 2006, p. 2). The new wars can be characterized as postmodern wars, or degenerate wars, in the sense that they evince the decay of national frameworks (Baudrillard, 1995 and Shaw, 2000, as discussed in Kaldor, 2006). Indeed, national frameworks are breaking down and at least refiguring. The gender implications and opportunities are of interest here as nationalisms and particularly wars and patriotisms have called on gendered alignments to do their work; for example, World War II and its aftermath in Germany and the United States, the Vietnam War, and particularly the peace movement's use of gender ('girls say yes to guys who say no!'), but also in the broader support for male soldiers to be drafted. The interesting exception was Rostker v Goldberg (1981) in which the Supreme Court ruled that it was unconstitutional for the US to conscript only males. If a draft for the US military is ever reinstated, females will also be subject to it.

The blurring of the boundaries of the battlefield in the first Persian Gulf War in 1991 led to the clear argument against excluding females from the benefits of having their billets classified as combat exposed. Females were communication specialists at the front line, refueled combat jets in the combat theater and were trapped in combat situations in their convoys. US Rep. Patricia Schroeder (D-CO) articulated this with her testimony that the presence of females in communication vans within the combat zone obliterated the notion of a non-combat area in war (Feinman, 2000).

Gender shapes militarism. To understand this influence it is useful to employ a feminist critique of the alignment between masculinism and war, and, in parallel fashion, feminism and peace. Transnational work on gender and war has brought to our attention the use of rape as a war crime, the (historic and contemporary) use of females to mobilize males, and the use of females' safety and 'rights' discourse to mobilize for war.

The use of females' inclusion in militaries as a civilizing force has also worked to continue to set war as the appropriate venue for achieving justice and peace.

R.W. Connell, as Cynthia Cockburn reminds us, thinks carefully about gender in relation to militarism. Connell suggests that the gender question is answered by noting that 'men predominate across the spectrum of violence. A strategy for demilitarization and peace must concern itself with this fact, with the reasons for it, and with its implications for work to reduce violence' (Connell, 2002, p. 34, quoted in Cockburn, 2010a). Connell qualifies this statement with an acknowledgement that '[e]vidently, then, a strategy for demilitarization and peace must include a strategy of change in masculinities' (Connell, 2002, p. 38, as quoted in Cockburn, 2010a). While gender may not be essential to a military enterprise, the practices of warring have accrued to the masculine and not to the feminine in most world cultures. The question of whether or not females can engage in violent militarism in the same ways as males is as hard to answer as the core questions of nature versus nurture in gender studies. Rada Ivecovic suggests that 'the whole framework which permits or calls for war is organized in such a way that it favors the stronger, whether socially, politically, historically, or militarily stronger. The political and social systems are socially "male" only because the historically dominant gender is male' (Ivecovic, in Banerjee, 2008, p. 115). Will we find that militaries can continue to reproduce their brutalities without relying on masculinist tropes of domination to feed them? Indeed, there is ample evidence in recent history (for example, Herbert, 1998; Nordland, 2011) that masculinism persists as the organizing principle even where it is countered by feminine gender performances, that toughness of a particular masculine type is glorified and fully expected, and that to 'feminize' a prisoner through sexual domination is the way to humiliate and defeat them (Feinman, 2007). Thus, the policing of gender performance and engendering of violence as a masculine enterprise persists.

United Nations Security Council Resolution 1325 on Women, Peace and Security (2000) called for a reform across the board in female participation in peacemaking efforts and drew attention to the various impacts of war on females. The resolution was a promising landmark in its claims for females' rightful participation in processes toward peace. Framed from females' perspectives and largely by females' input and authorship, it called on nation-states to acknowledge the importance of including females at the table and respecting their experiences and contributions. It was a landmark in scope and promise, and still remains unfulfilled in practice. Formal governmental and intergovernmental feminist peace efforts, as well as feminist peace activism from non-governmental organizations such as the Women's International League for Peace and Freedom (WILPF) to the kinds of street action organized by CODEPINK, persist in marking the issues, but have yet to make significant headway in resolving them.

In my book, *Citizenship Rites* (2000), I argued that motivations for war 'are lodged in the traditional modalities of economic and political domination and sexual conquest, and the masculinist dynamic of militarist discourse' and that

> feminist antimilitarist analyses and activism uncover the violence of military diplomacy as it affects civilians, as it shapes the sex-workplace around military bases, and as it destroys communities and ecosystems. Feminist antimilitarism connects peace activism more precisely to justice struggles and, last but in no way least, feminist antimilitarist direct action has also influenced policy via participation in broad public opposition to the nuclear industries and to war. (Feinman, 2000, p. 2)

Unfortunately, the promise of a cultural shift caused by American females taking their places more easily in the MOSs and the public eye as legitimate citizen-soldiers has not been fulfilled; more than a decade later we still suffer the sexism that undergirds military culture.

FEMINIST ANTIMILITARISM AND THE PEACE MOVEMENT

The contemporary peace movement expresses in inherent ways lessons of feminist antiwar and social justice movements but does not feature a feminist sensibility in its public discourse. There is an abundance of lively feminist critique, but it exists in the feminist antiwar scholarship and reportage and in particularly *feminist* antiwar organizations, for example Women's Network Against Militarism, Women's International League for Peace and Freedom, Women in Black (WiB) and CODE-PINK, as well as multiple regional organizations of females fighting to end local wars. All of these instances of organization and contemplation of feminist and female-centered approaches to end war and bring peace continue to push at the margins of more mainstream justice and peace movements to include females' agendas and issues, to engage females' voices. Feminist approaches are also present in the international and multivalent organizing elsewhere against war's effects on females' spheres of work and in international and precise regional organizations against wars local, regional and global. There are indeed paradigmatic representations and activisms that invoke and engage females as central figures in the shape and effects of war and of peace, but they are as marginalized as has historically been the case. In other words, while feminism is a strong inflection in the form and substance of many movements, it goes unnamed save for specifically feminist loci. In the 1970s and 1980s, anti-nuclear movements and some of the anti-intervention movements were shaped by feminist and civil rights movement inspired models for organizing, such as non-hierarchical decision-making practices and a widespread discourse on the many modalities of domination. By the 1990s, movements engaged in peace and justice had largely submerged feminism or references to the civil rights movement. At that point, explicitly feminist antiwar and social justice movements became the only spaces articulating feminist claims for peace and justice.

Feminist antimilitarist theorizing and practice continues to contribute critical insights to antiwar activisms and strategizing, though is often unheard in the mainstream movements. It has evolved from Eurocentric sensitivities through significant challenges to a more geopolitically nuanced set of insights and practices. The construct of feminist antimilitarism has to be, as Peterson suggests, read through an intersectional framework to develop a nuanced view of the operations of militarism as it adapts to accommodate gender and racial diversities and across national boundaries (Sjoberg and Via, 2010). For instance, the racialized operations of the US military work differently within the US than they do once deployed in an Arab country. How we use racist tropes changes in the context of the country we are engaged with. Witness the use of white females as powerful over Arab males in interrogation contexts.

Feminist antimilitarist scholarship gives us ways to view globalized militarisms and the contributions that feminists can make to those discussions. As Cockburn suggests, feminist antimilitarism

> involves a critique of the meaning and operation of power itself – women often choose to organize in prefigurative ways that exchange 'power over' (domination) for 'power to' (capability). It is necessarily a transnational feminism, for our movements are in touch with each other over many borders. And it has a healthy old-fashioned respect for the reality and significance of structures and systems of power – a lot of antiwar feminists refuse to drop the concept of 'patriarchy'. (2010b)

Feminist antimilitarism articulated a shift from 'power over' to 'power with', or 'empowerment', connoting a particularly egalitarian notion of directly disrupting hierarchy. The way feminist antimilitarism influences broader antiwar work is twofold. First, feminist antimilitarist autonomous work addresses particularly gendered female impacts of warring and its aftermath, such as the damage to reproductive activities of shelter, food and care of children, not to mention the violence of rape as a tool of war on women and children. Second, the presence of feminist-informed or directly feminist versions of antimilitarist action includes everything from CODEPINK activist strategies to attempts, more and less successful, to infuse broad antiwar organizations with feminist perspectives and priorities. In each broad case, there are many internal permutations in the definitions and value of feminism. Cockburn teaches us that the unifying factor is, as quoted above, focused on patriarchy and power systems. We need to move further than Cockburn here and note the parallel and mutually influential effects of race and ethnicity as they shift the meanings and practices of feminisms as they are localized.

Feminist antimilitarisms have become increasingly sophisticated as feminist transnational attentions to the ways that militarism unfolds have become more fully developed. A piece of this development is precisely the specificity of geopolitical organization of race and gender power. Organizations have proliferated and accounts of activism and theorizations of its meanings abound. Indeed, a number of anthologies have been published engaging the questions of females, gender and war from multiple feminist standpoints and delivering accounts of the contours of war and its effects on females as civilians and in their roles as reproductive workers in home and community. Sjoberg and Via suggest we attend to two main issues: First, 'the impacts of war and militarism on people', especially females, and second, that 'gendered construction of war and militarism [are] linked to systems of power and inequality based on race, class, nation' (Sjoberg and Via, 2010, p. 10). They likewise argue that '[e]xamining the gendered construction ... shows that gender is a linchpin not only of how war and militarism affect people, but also of the very existence of the war system' (p. 10). In her contribution to the same volume, V. Spike Peterson uses this framework to suggest that to understand militarism we need an intersectional approach looking at femininity as demeaned and masculinity as privileged. Then, engaging the structure of the military, we can see how 'diverse hierarchies are linked and ideologically "naturalized" by feminizing those who are subordinated' (2010, p. 19). She argues further that '[b]y obscuring the reciprocal constitution of valorized masculinity and vilified femininity, these [official war] stories avoid critique of gender itself, with the effect of reproducing multiple forms of subjection and violence' (p. 28).

Giles and Hyndman in *Sites of Violence* (2004) explain that 'gender relations have been deployed in sites of militarized conflict to incite, exacerbate, and fuel violence' and that there has been 'widespread incorporation of civilians into war. Very little attention to date has been paid to this highly gendered and racialized phenomenon, and the massive scale of people's displacement due to conflict and subsequent research on the gendered experience of both conflict and asylum' (p. 4). This all points to the way that masculinism and racism are utilized in the organizing assumptions of war as well as the ways in which females, by their assumed and widely practiced biological and social reproductive work, are implicated in every way that civilians are impacted by war.

In *Women in Peace Politics* Banerjee (2008) explains, '[w]omen's fight for peace in South Asia is a fight against all forms of oppression' (p. xv). For Anuradha Chenoy the issue is to explore 'the gendered aspect of military violence by emphasizing that sexual violence continues to be the specific experience of women during war' (Chenoy in Banerjee, 2008, p. 28). Samir Kumar Das cautions us against

> making gender-just peace a synonym for privileging women and their biological presence. Many run-of-the-mill feminist writings ironically are premised on this 'metaphysics of presence'. As the meaning of security gets demystified and disentangled from the mega project of state security, it ... gets linked up with the struggle for gender equality and justice. (Kumar Das in Banerjee, 2008, p. 6)

Indeed, while feminist antimilitarists are engaged in building gender-just and, for that matter, race-just peace projects we also need to tread carefully in the articulations of this peace as inclusive, non-hierarchical (power with), and non-dominating via gender, race and nation-state.

It is impossible to escape the fact that 'war and nationalism are also practically anti-feminine in many respects. As real and not only symbolic victims (and they are most often real victims), women are "entitled", once again, to specific types of suffering, atrocities, rape, etc.' (Ivecovic, in Banerjee, 2008, p. 121). Indeed, in most wars the targeting of female sovereignty is endemic and precisely strategic. While it is important not to fix this observation as universal, especially at the cost of being unable to address militarist projects inclusive of females in domineering and oppressive roles, still we see the enactment of a refigured violent masculinist racist body, for example, in the form of Lynndie England, who is perhaps the most notorious of the US military females who took part in prisoner abuse at Abu Ghraib.

These anthologies have sometimes also looked critically at females' roles as soldiers, especially in the wake of the Abu Ghraib revelations about torture in Iraq. Some of the arguments fall into the category of the classic equation of war with masculinism while others provide more nuanced accounts of the ways war continues to be fastened to a culture of masculinist racism but is not necessarily wedded to it. Likewise, the lion's share of international feminist attention is on the impacts of war and militarism on females' lives in relation to the productive and reproductive work they attempt to sustain in war and post-war zones, as well as the precise local peace activist interventions they take, for example in many of the recent conflicts and civil wars.

As feminist antimilitarists engage the more recent developments of the inclusions of female soldiers and of gay and lesbian soldiers, a more nuanced reading of militarism in the US context is needed in order to continue to make visible both the ways that masculinism remains entwined and the ways it is dispensable, as it is replaced by other tropes of domination. Certainly the Abu Ghraib revelations were a prime example of these new moves. The female soldiers at Abu Ghraib were clearly subordinate to their male colleagues, yet they were being used to dominate others. Likewise, the female generals involved, albeit from the outside, participated as dominant figures over a racially subordinated group of prisoners, male and female. The explicitly cultural, gendered and racialized references to humiliation and domination used by the male and female guards, both at Abu Ghraib and repeated at sites elsewhere, demonstrate the importance of recognizing the racialized dimension of these abuses. Incidents of using females' body exposure, simulated menses, and manipulation to humiliate Muslim male prisoners are documented at length in the Report of the International Committee of the Red Cross on the Treatment by Coalition Forces (February 2004 White paper), the Taguba Report (2004), the Schlesinger Report (2004), and the Fay/Jones Report (Danner, 2004). The last three were commissioned directly by the US government to investigate Abu Ghraib once the photos showing the abuse of prisoners had leaked to the press. Reports of the concurrent rape and humiliation of female prisoners at Abu Ghraib and perhaps elsewhere were suppressed. These accounts came largely from Iraqi female attorneys interviewing prisoners and ex-prisoners.[3]

ANTIWAR FEMINISMS

As I have argued elsewhere, the critical insight of feminist antimilitarists is that they have 'both identified and opposed what they articulated as the masculinist construction of militarism' (Feinman, 2000, p. 27). Indeed the challenge for feminist antimilitarism remains 'to develop its analysis of militarism to mark the resilience of masculinist militarism in the face of pressure to incorporate women, without dismissing the possibility that militarism could function without masculinism' (Feinman, 2000, p. 30).

This challenge is especially relevant in light of developments over the last decade and two major US-led wars, as well as countless other regional wars. Perhaps simply because of the persistence of masculinist militarism and its forms within and impacted by military action, it is difficult to imagine militarism functioning without masculinism. I believe it is very important that our attention not waiver from the possibility that militarism could function without masculinism.

I see this as a refined version of the essentialist argument about the ways that the female–male binary is reified in war. It is hard to argue against such a claim in feminist antimilitarism given the overwhelming recurrence of violence against females in war. Even where the situation, for instance, Abu Ghraib, creates new tropes of gendered domination, they still revert to familiar patterns of male gender performance of domination. The prevalence of rape, of violent disruption of females' traditional spheres of influence (home, school, community) in most geopolitical situations speaks to ongoing masculinism in larger society and replicated in war. (See Cockburn's argument earlier that it is a basic condition of warring.)

Kalpana Kannabiran provides us with some guidance in thinking through what is at stake for a transnational feminist analysis of conflict and peace activism.

> Work on conflict in the past two decades has looked at the specific implications of conflict for women. Feminist writing has attempted to understand the politics of mothers' fronts; the specific mobilizations by women to promote peace and resist war; the ways in which family and community lock women into inescapable custody, through non-consensual marriage, the denial of choice in widowhood and remarriage practices; the experience of combatant women within militant movements and resistance struggles; the relationship between the violent masculinity of the armed forces and women at contested boundaries or on the borders of nations to cite a few concerns on the subcontinent. (In Banerjee, 2008, p, 134)

NEXT STEPS FOR FEMINIST ANTIMILITARISMS?

As personnel patterns and structures shift within the US military, feminist antimilitarists need to ask new questions. What does it mean to see females in roles as perpetrators of classically masculinist violence or in broad leadership roles inclusive of leading militaries, or state diplomatic missions, at the nation-state level (for example, Albright, Rice, Bachelet, Clinton, Merkel)? Does it change essential notions of the martial? Does statecraft leadership equate to military leadership? If, in fact, dominance is a historically masculinist trope is it always that, even when 'alienated' from males as such? How does the meaning change? We know from Butler that gender is a performance; is it one that anyone can try? Does it change an essential characteristic of war if female is dominator?

The US peace movement, represented by the organizations and episodes of peace activism that existed prior to 9/11 and those that have coalesced since, have complex relationships to feminist antimilitarism. The large organizations that are not explicitly feminist or female centered are often coalitions of smaller focus groups loosely affiliated, for example, Act Now to Stop War and End Racism (ANSWER) and United for Justice and Peace (UFPJ). ANSWER was founded in response to the advent of the War on Terror, and UFPJ against the Iraq War. Neither is explicitly feminist though both have their roots in the social justice and anti-oppression movements such as the feminist liberation movements, and feminist antiwar and justice movements. These two in particular, skirting for the purposes of this chapter their cross-organizational conflict, are umbrella organizations that have been able to engage large numbers of demonstrators professing feminist analyses of war via their signs and side actions. They are not typically focused via their speakers or their outreach toward feminist articulations.

There are feminist movement organizations that have come and gone, some that persist, and many individual feminist antimilitarists working within broader organizations. This is true in the United States, and elsewhere around the world. It is more common elsewhere for feminist and/or female-centered organizations to be concerned more broadly with the conditions of life for females in war and post-war zones. This is often because such groups are located within or proximal to the war zone itself. For instance, Women in Black got its start in 1988 when Jewish Israeli women held a silent vigil in a public square in Jerusalem to protest the occupation. Organizations within the US have based their arguments on the assumptions that females are peacekeepers and the less violent sex. Since at least Lysistrata, who organized the females of her community to refuse sex with their males until they agreed to end the Peloponnesian War, some females have argued that as mothers and caregivers females are responsible for protecting their progeny from war. Although few feminist actions have since included refusing sex with males, basing opposition to war on a precisely feminine standpoint and responsibility has been a recurring theme in feminist antiwar work. These arguments were expressed in actions against nuclear proliferation, testing and potential war. The Mothers and Others Day Action at the Nevada Test Site in 1987 is a prime example of this kind of organizing (Sturgeon,

2007; Feinman, 2000) and is perhaps the best example of a twentieth-century version of the argument. When planning their action the organizers resisted the implicit and explicit exclusions of a Mother's Day action, and instead modified the call to include 'others', that is, anyone who was opposed to war and chose to participate without identifying as a mother. The association of mothers and motherhood with peace was nevertheless a dominant feature of the protest, with birth canals constructed out of fabric and wire to enable protesters to trespass the test site and some of the male participants wearing pregnancy costumes and professing to be mothers for peace.

Contemporary organizations that are explicitly feminist and antiwar include CODEPINK (US); Women in Black (international); Women's International League for Peace and Freedom (international) and its web action site PeaceWomen; institutional affiliations like the NGO Working Group on Women, Peace and Security (which is working specifically for females' human rights and produces an annual report 'MAP' to guide and pressure UN work for females); International Network for Women Against Militarism (INWAM); and Women for Genuine Security (US affiliate of INWAM).

CODEPINK, Women in Black and Women's International League for Peace and Freedom are the feminist organizations most often visible in peace movement rallies and actions. Institutions like the NGO Working Group and INWAM are more often in the inter-organizational networks directly advocating policy and institutional changes toward peace. The rest of this section will focus on CODEPINK, WiB and WILPF for what we can learn about their influence in movement practices.

While each of these organizations has explicitly feminist and often, even in the case of the older organizations which were once tremendously Eurocentric, transnational perspective and aspiration, as activist organizing in visible street actions, CODEPINK is the group that garners the most attention and thus also sets the tone for feminist inclusions in large demonstrations.

CODEPINK began in response to the Alert level codes of the Bush Administration's initiation of the War on Terror, as an antiwar organization specifically to call for an end to the Iraq War. Self-described as a

women-initiated grassroots peace and social justice movement working to end the war in Iraq, stop new wars, and redirect our resources into healthcare, education and other life affirming ... calls for policies based on compassion, kindness and a commitment to international law. CODEPINK women and men seek to activate, amplify, and inspire a community of peacemakers through creative campaigns and a commitment to non-violence. (CODEPINK website)

CODEPINK began with its trademark pink-clothed activists and the unfurling of a giant pink slip out of windows visible to the peace marchers below in the early San Francisco marches against the Iraq War within the War on Terror, with signs that said 'Give Bush a pink slip!' (Author's personal observation, March 2003).

Women in Black, which began in 1988 as a street protest in Jerusalem by Israeli Jewish women opposing the occupation of the West Bank and Gaza Strip, later spread around the world in protest against the Israeli occupation, and is now a worldwide network inspiring Women in Black actions wherever women and their allies want to take a stand against war. Weekly vigils are typical statements in some local communities, including my own. Women in Black 'have a feminist understanding: that men's violence against women in domestic life and in the community, in times of peace and in times of war, are interrelated. Violence is used as a means of controlling women' (Women in Black website). Women in Black posits itself as a nonviolent activist group, multicultural and multiracial, international, working together to support peace and justice. They are an explicitly feminist group and work precisely through women initiated actions (which men are welcome to support) to stake a claim for women's political voices, which they assert are more often drowned out in mixed gender organizations. Women in Black thus makes two kinds of particularly feminist claims in their position statement: one, that women are precisely situated to take a stand against men's violence that is perpetrated against women in war and peace, and two, that women's strategies and voices are more difficult to hear in mixed-sex peace groups.

Women's International League for Peace and Freedom, and its more recent offshoot PeaceWomen, is a long-standing organization devoted to peace. Founded in 1915 to promote peace over World War I, the organization has grown and maintained its international standing as a female organization committed to peace. An official NGO, WILPF holds consultative status with several sections of the United Nations. They are the organization with ties both institutional and in street organizations. PeaceWomen is a project of the WILPF organization working to hold the UN accountable to the Security Council Resolution 1325, by monitoring the compliance with the full and equal participation of females in efforts to create and maintain international peace and security. PeaceWomen's focus is precisely on international conditions for females in active and post-conflict zones. In this way PeaceWomen is active for females although it does not explicitly call itself feminist in its online literature (PeaceWomen website). This is a fairly common attribute of organizations doing work centered on the conditions of females' lives as it is perhaps a more neutral political space to occupy when negotiating for a group's survival.

CODEPINK, WiB and WILPF are regularly seen in actions for peace in the US and, in the case of WiB and WILPF, abroad. CODEPINK activists have traveled to conflict zones to demonstrate for peace, yet they are a largely US-based organization. As evident in the epigraph, CODE-PINK embraces its acting out of the 'female' role in society, albeit with irony. CODEPINK's initial interest was in countering the very specific-ally masculinist response of the Bush Administration to the attack on 9/11 and the subsequent call to war against Iraq. The coded threat levels were answered with a 'threat' of pink power, a more precise and unabashedly 'feminine' remark than the careful inclusivity of the decade earlier 'Mothers and Others'. Of course, on the street, males and females easily embraced the CODEPINK agenda, wearing pink, referencing it in actions around the US. CODEPINK was thus formed in explicit response to the amped up masculinist militarism, and not at a more nuanced, racially sensitized level of engagement.

WiB in Israel, on the other hand, was both a protest movement and a conciliatory movement aimed at cultivating transnational sensitivity between Israel and Palestine in a context of inter-racial and international assertions of peace. WiB continues to hold regular vigils in cities around the world, transmuting its agenda for peace to emergent and persistent geopolitical conflicts.

CONCLUSION

There are various focuses among the feminist peace organizations as seen in the examples above. Some are explicitly about demonstrations and actions that speak truth to power and in both broad and singular critiques of military engagements. Others are at or within the margins of major national and international organizations providing information and im-petus for those organizations to take opposition to war seriously, and to bring attention and action to the violations that females face as a result of war, from rape to community displacements, effects that linger long after war has officially ended. All have grown savvy about the ways that an analysis of militarism requires attention to the particulars of region, race, ethnicity, gender and class status in a way that earlier movements were unable to fully engage. In part because of the proliferation of local–global organizations for females' rights, there is a framework within which to place these expressions.

If the changing military, especially in the US, bodes a disengagement with masculinism as militarism's *raison d'être*, then what use will we make of feminist critiques? Would militarism be as, or at all, destructive without masculinist tropes? If so, then to what end do we struggle for a feminist antimilitarism as if that is the solution? Perhaps this brings us back to the quotation at the beginning of this chapter, Starhawk's observation that females struggle for peace because males are most frequently off planning and executing war. Certainly, the feminist and female-centered organizations and activisms do not wait for such an analysis or moment to take hold, they operate with the urgency that males are warring and females are bearing the brunt in its various and brutal iterations. Any transformations in military culture that are to bode well for peace would have to include cultivation of the kinds of conflict resolution skills and practices that are currently only mildly tolerated, if even employed, and certainly we can see that the domination modalities of militarism can be as easily effected by female soldiers as by males. After all, females and their allies continue to rise up against war and celebrate the creative embodiment of justice and peace.

NOTES

1. The use of 'female' and 'male' in this chapter is intentional so as not to reify the category 'woman' in the context of these challenges to traditional gender formations.
2. The National Defense Authorization Act, signed by House and Senate Armed Services Committees, included the language for repeal, and the House and Senate each voted on a stand-alone DADT repeal bill on 15 December and 18 December respectively. President Obama signed this bill into law on 22 December 2010.
3. There are extensive writings by now on the Abu Ghraib scandal and what it revealed about military culture. Some excellent analytical sources are Hersh (2004) and chapters in McKelvey (2007).

REFERENCES

Alwi, Malathi de (2009), 'Interrogating the "political": feminist peace activism in Sri Lanka', *Feminist Review*, **91**, 81–93.
Banerjee, Paula (ed.) (2008), *Women in Peace Politics*, Sage.
Baudrillard, Jean (1995), *The Gulf War*, Power.
Benedict, Helen (2008), 'The scandal of military rape', *Ms. Magazine*, Fall, accessed 15 July 2015 at: http://www.msmagazine.com/Fall2008/TheScandalOfMilitaryRape.asp.
Bhavnani, Kum Kum and Margaret Coulson (1986), 'Transforming socialist feminism: the challenge of racism', *Feminist Review*, **23**, 81–92.
Cockburn, Cynthia (2007), *From Where We Stand: War, Women's Activism and Feminist Analysis*, Zed Books.
Cockburn, Cynthia (2010a), 'Gender relations as causal in militarization and war: A feminist standpoint', *International Feminist Journal of Politics*, **12** (2), 139–57.

Cockburn, Cynthia (2010b), 'What kind of feminism does war provoke?', 25 August, accessed 15 July 2015 at: http://www.opendemocracy.net/5050/cynthia-cockburn/what-kind-of-feminism-does-war-provoke.

CODEPINK (2002), 'Call to action', accessed 15 July 2015 at: http://starhawk.org/Activism/activism%20writings/Iraq/2002-10-21-Code%20Pink.pdf.

Danner, Mark (2004), 'Fay/Jones Report on Abu Ghraib', *Torture and Truth: America, Abu Ghraib, and the War on Terror*, New York Review of Books, pp. 403–579.

Feinman, Ilene (2000), *Citizenship Rites: Feminist Soldiers and Feminist Antimilitarists*, New York University Press.

Feinman, Ilene (2007), 'Shock and awe: Abu Ghraib and racially gendered torture', in Tara McKelvey (ed.), *One of the Guys: Women as Aggressors and Torturers*, Seal, pp. 57–80.

Giles, Wenona and Jennifer Hyndman (2004), *Sites of Violence: Gender and Conflict Zones*, University of California Press.

Hawthorne, Susan and Bronwyn Winter (2002), *September 11, 2001: Feminist Perspectives*, Spinifex.

Herbert, Melissa (1998), *Camouflage isn't only for Combat*, New York University Press.

Hersh, Seymour (2004), *Chain of Command*, Harpers Perennial.

Kaldor, Mary (2006), *New and Old Wars: Organized Violence in a Global Era*, 2nd edn, Polity.

McKelvey, Tara (ed.) (2007), *One of the Guys: Women as Aggressors and Torturers*, Seal.

Military Leadership Diversity Commission (2011), *From Representation to Inclusion: Diversity Leadership for the 21st Century Military*, Government Printing Office.

Nordland, Rod (2011), 'For soldiers, death sees no gender lines', *New York Times*, 22 June, accessed 15 July 2015 at: http://www.nytimes.com/2011/06/22/world/asia/22 afghanistan.html?src=ISMR_AP_LO_MST_FB.

Park, Sandra S. (2010), 'Uncovering sexual assault in the military', ACLU Women's Rights Project, accessed 15 July 2015 at: http://www.aclu.org/blog/womens-rights/uncovering-sexual-assault-military.

Peterson, Spike V. (2010), 'Gendered identities, ideologies, and practices in the context of war and militarism', in Laura Sjoberg and Sandra Via (eds), *Gender, War and Militarism: Feminist Perspectives*, Praeger, pp. 17–29.

Schlesinger, James R. et al. (2004), *Final Report of the Independent Panel to Review DoD Detention Operations*, August, Department of Defense.

Sjoberg, Laura and Sandra Via (eds) (2010), *Gender, War and Militarism: Feminist Perspectives*, Praeger.

Sturgeon, Noël (2007), *Ecofeminist Natures: Race, Gender, Feminist Theory and Political Action*, Routledge.

Taguba, Major General Anthony (2004), *Taguba Report: Article 15-6 Investigation of the 800th Military Police Brigade*, Government Printing Office.

US Department of Defense (2014), *Base Structure Report: Fiscal Year 2014 Baseline*, accessed 15 July 2015 at: http://www.acq.osd.mil/ie/download/bsr/Base%20 Structure%20Report%20FY14.pdf.

US Department of Defense, Sexual Assault Prevention and Response (2014), *Annual Report on Sexual Harassment and Violence at the Military Service Academies: Academic Program Year 2013–2014*, Government Printing Office.

Websites

CODEPINK website, accessed 15 July 2015 at: http://www.codepink4peace.org/.

Nobel Women's Initiative website, accessed 15 July 2015 at: http://www.nobelwomens initiative.org/about-us.

PeaceWomen website, accessed 15 July 2015 at: http://www.peacewomen.org/.

Women for Genuine Security website (n.d.a), accessed 15 July 2015 at: http://www.genuinesecurity.org/aboutus/transnational.html.
Women for Genuine Security website (n.d.b), accessed 15 July 2015 at: http://www.genuinesecurity.org/aboutus/framework.html.
Women in Black website (n.d.), accessed 15 July 2015 at: http://womeninblack.org/.
Women's International League for Peace and Freedom website (n.d.), accessed 23 May 2016 at: http://wilpfinternational.org/.

17. Iraq Veterans Against the War: 'that whole gender paradigm'

Cami Rowe

INTRODUCTION

In a statement at the National Labor College in Silver Spring, Maryland in 2008, Iraq War Veteran Jeff Key drew attention to the issue of gender hierarchy in the US military and the link to wider issues of unwarranted military violence and inhumanity:

> At the core of this war machine is an ideology that is based on the gender paradigm and homophobia ... This idea that men are beings devoid of feelings and compassion and that women are weak and a ball of emotion is at the centre of all this ... It's got to stop ... My highest idea of someone who serves in our military, the code of conduct that they would bring to the battlefield, has everything to do with dispelling these old ways of thinking around gender and sexuality. (Key, 2008)

Key's statement suggests that an attention to gender inequality may go a long way toward undoing the structures of the military that perpetuate both institutional and interpersonal injustices within the context of the War on Terror. Surprisingly little scholarly attention has been paid to the role of military men and women as a distinct group of political actors who share key identity traits alongside strictly imposed limitations on their political agency. While some key studies have established the military sphere as an arena of biopolitical ordering that upholds sovereign authority,[1] few have undertaken to critically evaluate the contributions of individuals who speak from their experiences within the military ranks, but outside of and often contrary to the institutional military agenda. This is a particularly pressing issue for war veterans in the United States, who are frequently operating simultaneously on behalf of, and against, the world's largest military power. In the spirit of Key's exhortation, this chapter focuses on the antiwar activism of Iraq Veterans Against the War (IVAW), an organization comprised of American military veterans who have served since 11 September 2001. In an analysis of the social performance of disaffected veterans, I examine the extent to

361

which IVAW successfully challenges the cultural gender norms that underpin militarization and war.

Since the inception of the War on Terror a new wave of dissenting soldiers has come to the forefront of the American antiwar movement. Veterans of military actions in Iraq and Afghanistan have launched campaigns to alter American foreign policy and tip public opinion in favor of ending US military intervention there. From the American Civil War onwards, military service members and veterans have organized in opposition to war and in various political campaigns relating to war's domestic aftermath. Since the nineteenth century, enlisted members of the military have been speaking out against their superiors' orders and policies, often paying a hefty price for their actions (Cortright, 2005). While opposition to war by American veterans is perhaps most vividly associated with the Vietnam Era, the intensification of military dissent in the mid-twentieth century would probably not have been so forthcoming without the historical precedence of the veterans who opposed American interventionism in the midst of the Spanish–American War, or the anti-Hoover march of the Bonus Army in 1932.

However, despite this long history of military dissent in the United States, antiwar campaigns by veterans remain a primarily fringe aspect of the broader antiwar 'movement', and have, like antiwar campaigns more generally, lacked a significant impact on foreign policy. It is my suggestion that this stems in part from the fact that, like their Vietnam Era counterparts, American War on Terror veterans must engage with the stereotypical role assigned to them by society and the media – the symbolic social role of the sacrificial, heroic Soldier (indicated herein by an uppercase 'S'), a figure in a position of loyal service for the sake of his or her country's welfare. In general, military dissent has made little headway into the popular characterization of The Soldier, a figure which largely endures in the public imaginary as an unassailable sacrificial hero. While some popular culture products reveal the public appetite for stories of Soldiers as defiant rebels, overall these narratives retain a sense of The Soldier as sacrificial hero, as illustrated by the depiction of Ron Kovic in the film *Born on the Fourth of July* (1989) or the fictional Brandon King in *Stop-Loss* (2008).

In this chapter, I probe the complexities behind the frequent appearance of The Solider in popular culture on the one hand, and the apparent lack of political impact by military dissenters on the other. By explicating the gap between the celebrated stereotype of The Soldier versus the political marginalization of disaffected military veterans, I show how members of the US military occupy a unique position with regard to sovereign authority and biopolitical marginalization, and that gender is a foundational component of the social performances that underpin these processes.

At the heart of this analysis is a concern with the way that sovereign authority and biopolitics are innately performative, in the theatrical sense of the term. Crucially, theater and performance scholars have demonstrated the extent to which resistant performances can be derived from positions of institutional marginalization and from identification with quasi-mythic political tropes. By engaging in social performances that provoke associations with the familiar cast of characters in the dominant social imaginary, actors can go on to display critical differences that result in a capacity to challenge the logics of sovereign authority (Hughes, 2011; McKenzie, 2001). One way that this can be accomplished is through strategic approaches to mimesis, that is, attempts to enact representations of the world. In the case of American war veterans who seek to oppose war, I argue their success can be derived from an interweaving of normative mimetic renditions of Soldierhood with critical ironic or parodic enactments.[2] In the following analysis, I begin with a discussion of the particular ways that The Soldier character is constructed as a strictly delimited social role, and the centrality of gender to this construction. Following this I provide a brief account of IVAW's history before analyzing some specific IVAW actions. I discuss the group's 2008 Winter Soldier event, as well as their engagements with the Don't Ask Don't Tell (DADT) policy and campaigns in support of WikiLeaks whistleblower Chelsea Manning, probing each example for its critical counter-mimetic potential.

GENDERED MILITARY AND GENDERED ANTIWAR DISSENT

A common theme in scholarly analyses of protest performance is the risk that activism might inadvertently uphold political and cultural norms in its efforts to reveal social injustices. Protesters must confront the constant possibility that their activities might be co-opted back into the mechanisms of state power, effectively celebrated as hallmarks of democratic free speech while being simultaneously relegated to the sidelines of political debate. Furthermore, the content of protests can often simply represent the hierarchical ordering of society without prompting sufficient public critique of the social mechanisms that underpin inequalities. For military veterans wishing to speak out against war, these risks are heightened. Due to the special way that The Soldier character is constructed politically and culturally, military veterans are especially constrained in their opportunities for efficacious protest.

Political and cultural forces combine in the United States to construct the social role of The Soldier as an entity that strictly defines the acceptable behavior and beliefs of members of the United States armed forces. Military and judicial regulations and cultural traditions give rise to a set of characteristics that coalesce into the mask of the Solider, a mask which military enlistees are compelled to don and which they will find difficult to remove. The Soldier character is notably a representative of state political aims, and an object for public reverence which contributes to public support for war. Members of the military are therefore subject to an inscribed character that upholds the ideals of The Soldier as a figure that is universal, apolitical and removed from the public sphere.

To further understand these constraints, it is helpful to frame an account of military dissent with reference to notions of sovereign power and biopolitical exclusions. Giorgio Agamben's philosophies have proven foundational to much thinking around marginal identity categories, and feminist scholars have demonstrated the ways that gender is implicit in the construction of sovereignty and *homo sacer*[3] (e.g., Masters, 2009; Pratt, 2005; Smith, 2010). In an analysis of the gendered exclusions apparent in military institutions, Veronique Pin-Fat and Maria Stern have noted that the military gives rise to bare life within its ranks, as its members become depoliticized fighting machines (2005). Furthermore, Slavoj Žižek reminds us that that the figure of *homo sacer* can be constituted by the different treatment experienced by individuals in varying circumstances (2002). While they may possess certain rights or degrees of citizenship in one context, that position can equally be threatened in another. War veterans are a prime example of this, as they simultaneously have the potential to embody sovereign authority, and also experience severe restrictions on their individual political agency.

I concentrate here on the ways that the bare life-sovereignty dynamic is manifested in the construction of The Soldier character and the subsequent differentiated treatment of war veterans. I suggest that members of the US military are often likely to be excluded from ordinary social and political mechanisms. This is facilitated because their individual selves – actors possessing personal embodied experiences and perceptions – are obscured by the vividness and rigidity of The Soldier mask. Within the military realm, their speech and actions are strictly regulated; in the realm of popular culture their characteristics and motivations are only readable when consistent with social norms relating to Soldierhood. In both environments, veterans will find that the surest way to speak with visibility and authority is through reference to The Soldier trope, but this risks further reinforcing sovereign authority – a risk that will be further explicated below. As a result, the individual war veterans who oppose war violence, exemplified here through the case of IVAW, demonstrate the difficulty of becoming a recognized political being when their personal, embodied individuality becomes visible.

Importantly, the difficulties of effective social performance by disaffected veterans are intertwined with social gender norms. The cultural reluctance to recognize former members of the military as critical political agents is rooted in a minefield of gender stereotypes that dissenting veterans must navigate. This can be further elucidated through a more sustained focus on the two realms of veterans' marginalization discussed above, and the specific ways that gender constructions are in play here.

It is first useful to address the codified rules that constrain the behavior of those enlisted in the US military. These regulations stem from both internal military procedures and federal legislation. In general, veterans in the United States are disproportionately restricted by legal provisions that regulate their speech and actions, in some cases even following their discharge. Articles 133 and 134 of the Uniform Code of Military Justice (UCMJ) have most frequently been used to regulate the social and political conduct of American soldiers. Dating to 1775, these articles have only recently been called upon to discipline and punish soldiers who speak out against wars, being cited with increasing frequency from the early Cold War period onward. Article 133 prohibits 'conduct unbefitting an officer and a gentleman', and includes the offence of insulting or defaming other members of the military. Article 134 prohibits conduct that might disrupt good order and discipline or that in any way 'discredits' the armed forces. It also forbids the misuse of military uniforms, including wearing them in a way that brings dishonor to the military (United States Government, 2010). Significantly, in 1974 the Supreme Court upheld the military's authority to invoke these articles against antiwar commentary by soldiers, issuing a decision that supports restrictions on the First Amendment for US soldiers in light of the special character of the military community and military missions. This decision still applies today (Noone, 2007). Punishment for violating the UCMJ can extend to the revocation of pay and benefits as well as prolonged imprisonment under the military court-martial system. The fact that up until 2009 military service was compulsorily extended under Stop-Loss orders meant that more than 13 000 soldiers faced involuntary restrictions to their First Amendment rights. These legal restrictions should not be underestimated – charges have been brought against several members of IVAW and some have suffered reductions in rank and even imprisonment.

Significantly, in many cases these charges have related to political speech made whilst the actor is in military uniform, contradicting the social character of The Soldier as a universal embodiment of state policies.[4]

We begin to get a sense of the way that gender is involved in these regulations from the language referring to officers and gentlemen and fears of defamation or dishonor. This becomes clearer when these regulations are read alongside a history of military practices that proscribe who may take part in the military, and in what roles. Recent legislative changes demonstrate some advances here with regard to sex and gender equality. Since the mid-1970s legislative changes have allowed a much greater range of assignments for women in the armed forces. In 2010 the Don't Ask Don't Tell policy that prohibited openly gay individuals from serving in the military forces was repealed by the US Senate, and in 2013 the ban on women in combat roles was removed. Yet despite these advances, the military continues to aggressively police the gender and sexuality of its recruits. While the military has issued 'moral waivers' to would-be recruits guilty of murder, child abuse and sexual offences, transgenderism is still a dischargeable offence (IVAW, 2013). This is despite the fact that transgender people are twice as likely to enlist in the military compared to the general US population (Harrison-Quintana and Herman, 2013). In addition, basic training and the discipline of military units still rely on accusations of homosexuality and femininity aimed at underperforming recruits. Rape and sexual abuse are not only frequent, but common. Researchers and former military officers have mostly attributed this to a culture that promotes gendered violence and inequality (Benedict, 2009; Wright, 2009). These facts suggest that the gendered subtext of the UCMJ is actually reflective of the extent to which gender is complicit in the construction of The Soldier as a highly regulated and often excluded social role.

These political and legal restrictions support the characterization of Soldiers as figures outside of everyday civic life, and place them in a position removed from the polis. This contributes to the construction of sovereign authority in its ability to differentiate and exclude members of the military. Importantly though, cultural norms facilitate the elevation of this exceptional treatment into a celebrated popular tradition. These cultural norms also add convincing depth to the character of The Soldier, and it is helpful to touch upon some of the more subtle ways that gender is in play here.

To begin with, voluntary enlistment in the military is one of the most celebrated characteristics of The Soldier in American culture. Although the actual degree to which the American military is comprised of willing volunteers is highly debatable,[5] it remains a pervasive cultural myth that impacts perceptions of individual war veterans. The Soldier's death is assumed to follow from an individual's free and willing decision to put his or her life at risk, and the legal and political limitations discussed above are also largely assumed to be a voluntary sacrifice. Soldiers – bearing the uniform masks of the institutional military – are publicly celebrated for their willing sacrifice of individual agency and, if killed in action, are mourned for their sacrifice for national ideals. Existing scholarship convincingly elucidates the function of this soldier-sacrifice myth and the way that it not only demands public deference to past and current members of the military, but also obliges soldiers to unquestioningly follow orders so that the historical trajectory of patriotic heroism can be preserved (Grant, 2005; Harrison, 2003). Significantly, the popular understanding of solider-sacrifice is predominantly centered on male volunteers who heroically leave behind their women-and-children, in the interest of protecting the feminized nation at large. However, the concept of volunteerism itself is also beset by gendering. In the first instance, military regulations prohibit the enlistment of would-be recruits who are deemed to have too many dependent children, something which is likely to impact women disproportionately to men (Hillman, 2010). Additionally, several recent cases of high profile female Soldiers have revealed the uneasiness with which this concept of the volunteer sits alongside gender norms. Particularly for women who have children, it would appear that the public is culturally less inclined to celebrate their voluntary choice to temporarily remove themselves from the home space and family relationships, with those who do so typically configured as transgressive or abnormal. This is evidenced in part by the depiction of women in military recruitment materials, wherein they are typically shown in non-war roles; and also in the personal accounts of women in the military (Brown, 2012; GoArmy.com, 2010; Scott, 2010).

William Astore has made the point that individuals who willingly join the armed forces are thenceforth considered heroes simply on the basis of that action alone. All Soldiers who uphold the ideals of volunteerism are therefore considered to be heroic figures whose actions are morally and politically unassailable (Astore, 2010). The gendered aspects of volunteerism combine with the heightened gendering of heroism and victimhood that was evident in post-9/11 American culture. James Messerschmidt links this to what he deems a 'global dominate masculinity' constructed by the George W. Bush administration and facilitative of the narratives of rescue, diplomacy and voluntary suffering that justified the early War on Terror (Messerschmidt, 2010). What all of this adds up to is that only some actors can fit the culturally constructed mask of The Soldier. On the one hand, social gender norms and narratives create confined characterizations to which veterans must to some degree conform if they seek to lay claim to their military backgrounds as a means for political agency. On the other hand, some veterans are kept backstage entirely and deemed wholly unfit to act as Soldiers in public. This point will be returned to later, but for now it is sufficient to point out that The Soldier character, as representative of the military institution, is one rooted in cultural associations with voluntary sacrifice and heroism, and that these characteristics are reliant on social gender norms to gain purchase in the public imagination. This amplifies the difficulties for individual members of the military to exercise personal agency or gain recognition for their unique embodied voices and perspectives.

Despite these clear obstacles to voicing individual political opinions, the United States has a long history of military dissent, and of course, antiwar dissent more broadly. Historically, gender stereotypes have been prominent in antiwar discourses globally. From the apron-clad women of Women Strike for Peace in the 1960s, to the nurturing home-spaces created at the influential Greenham Common Women's Peace Camp in the UK in the 1980s, much historical anti-militarist activism by women sought to gain authority by overtly performing 'feminine' stereotypes as a basis for political beliefs. Similarly, activism by US war veterans has tended to obscure female veterans, in favor of uniformed marches, aggressive throwing-away of combat medals and an overall adherence to cultural ideals of heroic masculinity. In more recent years, since antiwar activism has been reinvigorated by the War on Terror, protesters have largely embraced more nuanced approaches to gender and identity. With the emergence of groups such as Code Pink and Missile Dick Chicks, the antiwar contingent has increasingly sought to challenge gender norms with parodic depictions of hyper-gendering alongside its anti-militarist messages. Iraq Veterans Against the War sits alongside other military dissent organizations in the United States, such as Veterans for Peace and the Service Women's Action Network, which seek to complicate social gender norms and campaign for gender equality.

However, despite the evidence that suggests that antiwar activists are increasingly aware of the complicity of gender in the construction of global violence and militarization, there remains reluctance in the antiwar movement at large to tackle the characteristics of The Soldier trope head-on. Indeed, the conflation of Soldierhood with voluntary heroism has been extensively embraced by the American antiwar community in the post-9/11 era. This stems in part from a concern with the treatment of returning Vietnam War veterans by an American public that was increasingly opposed to that conflict. From my observations of the antiwar community in 2008 it became clear that many individuals felt a need to correct the perceived historical error of persecuting soldiers for their participation in an unjust war. As a result, many antiwar messages were carefully crafted to ensure that the message, 'Love the troops, hate the war' was lucidly conveyed (Rowe, 2013). While most antiwar activists would emphasize the financial and political pressures that underlie military enlistment, the danger here is that activists unintentionally reinforce the message that Soldierhood is a reified category from which individual agency and responsibility are substantially diminished, a position that serves to further marginalize the potential contributions from antiwar veterans. I contend that IVAW is uniquely positioned to grapple with this. Specifically, by engaging directly with the gendering of the military and The Soldier character, IVAW demonstrates the potential to wrest the figure of The Soldier back into a realm of cultural negotiation, where political critique of the military becomes possible. Crucially, this challenge to the established characteristics of Soldierhood is effectively enacted through a fluid interweaving of normative representations of The Soldier with more parodic theatricality. In the remainder of this chapter I offer a discussion of the ways that IVAW exemplifies the potential of social performance to challenge the gender norms that underpin constructions of war. This entails a discussion of their organizational background, as well as specific campaigns that engage directly with gender inequalities.

ENTER IVAW

IVAW was formed in 2004 at the annual convention of Veterans for Peace. From a small band of members scattered throughout the country, IVAW grew in their first year into an organization with thousands of members. Local chapters exist throughout the United States and at military bases around the world (IVAW, 2010). Over the past twelve years the organization has engaged in an array of activist actions, ranging from testimonial congressional hearings to guerrilla street theater.

In many of its actions, IVAW performs faithful depictions of the popular Soldier stereotype. For example, particularly in their early bids to gain political visibility, IVAW members frequently made reference to their service histories in Iraq and Afghanistan and spoke of fellow soldiers as honorable individuals faced with the impossibly complex ethical and emotional pressures of war (IVAW, 2008). Like their Vietnam counterparts, they staged events in which they ritualistically threw their service medals away in contempt, suggesting that they uphold the values believed to be inherent to Soldierhood, but that these values had been betrayed by elite leaders. However, at other times IVAW has demonstrated an innate capacity for parodic enactments of Soldierhood. In *Operation First Casualty*, first staged in 2007, IVAW took to the streets of American cities in a guerrilla theater enactment of War on Terror combat in the midst of the unsuspecting urban public. This performance depicted armed patrol of public spaces, stop-and-search activities, and the hooding and handcuffing of terrorized detainees. Similarly, in 2008, IVAW members scaled the façade of the National Archives building in Washington, DC, and announced to the gathered tourists that they were seizing the building to 'protect and defend the United States Constitution' housed within – alleging that George W. Bush, Dick Cheney and Donald Rumsfeld were war criminals and demanding their arrest under the authority granted to them by their oaths of military service (Rowe, 2013). These acts relied on ironic citations of The Soldier stereotype, seemingly conforming to the confines of the role but enacting it with a hyper-realization that rendered the performances parodic. Indeed, when considered in terms of performance efficacy, I believe that IVAW is at its most successful when there is evident seepage between these two performative approaches – when imitative representations of Soldierhood dissolve into irony or parody, and vice versa. At issue here is what Jon McKenzie refers to as 'normative repetition' on the one hand and 'countermimesis or countermimicry' on the other, the latter terms relating to the capacity for performance to present 'mutational repetition' in which the notion of a presumed original is present but difference is highlighted (McKenzie, 2001).[6] To understand this in relation to IVAW's gender activism, a more detailed examination of some of their campaigns is required.

While the focus here is on IVAW campaigns that have been directly aimed at gender equality, it should be acknowledged that their inception and ongoing public presence has a performative force of its own. From IVAW's founding, the organization already offered challenges to the social construction of the military and The Soldier character. In the first instance, the very existence of veterans who espouse pacifism contradicts the biopolitical characterization of members of the military and the logics of sovereignty that follow. In an analysis of masculinities in social performance, Victoria Robinson and Jenny Hockey refer to Esther Newton's foundational works on Camp and Drag performance, and posit that the social environment that men appear within may function as the one accessory or sartorial item that can impinge on their masculine identity (Robinson and Hockey, 2011, p. 117). If this is so, and environments, or social stages, can function in this manner, then it follows that the very appearance of soldiers in pacifist arenas – at protests, in

Congressional caucuses, at vigils mourning the loss of enemy life – can operate in a way that calls masculinity into question, and particularly, calls the hyper-gendering of militarized culture into question in a way that might challenge the underpinnings of popular support for war.

In addition, IVAW's existence has countered the gender norms of the military through its organizational and management practices. The founding executive director of IVAW was a woman, Kelly Dougherty. While specific data on the sex and gender identity of all IVAW members is not available, the testifiers at the 2008 *Winter Soldier, Iraq and Afghanistan: Eyewitness Accounts of the Occupation* (perhaps IVAW's most high-profile action in terms of mainstream media attention) included a larger percentage of women than the percentage of women in the US military as a whole that year (IVAW, 2008; Rutgers Institute for Women's Leadership, 2009).[7] Leslie Hill contends that the early feminists were the first to understand and actively embrace the notion that 'the medium is the message'. By marching collectively in the streets they shattered the widespread notion that women had no place in politics, both physically and philosophically (Hill, 2000). In the same way, the gathering of IVAW members in non-military events that highlighted their Soldierhood while espousing an antiwar ideology was a clear show of strength; the fact that they exhibited greater sex and gender equality at an institutional level added to the potential for their very presence to operate as a performative challenge to the Solider characterization. Beyond its presence alone though, IVAW has been notable for its campaigns that link gender inequality and what Key describes as 'the war machine'.

Although IVAW was founded in 2004, it was nearly four years later that the organization attracted mainstream media attention as a result of the testimonies presented at the Winter Soldier event. Over four days in March 2008, IVAW members provided detailed accounts of their experiences of war in Iraq and Afghanistan, to selectively invited members of the media and various supporters. The testimonies were organized into panels relating to particular aspects of the repercussions of war and militarization. For the most part, this event took the form of a ritualized normative repetition of The Soldier figure, drawing on characterizations of The Soldier as a bearer of truth and justice in order to underscore the sincerity and authenticity of the testimonies on offer. Of particular interest for this study is the panel entitled, 'Divide to Conquer: Gender and Sexuality in the US Military'. This panel, which included the opening statement by Jeff Key cited above, was comprised of both men and women and covered a range of topics relating to gendered violence and inequality in the armed forces (IVAW, 2008).

Despite the overall faithful imitation of The Soldier character by Winter Soldier testifiers, countermimetic difference can be found in the content of the testimonies themselves. For example, on the Divide to Conquer panel female testifiers spoke with some consistency about their experiences of sexual harassment and discrimination. They alleged harassment in basic training, and frequent aggressive sexual advances by their male counterparts. Some testifiers spoke of extremes of sexual violence, and the likelihood of sex crimes in this sphere due to the environment of gender inequality propagated by the military. Most of the stories of rape emphasized the difficulty of seeking support or justice in the aftermath of the crime, due to the ways the various branches of the military handle rape allegations. One common theme among most of the testimonies was the sense of betrayal felt by the testifiers, who had joined the military out of respect for its morals and ideals. Many stressed the incompatibility of their ideals of Soldierhood with what they actually experienced once enlisted. For the most part this approach leaves The Soldier characterization unchanged. Although testifiers made numerous and detailed accounts of the way that some members of the military behaved in un-Soldier-like ways, they didn't fully undo the making of Soldierhood itself, and rather left their accounts open to interpretation as exceptions to the rule (IVAW, 2008).

One of the testimonies, delivered in absentia by an anonymous member of the US Coast Guard, was particularly revealing with regard to the intertwining of The Soldier stereotype and issues of gender inequality. In this account, in which the testifier described being raped by one of her shipmates, the normative Soldier characterization is dominant but ironic elements also appear. The testifier detailed the many obstacles that she faced in reporting the rape and seeking justice, and among those were the fact that no member of the military could be believed capable of committing such a heinous act, due to the thorough vetting of would-be recruits. The testimony includes the following details:

> A lieutenant commander from District 1 legal team was assigned to be my legal advocate. According to him, it is dishonorable to 'report a rape'. According to the Coast Guard's core values of honor, respect, and devotion to duty, how am I honoring and respecting my shipmate for bringing a rape allegation against him? He also said he didn't believe that I was assaulted, given that 'One undergoes a security, background check to be able to serve in the Coast Guard. Only those that passed the criminal background check are able to serve and if he did not have a history of raping women in the past why would he be doing it now?' (Glantz, 2008, p. 135)

This account reveals the way that the characterization of Soldierhood complicates gender inequalities. In the first instance, a good Soldier should not report a rape, as this reporting is a dishonorable and disrespectful act. Secondly, it is not even possible for a Soldier to commit rape, because to become a Soldier in the first place is to have proven oneself incapable of such acts. Clearly, The Soldier character is so robustly constructed that its associations with honor and respect can be deployed to cloak all manner of behaviors. In some ways the irony that is invoked here brings this depiction of Soldierhood into the realm of parody, although overall the testimony remained couched in references to normative ideals.

The Winter Soldier hearings evidenced IVAW's broad commitment to gender justice, and this commitment is further apparent in other acts of activism by members of the group. From its inception, IVAW campaigned strongly against the Don't Ask Don't Tell policy. To some extent, these campaigns demonstrated a worrying tendency to uphold the universal, heroic characterization of The Soldier. For example, their 2009 resolution opposing the policy includes the following language: '... LGBT service members have given honorable military service to our country during peacetime and war and continue to serve honorably in Iraq, Afghanistan, and wherever the United States military is currently deployed or stationed' (IVAW, 2009).

Although the resolution goes on to emphasize issues of discrimination against 'LGBT service members', the assertion of honorable military service among all LGBT members – 'wherever the United States military is currently deployed' – seems to uphold a view of military members as uniformly honorable and dedicated to their military roles. This leaves little scope for expanding the frameworks of identity that limit veterans' abilities to critique war.

However, it is clear that celebrations of the traditional characteristics of Soldierhood are not inevitable in bids to challenge DADT, as some individual acts have demonstrated. Although there are several potential examples that illustrate this, this chapter will examine one particular action by Retired Marine Lance Corporal Jeff Key. Prior to the Winter Soldier event in 2008, Key made national headlines on an individual basis when he declared his homosexuality openly on CNN during an interview with Paula Zahn. Key is a tall, broad-shouldered southerner, perhaps a good example of the stereotypical Marine figure in the social imaginary. In 2004 he was invited to appear as a commentator in a CNN broadcast about Iraqi violence against US civilian contractors. The intent was to have Key, recently returned from service in Iraq, describe the potential impact of the violence on the morale of US service members.

Instead, he seized the opportunity to perform according to his own script (Paula Zahn Now, 2004).

At the time, Key hoped that coming out to an international television audience would force the US Marines to discharge him from the military, under the provisions of the Don't Ask Don't Tell policy. Although this proved not to be the case due to the precise legal provisions of DADT, the action by Key was significant for the way that it made use of gender norms in parallel normative and countermimetic approaches to The Soldier character. On the one hand, Key ostensibly embodied the role of The Soldier in every way except in his sexuality, in a manner that would force the military to recognize his individuality and discharge him due to his innate nonconformity. This aspect of his performance fully upheld the overall characterization of The Soldier figure, but simply suggested that this decorated Marine wasn't quite appropriate for the role. However, there is also a strong suggestion here that Key was aware of having dual audiences for this media performance, leading to the possibility of dual interpretations. While his declaration of his sexuality seemed to uphold the Soldierhood characteristics for the audience of military authorities, at a parallel level his public performance suggested a parody of the rigidly defined Soldier.

This performance exhibited an interweaving of theatrical modes in which the social performer is seemingly aware of the multiple audiences to which their social selves are performed. In the case of Key's coming-out statement, the performance gains its political currency by attempting to authentically imitate the characteristics of The Soldier mask and its associated values – a characterization that proves useful to the military audience it purports to address; but I would argue that its efficacy as political resistance stems from Key's obvious awareness of the public audience that is witnessing this address, and interpreting the characterization of Soldierhood as a subtle parody that mocks established military values.

More recently, IVAW members have campaigned on behalf of WikiLeaks whistleblower Chelsea Manning, and in support of transgender veterans more broadly. One particular aspect of this is notable with regard to the blending of normative representations and counter mimesis. In May 2013, IVAW joined other LGBT organizations to support the election of Private Manning to the position of Grand Marshal of the San Francisco Gay Pride Parade. Manning had been nominated by Gay Pride committee members, but was subsequently dis-invited by the organizers, who condemned the whistleblower's actions and suggested that she was unsuitable to represent members of the military:

... even the hint of support for actions which placed in harms [sic] way the lives of our men and women in uniform – and countless others, military and civilian alike – will not be tolerated by the leadership of San Francisco Pride. It is, and would be, an insult to everyone, gay and straight, who has ever served in the military of this country. (Williams, 2013)

This is a fascinating celebration of The Soldier stereotype by a figurehead of San Francisco Gay Pride, and IVAW countered it, along with other veterans' organizations, in a vigorous defense of Manning's heroism. IVAW member Stephen Funk read a statement which outlined the sacrifice Manning had made in service to the people of the United States, and depicted the US military as an immoral and inhumane institution (Funk, 2013). This statement blurred the distinction between the idealized Soldier mask and an ironic portrayal of Soldierhood in which heroism means revealing state secrets in the interest of safeguarding national values. This alone has the performative potential to undermine the characterization of military members as universal, apolitical, excluded beings. While IVAW and its allies were not successful in this campaign in 2013, one year later Chelsea Manning was appointed as an honorary Grand Marshal of the 2014 San Francisco Gay Pride Parade. The representation of Manning amongst the other figureheads of the Gay Pride parade certainly pulled the role of The Soldier into muddled territory. Manning is a transgressive soldier, and so perhaps a gay pride parade is where she belongs. But the fact that gay and antiwar activists had to campaign for her inclusion (and this was widely publicized in mainstream media) makes this social drama more complex. Here we see a military figure who has been multiply excluded, laid claim to by antiwar veterans, and imprisoned by the military itself. This creates a multiply layered character with the potential to destabilize The Soldier mask in many ways.

CONCLUSION

In this chapter I have provided an account of war veterans' activism as it relates to social gender roles and their complicity in processes of war. The discussion of gender activism by IVAW has been framed by a reading of the war veteran as a social role bound up with the more rigid but popular social character of The Soldier. This reading considers The Soldier as a character mask that upholds military power and the ability of the state to differentiate the political lives of military enlistees and veterans. By paying close attention to the way that this Soldier stereotype is gendered in military and cultural processes, we can begin to understand the problematics faced by veterans who wish to campaign against war and militarization, and the pressing need to address gender injustice as a key component of these.

There can be no doubt that IVAW still has a long and difficult road ahead if it wishes to give due consideration to the intersection of gender norms with the machinery of war violence. Organizationally it might carry on its campaigns for gender equality within the military, particularly paying attention to the current rules that compel discrimination against transgender recruits. However, it must also engage with the issue of whether or not such campaigns are really useful in undoing the gender–military–sovereignty paradigm: might it not be the case that campaigning for the inclusion of multiple identities would simply result in more sectors of society becoming eligible for the indelible characterization by The Soldier mask? As one IVAW member, Ryan Holleran, writes: 'Some of the most well-funded mainstream queer organizations focus on permitting queers to join heterosexual society rather than solidifying whatever counter-culture still exists. Instead of defending our identity, they are aggressively prioritizing its assimilation' (Holleran, 2013).

However, the performance of normally excluded characteristics against symbolic indicators of the military realm clearly offers the potential to disrupt the dominant gendering of the military itself. These performances threaten the carefully constructed image of the gendered heroic Soldier, and therefore the politics of exceptionality that uphold sovereign authority. The risk though is that in performing these transgressive characteristics, veterans will fall into one of two traps: either their performances will largely uphold The Soldier character – sometimes simply through reinforcing expectations of what a Soldier should *not* be – and therefore reinforce the construction of the military sphere itself; or they will stray too far from the acceptable script for Soldiers and therefore be deemed non-Soldierly, and not deserving of political and cultural respect.

Although it is not possible to provide an in-depth analysis of the performance examples mentioned above, this chapter has attempted to illustrate the promise of IVAW's activism when modes of social performance are blended. It could perhaps be argued that all of IVAW's actions challenge The Soldier stereotype and its subsequent rendering of veterans into *homo sacer*. By simply appearing in venues where 'Soldiers' don't belong, and by acting and speaking against military action, these actors explode the myth of Soldierhood as a homogenous, apolitical characterization. However, I suggest that war veterans in the United States must go further if their actions are to achieve public political validity on one hand, and resist dominant biopolitical characterizations on the other. Actions in which IVAW emphasizes The Soldier stereotype no doubt gain purchase in the social imaginary as they represent familiar themes relating to the mask of The Soldier. However, these actions are best viewed as foundational bids for visibility from which subsequent parodic acts could emanate. As the examples above illustrate, consistent engagement with alternative mimetic approaches, including critical parody and mimicry, might provide a pathway to more efficacious challenges of 'that whole [gender-war] paradigm'.

NOTES

1. See Pin-Fat and Stern (2005) in particular.
2. The concept of mimesis has attracted a great deal of scholarly attention in recent decades. Broadly understood as the act of representing 'reality', scholars and artists have variously explored alternative approaches to mimesis, including those that normatively uphold dominant world views as well as those that seek to challenge social norms through various means including mimicry and parody. For more thorough discussions of the concept see Borowski and Sugiera (2007) and Diamond (1997).
3. Agamben's treatment of *Homo sacer* derives from the historical figure in Roman law which could be 'killed but not sacrificed'. This figure illustrates the inclusion-through-exclusion that is central to the perpetuation of sovereign power through obviation of the sovereign authority to differentiate or exclude some subjects from the legal or political order (Agamben, 1998).
4. See, for example, the military cases of Adam Kokesh and Ehren Watada, both discussed in Rowe (2013).
5. There are multiple pressures that might compel young men and women to join the military – these frequently include the financial benefits granted to members of the armed forces, including health care, education and housing. In addition, recruitment practices often target the young or vulnerable. For more see American Civil Liberties Union (2008) and Appy (2003).
6. McKenzie speaks of two types of performative repetition, or mimesis, and characterizes them as 'on the one hand, the normative repetition of traditional mimesis, which tends to erase differences and anomalies in order to create the *appearance* of a unified, coherent, and originary presence, and, on the other, the mutational repetition of countermimesis or countermimicry, in which repetition is exaggerated to the point that differences proliferate and disseminate themselves' (2001, p. 214).
7. Roughly 16 percent of the testifiers at *Winter Soldier* were women. In the same year, 2008, 14 percent of US armed forces personnel were women.

BIBLIOGRAPHY

American Civil Liberties Union (ACLU) (2008), 'Soldiers of misfortune: abusive US military recruitment and failure to protect child soldiers', 1st edn [pdf] ACLU, accessed 25 April 2015 at: https://www.aclu.org/files/pdfs/humanrights/crc_report_20080513.pdf.

Agamben, Giorgio (1998), *Homo Sacer*, trans. David Heller-Roazen, Stanford University Press.

Appy, Christian G. (2003), *Patriots*, Viking.

Astore, William J. (2010), 'Our American heroes', *The Nation* [online], accessed 30 October 2015 at: http://www.thenation.com/article/37873/our-american-heroes.

Benedict, Helen (2009), *The Lonely Soldier*, Beacon.

Born on the Fourth of July (1989), Film, directed by Oliver Stone.

Borowski, Mateusz and Malgorzata Sugiera (eds) (2007), *Fictional Realities/Real Fictions: Contemporary Theatre in Search of a New Mimetic Paradigm*, Cambridge Scholars.

Brown, Melissa T. (2012), *Enlisting Masculinity*, Oxford University Press.

Cortright, David (2005), *Soldiers in Revolt*, Haymarket.

Diamond, Elin (1997), *Unmaking Mimesis: Essays on Feminism and Theatre*, Routledge.

Funk, Stephen (2013), 'They say "court-martial"? we say "grand marshal"!', *The Huffington Post*, accessed 30 October 2015 at: http://www.huffingtonpost.com/stephen-funk/they-say-court-martial-we-say-grand-marshal_b_3275470.html.

Glantz, Aaron (2008), *Winter Soldier, Iraq and Afghanistan*, Haymarket.

GoArmy.com (2010), 'Ask a soldier: moms joining the army', accessed 17 July 2012 at: https://forums.goarmy.com/thread/204600.

Grant, Susan-Mary (2005), 'Raising the dead: war, memory and American national identity', *Nations and Nationalism*, **11** (4): 509–29.

Grindley, Lucas (2014), 'San Francisco Pride apologizes, honors Chelsea Manning', Advocate.com, accessed 30 October 2015 at: http://www.advocate.com/pride/2014/04/13/san-francisco-pride-apologizes-honors-chelsea-manning.

Harrison, Robert Pogue (2003), *The Dominion of the Dead*, University of Chicago Press.

Harrison-Quintana, Jack and Jody L. Herman (2013), *Still Serving in Silence: Transgender Service Members and Veterans in the National Transgender Discrimination Survey*, 1st edn [ebook], accessed 11 June 2015 at: http://www.hkslgbtq.com/still-serving-in-silence-transgender-service-members-and-veterans-in-the-national-transgender-discrimination-survey/.

Hill, Leslie (2000), 'Suffragettes invented performance art', in Lizbeth Goodman and Jane de Gay (eds), *The Routledge Reader in Politics and Performance*, Routledge, pp. 150–56.

Hillman, Elizabeth (2010), 'The female shape of the all-volunteer force', in Linda K. Kerber, Jane De Hart and Cornelia Hughes Dayton (eds), *Women's America*, 7th edn, Oxford University Press, pp. 689–99.

Holleran, Ryan (2013), 'Queer identity in military culture', *IVAW Dispatches*, pp. 10–11.

Hughes, Jenny (2011), *Performance in a Time of Terror*, Manchester University Press.

Iraq Veterans Against the War (IVAW) (2007), 'Operation first casualty II (New York City) a success!' [no longer available online] IVAW.org.

Iraq Veterans Against the War (IVAW) (2008), 'Divide to conquer: gender and sexuality in the US military', testimonies delivered at Winter soldier hearings, National Labor College, Silver Spring, MD, 16 March, documented by the author.

Iraq Veterans Against the War (IVAW) (2009), *IVAW Resolution on DADT*, 1st edn [ebook], accessed 30 October 2015 at: http://www.ivaw.org/sites/default/files/public/documents/IVAW%20Resolution%20on%20DADT%20%28AUG%202009%29.pdf.

Iraq Veterans Against the War (IVAW) (2010), 'History of IVAW', [online] IVAW.org, accessed 30 October 2015 at: http://www.ivaw.org/history.

Iraq Veterans Against the War (IVAW) (2013), 'IVAW's statement in support of Chelsea Manning', [online] IVAW.org, accessed 9 June 2015 at: http://www.ivaw.org/blog/ivaws-statement-support-chelsea-manning.

Key, Jeff (2008), 'Divide to conquer: gender and sexuality in the US military', testimony delivered at winter soldier hearings, National Labor College, Silver Spring, MD, 16 March, documented by the author.

Leff, Lisa (2011), 'Transgender vets want military access for own', *The Boston Globe*, [online], accessed 30 October 2015 at: http://www.boston.com/news/nation/articles/2011/01/11/transgender_vets_want_military_access_for_own/.

Masters, Cristina (2009), 'Femina sacra: the "war on/of terror", women and the feminine', *Security Dialogue*, **40** (1): 29–49.

McKenzie, Jon (2001), *Perform or Else*, Routledge.

Messerschmidt, James W. (2010), *Hegemonic Masculinities and Camouflaged Politics*, Paradigm.

Noone, Michael (2007), *Political Dissent in the U.S. Military* [online], ABC News, accessed 30 October 2015 at: http://abcnews.go.com/Politics/story?id=2857017&page=1/.

Paula Zahn Now (2004), *American Civilians Killed in Iraq* [online], CNN.com, accessed 30 October 2015 at: http://transcripts.cnn.com/TRANSCRIPTS/0403/31/pzn.00.html.

Pin-Fat, Veronique and Maria Stern (2005), 'The scripting of Private Jessica Lynch: biopolitics, gender and the "feminization" of the US military', *Alternatives*, **30** (1): 25–53.

Pratt, Geraldine (2005), 'Abandoned women and spaces of the exception', *Antipode*, **37** (5): 1052–78.

Robinson, Victoria and Jenny Hockey (2011), *Masculinities in Transition*, Palgrave Macmillan.

Rowe, Cami (2013), *The Politics of Protest and US Foreign Policy*, Routledge.

Rutgers Institute for Military Leadership (2009), 'Women's leadership fact sheet' [pdf], accessed 10 June 2015 at: http://iwl.rutgers.edu/documents/njwomencount/Women%20in%20Military%202009%20Final.pdf.

Schor, Elana (2008), 'US Army increases use of moral waivers to meet demand for troops' [online], *The Guardian*, accessed 30 October 2015 at: http://www.theguardian.com/world/2008/apr/21/usa1.

Scott, Jessica (2010), 'Mothers in the military: punishing mothers who serve | POV – regarding war | PBS' [online], PBS.org, accessed 30 October 2015 at: http://www.pbs.org/pov/regardingwar/conversations/women-and-war/mothers-in-the-military-punishing-mothers-who-serve.php.

Smith, Anna Marie (2010), 'Neo-eugenics: a feminist critique of Agamben', *Occasion: Interdisciplinary Studies in the Humanities* [online] 2, accessed 30 October 2015 at: http://arcade.stanford.edu/sites/default/files/article_pdfs/Occasion_v02_Smith_122010_0.pdf.

Stop-Loss (2008), Film, directed by Kimberly Peirce.

Swerdlow, Amy (1993), *Women Strike for Peace*, University of Chicago Press.

United States Department of Defense (1993), *Directive 1304.26*.

United States Government (2010), *10 U.S. Code Chapter 47 – UNIFORM CODE OF MILITARY JUSTICE | US Law | LII / Legal Information Institute* [online], Law.cornell.edu, accessed 30 October 2015 at: http://www.law.cornell.edu/uscode/10/stApII ch47.html.

Williams, Lisa L. (2013), 'San Francisco Pride statement about Bradley Manning', *Facebook* [online], accessed 30 October 2015 at: https://www.facebook.com/SanFranciscoPride/posts/622822351079480.

Wright, Ann (2009), 'With its record of rape don't send the US military to the Congo', *The Huffington Post* [online], accessed 30 October 2015 at: http://www.huffingtonpost.com/ann-wright/with-its-record-of-rape-d_b_264980.html.

Žižek, Slavoj (2002), *Welcome to the Desert of the Real!* Verso.

18. Gender and resistance to political violence in Palestine and Israel

Simona Sharoni

INTRODUCTION

In this chapter, the term 'political violence' is used to address the Israeli–Palestinian conflict because the term 'war' can be misleading, implying a confrontation involving two parties on an equal playing field. The literature on women in conflict zones, in general, and on women in Palestine and Israel, in particular, has been dominated by a focus on women's ability to transcend their differences and build alliances, as well as on joint peace initiatives. Notwithstanding the importance of women finding ways to work together, especially amidst political violence, the Israeli–Palestinian conflict is a deep-rooted asymmetrical conflict between occupiers and occupied and not a war between two equal parties.

Although women in both Israel and Palestine were involved in political protest earlier, the 1987 Palestinian uprising, known as the first intifada, triggered an unprecedented level of political participation on the part of Palestinian and Israeli-Jewish women. Women took to the streets in Israel and Palestine calling for an end to the illegal Israeli occupation. Through separate, parallel and joint initiatives, women began to explore and to articulate connections between gender inequalities and political violence. Over decades of activism, significant changes occurred in forms of organizing, as well as in the broader vision of the movements and their key strategies. The changes in women's opposition to political violence, which coincide with significant turning points in the history of the Israeli–Palestinian conflict, not only complicate conventional understandings of gender-based opposition to violence but also offer a unique perspective on the root causes of the conflict and the prospects for its resolution.

This chapter examines gendered resistance to political violence in Israel and Palestine, with a particular emphasis on grassroots organizing that occurred between December 1987 (the start of the first intifada) and December 2014 (the aftermath of the Israeli attack on Gaza). A key theme involves a shift from joint ventures, based on dialogue and an emphasis on similarities between Israeli-Jewish and Palestinian women, to parallel initiatives, based on recognition of the unique needs and expectations of various constituencies within the Palestinian and Israeli collectivities. Finally, the chapter analyzes the transformative potential of solidarity initiatives, including the growing global support for the Boycott, Divestment and Sanctions (BDS) movement that is modeled after the anti-Apartheid movement in South Africa.

WOMEN AND POLITICAL PROTEST

Prevailing gender stereotypes suggest that women are often assumed to be able to make unique contributions to peacemaking, nonviolence, and conflict resolution (Sharoni, 2010). The involvement of women in opposition to political violence around the world, however, must not be taken for granted or interpreted merely as a natural extension of their womanhood or maternal instinct. In the Palestinian–Israeli context, analyses of women's opposition to military occupation and the political violence it has unleashed paint a more complicated story. Few feminist scholars and activists worldwide were aware of the nuances underscoring women's resistance to political violence when they applauded as women on both sides of the Palestinian–Israeli divide took to the streets with the outbreak of the first intifada in the late 1980s. Although the mainstream media during the first intifada took notice of the active participation of women in Palestinian–Israeli politics, journalists as well as feminist scholars were largely unaware that, for Palestinian women, political participation was not new; their experience and long history of political involvement and organizing at the community level and within the national liberation movement enabled them to mobilize quickly and claim a prominent role in the uprising. The intifada provided Palestinian women in the West Bank and Gaza Strip, who had participated in literacy programs and skill-training courses, with both an opportunity and an excuse to join the women's movement and put to use knowledge and skills previously acquired. While only a minority of Palestinian women were actively involved in the national liberation struggle, the majority of women in Palestine became politically involved as a way to protect their homes, families and communities. In the course of this involvement, women learned crucial skills, which prompted them to challenge the exclusion of women from the official decision-making levels in the political arena (Abdulhadi, 1998).

Israeli-Jewish women, whose political involvement was previously marginalized in the name of national security, were inspired by the visibility of Palestinian women at the forefront of the intifada. The result was a plethora of women-only actions that were implicitly, if not explicitly, feminist initiatives calling for justice and peace. Groups like Women in Black, the Women's Organizations for Women Political Prisoners (OPFPP), Israeli Women Against the Occupation (SHANI), the Women's Peace Coalition and the Israeli Women's Peace Net (RESHET) burst onto the Israeli political scene in the late 1980s and early 1990s, initiating numerous demonstrations, petition and letter-writing campaigns, solidarity visits to the West Bank and Gaza Strip, and a series of local and international peace conferences (Sharoni, 1995). These grassroots initiatives, which also involved Palestinian women who reside within Israel, were designed to influence public opinion in Israel and to put pressure on its political leaders to engage in peace negotiations.

Palestinian and Israeli women did not wait for their elected representatives to embark on the path of peace. Long before the Madrid and Oslo processes were underway, women engaged in a series of international peace conferences. The first such conference was held in Brussels in May 1989 under the title, 'Give peace a chance: women speak out'. About 50 women, including Palestinian women from the Occupied Territories, Israeli-Jewish women, and official representatives of the Palestinian Liberation Organization (PLO), met for the first time in such a format to discuss the Israeli–Palestinian conflict and the prospects for its resolution. At the time, Israelis who met with Palestinians officially affiliated with the PLO were breaking a 1986 Israeli law forbidding such contact. These events were designed to provide women participants with a hands-on experience in negotiation and with the impetus to continue the efforts by mobilizing support for peace-building within their own communities. Indeed, following the conference, in December 1989, representatives of the Palestinian Women's Working Committees and the Israeli Women's Peace Coalition coordinated a women's day for peace in Jerusalem, which culminated in a march of 6000 women from West to East Jerusalem under the banner: 'women go for peace'.

The first intifada provided Palestinian women with the opportunity to make public an earlier realization: that their national liberation struggle is intertwined with their struggle for gender equality. Palestinian women were no longer willing to accept the promise that gender issues would receive careful attention once the occupation is over. Palestinian women activists refused to make their struggle for gender equality secondary to their participation in the national struggle; this triggered critical debates within Palestinian society and opened a new chapter in the history of the

Palestinian women's movement. As a result of critical deliberations, in 1989 the women's committees established the Higher Women's Council and resolved to work closely together. Another important development in the mobilization of Palestinian women during this period involved the establishment of new women's centers throughout the West Bank and Gaza Strip (Jad, 2010). Determined not to place 'women's issues' on the backburner and to take advantage of the momentum for change created by the intifada, Palestinian women initiated numerous forums, research projects and publications to explore strategies for addressing women's issues. The premise of these initiatives was that all issues are women's issues, and that Palestinian women's issues are shaped by the social and political fabric of a society living under Israeli military occupation. A case in point is a 1990 conference held under the banner 'The intifada and some women's social issues'. Featuring prominent Palestinian women and men, the conference was designed to send an explicit message to both the national leadership and to the society at large: the lives and struggles of Palestinian women deserve public attention (Sharoni, 1995).

For women in Israel, one of the most significant turning points during this period involved the emergence of feminist anti-violence discourse, reflecting the links between issues that had been narrowly defined and marginalized as 'women's issues' and the politics of the Palestinian–Israeli conflict. The new discourse, articulated in slogans and public debates, made explicit the connections between violence against women and the violence of the conflict, and between the treatment of women as subordinate 'others' and the treatment of Palestinians under occupation (Sharoni, 1995). Informed by implicit, if not explicit, feminist principles, women peace activists in Israel articulated important connections between: (1) different systems of domination and structured inequalities; (2) practices of violence used against Palestinians and the unprecedented rise in violence against women in Israel; and (3) the struggles of Palestinians for liberation and self-determination and those of women throughout the world including Israel (Sharoni, 1995). The emergence of feminist perspectives on the conflict provided women who were not members of existing political parties in Israel with a political standpoint and platform. For women who were already politically aware and involved, the newly articulated links between gender issues and the politics of the conflict infused their activism with a new vision and creative strategies. Moreover, the new political discourse reflected an emerging adoption of feminist intersectional analysis, based on a critical examination of multiple forms of systemic oppression.

GENDER, RESISTANCE AND THE POLITICS OF DIFFERENCE

The emergence of a gendered analysis of the Palestinian–Israeli conflict – informed by a feminist examination of power, privilege and structured inequalities – was celebrated by feminists globally because of its potential to change dramatically the landscape of peace-building and conflict transformation in the region. However, the effort of the mainstream Israeli-Jewish women's movement to articulate a unique feminist perspective in general and a coherent vision for peace in Israel and Palestine in particular came at the expense of addressing differences among women. Like their counterparts in North American and other settler-colonial societies, the women who led both the feminist movement and the women's peace movement in Israel were by and large upper middle class, college educated, Jewish women whose cultural and ethnic origins could be traced to Europe and North America. Largely unaware that their interpretations of feminism, gender equality and, to a large extent, peace, reflected their own privileged social locations, many Israeli-Jewish feminists responded defensively to criticism from women who traced their ancestry to Arab countries (also known as Mizrahi women), lesbians and Palestinian women, both from within 1948 borders and from Palestine (Dahan-Kalev, 2001; Frankfurt-Nachmias and Shadmi, 2005; Kannneh and Nusair, 2010). By focusing primarily on their oppression as women and by accepting the premise that their experiences of and perspectives on sexism, violence and peace have universal currency, many Israeli-Jewish women refused to engage when their power, privilege and narrow interpretations of feminism were called into question. At the time, few feminists in the women's peace movement in Israel had the analytic and political skills required to engage in political discussions, let alone to build and sustain coalitions with women of different backgrounds. In those early days, only a minority among Israeli feminists acknowledged publicly the fact that regardless of their personal views on the conflict, as Israeli citizens, they were implicated in the policies and practices of the Israeli government and military. As a result, feminist peace activists continued to promote projects with Palestinian women that were based merely on similarities and thus perpetuated the illusion of symmetry in power relations between Palestinians and Israel.

Indeed, Israeli-Jewish women and their international sponsors celebrated women's involvement in peace-building and conflict resolution but devoted little or no attention to the fundamental disparities between

Palestinian and Israel-Jewish women as members of occupied and occupier collectivities respectively. This period in the history of women's mobilization against political violence in Israel and Palestine also exposed a clear bias on the part of Israeli-Jewish women against their Palestinian counterparts. The prevailing bias of Israeli-Jewish women reflected a persistent assumption among feminists in the Global North that national liberation movements are the least hospitable places for women (Yuval-Davis, 1997; Yuval-Davis and Anthias, 1989).

Conventional feminist critiques of nationalism overlooked the fact that women in national liberation movements, compared to women in the military or in state politics, often offer women (and men) more space to raise questions about gender inequalities (Sharoni, 2002). The common argument is that national liberation movements use women in the course of the struggle but overlook their contribution to the revolution and embrace conventional conceptions of femininity, masculinity and gender relations once the struggle is over. This argument overlooks women's agency and their ability to use strategically their involvement in the national struggle to safeguard their gains during and after the revolution (Jayawardena, 1986; West, 1997; Ibanez, 2001). Inspired by the prevalent Western critique of nationalism described above, women peace activists in Israel, who developed a critique of, and began to distance themselves from, Zionism and militarization, expected their Palestinian counterparts to do the same. Unaware of debates within Palestinian society about the interconnectedness of the struggles for national liberation and gender equality, many Israeli-Jewish women failed to understand both the vision and strategies of Palestinian women who were engaged in articulating a gender-sensitive analysis of repression and resistance (Sharoni, 1995).

Despite these obstacles, joint initiatives involving Palestinian and Israeli-Jewish women emerged in early 1988 and flourished during the first intifada. While most initiatives dissipated with the outbreak of the first Iraq War in 1990, some projects continued, on a smaller scale and with limited success, through the signing of the Oslo Accords in 1993, mostly at the insistence of the North American and European funders. During that period, joint projects of Jewish and Palestinian women, often made possible by external funding, were embraced uncritically by feminist organizations and individuals located almost exclusively in the Global North. In these joint ventures, little attention was given to structured inequalities and questions of power and privilege that have shaped the fundamental differences between Palestinian and Israeli-Jewish women in both the expectations and political agendas.

The participation of many Israeli-Jewish women in such encounters was encouraged primarily by liberal positions on both the Palestinian–

Israeli conflict and feminism. The majority of women at the time believed that through dialogue they could find ways to transcend cultural, historical and political differences. Empowered by the inroads they made into the Israeli political scene through protest, liberal feminists embraced uncritically the promise of global sisterhood, which they believed would help them mobilize many Israeli women and in turn would peacefully transform the course of the Israeli–Palestinian conflict. Palestinian women, in contrast, had very different expectations from such encounters. Their participation in dialogue groups and various other encounters with Jewish women were inspired by feminist convictions shaped in the context of a national liberation struggle and intense grassroots activism. Palestinian women viewed their meetings and strategic alliances with Jewish women as an important vehicle for influencing public opinion in Israel and getting them closer to their ultimate goal of ending the Israeli occupation. In other words, Palestinian women did not perceive such encounters as means for overcoming differences and establishing personal relationships or professional collaborations with their Jewish counterparts, but rather as a tool of social transformation and political change. Understanding the short-lived fragile alliances between Palestinian and Israeli-Jewish women requires paying close attention to the context in which these alliances emerged and to the different expectations of the women who joined them.

GENDERED RESISTANCE IN TIMES OF CRISIS

Unfolding political crises changed the dynamics of women's organizing on both sides of the Palestinian–Israeli divide. In many instances, women, like everyone else, were caught unprepared as political violence escalated. This is especially true for Israeli-Jewish women, whose commitment to justice and peace was tested whenever political violence escalated and the space available for protest in Israel closed. Indeed, when the 1990 US bombing of Iraq started and Iraqi Scud missiles were fired at Israel, many in the women's peace movement in Israel remained silent. Women peace activists overlooked the fact that Palestinians in the Occupied Territories also were at risk, given the inaccuracy of the missiles, and that unlike Israeli citizens, they had neither shelters nor state-issued gas masks. Moreover, the women's peace movement did not challenge the larger peace movement in Israel when it expressed its support for the US-led first Iraq war (Sharoni, 1995). This troubling silence reflects a persistent institutionalized response to political crisis in Israel. Whenever confronted with an external threat or an attack, Israeli

Jews, including those who self-identify as advocates of peace, tend not to question government propaganda and instead forget their differences and unite under the banner of 'national security'.

The failure of the Israeli women's peace movement to oppose the war did not go unnoticed by Palestinian women. Disappointed and betrayed, many Palestinian women activists resolved not to participate further in joint initiatives with Israeli-Jewish women. Instead, Palestinian women focused their work at the grassroots level to raise awareness of gender issues while alleviating the hardships caused by the occupation and exacerbated by the Gulf War.

Following the crisis of war, Palestinian and Israeli women activists were confronted with the crisis of 'peace' that resulted from the signing of the Oslo Accords in 1993. Palestinians were deeply divided about the Oslo Accords, with few people viewing them as actual peace accords. With mounting pressure from the United States, Egypt and most of the international community, two factions of the Palestinian Liberation Organization (PLO), Fatah and the Communist Party endorsed the agreement. The Popular Front for the Liberation of Palestine (PFLP) criticized the accords. The Democratic Front for the Liberation of Palestine (DFLP) split, with one group supporting Oslo and another opposing it. The divisions over the Oslo Accords also impacted Palestinian women because many became active in the women's movement through their work with women committees that were affiliated with particular factions of the PLO. The fragile unity forged among Palestinian women activists with the outbreak of the first intifada was on the brink of collapse. Moreover, sanctions were attached to opposition to Oslo. Groups that did not endorse the accords lost both their financial support because all funding for non-governmental organizations had to be funneled through the headquarters of the Palestinian National Authority (PNA). Historically, the women's committees affiliated with PFLP and DFLP held more progressive positions on women and gender issues than did other segments of the Palestinian national movement, and the loss of funding and the erosion of their influence were serious setbacks for the struggle for gender equality in Palestine. The Oslo Accords sidelined Palestinian women and men who had worked toward a vision of an independent, pluralistic Palestine with gender equality enshrined in both its founding documents and social institutions (Rubenberg, 2001).

The Israeli women's peace movement was also deeply divided about the Oslo Accords. While some were convinced the agreement was an important step towards a comprehensive peace with the Palestinians, others argued that these were far from representing a move towards just and lasting peace. In fact, the more radical women insisted that the accords perpetuated Israeli domination of Palestinians. As a result of these divisions and unable to reach consensus, the women's peace movement began to flounder, and the most visible segments of the Israeli peace movement, such as Women in Black and the Women for Peace Coalition halted their work (Sharoni, 2002).

THE FAILURE OF DIALOGUE AND JOINT INITIATIVES

The political impact of the encounters between Israeli-Jewish and Palestinian women during the first intifada was limited and short-lived. As a result, prominent leaders in the Palestinian women's movement began to limit their participation in conferences and joint speaking tours that had no specific political objective. Unlike their Jewish counterparts, who saw their dialogues with Palestinian women as a radical departure from political consensus in Israel, Palestinian women viewed dialogue as means to an end; their primary interest was in joint actions, including those that are not limited to so-called 'women's issues'.

The signing of the Oslo Accords in 1993 accelerated the establishment of the Jerusalem Link. Founded in 1994, the Jerusalem Link was the culmination of a series of meetings between prominent Israeli and Palestinian women peace activists. It was composed of two women's organizations – *Bat Shalom* ('Daughter of Peace' in Hebrew) on the Israeli side and *Markaz al-Quds la l-Nissah* ('Jerusalem Center for Women' in Arabic), on the Palestinian side. The two organizations shared a set of political principles, designed to serve as the foundation for a cooperative model of Palestinian and Jewish co-existence. According to the rationale of the Jerusalem Link, each organization was autonomous and directed its work towards its own national constituency. Yet both organizations agreed in principle to promote a joint vision of a just peace, democracy, human rights and women's leadership. The two groups affirmed their support for a viable solution to the conflict based on recognition of the right of the Palestinian people to self-determination and an independent state alongside the state of Israel, Jerusalem as the capital of both states, and a final settlement of all relevant issues based on international law (Daniele, 2011).

Funded mostly by European donors and showcased as a model for women's peace activism and feminist conflict resolution, the Link has received extensive scholarly and media attention (Cockburn, 2007; Powers, 2006; Richter-Devroe, 2009). It was often hailed as the main prototype for feminist collaboration and cross-community reconciliation in Israel and Palestine. A critical examination of the project underscores its limitations, however, by shedding light on both the potential and the pitfalls of women's alliances in the Palestinian–Israeli context. A report commissioned by Norwegian Church Aid evaluated various joint peace-building projects implemented by the Jerusalem Link before 2000 and restarted after 2005. The report also assessed the organization's activities in response to political crises and human rights violations. Raising some critical questions about the work of this unique enterprise and highlighting its limited impact in both the Palestinian and Israeli-Jewish communities, the evaluators concluded that projects and initiatives within the current political context in Palestine and Israel require more careful planning and better preparation (Hilal and Touma, 2008). Others have argued that such preparation must involve close attention to such key issues framing the conflict as refugees and Jerusalem as well as to the significantly divergent needs and expectations that Israeli-Jewish and Palestinian women carry with them to joint initiatives (Abdo and Lentin, 2002; Byrne, 2009).

Ironically, such contested political issues as the right-of-return for Palestinian refugees or the status of Jerusalem, which have been identified by scholars and politicians alike as key to a just and lasting resolution of the conflict, seldom were prominent on the agenda of cross-community encounters. Furthermore, the significant differences in needs and expectations between Palestinian and Israeli-Jewish women, as well as among the collectivities themselves, were often overlooked in the planning and implementation stages of joint projects. As a result, cross-community encounters often reflected a tendency on the part of Israeli-Jewish participants to focus on their shared experiences as women and to downplay or overlook the asymmetry of the conflict and differences altogether. Third-party organizers and mediators tended to acquiesce to Jewish participants, who were generally unwilling to account for their power and privilege vis-à-vis Palestinian women. As a result, Jewish women were allowed to dictate the terms of collaboration and to frame the boundaries of the discourse. With time, Palestinian women who participated in these encounters in the region and abroad grew impatient with the patronizing approach of their Israeli counterparts. During their reluctant participation in many cross-community conflict-resolution and peacemaking initiatives, Palestinian women have consistently expressed their skepticism regarding both the nature and objectives of such encounters (Daniele, 2011; Richter-Devroe, 2009).

The ongoing enthusiastic support of outside donors and sponsors notwithstanding, alliances and joint ventures between Palestinian and Israeli-Jewish women have remained fragile, suffering major setbacks since their inception, especially during such crisis periods as the first

Gulf War (1990), the second intifada (2000), and the devastating Israeli attacks on Gaza (2008–2009, 2012 and 2014), to name just a few. With the exception of the early years of the first intifada, joint initiatives between women in Israel and Palestinian women from the West Bank and Gaza Strip have been few and far between. Even at the height of the first intifada, such encounters were always fraught with trouble and contradictions. However, the fragility of the alliances between Palestinian and Jewish women became evident during times of political crises. The escalation of political violence made it impossible to ignore the fundamental differences between Palestinian women who live under military occupation and Israeli-Jewish women who in times of crisis are silenced in the name of 'national security' and often become complicit with a system of domination and oppression that they previously criticized. Although Palestinian and Israeli women engaged in more substantive discussions of the conflict than their male counterparts in the late 1980s and early 1990s, the Israeli women's lack of readiness to acknowledge their relative power and privilege and to hold their government and military accountable for their violence and oppressive practices against Palestinians was the ultimate demise of the women's dialogue enterprise.

WOMEN CONFRONT MILITARIZATION

Women's anti-militarism and peace efforts in Israel have been both trivialized and marginalized unless they have used motherhood as a platform. Filling the post-Oslo vacuum in women's peace organizing in Israel, two new groups burst onto the scene in the late 1990s: Women and Mothers for Peace and Four Mothers. Comprised mostly of women with no previous involvement in the women's peace movement or in official Israeli politics, these groups, which did not identify as feminist, received prominent coverage in both Israeli and international media and a relatively warm reception from Israelis, including many elected officials. Led primarily by mothers of sons then serving in Lebanon, these groups successfully mobilized the discourse of motherhood to challenge Israeli government policies. The mothers' peace groups played a key role in shifting the national consensus in Israel about its occupation of southern Lebanon. They were the most visible representatives of the public campaign that eventually resulted in the Israeli military withdrawal from Lebanon in May 2000 (Sharoni, 2002).

In September 2000, the *Al-Aqsa Intifada* erupted. Provoked by a visit to the Al-Aqsa mosque compound by former Prime Minister Ariel Sharon, accompanied by 1000 Israeli policemen, the uprising gained momentum at least in part due to the failure of the Oslo agreements to end the Israeli occupation of the West Bank and Gaza. Also known as the second intifada, the popular uprising's message was similar to the one articulated by anti-occupation activists in Israel and Palestine during the first intifada: an end to the illegal Israeli occupation is a necessary condition for a just and lasting peace in the region. However, unlike the bottom-up popular character of the first uprising, the *Al-Aqsa Intifada* resembled more a guerilla war. Because of its militarized aspect, the Israeli military's unprecedented repression and the risks associated with armed struggle, fewer Palestinian women assumed leadership positions during the *Al-Aqsa Intifada*. The same is true for the participation of women at the grassroots level because the key avenues of organized resistance did not involve widespread community participation. The mainstream global media quickly focused on the escalation in violence in the region, highlighting such desperate acts of violence as suicide bombings carried out by Palestinians. Journalists analyzed neither the context that precipitated the uprising nor the fact that Palestinians who condoned the use of armed struggle did so because of their deep disappointment with the failure of both Israeli society and the international community to grasp the message of the first intifada, which was mostly nonviolent in both principle and practice (Pressman, 2003). Also missing from dominant media representations of the second intifada were analyses of the systemic repression and violence stemming from the Israeli military occupation, including home demolishing, checkpoints, targeted killings and an economic crisis.

One form of gendered resistance of Palestinian women during the second intifada was research and documentation of the effects of political violence on women and other vulnerable populations and on the community as a whole. Feminist researchers and scholars in Palestine were key in documenting the second intifada. They examined critically such issues as the impact of checkpoints on women's mobility, work patterns and support systems, as well as the impact of the ongoing political and economic crisis on family structures and on violence against women (Taraki, 2006; Shalhoub-Kevorkian, 2009). This impressive body of literature also includes analysis of the erosion of space for women's autonomous political organizing after the establishment of the Palestinian Authority and the contradictions and problems associated with the proliferation of non-governmental organizations in Palestine (Abdulhadi, 1998; Hasso, 2005; Jad, 2010). The issues examined included the politics of funding, which often involved imposing an agenda that reflected the interests of external entities, rather than the priorities of Palestinian women's organizations (Hammami, 2002; Jad, 2010). The impressive body of literature authored by Palestinian feminists about Palestinian women and contemporary gender issues within Palestinian society constitutes an important contribution to peace-building and conflict transformation. They ought to be both considered by scholars in the field and taken into account by political actors crafting the next peace agreement.

In Israel, the outbreak of the second intifada prompted some women to engage in actions directed at their own society and especially the mechanism associated with Israel's military occupation. The result was the establishment of several new groups addressing the escalating political violence and the grave violations of Palestinian human rights, including Machsom Watch, New Profile and the Coalition of Women for Peace (CWP). Founded in 2001 in response to repeated press reports about human rights abuses of Palestinians crossing army checkpoints, Machsom Watch involved mostly middle-aged and college-educated, Israeli-Jewish women divided into small groups who positioned themselves as observers at key checkpoints in the West Bank. They have documented human rights violations and periodically disseminated these to the press. When necessary, the women of Machsom Watch have confronted Israeli soldiers, using their moral authority as mothers and grandmothers to question inhumane practices and behaviors (Halperin, 2007).

New Profile, which describes itself as feminist and anti-militaristic, goes beyond challenging the Israeli national consensus on questions of war and peace. They challenge the social and political culture and educational system within which Israeli-Jewish men are socialized and they work to convince their own sons and others to refuse on moral grounds to serve in the Occupied Territories. Despite attempts by the Israeli public and mainstream media to portray New Profile as extreme, their anti-militaristic stance and efforts to destabilize conceptions of masculinity and femininity have struck a chord in Israeli society. In so doing, New Profile has triggered unprecedented public discussions about the interplay of gender and politics, suggesting that a true commitment to peace must be rooted in antimilitarism (Sharoni, 2002).

In November 2000, a month after the outbreak of the second intifada, a group of leading feminist peace activists met to discuss possible responses to the crisis. Outraged by the rise in violence stemming from Israeli occupation and Israeli government propaganda that blamed the escalation on the resurgence of Palestinian resistance, they agreed to establish an organizing platform for feminist peace and human rights organizations. They established the Coalition of Women for a Just Peace, which later was shortened to the Coalition of Women for Peace (CWP). The sense of urgency that triggered the establishment of the Coalition has continued to inspire its dynamism and prolific activities over the years. CWP's leaders have overcome many of the key obstacles of previous Jewish-led women's peace initiatives in Israel, including making explicit the structured power asymmetry between Palestinians and Israelis and a reluctance to confront differences and conflicts within organizations. The new organization brought together nine feminist organizations including such veteran groups as Women in Black, Movement of Democratic Women in Israel (TANDI), the Israeli branch of Women's International League for Peace and Freedom (WILPF), Women for Coexistence (Neled), and *Noga Feminist Journal*. In addition, the coalition worked closely with such newer groups as Women and Mothers for Peace, New Profile and Machsom Watch. Many women not involved in existing organizations also joined CWP.

The CWP's commitment to formulating feminist responses to political violence was repeatedly tested as a result of Israel's military attacks on Jenin in 2002, Lebanon in 2006 and Gaza in 2008–2009, 2012 and 2014. Although the coalition's response involved primarily demonstrations and statements to the Israeli press, it was important in the Israeli political landscape, given the shift to the right in Israeli politics and limited opportunity for dissent during military operations. Moreover, CWP provided the space for feminist activists to strategize about future feminist responses to both crises and opportunities. Over the years, a small but dedicated group of feminist peace activists in Israel, both Jewish and Palestinian, understood the urgency of active solidarity with Palestinians, especially during crisis. These women who had played leading roles in the anti-occupation movement since the first intifada were determined to infuse the new political reality with feminist perspectives, new strategies of struggle, and bold initiatives. Gradually, the more radical feminist peace activists sharpened their critique of Israel's aggression as they shifted their interactions with Palestinians from those based on dialogue to those based on unequivocal critiques of Israel's occupation and settler colonialism, coupled with solidarity initiatives.

FEMINIST SOLIDARITY AS A RESPONSE TO POLITICAL VIOLENCE

Feminist resistance to war and political violence often called into question the 'us' versus 'them' distinctions that have been used to demonize the enemy and legitimize the use of violence against them. In Israel, gender-based resistance to political violence often involved critiques of militarism and the treatment of Palestinians. Notwithstanding initiatives geared at dialogue and reconciliation and the ongoing public protest against Israeli aggression, feminist actions or campaigns originating in Israel as expressions of solidarity with Palestinians in the West Bank and Gaza Strip are rare. The call for Boycott, Divestment and Sanctions (BDS), issued in July 2005 by a broad coalition of Palestinian trade unions, political parties, community networks and non-governmental organizations, many of them led by women, created a new momentum for solidarity with Palestinians. The historic call was inspired by the success of the South African anti-apartheid movement of the 1980s and recognition that the Palestinian struggle for human rights, equality and the enforcement of international law needed international support, and that civil society organizations have an important role to play in such a campaign (Bennis, 2010). The language of the call for BDS and the unity at the grassroots level in Palestine created the impetus for dramatic change in the dynamics and strategies of resistance to the Israeli occupation.

For Palestinian activists, the BDS movement created space to engage in nonviolent resistance, using new modes of organizing, diverse coalitions, and campaigns, including some featuring constituencies and messages that have been previously relegated to the margins of the political scene in the region. While Palestinian women continue to be involved in projects addressing the gendered aspects of the conflict and to challenge the political status quo, the most exciting examples of feminist responses to political violence in Palestine involve Palestinian Queers for BDS (PQBDS) and *al-Qaws* (Arabic for 'rainbow'). These newer groups advance sexual and gender diversity in Palestine while simultaneously addressing the political violence and engaging in solidarity efforts abroad. Palestinian Queers for BDS (PQBDS) was launched in response to the Palestinian civil society call for BDS against Israel. In June 2010, PQBDS issued a call to queer activists around the world, explicitly articulating connections between their oppression as members of the LGBTQI (lesbian, gay, bisexual, trangender, queer and intersex) community and as Palestinians. The group insisted that the rights of oppressed and marginalized queer minorities cannot be separated from fighting against all forms of oppression around the world (Palestinian Queers for BDS website).

Highlighting the proud history of the queer movement worldwide, which has joined numerous global socio-political struggles against manifestations of oppression, imperialism, injustice and discrimination around the world, PQBDS urges LGBTQI activists around the world to stand for justice in Palestine through adopting and implementing broad boycott, divestment and sanctions against Israel until the latter has ended its multi-tiered oppression of the Palestinian people, in line with the 2005 Palestinian civil society call for BDS. In addition to the statement, the group launched Pinkwatching Israel, an online resource and information hub for activists working on BDS within queer communities to expose and resist Israeli pinkwashing – the cynical use of gay rights to distract from and normalize Israeli occupation, settler colonialism, and apartheid (see Pinkwatching Israel website). The coalition has used online activism and social media both to educate and mobilize, usually through targeted Calls for Action. For example, early in 2012, PQBDS activists learned that The Equality Forum, an annual LGBTQ conference held in Phila-delphia, had identified Israel as its featured nation for 2012, and had invited the Israeli Ambassador to the United States, Michael Oren, to deliver the keynote speech. In response, PQBDS released a statement calling for a boycott of the Equality Forum 2012, which it cleverly renamed: the (In)Equality Forum. The coalition coordinated a multi-front public campaign, including letter-writing, op-ed pieces, and numerous media appearances. The success of these efforts notwithstanding, the strength of PQBDS lies in the strong bonds of solidarity it has forged with queer activists around the world. In Toronto, local activists founded Queers Against Israeli Apartheid (QuAIA), organizing community events and assembling large contingents in the annual gay pride marches. No Pinkwashing, a British group that had just formed, made a splash at the 2012 World Pride in London.

Like PQBDS, *al-Qaws* has loudly criticized Israel's pinkwashing campaign, which it views as an example of Israeli propaganda designed to create an image of Israel as an enlightened democracy when actually it legitimizes political violence perpetrated by the state. From its inception in 2006, the group's founders refused to limit their focus to challenging social attitudes and religious taboos about sexuality and gender in Palestine. Instead, *al-Qaws* insists that 'LGBTQ Palestinians face pres-sures, not just from Palestinian society, but from the wider context of the Israeli–Palestinian conflict. LGBTQ Palestinians' struggles are a complex result of problems internal to Palestinian society and the harsh realities of the Israeli–Palestinian conflict' (Maikey, 2008).

In Israel, a mixed-gender direct action group, Anarchists Against The Wall (AATW), exemplifies solidarity as a mode of resistance to political violence. The group emerged in 2003 after Israeli-Jewish activists joined Palestinian villagers in the West Bank in resisting the construction of the 'Apartheid Wall', which Israel refers to as a 'security fence'. Although the group does not describe itself as feminist and many of its prominent members are men, their practices offer numerous insights about gender, resistance, solidarity and opposition to political violence. AATW solidarity actions with Palestinian villagers across the West Bank show coalition building across significant differences: young anarchists in their late teens and early twenties marching alongside Palestinian villagers who previously had no contact with Israelis except soldiers. Moreover, AATW activists used their power and privilege as Israeli Jews to confront Israeli soldiers and attempt to shield Palestinians from the violence unleashed against them, even when engaged in nonviolent resistance. Although AATW's resistance to Israel's violent practices was not gender-based, their successful strategies highlight what has been missing from the opposition mounted by the women's movement in Israel. By disrupting, or at least temporarily halting, the repressive measures used by the Israeli military and border police against Palestinians, AATW activists made clear that solidarity with the oppressed involves the willingness of members of the oppressors to take risks. Because the presence of AATW activists attracted both Israeli and international media attention, they too became targets of political violence, with members injured and arrested during the protests. Although AATW only has about 100 active members, the group's existence, actions and international visibility are hopeful signs that solidarity is possible and a model of how to practice solidarity amidst repression and violence.

CONCLUSION

Palestinian and Israeli women and queer activists have faced numerous challenges in the course of their struggles to advance gender equality while at the same time resisting political violence. Despite the escalation of the political conflict, however, women on both sides of the Palestinian–Israeli divide have made considerable gains. First and foremost, their active involvement in the resistance to the occupation and the violence unleashed by the Israeli military has had a transformative effect on their own lives. Through their activism, many women have grown more confident and have developed feminist consciousness and an overarching political perspective. As a result, these activists now constitute a critical mass that is likely to continue to impact the course of the conflict and shape its aftermath. Second, by exposing the gendered dimensions of the conflict and bringing this analysis into the media and popular culture, activists have begun to transform the cultures of their respective collectivities, ensuring that gender, sexuality and other inequalities and oppressions are not overlooked.

As the case of the Coalition of Women for Peace (CWP) underscores, overcoming the problems facing women's alliances requires a dramatic shift in both orientation and framework. Such a shift requires moving away from dialogue and sporadic protests to a framework of solidarity. The call issued by a diverse coalition of Palestinian Civil Society to the international community to support the Boycott, Divestment and Sanctions movement created a momentum for radical transformation in modes of resistance. Although many in the women's movement in Israel remain reluctant to move beyond dialogue and protest as the main modes of opposing political violence, the failure of these avenues to bring about a just and lasting solution to the conflict may convince them to explore a different approach. The unprecedented mobilization of queer activists in Palestine highlights the promise of the global Boycott, Divestment and Sanctions campaign. The international attention and support for such groups as PQBDS, *al-Qaws* and Anarchists Against the Wall on the global stage, underscores the power of solidarity to resist political violence and to transform the course of the conflict. Taken together, these new initiatives reflect a new approach of resistance to political violence in the region. Rooted in an understanding of multiple and intersecting oppressions as the basis for cross-community and transnational solidarity, they provide a coherent discourse and a more radical platform for action.

In recent years, feminist scholars and activists have insisted that by joining the BDS movement, feminists engage in transnational solidarity (Sharoni and Abdulhadi, 2015). The BDS movement has provided feminists and other activists in Palestine, Israel and worldwide with a clear vision and manifold opportunities to mobilize the international community to confront Israeli apartheid in support of the struggle to bring about a just and lasting resolution of the conflict. Despite the Israeli government's hostility to the growing momentum of the BDS movement worldwide, BDS has clearly changed dominant representations of the Palestinian–Israeli conflict. The nonviolent solidarity movement with Palestinians has made clear that the conflict is not between two parties on an equal playing field and that ending violence requires addressing its root causes.

REFERENCES

Abdo, Nahla and Ronit Lentin (eds) (2002), *Women and the Politics of Military Occupation: Palestinian and Israeli Gendered Narratives of Dislocation*, Berghahn.
Abdulhadi, Rabab (1998), 'The Palestinian women's autonomous movement', *Gender and Society*, **12** (6): 649–73.

Bennis, Phyllis (2010), 'Waging peace from afar: divestment and Israeli occupation', *Yes!*
Magazine, 20 August, accessed 10 July 2012 at: http://archive.truthout.org/phyllis-
bennis-waging-peace-afar-divestment-and- israeli-occupation62605.

Byrne, Siobhan (2009), 'Beyond the ethnonational divide: identity politics and women in
Northern Ireland and Israel/Palestine' (Doctoral dissertation), Queens University,
Ontario.

Coalition of Women for Peace, accessed 18 July 2012 at: http://www.coalitionof
women.org/.

Cockburn, Cynthia (2007), *From Where We Stand: War, Women's Activism and Feminist
Analysis*, Zed Books.

Dahan-Kalev, Henriette (2001), 'Tensions in Israeli feminism: the Mizrahi–Ashkenazi rift',
Women's Studies International Forum, **24**: 1–16.

Daniele, Giulia (2011), 'The road not taken: women, reconciliation and Israeli–Palestinian
conflict' (Doctoral dissertation), University of Exeter and Scula Superiore Sant'Anna.

Frankfurt-Nachmias, Chava and Erela Shadmi (2005), *Sappho in the Holy Land: Lesbian
Existence and Dilemmas in Contemporary Israel*, SUNY.

Halperin, Irit (2007), 'Between the lines: the story of Machsom Watch', *Journal of
Humanistic Psychology*, **47** (3): 333–9.

Hammami, Rima (2002), 'Palestinian NGOs since Oslo: from NGO politics to social
movements?', *Middle East Report*, **214** (Spring): 16–19.

Hasso, Frances (2005), *Resistance, Repression, and Gender Politics in Occupied Palestine
and Jordan*, Syracuse University Press.

Hilal, R. and Aida Touma (2008), 'Jerusalem Link, Bat Shalom and the Jerusalem Center
for Women: evaluation report', accessed 28 November 2011 at: http://www.norad.no/en/
tools-and-publications/publications/publication?key=132926.

Ibanez, Ana (2001), 'El Salvador: war and untold stories – women guerrillas', in Cynthia
Moser and Fiona Clark (eds), *Victims, Perpetrators or Actors? Gender, Armed Conflict
and Political Violence*, Zed Books, pp. 117–30.

Jad, Islah (2010), 'The demobilization of a Palestinian women's movement: from
empowered active militants to powerless and stateless citizens', in Amrita Basu (ed.),
Women's Movements in the Global Era: The Power of Local Feminisms, Westview,
pp. 343–74.

Jayawardena, Kumar (1986), *Feminism and Nationalism in the Third World*, Zed Books.

Kannneh, Rhoda and Isis Nusair (2010), *Displaced at Home: Ethnicity and Gender among
Palestinians in Israel*, SUNY.

Maikey, Haneen (2008), 'Rainbow over Palestine', *The Guardian*, 10 March, accessed 21
May 2015 at: http://www.theguardian.com/commentisfree/2008/mar/10/rainbowover
palestine.

Palestinian Queers for BDS website, http://www.pqbds.com, accessed 9 July 2015.

Pinkwatching Israel website, http://www.pinkwatchingisrael.com/, accessed 9 July 2015.

Powers, Janet (2006), *Blossoms on the Olive Tree: Israeli and Palestinian Women Working
for Peace*, Praeger.

Pressman, Jeremy (2003), 'The second intifada: background and causes of the Israeli–
Palestinian conflict', *The Journal of Conflict Studies*, **23** (2), accessed 19 June 2015 at:
https://journals.lib.unb.ca/index.php/jcs/article/view/220/378.

Richter-Devroe, Sophie (2009), '"Here, it's not about conflict resolution – we can only
resist": Palestinian women activism in conflict resolution and non-violent resistance', in
Nadje Al-Ali and Nicola Pratt (eds), *Women & War in the Middle East*, Zed Books,
pp. 158–90.

Rubenberg, Cheryl (2001), *Palestinian Women: Patriarchy and Resistance in the West
Bank*, Lynne Rienner.

Shalhoub-Kevorkian, Nadera (2009), *Militarization and Violence Against Women in
Conflict Zones in the Middle East*, Cambridge University Press.

Sharoni, Simona (1995), *Gender and the Israeli–Palestinian Conflict: The Politics of Women's Resistance*, Syracuse University Press.

Sharoni, Simona (2002), 'Gendering conflict and peace in Israel/Palestine and the North of Ireland', in Louisa Odysseos and Hakan Seckinelgin (eds), *Gendering the International*, Zed Books, pp. 174–207.

Sharoni, Simona (2010), 'Conflict resolution: feminist perspectives', in Robert Denemark (ed.), *The International Studies Compendium Project*, Blackwell.

Sharoni, Simona and Rabab Abdulhadi (2015), 'Transnational feminist solidarity in times of crisis: Boycott, Divestment and Sanctions (BDS) movement and justice in/for Palestine', *International Feminist Journal of Politics*, **17** (4), http://www.tandfonline. com/doi/full/10.1080/14616742.2015.1088226.

Taraki, Lisa (ed.) (2006), *Living Palestine: Family Survival, Resistance, and Mobility Under Occupation*, Syracuse University Press.

West, Lois (1997), *Feminist Nationalism*, Routledge.

Yuval-Davis, Nira (1997), *Gender and Nation*, Sage.

Yuval-Davis, Nira and Floya Anthias (eds) (1989), *Women-Nation-State*, Macmillan.

19. In the rain and in the sun: women's peace activism in Liberia
Jennifer Pedersen

INTRODUCTION

It is widely recognized in the literature on women, war and peace that women are regularly excluded from formal political decision-making processes, especially peace processes. Women are generally perceived to be peaceful, apolitical victims, and their identities are frequently appropriated as symbols of the nation (Anderlini, 2007; Porter, 2007; Kaufman and Williams, 2010). Yet, as feminist literature has shown, women's actual experiences of conflict are often much more complex than stereotypes convey; women play many roles in wartime, including those of 'victims, perpetrators, and actors' (Moser and Clark, 2001).

The case of Liberia in 2003 is one such complicated example. Beginning in the 1980s, Liberia suffered a series of violent conflicts and civil wars that were characterized by the extensive use of child soldiers, sexual violence, mass displacement and extreme hardship (Moran, 2008; Moran and Pitcher, 2004; Cain, 1999; Klay Kieh Jr, 2003; Hoffman, 2004). Some women participated in the conflicts as fighters or bush wives,[1] and many women were displaced.[2] Yet Liberia was also the site of a unique peace movement made up entirely of women, many of whom came from the grassroots, which both embraced and manipulated stereotypes about 'peaceful' women.

This chapter examines the case of the Women in Peacebuilding Network (WIPNET), which mobilized thousands of women for peace at the height of the Second Civil War in 2003. Through a culturally-specific strategy of 'women's peace activism' the participants in this movement challenged the commonly-held belief that women were apolitical and passive victims of conflict. They questioned militarism through a feminist lens, and aimed to create new space for women within a highly patriarchal context. One of the founders of this movement, Leymah Gbowee, was recognized with the Nobel Peace Prize in 2011 for her work to advance women's roles in peacebuilding. As a movement, WIPNET's Women Mass Action for Peace included standard nonviolence tactics such as sit-ins, marches and press conferences that were designed to put a woman's face to the war and call for an end to the violence that had engulfed their country for 14 years. The chapter focuses first on how this movement was built, then explores how the movement operated and finally discusses its main achievements, including forcing an end to the conflict and encouraging women to claim their rightful place in peace-building processes. As a case study this is one example of the strategic and deliberate use of women's identities and gendered roles often employed by women peace activists – in this case, to great success.

BUILDING A MOVEMENT

While Liberia is a highly patriarchal country where gendered power relations generally allow men to dominate socially, economically and politically, Liberian women have at times mobilized together to achieve political goals outside periods of conflict (Moran and Pitcher, 2004; Moran, 2008). This form of activism is one way that Liberian women, subordinate when it came to formal politics, were able to give voice to their concerns and to 'act collectively in order to counter the power of a political hierarchy in which they are junior partners' (Moran, 2008, p. 48). During the First Civil War in Liberia in the 1990s, several women's groups organized around peace issues, including the Liberian Women's Initiative and the Mano River Union Women's Peace Network (Aisha, 2005; Solomon, 2005; African Women and Peace Support Group, 2004; Cockburn, 2007).

The Women in Peacebuilding Network of Liberia (WIPNET), founded in 2001, was part of a larger network of women peace activists in West Africa who operated through their parent organization, the West Africa Network for Peacebuilding (WANEP). WIPNET was the brainchild of Thelma Ekiyor, a Nigerian lawyer and conflict resolution specialist who was concerned about the absence of women from peacebuilding processes in Africa. Ekiyor worked closely with Leymah Gbowee, a Liberian social worker who had worked with child soldiers and women from neighboring Sierra Leone. When conducting trauma-healing workshops, Gbowee had noticed that few women would speak when men were in the room, and instigated women-only sessions where women could speak openly about their experiences of war. Gbowee was also an avid reader of literature on social transformation, citing Martin Luther King Jr, Gandhi and Kenyan reconciliation expert Hizkias Assefa as inspirational leaders who transformed the way she thought about conflict. Like Ekiyor, Gbowee was struck by the absence of women in public life and the silence of women when it came to war and peace: 'Why were women, who bore the brunt of war, expected to remain quiet while men debated how to make peace?' (2011, p. 100).

Nira Yuval-Davis has argued that 'some women's antimilitaristic and antiwar groups see their work as a spearhead in the fight against the patriarchal social system as a whole that they see as dominated by male masochism and violence' (2004, p. 186). This was certainly the case with WIPNET. In their vision statement, Ekiyor and Gbowee drew on Galtung's (1996) concept of 'positive peace' by linking their antiwar activism to 'the deconstruction of structural forms of violence in everyday (African) society' (Ekiyor and Gbowee, 2005). They argued that widespread violence against women 'was an expression of a deeper systemic disregard for women existing in West African societies'. The way to combat these attitudes was through mass-mobilization of women 'around key issues' of peace and security (Ekiyor and Gbowee, 2005). WIPNET, which operated in several countries in the West African sub-region, focused on building the capacities of women at the grassroots level. Ekiyor wrote a training manual for women in peacebuilding that was tailored to the West African context. In 2001 Gbowee was named the head of the Liberian chapter of WIPNET, and set out to train a network of women capable of working for peace in their respective communities across Liberia.

WIPNET did not begin as a formal peace movement but as a network focused on training women to resolve conflicts within their local contexts (Gbowee, 2011, p. 123). The grassroots approach, which involved training-of-trainers workshops that encouraged women to take what they learned back to their communities, quietly worked to energize women across different parts of Liberia to begin to focus on women's roles in peacebuilding. Despite the history of women's organizing in Liberia, WIPNET's focus on the grassroots was unique. WIPNET developed a different approach that avoided the traditional elitism that had previously excluded young and poorer women from the activist women's community and peace activism during the first Liberian war.

A key part of WIPNET's strategy was uniting women of different religious faiths. With the support of her colleague Asatu Bah Kenneth, a prominent Liberian policewoman, Gbowee brought together Christian and Muslim women for the first time. As the situation in Liberia deteriorated throughout 2002 during the Second Civil War, the women of WIPNET narrowed their focus to the ongoing conflict. They launched a Peace Outreach Project where, for six months, their members went to mosques, churches and markets to campaign to make Liberian women 'awake for peace' (Gbowee, 2011, p. 126). They campaigned for women to be part of the peace process – a process that had not yet started at any official level. The overall strategy was to campaign wherever women were:

> We worked in a world inhabited by women and we used women's networks to communicate. When the market women bought fruits and vegetables from women in rural areas, they passed along our message, and when they sold their goods in the city, they shared it with the women who were the customers. (Gbowee, 2011, p. 127)

The differing identities of the women were a source both of strength and of strain for the growing movement. Christian women and Muslim women continued to meet to discuss peacebuilding work, although it was challenging to convince some that working with the other group was a positive step due to long-standing distrust between the communities and the fact that one of the major rebel groups, LURD, was predominantly Muslim. In an attempt to bring Christian and Muslim women together, Gbowee started a new workshop titled 'Being a Woman' that encouraged the participants to leave their differences aside (Gbowee, 2011, p. 128).

In 2003, as the conflict drew closer to the capital Monrovia and became more deadly in the countryside, WIPNET launched a new initiative called the 'Women's Mass Action for Peace', outlining three demands: an immediate unconditional ceasefire; peace talks between government and rebel forces; and the deployment of an international intervention force. The Mass Action called on women from across Liberia to join in a 'sit-in', or public vigil, at an airfield on the outskirts of Monrovia. Women sat together praying and fasting for days to protest against the ongoing war. The vigil required a serious level of commitment on the part of the women. As WIPNET member Asatu Kenneth recalled:

> (A)t first it was frustrating, and we had to be focused ... We weren't wearing makeup, we weren't eating, we were fasting, we were praying, we spent the whole day in the heat, and people were frustrated, because it was like every day wearing the white t-shirt and tying our hair back ... it was challenging because most of us were tired ... (but) we all benefited from it. (Author's interview with Asatu Kenneth, 2006)

The persistence of the women going daily to the airfield despite public criticism helped to change public attitudes towards the women and earn popular support for their movement; with daily media coverage and increasing numbers of women participating in the vigil, the women's message spread and gained legitimacy in the eyes of the public. The women's sacrifices – leaving their jobs, families and lives to demonstrate for peace – took their toll. But as Vaiba Flomo remembered,

> [W]e were sitting in the sun, we were sitting in the rain. So our sit-in is the one that really caught the people's hearts. They would say to us, 'when you leave your children, when you leave your husbands, leaving your daily activities' – because I left my job, I was saying to my boss, if war should come, I wouldn't have a job! Definitely I'd be dead! ... It was one of the strategies that really worked for us, the sit-in. (Author's interview with Vaiba Flomo, 2006)

During the daily vigil hundreds of women, many of whom did not know each other, shared their stories and experiences of the war. The very act of hearing each other's stories renewed their sense of purpose. As Vaiba Flomo recounted, 'Every morning we went there, we got to know one another. We started to empathize with each other' (*Pray the Devil Back to Hell*, 2008). These activities of speaking and listening fostered the idea of a collective of 'Liberian women', no longer divided along lines of politics, race or class, but united in a common experience.

A noted characteristic of many women's peace groups is their choice of dress, which not only serves to identify the group to the public and power-holders but also helps to build a sense of collective identity within the group. In Liberia the women of the Mass Action wore white t-shirts that were marked only with the WIPNET logo on the front and a variety of peace slogans on the back. They also wore identical *lappas*, traditional dresses or skirts worn by Liberian women. The *lappa*

> is often associated with illiterate or less-educated women who are either petty traders or peasant farmers ... in indigenous Liberian societies, tying a *lappa* around the torso was considered quite significant. It was a 'sacred and prayerful beginning to a new day' for women, who considered the act as symbolizing encircling the living and dead members of their immediate and extended family, a statement of the continuity of life. (Olukoju, 2006, p. 86)

Mary Moran notes a strong connection between clothing and communal perceptions of women, arguing that the *lappa*, while worn by women in all social categories, can be used to symbolize differences between 'native' and 'civilized' (that is, 'Westernized' or 'elite') Liberian women (2008, p. 82). The choice to wear the *lappa*, rather than Western-style dress, helped to create a collective image that associated the WIPNET women with the traditional Liberian woman who had suffered as a result of years of war. In addition to wearing identical clothing, the women also banned the wearing of jewelry and makeup in order maintain an austere appearance, as they argued that their message would be best communicated if visible class differences among them were suppressed. Women were also issued with WIPNET ID cards, complete with their name and photo, to emphasize that this was an official movement with a committed membership.

In a violently divided society such as Liberia, where divisions between groups of people were exacerbated by nearly fifteen years of conflict and exploited by fighters on all sides, the choice to identify as a collective of Liberian *women* was key to being perceived as a new and *nonviolent* political force. The women's focus on reconciliation contrasted with the aggressive and divisive politicking of the warring parties and challenged the religious, class and ethnic hierarchies that had been exploited during the conflict.

The women also engaged in a sex strike for several months in 2003 to accompany their daily prayers and silent vigils. As Cecelia Danuweli recalled,

> Some of us denied our husbands from having any relations with us, because we were fasting and praying. And the husbands do suffer it, because we were not to carry anything for them, we told them, 'it is *you* who are fighting the men! So we will suppress you until your friends begin to listen to us …!' So that was how we engaged our own husbands, so that they will get involved in the Mass Action for Peace … and some of them supported us! They marched with us! They cried with us! They gave us all support: 'Women, we are with you!' (Author's interview with Cecelia Danuweli, 2006)

The use of this tactic in Liberia is especially significant when we consider the levels of sexual violence against women during the conflict, where some estimate that upwards of 75 percent of Liberian women were raped (Murray, 2009). Liberian women's bodies were frequently sites of violence, and for the Liberian women to take back that power, to reclaim their bodies as their own, was a serious political statement. Gbowee explained this tactic by connecting men's responsibilities for the war. As she said, 'Men were the perpetrators of violence, so either by commission or omission, you (men) were guilty' (*Pray the Devil Back to Hell*, 2008). Yet it is interesting to note in Danuweli's testimony that some male partners of the Liberian peace women were generally supportive of their action. This may be attributed to the fact that these men did not see the sex strike as a personal punishment but rather as part of a nationwide struggle for peace in which they were invited to participate; just as the women were praying and fasting daily, their partners could show their own commitment to the cause by supporting their struggle. The sex strike also worked better in the rural areas, where women associated the strike with their religious beliefs: 'Bringing God into it made their men fearful of opposing them' (Gbowee, 2011, p. 147). At the same time, Gbowee wrote, 'The strike had little or no practical effect, but it was extremely valuable in getting us media attention' (Gbowee, 2011, p. 147).

The initial reaction to the women's organizing was less than positive as it inspired a wave of criticism from members of the public who questioned the appropriateness of their behavior. Women were criticized for leaving their families and jobs behind. Criticism also came from angry government representatives; Gbowee recalled how the Speaker of Parliament once asked her, 'why in the hell do you want to embarrass the government?' (United States Institute of Peace, 2007). The initial reaction from the public and government underlined the difficulties in challenging notions of what was 'appropriate' political activity for women. In front of the international media, President Charles Taylor spoke of respect for the mothers of Liberia, and even invited them to speak to him publicly about their concerns, but privately Taylor had ordered his supporters to attack the women, and he had allegedly declared 'even if my mother got on the street, keep her off the street!' As Gbowee recalled, 'he actually didn't believe that the women of Liberia would defy him' (United States Institute of Peace, 2007). As Cecelia Danuweli remembered,

> Taylor once sent his boys to the airfield with some whips, to whip us where we were doing our sitting. But then the boys came and they said, 'Ah, no! We can't! We won't do it!' One told his friend and said, 'If you don't have a mother, go and touch one woman … If you touch them, you've touched all of us.' So they all left. (Author's interview, 2006)

It is clear from this example that their collective identity as 'the women of Liberia' offered the WIPNET women a certain amount of protection from public reprisals. It is likely that if men had been on the field with them, the group would have been attacked. Thus WIPNET's identity as apolitical sisters, mothers and wives worked to their advantage, as it offered both protection from attack and an opportunity to articulate their concerns in a very public way

TAKING THE PROTEST TO THE PEACE TALKS

WIPNET's constructed identity as 'the women of Liberia' also gave the movement unique access to power-holders. When it appeared that one of the rebel groups, Liberians United for Reconciliation and Democracy (LURD), were refusing to attend peace talks in Accra in 2003, WIPNET sent a delegation of women to the LURD base across the border in Sierra

Leone to convince the rebels to commit to the peace process. In Freetown WIPNET mobilized Liberian women from the refugee camps before confronting LURD leaders outside their hotel. 'We told them "we are your wives, we are your mothers, we are your sisters"', recalled Grace Jarsor (Author's interview, 2006). As Asatu Kenneth remembers,

> At first they were bitter, they were resisting us, but the fact [is] that they thought we were supporting Taylor, and then they said, 'Why did you come here to us?'... And I said this was for our country and the future of our children. I spoke in tears, and all the women were crying, and I think from there they saw it, and then they decided to give in, and some of them said, 'Oh, we didn't expect people like you to represent the government of Liberia,' and we said, 'no, we are not representing the government of Liberia, we are representing the *women* of Liberia!' and from that point we had a breakthrough. (Author's interview with Asatu Kenneth, 2006)

WIPNET then sent a delegation of women to sit outside the Peace Talks in Accra, Ghana, where the Liberian government and rebel groups were meeting under the supervision of the international community. After several weeks, the women demonstrating outside the talks in Ghana grew frustrated with the slow pace of negotiations and increasingly concerned with the deteriorating humanitarian situation at home in Liberia. LURD was closing in on Monrovia and began to shell the centre of the city. Civilians were caught between the rebels at one end of the city and the Government of Liberia fighters at the other, facing starvation and brutal violence (O'Neill and Ward, 2005).

The women tried to engage the warlords 'behind the scenes', as Etweda 'Sugars' Cooper recalled, but the warlords continued to direct the fighting in Liberia, telephoning their subordinates from their hotel rooms in Accra in between the talks (*Pray the Devil Back to Hell*, 2008). The increase in violence in Monrovia spurred the women to develop a 'harsher nonviolent strategy' (Ekiyor and Gbowee, 2005). Leymah Gbowee was 'angrier and more bitter. I was just raging inside. So I told Sugars, today is showdown. Send for more women!' (*Pray the Devil Back to Hell*, 2008). The women barricaded the assembly hall, preventing all parties from leaving for several hours. Refusing to accept any further delays to the negotiations, they demanded the delegates take the process seriously and commit to a peace agreement. As Cecelia Danuweli recalled,

> We closed them up in the house, we said they were not coming in or going out until the ceasefire was signed ... We barricaded the doors ... They were scared of the women! They started jumping through the windows ... because they knew we were serious and the chief mediator came out, he pleaded with

us and we said no, we were not listening to him until the ceasefire was signed. And he got angry, he went in and blasted them. He told them, 'if those women out there continue ... because they are angry, they will come in here and they will do just what they please, so please, we have to do something, so that those women can leave the place.' ... At the time, they were fighting in Monrovia. We were watching it on CNN, seeing our people dying ... so it got us all angry, for us to bellow and do what we were doing. (Author's interview with Cecelia Danuweli, 2006)

As police came to arrest her for obstructing justice, Gbowee began stripping her clothes off, shocking those present. The cultural significance of her action should not be underestimated. As one of the Liberian women at the talks remembered, 'For a son to see his mother's nakedness – it's considered a curse. And to do it in public! So the men were saying, "we better do something because they're threatening to take their clothes off!"' (Hayner, 2007, p. 13).

Gbowee's actions and the barricade finally forced the delegates to agree to go back to the table. Sanam Anderlini has argued that the 'informal and behind-the-scenes mediation' (2007, p. 15) by the Liberian women made a critical difference to the outcome of the peace process. The sit-ins, lobbying of rebels and government officials and the barricade actions worked together to put pressure on power holders, raise the public profile of the women's action, illustrate their concerns about the ongoing war and counteract assumptions both in society and among male holders of power that women cannot play a role in resolving issues of peace and security. The women's barricade and demonstrations also secured them a place in meetings with the rebels and mediators. As Ekiyor and Gbowee observed,

> For WIPNET, attendance at these meetings, where the basic issues concerning the future of Liberia were discussed, represented one of the great successes of the Mass Action for Peace campaign. It had shown that the women were stakeholders in the conflict and had a role to play in the peace process. (Ekiyor and Gbowee, 2005, p. 138)

As the Comprehensive Peace Agreement was negotiated, the WIPNET women united with MARWOPNET delegates[3] and sponsors from the United Nations Development Fund for Women (UNIFEM) to release a women's declaration, later known as the Golden Tulip Declaration (after the hotel in which they met). Referring to UN Security Council Resolution 1325 on Women, Peace and Security,[4] the women's declaration demanded greater participation of women in the peace process and disarmament processes and a quota of 50 percent for the inclusion of women in the transitional government (Golden Tulip Declaration, 2003).

The women advocated a war crimes tribunal, emphasizing their concerns about war rape and their fear that warring factions would be offered a blanket amnesty in return for signing the peace agreement.[5] Along with other members of civil society such as the Association of Female Lawyers of Liberia (AFELL), the women informally demanded that the warlords not be included in the transitional government (Hayner, 2007). But the final peace agreement did not live up to the women's expectations; it did not include the quotas for women, and it allowed the rebel leaders to secure positions of authority within the newly-created transitional government. Etweda Cooper recalls how differently the women and the rebel leaders understood the peace process:

> That is what it was all about at the end of the day. It was about jobs. 'I want to be the Minister of Justice, I want to be the Minister of Finance, so I can steal.' So are we supposed to pay you for killing us? And then one of the LURD members had come to me and said, 'Well, we're going to kill the people in Monrovia, and then we'll go back there, and we'll bring women with us, and we will replenish the population.' That was the foolishness he said to me. He became Deputy Minister of Defense. (*Pray the Devil Back to Hell*, 2008)

Despite the failures to incorporate all of the women's demands into the final agreement, the Mass Action for Peace played a key role in achieving the Comprehensive Peace Agreement (CPA). Following the signing of the CPA, Charles Taylor resigned and went into exile in Nigeria. Taylor's departure created a temporary absence of authority and an increase in violence, with both rebels and government soldiers engaging in a 'frenzy of rape', targeting thousands of women and girls (African Women and Peace Support Group, 2004). By September 2003, the arrival of peacekeepers from the Economic Community of West African States (ECOWAS) allowed for the establishment of Gyude Bryant's transitional government, reinstated order and marked the formal end of the war.

The Mass Action for Peace served to build a strong movement of women who were prepared to be vocal and visible political actors. Strategizing, recalled Gbowee, was key to the success of the movement:

> The movement we called the 'Mass Action for Peace' would later appear to be a spontaneous uprising. It was prompted by emotion – by women's exhaustion and desperation – but there was nothing spontaneous about it; managing a huge daily public protest was a complicated task and we planned every move we made ... We formed committees to handle different jobs, such as finding buses to bring women to the protest from the internally displaced persons camps. Every night a core of us, the WIPNET 21, met at the office and spent hours going over what had happened that day. (2011, p. 139)

The success of the movement came from hard work, planning and commitment. But in the post-conflict period there was still much work to be done. Gains achieved by women in times of conflict are always fragile; in every country experiencing a conflict to post-conflict transition, women are generally excluded from peace processes and post-conflict reconstruction efforts. It is also true that women who are very active during conflict are often relegated to their pre-conflict roles when wars end (Meintjes et al., 2001; Anderlini, 2007). The conflict to post-conflict transition is the crucial moment for women to build on their gains and prevent further losses.

The implications of these patterns were clear to Leymah Gbowee, who noted that after the peace agreement was signed, the women asked, 'have we really achieved what we thought we started to do? And the answer was a resounding "No. We need to do something more"' (United States Institute of Peace, 2007). In September 2003, WIPNET and MARWOPNET, together with the Liberian Women Initiative, educated over eighty women about the content and expected implementation of the peace agreement. They asked the women activists to keep their placards ready and remain vigilant should the parties not adhere to the agreement. 'Maintaining and sustaining the peace' became their new catchphrase (WIPNET, 2004; United States Institute of Peace, 2007).

'MAINTAINING AND SUSTAINING THE PEACE': REMAINING RELEVANT IN THE POST-CONFLICT PERIOD

A challenge common to many women's peace organizations forged in wartime is how to remain relevant once the 'peace' is achieved, as 'the return to peace is invariably conceptualized as a return to the gender status quo, irrespective of the nontraditional roles assumed by women during conflict' (Meintjes et al., 2001, p. 9). In Liberia, the women who had called for peace throughout the conflict were told that once the agreement was signed they should 'go back home and sit'. WIPNET's leaders, however, resisted this: 'Do we go back and sit? Hell, no!' declared Gbowee (United States Institute of Peace, 2007). They identified the disarmament process as their first key area of opportunity for continued engagement in peace and security issues.

The United Nations Mission in Liberia (UNMIL) was tasked with securing a country that had been completely destroyed by the previous fourteen years of war. It was UNMIL's responsibility to support the implementation of the Comprehensive Peace Agreement signed in Accra, facilitate humanitarian assistance and the return of refugees and Internally Displaced Persons (IDPs), protect civilians, disarm combatants – many of whom were children – and prepare for elections. In order to achieve these aims, the UN was to work alongside the National Transitional Government of Liberia (NTGL), headed by Gyude Bryant, a Monrovia businessman with no ties to any of the warring parties (Reno, 2007).

One of the first tasks of the UN Mission in Liberia was to set up the Disarmament, Demobilization, Rehabilitation and Reintegration (DDRR) process, which was central to establishing security. The Comprehensive Peace Agreement required combatants to disarm and demobilize. Disarmament generally happens at camps, also known as 'cantonments', where combatants are offered food, aid, shelter, education, skills training and sometimes money in exchange for their weapons (Anderlini, 2007, p. 96). In Liberia, Phase One of this process was to disarm Government of Liberia forces at Camp Scheffelin. The first attempt at disarmament, which took place on 7 December 2003, failed miserably; a near-riot forced the UN to suspend the program and led the International Crisis Group to call the first phase of the disarmament process a 'fiasco' (Cleaver and Massey, 2006; Spear, 2006).

The UN was accused of having failed to engage Liberians in the design of the first phase of the DDRR process, relying only on outside knowledge. While 'best practices' from the neighboring mission in Sierra Leone were applied, the experts who were brought in from outside conflicts such as Kosovo were not equipped to deal with the local context (Cleaver and Massey, 2006). As one of many civil society organizations asking to be part of the DDRR process, WIPNET were critical of UNMIL's ignorance of the situation on the ground and their lack of consultation with women's groups. The day after the riot, the WIPNET women met with Jacques Klein, the head of UNMIL, and issued a statement criticizing the UN effort. They called for calm among the fighters and urged people to trust in the disarmament process. As Gbowee observed, 'This failure was based on the UN's failure to get local knowledge on a lot of important issues. As a matter of fact, in consultation with them, we asked them, "Can you get local knowledge?", and they said no' (Gbowee and Gautam, 2006). UNMIL, which at the time did not have a gender unit or a gender advisor on staff, initially refused to include women peace activists in the disarmament process. This frustrated the women, as some had previously participated in disarmament processes following the First Civil War in Liberia in the 1990s, and they knew the fighters and the local context much better than the UN. Gbowee likened the UN's response to WIPNET to being told, 'your protest and other form of non violent protest actions were great but we think its [*sic*] time to go back home and take care of the kids' (Gbowee, 2005).

The failure of the first phase of the process led to an overhaul of the DDRR program (Aboagye and Bah, 2004). By April 2004 UNMIL attempted a second phase of disarmament and this time included the women (Gbowee and Gautam, 2006). UNMIL embarked on a partnership with WIPNET through their Public Information Office, attempting a new kind of 'door to door sensitization'. The goal of the sensitization program 'was to create the awareness amongst the combatants on the DDR package and the need for their involvement in the entire process' (WIPNET, 2004). WIPNET, as 'harmless and armless'[6] women, engaged in one-on-one dialogue with some of the rebels and appealed to the emotions of the ex-combatants, saying 'I'm your mother, I'm your sister.' The ex-combatants appeared to respond positively to the women (Author's interview with Kingsley Ighobor, 2006). A former fighter said the women were 'crying on us. So we listened to them.' Another later said, 'We appreciate them a lot and we are still there for them. They are our mothers' (*Pray the Devil Back to Hell*, 2008). This example shows how women's involvement in disarmament processes may be an effective way to get ex-combatants onside and willing to disarm, since they are more willing to listen to respected members of their community than to foreign and militarized UN peacekeepers. As Lindora Howard explained, 'we gained so much respect that even the ex-combatants, when time came that they didn't want to listen to UNMIL, when they didn't want to listen to the government, they were willing to listen to us' (Author's interview with Lindora Howard, 2006).

Anderlini suggests that women's involvement in disarmament can be helpful in convincing the combatants that *disarmament* does not denote *disempowerment* – as many disarmed fighters might 'feel stripped of their means of protection, their livelihood, and their identity' (2007, p. 106). In Liberia, the women sat with the combatants and took time to explain the process to them, showing them why disarmament was important to their community and their future. More than 3000 combatants benefited from this process (Gbowee, 2005).

WIPNET's involvement in the disarmament process may have contributed to changing attitudes regarding the inclusion of women in DDRR, at least within this mission. This was the view of an UNMIL Public Information official, who told the author in 2006 that the women's participation in the disarmament process had been essential to its success. As Gbowee has noted, DDRR is a highly patriarchal field: 'For peacekeepers from those areas it was unheard of for women to be in the frontline of DDRR' (Gbowee, 2005). Following the initial disarmament stage, the women were also asked to assist with the reintegration of ex-combatants in communities. Their experience with DDRR highlights the challenges for women peacebuilders to remain relevant in the post-conflict period, where women's concerns are considered secondary to 'hard' security issues. Yet, as this example shows, there are clear benefits to including women's civil society organizations in both the design and implementation of DDRR processes. The Liberian women's participation challenged their exclusion from the process, showing how they manipulated their status as women and particularly as mothers to play an important and essential role in ensuring the UN's approach to DDRR reflected the needs and interests of the entire community.

Promoting women in decision-making on issues of peace and security became one of WIPNET's priorities in the post-conflict period and the 2005 elections provided an opportunity for the organization to encourage women to participate in politics. WIPNET chose to be politically neutral during the electoral process and refused to support any political parties despite multiple requests for support or endorsement from candidates. Although WIPNET encouraged women to put themselves forward as candidates, members of the organization who decided to run in the elections were asked to submit letters withdrawing from WIPNET for the duration of the campaign.

When the electoral process began in 2005, WIPNET approached the United Nations Development Programme with concerns over low levels of voter registration among certain groups of women. As a result, UNDP asked WIPNET to engage in voter registration in market areas. Hundreds of volunteers watched market stalls, did laundry and cared for children to enable market women to register to vote. Over the course of five days, WIPNET registered 7477 women voters and at the end of the registration period women made up more than half of Liberia's registered voters (Gbowee and Gautam, 2006).

Women were highly visible in the election campaign that pitted Harvard graduate and economist Ellen Johnson-Sirleaf against million-aire footballer George Weah in the race for the Presidency, with support for Johnson-Sirleaf culminating in the tongue-in-cheek campaign slogan 'Ellen is our Man!' Johnson-Sirleaf's victory was widely seen as a victory for women; as Gbowee later said, 'I know that we laid the foundation [for Ellen's victory]' (*Pray the Devil Back to Hell*, 2008). WIPNET member Louise Tucolon explained, 'we have changed greatly ... Anything a man does, a woman is capable of doing it' (Author's interview with Louise Tucolon, 2006). There was a feeling among Liberian women that 'this is our time' (United States Institute for Peace, 2007).

Despite Johnson-Sirleaf's symbolic victory, some had reservations about Liberia's 'Iron Lady', who was seen as the establishment candidate – another elite woman who would ultimately maintain the status quo. Although she sponsored initiatives to aid market women and to promote women's education, one year into her term Johnson-Sirleaf was not making women's empowerment enough of a priority to satisfy some of the women activists. At a 2007 donor conference in Monrovia, women activists were dismayed to see that the President had excluded gender issues from her list of priority areas. As Gbowee commented,

> Liberian women are like, 'we have a woman President, and she will do it all for us!' but this is not the case ... Women need to understand that this is not a woman's President. She is a woman but she is the President of a nation ... We need to continue our advocacy, we need to continue to develop policies, we need to continue to be in the limelight. Unfortunately we are not. (United States Institute for Peace, 2007)

By 2011, however, Johnson-Sirleaf's work as President prompted Gbowee to support her in her bid to run for a second term as Liberian president. As Gbowee noted in her 2011 memoir,

> Under President Sirleaf, we've gotten the National Gender Policy to promote equality, a new sex crimes unit within the Ministry of Justice, and one of the strongest anti-rape laws in Africa ... Parliament is considering affirmative action legislation that would mandate 30 percent female representation in government, and more women than ever are in key positions. (p. 220)

Yet this was not all due to the work of 'Ma Ellen', as she is known; as Gbowee wrote, 'Oddly enough, the war did this for us – or rather, the widespread recognition that we helped bring the war to an end. We might have made progress anyway, but if we hadn't felt compelled to step into the public arena, it might have taken us a lot longer' (Gbowee, 2011, p. 220).

In the post-conflict period WIPNET continued to focus on the empowerment of rural women by developing peacebuilding programs in different communities where women-only spaces are being created for women to discuss issues of peace and security. WIPNET's education programs and the mobilization of thousands of women at the grassroots level are in themselves challenges to the marginalization of women in politics. In 2006 Gbowee left WIPNET and, wanting to increase women's participation in higher-level decision-making, launched the Women in Peace and Security Network (WIPSEN-Africa), a women-led organization promoting the participation and leadership of women in peace and security in Africa.

In 2008 the Liberian women's story became the focus of a major documentary film, *Pray the Devil Back to Hell*, produced by American Abigail Disney and directed by Gini Reticker. As a result of this film, the story of the Liberian women's struggle has been shown to women's groups in many countries, beginning with a screening in Srebrenica on International Women's Day 2008, followed by screenings to women activists in Peru, Ramallah, Jerusalem, Georgia, Afghanistan, Iraq and Sudan. According to Disney, '[women peace activists in other countries] see themselves in the film and they identify strongly with Leymah (Gbowee), because there's a Leymah in every room' (Sherr, 2008). Gbowee attends many of the international screenings and encourages other women to start their own peace campaigns. She says,

> This is a huge responsibility… I need to be that encouragement, not go into any conflict and to say to my sisters, 'I am here to teach you,' but to say 'I am here to walk with you … I feel your pain. I've been down this road. And I'll walk this walk with you. … I feel that is the fulfillment of my life'. (Sherr, 2008)

In 2011, Gbowee was awarded the Nobel Peace Prize alongside Ellen Johnson-Sirleaf and Yemen's Tawakkul Karman, 'for their non-violent struggle for the safety of women and for women's rights to full participation in peace-building work' (Nobel Peace Prize, 2011). Gbowee, who continues to work on gender, peace and security issues globally, has founded the Gbowee Peace Foundation Africa, based in Liberia, with a mission to help girls, women and youth develop leadership skills and become agents of change.

As noted in the introduction to this chapter, dominant stereotypes about women in wartime reflect a simplistic belief that women are peaceful and apolitical. Yet as the Liberian example shows, women can manipulate and exploit these stereotypes in order to become political – and powerful – actors, and to influence the peace process. The peace women of Liberia used their public identities as sisters, wives and mothers to articulate their alternative visions of peace and security based on social justice and an end to patriarchy. They emphasized the values of collaboration, solidarity, reconciliation and nonviolence and demanded that women be full and equal partners in decision-making. As Gbowee told the media after being awarded the Nobel Peace Prize, 'this … is a loud call that no more can we negotiate peace and leave fifty per cent of the world's population out' (Huffington Post, 2011).

NOTES

1. Bush wives were women taken against their will and forced to fight, cook and be spouses of soldiers.
2. For background and analysis of the origins and course of the conflicts in Liberia, see Ellis (1995); Utas (2005); Amnesty International (2008); Pan (2003); Cleaver and Massey (2006); Reno (2007).
3. These were the women delegates from the Mano River Union Women's Peace Network, who had been granted official observer status at the talks.
4. See http://www.un.org/womenwatch/osagi/wps/ for more information on this landmark resolution on women, peace and security.
5. A compromise between the warring factions and civil society resulted in the CPA-mandated Truth and Reconciliation Commission. See James-Allen et al. (2010).
6. This phrase was used by UNMIL Public Information Officer Kingsley Ighobor in an interview with the author.

REFERENCES

Aboagye, Festus and Alhaji M.S. Bah (2004), 'Liberia at a crossroads: a preliminary look at the United Nations mission in Liberia (UNMIL) and the protection of civilians', Occasional Paper No. 95, Institute of Security Studies, accessed 14 September 2015 at: https://www.issafrica.org/acpst/papers/liberia-at-a-crossroads-a-preliminary-look-at-the-united-nations-mission-in-liberia-unmil-and-the-protection-of-civilians.

African Women and Peace Support Group (2004), *Liberian Women Peacemakers: Fighting for the Right to be Seen, Heard and Counted*, Africa World Press.

Aisha, Fatoumata (2005), 'Mainstreaming gender in peace support operations: the United Nations Mission in Liberia', in Festus Aboagye and Alhaji M.S. Bah (eds), *A Tortuous Road to Peace: the Dynamics of Regional, UN and International Humanitarian Interventions in Liberia*, Institute for Security Studies, pp. 147–63.

Amnesty International (2008), 'Women of Liberia: fighting for peace', accessed 14 September 2015 at: http://peacemedia.usip.org/resource/women-liberia-fighting-peace.

Anderlini, Sanam Naraghi (2007), *Women Building Peace: What they do, Why it Matters*, Lynne Rienner.

Cain, Kenneth (1999), 'The rape of Dinah: human rights, civil war in Liberia, and evil triumphant', *Human Rights Quarterly*, **21** (2): 265–307.

Cleaver, Gerry and Simon Massey (2006), 'Liberia: a durable peace at last?', in Oliver Furley and Roy May (eds), *Ending Africa's Wars: Progressing to Peace*, Ashgate, pp. 179–99.

Cockburn, Cynthia (2007), *From Where we Stand: War, Women's Activism and Feminist Analysis*, Zed Books.

Ekiyor, Thelma Aremiebi and Leymah Roberta Gbowee (2005), 'Women's peace activism in West Africa: the WIPNET Experience', in Paul Van Tongeren, Malin Brenk, Marte Hellema and Juliette Verhoeven (eds), *People Building Peace II: Successful Stories of Civil Society* (European Centre for Conflict Prevention), Lynne Rienner.

Ellis, Stephen (1995), 'Liberia 1989–1994: a study of ethnic and spiritual violence', *African Affairs*, **94** (375): 165–97.

Galtung, Johan (1996), *Peace by Peaceful Means: Peace and Conflict, Development and Civilization*, International Peace Research Institute.

Gbowee, Leymah Roberta (2005), 'Women building peace through Disarmament, Demobilisation and Reintegration', Speech to UNIFEM Panel on DDRR at the Beijing+10 CSW Conference, 9 March, speech no longer available online, summary of proceedings accessed 14 September 2015 at: http://www.peacewomen.org/assets/file/Resources/UN/unifem_buildingpeaceddr_2005.pdf.

Gbowee, Leymah (with Carol Mithers) (2011), *Mighty be our Powers: How Sisterhood, Prayer, and Sex Changed a Nation at War*, Beast Books.

Gbowee, Leymah and Shobha Gautam (2006), 'A conversation with women peacebuilders: Leymah Gbowee and Shobha Gautam', Boston Consortium on Gender, Security and Human Rights, 8 March, accessed 14 September 2015 at: http://genderandsecurity.org/projects-resources/consortium-lectures/conversation-women-peacebuilders-leymah-gbowee-and-shobha.

Golden Tulip Declaration (2003), accessed 14 September 2015 at: http://www.peace women.org/e-news/golden-tulip-declaration-liberian-women-attending-peace-talks-accra-ghana.

Hayner, Priscilla (2007), 'Negotiating peace in Liberia: preserving the possibility for justice', Centre for Humanitarian Dialogue and the International Center for Transitional Justice.

Hoffman, Danny (2004), 'The civilian target in Sierra Leone and Liberia: political power, military strategy, and humanitarian intervention', *African Affairs*, **103**: 211–26.

Huffington Post (2011), 'Leymah Gbowee: an interview with the 2011 Nobel Prize Winner', 8 October, accessed 14 September 2015 at: http://www.huffingtonpost.com/2011/10/07/leymah-gbowee-nobel-prize_n_1000887.html.

James-Allen, Paul, Aaron Weah and Lizzie Goodfriend (2010), 'Beyond the Truth and Reconciliation Commission: transitional justice operations in Liberia', International Centre for Transitional Justice.

Kaufman, Joyce and Kristen Williams (2010), *Women and War: Gender Identity and Activism in Times of Conflict*, Kumarian.

Klay Kieh Jr, George (2003), 'Liberia: legacies and leaders', in Chandra Lekha Sriram and Karin Wermester (eds), *From Promise to Practice: Strengthening UN Capacities for the Prevention of Violent Conflict*, Lynne Rienner, pp. 307–26.

Meintjes, Sheila, Anu Pillay and Meredeth Turshen (2001), 'There is no aftermath for women', in Sheila Meintjes, Anu Pillay and Meredeth Turshen (eds), *The Aftermath: Women in Post-Conflict Transformation*, Zed Books, pp. 3–18.

Moran, Mary (2008), *The Violence of Democracy*, University of Pennsylvania Press.

Moran, Mary and Anne Pitcher (2004), 'The "basket case" and the "poster child": explaining the end of civil conflicts in Liberia and Mozambique', *Third World Quarterly*, **25** (3): 501–19.

Moser, Caroline and Fiona Clark (eds) (2001), *Victims, Perpetrators or Actors? Gender, Armed Conflict and Political Violence*, Zed Books.

Murray, Rebecca (2009), 'The fight against rape a brutal wait', *AllAfrica*, 14 September, accessed 13 September 2015 at: http://allafrica.com/stories/200909141478.html.

Nobel Peace Prize (2011), accessed 14 September 2015 at: http://www.nobelprize.org/nobel_prizes/peace/laureates/2011/gbowee.html.

Olukoju, Ayodeji (2006), *Culture and Customs of Liberia*, Greenwood.

O'Neill, April and Leora Ward (2005), 'Building peace on fragile foundations: the Liberian challenge', Occasional Paper No. 6, Kofi Annan International Peacekeeping Training Centre.

Pan, Esther (2003), 'Liberia: child soldiers', *Council on Foreign Relations*, 29 August, accessed 14 September 2015 at: http://www.cfr.org/publication/7753/.

Porter, Elizabeth (2007), *Peacebuilding: Women in International Perspective*, Routledge.

Pray the Devil Back to Hell (2008), Documentary, produced by Abigail Disney and directed by Gini Reticker, Fork Films.

Reno, William (2007), 'Liberia: the LURDs of the New Church', in Morten Boas and Kevin C. Dunn (eds), *African Guerrillas: Raging Against the Machine*, Lynne Rienner, pp. 69–80.

Sherr, Lynn (2008), 'Interview with Leymah Gbowee and Abigail E. Disney', *Bill Moyers Journal* (Public Affairs Television), available on *Pray the Devil Back to Hell* DVD (Fork Films).

Solomon, Christina (2005), 'The Mano River Union sub-region: the role of women in building peace', in Rawwida Baksh, Linda Etchart, Elsie Onubogu and Tina Johnson (eds), *Gender Mainstreaming in Conflict Transformation: Building Sustainable Peace*, Commonwealth Secretariat, pp. 171–80.

Spear, Joanna (2006), 'Disarmament, demobilization, reinsertion and reintegration in Africa', in Oliver Furley and Roy May (eds), *Ending Africa's Wars: Progressing to Peace*, Ashgate, pp. 63–80.

United States Institute of Peace (2007), 'Women's role in the reconstruction of Liberia', 23 April, audio, accessed 14 September 2015 at: http://www.usip.org/events/womens-role-in-the-reconstruction-liberia.

Utas, Mats (2005), 'Victimcy, girlfriending, soldiering: tactic agency in a young woman's social navigation of the Liberian war zone', *Anthropological Quarterly*, **78** (2): 403–30.

WIPNET (2004), 'Women in Peacebuilding Network – Liberia annual report', Monrovia.

Yuval-Davis, Nira (2004), 'Gender, the nationalist imagination, war, and peace', in Giles and Hyndman (eds), *Sites of Violence: Gender and Conflict Zones*, University of California Press, pp. 170–91.

Interviews – Conducted in Monrovia, Liberia in March 2006

Asatu Bah-Kenneth
Etweda 'Sugars' Cooper
Cecelia Danuweli
Vaiba Flomo
Lindora Howard
Kingsley Ighobor
Grace Jarsor
Louise Tucolon

20. Gender and the Campaign for Nuclear Disarmament in the 1960s

Jodi Burkett

INTRODUCTION

The gendered history of war and peace is a thriving area of research, as is clearly demonstrated by this volume. This chapter is concerned with gender and gendered concepts within one, rather atypical, peace organization. The Campaign for Nuclear Disarmament (CND), formed in 1958 in the United Kingdom, was not, by its own definition, a peace organization but a group focused on opposing nuclear weapons. However, it was the largest and best-known organization of the 1960s that advocated peaceful solutions to international problems. CND has gone through a number of manifestations and continues to function as an anti-nuclear campaigning organization. Its fortunes have been very much tied to the Cold War, attracting more supporters in times of heightened tension. During the first four years after its founding, CND grew to many thousands before its membership dropped off from the mid-1960s. It then went through a great revival in the early 1980s before its membership again subsided in the aftermath of the Cold War. This chapter focuses on the first phase of the organization throughout the 'long 1960s' from its creation in 1958 to the early 1970s. Officially, CND was interested only in opposing nuclear weapons, but in practice the majority of its members and supporters saw nuclear weapons as a symptom of the wider problem of war to which they were fundamentally opposed. The focus on nuclear weapons alone was a tactical move rather than one that reflected the political stance of its membership and was constantly a matter of debate within the organization itself. This chapter examines the dynamics of gender within CND, exploring both how the actions and activities of the organization were structured and informed by gendered attitudes and ideas, and also how the rhetoric of the organization used gendered norms to appeal to its audience and provide its own interpretation of the major issues of the day. First, however, we examine the scholarship in three key areas within which CND must be understood: gender and peace; gender and the Cold War; and shifting attitudes towards gender in post-war Britain.

CND IN ITS HISTORICAL CONTEXT

There is a longstanding and often repeated link between women, feminism and pacifism. Jill Liddington asserts strongly that 'any history of peace politics which ignores the issue of gender and ignores the powerful language and imagery of women and peace remains inadequate and misleading; so is any history of feminism in Britain which omits peace ideas and campaigns' (Liddington, 1989, p. 5). For Liddington, peace and gender, or more particularly, peace and women, are inseparable. Liddington was certainly not the first person to assert this connection. Heloise Brown demonstrates the relationship between pacifism and feminism at the end of the nineteenth century, and points out that women often used this connection to put forward their arguments for greater equality. She begins her book on pacifist feminism in Britain by quoting Lydia Becker, a feminist and pacifist who wrote in 1870 that 'War is an essentially masculine pursuit. Women do not as a rule seek to quench their differences in blood. Fighting is not natural to them' (Brown, 2003, p. 1). As Brown illustrates, many women in the late nineteenth and early twentieth centuries played up this perceived connection between women and peace to argue that women are inherently different from men. This, they claimed, made female input into all aspects of politics and society a necessity (Brown, 2003, p. 1). This connection also helped to bolster the argument that women were moral agents and that their different view of the world and different strengths should be recognized, honored and utilized. Lucy Noakes agrees with Brown, saying that while the first widely recognized 'feminist-pacifist' organization was the Women's International League for Peace and Freedom created in 1915, 'female pacifist activism existed long before this' (Noakes, 2001, p. 316).

Noakes further points out that not only was pacifism used to bolster feminist ideas, but that feminism was also used to give added strength to pacifist objectives. As she states, 'women in peace groups have often chosen to project a particular representation of femininity in order to stress their opposition to man-made wars' (Noakes, 2001, p. 319). Thus it was not just a link between pacifism and feminism that was being constructed, but also a notion of femininity that would support and conform to this ideal. As Joan Scott has demonstrated, gender is itself culturally constructed and so is the perceived 'naturalness' of the association between women and pacifism (Scott, 1999, pp. 43–4). As Inger Skjelsbaek and Dan Smith point out, this construction was largely done in opposition to the construction of military masculinity. Holding men responsible for wars has allowed for a line of argument that sees women as 'inherently peaceful' (Skjelsbaek and Smith, 2001, p. 2). Heloise Brown and Bernice Carroll, amongst others, have also taken up this point. They too argue that the connection between women and peace is not natural but constructed. Carroll asserts that this is not necessarily positive, as it 'is a connection imposed upon women along with their subordination, their disarmed condition, and their stereotyped roles' (Carroll, 1987, pp. 15-16; Brown, 2003, p. 2). Michael Salla also finds that this may not be a positive construction, warning that it is an essentialized understanding of men and women, which argues that men and women think differently, that perpetuates the connection between women and peace (Salla, 2001, p. 70).

Mary Burguieres (1990) has explored the ways in which feminists have criticized these essentialist notions by undermining both sides of the dichotomy – the 'women and peace' connection and the 'men and war' connection – or by abandoning both (Burguieres quoted in Salla, 2001, p. 71). The danger of this essentialized position, according to Emily Rosenberg, is that it conveys the impression that biology rather than culture explains women's marginality (Rosenberg, 1990, p. 117). This highlights a fundamental argument within women's organizations about whether they should stress women's differences from men, which could seem inherent and therefore justify women's marginal place in society, or stress equality, which could then encourage women to mimic male behaviors rather than challenge them. This is a longstanding debate amongst feminists and is often manifest in the debate about whether they should promote women as different from, but equal to men, or indeed argue that men and women are more similar than different. These arguments often coexist within the same organizations at the same time. CND was not a specifically feminist-pacifist organization, but it was certainly informed and defined in part by the perceived connection between women and pacifism. This chapter takes as its starting point the constructed nature of this connection and examines how anti-nuclear activism and gender identities helped define each other within this context.

Unlike many earlier feminist-pacifist organizations, CND was decidedly mixed in its gender makeup. Examining the gendered dynamics at work within CND therefore allows us to examine both sides of the traditional dichotomy. The men who were part of this organization certainly did not fit the masculine ideal that associated men with war.

The gendered dynamics of CND were complicated, encompassing both traditional notions of gender roles and newer, sometimes subversive attitudes. During the period on which this chapter focuses, CND was very much a product of its time, reflecting attitudes towards gender norms in Britain in the late 1950s and early 1960s. But these norms and ideas were not static or homogeneous. As many scholars have shown, gender norms had been under stress and the subject of significant transformation in the first half of the twentieth century. Both world wars had a substantial impact on notions of masculinity and femininity and these were used to promote a variety of actions and activities both during war and in peacetime. After the Second World War there was a renewed emphasis on domesticity for both men and women. As men returned from combat women were encouraged to return to the home and focus on bearing and bringing up children. The welfare state that was created by the new Labour government under Clement Attlee was based on the assumption that a family was composed of a husband who went out to work and a wife who stayed home and looked after children (Hall, 2000, p. 146). However, the extent to which this assumption matched reality is highly debatable (Kingsley-Kent, 1999, p. 319). The post-war baby boom attests to the fact that many women did indeed have children in the late 1940s and early 1950s. However, it was also clear that attitudes and ideas about gender, marriage and the family were changing (Brooke, 2001). With the increasing affluence of the late 1950s and early 1960s men too were encouraged to focus on the family and home, especially as a growing number of working class families were able to buy their own homes. Contemporary commentators remarked on the domestication of the 'new man' who would rather spend his spare time doing odd jobs around the house than drinking in the pub (Zweig, 1961). There has been a move within historical scholarship to see the 1950s not as a period of stability before major changes in gender identity and relations took place in the 1960s, but rather as a time when fundamental shifts were taking place below the surface, when a sense prevailed 'that old constraints were falling away' (Hall, 2000, p. 166).

While the focus of many ordinary people in Britain was overwhelmingly domestic, CND was concerned with the international situation and Britain's place in the Cold War world order (Burkett, 2010). The organization therefore had to bridge the gap between the domestic and the international, and put a great deal of effort into trying to convince British society of the need to be interested in and concerned about foreign affairs and Britain's international policies. The significance of nuclear weapons to politics and the fate of humanity was demonstrated just a few years after the founding of CND, when the Cuban Missile

Crisis arguably brought the world as close as it has ever come to nuclear annihilation. But while CND was part of a tradition of peace groups which were largely gendered feminine, it also worked to influence a very male dominated sphere of foreign policy and international diplomacy: the high international politics of the Cold War (Tickner, 2001, p. 37). CND was thus defining itself against established norms that were understood to be masculine. This helps to reinforce the notion that pacifist groups are associated with femininity or feminism but raises the question what impact this gendered identification had on the masculinity of those men who were involved in CND, either in the leadership or among the rank and file. As John Tosh has reminded us, the gendered structure of society is not only made up of unequal power relations between men and women, but also between men. The term 'hegemonic masculinity' has been most often used to refer to the culturally established assumptions that create a 'common sense' about what it is to be a man (Tosh, 2004, pp. 42–3). As Tosh shows, many different types of men do not fit into this norm, particularly homosexual men. This 'deviant' sexuality, he argues, 'is systematically employed to discipline not only sexual deviants but other marginal masculinities'. In particular, male pacifists have often been branded as homosexuals as a way of questioning their manhood (Tosh, 2004, p. 46), a subject to which we will return below.

Key to the understanding of hegemonic masculinity, as with all gender constructions, is that it is not static but is in a continual process of adaptation. A number of studies of the Second World War have shown, perhaps unsurprisingly, the importance of military service to the construction of masculinity. Despite the fact that large numbers of men were in protected occupations and never served in the military, as Sonya Rose has argued, 'being visibly a member of the fighting services was necessary to the performance of wartime masculinity' (Rose, 2003, p. 178). Penny Summerfield too has argued that policy-makers during the war emphasized 'the young fit male' in an effort to rehabilitate military masculinity after the damage that was done to it during the Great War. By implication, then, those men who were not at the front during the war were 'either too young, or too old, or unfit' (Summerfield, 1998, p. 177). While this was clearly not the case, it was widely assumed and widely believed. During the Second World War, and continuing in the post-war period, pacifism was associated with being unmanly. However, as Salla has pointed out, this was successfully challenged in the post-war period by a number of prominent men using non-violent tactics including Mahatma Gandhi and Martin Luther King (Salla, 2001, p. 76). Although Salla does not discuss them directly, the leadership of CND was at the forefront of the challenge to the assumed link between militarism and masculinity in Britain. Many of the male members and leaders of CND had lived through the Second World War and their wartime experiences had not necessarily fit this hegemonic notion of masculinity. During the war, J.B. Priestley, whose writing later spurred the creation of CND and who was on its first Executive Committee, presented a number of radio broadcasts in which he articulated this dominant military masculinity, although Priestley depicted himself as too old to fight, having done his bit in the previous war (Summerfield, 1998, p. 119). Another key figure in the early phase of CND, Bertrand Russell, a mathematician and philosopher who was CND's first President, had been a conscientious objector during the First World War and spent the majority of the Second World War in the United States (Ryan, 1988).

The first phase of CND also coincides with a period – the 1960s – that is widely associated with dramatic social and cultural transformations in Britain and throughout the West (McWilliams, 2000; Marwick, 1998; DeGroot, 2009). The 1960s are popularly seen as a time when gender roles were subverted and transformed. However, many of the key legislative and social changes that impacted on gender norms occurred only very late in the 1960s or in the early 1970s. For the majority of people in Britain, traditional gender norms and stereotypes were remarkably persistent throughout the 1960s. Yet it is clear that the transformations associated with this decade could not have occurred without profound social and cultural changes taking place, if only subtly, throughout the 1950s and 1960s. CND reflects both the continuity and the stirrings of change in gender norms during this period. The leadership of CND was made up of a number of important, powerful and well-known men. The first Chairman, John Collins, was the Canon of St Paul's Cathedral. The vast majority of those on the first Executive Committee were listed in *Who's Who*, an annual publication providing bibliographies of notable Britons. These included J.B. Priestley, Professor Joseph Rotblatt, a prominent scientist who was awarded the Nobel Peace Prize for his work opposing nuclear weapons, and Michael Foot, long-time Labour MP (Driver, 1964, p. 44). There were, of course, a number of women involved in the organization at this early stage, although, as in the majority of organizations at this time, they were in supporting roles. The most important of these was Peggy Duff, a long-time activist and the first general secretary of the organization. It was Duff's energy and hard work that made the organization a success in this early period. By the mid-1960s the top leadership positions in CND were no longer occupied by men: Russell resigned from the Presidency in 1961, followed by Collins's resignation in 1964. The next two chairmen of CND were women: Olive Gibbs took over in 1964 and was replaced by Sheila Oakes in 1967. In turn, when Duff left the position of General Secretary in 1967 the position was taken up by Dick Nettleton. The traditional gendered division between the male face of the campaign and the female working behind the scenes was, therefore, reversed by the end of the decade.

The subtle changes of attitude towards gender in the 1950s and 1960s came to fruition in the late 1960s and early 1970s. The Women's Liberation movement emerged in Britain in 1969 and was, in part, built on women's experiences in organizations like CND. Many young women who had been active in the peace movement, and particularly CND, developed skills that they used to advance other causes, such as women's liberation. According to Lawrence Wittner, the importance of nuclear weapons in changing attitudes towards gender has largely been over-looked. The bomb changed the world so fundamentally that 'gender roles could hardly remain unaffected'. It is nuclear weapons and nuclear culture to which scholars should turn if they are looking for 'the missing link between the conventional gender norms of the immediate post war decade and the emerging women's liberation movement of the late 1960s' (Wittner, 2000, p. 197). CND was implicated in and participated in this wider transformation. The next part of this chapter explores in detail how gender dynamics played out within CND.

THE GENDERED MAKEUP OF CND

In the early 1950s much of the work against nuclear weapons and nuclear weapon testing was being done on a local level and often by women's organizations. One of the most famous of these, as discussed by Jill Liddington and Adam Lent, was the Golders Green Committee for the Abolition of Nuclear Weapons founded by Gertrude Fishwick, a former suffragette (Liddington, 1989, p. 178; Lent, 2001, p. 40). These women's groups had a great deal of experience of protest and formed the basis of many local CND groups. The first mixed-sex anti-nuclear groups fol-lowed rather traditional gender norms (Wittner, 2000, p. 197). Wittner found that while men tended to dominate mixed gender demonstrations, when it came to the actual membership of organized groups, it was women who outnumbered men (Wittner, 2000, p. 198). As an example of this phenomenon, he uses the National Council for the Abolition of Nuclear Weapon Tests (NCANWT), an organization that preceded CND and in fact wound up its activity and donated all remaining resources to CND when the latter was created. The NCANWT had a male chair, but it also had some prominent women members including Sheila Jones, who was the secretary of the group, and Peggy Duff, who worked as the chief of staff. The majority of members were also women (Wittner, 2000, p. 199).

As discussed above, the early leadership of CND was made up of prominent men. It is thus relatively easy to gather information about them, their lives and attitudes. However, the vast majority of the organization's members and activists are largely hidden from the historical record. CND did not have an official membership register until 1967. For its early years, therefore, there are no records about who was involved and their backgrounds, attitudes and ideas. In the late 1960s sociologist Frank Parkin undertook a survey to determine the makeup of the organization (Parkin, 1968). However, he, like many of the scholars of CND who followed him, was much more interested in determining the class background of those involved rather than the gendered makeup of the organization. Paul Byrne too was particularly interested in the middle class identity of the CND membership (Byrne, 1988, p. 1). Others who published early work on the composition of CND were concerned with the age profile of the organization's membership. Christopher Driver, writing in 1964, was particularly taken with the youthful makeup of participants in the Aldermaston marches (Driver, 1964, p. 55). The gender of participants or members, however, was simply not deemed a topic worthy of discussion by these scholars. This attitude was not unique to male writers. Peggy Duff herself did not treat gender as an important topic in her autobiographical work on CND and the other protest organizations of which she was a member (Duff, 1971). As Liddington comments, 'the popular impact of feminism and the peace–gender debate was extremely limited' within CND. Instead, Liddington continues, 'the inherited image of CND is predominantly one of angry young men' rather than representing the feminists who were so fundamental to its foundation (Liddington, 1989, pp. 175, 189). But while there are no substantive studies of the gendered makeup of CND from this period, much of the published work does not support the popular image of CND as dominated by 'angry young men' but shows that women were the backbone of the organization, if not its official public persona.

As mentioned above, the domination of men at the top of the organization did not last. It was an important feature of the first six years of the organization, but from 1964, when Canon Collins resigned, the next two chairs of CND were women. While the chairperson was certainly an important figure within CND it was the general secretary Peggy Duff who did most of the day-to-day work of the organization. Within local CND groups it also seems it was women who, in the main, were the driving force. This was at odds with the image that CND itself wanted to portray of an organization that was open to anyone and the responsibility of everyone. CND promoted its membership as 'factory workers, some white-collar men, some ordinary wives and mothers' ('Introducing CND', 1962). Throughout the 1960s and into the 1970s CND continued to depict itself as an organization that united men and women. In fact one of the most popular songs at the first Aldermaston march in 1958 clearly stated 'Men and women stand together!' However, it did continue by imploring them 'do not heed the men of war' (Wittner, 2000, p. 211; 'Seven years of marching against the bomb', 1965). While CND depicted its membership as men and women united in opposing nuclear weapons, CND members were also seen to be opposing men and men's desire to propagate these weapons. In 1962 when the CND newspaper *Sanity* printed an article introducing the organization and its aims, it clearly stated that the campaign 'consists of men and women'. The article tried to show their members' 'ordinariness', their desire to know the truth and their rational character ('This is your campaign and these are its aims', 1962). A decade later *Sanity* continued to print articles which referred to 'a new generation of ordinary men and women' who were joining CND and other protest groups and who were 'less inclined than their fathers and predecessors to accept the old myths at their face value' (Heelas, 1972). It is important to note that this new generation of supporters was described as different from their fathers. Their mothers, apparently, did not figure.

CND was composed not only of local groups, but also of groups organized around particular identity markers. For example, there were active Christian and Youth CND groups throughout the 1960s. Early in 1958 a Women's Group was also set up (Minutes of CND Executive Committee Meeting, 1 June, 1958). Women's meetings were held, women's deputations were sent to talk to women MPs, and specific literature was created for women supporters (Minutes of CND Executive Committee Meeting, 15 December, 1958 and 29 June, 1958). According to Wittner, they also 'revised CND's unilateralist slogan ["Let Britain Lead"] into: "Let Britain's Women Lead"' (Wittner, 2000, p. 199). Some scholars have pointed to this group to show the importance of women to CND in this period (Noakes, 2001, p. 318). However, the reasons why such a group was wanted or needed were never really discussed within the organization or by scholars. Diana Collins, one of the founding members of the CND Women's Group, did comment that when planning a 'women-only meeting' in 1958 one of the reasons for excluding men was 'perhaps [that] we feared they [men] might be tempted to mock us' (Collins, 1992, p. 234). Unfortunately, she does not develop this idea any further. It is difficult to determine if this sentiment was widely shared and whether it reflects the women's concerns about men outside of the organization or equally applied to men inside CND. It is, however, certainly reminiscent of comments from many women's activists in the late 1960s and early 1970s, who complained about men laughing at them when they tried to raise serious points about their treatment (Rowbotham, 2002, p. 251).

There are many reasons why specialist groups were created within CND. Some, like Youth CND, were designed to represent an ignored or under-represented aspect of the membership to the Executive Committee. The creation of a women's group could therefore suggest that many women members felt alienated from a male-dominated organization. However, there are also examples of groups organized not to represent people who were perceived as marginal but to better speak to a community who, it was assumed, had an affinity with CND and would be more inclined to support the organization if it appealed to them directly. This was the case with Christian CND and the same logic may have been at work in the decision to create the Women's Group.

To further complicate matters, the Women's Group did not last long. There were representatives from the Women's Group of CND at the National Co-ordinating Committee meetings sporadically in 1959 and 1960 but not consistently enough to suggest that it was an active and involved member of the CND community during these years (Minutes of CND National Co-ordinating Committee, 15 May, 1958). By 1960 it would appear that the Women's Group was largely defunct, although there continued to be efforts in the following years to organize specific events targeted at women (Minutes of CND National Council Meeting, 29 October, 1961). In the late 1960s CND resumed its interest in targeting women directly. In late 1967, after Sheila Oakes had taken over as Chairman and Dick Nettleton as General Secretary, CND's newspaper *Sanity* began to run a regular feature on the 'Women's Campaign' ('Women's Campaign', 1967). This feature was very short-lived but did continue briefly into 1968 and included items that the editor evidently believed would interest CND's women members, such as a recipe from Vietnam ('Women's Campaign', 1968). CND's Women's Group was not tied to the new, more radical groups associated with the women's liberation movement or reflect these attitudes. Instead it continued to put forward more traditional notions of femininity based on women's domestic activities (Wittner, 2000, p. 205).

CND was not the only anti-nuclear organization in Britain in this period and each one had specific gendered dynamics. There were divisions between the groups based largely on the question of tactics, specifically the use of direct action or civil disobedience (Burkett, 2009).

The Direct Action Committee Against Nuclear Weapons Tests (DAC) predated CND and, as can be seen from its name, advocated a direct action approach. The DAC managed to work well alongside CND for the first three years of its existence with a great deal of overlap in membership between the two organizations. However, this dynamic changed in 1961 with the formation of the competitor organization that posed the greatest challenge to CND, the Committee of 100, and the dissolution of the DAC, which was heavily in debt and decided to wind up its activities and join the Committee of 100 en masse. The Committee of 100 was set up in 1961 by Bertrand Russell and Michael Scott and precipitated Russell's resignation as President of CND and a rift between him and Canon Collins that never really healed (Russell, 1969; Collins, 1966). It was the opinion of Russell, and others, that CND was moving too slowly and that the urgency of the anti-nuclear argument required a more direct approach including civil disobedience.

The creation of the Committee of 100 did not end the debate within CND about the use of direct action tactics (Byrne, 1988, p. 45). This divide continued and seemed to line up with a number of other divisions within the organization, particularly those of geography and generation. The evidence, which is limited, suggests that in the main arguments for keeping CND a pressure group which used only legal means came from suburban areas and from middle-aged supporters, while arguments for the use of direct action came more strongly from urban groups and younger supporters (Boulton, 1963). Other discussions of these divisions within CND also suggest that they may illustrate a gendered division. The suburban middle-aged groups tended, in the main, to be dominated by women, while young men tended to be predominant in urban groups. It may not be surprising that young men were more vocal in supporting potentially dangerous and illegal activities, but it does raise some interesting questions for the scholarship of these tactical discussions that have not yet been examined.

The differences between the gendered dynamics of CND and the Committee of 100 may shed some light on this topic. Sam Carroll (2004) has written a fascinating article based on interviews with some of those who belonged to the Committee of 100 in the 1960s to explore their perceptions of the gender dynamics of that organization. Carroll found that the Committee of 100 organized itself in a way that was deliberately opposed to CND's structure. Although women's issues were largely absent from the Committee of 100's agenda, which is not surprising given the time period, its different organization created 'a more egalitarian environment for political activism by women as well as men'

(Carroll, 2004, pp. 10–11). While CND functioned using a strict hier-archy both within groups and between local groups and the London based executive, the Committee of 100 'established itself on the princi-pals [*sic*] of anti-hierarchy and consensus', which Carroll argues meant that 'gendered discrimination for women in the groups was less extreme than in other radical campaigns of the time', specifically CND, and in relation to the wider society (Carroll, 2004, pp. 11–13). While in the main Carroll found that women members of the Committee of 100 felt that the organization had been 'inclusive and fair', some also recalled 'a lingering sense of intimidation resting on gender' (Carroll, 2004, p. 14). The legacy of the Committee of 100's organization and tactics may further reveal the gendered nature of this division. One of the women Carroll interviewed, Sasha Roseneil, reminds us that it was 'the Commit-tee of 100's stress on the responsibility of individuals to oppose nuclear weapons and their opposition to the parliamentarian "Labour-path" strategy of the Campaign for Nuclear Disarmament (CND), [which] were precursors of Greenham's ethos and mode of action in the 1980s' (Carroll, 2004, p. 24).

Greenham Common was an RAF base in Berkshire at which a women's peace camp was established in 1981 and where a protesting presence remained for the next 19 years. What is particularly relevant to this chapter is that when women in the 1980s were looking for appropri-ate and authentic tactics to adopt, they turned to the Committee of 100 rather than to the CND ethos. This could simply tell us about the perceived effectiveness of the two groups, but may indeed say something more about the assessment of these women that they would be happier and more comfortable working within a more egalitarian process.

CND AND THE RHETORIC OF GENDER

Despite the reluctance within CND, and by many scholars of CND, to engage with issues of gender it is clear that the organization put forward particular ideals of both masculinity and femininity. The identity of CND as a whole was firmly rooted in a Christian morality that informed its actions and activities. James Hinton argues that this ability to meld morality and politics was at the root of their success (Hinton, 1989, p. 161). This meant that CND fitted very well into the traditions of pacifist feminism that was strongly moralistic in character (Brown, 2003, p. 7) but it put male members of the organization more firmly outside the bounds of hegemonic masculinity. The latter had to contend with accusations that their anti-nuclear activities meant they were unpatriotic, an important aspect of manliness in this period (Brandon, 1987, p. 42). Wittner agrees with the assessment that 'male nuclear disarmament proponents could hardly help noticing that their masculinity was sometimes in question'. As mentioned above, 'at demonstrations, they were baited not only as "commies", but as "fags"' (Wittner, 2000, pp. 206–7). However, there is little sense from the CND literature that male members were particularly concerned with these aspersions cast on their masculinity. Instead, they appeared to embrace an alternative type of masculinity which partly looked back to that of the war and earlier with its connections to the conscientious objector, but also showed the growth of the new 'domesticated' post-war male (Minutes of CND Executive Committee Meeting, 21 February, 1963; Zweig, 1961). For example, while child care was still largely the purview of women in the late 1950s and 1960s, children were often a primary concern of CND. This was an interesting and important choice for a male-dominated organization (Wittner, 2000, p. 207). And CND's interest in child welfare was not limited to the impact of nuclear weapons and nuclear fallout on children. There was a group within CND known as the CND Constructive Service that participated in work such as clearing an area near King's Cross in London to create a children's playground ('Building instead of Blasting', 1962). CND's notion of masculinity, however, came under criticism during discussions of non-violence. Manliness was used on both sides of the debate to argue, on the one hand, that CND should be involved in physically and directly opposing nuclear weapons and, on the other, that CND should remain a pressure group focusing on gaining publicity and symbolically opposing nuclear weapons. This first side of the debate was voiced in 1966 in relation to the Vietnam War. One CND supporter argued in the organization's newspaper that they could not simply cheer the Vietnamese National Liberation Front into battle from the safety of Great Britain. This, he said, was what Bertrand Russell was doing and 'from an old man it's just pathetic'. Instead, it was 'the job of the Peace Movement to get them [the United States] out' of Vietnam. How exactly they should do that, was unclear (Leaver, 1966). While the organization officially stood for non-violence, it was acknowledged that violence was necessary in certain circumstances and the 'heroes' of those within the movement, especially the youth, were seen to be men of violence including 'Che Guevara, Ho Chi Minh, Stokely Carmichael' (Jones, 1968). Thus the generational divide within CND that seemed to open in the late 1960s also included a move towards embracing a more traditionally violent masculinity.

While the masculinity espoused by CND in the early 1960s did not fit into the norms of hegemonic masculinity, neither did the ideal femininity espoused by the organization fit neatly into established norms (Wittner, 2000, p. 206). It is certainly true that a maternal femininity was accepted and put forward by CND, but this was not an entirely domesticated maternal identity. Women participants in CND activities were also involved in political action, and more particularly political activism, to a greater extent than was the contemporary norm for British women (Carroll, 2004, p. 10). Invoking the traditional female role as mother can thus be seen as a way of combating the impression that CND was outside gender norms. It was not uncommon for women within CND to present themselves as mothers in appealing to potential supporters as well as to apply further pressure to those in power (Wittner, 2000, p. 203). The imagery of motherhood was used extensively in CND publications. In 1964 the front cover of *Sanity* carried a photo of a breastfeeding baby to accompany a story on the Youth declaration that year titled 'For life' ('For life: declaration of youth', 1964). Images of children were used to symbolize the unity of the peace movement ('Rhodesia: the threat we must face', 1965), and highlight the impact of war and inequalities around the world (Caldwell, 1967). Children were also used by CND to highlight problems such as racism, which was a contentious issue within the organization during the 1960s when CND debated whether it should address issues beyond nuclear weapons ('My God! How did you get passes?', 1969; Allaun, 1969; Jones, 1968). CND also used motherhood in its campaigns to try and stir international sympathies. For example, in 1971, *Sanity* reminded its readers that 'it hurts a Pakistani mother to see her child die in her arms as much as it would hurt an English mother' (Allaun, 1971). Images of women and children suffering were most often used by *Sanity* to depict the conflict in Vietnam, and Vietnam as a country was imagined in a victimized female role in relation to the United States' aggressive masculinity (Gibbs, 1966; Uncaptioned photograph, January 1968; 'The Children will weep', 1971).

Most often, of course, it was the impact of nuclear fallout and radiation on children that was the subject of CND concern. In the summer of 1969 CND reported on the findings of an American scientist which showed that 'Every time an atomic blast takes place the lives of countless thousands of children, not only unborn but unconceived, are in deadly jeopardy' (Caldwell, 1969). In the next edition of the CND newspaper the warnings were given in even more dire language with such headlines as '375,000 babies are missing' and 'The end of all children' (September 1969). These reports were designed to shock, to galvanize members into action and entice others to join the campaign. But they did not require female supporters to stray beyond accepted traditional gender norms. In fact, they depended on traditional notions of femininity to encourage both supporters and new recruits ('The First Time', 1972). Thus, they used traditional forms of femininity – namely motherhood and its associated caring, nurturing roles – to encourage their female members to do something that was not traditionally seen as feminine: to participate in the national security debate. And, as Wittner points out, they were asking women to become involved 'in an increasingly "unladylike" way – by leafleting, picketing, and public speaking. Consequently, they began to undermine "the feminine mystique" and to develop a sense of women's empowerment' (Wittner, 2000, p. 206).

It is also important to point out that CND's use of children to appeal to supporters was not strictly limited to mothers. The organization did also explicitly appeal to fathers ('This is your campaign and these are its aims', 1962). The reference to fathers was decidedly uncommon, however, and in fact only occurred on one occasion.

The language used by the organization in its official pronouncements and publications, as we have seen, continued to use stereotypical gender norms. It was 'man' who was responsible for both nuclear weapons and war in general (Minutes of CND National Co-ordinating Committee, 28 November, 1958; Calder, 1964). Articles in *Sanity* also often used the male pronoun to refer to the general public. When discussing 'the permissive' (that is, progressive) person in the abstract in 1965, a CND supporter used 'he' throughout his article (Jones, 1965). Similarly, society in general was still rhetorically depicted as a male construction. When Mervyn Rice, another longstanding CND supporter, wrote about society it too was in male terms. Humanity had been given 'a world in which to build a society based on human brotherhood' and the under-mining of this was also down to the work of men (Rice, 1965). The British government was shown to be 'a group of men who are not ashamed to lie their way into power' (Boulton, 1963). This sort of terminology continued into the 1970s, with nuclear weapons described as 'the most evil and destructive machine ever known to mankind' ('The most evil machine in the world is now in Holy Loch ... and Britain should throw it out', 1971) and nuclear proliferation described by the headline 'Poor man's bomb is nearly here' (1972). Regardless of the actual gender makeup of CND in this period, the world-view of its supporters, or at least those who wrote for its newspaper, decidedly embraced traditional gender norms and stereotypes. The men in the organization, who largely made up the editorial team of *Sanity*, saw a world in which men were responsible for all that was destructive and all that they opposed. The rhetorical construction of the gendered dynamics of the international situation clearly shows CND to be a product of traditional gender norms and of Britain before the women's liberation movement took hold.

CONCLUSION

Lawrence Wittner argues that the nuclear bomb could not help but undermine and disturb existing gender norms (Wittner, 2000, p. 214). Certainly it is clear that gender identity and dominant views of both masculinity and femininity underwent a radical transformation after the Second World War. Many scholars have looked for the origins of these changing gender norms. It has often been a matter of popular agreement that the 1960s were the decade responsible for these radical transformations. More recently, however, some scholars have argued that the movement of the tectonic plates of gender norms was visible in the 1950s and even earlier. These transformations did not occur overnight but were part of a long process of transformation. Wittner makes a persuasive argument that nuclear weapons forced these transformations as 'Women could no longer protect children by caring for them at home and men could no longer guarantee their safety by soldiering' (Wittner, 2000, p. 214).

It is certainly true that both men and women involved in the work of the Campaign for Nuclear Disarmament did not simply abide by the existing strictures of their gender. Women were called on to do many things which were considered 'un-lady-like' or falling within the purview of men, while the manhood and virility of male CND supporters were often called into question. The rhetoric of the organization, however, did not match this progressive attitude. The gendered dynamics of CND are therefore complicated and multi-faceted. The organization clearly espoused traditional roles for both men and women at specific times while sometimes simultaneously accepting and expecting that they not conform to these traditional modes. The popular link between peace and women was often used by CND in order to try to attract new supporters. And many of those who participated in CND and other organizations that opposed nuclear weapons strongly believed that they would have an important impact in changing gender stereotypes and ultimately society. As activist Alison Assister argued, 'the participation of women in the disarmament movement will contribute to other alterations in society; their participation in the movement will help break down gender divisions outside CND' (Assister, 1983, pp. 204–5). Many women, and men, who participated in the activism of 1968 and the feminist movement beginning in the early 1970s, referred to the work of CND as awakening their activist spirit. The extent to which CND's complication of traditional gender norms helped lead to the radical transformations of these norms in the 1960s, 1970s and 1980s is difficult to pinpoint exactly, but should be seen as an important contributing factor.

REFERENCES

CND Archive, London School of Economics

Minutes of CND Executive Committee Meetings, 1958–1972, LSE/CND/1.
Minutes of CND National Co-ordinating Committee, 1958–1972, LSE/CND/1.
Minutes of CND National Council Meetings, 1958–1972, LSE/CND/1.

CND Newspaper, *Sanity* 1962–1972

'375,000 babies are missing' (1969), September.
Allaun, Frank (1969), 'Biafra's children – the victims', April.
Allaun, Frank (1971), 'This is the final result of arms and war', September.
Boulton, David (1963), 'The traitors', May.
'Building instead of blasting' (1962), July.
Calder, Ritchie (1964), 'Memo to the next Prime Minister', September.
Caldwell, Malcolm (1967), 'China's bomb – Caldwell replies', October.
Caldwell, Malcolm (1969), 'The threat to our children', August.
'For life: declaration of youth' (1964), January.
Gibbs, Olive (1966), 'The vital choice for CND', October.
Heelas, Terence (1972), 'Saint George and the dragon', September.
'Introducing CND' (1962), September.
Jones, Mervyn (1965), 'What! Said the Colonel', September.
Jones, Mervyn (1968), 'So let them starve', August.
Leaver, Alec (1966), 'Letter to the editor', October.
'My God! How did you get passes?' (1969), caption of cover photo, January.
'Poor man's bomb is nearly here' (1972), January/February.
'Rhodesia: The threat we must face' (1965), December.
Rice, Mervyn (1965), 'The future belongs to US', January.
'Seven years of marching against the bomb' (1965), April.
'The children will weep' (1971), November/December.
'The end of all children' (1969), September.
'The first time' (1972), January/February.
'The most evil machine in the world is now in Holy Loch ... and Britain should throw it
    out' (1971), June.
'This is your campaign and these are its aims' (1962), October.
Uncaptioned photograph (1968), January.
'War on the children' (1967), April.
'Women's campaign' (1967), December.
'Women's campaign' (1968), February.

Published Sources

Assister, Alison (1983), 'Womanpower and nuclear politics: women and the peace movement', in D. Thompson (ed.), *Over Our Dead Bodies: Women against the Bomb*, Virago, pp. 199–206.

Brandon, Ruth (1987), *The Burning Question: The Anti-Nuclear Movement since 1945*, Heinemann.

Brooke, Stephen (2001), 'Gender and working class identity in Britain during the 1950s', *Journal of Social History*, **34** (4): 773–89.

Brown, Heloise (2003), *Truest Form of Patriotism: Pacifist Feminism in Britain, 1870–1902*, Manchester University Press.

Burguieres, Mary K. (1990), 'Feminist approaches to peace: another step for peace studies', *Millennium – Journal of International Studies*, **19** (1): 1–18.

Burkett, Jodi (2009), 'Direct action and the Campaign for Nuclear Disarmament, 1958–62', in Nick Crowson, Matthew Hilton and James McKay (eds), *NGOs in Contemporary Britain: Non-state Actors in Society and Politics Since 1945*, Palgrave Macmillan, pp. 21–37.

Burkett, Jodi (2010), 'Re-defining British morality: "Britishness" and the Campaign for Nuclear Disarmament 1958–1968', *Twentieth Century British History*, **21** (2): 184–205.

Byrne, Paul (1988), *The Campaign for Nuclear Disarmament*, Croom Helm.

Carroll, Bernice (1987), 'Feminism and pacifism: historical and theoretical connections', in R.R. Person (ed.), *Women and Peace: Theoretical, Historical and Practical Perspectives*, Croom Helm, pp. 2–28.

Carroll, Sam (2004), '"I was arrested at Greenham in 1962": investigating the oral narratives of women in the Committee of 100', *Oral History*, **32** (1).

Collins, Canon L. John (1966), *Faith under Fire*, Leslie Frewin.

Collins, Diana (1992), *Partners in Protest: Life with Canon Collins*, Victor Gollancz.

DeGroot, Gerard (2009), *The Sixties Unplugged*, Pan Macmillan.

Driver, Christopher (1964), *The Disarmers: A Study in Protest*, Hodder & Stoughton.

Duff, Peggy (1971), *Left, Left, Left: A Personal Account of Six Protest Campaigns 1945–65*, Allison & Busby.

Hall, Lesley A. (2000), *Sex, Gender and Social Change in Britain since 1880*, Macmillan.

Hinton, James (1989), *Protests and Visions: Peace Politics in Twentieth-Century Britain*, Hutchinson Radius.

Kingsley-Kent, Susan (1999), *Gender and Power in Britain, 1640–1990*, Routledge.

Lent, Adam (2001), *British Social Movements since 1945: Sex, Colour, Peace and Power*, Palgrave Macmillan.

Liddington, Jill (1989), *The Long Road to Greenham: Feminism and Anti-militarism in Britain since 1820*, Virago.

Marwick, Arthur (1998), *The Sixties: Cultural Revolution in Britain, France, Italy and the United States, c.1958–1974*, Oxford University Press.

McWilliams, John C. (2000), *The 1960s Cultural Revolution*, Greenwood.

Noakes, Lucy (2001), 'War and peace', in Ina Zweiniger-Bargielowska (ed.), *Women in Twentieth-Century Britain*, Pearson, pp. 307–20.

Parkin, Frank (1968), *Middle Class Radicalism: The Social Bases of the British Campaign for Nuclear Disarmament*, Manchester University Press.

Rose, Sonya (2003), *Which People's War? National Identity and Citizenship in Britain 1939–1945*, Oxford University Press.

Rosenberg, Emily S. (1990), 'Gender', *The Journal of American History*, **77** (1): 116–24.

Rowbotham, Sheila (2002), *Promise of a Dream: Remembering the Sixties*, Verso.

Russell, Bertrand (1969), *The Autobiography of Bertrand Russell. Volume III 1945–1967*, Allen & Unwin.

Ryan, Alan (1988), *Bertrand Russell: A Political Life*, Penguin.
Salla, Michael (2001), 'Women & war, men & pacifism', in I. Skjelsbaek and D. Smith (eds), *Gender, Peace and Conflict*, Sage, pp. 68–79.
Scott, Joan W. (1999), *Gender and the Politics of History*, Columbia University Press.
Skjelsbaek, Inger and Dan Smith (2001), 'Introduction', in I. Skjelsbaek and D. Smith (eds), *Gender, Peace and Conflict*, Sage, pp. 1–13.
Summerfield, Penny (1998), *Reconstructing Women's Wartime Lives: Discourse and Subjectivity in Oral Histories of the Second World War*, Manchester University Press.
Tickner, J. Ann (2001), *Gendering World Politics: Issues and Approaches in the Post-Cold War Era*, Columbia University Press.
Tosh, John (2004), 'Hegemonic masculinity and the history of gender', in S. Dudink, K. Hageman and J. Tosh (eds), *Masculinities in Politics and War: Gendering Modern History*, Manchester University Press.
Wittner, Lawrence S. (2000), 'Gender roles and nuclear disarmament, 1954–1965', *Gender & History*, **12** (1): 197–222.
Zweig, Ferdynand (1961), *The Worker in an Affluent Society: Family Life and Industry*, Heinemann.

21. Gendered dimensions of anti-war protest in Japan

Jennifer Chan

INTRODUCTION

The subject of war is always contentious in Japan. The modern state of Japan was founded upon the imperial conquests of two indigenous peoples (the Ainu and the Okinawans) and two neighboring countries (Korea and Taiwan). Japanese aggression during the Second World War has left a legacy of complex war crime responsibility issues that Japanese society continues to grapple with more than 60 years after the fighting ended. Postwar Japanese history has been punctuated by social movements protesting against a range of issues connected with war, militarism, nuclearism (the use of nuclear technologies both to create weapons and to provide energy), and the close connections constructed between the security of Japan and that of the United States. This chapter provides an overview of antiwar protests in Japan from a gender perspective. I discuss how Korean and other Asian feminist networks together with minority feminist movements in Japan challenge the mainstream gender equality paradigm and bring a diversity of women's war experiences and narratives from intersectional perspectives of gender, race, colonialism and class. Feminist antiwar mobilization has enabled a rewriting of history and international law concerning women's specific wartime experiences and, in particular, those of colonized and racialized minority women.

Using a poststructuralist narrative approach,[1] I critically question each of the four core constructs in the chapter title: war, gender, protests and Japan. The first section deconstructs the notions of war and nation in the Japanese context from the multiple antiwar protest movements spanning the last six decades. This is followed by an examination of the predominant gender equality narrative in Japan and the proposal of an alternative approach to gender, namely intersectionality, which allows us also to consider the factors of nation, colonialism, race and empire. The third section of the chapter focuses on the two examples of war crime responsibility and anti-base activism to discuss the gender dimensions of antiwar protest in Japan. I conclude by discussing the implications of feminist interventions in renewed peace movements in Japan. This chapter raises several issues including the signification of gender in Japan (who has the power to challenge the predominant gender equality paradigm), the emergence of alternative gender narratives from indigenous and minority perspectives, and new understandings of war and antiwar protests from women's experiences.

(RE)NARRATING WAR AND NATION

In a country known for its postwar peace constitution, the notion of war in Japan has been narrated and re-narrated in different fashions that go well beyond specific acts of international aggression. Article 9 of the Japanese Constitution states that 'the Japanese people forever renounce war as a sovereign right of the nation and the threat or use of force as means of settling international disputes' (Constitution of Japan, 1947). In this context, many Japanese feel very strongly about keeping their pacifist constitution. Antiwar mobilizations in postwar Japan have centered on a range of specific issues. During the period from the 1950s through to the 1970s, opposition was focused in particular on nuclearism, on the conclusion of a security treaty with the United States and on US military involvement in Vietnam. Activists have mobilized against the presence of US military bases in Okinawa more or less continuously since 1945, while several issues have emerged since the 1990s as the focus of protests: Japan's responsibility for war crimes during the Second World War; the preservation of the Japanese constitution; and global peace activism.

Pacifism in Japan (*heiwa shugi*) is a consciousness based on the direct experience of war-weariness and the repudiation of wartime ideology (Yamamoto, 2004). The antiwar protests that developed in the three decades immediately following the Second World War clustered around the triple issues of nuclear power and weapons, the creation of a security treaty with the United States, and the Vietnam War. One of the consequences of the Japanese experience of the atomic bombs is the emergence of an anti-nuclear movement that encompasses opposition both to nuclear weapons and to the use of nuclear technologies for generating energy. In 1954, a national ban-the-bomb movement developed in Japan when the US conducted a hydrogen bomb test at Bikini Atoll in the Marshall Islands in the South Pacific with radiation fallout on a Japanese tuna boat, the Lucky Dragon (Yamamoto, 2004). The Japan Council against Atomic and Hydrogen Bombs (*Gensuikyo*) was formed in 1955 to advocate for a total ban on nuclear weapons as well as to support victims of the atomic bombs. Since then, this residents' and citizens' movement has continued to mobilize around issues of nuclear power plant construction, accidents, testing and the stockpiling of nuclear weapons at US military bases in Okinawa and mainland Japan. Many local Japanese city governments have joined a global movement to legislate nuclear free zones, legally banning the production, testing, transportation and storage of nuclear weapons and nuclear waste. Internationally, the Nuclear Non-Proliferation Treaty (NPT) serves as a platform for Japanese non-governmental organizations (NGOs) such as Mayors for Peace (created by the then Hiroshima Mayor Takeshi Araki in 1982, now a network of 1002 cities in 120 countries) to connect to global movements such as Abolition 2000, a network of 2000 organizations in 90 countries for the abolition of nuclear weapons (Mayors for Peace, 2015; Abolition 2000, 2015). The incident at the Fukushima nuclear power plant as a result of the earthquake and tsunami in March 2011 provided another opportunity for anti-nuclear activists in Japan to oppose nuclear power. One of the fifteen largest nuclear power plants in the world, the Fukushima plant began to leak radiation when a 9.0 earthquake disabled the reactor cooling systems. Over 1500 people marched in downtown Tokyo on 20 March 2011, followed by other similar anti-nuclear protests in Europe, notably in Germany. The catastrophe confirmed longstanding fears of Japanese anti-nuclear activists about nuclear safety.

Besides anti-nuclearism, the other longstanding pillar of postwar Japanese pacifist movements is the *AMPO tôsô* (anti-US–Japan Security Treaty protests). Signed originally in 1950 at the end of the occupation of Japan by the Allied Forces, the security treaty was re-opened for negotiations in 1959. The treaty provided the basis for mutual security cooperation between the United States and Japan. Two issues were particularly contentious. The first one pertained to the obligation to assist each other in case of armed attack. Japanese citizens were concerned about the eventual possibility of sending Japanese armed forces overseas to the defense of the United States, which was against its Constitution. The second concern was about the stationing of US Armed Forces in Japan, and, in particular, in Okinawa. In June 1959 a mass movement made up of major labor unions, student groups, women's organizations, the Japan Communist Party and the Japan Socialist Party mobilized over 330 000 people to become the largest-ever popular protest in Japan to block the revision of the Japan–US Security Treaty. This movement of movements was plagued with differences over goals (whether to link the anti-US protest with the removal of the Kishi government at the time) and tactics (the student group, *Zengakuren*, was criticized for its radical action) (Yamamoto, 2004). In May 1960, the security treaty bills were forced through the lower house by the Kishi government.

The same decade also saw the development of *Beiheiren* (Anti-Vietnam War Alliance) that protested against the US bombing of North Vietnam in February 1965. The anti-security treaty as well as anti-Vietnam War protests were marked by strong labor union leadership, a radical student movement (Takagi, 1990), close links to left-wing political parties and women's participation. Though traditionally not the bread and butter of union business, Japanese labor unions nonetheless took up leadership roles in antiwar protests, since they saw 'peace as an extension of their economic well-being' (Yamamoto, 2004, p. 104). Although this period of antiwar activism was short-lived due to the violence among New Left sects, ideological differences and state repression that led to the demise of these movements, it left an indelible mark on many subsequent new social movements that campaigned on a wide range of human rights issues in terms of direct action and challenging Japanese state authority (Shirakawa, 1999 and Yamamoto, 2004). For example, we see remnants of antiwar activism of this period in the subsequent emergence of antiwar coalitions during the protests against the war in Iraq in 2003. As in the 1960s and 1970s, the labor unions once again took up a leadership role in these protests. Veteran antiwar activists from the *AMPO tôsô* and *Beiheiren* era also took the lead in the coalition called World Peace Now (Chan, 2008).

If Japanese pacifist consciousness is based on Japanese society's direct experience of war, these early protests against nuclear power, the security treaty and the Vietnam War nonetheless reflect a racial bias in antiwar activism. Okinawa has continuously suffered disproportionately from the US–Japan Security Treaty: Okinawa provides the territory for 75 percent of all US military base area in Japan even though it represents only 1 percent of the total population and 0.6 percent of total land area in the country (Arasaki, 1996). Further, Okinawans continue to suffer from land confiscation, military rape and ecological damage. Nonetheless, few peace activists in mainland Japan made the connection between their antiwar activities and the situation in Okinawa. Several antiwar activists have suggested this is a result of blatant racism within Japanese media. One of the reasons why the anti-US military base movement in Okinawa has not developed into a national antiwar movement is the lack of national media coverage and public attention (Chan, 2008). For Okinawans, war was not something that had happened 'over there'. The island archipelago saw the only ground battle in Japan during the Second World War, with a staggering death toll of 240 000 including 140 000 civilians (about a quarter of the Okinawan population) between March and August 1945. It is also important to point out that the end of the war in mainland Japan did not bring peace in Okinawa. Article 3 of the 1951 San Francisco Peace Treaty, which marked the formal end of hostilities in the Asia Pacific region following the Second World War, specified that 'the United States will have the right to exercise all and any powers of administration, legislation and jurisdiction over the territory and inhabitants of these Ryûkyû islands, including their territorial waters' (San Francisco Peace Treaty, 1951). Until its reversion to Japan in 1972, Okinawa had been under direct US military rule for 27 years, during which time (mostly private) land was confiscated for military base construction with only nominal compensation paid to the landowners (Hein and Selden, 2003). Anti-base activists in Okinawa began their protests against arbitrary land seizure and inadequate compensation as early as the mid-1950s (Arasaki, 1996). The well-known national network *Hitotsubo hansen jinushi kai* (Hitotsubo Antiwar Landlords Association) was created in 1982 with over 3000 members, each buying and owning one or more *tsubo* (equivalent to 40 square feet) as a symbolic gesture to defy land lease for the US military bases in Okinawa. The other pillar of antiwar activism in Okinawa was peace education, which was spearheaded by the Okinawan Teachers Association (*Okikyôso*) and later institutionalized by the so-called peace administration of the prefectural government. Through people's own war narratives, battle site visits, a youth peace forum, exchange peace programs between universities, participation in protests and the construction of sites such as the Okinawa Prefectural Peace Memorial Museum and the Himeyuri Memorial, peace education in Okinawa focuses on the Battle of Okinawa, the military bases and minority culture (Figal, 2003). For Okinawans, postwar anniversary celebrations in mainland Japan are insulting. Through activism, they try to forge an alternative subaltern discourse of postwar zero year (Syun, 2005); that is, while Japanese celebrated the 60th anniversary of the end of war in 2005, Okinawans lamented the fact that military occupation of their islands had not yet come to an end. For them, Japanese imperialism is not something of the past; they continue to challenge the predominant narrative of the Japanese nation from their ongoing colonial experiences. While mainstream Japanese antiwar activists challenge the Japanese state from a peace perspective, Okinawan activists have been doing so from an intersectional perspective of anti-militarism and colonialism. From an indigenous perspective, continuous US military presence represents dual colonization of the US and Japan.

Since the early 1990s, antiwar activism in Japan has focused on demands that Japan accept responsibility for war crimes committed during the Second World War, that key elements of the Japanese constitution be preserved (particularly Article 9, which renounces the use of war and threat of violence) and that Japan pursue the goal of global peace (Chan, 2008). Several factors facilitated the emergence of a range of war crime movements in Japan and Asia that challenge Japanese government denial of and public amnesia about Japan's conduct in the Second World War. An intellectual movement led by Japanese historians, philosophers and political theorists such as Oda Makoto reversed the Japan-as-war-victim narrative to look at the complicity of the Japanese nation as war aggressors (Avenell, 2010). New evidence unveiled by South Korean and Japanese historical and feminist researchers reopened issues of Japanese war crime responsibility that were left out by the Tokyo Tribunal (which tried and convicted a number of Japanese officials in the years immediately following the war), such as the 'comfort women' issue. It was believed that Emperor Hirohito, as the Supreme Commander in Chief, knew what was going on and was responsible for the various war crimes. As long as he was still alive, it was difficult to bring up the issue in Japanese society. The death of Emperor Hirohito in 1989 removed one of the last obstacles for various national and regional social movements (Dudden, 2006). Finally, the emergence of international human rights discourses and movements since the 1990s has lent considerable normative as well as organizational weight to various war crime social movements in Japan and the Asia-Pacific region (Tsutsui, 2009). These movements are characterized by domestic, regional and international activism on a range of differentiated issues from forced slave labor to military sexual slavery. Other antiwar movements that can be grouped under this larger rubric of war crime responsibility include longstanding anti-Emperor activism (the Emperor is perceived by these activists to be responsible for Japanese aggression in Asia including the colonization of Korea and Taiwan and various war crimes during WWII), opposition to the censorship of history and civics textbooks, resistance to the reinstatement of the *Hinomaru* and 'Kimigayo' as the national flag and national anthem in 1999 and the amendment of the Fundamental Law on Education to instill patriotism (see Chan, 2008). The *Hinomaru* and 'Kimigayo' were adopted as the national flag and national anthem in 1999. In the Japanese Diet (Parliament), the government maintains that the law does not mandate people to observe the national flag and the national anthem. However, boards of education have made it compulsory for teachers and students to observe them during school ceremonies. In 2004, there were over 200 cases in which teachers who did not sing 'Kimigayo' or stand up while it was being sung were punished by the Board of Education (Nishihara, 2008). Further, since the early 2000s, there has been a conservative movement to amend the Fundamental Law on Education. The 1947 Fundamental Law on Education lays out the general principles in education. On 20 March 2003, the Central Council of Education submitted a report entitled 'The modality of a new fundamental law of education befitting to the new times and a basic plan for education' to the Ministry of Education, Culture, Sports, Science and Technology (MEXT) in which several changes were proposed including the 'restoration of the ability of the home to educate children' and fostering 'respect for tradition and culture, and a sense of love and respect of the country and home and internationalism' (Nishihara, 2008).

Another strong antiwar movement that developed in the early years of the twenty-first century pertained to constitutional preservation in response to a renewed movement within the ruling Liberal Democratic Party to amend the Constitution to allow Japanese forces to be sent overseas. In Japan, the political move to revise the Constitution has been around since the 1950s. Though the revision movement was defeated by the end of the 1950s due to strong popular opposition, the idea has lingered on in the minds of some politicians within the Liberal Democratic Party. In 2005, the former Prime Minister Nakasone Yasuhiro (1982–87) reiterated his ideas on the topic. In his draft, the first article of the amended constitution stipulates the emperor to be the 'head of state of Japan'. He wanted to rename the Self Defense Forces as Defense Forces and allow the forces to be dispatched overseas (Takada, 2008). In 1999, 100 Japanese citizens' groups came together to form the 'No to Constitutional Revision! Citizens' Group' to oppose the political trends to amend the constitution. The Article 9 Association (*9-jô no kai*) was founded in June 2004 by nine Japanese intellectuals: Inoue Hisashi (novelist), Katô Shûichi (commentator and doctor), Miki Mutsuko (UN Women's Society), Oda Makoto (writer), Ôe Kenzaburô (novelist and Nobel Laureate), Okudaira Yasuhiro (constitution scholar), Sawachi Hisae (writer), Tsurumi Shunsuke (philosopher) and Umehara Takeshi (philosopher). There are now over 2700 *9-jô no kai* throughout Japan and worldwide (Nara and Brock, 2004). A significant dimension of the Article 9 movement is its appeal to globalism. The intellectual leaders and the citizen supporters frame this pacifist movement as Japan's unique contribution to global peace. According to this global movement, 'Article 9 of the Japanese Constitution renounces war as a means of settling international disputes and prohibits the maintenance of armed forces and other war potential. Article 9 is an international oath declaring No to War, a shared property of all the world's citizens who wish for peace' (Global Article 9 Campaign, 2008). Since 2005, the network has over 190 institutional and individual supporters and has been active in global peace building through a wide range of activities including public seminars, press conferences, rallies, and lobbying at the UN for a declaration on the human rights to peace.

Finally, the US-led military invasions of Afghanistan in 2001 and Iraq in 2003 spurred the creation of a new kind of youth-based antiwar coalition in Japan. Peace activists in Japan vehemently opposed the successive passage of many bills by the Japanese government including the Special Measures against Terrorism in 2001, the Iraqi Reconstruction Special Measures Law in 2003, and seven war-contingency laws in 2004 to allow the dispatch of the Japanese Self Defense Forces to Iraq. World Peace Now (WPN) came into being as an amorphous network led by youth groups like CHANCE Pono2 and other civic groups. WPN operates on four principles: no more war; opposition to the attack on Iraq; opposition to the Japanese government's support and cooperation for the attack on Iraq; and non-violent action. Until WPN was formed, many nongovernmental groups in Japan focused on a single theme and acted separately (Hanawa et al., 2008). The coalition organized its first demonstration on 26 October 2002. On 18 January 2003, before the start of the attack on Iraq, 7000 people participated in the demonstration in Tokyo, and then 50 000 people joined on 21 March 2003 right after the attack was started. In March 2004, the first anniversary of the US invasion of Iraq, 130 000 people in 120 places across Japan marched on the streets as part of an international antiwar action.

All three movements that have emerged since the 1990s pertaining to war crime responsibility, constitutional preservation and global peace play a role in challenging Japanese militarism. Antiwar activism in Japan has been part and parcel of a global peace movement. For these Japanese activists, the notion of war is less about Japanese aggression abroad, as it is prohibited by Japan's constitution, and more about any threat to peace such as constitutional revision and Japanese contribution to war efforts overseas.

(RE)NARRATING GENDER

If the notions of war and nation have been continually re-narrated in Japan, the category of gender is under no less scrutiny. Gender is, of course, a modern and arguably Western construct, even though women's movements clearly developed their own trajectory in Japan (Chan-Tiberghien, 2004a). An equality paradigm has been the predominant approach to gender relations in postwar Japan by activists and government alike. In terms of formal, legal equality, Article 14 of the Japanese

Constitution guarantees equality before the law and prohibits discrimination based on 'political, economic or social relations' or 'race, creed, sex, social status or family origin' (Constitution of Japan, 1947). Subsequently, through women's activism, a gender equality approach was institutionalized step by step in Japan: first in the form of national machinery consisting of the Headquarters for the Planning and Promotion of Policies Relating to Women, the Office for Women's Affairs, and the Advisory Council to the Prime Minister on Women after the UN World Conference of the International Year of the Woman in 1975; then in the passage of the Equal Employment Opportunity Law as part of Japan's legal obligations to ratify the UN Convention on the Elimination of All Forms of Discrimination against Women (CEDAW); and finally in the enactment of the first Basic Law on Gender Equality in 1999 as a result of Japanese women's mobilization after the Beijing Conference.

Without diminishing the hard-won gains achieved by women's movements in Japan since the Second World War, however, it is important to understand that the predominant gender equal approach reflects a racial bias in Japanese feminist activism. The mobilization that resulted in the women's liberation movement in the 1960s and 1970s and led to a series of pieces of legislation (for example, the Anti-Prostitution Law in 1956, the amendment of the Equal Employment Opportunity Law to mandate sexual harassment prevention in the workplace in 1997, the legalization of the contraceptive pill in 1999, the Anti-Stalking Law in 2000 and Domestic Violence Prevention Law in 2001) failed to make the connection between activism and the compound discrimination faced by women affected by multiple social locations such as race, colonialism class, disability and immigrant status (Chan-Tiberghien, 2004b). The dominant gender equality narrative eclipses differences among women such as minority women living in Japan including the Ainu, Okinawan, Korean and other foreign women residents. In the area of antiwar activism, the issues of the complicity of Japanese women in supporting Japan's aggression in Asia and of reparation for 200 000 comfort women (the majority of whom are not Japanese) surfaced in discussions among Japanese feminist academics and activists only in the early 1990s (Chan-Tiberghien, 2004a). A similar charge of omission can be made against Japanese mainstream feminists for their failure to become involved in antiwar mobilization in Okinawa.

Looking at the gender dimensions of antiwar protests in Japan in their multiplicity necessarily requires alternative gender narratives. Approaching gender as 'differences that matter' (Ahmed, 1998) allows us to deconstruct the power mechanisms within not only mainstream Japanese women's movements, but also various antiwar movements. As Crenshaw argues,

> Intersectionality is a conceptualization of the problem that attempts to capture both the structural and dynamic consequences of the interaction between two or more axes of subordination. It specifically addresses the manner in which racism, patriarchy, class oppression and other discriminatory systems create background inequalities that structure the relative positions of women, races, ethnicities, classes, and the like. (2000, p. 7)

By insisting on difference, a poststructuralist narrative approach to gender such as the one advocated by Butler (1999) refuses any one particular hegemonic definition of gender. Instead, gender is understood as an ongoing discursive practice open to intervention and resignification. In the case of antiwar activism in Japan, Korean and other Asian feminist networks in conjunction with minority feminist movements in Japan challenge the mainstream gender equality paradigm and bring a diversity of women's war experiences and narratives to the forefront.

GENDER AND ANTIWAR PROTESTS IN JAPAN

While women participated in the activism against nuclearism, the US–Japan Security Treaty and the Vietnam War in postwar Japan, the gender dimensions of antiwar activism are arguably the strongest in the war crime movements and the anti-base activism in Okinawa. These two prime examples illustrate how feminist interventions contribute to the re-narrations of gender, nation, war and protests.

One of the most significant turnarounds in war crime narration in postwar Japan pertains to the issue of comfort women. Between 1932 and 1945 an estimated 200 000 women (80 percent of whom were Korean with the rest Japanese, Korean, Taiwanese, Chinese, Filipino, Indonesian, Vietnamese, Burmese, Dutch and Australian) were sent to several hundred comfort stations throughout the Asia-Pacific region to serve Japanese soldiers (Yoshimi, 1995). With the exception of a few cases, the issue was mostly left out of the scope of the Tokyo Tribunal (Totani, 2008). Neither was it a concern in the subsequent bilateral treaties between the Japanese government and the Korean and Chinese governments. Postwar citizens' movements that focused on Japanese war crime responsibility in Korea, China and Japan did not find the issue important enough to warrant mobilization. Mainstream Japanese women's movements picked up the cause only in the late 1980s and early 1990s upon the instigation of their Korean counterparts. The experiences of comfort women are perfect examples of multiple discrimination at the intersections of gender (omitted by the male-dominated nationalist movements in Korea, Taiwan and China), race (neglected by the mainstream Japanese women's movements), colonialism (over 80 percent of the women drafted were colonial subjects of Japan) and class (these women were lured into becoming sexual slaves due to their poverty).

The redress movement for comfort women since the early 1990s is a remarkable feminist mobilization story that involves a delicate dance between domestic, regional and international nongovernmental networks, the Japanese state and intergovernmental organizations. It began with the publication of new research materials by Korean and Japanese historians. Led by the Korean feminist historian Yun Chung-Ok, the Korean Council for the Women Drafted for Sexual Slavery by Japan (hereafter known as the Korean Council) was created in 1990 and made specific demands to the Japanese government including acknowledgment of the war crime; revealing the truth in its entirety about the crimes of military sexual slavery; making an official apology; making legal reparations; punishing those responsible for the war crime; accurately recording the crime in history textbooks; erecting a memorial for the victims and establishing a war museum (Korean Council for the Women Drafted for Sexual Slavery by Japan). The Japanese government denied responsibility for the problem by arguing that the comfort system was run by civilians. In 1991, the Korean Council supported the public appearance and speaking out of one comfort woman, Kim Hak-Shun, in Japan, which then led to the formation of a Japanese feminist coalition of 15 nongovernmental groups, the Action Network for the Issue of Military Sexual Slavery Japan, which filed the first comfort women lawsuit in Tokyo. The publication of six pieces of evidence by Japanese historian Yoshimi Yoshiaki in *Asahi Shimbun* on 11 January 1992 led to the groundbreaking Japanese government admission of the Japanese army's involvement in setting up the comfort system. One week later, on 17 January, Prime Minister Miyazawa Kiichi made a public apology at the Japan–Korea Summit: 'I would like to once again express a heartfelt remorse and apology for the unbearable suffering and sorrow that you experienced during this period because of our nation's act. Recently the issue of the so-called 'wartime comfort women' is being brought up. I think that incidents like this are seriously heartbreaking, and I am truly sorry.'[2] A year later, in August 1993, the Japanese government made a series of further admissions. The government acknowledged that the Japanese army was directly or indirectly involved in the establishment, management and moving of the comfort stations. It admitted that, in many cases, the women were recruited by deception or force, in some cases with the involvement of Japanese officials. The women at the comfort stations were subject to force and control and, in the case of Korean comfort women, most were recruited, moved and managed against their will, by deception and force. The Japanese government accepted that the military comfort system run by the Japanese army deeply hurt the respect and dignity of these women and issued an apology to them (Yoshimi, 1995). A private Asian Women's Fund was established in July 1995 with donations from the public to provide atonement funds to the victims and to promote research and education about the comfort women as well as about other contemporary women's human rights issues. Between 1995 and 2003, when the Fund ceased to pay out atonement, only 266 individuals in South Korea, Taiwan, the Philippines and the Netherlands accepted money from the Fund. Since 2003 the Fund has focused primarily on contemporary issues of women's human rights such as violence against women (Asian Women's Fund, 2007).

The redress movement for comfort women also reflects the gender and racial biases of international law, the UN human rights system and the international women's movement. Though rape was clearly defined as a war crime in The Hague Conventions and the Geneva Conventions and so could have been included in the war crimes charges considered by the Tokyo Tribunal, the issue of comfort women was virtually ignored by that forum. An extensive body of international human rights law including the International Convention on Civil and Political Rights, the International Convention on Economic, Social and Cultural Rights, the Convention against Torture, and most importantly, CEDAW failed to provide any redress mechanism for the comfort women. The issue was also not picked up by the international women's movement in the First World Conference on Women in Mexico City (1975), the Second World Conference on Women in Copenhagen (1980), or the Third World Conference on Women in Nairobi (1985). It was not until the early 1990s that Korean and Japanese women's groups could mobilize at the UN level using the discourse that women's rights are human rights. The 1993 Vienna Declaration and Platform for Action states that 'violations of the human rights of women in situations of armed conflict are violations of the fundamental principles of international human rights and humanitarian law. All violations of this kind, including in particular murder, systematic rape, sexual slavery, and forced pregnancy, require a particularly effective response' (Vienna Declaration, 1993). Further, the 1995 Beijing Declaration and Platform for Action specifically prohibits violence against women in armed conflicts. Between 1994 and 1998, the redress movement took a number of important steps. In 1994 it supported

11 comfort women to file a case with the UN Permanent Court of Arbitration upon the suggestion of the UN Working Group on Contemporary Forms of Slavery. The movement lobbied the influential NGO, International Commission of Jurists, to issue a damning 208-page Report on Comfort Women, concluding that 'the Japanese government has responsibility for the sexual abuses suffered by the women under the Japanese army and government of the time' (Dolgopol and Paranjape, 1994). It succeeded in getting the UN Special Rapporteur on Violence Against Women to issue a mission report in 1996 on the issue of military sexual slavery in wartime.[3] As a result of the movement's efforts a 1997 International Labor Organization Committee of Experts report framed the comfort women issue also as forced labor, in contravention of the 1930 Convention No. 29 that the Japanese government had ratified in 1932. Perhaps most significantly, it managed to get the comfort women issue redefined as military sexual slavery through a 1998 report by the UN Special Rapporteur on Systematic Rape, Sexual Slavery, and Slavery-like Practices during Armed Conflicts (see Chan-Tiberghien, 2004a). The issue of violence against women in conflicts was finally brought to the forefront in the worldwide mobilization for the establishment of the International Criminal Court in the Rome Conference in 1998, largely thanks to the mobilization of feminist networks such as the Women's Initiatives for Gender Justice (2015).

What has emerged in this decade of feverish feminist mobilization is a body of subjugated knowledge – narratives of the comfort women themselves recorded in videotapes, publications and online resources – a rewriting of history and international law to take into account women's specific wartime experiences and also a resignification of gender in the international, regional and national women's movements to challenge previous exclusions of the experiences of colonized and racialized minority women. These achievements were best reflected in the 2000 International War Crimes Tribunal on Japan's Military Sexual Slavery, a people's tribunal organized by three Asian feminist networks: the Violence against Women in War Network – Japan; the Korean Council for the Women Drafted for Military Sexual Slavery by Japan; and the Philippine-based Asian Center for Women's Human Rights. For the first time, the judges clearly pronounced that rape and sexual slavery, when committed on a widespread, systematic or large-scale basis, constituted crimes against humanity and that Emperor Hirohito was criminally responsible for crimes against humanity (see Women's International War Crimes Tribunal, 2001).

The other example of strong gender dimensions of antiwar protests in Japan is undoubtedly the issue of anti-base activism. Postwar peace activism in Okinawa has primarily focused on the seizure of land for the creation of US military bases. Although prostitution on these military bases was raised as a concern during the anti-base protests in the 1960s, earlier anti-base activism was by and large a male-dominated movement. Okinawan women had certainly been involved in anti-base activism, but women activists had been accused of diminishing the peace movement with their gender concerns (Author interview with Okinawa Women Act Against Military Violence, 2005). It was not until the rape of a twelve-year-old Okinawan schoolgirl by two US marines and a sailor in September 1995 that issues of violence against women were brought to the mainstream Okinawan peace movement. The attack on this girl represented the structural violence in the military (Takazato, 1996), a pattern ignored, if not condoned, at the highest levels of the American military hierarchy (Johnson, 1999). Violence against women is structural in the sense that it is an inherent feature of the male-dominated military institution that has been present in Okinawa since 1952, seen in the use of force, and continuous threat of rape and sexual aggression faced by Okinawan women. The incident and the subsequent mass rally attended by 85 000 in October 1995 opened a new chapter in the contemporary Okinawan peace movement; finally, violence against women was recognized as a legitimate peace issue. A few days before the rape occurred, 71 women from Okinawa had organized 11 workshops concerning violence against women in Okinawa at the Fourth World Conference on Women in Beijing. Armed with the newly adopted Beijing Platform for Action, which called for the elimination of violence against women in armed conflicts and wars, feminist leaders in Okinawa created a network called Okinawa Women Act Against Military Violence and mobilized around the global discourse of women's human rights (Author interview with Okinawa Women Act Against Military Violence, 2005).

The protests spurred the establishment of the Japan–US Special Action Committee on Okinawa (SACO) to look into ways to reduce the burden that US military bases placed on the people of Okinawa. In December 1996 the SACO Final Report outlined 27 recommendations concerning the return of 21 percent of US base properties on the island including the controversial Futenma Marine Corps Air Station (discussed below). The protests also forced the Okinawan prefectural government to take a more proactive stand on peace issues. For example, in 1995 the prefectural governor Ota Masahide refused to renew expired leases on land used for US military bases. The land occupied by the American military in Okinawa is legally owned by about 31 000 families and leased by the United States. In order for the bases to continue to operate legally, the leases must be renewed periodically. The governor's refusal to act forced the Prime Minister of Japan to renew the lease himself and the case was taken to court to challenge the Prime Minister's forced decision without the consent of the Okinawan prefectural governor (Johnson, 1999). Although the Supreme Court dismissed the case, the bravura of Governor Ota captured the attention of the Japanese public. Further, on 8 September 1996, the Okinawan prefectural government organized a prefecture-wide vote on the continued presence of US bases on Okinawa in which the majority was in favor of reducing the number of bases (about 60 percent of eligible voters cast ballots; 482 000 supported reducing the number of bases while 46 000 opposed). Although the vote was non-binding, the overwhelming nature of the majority in favor of base reductions combined with the recommendations of the SACO Final Report led to widespread outrage in December 1999 when the Nago City Mayor Kishimoto Tateo accepted US plans to move the Futenma Marine Corps Air Station to a 1500-meter sea-based facility off the east coast of the main island of Okinawa near the village of Henoko (Makishi, 2000). Since boring tests began off the coast of Henoko in 2004, local villagers, supported not only by peace activists in Okinawa and on the mainland, but also by the international NGO Greenpeace (through a campaign entitled 'Save the Dugong in Okinawa and Stop the Air Base') have been participating in a sit-in the Henoko harbor, joining campaigners who have maintained a presence at the harbor since 1996 (Yui, 2004). Okinawan *obâ* (elderly women) also tried media-savvy tactics including underwater demonstrations (Author interview with Grassroots Movement to Remove US Bases from Okinawa and the World, 2004).

Since the Beijing conference, Okinawan feminists have been networking with their counterparts in East Asia, Puerto Rico and the US against militarism. In addition to campaigning for the recognition of gender-based violence, feminist anti-base activism in Okinawa since the 1990s has also tried to make explicit the connections between gender, race, colonization, imperialism and ecology (Nomura, 2005). The continuous violence perpetuated by the US military is believed by many Okinawans to be a result of the actions of Emperor Hirohito, who is regarded as having sacrificed the people of Okinawa twice over. The first such occasion was the horrendous Battle of Okinawa, which was fought in order to delay Japan's surrender to the Allies in the Second World War. The second occasion was the agreement in 1952 to permit US military bases to be located in Okinawa. The existence of the bases enabled Japan to regain its independence from the Allied Occupation Force while their location away from the mainland allowed most Japanese to feel comfortable with the Japan–US Security Treaty (Johnson, 1999). Many Okinawans have also become aware of the continuous colonization of

Okinawa by mainland Japanese, whether through state economic policy or mass tourism to the beautiful tropical archipelago (Syun, 2005; Nomura, 2005). The large-scale protests following the 1995 rape incident created an impetus for the formation of many youth-led groups such as the Association of Indigenous Peoples' Rights in the Ryukyus. They mobilize at the UN level from the perspective of indigenous peoples' rights and try to redefine Okinawan issues from an indigenous peoples' point of view. For example, the nongovernmental group, Association of Indigenous Peoples in the Ryukyus (AIPR), was established in 1996 in the context of Okinawan citizens' movements. AIPR declares Okinawan people as 'indigenous peoples' defined by international law. The aim of the movement is 'the recovery of the "self-determination" of Okinawan people, and to achieve the solution of Okinawan problems by Okinawan people themselves through the human rights regime of the United Nations' (Taira, 2008). Every year, AIPR members attend the Permanent Forum on Indigenous Issues in May and the UN Working Group on Indigenous Populations in July. They also monitor and make position statements concerning the impact of military bases in Okinawa on various UN human rights conventions including the UN Convention on the Rights of the Child (CRC), Convention on the Elimination of All Forms of Discrimination against Women, and International Convention on the Elimination of Racial Discrimination from Okinawan perspectives. Finally, more and more Okinawan peace activists including feminists have begun to use an environmental frame for their cause as well, that is, they lobby for the removal of military bases on ecological grounds. The Okinawa Environment Network, for example, was formed in 1997 to link the protection of the environment with the promotion of peace. A loose national network comprising the Save the Dugong Fund Committee, Dugong Network Okinawa, the Okinawa Environment Network and Dugong Conservation Campaign Center, with the support of the Japan Federation of Bar Associations, the Japan Environment Lawyers Federation, the Mammological Society of Japan, the Wild Bird Society of Japan, and the Worldwide Fund for Nature Japan has also used a variety of tactics to lobby against the construction of a new heliport in Henoko. In 2000, they managed to get the World Conservation Union to issue a Recommendation concerning the 'Conservation of Dugong, Okinawa Woodpecker, and Okinawa Rai in and around Okinawa Island'. Further, a coalition of US and Japanese environmental NGOs have also filed a lawsuit in a San Francisco District Court demanding that the US Department of Defense comply with the US National Historic Preservation Act to protect the endangered Dugongs in the proposed heliport site (Author interview with Dugong Network Okinawa, 2005).

CONCLUSION

This chapter provides an overview of antiwar protests in Japan from feminist perspectives. Antiwar activism in postwar Japan centered upon a wide range of issues including opposition to nuclearism, opposition to US military bases in Japan and the preservation of Article 9 of the Japanese constitution preventing Japan from using or threatening military forces. Through the two examples of war crime responsibility and anti-base activism, I use a poststructuralist narrative approach to analyze feminist resignification of gender, war, nation and protests.

In the Japanese wartime sexual slavery redress movement, feminist activists expanded the definition of war crimes and the scope of the war reparation movements, traditionally focused on the issues of forced labor and the responsibility of the Emperor, by revealing new forms of military violence from the perspectives of gender, race and colonialism. Similarly, feminist interventions have renewed peace movements in Okinawa. Besides the obvious fact of engendering traditionally male-dominated peace movements, feminist antiwar activism has led to a redefinition of the concepts of gender, nation, peace and protests. Okinawan feminists press mainland Japanese feminists to go beyond a gender equality approach and to recognize intersectional forms of discrimination and the specific forms of violence experienced by women in Okinawa. Okinawan antiwar activists also refuse the statist narratives that depict the US–Japan Security Alliance as being in the interests of the Japanese nation. They challenge the Japanese state from indigenous and feminist perspectives. The issue of the presence of US military bases is obviously not unique to Okinawa, it is a global peace issue. Further, peace is linked to land, ecology, racism, colonialism, gender, youth and class. Hence antiwar activism requires local, national, regional and global networking of a broad spectrum of women's, youth, environmental and peace networks. Finally, protests also take up new forms and expressions to foster inclusive participation beyond the traditional leadership of labor union and civic groups. In addition to the traditional protest repertoire of peace parades and signature campaigns, these renewed peace movements experiment with a wide range of cultural, artistic and political means including popular concerts, people's tribunals and arts exhibitions.[4]

The attacks on the United States on 11 September 2001, the subsequent invasions of Afghanistan and Iraq, the passage of anti-terrorism special measures by the Japanese government to allow the dispatch of Japanese Self Defense Forces overseas and the 2011 Fukushima nuclear crisis provide a whole new context for antiwar activism in Japan. The gender dimensions of the newer youth-focused peace coalitions are yet to be studied. What we do know is that women are active participants in these movements, feminist groups are part of these networks, the mobilizing frame is one of global peace, and the repertoire of activist actions is much broader than those of the older peace movements. More research needs to be done, however, to understand what gender signifies in these emerging overlapping networks that continually call our understandings of the Japanese nation and of war itself into question.

NOTES

1. A post-structuralist narrative approach draws upon the works of Michel Foucault in examining how certain narrative knowledges arise and become dominant. The key is to unpack power dynamics behind predominant narratives in a wide range of social institutions.
2. 'Policy speech at the occasion of the visit to South Korea', *The World and Japan Database Project*, Institute of Oriental Culture, University of Tokyo, pp. 383–88.
3. 'For the purpose of terminology, the Special Rapporteur concurs entirely with the view held by members of the Working Group on Contemporary Forms of Slavery, as well as by representatives of nongovernmental organizations and some academics, that the phrase "comfort women" does not in the least reflect the suffering, such as multiple rapes on an everyday basis and severe physical abuse, that women victims had to endure during their forced prostitution and sexual subjugation and abuse in wartime. The Special Rapporteur, therefore, considers with conviction that the phrase "military sexual slaves" represents a much more accurate and appropriate terminology' (UN Special Rapporteur on Violence Against Women, 1996).
4. For example, see the work of Feminist Art Action Brigade.

REFERENCES

Abolition 2000: Global Network to Eliminate Nuclear Weapons (2015), accessed 13 July 2015 at: http://www.abolition2000.org/.
Ahmed, Sara (1998), *Differences that Matter: Feminist Theory and Postmodernism*, Cambridge University Press.
Arasaki, Moriteru (1996), *Okinawa Hansen Jinushi* (Okinawan Antiwar Landlords), Kôbunken.
Asian Women's Fund (2007), 'To our visitors', accessed 13 July 2015 at: http://www.awf.or.jp/e-preface.htm.
Avenell, Simon Andrew (2010), *Making Japanese Citizens: Civil Society and the Mythology of the Shimin in Postwar Japan*, University of California Press.
Butler, Judith (1999), *Gender Trouble: Feminism and the Subversion of Identity*, Routledge.
Chan, Jennifer (ed.) (2008), *Another Japan is Possible: New Social Movements and Global Citizenship Education*, Stanford University Press.
Chan-Tiberghien, Jennifer (2004a), *Gender and Human Rights Politics in Japan: Global Norms and Domestic Networks*, Stanford University Press.

Chan-Tiberghien, Jennifer (2004b), 'Gender as intersectionality: multiple discrimination against minority women in Japan', in M. Nakamura and P. Potter (eds), *Comparative International Studies of Social Cohesion and Globalization in Asia: Japan*, Palgrave Macmillan, pp. 158–81.

Constitution of Japan (1947), accessed 14 July 2015 at: http://japan.kantei.go.jp/constitution_and_government_of_japan/constitution_e.html.

Crenshaw, Kimberlé (2000), 'Gender-Related Aspects of Race Discrimination', paper delivered at the Expert Group Meeting on Gender and Racial Discrimination, Zagreb, 21–24 November.

Dolgopol, Ustinia and Snehal Paranjape (1994), *Comfort Women: an Unfinished Ordeal: Report of a Mission*, International Commission of Jurists.

Dudden, Alexis (2006), 'Japan's political apologies and the right to history', USJP Occasional Paper 06/01, Program on US Japan Relations, Harvard University.

Feminist Art Action Brigade website, accessed 15 July 2015 at: http://home.interlink.or.jp/~reflect/GAAP/FAABe.html.

Figal, Gerald (2003), 'Waging peace on Okinawa', in Laura Hein and Mark Selden (eds), *Islands of Discontent: Okinawan Responses to Japanese and American Power (Asian Voices)*, Rowman & Littlefield.

Global Article 9 Campaign (2008), Global Article 9 Campaign to Abolish War website, accessed 13 July 2015 at: http://www.article-9.org/en/index.html.

Hanawa, Machiko, Tsukushi Takehiko and Cazman (2008), 'World peace now', in Jennifer Chan (ed.), *Another Japan is Possible: New Social Movements and Global Citizenship Education*, Stanford University Press.

Hein, Laura and Mark Selden (eds) (2003), *Islands of Discontent: Okinawan Responses to Japanese and American Power*, Rowman & Littlefield.

Johnson, Chalmers (ed.) (1999), *Okinawa: Cold War Island*, Japan Policy Research Institute.

Korean Council for the Women Drafted for Military Sexual Slavery by Japan website, accessed 15 July 2015 at: https://www.womenandwar.net/contents/general/general.nx?page_str_menu=2101.

Makishi, Yoshikazu (2000), *Okinawa Wa Mô Damasarenai: Kichi Shinsetsu=SACO Goi No Karakuri Wo Utsu* (Okinawa won't be Cheated Anymore: Taking a Shot at the SACO Agreement), Kobunken.

Mayors for Peace (2015), website, accessed 13 July 2015 at: http://www.mayorsforpeace.org/english/index.html.

Nara, Katsuyuki and Sarah Brock (2004), Article 9 Association English website, accessed 13 July 2015 at: http://www.9-jo.jp/en/index_en.html.

Nishihara, Nobuaki (2008), 'Fundamental law in education, peace and the marketization of education', in Jennifer Chan (ed.), *Another Japan is Possible: New Social Movements and Global Citizenship Education*, Stanford University Press.

Nomura, Kôya (2005), *Muishiki no Shokuminchi: Nihonjin no Beigun Kichi to Okinawajin* (Unconscious Colonialism: Japanese US Military Bases and the Okinawans), Ochanomizu Shobo.

San Francisco Peace Treaty (1951), accessed 13 July 2015 at: http://www.taiwandocuments.org/sanfrancisco01.htm.

Shirakawa, Masumi (1999), 'Shinsayoku to Bôryoku' (The new left and violence), in Watanabe Ichie, Shiokawa Yoshinobu and Oyabu Ryusuke (eds), *Shinsayoku undo 40-nen no Hikari to Kage* (The Light and Shadow of Forty Years of History of the New Left), Shinsensha.

Syun, Medoruma (2005), *Okinawa 'Sengo' Zero Nen* (Okinawa 'Postwar' Year Zero), NHK Shuppan.

Taira, Satoko (2008), 'I would like to be able to speak Uchinaguchi when I grow up!', in Jennifer Chan (ed.), *Another Japan is Possible: New Social Movements and Global Citizenship Education*, Stanford University Press.

Takada, Ken (2008), 'Article 9 and the peace movement', in Jennifer Chan (ed.), *Another Japan is Possible: New Social Movements and Global Citizenship Education*, Stanford University Press.

Takagi, Masayuki (1990), *Shin Sayoku Sanjunenshi* (Thirty Years' History of the New Left), Doyoubijutsusha.

Takazato, Suzuyo (1996), *Okinawa no Onnatachi: Jose no Jinken to Kichi, Guntai* (Women in Okinawa: Women's Human Rights and Military Bases/Army), Akaishi Shoten.

Totani, Yma (2008), *Tokyo War Crimes Trial: The Pursuit of Justice in the Wake of World War Two*, Harvard University Press.

Tsutsui, Kiyoteru (2009), 'The trajectory of perpetrators' trauma: mnemonic politics around the Asia-Pacific War in Japan', *Social Forces*, **87** (3): 1389–422.

UN Special Rapporteur on Violence Against Women (1996), 'Report on the mission to the Democratic People's Republic of Korea, the Republic of Korea, and Japan on the issue of military sexual slavery in wartime', accessed 14 July 2015 at: http://www1.umn.edu/humanrts/commission/country52/53-add1.htm.

Vienna Declaration and Programme of Action (25 June 1993), accessed 15 July 2015 at: http://www.ohchr.org/EN/ProfessionalInterest/Pages/Vienna.aspx.

Women's Initiatives for Gender Justice (2015) website, accessed 13 July 2015 at: http://4genderjustice.org/.

Women's International War Crimes Tribunal (2001), 'Judgement', available at: http://www.asser.nl/upload/documents/DomCLIC/Docs/NLP/Japan/Comfort_Women_Judgement_04-12-2001_part_1.pdf.

Yamamoto, Mari (2004), *Grassroots Pacifism in Post-War Japan: The Rebirth of a Nation*, Routledge/Curzon.

Yoshimi, Yoshiaki (1995), *Jugun Ianfu* (Military comfort women), Iwanami Shoten.

Yui, Akiko (2004), 'The Okinawan anti-base movement regains momentum: new U.S. base project off Henoko Beach met with effective non-violent resistance on the sea', *Europe Solidaire Sans Frontières*, 31 December, accessed 14 July 2015 at: http://www.europe-solidaire.org/spip.php?article5147.

Author Interviews

Dugong Network Okinawa, October 2005.

Grassroots movement to remove US bases from Okinawa and the world, December 2004.

Okinawa women act against military violence, October 2005.

PART IV

GENDER AND THE AFTERMATH OF WAR

Part IV Introduction: Gender and the aftermath of war

Simona Sharoni

Although feminists have long pointed out that wars seldom have neat beginnings and ends, the attention of scholars and policy-makers alike to the aftermath of war and political violence, let alone their gendered dimensions, is relatively new. The result is an interdisciplinary body of literature that examines war as a continuum, with careful attention to the multiple impacts of its escalation and de-escalation. At the same time, the conceptual shift to viewing war on a continuum rather than as an event with a distinct beginning and end presents an important challenge for those interested in understanding the aftermath of war. Feminist scholars embraced the challenge as an opportunity to explore the complex and fluid dynamics in gender identities, roles and relations. Policy-makers and practitioners, however, arbitrarily defined the length of the aftermath of war, often in order to determine when to end their funding of a particular operation and shift their attention to a different conflict zone. In most societies, however, key issues persist after fighters put down their weapons and a truce is reached or peace accord signed.

The chapters in this part coalesce around the centrality of gender into three overarching themes: the changing definitions of peace, security and justice in the aftermath of war; the demilitarization and reintegration of soldiers; and the opportunities and challenges facing the post-conflict society.

THE CHANGING DEFINITIONS OF PEACE, SECURITY AND JUSTICE

The literature on the aftermath of war reflects a critical rethinking and re-definitions of such concepts as peace, security and justice. Whereas peace has been broadly defined as the opposite of war and viewed as an event, or a moment that signaled war's end, scholars focused on post-conflict societies have used such terms as 'peacebuilding' or 'conflict transformation' to examine the complex processes that unfold once political violence officially ends (Jacobson, 2013; Douglas, 2015).

461

In Chapter 22, Laura Shepherd and Caitlin Hamilton provide an overview of the academic literature on gender and peacebuilding, including a clear articulation of why and how the process of peacebuilding is inherently gendered. They describe how the gender identities, roles and relationships of the individuals involved in peace processes shape both the policies and the outcomes of peacebuilding efforts. Shepherd and Hamilton identify three central themes in the growing bodies of feminist scholarship on gender and peacebuilding. The first theme involves the intersection of gender with other such markers of identity as race, sexuality, ethnicity, class, age and ability that can be used to divide people and communities. The second theme consists of a careful analysis of the gendered language that underlies the conceptual architecture of peace agreements, while the third theme examines the gendered aspects of policy documents with particular attention to how they address women's agency in post-conflict societies.

Some of the themes identified by Shepherd and Hamilton also inform Megan Mackenzie's feminist exploration of the shifting definitions of security in the aftermath of war. In Chapter 23, Mackenzie examines critically contending definitions of security in the context of the emergence of 'post-conflict' as a sub-field of study within International Relations and Security Studies, and as a distinct focus for policy-makers. She explores such questions as: what conditions need to be in place to allow women and men to feel more secure in a postwar period compared to during and before the war? In doing so, Mackenzie reminds us that a gendered approach to post-conflict security does not mean simply 'looking for women'. Rather, it requires an examination of how security itself is defined in relation to gender norms and identities.

Transitional justice – a relatively new area of feminist engagement – has been mostly associated with truth and reconciliation commissions and sexual violence in times of conflict, but its scope is much broader. Catherine O'Rourke explores, in Chapter 24, the transformative potential of transitional justice for women and gender relations. She argues that paying careful attention to the gendered aspects of transitional justice recognizes not only women's gendered experiences of conflict but also their differential needs for accountability. Moreover, a transitional justice framework is designed to ensure that gender equality and the protection of women's human rights are enshrined in the post-conflict society. One of the chapter's significant contributions is the focus on the relationship between scholarship on gender and transitional justice, and the practical and policy-relevant applications of this work.

DEMILITARIZATION AND REINTEGRATION

The literature on the processes of demilitarization and reintegration of soldiers is an excellent example of the nexus between scholarship and practice. Indeed, most of the scholarly and policy debates on the topic are related to the efforts of the United Nations to deal with large numbers of former soldiers and weapons in post-conflict zones. The process of demilitarization in post-conflict societies is currently referred to, especially in policy circles, as Disarmament, Demobilization and Reintegration (DDR). More recently, in some cases, a second 'R' was added, to stress the importance of rehabilitation. The most significant contribution of research on demilitarization and reintegration is in addressing the gap between 'best practices' and the actual implementation of DDR initiatives in conflict zones. Focusing on DDR programs in Liberia, in Chapter 25 Christopher Hills situates the implementation of demilitarization and reintegration initiatives in the region in a historical context that is crucial to understanding their successes and shortcomings. The failures of UN officials to consult with local women's groups and to successfully address sexual and gender-based violence are among the shortcomings discussed in Hills' chapter.

In Chapter 26, Myriam Denov, Alexandra Ricard-Guay and Amber Green also address demilitarization and reintegration with a focus on child soldiers, and former girl soldiers in particular. Some of the problems they examine include the exclusion of former girl soldiers from programs of assistance, the social stigma that complicates their reintegration, economic hardship and the post-traumatic impacts of war and its outcomes on their sense of self and identity. Using excerpts from interviews conducted with former girl soldiers from Colombia and Sierra Leone, the authors highlight the importance of a gendered approach to studying war and child soldiers, stressing that girls' options, roles and agency, both during conflict and following demobilization, are embedded within broader gendered power structures and identities.

THE POST-CONFLICT SOCIETY: OPPORTUNITIES AND CHALLENGES

The UN has been the largest and most influential body involved in post-conflict peacebuilding, demilitarization and reintegration efforts around the world. The passage of UNSCR 1325 by the Security Council in 2000 has been viewed widely as a key turning point in the struggle to make gender central to peacebuilding efforts in post-conflict societies. The resolution affirmed that political conflicts and their aftermaths are gendered processes, focusing attention on the lives and experiences of women and girls in conflict zones, and making visible the active role of women in the prevention and resolution of armed conflicts. Additionally, the resolution addressed violence against women, especially sexual and gender-based violence, both during war and in its aftermath.

Soumita Basu's analysis of the UN's women, peace and security agenda in Chapter 27 focuses on the significance of UNSCR 1325 in relation to other Security Council resolutions that have addressed women and gender issues in times of conflict and post-conflict. Some feminist scholars, however, have been critical of UNSCR 1325 and of gender mainstreaming initiatives in post-conflict societies more generally (McWilliams and Kilmurray, 2015). The critics have warned against simply adding 'women' or 'gender' to existing frameworks of development, peacebuilding and transition. Instead they call for context-specific models that view gender not only as an identity but also as central to power relations in any give society (McWilliams and Ni Aoláin, 2013; Pratt, 2013). Although Basu is well aware of feminist critiques of both UNSCR 1325 and the role of the UN in post-conflict reconstruction more generally, she concludes that the UN has an important role to play in ensuring that post-conflict concerns relating to the gendered aspects of armed conflict are addressed.

The conventional framework used by the UN and many NGOs and INGOs for gender-sensitive projects in post-conflict societies include three broadly defined areas: women-focused activities, gender-awareness programing and gender-oriented social transformation (Omonaa and Aduob, 2013). Some authors in this part are critical of the implementation of gender-sensitive initiatives in post-conflict societies. For example, reflecting on the Liberian case, Christopher Hills calls into question the tendency of UN officials to impose one-size-fits-all programs with little or no consultation with local women's groups and gender experts. Along the same lines, Denov, Ricard-Guay and Green insist that DDR initiatives must pay closer attention to the special needs of former girl soldiers and their short-term needs. To address these and other critiques and challenges, the UN and NGOs must develop context-specific models in close consultation with individuals and groups on the ground. Additional research in this area, focusing both on the promise and shortcomings of particular interventions in post-conflict societies, may enhance the success of future programs.

Taken together, the chapters in this part make significant contributions to the understanding of how gender impacts and is in turn impacted during the aftermath of war. Their theoretical innovation notwithstanding, contributors also raise critical questions about the implementation of gender-sensitive policies and programs in conflict zones around the world. Authors in this part agree that more research and careful examination of existing initiatives are needed in order to address the gendered issues confronting people during the aftermath of war. In particular, authors call for closer consultation between scholars and practitioners and especially between outside agents and those involved in struggles for gender equality and justice in the local post-conflict community.

REFERENCES

Douglas, Sarah (2015), '"What gets measured gets done": translating accountability frameworks into better responses for women and girls in peacebuilding contexts', *Journal of Peacebuilding & Development*, **10** (1): 90–96.

Jacobson, Ruth (2013), 'Women "after" wars', in Carol Cohn (ed.), *Women and Wars*, Polity Press, pp. 215–42.

McWilliams, Monica and Avila Kilmurray (2015), 'From the global to the local: grounding UNSCR 1325 on women, peace and security in post conflict policy making', *Women's Studies International Forum*, **51**: 128–35.

McWilliams, Monica and Fionnuala Ni Aoláin (2013), 'There is a war going on you know: addressing the complexity of violence against women in conflicted and post conflict societies', *Transitional Justice Review*, **1** (2): (Article 2).

Omonaa, Julius and Jennifer Rose Aduob (2013), 'Gender issues during post-conflict recovery: the case of Nwoya district, northern Uganda', *Journal of Gender Studies*, **22** (2): 119–36.

Pratt, Nicola (2013), 'Reconceptualizing gender, reinscribing racial–sexual boundaries in international security: the case of UN Security Council Resolution 1325 on "Women, Peace and Security"', *International Studies Quarterly*, **57** (4): 772–83.

22. Gender and peacebuilding
Laura J. Shepherd and Caitlin Hamilton[1]

INTRODUCTION

In his 1992 *Agenda for Peace*, then-Secretary-General of the United Nations Boutros Boutros-Ghali insisted that, having overcome the 'immense ideological barrier' that characterized the era of 'Cold War', the organization must 'stand ready to assist in peacebuilding in its different contexts; rebuilding the institutions and infrastructures of nations torn by civil war and strife; and building bonds of peaceful mutual benefit among nations formerly at war' (United Nations, 1992).

The concept and practices of peacebuilding have been distinguished from peacemaking and peacekeeping, both operationally (United Nations, 1996; Brahmini et al., 2000; Panyarachun et al., 2004) and in scholarly literature (Galtung, 1969, 1975; Doyle and Sambanis, 2000; Gawerc, 2006; Denskus, 2007). Though clearly and inextricably related to both peacemaking and peacekeeping, peacebuilding activities have come to represent 'the front line of preventative action' (Doyle and Sambanis, 2000, p. 779) through the production of stable political, social and economic institutions in the aftermath of war.

Despite the recognition among peacebuilding agencies of the need 'to integrate a gender perspective' into their operations (UNSC, 2005, Art. 20), some scholars in the field of peace research and research on peacebuilding still tend to assume that peacebuilding activities are experienced similarly by all, irrespective of gender identity and performance. To illustrate the gender-blind approach to peacebuilding Mary Moran notes that '[Roland] Paris's influential book *At War's End: Building Peace After Conflict* (2004) ... contains no index entries for "women", "men", or "gender"' (2010, p. 262). At the same time, a significant body of literature has developed that specifically engages with gendered logics and practices of peacebuilding. Scholarship on gender and conflict more broadly insists that to seek to understand the socio-political dynamics of war and peace without paying attention to gender is to construct a partial and thin account. This view is shared by a number of highly influential collections that address peacebuilding from a variety of feminist perspectives (see, for example, Mazurana et al., 2005;

Sweetman, 2005b; Afshar and Eade, 2004; Cockburn, 2001; Moser and McIlwhaine, 2001; Meintjes et al., 2001). This collection of literature contributes to a more holistic understanding of peacemaking, peacebuilding and post-conflict reconstruction than that allowed within conventionally gender-blind academic literature.

Weaving together insights from a range of disciplinary perspectives (including Peace Studies, Development Studies, International Relations, Anthropology and Economics), these scholars remind us not only that the individuals involved in peace processes are embodied agential subjects, but also that the concepts deployed in policies aiming to facilitate peacebuilding, including 'peace' itself, are inherently gendered. We begin this chapter with an overview of the academic literature on gender and peacebuilding, before moving on to discuss the institutional architecture supporting gender-sensitive peacebuilding efforts. We conclude with some suggestions for future research in this area.

CONTRIBUTIONS FROM THE ACADEMY

Feminist scholarship on peacebuilding tends to pay close attention to the specificities of national and local contexts of peacebuilding-related activities, an ethos that underpins much research in this area. Evaluating the efficacy of peacebuilding activities in specific geographical contexts not only provides valuable empirical information about the case at hand, but also centralizes a focus on local ownership of peacebuilding practices and the everyday politics of peace. Examples of this include research focused on Rwanda (Hudson, 2009; Rostegui, 2013), Côte d'Ivoire (Hudson, 2009), Uganda and South Sudan (Rostegui, 2013), the Pacific Islands (George, 2014), Bosnia-Herzegovina (O'Reilly, 2012), Kenya and Nepal (Myrttinen et al., 2015) and the Solomon Islands (Westendorf, 2013). The first strand of feminist peace research on peacebuilding was grounded in an understanding of women involved in peacebuilding-related activity as scholars and theorists of peace (cf. Brooke Ackerly's construction of 'women's human rights activists as cross-cultural theorists', 2001). These studies have drawn attention to the local sociopolitical contexts of peace, the everyday practices of peace, and the gendered dimensions of both.

Feminist analyses of peacebuilding have also challenged and contributed to academic and policy debates about peacebuilding; three particular thematic contributions stand out. First, feminist works on peacebuilding emphasize equality in both formal and informal institutional access. Caroline Sweetman, for example, argues that '[i]ntegrating a gender perspective into peacebuilding and reconstruction is an essential step in the process of ensuring democratic decision making at all levels of society' (2005a, pp. 6–7). Similarly, based on their study of gendered peacebuilding, Cheryl de la Rey and Susan McKay insist that '[a]dvancing women's global status demands that they be co-architects with men of re-emerging post-conflict societies' (2006, p. 150). Feminist scholars examining these issues make explicit the links between formal gender equality in governance institutions, resource allocation and decision-making forums and the formation of a society that values the voice and activities of all its members equally.

This research agenda also draws on the concept of intersectionality to stress that gendered approaches to peacebuilding must consider the 'dialogue necessary for recognizing and moving beyond historical differences that have so violently excluded different ethnic groups in the past' (Baines, 2005, p. 221). In other words, feminist scholars of peacebuilding recognize the salience not only of gender difference but also of other such markers of identity as race, sexuality, ethnicity, class, age and ability that can be used to divide people and communities; thus, they insist that true equality must negotiate these differences and mediate the multiple ways in which these markers can be mobilized to silence or marginalize individuals or social collectives. Lesley Pruitt (2014), for example, has looked at how gender and age intersect (along with other identity markers) in the context of peacebuilding. While peacebuilding policies and initiatives have been directed to both women and youth as groups marginalized in peacebuilding practices, Pruitt's work looks specifically at girls, who often 'remain the group most excluded from peace processes and least recognized in political participation' (2014, p. 486). Being sensitive to the needs of women is therefore not enough; researchers, policymakers and those working in (post-)conflict contexts need to be aware of and attentive to the multiple axes of exclusion that exist, to ensure that the voices of all participants in the peacebuilding process are taken into account.

The second important trend within the growing body of feminist literature on peacebuilding has focused on the conceptual architecture of peace agreements and policy documents. In her analysis of Angolan peace processes, Zoë Wilson concludes 'that peacemaking and peacebuilding efforts have reiterated rather than addressed distinctive vulnerabilities Angolan women experience today because such efforts are undergirded by gender-biased assumptions' (2005, p. 242). Feminist scholars have sought to understand the ways in which the language used to write policy has implications beyond textual representation and can be seen as constitutive of the reality of which it purports to speak (see

Puechguirbal, 2010; Otto, 2009). This body of research includes engagements with United Nations Security Council (UNSC) Resolution 1325 (frequently represented as the first international policy document directly addressing gender in conflict prevention and conflict resolution, as we discuss further below) (see, for example Willett, 2010; Shepherd, 2008; Cohn et al., 2004). It also encompasses studies of gender and security sector reform (see Mobekk, 2010; Shepherd, 2010).

Feminist scholarship on gender and representation in peacebuilding examines not only the assumptions about the inherent or biologically determined capacity of women to facilitate peace but also the ways in which writing gendered bodies into policy documents can pre- and proscribe engagement with the political agenda enshrined within the document itself (see Pankhurst, 2004; Cohn, 2004; Cohn and Ruddick, 2004). Such analyses allow researchers to explore the ways in which a peacebuilding actor is 'positioned as a subject ... what its priorities are, and how its activities – including the production of peacebuilding-related policy materials – function to reproduce its identity as a particular kind of peacebuilding actor ... . [This] then produces (and is in turn reproduced by) modes of engagement in peacebuilding contexts on the ground' (Hamilton and Shepherd, 2015, p. 5).

The third trend in feminist research on the gendered politics and practices of peacebuilding examines agency, particularly women's agency in post-conflict societies. One influential line of research into women's agency in peacebuilding stresses the importance of reframing women as agents of change, instead of the reiteration of a narrative that focuses on vulnerability or victimhood. This research agenda sees women 'as potential contributors to all collaborative measures to achieve peace' (Porter, 2003, p. 251) (see also Pratt and Richter-Devroe, 2011; Hamilton and Shepherd, 2015). Research on agency has also seen the identification of the multiple ways in which women act as agents; as Manchanda (2005, p. 4741) notes, '[w]omen's agency is visible in spontaneous and sporadic interventions to protect their families from immediate violence, in campaigns against human rights abuse and for justice; in building trust and reconciliation across the conflict divide'. However, importantly, she also notes that '[t]here is [an] agentive moment produced by women transcending traditional social roles and joining the fighting ranks' (p. 4741). Conflict and post-conflict scenarios see women occupy multiple roles, and this research on agency contributes to a fuller understanding of how we might start to bring about women's increased involvement in peace negotiations and in post-conflict governance.

Derived from situated, contextual and sympathetic research conducted all over the world, feminist accounts of peacebuilding from Afghanistan

(Kandiyoti, 2005) to Zimbabwe (Meintjes, 2001) remind us of the importance of paying attention to both the differences and commonalities in the gendered experiences of peacebuilding (see Afshar, 2004). Such comparative analysis could not occur without the nuanced field accounts of the minutiae of peace negotiations, socio-political reconstruction and community rebuilding provided by feminist activists, academics and advocates who take gender as a primary analytical focus.

THE INSTITUTIONAL ARCHITECTURE OF PEACEBUILDING

UNSC Resolution (UNSCR) 1325 is widely acknowledged as the foundation of gender-sensitive policy formulation in the sphere of peace and security (see Moran, 2010, p. 262), although the resolution itself owes a debt to a number of previous UNSC Resolutions as well as other UN Declarations and Reports including 'the Windhoek Declaration and the Namibia Plan of Action' (UNSC, 2000, Preamble). UNSCR 1325 'called for, *inter alia*, the increased participation of women in decision-making related to the prevention, management and resolution of conflict' (Otto, 2006–2007, p. 116, emphasis in original). At the time of writing, UNSCR 1325 has been translated into many languages, from Albanian to Zulu, and 48 countries have adopted National Action Plans to facilitate the implementation of UNSCR 1325 in peace operations and conflict prevention (see PeaceWomen.org). UNSCR 1325 is the first of eight 'Women, Peace and Security' resolutions issued since 2000: UNSCR 1820 (2008); UNSCR 1888 (2009); UNSCR 1889 (2009); UNSCR 1960 (2010); UNSCR 2016 (2013); and UNSCR 2122 (2013). The core provisions of each resolution are summarized in Table 22.1.

UNSCR 1325 has been subject to significant critical scrutiny from academics and policymakers alike. Jasmine-Kim Westendorf (2013, pp. 459–60), for example, notes that there are fundamental challenges that undermine the effectiveness of the resolution, spanning its enforcement, operationalization, and its implementation. Sarah Douglas (2015, p. 91) agrees that, despite the

> bevy of policies adopted by the UN, gender advisory teams deployed globally, and application of the women's rights vocabulary in peace and security arenas … the resounding consensus around the tenth anniversary of the resolution was that policy and rhetoric were yet to have sufficient impact on women and girls living in conflict and post-conflict zones.

Table 22.1   Key issues and core provisions in the UN SC 'Women, Peace and Security' resolutions

Resolution/year	Key issues and core provisions
S/RES/1325 (2000)	Representation & participation of women in peace and security governance; protection of women's rights and bodies in conflict & post-conflict situations.
S/RES/1820 (2008)	Protection of women from sexualized violence in conflict; zero tolerance of sexualized abuse and exploitation perpetrated by UN Department of Peacekeeping Operations personnel.
S/RES/1888 (2009)	Creation of office of Special Representative of the Secretary-General on Conflict-Related Sexual Violence (CRSV); creation of UN Action as an umbrella organization addressing issues related to CRSV; identification of 'team of experts'; appointment of Women's Protection Advisors (WPAs) to field missions.
S/RES/1889 (2009)	Need to increase participation of women in peace and security governance at all levels; creation of global indicators to map implementation of UNSCR 1325.
S/RES/1960 (2010)	Development of CSRV monitoring, analysis and reporting arrangements; integration of WPAs to field missions alongside Gender Advisors.
S/RES/2106 (2013)	Challenging impunity and lack of accountability for CRSV.
S/RES/2122 (2013)	Identifies UN Women as key UN entity providing information and advice on participation of women in peace and security governance; whole-of-UN accountability; civil society inclusion; 2015 High-level Review of implementation of UNSCR 1325.

Note: This table is reproduced with minor edits from Shepherd (2014).

Despite these issues, UNSCR 1325 remains a profoundly influential document that continues to shape gender-sensitive policy on peace and security.

In the area of peacebuilding, there is a range of policy documents governing operations and activities, many of which draw on or acknowledge a debt to UNSCR 1325. Initial engagement with conflict resolution and post-conflict reconstruction was governed by 'DDR' programmes: processes aimed at the Disarmament of individuals or combatant collectives, the Demobilization of combatants and their Reintegration into society. 'First generation' or traditional DDR programmes tended to focus on dismantling formal military structures and building sustainable socio-political institutions to facilitate peace processes, whereas 'second generation' DDR programmes have extended their remit to include communities affected by armed conflict (United Nations, 2010). In both cases, however, the commitments upheld by practitioners in DDR programmes, often but not exclusively (see Muggah et al., 2003, p. 9 and *passim*) under the auspices of the United Nations, relate explicitly to the strategic aims of DDR more broadly: 'to support the peace process, create political space and contribute to a secure environment' (United Nations, 2010, p. 3).

The United Nations Secretary-General, alongside other actors, represents DDR as foundational to effective peacebuilding; in a recent report the Secretary-General noted the central importance of DDR to 'basic safety and security', a precondition of peacebuilding activities (United Nations, 2009, p. 6; see also United Nations, 2010, p. 10). However, 'the policies and programmes of international funding agencies typically concentrate upon reconstruction of physical, political, educational, and economic infrastructures, not people's lives' and, as a consequence, gender has historically been represented as being of secondary importance in DDR programmes (McKay, 2004, p. 20). Recent UN publications, however, indicate a shift in orientation by the key institutions involved in DDR practices, containing an entire chapter devoted to 'Women, gender and DDR' (United Nations, 2006). The United Nations' 'Integrated Disarmament, Demobilisation and Reintegration Standards' explicitly engage 'stereotypical beliefs' about gender and articulate a willingness to institutionalize the 'gender-aware interventions and female-specific actions that should be carried out in order to make sure that DDR programmes are sustainable and equitable' (United Nations, 2006, 5.10, p. 2). Only if DDR programmes are 'gender-responsive' will post-conflict communities be able to create durable peace.

In addition to DDR programmes, other policy initiatives facilitating the creation of gender-sensitive peacebuilding include Security Sector Reform (SSR). SSR intersects with DDR and also engages questions of legitimacy and authority in the security sector of post-conflict societies, in an effort to ensure that 'forces do not regroup ... ; bribery and corruption are eliminated; and the sector (including leadership structures) is fully transformed so as to gain credibility, legitimacy and trust in the public eye' (Anderlini and Conaway, 2004, p. 31). Peacebuilding efforts are often grounded in both DDR and SSR programmes, and multiple policy platforms and toolkits exist to enshrine the centrality of gender-awareness in these practices (see, for example, Hunt Alternatives Fund and International Alert, 2004; Bastick and Valasek, 2008; United Nations, 2008). Scholarly work on SSR, however, suggests that '[t]he gap between policy and practice persists and gender issues are still treated as an afterthought' (Mobekk, 2010, p. 288), which may be an obstacle to the creation of sustainable peace.

In 2010, under the auspices of the Women, Peace and Security agenda deriving from UNSCR 1325, the UN Secretary-General produced a report titled 'Women's Participation in Peacebuilding' (UN SC, 2010). The report specifically relates women's participation in peacebuilding back to the core provisions of the Women, Peace and Security Agenda (UN SC, 2010, para. 3). It further discusses DDR and SSR explicitly throughout, and thus now forms the foundation of much gender-sensitive programming in the area of peacebuilding-related activity. Articulating a clear commitment to the systematic protection of women's rights at all stages of peacebuilding, from negotiation through to development and democratization, the Secretary-General outlines the seven-point action plan for gender-responsive peacebuilding (UN SC, 2010, para. 26 and *passim*), the key commitments of which are:

1. the inclusion of women and gender experts in mediation and conflict resolution;
2. the inclusion of women in post-conflict planning to ensure the needs of women and girls are met;
3. gender-sensitive post-conflict financing;
4. ensuring gender training for development and humanitarian workers;
5. women's representation in post-conflict governance and participation in political reform processes;
6. commitment to the rule of law and access to justice for women and girls;
7. ensuring women's participation in economic recovery.

This framework now informs much UN action, particularly when undertaken by the UN Peacebuilding Commission.

Recognizing that efforts toward peacebuilding needed to be integrated to maximize efficiency, the United Nations Peacebuilding Committee (UN PBC) was inaugurated as an intergovernmental advisory body in 2005 following the adoption of Resolutions by both the UN Security Council and the UN General Assembly (1645 and 60/180 respectively). As explained in an addendum to the 2005 report *In Larger Freedom: Towards Development, Security and Human Rights for All*, then-Secretary General Kofi Annan suggested that the Commission should

> provide a central node for helping to create and promote comprehensive strategies for peacebuilding both in general terms and in country situations. It

should encourage coherent decision-making on peacebuilding by Member States and by the United Nations Secretariat, agencies and programmes. ... It must also provide a forum in which representatives of the United Nations system, major bilateral donors, troop contributors, relevant regional actors and organizations, the international financial institutions and the national or transitional authorities of the country concerned can share information about their respective post-conflict recovery activities. (UN General Assembly, 2005)

Under normal circumstances, 'client' countries, or countries that seek to include their peacebuilding activities on the agenda of the Commission, must submit a request first to the Security Council and the General Assembly, the former of which then refers the case to the UN PBC. Since its inception, the UN PBC has provided advice and support on peace-building activities in six countries, all of which are still on the agenda: Burundi, Sierra Leone, Guinea-Bissau, Central African Republic, Liberia and Guinea (UN PBC, n.d.).

Due to its relatively recent establishment, the PBC is under particular pressure 'to embody the dominant norms and ideas that currently apply to UN thinking on peacebuilding' (Tryggestad, 2010, p. 160), including those relating to the 'Women, Peace and Security' agenda. As noted in the founding Resolution, and building on the institutional architecture outlined above, the UN PBC is called upon 'to integrate a gender perspective into all its work' (UN SC, 2005, Article 20). Evidence of this commitment can be found in some of the annual reports submitted by the Commission; in 2007, for example, the UN PBC noted that '[g]ender equality was identified as a critical cross-cutting issue for peace consoli-dation in both Burundi and Sierra Leone' (UN PBC, 2007, p. 6). The Commission also held a workshop titled 'Gender and Peacebuilding: Enhancing Women's Participation' under the auspices of its Working Group on Lessons Learned, which aims to consolidate information and experience from previous activities relevant to the agenda of the Com-mission (UN PBC, 2008a; UN PBC, 2008b; UN PBC, 2008c).

In a key document provided to workshop participants Jennifer Klot notes that '[a]lthough women's participation and gender equality is a "predictable" peacebuilding gap, it is striking how far this core issue is lacking in institutional capacity, policy and operational guidance, pro-gramme implementation, data, monitoring and evaluation, knowledge and resources' (UN PBC, 2008b, p. 9). Klot makes five specific recommenda-tions to the Commission to ameliorate the situation (UN PBC, 2008b, p. 11):

1. increase women's participation in peacebuilding;
2. strengthen institutional capacity for gender equality and peacebuilding;
3. respond to gaps in knowledge and information on gender and peacebuilding;
4. increase coherence of UN actions in support of gender equality and peacebuilding;
5. ensure adequate resources to mainstream gender equality into peacebuilding.

These recommendations, alongside a need to monitor gender mainstreaming mechanisms and other avenues designed to increase women's access to justice and full participation in public life, including formal political activities, were also highlighted in the Summary Notes of the Chair (UN PBC, 2008c, p. 4).

More recently, the UN Peacebuilding Commission Working Group on Lessons Learned held a further workshop titled 'Enhancing Gender-Responsive National Reconciliation Processes', focusing on the gendered dimensions of peacebuilding and reconciliation. This workshop followed a Declaration from the Peacebuilding Commission on the importance of women's economic empowerment for the building of sustainable peace (UN PBC, 2013a). The issues discussed at the workshop included increased women's participation in reconciliation, mediation and conflict resolution, and the need for transformative transitional justice mechanisms to ensure that the post-conflict society is characterized by gender equality rather than returning to a *status quo ante* of gender discrimination, where that was the case. The explicit commitment to the implementation of UNSCR 2122, the most recent Women, Peace and Security resolution, as well as linking to the UN Secretary-General's 2010 report outlining the seven-point action plan discussed above (UN PBC, 2013b), suggests a significant institutional change aimed at encouraging gender-responsive peacebuilding and gender-sensitive planning, which is likely to have positive outcomes in peacebuilding contexts.

FUTURE DIRECTIONS

Future research in the field of gender and peacebuilding should consider the methods used to analyze data relating to gender and peacebuilding. For example, a form of process-tracing could be used to investigate how and under what circumstances gender is written into and out of various iterations of the policy process at the UNPBC. Process-tracing can be separated from its roots as a positivist approach to social research that seeks to uncover 'the causal chain and causal mechanism ... between an independent variable (or variables) and the outcome of the dependent variable' (George and Bennett, 2005, p. 206). In this context, process-tracing that takes seriously embodied subjectivity and the politics of positioning could shed light on how different agential subjects have differing abilities to speak to and influence policy in various different situations. Such a process would consider, for example, how and why did gender, which was deemed a key issue to peacebuilding in Sierra Leone in the original strategic framework produced by the UN Peacebuilding Commission, disappear entirely from the review published a year later? What circumstances – or which actors – had changed? What are the narratives recounted by the actors involved and how did they shape or influence the iterated policy formulation? What constraints did they perceive and what opportunities did they identify? Addressing these questions is central to the institutionalization of a holistic understanding of gender in peacebuilding activities. Another fruitful area of future research might consider the methods used to evaluate the efficacy of gender-mainstreaming in UN missions; Kiril Sharapov, for example, suggests that 'an all-inclusive, qualitative perspective rooted in feminism, gender analysis and localized forms of political participation' can be useful to measure the success (or otherwise) of UN policies on-the-ground (2005, p. 99).

Future research might also engage with the problematic representations of gender and Civil Society Organizations (CSOs) in countries engaged in peacebuilding and post-conflict reconstruction to find out how and in what ways political participation at the sub-state level is perceived as authentic and a site of legitimate action. If 'women's organizations' are being tasked with ensuring that peacebuilding activities are undertaken with a sensitivity to gender, then this is an area to which scholarship can contribute, not least to ensure that a link between women and CSOs is not forged with the effect of displacing women from formal political arenas and reducing their formal political capital. The tendency of resources to flow to domains of 'high politics' is well documented, and these domains frequently exclude women and certain men. If peacebuilding is to proceed in an authentically inclusive and democratic modality, then documenting the support given to CSOs and the extent of the 'stakes' that they 'hold' in the peacebuilding process may be illuminating.

Further, while the concepts and language of gender-sensitive approaches to peacebuilding have been adopted by national governments and international institutions alike, there remains a schism between policy and practice; there is a real need for us to be more attentive to 'the lived experiences of peacebuilders working in contexts of protracted and often recurring cycles of violence and conflict' (Noma et al., 2012, p. 17).

Although institutional policies rightfully constitute an important aspect of literature on peacebuilding, we should also '[allow] women peacebuilders to tell their own stories' (Noma et al., 2012, p. 7). Projects such as the 'Women PeaceMakers Program', which offers women peacebuilders 'a protected space to examine their life trajectory and reflect on how they came to be agents of peacebuilding in their own communities' (Noma et al., 2012, p. 8), are particularly valuable in this regard.

Additionally, future research should examine how gender and peace-building intersect with other potential indicators of conflict. Recent research looks at gender, natural resources and peacebuilding. Scholars have noted that researchers and policymakers had looked at gender and peacebuilding, and natural resources and peacebuilding, but that there was a much more limited body of research that paid attention to the three concepts together (Myrttinen et al., 2015, p. 2). By doing so, the researchers demonstrate that gender needs to be taken into account in multiple settings across peacebuilding contexts; failing to do so means 'missing fundamental, gendered conflict dynamics and peacebuilding opportunities' (Myrttinen et al., 2015, p. 11). By expanding the focus on gender and peacebuilding to include other pertinent areas in post-conflict and development contexts, a broader demographic may become aware of the role of gender in all aspects of peacebuilding and post-conflict development contexts, including access to health services and education as well as to areas that have not received as much attention, such as natural resources or technological innovation (Llamazares and Mulloy, 2014).

Finally, future research should continue to engage with the tricky question of meaning and the politics of representation. As Dvora Yanow points out, '[i]nterpretations [...] are more powerful than "facts". That makes the policy process, in all its phases, a struggle for the determination of meanings' (1996, p. 19). Policy formulation and even implementation is an ongoing process requiring metaphorical and sometimes literal translations at every stage (see Shepherd, 2010, pp. 15–16). *How* a policy means (Yanow, 1996) as well as *what* a policy means are crucial considerations, particularly in relation to gender.

Decades of feminist scholarship sought not only to include women – and recognize men as gendered subjects – in official and unofficial accounts of social and political life but also to question and problematize the conflation of 'gender' with women, the representation of women as vulnerable victims in need of protection and the corollary stereotypical association of women with pacifism. Future research on gender and peacebuilding could engage with the relevant institutional architecture to demand that conceptual space is made for *all* gendered subjects to be represented as fully agential, complex and multifaceted, while simultaneously demanding that physical space is made for these same subjects to contribute to every stage of peacebuilding activity. We must be attentive to nuance, acknowledge the multiple ways in which language functions to both include and exclude subjects and objects of knowledge, and conscious of the constitutive effects of both material and discursive interventions, if we are to support truly gender-sensitive peacebuilding efforts.

NOTE

1. Research for this chapter was funded by the Australian Research Council (DP130100707).

REFERENCES

Ackerly, Brooke (2001), 'Women's human rights activists as cross-cultural theorists', *International Feminist Journal of Politics*, **3** (3): 311–46.
Afshar, Haleh (2004), 'Women and wars: some trajectories towards a feminist peace', in Haleh Afshar and Deborah Eade (eds), *Development, Women and War: Feminist Perspectives*, Oxfam GB, pp. 43–59.
Afshar, Haleh and Deborah Eade (eds) (2004), *Development, Women and War: Feminist Perspectives*, Oxfam GB.
Anderlini, Sanam Naraghi and Camille Pampell Conaway (2004), 'Security sector reform', accessed 9 June 2011 at: http://www.international-alert.org/sites/default/files/library/TKSecuritySectorReform.pdf.
Baines, Erin (2005), 'Les femmes aux milles bras: building peace in Rwanda', in Diane Mazurana, Angela Raven-Roberts and Jane Parpart (eds), *Gender, Conflict and Peacekeeping*, Rowman & Littlefield, pp. 220–41.
Bastick, Megan and Kristin Valasek (eds) (2008), *Gender and Security Sector Reform Toolkit*, DCAF, OSCE/ODIHR and UN-INSTRAW.
Brahmini, Lakhdar et al. (2000), 'Report of the Panel on United Nations peace operations', accessed 9 February 2013 at: http://www.un.org/peace/reports/peace_operations/.
Cockburn, C. (2001), 'The gendered dynamic of armed conflict and political violence', in Caroline Moser and Fiona Clark (eds), *Victims, Perpetrators or Actors? Gender, Armed Conflict and Political Violence*, Zed Books, pp. 13–29.
Cohn, Carol (2004), 'Feminist peacemaking', *The Women's Review of Books*, **11** (5): 8–9.
Cohn, Carol and Sara Ruddick (2004), 'A feminist ethical perspective on weapons of mass destruction', in Sohail H. Hashmi and Steven P. Lee (eds), *Ethics and Weapons of Mass Destruction: Religious and Secular Perspectives*, Cambridge University Press, pp. 405–35.
Cohn, Carol, Helen Kinsella and Sherri Gibbings (2004), 'Women, Peace and Security: Resolution 1325', *International Feminist Journal of Politics*, **6** (1): 130–40.
De la Rey, Cheryl and Susan McKay (2006), 'Peacebuilding as a gendered process', *Journal of Social Issues*, **62** (1): 141–53.
Denskus, Tobias (2007), 'Peacebuilding does not build peace', *Development in Practice*, **17** (4): 6546–662.

Douglas, Sarah (2015), '"What gets measured gets done": translating accountability frameworks into better responses for women and girls in peacebuilding contexts', *Journal of Peacebuilding and Development*, **10** (1): 90–96.

Doyle, Michael W. and Nicholas Sambanis (2000), 'International peacebuilding: a theoretical and quantitative analysis', *The American Political Science Review*, **94** (4): 779–801.

Galtung, Johan (1969), 'Violence, peace and peace research', *Journal of Peace Research*, **6** (3): 167–191.

Galtung, Johan (1975), *Essays in Peace Research, Volume 1*, Eljers.

Gawerc, Michelle I. (2006), 'Peace-building: theoretical and concrete perspectives', *Peace & Change*, **31** (4): 435–78.

George, Alexander and Andrew Bennett (2005), *Case Studies and Theory Development in the Social Sciences*, Belfer Centre for Science and International Affairs.

George, Nicole (2014), 'Promoting women, peace and security in the Pacific Islands: hot conflict/slow violence', *Australian Journal of International Affairs*, **68** (3): 314–32.

Hamilton, Caitlin and Laura Shepherd (2015), 'The construction of gender-sensitive peacebuilding in Australia: "Advance Australia Fair"', *Australian Journal of International Affairs*, **69** (4): 379–99.

Hudson, Heidi (2009), 'Peacebuilding through a gender lens and the challenges of implementation in Rwanda and Cote d'Ivoire', *Security Studies*, **18** (2): 287–318.

Hunt Alternatives Fund and International Alert (2004), *Inclusive Security, Sustainable Peace: A Toolkit for Advocacy and Action*, accessed 9 February 2013 at: http://www.huntalternatives.org/pages/87_inclusive_security_toolkit.cfm.

Kandiyoti, Deniz (2005), *The Politics of Gender and Reconstruction in Afghanistan*, UNRISD.

Llamazares, Monica and Katie Mulloy (2014), 'Unicef in Uganda: using technology-based innovations to advance peacebuilding', *Journal of Peacebuilding & Development*, **9** (3): 109–15.

Manchanda, Rita (2005), 'Women's agency in peace building: gender relations in post-conflict reconstruction', *Economic and Political Weekly*, **40** (44/45): 4737–45.

Mazurana, Diane, Angela Raven-Roberts and Jane Parpart (eds) (2005), *Gender, Conflict and Peacekeeping*, Rowman & Littlefield.

McKay, Susan (2004), 'Reconstructing fragile lives: girls' social reintegration in Northern Uganda and Sierra Leone', in Caroline Sweetman (ed.), *Gender, Peacebuilding and Reconstruction*, Oxfam GB, pp. 19–30.

Meintjes, Sheila (2001), 'War and post-war shifts in gender relations', in Sheila Meintjes, Anu Pillay and Meredith Turshen (eds), *The Aftermath: Women in Post-Conflict Transformation*, Zed Books, pp. 63–77.

Meintjes, Sheila, Anu Pillay and Meredith Turshen (eds) (2001), *The Aftermath: Women in Post-Conflict Transformation*, Zed Books.

Mobekk, Eirin (2010), 'Gender, women and security sector reform', *International Peacekeeping*, **17** (2): 278–91.

Moran, Mary H. (2010), 'Gender, militarism and peace-building: projects of the post-conflict moment', *Annual Review of Anthropology*, **39**: 261–74.

Moser, Caroline and Cathy McIlwhaine (2001), 'Gender and social capital in contexts of politics violence: community perspectives from Colombia and Guatemala', in Caroline Moser and Fiona Clark (eds), *Victims, Perpetrators or Actors? Gender, Armed Conflict and Political Violence*, Zed Books, pp. 178–200.

Muggah, Robert, Philippe Maughan and Christian Bugnion (2003), 'The long shadow of war: prospects for generation disarmament, demobilisation and reintegration in the Republic of Congo', accessed 10 February 2013 at: http://www.oecd.org/dataoecd/49/32/35113279.pdf.

Myrttinen, Henri, Jana Naujoks and Janpeter Schilling (2015), 'Gender, natural resources, and peacebuilding in Kenya and Nepal', *Peace Review: A Journal of Social Justice*, **27** (2): 181–7.

Noma, Emiko, Dee Aker and Jennifer Freeman (2012), 'Heeding women's voices: breaking cycles of conflict and deepening the concept of peacebuilding', *Journal of Peacebuilding and Development*, **7** (1): 7–32.

O'Reilly, Maria (2012), 'Muscular interventionism', *International Feminist Journal of Politics*, **14** (4): 529–48.

Otto, Diane (2006–2007), 'A sign of "weakness"? Disrupting gender certainties in the implementation of Security Council Resolution 1325', *Michigan Journal of Gender and Law*, **13**: 113–75.

Otto, Diane (2009), 'The exile of inclusion: reflections on gender issues in international law over the last decade', *Melbourne Journal of International Law*, **11** (10): 11–26.

Pankhurst, Donna (2004), 'The "sex war" and other wars: towards a feminist approach to peacebuilding', in Haleh Afshar and Deborah Eade (eds), *Development, Women and War: Feminist Perspectives*, Oxfam GB, pp. 8–42.

Panyarachun, Anand et al. (2004), *A More Secure World: Our Shared Responsibility*, United Nations.

Porter, Elisabeth (2003), 'Women, political decision-making, and peace-building', *Global Change, Peace & Security*, **15** (3): 245–62.

Pratt, Nicola and Sophie Rickter-Devroe (2011), 'Critically examining UNSCR 1325 on women, peace and security', *International Feminist Journal of Politics*, **13** (4): 489–503.

Pruitt, Lesley (2014), 'The Women, Peace and Security agenda: Australia and the agency of girls', *Australian Journal of Political Science*, **49** (3): 486–98.

Puechguirbal, Nadine (2010), 'Discourses on gender, patriarchy and Resolution 1325: a textual analysis of UN documents', *International Peacekeeping*, **17** (2): 172–87.

Rostegui, Julie (2013), 'Gender, conflict, and peace-building: how conflict can catalyse positive change for women', *Gender & Development*, **21** (3): 533–49.

Sharapov, Kiril (2005), 'Methodological approaches to assessing United Nations gender mainstreaming policies in Kosovo', *Journal of Peacebuilding & Development*, **2** (2): 99–106.

Shepherd, Laura J. (2008), *Gender, Violence and Security: Discourse as Practice*, Zed Books.

Shepherd, Laura J. (2010), 'Women, armed conflict and language/gender, violence and discourse', *International Review of the Red Cross*, **92** (877): 143–59.

Shepherd, Laura J. (2014), 'Advancing the Women, Peace and Security agenda: 2015 and beyond', *NOREF Norwegian Peacebuilding Resource Centre*, available at: http://www.peacebuilding.no/Themes/Inclusivity-and-gender/Publications/Advancing-the-Women-Peace-and-Security-agenda-2015-and-beyond.

Sweetman, Caroline (2005a), 'Editorial', in Caroline Sweetman (ed.), *Gender, Peacebuilding and Reconstruction*, Oxfam GB, pp. 2–7.

Sweetman, Caroline (ed.) (2005b), *Gender, Peacebuilding and Reconstruction*, Oxfam GB.

Tryggestad, Torunn L. (2010), 'The UN Peacebuilding Commission and gender: a case of norm reinforcement', *International Peacebuilding*, **17** (2): 157–71.

United Nations (1992), 'Agenda for peace: preventative diplomacy, peacemaking and peace-keeping', accessed 9 June 2011 at: http://www.un-documents.net/a47r120a.htm.

United Nations (1996), 'An inventory of post-conflict peace-building activities', accessed 10 February 2013 at: http://www.un.org/esa/peacebuilding/Library/st_esa_246.pdf.

United Nations (2006), 'Integrated disarmament, demobilisation and reintegration standards', accessed 9 June 2011 at: http://www.unddr.org/iddrs.aspx.

United Nations (2008), 'Securing peace and development: the role of the United Nations in supporting security sector reform', A/62/659-S/2008/39, accessed 9 February 2013 at: http://www.un.org/Docs/sc/sgrep08.htm.

United Nations (2009), 'Report of the Secretary General on peacebuilding in the immediate aftermath of conflict', A/63/881–S/2009/304, accessed 9 February 2013 at: http://www.unrol.org/doc.aspx?n=pbf_090611_sg.pdf.

United Nations (2010), *Second Generation Disarmament, Demobilisation and Reintegration Practices in Peace Operations*, United Nations.

United Nations General Assembly (2005), 'In larger freedom: towards development, security and human rights for all', A/59/2005/Add.2, accessed 9 February 2013 at: http://www.un.org/largerfreedom/contents.htm.

United Nations Peacebuilding Commission (2005), 'Resolution 1645', S/RES/1645, accessed 9 February 2013 at: http://www.un.org/Docs/sc/unsc_resolutions05.htm.

United Nations Peacebuilding Commission (2007), 'Report of the Peacebuilding Commission on its first session', A/62/137-S/2007/458, accessed 9 February 2013 at: http://www.un.org/peace/peacebuilding/docsandres.shtml.

United Nations Peacebuilding Commission (2008a), 'Concept note', accessed 9 June 2011 at: http://www.un.org/peace/peacebuilding/Working%20Group%20on%20Lessons%20Learned/MWGLL%20Concept%20note%20Jan%2029.08.pdf.

United Nations Peacebuilding Commission (2008b), 'Background note', accessed 9 February 2013 at: http://www.un.org/peace/peacebuilding/Working%20Group%20on%20Lessons%20Learned/WGLLbackgroundpaper%2029.01.08.pdf.

United Nations Peacebuilding Commission (2008c), 'Summary notes of the Chair', accessed 9 February 2013 at: http://www.un.org/peace/peacebuilding/Working%20Group%20on%20Lessons%20Learned/WGLL290108GenderPBCSummary.pdf.

United Nations Peacebuilding Commission (2013a), 'Declaration: women's economic empowerment for peacebuilding', PBC/7/OC/3, accessed 8 June 2015 at: http://www.un.org/en/peacebuilding/pdf/oc/Declaration%2026%20Sept%2013.pdf.

United Nations Peacebuilding Commission (2013b), 'Peacebuilding Commission Working Group on lessons learned: enhancing gender-responsive national reconciliation processes: concept note', accessed 8 June 2015 at: http://www.un.org/en/peacebuilding/wgll/WGLL%20Concept%20Note%20on%20reconciliation21November.ed.pdf.

United Nations Peacebuilding Commission (n.d.), 'The Peacebuilding Commission (PBC)', accessed 5 August 2015 at: http://www.un.org/en/peacebuilding/.

Westendorf, Jasmine-Kim (2013), '"Add women and stir": the Regional Assistance Mission to Solomon Islands and Australia's implementation of United Nations Security Council Resolution 1325', *Australian Journal of International Affairs*, **67** (4): 456–74.

Willett, Susan (2010), 'Introduction: Security Council Resolution 1325: assessing the impact on security', *International Peacekeeping*, **17** (2): 142–58.

Wilson, Zöe (2005), 'State making, peace making and the inscription of gendered politics into peace: lessons from Angola', in Diane Mazurana, Angela Raven-Roberts and Jane Parpart (eds), *Gender, Conflict and Peacekeeping*, Rowman & Littlefield, pp. 242–64.

Yanow, Dvora (1996), *How Does a Policy Mean? Interpreting Policy and Organizational Actions*, Georgetown University Press.

23. Gender and post-conflict security
Megan MacKenzie

INTRODUCTION

In recent times, the post-conflict period has garnered increased attention from political scientists, International Relations (IR) and development scholars and policy-makers. This new focus represents a shift in the disciplinary boundaries within some of the social sciences. Historically, Political Science and International Relations were more concerned with war itself, rather than its aftermath. The prevailing tendency was to focus on the strategies, causes and impacts associated with war and insecurity. As a result, the immediate and long-term impacts of conflict on individuals and societies, including issues of social rehabilitation and reintegration, economic development and national healing have often been relegated outside the boundaries of IR. Thus, until recently, it was not IR scholars, but mostly scholars in such fields as development, anthropology, sociology and psychology that examined the aftermath of war and political violence.

The surge in attention to post-conflict security within IR reflects broader shifts within both the academic field of IR as well as policy trends within Western nations. Within the academy, there has been growing attention to the relationship between development and security issues, which is often referred to as 'the security/development nexus' (Duffield, 2001). This also came at a time when numerous universities began emphasizing (arguably paying lip service to) the value of interdisciplinary work. Scholars promoting a security/development nexus approach argue that separating development and security does not do justice to either field. Rather than segregate the methods and approaches of these fields of study, scholars like Mark Duffield and Rita Abrahamsen argue that in order to understand development one must consider security and vice versa (Abrahamsen, 2005). Attention to the development/ security nexus in academia, or the 'radicalization of development' reflects policy trends supported largely by Western nations (Duffield, 2007). In particular, it reflects the growing tendency both to assume that underdevelopment in the so-called Global South negatively impacts global insecurity and to paint developing nations as hotbeds of potential insurgents or sources of insecurity for those in the Global North.

Regardless of the rationale or the newness of this security/development nexus and the policies associated with it, there has been a significant amplification in attention to post-conflict security. There is a growing body of literature focused on 'post-conflict', and policy discourses from both development and security actors are riddled with talk of post-conflict security and stability. Moreover, sub-fields linked to the aftermath of conflict have emerged, including transitional justice and security sector reform. With the growth of post-conflict as a sub-field of study within International Relations and Security Studies, as well as its emergence as a distinct focus for policy-makers, it has become essential to reflect on the relationship of gender to post-conflict security.

This chapter addresses this relationship; it begins by posing several important questions related to gender and post-conflict security. Specifically, it is necessary to question and critique key concepts related to post-conflict and to consider if they are indeed gender-neutral; these concepts include 'security', 'peace', 'reintegration' and 'the return to normal'. In a highly securitized moment such as the so-called transition from war to peace, it seems pertinent to ask what forms of gendered ordering take place in the name of 'reconstruction' and 'rehabilitation'. It is also essential to analyze the types of gendered security issues that might arise during the post-conflict period. Considering these aspects of gender and security raises several particular questions, including:

- What does reintegration mean for men and women?
- Can the process of stabilization and reconstruction be a hierarchical and gendered process?
- How do men and women experience the transition from war to peace and how are their security needs and concerns similar and different?
- What kinds of 'conflicts' and insecurities continue for men and women post-conflict?
- How can a gender analysis broaden and deepen our understanding of post-conflict realities?
- What conditions need to be in place to allow women and men to feel more secure in a postwar period compared to during and before the war?
- If women make some gains during the conflict, such as greater earning capacity or otherwise becoming more independent, do those gains disappear when 'peace' returns?

Answering these questions requires paying close attention to how gender is constructed in war and in the postwar period and to the experiences of women *and* girls and boys and men before, during and after the formal ending of war. A gendered approach to post-conflict security does not mean simply 'looking for women'. Rather, it requires an examination of how security itself is defined in relation to gender norms and identities. 'Idle men', 'returning home', and 'family stabilization' are all highly gendered terms used in reference to post-conflict security. Assumptions about security often depend on gender stereotypes that see men as naturally more prone to violence and women as inherently peaceful. These gendered stereotypes about women's and men's 'place' during war continue to inform policies associated with post-conflict security. Men are often seen as naturally more violent, more prone to participating in conflict, and more likely problematized as 'idle' and potential spoilers of post-conflict peace. In turn, men are often categorized as security 'problems' post-conflict. By contrast, women and girls, with some justification, tend to be characterized as the biggest losers of war; they are defined by their victimization and the way that war has impacted them rather than the ways that they may have actively participated in or engaged with war. As such, women and girls tend to be delinked from security considerations post-conflict; they are viewed as social 'problems' rather than security threats or concerns. A critical analysis of post-conflict security requires untangling these assumptions. Because the study of war and security so often ignores the experiences of women and girls, paying attention to their lives and struggles in the post-conflict period can help broaden our understanding of post-conflict security.

With attention to the above research questions as well as to broader scholarly and policy shifts, this chapter encourages long-term and complex analysis of the impacts of war. There has always been a great deal of attention paid to security matters that arise during war. Activities associated with war, such as casualties, border infringements and allies, are central to thinking about international security. Perhaps less attention has been paid to the types of security issues that arise in the post-conflict period, or once armed conflict has formally ceased. This chapter explores some of the different questions, debates and issues that are associated with post-conflict security from a gendered perspective. That is, it examines these issues with constant attention to, and consideration of, social hierarchies, gendered identities and constructs, as well as the ways that individuals might experience this period differently. In turn, rather than viewing the post-conflict period as a time of increased security and a positive linear transition point following war, this chapter will demonstrate the need for further investigation into the restrictions placed on behavior and identities in the name of 'returning to normal'. The following section expands on the security/development nexus before exploring the concepts of security, war and militarism with attention to how questions of gender broaden our understanding of these key international relations concepts. Three specific assumptions associated with post-conflict security are then explored: the myth of post-conflict security, the myth of a finite post-conflict period, and the myth of post-conflict as a time of progress for all. Finally, disarmament programs, transitional justice, and sexual violence are discussed as three particular gendered post-conflict issues that help illustrate the broader themes through the chapter.

THE RADICALIZATION OF DEVELOPMENT

An examination of post-conflict security requires a reflection on the merging of the academic fields of development and security studies as well as a fusing of policies in both these areas. This merging of security and development is of particular concern for those focused on gender because the shifts in attention and priority associated with the security/development nexus might present new opportunities and challenges to those wishing to get gender concerns and issues on the agenda. Certainly any turn from 'traditional' security studies, which have historically marginalized gender as either an afterthought or entirely irrelevant, presents possibilities. However, it remains to be seen if the turn towards a security/development nexus might indeed reproduce the same sorts of gender hierarchies and silences as traditional security. Increasingly, governments in the Global North are treating international security and development as two sides of the same coin, acknowledging that the security and long-term development of nations across the world directly impact their own prosperity and stability.[1] In particular, Western governments have increasingly become interested in so-called failed states, many of which are experiencing, or recently have experienced, civil conflict or war. There seems to have been a reframing of failed states as not just a potential threat to their own citizens but also a threat to international security. As a result, many Western donor governments and Western-based organizations and institutions have taken an active role in overseeing the process of post-conflict reconstruction and development.[2]

Duffield has referred to the security/development nexus as the 'radicalization of development', stressing the interdependency of these fields of study and practice (2001, p. 16). Duffield has argued that the Global

South has increasingly been viewed as a source of international instability 'through conflict, criminal activity and terrorism' (2001, p. 2). As a result, Western states have come to view the Global South not only as simply underdeveloped, but as a security threat.

Scholars have noted that one of the impacts of the security/development nexus has been that Western states are more interested in the internal governance and development of states in the Global South. Peace and stability have become linked to liberal social policies. As a result, successful development – particularly post-conflict development – policies become associated with Western liberal values and priorities: 'liberal values and institutions have been vested with ameliorative and harmonizing powers' (Duffield, 2001, p. 16). Post-conflict security is being equated to radical social transformation, including the instillation of liberal institutions and values. In turn, post-conflict development is strongly linked to particular types of security and governance reforms, including 'conflict resolution, reconstructing social networks, strengthening civil and representative institutions, and security sector reform in the context of a functioning market economy' (Duffield, 2001, p. 11). The security/development nexus represents a significant trend within the academic and policy fields, yet little attention has been paid to the relationship that gender has to it. In fact, there is growing evidence that ideals of liberal 'order' often involve strict gender roles and norms, including marriage, a gendered division of labor, and the promotion of family planning (MacKenzie, 2012). Marriage has long been viewed – by colonizers and by international organizations – as a source of social stability and order. In fact, 'idle men' are often defined not only as jobless young men, but particularly unmarried jobless men. Questions remain as to how the association of post-conflict security with liberal social values and institutions, including the nuclear family, might impact gender social hierarchies post-conflict.

SECURITY AS GENDER BLIND

The challenges associated with the so-called radicalization of development are compounded when one considers that many understandings of security remain gender blind. Within IR, security has traditionally been narrowly defined as threats to the nation state. Attention to security often emphasizes formal threats to state sovereignty, particularly through warfare. According to this view, 'the provision of security is entrusted to the state, with the assumption that states protect and secure the members of the political community from threats emanating from the dangerous, foreign realm outside state boundaries.' (Blanchard, 2003, p. 1289). There is little space within this understanding of security to consider the gendered impacts of war, or the various security threats that remain post-armed conflict. An expanded understanding of security that moves beyond state borders, military activity and sovereignty is essential to an analysis of security in the post-conflict period (Wibben, 2009). Many of the issues that individuals and communities face post-conflict, including displacement, sexual violence and economic uncertainty, are sources of great insecurity; however, traditionally most of these issues would have been considered 'low-level' politics not worthy of significant attention by Security Studies or International Relations.

For decades feminists and other critical IR scholars have worked to expand the way that security is defined. In doing so, these scholars have carved out space for theorizing and thinking about gender in relation to security. Members of the Copenhagen School, for example, have introduced a post-structural approach to security, arguing that security is not a fixed entity but rather a construct (Buzan and Wæver, 2003). According to this perspective, language and power relations are crucial factors in the determination of security priorities (Buzan and Wæver, 2003; Hansen, 2000, 2006).

Lene Hansen has drawn particular attention to the ways in which security policies and discourses are influenced by gendered power structures and norms. Hansen's work on bride burnings and sexual violence has been used to support her critique of the Copenhagen School's approach to security, which tends to ignore gender hierarchies. Hansen demonstrates that not all actors are equally able to voice their security concerns, both within and outside conflict settings (Hansen, 2000). Traditionally, the gendered dimensions of security have been overlooked because security concerns associated with gender, including gender-based violence, economic insecurity and social isolation have been classified as domestic issues or human security concerns rather than national security priorities (Hudson, 2005; MacKenzie, 2009b).

Feminist scholars are responsible for most scholarship on the relationship between gender and security. Much of this scholarship is not simply focused on 'women's' security issues; rather, it examines the power relations associated with security policies and discourses and considers the ways that social norms associated with masculinity and femininity might affect the types of issues and questions that are considered significant and 'legitimate' security matters. As Laura Sjoberg reminds us, 'feminists argue that gender is conceptually, empirically, and normatively essential to studying international security' (Sjoberg, 2009, p. 2).

Heidi Hudson echoes this position in her work on human security, stating that 'gender is intrinsic to the subject matter and politics of security' (Hudson, 2005, p. 156). She explains how considering gender can provide scholars with perspectives on both women's and men's experience of security and insecurity:

> gender not only personifies a specific relationship of power, but also serves as a dynamic analytical and political tool by means of which gender as a unit of analysis and women and men as identity groups are used in tandem (but not interchangeably). This means that statements about femininity are necessarily also claims about masculinity, and that a challenge to our understanding of women's security necessarily transforms our understanding of men's security. (p. 156)

Feminist IR scholars called into question the tendency of mainstream scholars to focus on narrow aspects of security, that is, military or national security issues that are largely disconnected from the everyday experiences of both men and women. Ann Tickner expressed frustration with the 'dysfunctional' focus on military aspects of security within IR (Tickner, 1992). For Tickner, violence at the international, national and domestic levels are interrelated. Tickner argued that distinguishing security studies as an elite field tasked with understanding 'high-level' threats to national security overlooks the relationship between different types of violence and insecurity and discounts the significance of 'low-level' domestic politics for international security (Tickner, 1992). Sylvester has also argued that security studies largely ignore the 'mundane' or the everyday sources of insecurity. She has noted that women in particular face multiple sources of insecurity, both structural and relational, as a result of their struggles with everyday patriarchy (Sylvester, 1994). As a result of these limitations to traditional security studies, the field seems to largely overlook the experiences, desires, fears and needs of women and girls.

Annick Wibben has identified Feminist Security Studies as a separate sub-field of study, marked by its methodological and epistemological distinction from the mainstream (Wibben, 2009). According to Wibben, feminist scholars have typically relied on interviews and interactions with their research subjects and topics, resulting in scholarship that is more reflexive and inclusive. She also argued that including different perspectives and narratives about security in scholarship is a powerful way to alter mainstream approaches and assumptions within security studies, which tend to remain fixated on national identity and national threats. The following sections explore aspects of security studies that are particularly gendered and consider how a gender analysis might shift the way we think about these security topics.

WAR AND MILITARISM

The very definitions of war, violence, peace and security matter and must be critiqued from a gendered perspective (Nikolic-Ristanovic, 2000; Allison, 2004). The way that war and conflict is defined shapes our understanding of post-conflict security. Labeling war as a time of public violence and political action characterized by hyper-masculinity, aggression and heroism tends by definition to exclude women from the study of war. Furthermore, such characterizations of war lead to an understanding of post-conflict security as activities that should be focused on containing and rehabilitating violent male perpetrators or offering resources to female victims of war. Liz Kelly argued that the narrow definition of war as simply the exchange of formal hostilities between state actors ignores multiple sources of violence and insecurity that affect significant cohorts of the world. She noted for example that 'neither patriarchal violence nor genocidal colonialism are termed war' (Kelly, 2000, p. 48). Without considering war, violence and insecurity as gendered practices, it is impossible to draw attention to post-conflict security issues relevant to both men and women.

One of the ways in which traditional definitions of war have been challenged is through discussions of militarism. Militarism can be defined as 'the manner in which the valorization of war and the military makes lasting and engrained impressions in society – regardless of whether a war is being fought or not' (MacKenzie, 2009a, p. 198). As Gusterson explains, 'in militarized societies, war is always on our minds, even if we are technically at peace' (Gusterson, 2007, p. 155). Militarism is a concept that helps us to understand the long-term impacts of war, including those effects and impacts that continue into the post-conflict period. Over the course of years of conflict the process of militarization reacts with and influences almost all aspects of society (Enloe, 2000). The legacies of militarism are something not often considered as security issues post-conflict; however, after years of conflict both explicit and implicit forms of militarism seep deep into societal structures.

Beyond the obvious examples of soldiering and military structures, the less explicit effects of militarism that remain post-conflict include the continued valorization of violence and the militarized social hierarchies that persist after the disarming of official military structures (Teaiwa, 2011). The valorization and legitimization of violence associated with militarization are embedded in values, identities and practices that do not simply end with the formal cessation of war (Enloe, 2007). As such, militarization as a concept is useful to identifying broader sources of insecurity post-conflict. Militarization as a process and militarism as a set of values demonstrate that the line between war and peace is not distinct; rather, these concepts help illustrate the continuities between war and post-conflict and draw attention to forms of insecurity that persist post-armed conflict.

POST-CONFLICT

There is no single definition of post-conflict, a concept that is often linked to peace, security, reintegration and reconstruction. The post-conflict period is generally understood as starting with the formal end of a conflict and continuing until social, economic and political order is re-established. In turn, post-conflict, by definition, is considered to be a finite period of time characterized by the cessation of violence and other forms of insecurity and the gradual 'return to normal'. Characterizations of post-conflict often ignore gender; it is assumed that men and women experience the post-conflict period in similar ways and that it is a positive period of increased stability for everyone. In fact, there is some evidence that the increased attention to the security/development nexus has in fact reinforced gender-blind understandings of the post-conflict period. Specifically, the rationale associated with the security/development nexus encourages policy-makers to focus on immediate security threats in the post-conflict era and to assume that development initiatives will necessarily enhance 'progress' and 'security' in particular regions. A gender analysis reveals that this assumption of the post-conflict period as a uniform transition from war and insecurity to peace and development leaves out the experiences and concerns of many individuals. The following section explores how the post-conflict period is gendered – from the signing of peace agreements to the establishment of disarmament programs – and how we might work to unravel militarism and gendered order.

The post-conflict period usually begins with peace agreements or cease-fire agreements that lead to the cessation of formal conflict. Interestingly, although these agreements are essential in ensuring immediate and lasting security and mark the beginning of the so-called post-conflict period, they are not gender-neutral. From decisions about who should be at the negotiating table to the types of concessions and resources committed to individuals and groups, there are intense gendered power relations associated with peace agreements. Women worldwide have had a significant role in pushing for peace agreements. For example, women activists in Liberia sat outside peace negotiations in protest, attempting to keep the negotiating parties at the table so that they would reach an agreement (Karam, 2000). Despite evidence that women's groups have played active roles in instigating and supporting peace and ceasefire agreements, historically, women have not been included as formal participants in peace negotiations. This exclusion is important when considering security because peace agreements are designed to appease the major actors in the conflict and to ensure that the agreement will last. Without women at the table, security issues that are important to them are often not included on the agenda. Peace agreements are often the first step towards post-conflict reconstruction. Ample evidence that these agreements are gendered and exclude women indicates that the post-conflict period is plagued by gendered power relations from the very start.

Before discussing examples of gender and security issues that arise post-conflict, it is crucial to examine critically some of the assumptions associated with the definitions of 'post-conflict' and 'post-conflict security'. First, there is an assumption that the post-conflict period is a time of relative peace, stability and calm. The term 'post-conflict' itself clearly implies that any armed conflict is over and that a new era, defined by a lack of violence, has been ushered in. This assumption is reinforced by traditional understandings of security, which are focused on formal armed violence (MacKenzie, 2012). From this perspective, once the formal conflict has ended there ceases to be an international relations 'problem'. What remain may be domestic issues of disarmament or reintegration, but the 'real' security threats – those associated with armed conflict – have been addressed (MacKenzie, 2009b).

Many sources of insecurity continue into the post-conflict era. Considering the relationship between gender and security allows for an analysis of multiple sources of insecurity for individuals post-conflict. For example, there is evidence that American soldiers returning from the wars in Iraq and Afghanistan face post-traumatic stress disorder, social isolation and are prone to high rates of suicide (Grieger et al., 2006). These are sources of grave insecurity for individuals who find themselves unable to cope with the experience and impacts of war post-conflict; however, these experiences are all too often left out of an analysis of post-conflict security. There is particular gendered significance to this oversight. Paying attention to gender and militarization points us to these varying and often unseen forms of insecurity. Simona Sharoni reminds us that if we ever hope to unravel militarization and establish peace 'one must begin to pay close attention to how masculinities have been constructed.' (Sharoni, 2008, p. 147). In particular, the preservation of militarized masculinities and hierarchies puts pressure on men and boys to 'man up' and may prevent them from seeking the emotional support they need when they return from war. Evidence indicates that this can reproduce social norms and practices that harm women. For example, there are extremely high rates of domestic violence committed by military veterans and active duty servicemen (Marshall et al., 2003). The violence that is valued and revered in war spills over into the domestic and puts wives and children at risk. Attention to masculinities also requires an examination of the ways that peacekeepers may reproduce military structure and values. Research on police-keepers (military peace keepers) in Timor-Leste indicates that military police were aware of militarized and racist 'cowboy' style peacekeeping that prioritized order and characterized locals as ignorant and immature (Bevan and MacKenzie, 2012).

In addition to the misperception that the post-conflict period is 'more secure', a second misunderstanding associated with post-conflict security relates to the time frame of 'the post-conflict'. The post-conflict period is presumed to be a relatively short, finite period of time. In policy circles, states are typically classified as post-conflict for a period of about two to four years. While it has been acknowledged that security issues remain after the cessation of formalized violence, there is still little understanding of how long the post-conflict period should last. Is a state still considered to be post-conflict two months after a conflict, a year, a decade later? This is an important question to consider when thinking about security matters and their gendered aspects. While a state is still considered to be 'post-conflict', it receives much-needed aid and international attention. The length of this support is limited, however, due to the limited time frame associated with 'post-conflict'. Indeed, post-conflict issues, including those associated with disarmament, transitional justice and sexual violence, linger long after a state is considered post post-conflict.

A third assumption about the post-conflict period is that it is a time of progress, political evolution and unity. In general, it is often understood that the post-conflict period – at minimum – represents a time in which individuals are not only more secure, but also have more opportunities for work and can envision a positive future. There is often the presumption that the new social roles that women and men take on during conflict can be leveraged post-conflict into more progressive social configurations, based on a more equitable division of power and labor. Changes to hierarchical structures that occur as a result of war are sometimes viewed as occasions for women specifically to renegotiate and hold power. In particular, women historically have participated in 'non-traditional' activities during war, including within the domestic workforce, as support staff in various militaries and as combatants. In theory, women's participation in 'unconventional' activities could have the potential to loosen longstanding patriarchal hierarchies within societies. The post-conflict period should 'provid[e] an opportunity for women to challenge traditional gender roles, create spaces for new identities and imagine new possibilities for themselves' (Baksh-Soodeen, 2005, p. 32).

In reality, the post-conflict period seldom ushers in gender equality. In fact, post-conflict reconstruction efforts such as the Disarmament Demobilization and Reintegration (DDR), which are aimed at re-establishing security and order by encouraging a 'return to normal', may serve to re-institute particular gendered orders. Those individuals who might be seen as taking on unexpected roles during the conflict, such as male civilians or female combatants, can find this process of the return to normal deeply insecure. Men who did not participate as combatants do not receive the same employment and reintegration opportunities provided to male combatants through programs such as the formal disarmament and reintegration process. For women who participated in the conflict, returning to normal post-conflict may entail to trade power and roles that they attained during the war for traditional social positions, largely within the domestic sphere. As Mari Caprioli explains: 'the national patriarchy begins to reassert itself after the war and expects women to return to "the way they were before the war"' or 'to their subordinate positions' (2001, p. 436). Susan McKay reiterates this position: 'the [post-conflict] reality usually proves that, regardless of culture and place, women's roles revert to traditional ones, and nationalistic loyalties are more highly valued than is gender equality' (McKay, 1998, p. 356).

For both men and women, returning to 'normal' can involve compromise, silence – or hiding or not talking about one's experience – and insecurity. Krug also notes,

> it is rarely considered that encouraging a return to what is considered 'normal' after a conflict may reflect the patriarchal order before the conflict where women's rights might have been routinely violated. Or that the international community's definition of 'normal' tolerates high levels of violence against women in their own societies. (Krug et al., 2002, p. 61)

In addition to marking the cessation of formal conflict, post-conflict security also often presumes a particular social order that is gendered. As a result, limitations and expectations are placed on both men and women post-conflict in the name of stability, security and the return to normal. Transitional justice, disarmament and sexual violence are three important aspects of post-conflict security that illustrate the centrality of gender in the aftermath of war and political violence.

TRANSITIONAL JUSTICE AND TRUTH AND RECONCILIATION COMMISSIONS

Transitional justice is increasingly being discussed as an essential element of lasting peace and security post-conflict. In particular, the number of Truth and Reconciliation Commissions (TRCs) initiated after conflicts or political turmoil has risen over the last two decades and truth commissions have now become established as a norm (Hirsch, 2013; Hirsch et al., 2012). That is, they are seen as a legitimate and necessary part of post-conflict peace and security. Truth and reconciliation commissions are one of several transitional justice tools; special courts are another example of transitional justice mechanisms. Rather than simply providing an account of the conflict or political transgression, special courts typically are punitive and are designed to prosecute those considered most responsible for human rights abuses and violence. There has been little attention to the gendered elements of transitional justice. Although both TRCs and special courts have been traditionally viewed as gender-neutral bodies and processes, feminists point out that there are important gender issues associated with transitional justice. For truth and reconciliation commissions there are questions of who is encouraged to participate, what stories are included in the formal account of the war and who controls the process (Shaw, 2007).

A detailed analysis of truth commissions highlights the saliency of the three myths associated with post-conflict security: the myth of post-conflict security, the myth of a finite post-conflict period, and the myth of post-conflict as a time of progress. With the aim of providing an account of political turmoil or war, truth commissions presume that the main activities of war are completed, that there is a finished story of war to tell. It is believed that acknowledging these past atrocities and events will contribute to lasting security. Again, this belief is based on the assumption that atrocities are in the past, thereby ignoring any forms of violence or insecurity that may be continuing for members of a community or nation. This makes it difficult to draw attention and resources to lasting forms of violence and security that continue post-war, including domestic violence, sexual violence, human trafficking, and unsafe or precarious labor conditions. Furthermore, the forms of insecurity, stigma and isolation that can result from an individual participating in a truth commission process have not readily been acknowledged. In Sierra Leone, for example, women were much more likely to face stigma in their local communities if they were known to have been assaulted or to have participated as combatants in the civil war (MacKenzie, 2012). Furthermore, truth commissions are often public events. Therefore, an individual who participates in the commission is publicizing his or her participation. Those women who came forward during the TRC may have put themselves in a particularly vulnerable position in terms of stigma and security. Moreover, the logistics of participating in TRCs often require risks to one's personal security. In order to participate in commissions, individuals must travel to specific locations, which can be a source of insecurity in the immediate aftermath of war, especially for women and girls. Participating in commissions may also highlight women's and girls' active participation in the conflict, which could cause vulnerability in the form of stigmatization or retribution.

Truth commissions also tend to reinforce the understanding of the post-conflict period as a restricted, relatively short period of time. Truth commissions are sometimes even planned before the formal cessation of war and are often initiated immediately following a ceasefire. Many commissions have completed their mandates before other signs of post-conflict stability have been established, such as refugee resettlement. Operating in this strict time frame could impede the ability of the commission to present a complete picture of the conflict. The timing of a TRC has particular gender implications in that it tends to attract and include evidence related to the immediate impacts of the war and overlooks the diverse and long-term impacts of war discussed earlier. In the case of Sierra Leone, the TRC only mentions women as victims of the war – not as combatants. This could be because women were scared to come forward and participate in the TRC, and it may also be due to the fact that the international community did not acknowledge and recognize women's role in the conflict until some time had passed and organizations and researchers began recognizing women's role. Furthermore, the presence of the commission and the responses of the public to the testimonies may reignite conflict and thereby jeopardize security.

Finally, truth commissions reflect the tendency to associate the post-conflict period more generally with progress, unity and social evolution. One of the objectives of most commissions is to create a unified narrative of political events and the conflict. It is believed that this singular story will unite communities and provide a complete and accurate account for future generations. Linking security and moving forward with a unified narrative of conflict may not be entirely realistic and certainly does not acknowledge the gendered dynamics of truth commissions. Not all members of society participate equally in this process; therefore, the commission presents one perspective – largely that of men – rather a unified cohesive view. Moreover, the logic of Western institutions intervening in the Global South to 'improve' society has its roots in colonialism. In her chapter, O'Rourke reminds us that 'transitional justice can be seen as one of the masculine human rights strategies that are reminiscent of imperial intervention in the lives of postcolonial subjects …' (Chapter 24, this volume). In turn, a critical gender analysis of post-conflict security and the role of transitional justice in achieving this security must pay attention to – and question – the power relations being imposed through justice processes as well as the assumptions about 'local' justice inadequacies and deficiencies.

DISARMAMENT DEMOBILIZATION AND REINTEGRATION

DDR programs reflect all three of the assumptions associated with post-conflict security discussed earlier. First, the programs generally operate assuming that fighting and major threats to security have ceased. By removing armed soldiers from society, DDR programs help to define the post-conflict period as one of increased peace and stability as well as the absence of violence. It is rarely considered that the disarmament process itself can pose a security threat to individuals. Because many DDR processes are designed with men as beneficiaries in mind, the buildings used to house former combatants often do not make provision for separate sleeping or lavatory facilities for women. This can cause a problem for women and girls who might be housed with men. Sexual violence has been a problem at DDR facilities in several countries including Sierra Leone and the Democratic Republic of Congo (DRC). The United Nations has acknowledged that, for children in particular, sexual abuse and exploitation is a threat 'at all stages of the DDR process' (UNDDR, 2005). Another source of insecurity for both men and women comes from stigma. DDR processes tend to be public events with participants receiving ID cards, being housed at facilities identified as DDR and participating in training programs specifically for former soldiers. In turn, participating in DDR publicly identifies oneself to the community as a soldier.

For many women in particular, the public acknowledgment of their role as soldiers brought stigma and shame to themselves as well as their families. While men also faced stigma, it seems that in many cases women were further stigmatized because they had betrayed their expected roles in society. As a result, participating in DDR could increase social insecurity for women and girls in the sense that they would be less able to function normally, less able to get married, potentially rejected by their families and find it more difficult to get a job (MacKenzie, 2012; Hills, 2015).

Disarmament programs are also affected by the restricted time frame that tends to define post-conflict. International funding directed at post-conflict initiatives such as the DDR often within a year or two after the conflict. International organizations such as the United Nations as well as smaller humanitarian bodies tend to move their focus to new areas of crisis. As a result, even though DDR programs have three distinct elements, funding, enthusiasm and attention often wane before the reintegration phase can be completed. This greatly impacts the success of these programs as well as prospects for lasting security. For example, in Sierra Leone, reintegration programs included training options for soldiers. Initially the training programs lasted a year; however, as funding for such programs dwindled, the training programs were shortened to nine months, then six months and eventually some training programs were offered for only three weeks (Mackenzie, 2012). This shows the limitation of viewing the post-conflict period in terms of strict time frames. There are particular gender implications for the limited time frames associated with the DDR. First, evidence from Sierra Leone and other countries indicates that women face a more difficult and longer reintegration process than men. Women face higher levels of stigma and women have fewer means to support themselves economically in a post-conflict environment. Moreover, women have particular health and psychosocial needs post-conflict – particularly those who survived rape – which reintegration programs could address if there was sufficient funding and will. Single mothers are also particularly vulnerable and require specific attention and programs in the reintegration phase, which largely remained unaddressed in existing programs.

The vocational training opportunities for former combatants was both limited and highly gendered. Women across a number of DDR programs were offered training in tailoring, weaving, gara tie-dying, soap making and catering, while men could choose between such trades as masonry, mechanics or working as a taxi driver. The limited training options and the truncated training programs greatly affect the economic insecurity of both men and women and interfere with their ability to fully reintegrate into their communities. For example, the surge in poorly trained taxi drivers operating in places like Freetown in Sierra Leone has meant that the drivers are operating at a risk not only to their own security, but also to the security of the entire community.

Critiques of DDR programs contradict depictions of the post-conflict period as a progressive and positive transition (MacKenzie, 2009a; MacKenzie, 2012). Feminists and other critics have pointed out that the 'return to normal' that is promoted by DDR programs can be disempowering sources of insecurity for individuals (Hills, 2015). In fact, there is evidence that women are often excluded from formal DDR processes because of stereotypes about men's and women's activities during war. As such, women do not benefit from the resources available through these initiatives. Those women who do participate face stigmatization based on these same gender stereotypes. In turn, some former soldiers achieve post-conflict security through silence, hiding their activities during war, and avoiding participating in public post-conflict activities (Baldi and MacKenzie, 2007).

SEXUAL VIOLENCE

Special envoy for sexual violence in the DRC, Margot Wallstroem, stated in 2010 that rampant sexual violence is the biggest obstacle to lasting peace in that country (Euro Coopération Ingénierie, 2010). More recent research has also revealed that female soldiers are particularly susceptible to sexual violence. Data on the civil war in Sierra Leone showed that between 70 percent and 90 percent of the female fighting forces experienced sexual violence during the conflict (MacKenzie, 2012). This data is valuable not only because it challenges the perception that sexual violence happens primarily to innocent female civilians, but also because it indicates the dire need for research into female participants in conflict and the policies, programs and resources available to them during and after the conflict.

It is difficult to think of a war or civil conflict that has not featured some form of gender-based violence. From the recent wars in Iraq and Afghanistan, to the mass rapes in Bangladesh in the 1970s (Habiba, 1998), to the comfort women taken by Japanese soldiers in China and Korea (Chung, 1995; Hyun-Kyung, 2000), gender-based violence – and particularly wartime rape (Wood, 2009) – has been used consistently as a tactic of war. While there has been an increased focus on wartime rape as a tool of war, including the recent enshrinement of wartime rape as a crime of war, there has not been significant examination of gender-based violence post-conflict (Olujic, 1998). Gender-based violence does not end with the formal cessation of armed conflict. In fact, in many post-conflict societies there is evidence that sexual and gender-based violence rates remain as high as they were during war. This results in a considerable security threat for many individuals.

Although women and men can be victims and perpetrators of gender-based violence both during and after conflict, women and girls continue disproportionally to experience sexual violence. Sexual and gender-based violence cause several lasting forms of insecurity, including stigmatization, health problems and social rejection and isolation. In many countries, women who have been raped during the war experience various forms of social stigma. Despite the widespread use of rape as a tactic of war, in many societies women who are victims of rape are blamed for the assault and ostracized from their families and communities. Stigma obliges individuals to stay silent about their experiences of rape and sexual assault. After the formal armed conflict ends, the lasting forms of insecurity associated with gender-based violence challenge dominant perceptions of the post-conflict period as a time of peace, security and the absence of all forms of violence. In Liberia today, for example, despite decades of 'peace', sexual violence remains one of the most common domestic crimes in the country. The local police have limited means to address this issue, and remain crippled by simple realities like a lack of vehicles (Boley, 2015). Women and men who experience sexual violence in and out of war often face stigma, the possibility of sexually transmitted diseases, and pregnancy. Without resources such as counseling, access to birth control, and medical care, these women and men face various forms of insecurity and hardship in the post-conflict environment.

CONCLUSION

Examining gender *and* post-conflict security complicates mainstream understandings of security, war and the post-war period and challenges key assumptions associated with post-war security. This chapter explored the definition of security and looked at several specific examples of post-conflict issues and programs and their relationship to gender and security. The chapter was framed around a discussion of the radicalization of development – or the security/development nexus. This frame was used to highlight the significance placed on 'security' in a post-conflict arena. Even after the cessation of formal conflict, post-conflict development programs and policies often remain fixated on a particular notion of security and order. The chapter drew attention to this, and asked the reader to consider how particular understandings of order and security might rely on – and reproduce – gendered assumptions and hierarchies.

The chapter also set out to demonstrate three key myths or presumptions about post-conflict security. These included the myth that the end of formal war necessarily means that citizens in a particular region are 'more secure' than they were before. It also included the 'time myth', or the notion that the post-conflict 'moment' is relatively short and finite. Finally, it included the 'moving forward myth', or the assumption that the post-conflict period is a time of progress for all, a time where human rights, security, opportunity and even happiness are all 'on the rise'. To illustrate the weakness and gendered nature of each of the three assumptions, the chapter focused on specific examples and programs, including the disarmament program, transitional justice, and addressing sexual violence. Women and girls and men and boys may experience various forms of insecurity, disorder, fear and uncertainty that are left out of dominant narratives and approaches to post-conflict security. For many individuals and communities, post-conflict security is a misnomer as multiple threats, insecurities and uncertainties that were present during war often prevail after a ceasefire is reached or a peace agreement signed. Furthermore, the transitions associated with the post-conflict period can bring new forms of insecurity, isolation and instability. Despite the undue attention to combat and ceasefires, the cessation of formal armed conflict is only one aspect of post-conflict security.

NOTES

1. For example, see former British Prime Minister Tony Blair's speech on 2 October 2001 in which he declared, 'The starving, the wretched, the dispossessed, the ignorant, those living in want and squalor from the deserts of Northern Africa to the slums of Gaza, to the mountain ranges of Afghanistan: they too are our cause' (Abrahamsen, 2005, p. 57).
2. See, for example, the increased attention by the United Nations on longer-term strategies of transitional justice.

REFERENCES

Abrahamsen, R. (2005), 'Blair's Africa: the politics of securitization and fear', *Alternatives: Global, Local, Political*, **30** (1): 55–81.

Allison, Miranda (2004),'Women as agents of political violence: gendering security', *Security Dialogue*, **35** (4): 447–63.

Baksh-Soodeen, Rawwida (2005), *Gender Mainstreaming in Conflict Transformation: Building Sustainable Peace*, Commonwealth Secretariat.

Baldi, Guilia and Megan MacKenzie (2007), 'Silent identities: children born of war in Sierra Leone', in Charli Carpenter (ed.), *Born of War: Protecting Children of Sexual Violence Survivors in Conflict Zones*, Kumarian Press, pp. 78–94.

Bevan, Marianne and Megan H. MacKenzie (2012), '"Cowboy" policing versus "the softer stuff"', *International Feminist Journal of Politics*, **14** (4): 508–28.

Blanchard, Eric (2003), 'Gender, international relations, and the development of feminist security theory', *Signs: Journal of Women in Culture and Society*, **28** (4): 1289–312.

Boley, Tecee (2015), 'War is over but rape goes on: many victims are children', New Narratives, accessed 3 August 2015 at: http://www.newnarratives.org/stories/tecee-boley/war-is-over-in-liberia-but-rape-goes-on-alarming-number-of-victims-are-children/.

Buzan, Barry and Ole Wæver (2003), *Regions and Powers: The Structure of International Security*, Cambridge University Press.

Chung, Chin Sung (1995), 'Korean women drafted for military sexual slavery by Japan', in Keith Howard (ed.), *True Stories of the Korean Comfort Women*, Cassell, pp. 11–30.

Duffield, Mark (2001), *Global Governance and the New Wars: The Merging of Development and Security*, Zed Books.

Duffield, Mark (2007), *Development, Security and Unending War*, 1st edn, Polity.

Enloe, Cynthia (2000), *Maneuvers: The International Politics of Militarizing Women's Lives*, 1st edn, University of California Press.

Enloe, Cynthia (2007), *Globalization and Militarism: Feminists Make the Link*, Rowman & Littlefield.

Euro Coopération Ingénierie (2010), 'Sexual violence can destroy DRC – UN', 8 October, available at: http://www.eci-ddr.org/en/united-nations/sexual-violence-can-destroy-drc-un/.

Grieger, Thomas A., Stephen J. Cozza, Robert J. Ursano, Charles Hoge, Patricia E. Martinez, Charles C. Engel and Harold J. Wain (2006), 'Posttraumatic stress disorder and depression in battle-injured soldiers', *American Journal of Psychiatry*, **163** (10): 1777–83.

Gusterson, Hugh (2007), 'Anthropology and militarism', *Annual Review of Anthropology*, **36**: 155–75.

Habiba, Shumi Umme (1998), 'Mass rape and violence in the 1971 armed conflict of Bangladesh: justice and other issues', in Indai Lourdes Sajor (ed.), *Common Grounds: Sexual Violence against Women in War and Armed Conflict Situations*, Asian Center for Women's Human Rights, pp. 257–67.

Hansen, Lene (2000), 'The Little Mermaid's silent security dilemma and the absence of gender in the Copenhagen School', *Millennium – Journal of International Studies*, **29** (2): 285–306.

Hansen, Lene (2006), *Security as Practice: Discourse Analysis and the Bosnian War*, 1st edn, Routledge.

Hills, Christopher (2015), 'Gendered reintegration in Liberia: a civilised "(Kwi)" failure?', *The Australian Review of African Studies*, **36** (1): 68–83.

Hirsch, Michal Ben-Josef (2013), 'Ideational change and the emergence of the International Norm of Truth and Reconciliation Commissions', *European Journal of International Relations*, **47** (3).

Hirsch, Michal Ben-Josef, Megan MacKenzie and Mohamed Sesay (2012), 'Measuring the impacts of Truth and Reconciliation Commissions: placing the global "success" of TRCs in local perspective', *Cooperation and Conflict*, **47** (3): 386–403.

Hudson, Heidi (2005), '"Doing" security as though humans matter: a feminist perspective on gender and the politics of human security', *Security Dialogue*, **36** (2): 155–74.

Hyun-Kyung Chung (2000), 'Your comfort versus my death: Korean comfort women', in Anne Llewellyn Barstow (ed.), *War's Dirty Secret: Rape, Prostitution, and Other Crimes Against Women*, Pilgrim, pp. 13–25.

Karam, Azza (2000), 'Women in war and peace-building: the roads traversed, the challenges ahead', *International Feminist Journal of Politics*, **3** (1): 2–25.

Kelly, Liz (2000), 'Wars against women: sexual violence, sexual politics and the militarised state', in Susie Jacobs, Ruth Jacobson, and Jennifer Marchbank (eds), *States of Conflict: Gender, Violence and Resistance*, Zed Books, pp. 45–65.

Krug, Etienne, Linda Dahlberg, James Mercy, Anthony Zwi and Rafael Lozano (2002), *World Report on Violence and Health*, World Health Organization.

MacKenzie, Megan (2009a), 'Empowerment boom or bust? Assessing women's post-conflict empowerment initiatives', *Cambridge Review of International Affairs*, **22** (2): 199–215.

MacKenzie, Megan (2009b), 'Securitization and desecuritization: female soldiers and the reconstruction of women in post-conflict Sierra Leone', *Security Studies*, **18** (2): 241–61.

MacKenzie, Megan H. (2012), *Female Soldiers in Sierra Leone: Sex, Security, and Post-Conflict Development*, New York University Press.

Marshall, Amy D., Jillian Panuzio and Casey T. Taft (2005), 'Intimate partner violence among military veterans and active duty servicemen', *Clinical Psychology Review*, **25** (7): 862–76.

McKay, Susan R. (1998), 'The psychology of societal reconstruction and peace: a gendered perspective', in Lois Lorentzen and Jennifer Turpin (eds), *The Women and War Reader*, New York University Press, pp. 348–62.

Nikolic-Ristanovic, Vesna (2000), *Women, Violence and War: Wartime Victimization of Refugees in the Balkans*, Central European University Press.

Olujic, Maria (1998), 'Embodiment of terror: gendered violence in peacetime and wartime in Croatia and Bosnia-Herzegovina', *Medical Anthropology Quarterly, New Series*, **12** (1): 31–50.

Sharoni, Simona (2008), 'De-militarizing masculinities in the age of empire', *Österreichische Zeitschrift für Politikwissenschaft*, **37** (2): 147–64.

Shaw, Rosalind (2007), 'Memory frictions: localizing the truth and reconciliation commission in Sierra Leone', *The International Journal of Transitional Justice*, **1** (2): 183–207.

Sjoberg, Laura, ed. (2009), *Gender and International Security: Feminist Perspectives*, 1st edn, Routledge.

Sylvester, Christine (1994), *Feminist Theory and International Relations in a Postmodern Era*, Cambridge University Press.

Teaiwa, Teresia (2011), 'Bleeding boundaries: gendered analyses of militarism in the Western Pacific', *Asia Pacific Viewpoint*, **52** (1): 1–4.

Tickner, J. Ann (1992), *Gender in International Relations: Feminist Perspectives on Achieving Global Security*, Columbia University Press.

United Nations Disarmament, Demobilization and Reintegration Resource Center (2005), 'National institutions for DDR' (United Nations), accessed 3 December 2010 at: http://www.unddr.org/iddrs/03/30.php.

Wibben, Annick (2009), *Feminist Security Studies: A Narrative Approach*, Routledge.

Wood, Elizabeth (2009), 'Armed groups and sexual violence: when is wartime rape rare?', *Politics & Society*, **37** (1): 131–61.

24. Gender and transitional justice
Catherine O'Rourke

From the popular feminist slogan of Latin American women's movements, 'Democracy in the Country and in the Home', to the contemporary feminist peace slogan of 'No to war that kills us. No to a peace that oppresses us', women living in conflict zones and under repressive rule have remained optimistic about the opportunity to link transitions from conflict to broader transformative objectives about gender equality (Cockburn, 2007; Waylen, 2007). The adoption of United Nations Security Council Resolution 1325 on Women, Peace and Security in 2000 marked formal political and legal recognition, at the highest international institutional level, that transitions from political violence should improve the lives of women and advance gender equality (Cohn et al., 2004; Swaine, 2009). The chapter's starting point is the enduring belief in the transformative potential of transitional justice for women and gender relations, to recognize women's gendered experiences of conflict and differential needs for accountability, to include women and men on a basis of equality and to advance the protection of women's human rights into the future. The reasons for this optimism are manifold. In settings of violent conflict and repressive rule, political violence causes ruptures in the traditional division between public and private life, between domestic and international law, and between traditional constructions of masculinity and femininity. For example, women enter the traditionally masculine public sphere en masse to engage in public protest and social mobilization (Navarro, 1989), while the private sphere can become increasingly militarized and subjected to public scrutiny, such as house and body searches (Ridd, 1986). These ruptures in the traditional public/private divide reveal the mutability of the divide and provide a basis for optimism that at least some of the more positive elements of this change can be retained post-conflict. There is also the suggestion of shifting gender norms and departure from established gender stereotypes of masculinity and femininity due to the exigencies of political violence. The absence of men from family and community due to participation in conflict can create greater space for women to take up leadership roles (McWilliams, 1995). Additionally, the relatively small numbers of women in armed groups can force men on the battlefields to assume such traditional 'female' roles as cleaning and food preparation that on the home front are typically reserved for women (Dietrich, 2012).

Transitions from conflict are increasingly negotiated in the shadow of international law, in particular in terms of requirements for criminal accountability of the most serious perpetrators of violence under international law, but also because international actors are often involved in the negotiation of accountability deals and peace agreements more broadly. These moments of transition therefore disrupt the traditional division between domestic and international law. In that vein, transitions from conflict and repressive rule may provide an opportunity to push for the domestic application of more progressive elements of international law, such as the Convention for the Elimination of All Forms of Discrimination Against Women, and the United Nations Security Council Resolution 1325 (2000) on Women, Peace and Security. It is for these reasons that, in the literature and more broadly, transitions and transitional justice can be characterized as 'critical junctures' or 'moments of opportunity' for gender relations and gender equality (Wills, 2007; Overseas Development Institute, 2013).

DEFINING AND CONTEXTUALIZING TRANSITIONAL JUSTICE

While there is no single agreed definition of transitional justice, most definitions pivot around the following points:

1. transitional justice should deliver a measure of accountability for widespread past human rights violations that have normally taken place in a setting of either violent conflict or repressive rule (Orentlicher, 1991);
2. transitional justice should be accompanied by some measure of redress for victims, in particular in the form of reparations (De Greiff, 2006);
3. transitional justice should support the development of new institutions to prevent the recurrence of past violations (United Nations Secretary-General, 2011).

Transitional justice is an area of study that involves multiple disciplines: anthropology, sociology, political science, history, area studies, political science, law and others.

The antecedents of transitional justice are typically traced to the post-WWII trials at Nuremberg and, to a lesser extent, Tokyo. In the aftermath of that genesis moment, transitional justice entered a period of abeyance. Overwhelmed by Cold War politics and the conduct of proxy conflicts in the Global South, the international consensus and state consent necessary for the development and support of a new regime of international law was simply unattainable. For political scientists exploring the nature of political transitions in southern Europe and South America in the 1970s and 1980s, accountability for past human rights violations was simply epiphenomenal: questions of transitional justice and legal accountability for past human rights violations were understood to be the outcomes of political bargains between elites, unconnected to normative or legal requirements of the international system. As such, backward-looking decisions around accountability motivated little interest or analysis from either feminist scholars or women's movements, who were more centrally concerned with forward-looking policy issues of domestic violence and abortion and levels of women's political participation in new democratic regimes. Against this ambitious feminist agenda for transformation, questions of accountability for human rights violations of prior non-democratic actors appeared peripheral and of relevance to only a very small constituency of direct (overwhelmingly male) victims and their immediate family members.

Contemporary transitional justice scholarship and practice is more clearly identified with normative work of human rights lawyers of the early 1990s, who argued that international human rights standards were applicable to and should be enforced during political transitions in order to hold perpetrators of serious violations to account. With the emergence of normative legal work in the study of transitions, articulating a duty on post-authoritarian states to prosecute perpetrators of the prior regime under international human rights law, the precise scope of the legal obligation – for what offences, in what circumstances – motivated very substantial doctrinal analysis. However, the advent of attention from international human rights lawyers to questions of accountability in democratization transitions did not at that early stage motivate feminist analysis, as human rights in transitional justice were almost exclusively concerned with men as political actors. Within this emerging conversation concerning legal obligations to prosecute past wrongdoers for a defined and narrow set of offences, feminist legal scholars were largely ignored.

Transitional justice has entered the broader study of gender and conflict relatively late in the day. The focus of early transitional justice scholarship on accountability for the deaths of overwhelmingly male victims presented little promise to feminist scholars (for example, Roht-Arriaza, 1995). Growing attention to demands for securing accountability and redress for human rights violations experienced by women, most notably sexual violence, began in the mid-1990s with the emergence of the 'women's rights are human rights' agenda (Reilly, 2009). Within contemporary transitional justice is a distinct stream of gender analysis. What is arguably unique and particularly important about gender and transitional justice is that it exists simultaneously as a field of scholarship and an area of concerted policy and practice. For example, the major international non-governmental organization (NGO) in the field, the International Center for Transitional Justice (ICTJ), has a dedicated Gender Justice Program with dedicated staff and extensive outputs in multiple country-settings. There are NGOs working exclusively on issues of transitional justice and gender, such as the Women's Initiatives for Gender Justice, which pursues criminal accountability for conflict-related crimes against women, principally through the International Criminal Court. Such activity is not limited to the non-governmental sphere. There is also substantial relevant inter-governmental activity; for example, one of UN Women's four priority areas is Peace and Security, which includes dedicated policy and programmatic activity on transitional justice. The Committee on the Elimination of All Forms of Discrimination Against Women's General Recommendation Number 30 (2013) on women in conflict prevention, conflict and post-conflict situations specifically enumerates transitional justice as a priority area for the protection and advancement of women's rights. Moreover, in 2014, the UN Secretary-General issued a Guidance Note on Reparations for Conflict-related Sexual Violence (United Nations Secretary-General, 2014a). Transitional justice matters in the aftermath of war, and it matters for women and gender relations.

An understanding of the potential and actual role of transitional justice in shaping changes in gender roles and relations is therefore critical for theorizing gender, conflict and the aftermath, as well as for informing policy and advocacy interventions to influence transitions positively. This chapter sets out to capture the key gender dynamics in the study and practice of transitional justice, its historical trajectory and the current state of the field. The latter part of the chapter identifies the most persistent research questions in gender and transitional justice, which are in need of greater theoretical and doctrinal reflection, as well as closer empirical and case study analysis.

FEMINIST CONTRIBUTIONS TO TRANSITIONAL JUSTICE THEORY AND PRACTICE

Gender Analysis, Harms and the Public–Private Divide

Feminist interventions aimed at shaping the field and scope of transitional justice have concentrated on widening the range of harms visible in the process of societal transformation.

The term 'harms' refers to women's lived experiences of political violence, and is to be distinguished from legal categories of criminal offences or human rights violations (Ní Aoláin, 2009). The identification of a public/private divide in harms and the distinction between harms falling within the purview of international law and those falling outside legal classifications, have been central to gender analysis of international law. Feminist legal scholars have pointed to the critical role that law plays in shaping the social understanding of harm (Conaghan, 1996). While harms experienced by women in contexts of political violence remain relatively consistent during the period under analysis, legal capture of those harms, as violations of international human rights law and offences under international criminal law and international humanitarian law, has evolved substantially over time (Askin, 2003).

Feminists have examined critically the gendered nature of the public–private divide – that women spend most of their lives in the private realm – and how, in turn, this division of public and private makes invisible a range of harms experienced by women within the private realm (Pateman, 1988). Continuing impunity around violence within the home, and the relatively unrestricted availability of pornography, are identified as the practical discriminatory outworking of the public/private divide (Fraser and Lacey, 1994).

Along these lines, the public/private divide may be one of the reasons for the gendered deficiencies of the human rights framework and the normative structure of international law. The prioritization of civil and political rights in the human rights canon reflects and perpetuates the prioritization of the public over the private: civil and political rights govern the relationship of an individual's 'public' life and their relationship with government. While women are also beneficiaries of this guarantee, the public is not the realm in which women most need this guarantee of protection. The traditional canon of human rights was the subject of heavy feminist critique for its focus on violations of civil and political rights of political activists, often presumed to be men, by state agents. Charlesworth has damningly characterized this approach to human rights as 'what men fear most will happen to them' (1993, p. 8).

The treatment of political violence as mostly a masculine domain implied that men were the focus of accounts of human rights violations and other harms inflicted in the context of political violence. Women's experience of harm on the other hand was treated as vicarious and only taken into account when women suffered because of a familial relationship to a male political actor. The *Madres of the Plaza de Mayo*, the iconic face of demands for justice and accountability in the Latin American Southern Cone, and politicized on the basis of their relationships to male relatives, are a powerful example of these gendered representations (Schirmer, 1988). Women's experiences of harm could therefore be characterized as secondary or 'indirect' – the absence and loss of a close family member, the disruption to family life and harmony caused by such loss, and the hardships encountered by those women in their campaigns for justice for the loss of a family member – and were therefore not prioritized for accountability or redress.

Gender, International Law and Transitional Justice

Feminist scholarship on transitional justice has examined the most prominent of justice initiatives involving selective prosecutions and wider amnesties, truth recovery and truth telling processes, reparations, and the reform of institutions most directly complicit in the human rights violations of the past (Buckley-Zistel and Stanley, 2012; Fineman and Zinstag, 2013). Notwithstanding the gendered dimensions of transitional justice, there are sound reasons to focus on law and legal aspects of transitional justice. Because substantial changes are often required to the law and legal institutions of transitional states, legal institutions can be instrumental in advancing (or not) transitions from conflict and repressive rule. Moreover, for comparative study of transitions, international law can provide a useful framework, both because it informs and shapes the domestic responses of states to post-conflict and post-authoritarian accountability and because women's movements and feminist civil society have invested much energy in making progressive international legal developments work on the ground in transitional settings (O'Rourke, 2013a). The recent flurry of United Nations Security Council Resolutions, the 2013 G8 Declaration, and the UK government's Preventing Sexual Violence in Conflict initiative, all posit an anti-impunity focus to women's experience of war that also privileges legal processes, especially evidence-gathering, investigation and prosecution (see for example the International Protocol on the Documentation and Investigation of Sexual

Violence in Conflict, 2014). The emphasis on legal process is influencing humanitarian interventions and resource targeting in sites of conflict, and is thus of much broader relevance.

Beyond 'Adding Women': Theorizing Women's Political Involvement

Women political actors have been subjected to similar forms of torture and extrajudicial killings as their male counterparts, and this has activated the same human rights concerns as in respect of male victims. Over time, international human rights law has been forced to acknowledge that in some instances women experience the same physical harms as men in contexts of political violence. Amnesty International's periodic issuance of 'women's action' circulars (to be contrasted with the routine urgent action circulars that consisted exclusively of men) is a convenient shorthand illustration of these broader gender dynamics to human rights activism of the period (O'Rourke, 2013a, pp. 63–82). In this way, women are recognized as enduring the same physical harms as men while performing roles traditionally held by men and within typically male domains. Feminists have called attention to the fact that some women experience different physical harms than their male counterparts in contexts of political violence (Ní Aoláin, 2006). In other words, although women political activists may perform similar roles to men, they may be subjected to gender-specific harms. The gendered analysis of political violence has marked an important expansion in the harms to women visible to international law and to transitional justice.

Most notable in the category of gendered harms is rape and other forms of sexual victimization, which women may experience during conflict and detention. The recognition of sexual violence perpetrated by state actors as torture was achieved in the 1990s through landmark jurisprudence of the regional human rights bodies. Energized by global campaigns asserting that 'women's rights are human rights', the gendered analysis of the institutions and doctrine of international human rights was critical to the prompting and shaping of feminist interventions into transitional justice. More specifically, the shattering revelations of widespread sexual violence against female civilian populations in the Balkans conflict motivated concerted feminist scholarship and advocacy seeking the prosecution of certain offences committed against women in contexts of political violence (Copelon, 1994; Askin, 1997). As Christine Chinkin observed:

> [R]ecent steps within the international community to ensure that women's rights are recognized as human rights and to enhance the accountability of

governments for violence against women are as much an integral part of the overall counter-attack on the war against women as are the more publicized and dramatic responses to events in the former Yugoslavia. (Chinkin, 1994, p. 341)

Ground-breaking work of the mid-1990s by feminist international legal scholars argued that it was possible to prosecute rape and sexual violence against women within the contemporary body of international criminal law and international humanitarian law, and also proposed substantial legal reform to better capture such violence under international law (Askin, 1997; Chinkin, 1994; Copelon, 1994; Gardam, 1997). Although principally linked to demands for accountability for past incidents of conflict-related sexual violence against women, this belated feminist engagement with questions of transitional justice was also motivated by a growing appreciation of the contemporary and possible future significance of improved accountability for these gendered harms against women. The potential significance of prosecutions for past conflict-related sexual violence was threefold: first, accountability for past conflict-related sexual violence could be symbolically and practically significant to broader initiatives to end impunity for violence against women in all settings; second, efforts to activate criminal accountability under international law for violence against women offered to advance broader normative developments in international law concerning women's rights; finally, the criminalization and prosecution of sexual violence under international law might foster similar developments in domestic law in states experiencing conflict or in the aftermath of conflict (O'Rourke, 2013b).

Recognition of the different physical harms women experience during political violence has longer antecedence in international criminal law and international humanitarian law. The post-World War II trials at Nuremberg did not address the sexual violence experienced by female civilians, despite significant evidence of rape by both Allied and Nazi forces during the war (Ní Aoláin, 2000). In the International Military Tribunal for the Far East, however, rape was included within war crimes charges (Ní Aoláin, 2000). More specifically, the shattering revelations of widespread sexual violence against women in civilian populations in the Balkans conflict motivated feminist campaigns seeking accountability for perpetrators of sexual and gender-based violence in contexts of political violence. Central to the changes secured in international law was the recognition of women's experiences of sexual violence in armed conflict as amongst the most serious crimes of war by including rape within the definitions of a 'grave breach' of the Geneva Conventions, of crimes against humanity and of genocide in the jurisprudence of the ad hoc criminal tribunals established for Rwanda and the former Yugoslavia in the mid-1990s (Askin, 1997). The 1998 Rome Statute established the International Criminal Court, and recognized explicitly rape, sexual slavery, enforced prostitution, forced pregnancy and sterilization and other forms of sexual violence as crimes against humanity and as war crimes (Rome Statute, 1998: articles 7 and 8). More recently, the Special Court for Sierra Leone recognized the abduction and assignment of women and girls to male combatants for domestic and sexual slavery as the separate crime of 'forced marriage' and as a constitutive act of crimes against humanity (*Prosecutor v. Brima, Kamara and Kanu*, Case No. SCSL-2004-16-A, Judgment, ¶ 202 (Feb. 22, 2008)). Importantly, the inclusion of sexual violence within the transitional justice framework has not been limited to violence against women. In recent years, increased attention has been devoted to the sexual victimization of men in conflict-settings (Sivakumaran, 2007). This work is showing greater policy traction, for example, the 2014 Guidance Note from the UN Secretary-General on Reparations for Conflict-related Sexual Violence specifically addressed the needs and entitlements of male victims, and the importance of including men who have been targeted in relevant reparations initiatives.

NEGOTIATING TRANSITIONAL JUSTICE

Peace agreements are the primary mechanism for the contemporary resolution of conflict: the scale of the practice is captured by the vast number of peace agreements documented, across all regions and almost all post-Cold War conflicts (Bell, 2008). Also, peace agreements set out agreed new political and legal arrangements; they therefore constitute power-maps for the post-conflict state (Bell, 2000). Peace agreements have played an important role in the shaping of the gendered contours of transitional justice. The significance of peace agreements for women and gender relations more broadly has been the subject of dedicated discussion and analysis (see especially Bell and O'Rourke, 2010). Peace agreements can be important sites for negotiating gender justice because in addition to focusing on the key element of the negotiated resolution of conflict, they also frequently outline post-conflict arrangements for accountability. Additionally, the range of actors involved in the negotiation process adds to the significance of peace agreements for understanding gender and transitional justice; peace agreement negotiations typically include violently opposed state and non-state actors, neighboring states, intergovernmental organizations such as the United Nations and the African Union and, very often, civil society organizations, if not in negotiations then in provisions for implementation (Bell and O'Rourke, 2007). Notwithstanding the prominence of peace agreements as sites for the negotiation of transitional justice, for years women and gender issues have been excluded from these important debates as from peace agreement negotiations more broadly (Bell and O'Rourke, 2010). Nevertheless, against this difficult backdrop, women's movements have crafted creative and resourceful strategies to influence both the process and scope of peace agreements as well as the contestations over their interpretation and implementation (Bell, 2005; McWilliams and Kilmurray, 2015).

Prosecutions

The requirement of justice in transition coheres around efforts to balance demands of criminal accountability for human rights violations committed under the former regime, with the exigencies of peace. In response to demands for peace, amnesties or partial amnesties can provide important incentives to violent actors ceasing their activities. The peculiarities of the transitional context are addressed through a more circumscribed notion of criminal accountability, involving the selective prosecution of the most serious offenders for the most serious crimes. The role of retributive justice in transition is argued to have important material and symbolic long-term implications for transitional societies (Osiel, 1997). By delivering retribution, the suffering of victims can be ameliorated, the recurrence of such crimes may be deterred, and broad societal moral condemnation of such acts is expressed. Extending these potential benefits of retributive justice to victims of gender crimes also has therefore been an important motivation for feminist interventions in the field (Copelon, 1994).

Women's movements and feminist lawyers have sought the inclusion of crimes of sexual violence within the range of offences that cannot be amnestied. The focus on sexual violence in both feminist mobilization and legal responses to feminist demands has informed critical debates within the field of transitional justice (Mertus, 2004). At the heart of these debates are two key concerns: (1) that the focus on sexual violence runs the risk of essentializing women's experiences of violence and political repression, ignoring the broader range of harms (socioeconomic and damage or destruction of familial relationships) experienced by women in such contexts; and (2) that the focus on women's sexual victimization obscures women's political agency and resistance during periods of conflict and repression. Taken together, these concerns with the lack of nuanced attention to varied experiences and roles of women as political subjects in conflict zones, point to possible implications for the longer-term citizenship of women in societies emerging from transition (O'Rourke, 2011).

Additional critiques followed ostensible successes in the prosecution of conflict-related sexual violence. Growing practice in the prosecution of sexual violence under international criminal law has prompted persistent introspection from feminist international lawyers as to the appropriateness of (international) criminal tribunals for delivering progressive gender outcomes (Zinsstag, 2013). Recurrent here is the failure of court processes to provide a forum for women to tell their stories, with the emphasis instead on proving an offence. Julie Mertus's identification of 'the legal counter-narrative' (2004: 110) is a particularly poignant characterization of what happens in court settings when women's stories of harm and survival meet legal exigencies of establishing the requisite action and intent by the perpetrator. Feminist critique of prosecutions has not ended with the ad hoc tribunals, but has been extended into more recent innovations, such as hybrid domestic-international tribunals and their inaccessibility to women's narratives of resistance and survival (Staggs Kelsall and Stepakoff, 2007) and gender bias in the Office of the Prosecutor of the International Criminal Court (Chappell et al., 2013).

Truth-recovery

The practice of official truth-recovery processes largely emerged from the political expediency of 'pacted' transitions in the Latin American Southern Cone, where the ongoing influence of former military regimes made the pursuit of prosecutions too politically dangerous (see generally Huntington, 1991). Despite these dubious origins, however, the principle of truth-recovery in transition is now broadly regarded as an important and appropriate element of contemporary transitions (Hayner, 2002) and has attracted considerable feminist interest and gender analysis (for example Ross, 2003). Because truth in transition is linked to the deterrence of future human rights violations, to promoting democracy and social healing, and to educating towards a human rights culture (Campbell and Turner, 2008), feminist interventions have sought to marshal these gains to support gender equality objectives also (International Center for Transitional Justice, 2006). Moreover, by providing a vehicle for a shared societal narrative of the wrongs of the past, and thereby establishing the foundations for a shared non-violent future, truth-recovery is linked to notions of reconciliation. Feminist interventions also have sought to ensure that shared societal narratives around past wrongs include strong moral opprobrium for gendered harms and that it is not shared commitments to gender hierarchies that underpin community reconciliation (Ross, 2003).

The scope of feminist analysis of truth-recovery has expanded greatly since the early truth commissions (TCs) of Chile (1991) and El Salvador (1993). As a result, significant advances have been made in securing accountability for gender-based violence through truth commissions. Nesiah (2006) notes that even though their mandates were formally gender-neutral, commissions in Guatemala, South Africa and Peru interpreted mandate language regarding torture and ill treatment as the legal channels to address sexual violence. In Haiti, Sierra Leone and East Timor/Timor Leste, gender-based or sexual violence was explicitly incorporated into commission mandates (Nesiah, 2006). Analysis of more general developments in the mandates of TCs indicates a positive trend, whereby the gender-neutral stance of the early Latin American commissions of Argentina and Chile can be contrasted with the comprehensive understanding of harms demonstrated by the recent East Timor/Timor Leste commission (International Center for Transitional Justice, 2006). A 2006 study by the World Bank confirmed this positive finding, noting the gradual improvements indicated by the decision of the South African Truth and Reconciliation Commission to hold gender hearings, then the establishment of a gender unit in the Peruvian Truth and Reconciliation Commission and the important role of the United Nations Development Fund for Women (UNIFEM) in delivering technical advice, training and other support, to staff and witnesses of the Sierra Leone Truth and Reconciliation Commission (World Bank, 2006).

There is, however, a more sustained conceptual gender critique of the truth-recovery format in transitional justice. Chiefly, this concerns the narrow scope of harms recognized by mechanisms such as truth commissions, and the resulting limitations of the 'truth' that emerges (Ní Aoláin and Turner, 2007). Truth commissions tend to focus on the past harms deemed 'most serious', privileging the legal standards of criminal liability and civil and political human rights violations. Thus, the gendered shortcomings of prosecutions tend to reassert themselves in these truth-recovery processes. The focus on bodily harms obscures the experiences of conflict and repression that tend to mark the lives of women in such periods: socioeconomic exclusions, the violation of the home, and damage or destruction of familial relationships. Worse still, the failure to account for such harms in official narratives of the past can create the impression that they simply did not occur, or do not merit explicit rebuke in transitional processes (Ní Aoláin and Turner, 2007). Fiona Ross's (2003) work on the South African Truth and Reconciliation Commission unarguably remains the most important feminist text on truth-recovery and commissions. Ross's text is a powerful caution regarding the limits of truth-telling for capturing a comprehensive picture of women's experience of political violence and the potential for women's individual narratives to be subsumed by broader agendas of victimhood and nation-building (Ross, 2003).

Problems stemming from the limitations of truth-recovery persist. Feminists continue to make robust claims for the recognition of harms against women in official truth-recovery processes. For example, Lia Kent (2014) called attention to the failure of truth-recovery in Timor Leste to capture the full breadth of sexual violence in the conflict. Evidencing the broader penetration of this feminist analysis of restorative approaches to transitional justice, whereas Priscilla Hayner's foundational work on truth commissions in 1994 and 2002 cited no feminist work and gave no specific attention to accounting for gender-specific harms against women, the 2011 revised edition included a specific chapter on gender, with extensive attention to the importance of accounting for sexual violence against women in truth commissions (Hayner, 1994, 2002).

Lofty claims around the relationship of truth to deterrence and reconciliation have received sustained critique from feminists and others. More policy-oriented interventions into gender and truth-recovery nevertheless emphasize that:

> Truth Commissions ... can provide an extraordinary window of opportunity to highlight neglected abuses, research the enabling conditions of gendered violations, provide a forum for victims and survivors, recommend reparations that redress injustices, and leave a long-term legacy that is responsive to women's history and quest for reform. (International Center for Transitional Justice, 2006, p. 2)

While there may be disagreement about the stakes involved, there is, at least, agreement that truth matters for women.

Feminist Perspectives on Reparations

Reparations constitute the most recent area of feminist interventions into transitional justice but limitations of the harms identified in feminist analysis of justice and truth measures in transition tend to be replicated in the area of reparations. While earlier reparations programs demonstrated little awareness of women's gender-specific experiences of conflict, contemporary reparations programs are increasingly including incidences of sexual violence within their mandate, as harms bringing monetary compensation and allowing access to a range of psycho-social services. Nevertheless, the deaths of male partners and the high levels of deprivation that tend to accompany conflict and repression, mean that reparations distributed to women on the basis of acts of sexual violence may provide little acknowledgement – or material assistance for addressing the consequences – of the most common aspects of women's gender-specific experiences of conflict and repression (Ní Aoláin et al., 2015). A key conceptual concern in gender analysis of reparations is the notion of restitution underpinning such programs: the objective to 'restore the victim to the original situation before the gross violations of international human rights law or serious violation of international humanitarian law occurred' (Basic Principles and Guidelines on the Right to a Remedy and Reparations, 2005, para 19). Understanding restitution as the desired outcome of reparation fails to consider the entrenched gender inequalities that existed before the violation to be repaired. Such a failure can legitimate these types of gender-based discrimination, and obscure the very factors that make individual women vulnerable to human rights violations in the first instance.

The shortcomings in prevailing approaches to reparations reflect many of the deficiencies surrounding gender and transitional justice. These shortcomings limit the transformative objectives of reparations, as potentially grounding equal citizenship in a renewed democratic polity (De Greiff, 2007). One of the most productive seams of feminist scholarship in transitional justice emerges as a result of the work on gender in reparations by the International Center for Transitional Justice (Rubio-Marin, 2006, 2009). The Center introduced a three-pronged feminist analysis that seeks the recognition of gendered harms, an understanding of structural gender inequalities and the participation of women (Rubio-Marin, 2006, pp. 21–49). Similar frameworks identify great feminist potential for reparations to bring attention and accountability for violations of women's sexual and reproductive rights, a quintessentially gendered harm experienced disproportionately by women and girls (Duggan et al., 2008). The increasing traction of a feminist focus on reparations within advocacy and policy circles evidences the practical dividends of ongoing critical scholarly work by feminists in the field (Couillard, 2007; Nairobi Declaration on the Right of Women and Girls to a Remedy and Reparation, 2007; UN Secretary-General's Guidance Note on Reparations for Conflict-Related Sexual Violence, 2014a).

Gender and Institutional Reform

Of all sites of transitional justice, institutional reform is undoubtedly the most opaque and nebulous. As a result, institutional reform in transition has been the aspect of transitional justice receiving the least concerted feminist attention. While there is broad agreement regarding the importance of reform to the institutions of the transitional state in securing the non-recurrence of past violations, including violations of women's human rights, there is little clear consensus as to what institutions should be prioritized for reform, or as to what shape these reforms should take. Widespread violence and human rights violations indicate the breakdown in the rule-of-law – the failure of the judiciary, police and armed forces to protect and uphold the human rights of individuals. Hence, reform to these institutions is often the priority concern in efforts to re-establish the rule of law. In practice, this type of institutional reform is being prioritized by international agencies, such as the United Nations (UNSG Report, 2011), including in the United Nations Security Council Women, Peace and Security Agenda (UNSG Report, 2014b).

Institutional reform in transition therefore has critically important implications for the capacity of transition to address women's gender-specific experiences of violence and injustice. Drawing on the contingent understanding of justice in transition, defined as 'what is deemed just is contingent and informed by prior injustices', institutional reform in transition can be seen to rest on a particular understanding of the violence and injustice of the past (Teitel, 2000, p. 6). Acknowledgements around what went wrong in the past structure priorities for what is to be addressed in the (re)formation of state institutions. Consequently, in designing institutional reform, there is clear danger for narrow understandings of harm, limited to serious civil and political rights violations, to prevail. The gendered shortcomings identified in the discussion of justice, truth and reparations in transition can easily be replicated in shaping reform to state institutions. An important feminist intervention into this conversation reveals the continuities between gendered violence before, during and after transitions (Swaine, 2016, forthcoming). Along the same lines, feminists point to the significant relationship between ostensibly 'private' violence – intimate partner violence – and 'public' violence directly connected to conflict and political repression (McWilliams and McKiernan, 1993).

NEW DIRECTIONS FOR FEMINIST RESEARCH ON GENDER AND TRANSITIONAL JUSTICE

As the final section of the chapter, this section profiles emerging important work in challenging the gendered boundaries of transitional justice and points to avenues for further theorization and empirical research.

Men and Masculinities in Transitional Justice

There is a rich and important seam of gender scholarship addressing men and masculinity in transitional justice (see, for example, Hamber, 2007). The core purpose of this work has been to explore the role of transitional justice in constructing and reinforcing key gendered binaries, most notably the binary opposition between the masculine warrior-perpetrator and the passive female victim-mother (O'Rourke, 2011). This exploration posits three important questions, worthy of both theoretical and empirical reflection, namely:

- What are the gender roles affirmed through inclusion and presence in transitional justice processes?
- What are the gender roles that are given most visibility in the testimony and documentation work of criminal trials and truth recovery mechanisms?
- What are the gender roles rewarded through reparations provision?

The intellectual and practical challenge of disarming masculinity has been a concerted area of activity, captured eloquently by Antje Krog in her discussion of the South African Truth and Reconciliation Commission: 'And how might maleness be reconstructed following periods of violence?' (Krog, 2001, p. 203). There are of course reasonable grounds to believe that other non-violent forms of masculinity also operate in these settings and might usefully be drawn on, buttressed and supported in the negotiation and implementation of transitional justice (Myrttinen, 2003; Sharoni, 2008). In particular, Theidon's study of Disarmament, Demobilization and Reintegration (DDR) of pro-state paramilitaries in Colombia reveals the importance of family in the daily and ongoing process of 'resocializing men', potentially into new ways of caring for, providing for, and protecting loved ones (Theidon, 2009).

Security

Discussion of security as gendered has been an extremely valuable line of inquiry in revealing the gendered limitations of transitional justice (see, generally, Ní Aoláin et al., 2011). The necessary corollaries of selected trials and criminal justice as sites of transitional justice are broader provisions for amnesty, accompanied by the Disarmament, Demobilization and Reintegration (DDR) of former combatants who are not captured by processes of criminal accountability. The notion of demilitarization, which large-scale amnesties are supposed to facilitate as the first step in the broader process of DDR into civilian life of violent actors, is currently undergoing heavy feminist scrutiny. Focused on ending the 'primary' conflict between state and/or non-state armed groups, demilitarization pays little attention to violent intra-group conflict which may alter form, though not necessarily prevalence, in the aftermath of violent conflict or repression. The continuation of intra-group violence and injustice, often occurring on the bodies of women, is identified as the main obstacle to achieving broader societal transformation through transition. Important empirical work from Colombia has revealed the harmful gendered outcomes in that setting of widespread impunity (Theidon, 2009), in which security is a 'private good', something one can have with sufficient resources to buy it or to leverage it. Consequently, the transition itself (the movement from violent to non-violent conflict) may be premised on the particular Faustian bargain that sees 'the state' trading public violence (or insecurity) for private violence (security).

Intersectionality

Efforts to apply insights from feminist theories of intersectionality to transitional justice also posit a potentially rich seam of analysis. Gender dynamics are closely imbricated within broader conflict dynamics over ethnic identities or political and material resource distribution. Intersectional analysis offers insights, therefore, for exploring which women are called into view in master narratives of gender and conflict (Rooney, 2006; Rooney and Swaine, 2012). In particular, as revealed in Rooney's work, these are the 'good' woman, the peaceful woman, the ethnic reconciler, the woman free of atavistic loyalties to divisive ethnic or sectional identities (Rooney, 2006). 'Feminist intersectionality theory is useful for assessing who gains what from transition' (Rooney and Swaine, 2012, p. 530). The manifold ways in which these selective invocations and inclusions of women work to further marginalize the most economically and politically marginalized women is an acutely important insight for thinking about how transitional justice might positively impact gender relations in the aftermath of conflict.

Postcolonial Challenges

Inspired by feminist legal theory and postcolonial literary studies, this work interrogates the 'transitional justice discourse' and coins critiques which re-examine the discipline's key tenets, namely: democracy, liberalism, rule of law and human rights. Feminist postcolonial scholars in transitional justice argue that transitional justice can usefully be examined as a masculine human rights strategy that is reminiscent of earlier colonial interventions into the lives of colonized peoples (Moyo, 2012, 2015). Given the geographic spread of transitional justice and the increasing centrality of postcolonial Africa to scholarship and practice in the field, these insights from postcolonial theory provide a critical next step to gender analysis of transitional justice. Dominant gender and feminist critique in the field, which focuses quite narrowly on the extent to which women's gender-specific experiences of harm are captured by transitional justice processes, is likely to be proven incomplete and unsatisfactory to deal with the full gendered legacies of conflict, transition and colonialism in Africa. This is a rich site and theme for further gender analysis.

CONCLUSION

The field of transitional justice has moved some distance from its origins in the Nuremberg trials. Burgeoning scholarly and policy activity in transitional justice has highlighted the importance of sustained gendered analysis. Feminist interventions aimed at shaping the field and scope of transitional justice have concentrated on widening the range of harms visible in the process of societal transformation. To this end, activating international accountability and deepening domestic criminalization of sexual violence in times of conflict and societal repression was an early priority. In a similar vein, the feminist agenda has also prioritized exploring the relationship of gender to truth-recovery, to amnesty, to reparations and to peacemaking. New questions and priorities now drive this research agenda – most urgently, how to constructively engage men and alternative (non-violent) masculinities. Observers and practitioners may be less sanguine about the potential of transitional justice to transform gender relations; recognition of transitional justice as an important site of gender analysis is, however, now established beyond doubt.

REFERENCES

Askin, Kelly (1997), *War Crimes Against Women: Prosecution in International War Crimes Tribunals*, Martinus Nijhoff.

Askin, Kelly (2003), 'Prosecuting Wartime Rape and Other Gender-Related Crimes under International Law: Extraordinary Advances, Enduring Obstacles', *Berkeley Journal of International Law*, **21**: 288–349.

Basic Principles and Guidelines on the Right to a Remedy and Reparation for Victims of Gross Violations of International Human Rights Law and Serious Violations of International Humanitarian Law, adopted and proclaimed by General Assembly resolution 60/147 of 16 December 2005.

Bell, Christine (2000), *Peace Agreements and Human Rights*, Oxford University Press.

Bell, Christine (2005), 'Women and the problems of peace agreements: strategies for change', in Radhika Coomaraswamy and Dilrukshi Fonseka (eds), *Peace Work: Women, Armed Conflict and Negotiation*, Women Unlimited.

Bell, Christine (2008), *On the Law of Peace: Peace Agreements and the Lex Pacificatoria*, Oxford University Press.

Bell, Christine and Catherine O'Rourke (2007), 'The people's peace? Peace agreements, civil society, and participatory democracy', *International Political Science Review*, **28** (3): 293–324.

Bell, Christine and Catherine O'Rourke (2010), 'Peace agreements or pieces of paper? The impact of UNSC Resolution 1325 on peace processes and their agreements', *International and Comparative Law Quarterly*, **59** (4): 941–80.

Buckley-Zistel, Susanne and Ruth Stanley (eds) (2012), *Gender in Transitional Justice*, Palgrave Macmillan.

Campbell, Colm and Catherine Turner (2008), 'Utopia and the doubters: truth, transition and the law', *Legal Studies*, **28** (3): 374–95.

Chappell, Louise, Rosemary Grey and Emily Waller (2013), 'The gender justice shadow of complementarity: lessons from the International Criminal Court's preliminary examinations in Guinea and Colombia', *International Journal of Transitional Justice*, **7**: 455–76.

Charlesworth, Hilary (1993), 'Alienating Oscar? Feminist analysis of international law', in D. Dallmeyer (ed.), *Reconceiving Reality: Women and International Law*, American Society of International Law.

Chinkin, Christine (1994), 'Rape and sexual abuse of women in international law', *European Journal of International Law*, **5**: 326–41.

Cockburn, Cynthia (2007), *From Where We Stand*, Zed Books.

Cohn, Carol, Felicity Hill, Maha Muna, Isha Dyfan, Helen Kinsella and Sherri Gibbings (2004), 'Women, peace and security: Resolution 1325', *International Feminist Journal of Politics*, **6** (1): 130–40.

Committee on the Elimination of All Forms of Discrimination Against Women (2013), *General Recommendation Number 30 on Women in Conflict Prevention, Conflict and Post-Conflict*.

Conaghan, Joanne (1996), 'Gendered harms and the law of torts: remedying (sexual) harassment', *Oxford Journal of Legal Studies*, **16**: 407–31.

Copelon, Rhonda (1994), 'Surfacing gender: re-engraving crimes against women in humanitarian law', *Hastings Women's Law Journal*, **5** (2): 243–66.

Couillard, Valerie (2007), 'The Nairobi Declaration: redefining reparations for women victims of sexual violence', *International Journal of Transitional Justice*, 1: 444–53.

De Greiff, Pablo (2006), *The Handbook of Reparations*, Oxford University Press.

De Greiff, Pablo (2007), 'Justice and reparations', in J. Miller and R. Kumar (eds), *Reparations: Interdisciplinary Inquiries*, Oxford University Press, pp. 153–75.

Dietrich, Luisa (2012), 'Looking beyond violent militarized masculinities: guerrilla gender regimes in Latin America', *International Feminist Journal of Politics*, 14 (4): 489–507.

Duggan, Colleen, Claudia Paz y Paz Bailey and Julie Guillerot (2008), 'Reparations for sexual and reproductive violence: prospects for achieving gender justice in Guatemala and Peru', *International Journal of Transitional Justice*, 2: 192–213.

Fineman, Martha and Estelle Zinstag (2013), *Feminist Perspectives on Transitional Justice: From International and Criminal to Alternative Forms of Justice*, Intersentia.

Fraser, Elisabeth and Nicola Lacey (1994), *The Politics of Community: A Feminist Critique of the Liberal–Communitarian Debate*, Harvester Wheatsheaf.

Gardam, Judith (1997), 'Women and the law of armed conflict: why the silence?', *International and Comparative Law Quarterly*, 46: 55.

Hamber, Brandon (2007), 'Masculinity and transitional justice: an exploratory essay', *International Journal of Transitional Justice*, 1 (3): 375–90.

Hayner, Priscilla (1994), 'Fifteen Truth Commissions: 1974–1994: a comparative study', *Human Rights Quarterly*, 16: 597–655.

Hayner, Priscilla (2002), *Unspeakable Truths: Facing the Challenge of Truth Commissions*, Routledge.

Huntington, Samuel (1991), *The Third Wave: Democratization in the Late Twentieth Century*, University of Oklahoma Press.

International Center for Transitional Justice (2006), *Truth Commissions and Gender: Principles, Policies, and Procedures*, ICTJ.

International Protocol on the Documentation and Investigation of Sexual Violence in Conflict (2014), *Basic Standards of Best Practice on the Documentation of Sexual Violence as a Crime under International Law*, accessed 23 August 2015 at: https://www.gov.uk/government/uploads/system/uploads/attachment_data/file/319054/PSVI_protocol_web.pdf.

Kent, Lia (2014), 'Narratives of suffering and endurance: coercive sexual relationships, truth commissions and possibilities for gender justice in Timor-Leste', *International Journal of Transitional Justice*, 8 (2): 289–313.

Krog, Antje (2001), 'Locked into loss and silence: testimonies of gender and violence at the South African Truth Commission', in Caroline Moser and Fiona Clark (eds), *Victims, Perpetrators or Actors? Gender, Armed Conflict and Political Violence*, Zubaan Books.

McWilliams, Monica (1995), 'Struggling for peace and justice: reflections on women's activism in Northern Ireland', *Journal of Women's History*, 6/7 (4/1): 13.

McWilliams, Monica and Joan McKiernan (1993), *Bringing it out in the Open: Domestic Violence in Northern Ireland*, Her Majesty's Stationery Office.

McWilliams, Monica and Avila Kilmurray (2015), 'From the global to the local: grounding UNSCR 1325 on women, peace and security in post conflict policy making', *Women's Studies International Forum*, 4 (1): 30–38.

Mertus, Julie (2004), 'Shouting from the bottom of the well: the impact of international trials for wartime rape on women's agency', *International Feminist Journal of Politics*, 6 (1): 110–29.

Moyo, Khanyisela (2012), 'Feminism, postcolonial legal theory and transitional justice: a critique of current trends', *International Human Rights Law Review*, 1 (2): 237–75.

Moyo, Khanyisela (2015), 'Mimicry, transitional justice and the land question in racially divided former settler colonies', *International Journal of Transitional Justice*, 9 (1): 70–89.

Myrttinen, Henri (2003), 'Disarming masculinities', *Disarmament Forum*, **4**: 37–46.

Nairobi Declaration on the Right of Women and Girls to a Remedy and Reparation (2007), accessed 7 March 2016 at: http://www.womensrightscoalition.org.

Navarro, Marysa (1989), 'The personal is political: las madres de Plaza de Mayo', in Susan Eckstein (ed.), *Power and Popular Protest: Latin American Social Movements*, University of California Press, pp. 241–58.

Nesiah, Vesuki (2006), 'Gender and Truth Commission mandates', International Center for Transitional Justice, accessed 7 March 2016 at: https://web.archive.org/web/20081121202356/http://ictj.org/static/Gender/0602.GenderTRC.eng.pdf.

Ní Aoláin, Fionnuala (2000), 'Sex-based violence and the Holocaust – a reevaluation of harms and rights in international law', *Yale Journal of Law and Feminism*, **12**: 43–84.

Ní Aoláin, Fionnuala (2006), 'Political violence and gender during times of transition', *Columbia Journal of Gender and Law*, **15** (3): 829–49.

Ní Aoláin, Fionnuala (2009), 'Exploring a feminist theory of harm in the context of conflicted and post-conflict societies', *Queen's Law Journal*, **35**: 219.

Ní Aoláin, Fionnuala and Catherine Turner (2007), 'Gender, truth and transition', *UCLA Women's Law Journal* **16**: 229.

Ní Aoláin, Fionnuala, Dina Haynes and Naomi Cahn (2011), *On the Frontlines: Gender, War and the Postconflict Process*, Oxford University Press.

Ní Aoláin, Fionnuala, Catherine O'Rourke and Aisling Swaine (2015), 'Transforming reparations for conflict-related sexual violence: principles and practice', *Harvard Human Rights Journal*, **28**: 97–146.

O'Rourke, Catherine (2011), 'Transitioning to what? Transitional justice and gendered citizenship in Chile and Colombia', in Susanne Buckley-Zistel and Ruth Stanley (eds), *Gender in Transitional Justice*, Palgrave Macmillan.

O'Rourke, Catherine (2013a), *Gender Politics in Transitional Justice*, Routledge.

O'Rourke, Catherine (2013b), 'International law and domestic gender justice: why case studies matter', in Martha Fineman and Estelle Zinstag (eds), *Feminist Perspectives on Transitional Justice*, Intersentia.

Orentlicher, Diane F. (1991), 'Settling accounts: the duty to prosecute human rights violations of a prior regime', *Yale Law Journal*, **100**: 2537–615.

Osiel, Mark (1997), *Mass Atrocity, Collective Memory and the Law*, Transaction.

Overseas Development Institute (2013), *Assessment of the Evidence of Links between Gender Equality, Peacebuilding and Statebuilding: Literature Review*, ODI.

Pateman, Carol (1988), *The Sexual Contract*, Polity.

Prosecutor v Brima, Kamara and Kanu, Case No SCSL-2004-16-A, Judgment, ¶ 202 (Feb 22, 2008).

Reilly, Niamh (2009), *Women's Human Rights: Seeking Gender Justice in a Globalizing Age*, Polity.

Ridd, Rosemary (1986), 'Powers of the powerless', in H. Callaway and R. Ridd (eds), *Caught Up in Conflict: Women's Responses to Political Strife*, Macmillan Education, pp. 1–24.

Roht-Arriaza, Naomi (1995), 'Introduction', in Naomi Roht-Arriaza (ed.), *Impunity and Human Rights in International Law and Practice*, Oxford University Press, pp. 3–10.

Rooney, Eilish (2006), 'Women's equality in Northern Ireland's transition: intersectionality in theory and place', *Feminist Legal Studies*, **14**: 353–75.

Rooney, Eilish and Aisling Swaine (2012), 'The "long grass", of agreements: promise, theory and practice', *International Criminal Law Review*, **12** (3): 519.

Ross, Fiona (2003), *Bearing Witness: Women and the Truth and Reconciliation Commission in South Africa*, Pluto.

Rubio-Marin, Ruth (ed.) (2006), *What Happened to the Women: Gender and Reparations for Human Rights Violations*, Social Science Research Council.

Rubio-Marin, Ruth (ed.) (2009), *The Gender of Reparations: Unsettling Sexual Hierarchies while Redressing Human Rights Violations*, Cambridge University Press.

Schirmer, Jennifer (1988), '"Those who die for life cannot be called dead": women and human rights protest in Latin America', *Harvard Human Rights Yearbook*, **1**: 41–76.

Sharoni, Simona (2008), 'De-militarizing masculinities in the age of empire', *Österreichische Zeitschrift für Politikwissenschaft*, **37** (2): 147–64.

Sivakumaran, Sandesh (2007), 'Sexual violence against men in armed conflict', *European Journal of International Law*, **18** (2): 253–76.

Staggs Kelsall, Michelle and Shanee Stepakoff (2007), '"When we wanted to talk about rape": silencing sexual violence at the special court for Sierra Leone', *International Journal of Transitional Justice*, **1**: 355–74.

Swaine, Aisling (2009), 'Assessing the potential of national action plans to advance implementation of United Nations Security Council Resolution 1325', *Yearbook of International Humanitarian Law*, **12**: 403–33.

Swaine, Aisling (2016), *Transforming Transitions: Understanding Conflict-related Violence Against Women*, Cambridge University Press.

Teitel, Ruti (2000), *Transitional Justice*, Oxford University Press.

Theidon, Kimberly (2009), 'Reconstructing masculinities: the disarmament, demobilization, and reintegration of former combatants in Colombia', *Human Rights Quarterly*, **31**: 1–34.

United Nations Secretary-General (2011), *The Rule of Law and Transitional Justice in Conflict and Post-conflict Societies*, United Nations.

United Nations Secretary-General (2014a), *Guidance Note on Reparations for Conflict-related Sexual Violence*, United Nations.

United Nations Secretary-General (2014b), *Report on Women, Peace and Security*, United Nations.

Waylen, Georgina (2007), *Engendering Transitions: Women's Mobilization, Institutions, and Gender Outcomes*, Oxford University Press.

Wills, Maria Emma (2007), *Inclusión sin Representación: Irrupción política de las mujeres en Colombia 1970–2000*, Grupo Editorial Norma.

World Bank (2006), *Gender, Justice and Truth Commissions*, World Bank.

Zinsstag, Estelle (2013), 'Sexual violence against women in armed conflicts and restorative justice: an exploratory analysis', in Martha Fineman and Estelle Zinsstag (eds), *Feminist Perspectives on Transitional Justice*, Intersentia.

Websites

International Centre for Transitional Justice, accessed 23 August 2015 at: www.ictj.org.

UN Women, accessed 23 August 2015 at: www.unwomen.org.

Women's Initiatives for Gender Justice, accessed 23 August 2015 at: http://4gender justice.org.

25. Gender and demilitarization in Liberia
Christopher Hills

INTRODUCTION

Since the end of the Cold War, the issue of what to do with large numbers of former members of armed groups in the aftermath of conflict has been a pivotal focus for the United Nations (UN). The process of demilitarization in post-conflict societies is currently referred to, especially in policy circles, as the Disarmament, Demobilization and Reintegration (DDR) of ex-combatants. On the African continent, DDR has been a major component of UN-led peacebuilding efforts over the past twenty-plus years (ECP, 2008). DDR, in its simplest iteration, has three major processes. First, DDR programs aim to remove and destroy weapons via disarmament – collecting light and heavy weapons from combatants and the civilian population. Second, the demobilization phase seeks to completely disband or downsize military structures and provide basic resettlement packages. Third, the reintegration phase offers educational and training opportunities as a means for alternative livelihoods to assist often huge swathes of individuals to reintegrate into communities of their choice after war. In the case of Liberia, the focus of this chapter, it had an additional 'R': rehabilitation. This phase espoused a concern for individuals' psychosocial needs via specialized counseling; however, as many individuals reported this aspect of the process was a non-event, most of this chapter's focus remains on the 'DD' and 'R' aspects.

Conventional DDR programs, though not exclusively, tend to follow the end of conflicts. Often designed and constructed at the time of peace talks – where women's representation is almost always lacking – the urgent nature of their application often means that many voices outside of the dominant military structures go unheard. DDR programs are pivotal to UN post-conflict peacebuilding efforts in the post-Cold War period, with the largest percentage of these having been prevalent on the African continent. The cost of these programs to the UN, in 2007, came to an estimated $US 1.569 billion (ECP, 2008, p. 4), not an insignificant amount. In the Liberian case, the 103 019 participants in official DDR(R) represented a huge 3 percent of the country's population and came at a cost of $US 110 million (Basini, 2013, p. 541). The seminal importance of these programs in post-conflict states remains obvious. DDR's influence – and specifically its gendered impact – therefore must be scrutinized.

Feminist scholars and practitioners have long argued the post-conflict moment is one which represents the possibility for a positive transformational agenda. Liberia promised to be one of the first real possibilities for the implementation of such an agenda. Sadly, however, DDR programs fell short of facilitating a shift towards gender equality in the country. Using the case study of Liberia to make feminist sense of why reintegration so often fails women and girls requires us not only to investigate what has happened in conflict and post-conflict settings, but also to understand the history of gender within the particular West African context.

The chapter provides an overview of gender and violence in the conflict and post-conflict settings and the existing literature on the implementation of the DDR(R) program in Liberia. Additionally, the chapter situates such resolutions as 1325 alongside the historical context of gender in order to bridge the gap between the rhetoric of such resolutions and reality. Finally the chapter questions notions of overall 'success' and highlights how a critical reading of post-conflict programs is needed to break a cycle of programmatic failures on the continent.

WAR AND 'PEACE' IN LIBERIA: A CONTINUUM OF VIOLENCE

DDR programs are centrally concerned with disbanding military structures. In order to engage in demilitarization, however, it is crucial to understand the origins of different military structures and the context that shaped their role in a particular setting, at a particular historical moment. In the case of Liberia, military structures gained prominence during the civil war. Though Liberia's conflict officially began on Christmas Eve 1989 via the incursion of the Charles Taylor-led National Patriotic Front of Liberia (NPFL), it is often considered to have much deeper roots that lay with the unique history of the country itself. One of only two African states never to be formally colonized, Liberia's unique experience with black settlers from North America beginning in 1822 shaped many political grievances – and indeed gender roles – throughout history (Moran, 1990, 2006; Hills, 2015). The American Colonization Society (ACS) was responsible for the settlement of free black men and women from the East coast of the United States as well as smaller numbers of repatriated slaves and those aboard slave ships heading to the US at the time. America's 'black colonizers', never making up more than 5 percent of the population of the small West African state, controlled politics in the country from 1822, to the formal declaration of independence in 1847, right up until the Samuel Doe-led coup of 1980. Doe's apparent grievances were that a 'native' born indigenous Liberian never held the highest position in his country, thus orchestrating a bloody coup murdering then President William Tolbert and members of his cabinet. Doe's noble claims for indigenous control of the state were soon exposed as a raft of corruption, and increasing intolerance for dissent soon led to a flight of Liberians, including Charles Ghankay Taylor, from the country (Ellis, 2007, pp. 65–74).

Doe met the same fate as his predecessor. He was murdered by Prince Y. Johnson in 1990 and his body paraded around the capital for all to see. Liberia subsequently endured over a decade of constant fighting. From late 1989 – the timeframe where the conflict is considered to have officially began – until 18 August 2003[1] it is estimated that approximately 200 000 to 250 000 people were killed and a quarter of the population of 4 million were either internally or externally displaced (African Women and Peace Support Group, 2004, p. 2).[2]

The war, as many others in post-Cold War sub-Saharan Africa, exacerbated inequalities between men and women (Aisha, 2005, p. 148). Although issues of trauma, displacement, injuries and killings affected the community, the violent conflict took a most devastating toll on women's and girls' bodies. Rape was cited as a 'weapon of war' and many instances of Sexual and Gender-Based Violence (SGBV) were reported, not only during the period between 1989 and 2003, but especially after the Comprehensive Peace Agreement (CPA) was signed and the guns were supposedly 'put down' (Fuest, 2008, p. 202). The post-conflict moment for many women and girls in Liberia represented merely a continuation of violence. As a result, what was defined as 'peace' was considered by many as a disappointment (Barth, 2002).

The gendered impacts of the conflict and post-conflict moment were devastating. Though statistics vary widely on the rates of SGBV, various estimates have stated that 40 percent of Liberian women were raped during the first part of the conflict (Specht, 2006, p. 46). As many as 75 percent of demobilized girls associated with the fighting forces had also suffered sexual abuse or exploitation (Specht, 2006, p. 45). That extended into the post-conflict environment, whereby women suffered from a period some scholars have labeled the 'militarization of intimate relations' (Liebling-Kalifani and Baker, 2010, p. 196), encountering sexual and domestic abuse at alarming rates.

At the same time, women and girls in the Liberian conflict were not just passive victims; they also played seminal roles in many of the major fighting forces (Specht, 2006). More accurately, women and girls showed extensive 'tactical agency' in navigating through the Liberian warzone, taking on a range of roles from frontline combatants, to spies, couriers, 'wives' and girlfriends (Utas, 2005; Aisha, 2005). It is generally considered that during the first part of the war (1989–97) a majority of women were forced to participate, whereas during the second phase (2000–2003) many more women volunteered, for reasons of security, to avenge the deaths of family members, for material needs or simply for survival (Amnesty International, 2009; Pugel, 2007, p. 41; Specht, 2006). Estimates hold the numbers of women and girls in the various fighting factions in the conflict to have been between 20 and 40 percent (Sherif, 2008). Studies completed in post-conflict Liberia have shown the importance in illuminating and problematizing the simplistic labels of 'victim' and 'perpetrator' especially for women and girls, something which gives the space for an analysis which recognizes their – albeit limited – agency throughout the conflict (Utas, 2003; McMullin, 2013; Nilsson and Thapar-Björkert, 2013; Specht, 2006).

Following the war, however, the contributions of many women and girls were overlooked and regardless of their roles they were referred to with such labels as 'bush wife' or 'female associated with the fighting forces' (Jennings, 2009, p. 482). The implications of not recognizing former women and girl fighters as 'ex-combatant' degraded and 'desecuritized' them and relegated them to the rear in many post-conflict programs (Jennings, 2009; MacKenzie, 2012). The crucial, heterogeneous roles played by women and girls throughout the war were overlooked, reducing their roles to their association with and support of men (Specht, 2006, p. 20). The lack of a genuine acknowledgement of the different entries of women and girls into armed groups, the diverse roles they played, the trauma experienced and skills gained during conflict limited their access to a specifically tailored and gender-responsive DDR process (Specht, 2006; Basini, 2013).

Liberian women have been recognized globally for their role in helping end the conflict. Groups such as the Mary Brownell-led Liberian Women's Initiative (LWI) prominent in fighting for peace all throughout the 1990s to the Mano River Union Women Peace Network (MARWOPNET), and later the Leymah Gbowee-led Women in Peacebuilding Network (WIPNET), all reflected a broader history of women's important place in the socio-political order in various contexts within the country (Moran, 2010, p. 267). Throughout the conflict, all of these organizations campaigned, forcefully, for the consistent male-dominated peace talks to act swiftly in ending their factions' disagreements and for an end to war. WIPNET's pressure was vital in forcing through the Comprehensive Peace Agreement (CPA), reached on 18 August 2003 in Accra, Ghana. It was at these talks that the United Nations Mission in Liberia (UNMIL) was conceived. UNMIL, quickly deployed, consisted of between 15 000 and 16 000 military and police staff and approximately 1500 civilian staff (Fuest, 2008, p. 205). A significant part of UNMIL's early responsibilities included the launching of one of the world's largest ever DDR programs.

LIBERIAN DDR(R)[3] – DISARMAMENT AND DEMOBILIZATION

DDR programs have been implemented in a wide spectrum of settings. They are common during an ongoing conflict, as in the Democratic Republic of Congo and Afghanistan, or at the end of liberation wars where the emphasis is on the downsizing of armed forces, as was the case in South Africa and Zimbabwe. Additionally, DDR programs also occur during – and after – the signing of official peace agreements following large-scale civil wars, as was the case in the small West African states of Sierra Leone and Liberia. Liberia's DDR(R) program was almost a replicate, both in form and structure, of the program already in place in Sierra Leone (Jennings, 2007, p. 338).

Liberia's Disarmament, Demobilization, Rehabilitation and Reintegration program indeed followed the Comprehensive Peace Agreement (CPA) of August 2003. Promisingly, the CPA made several specific references to women and children affected by the conflict (Aisha, 2005, p. 151). Further, provisions made within UN Security Council Resolution 1509 (2003) acknowledged the importance of promoting and protecting the rights of civilian groups, with specific reference to women and children. Perhaps most importantly, Liberia was the world's first program to mainstream gender concerns present within UNSCR 1325 (Basini, 2013).

Launched on 7 December 2003, Liberia's DDR(R) program remained under the guidance of a National Commission for DDRR (NCDDRR) and a Joint Implementation Unit (JIU) consisting of UNMIL, the United Nations Development Program (UNDP) and other governmental and non-governmental organizations (Nichols, 2005, p. 114). UNMIL was largely responsible for the DD stages of the process, whilst UNDP took charge during the later RR phases.

The program got off to a difficult beginning. Against the advice of many officials and stakeholders on the ground, UNMIL rushed the first foray into disarmament, at an army barracks called Camp Schefflin on the outskirts of Monrovia. Unprepared for the approximately three thousand ex-combatants quickly appearing at the Camp Schefflin cantonment site, supplies and personnel were insufficient to manage such a large number of individuals. Riots, looting and gunfights soon ensued. Over the course of two days, nine people died and disarmament was forced to be postponed (Basini, 2013, p. 544).

Disarmament and demobilization was restarted in April of the following year, due in a major part to the influence of the Leymah Gbowee-led WIPNET organization. Following the disastrous Camp Schefflin incident, UNMIL turned to civil society – and WIPNET in particular – and agreed to pay 20 women to assist with the restarting of DDR(R). A staggering 55 women agreed to take part in the important task, sharing the funds meant for 20 evenly between themselves (UNIFEM, 2005, p. 2). At this important juncture, WIPNET was seminal in restarting clear and concise communication with eligible ex-combatants, both men and women, about the imminent restarting of the process. In doing so, WIPNET reaffirmed the right of women who were involved in the Liberian conflict that they too were eligible for entry to fully participate in formal DDR(R) initiatives (Gbowee and Mithers, 2011). Though eventually representing approximately 23 percent of the total caseload, in the first week of the process women represented just 130 of a total of 1789 individuals registering for DDR(R) (UNMIL, 2010, p. 13).

Initially, the UN was hesitant to engage with Liberian women's NGOs in the DDR(R) process, even though they ultimately would prove to be an important aspect in all areas of post-conflict peacebuilding in the country. Though important in resurrecting the DD phases, sadly, women's organizations were not consulted during rehabilitation and reintegration (RR). Gbowee lamented how Liberian women's proposals in the later stages of the process were not considered 'expert' enough and instead outside 'experts' were brought into the country, people with experience from other situations such as Kosovo and Sierra Leone (Gbowee and Mithers, 2011, p. 169). In April of 2004, disarmament was restarted initially in five sites, including also Gbarngba, Buchanan, Tubmanburg and the Voice of America (VOA) camp. In July cantonment sites were established at Grand Gedeh, River Cess, Sinoe and Zwedru counties, targeting those from the Movement for Democratic Change in Liberia (MODEL) faction, whilst in Nimba county, camps targeted Government of Liberia (GOL) soldiers and in Voinjama a site was set up to target the Liberians United for Reconstruction and Democracy (LURD) caseload (Aboagye and Bah, 2005, p. 111). Though these sites highlight attempts to decentralize the process, due to the immediate need to disarm combatants and the dire state of infrastructure impacted by 'the Wet

Season', most individuals chose to settle within either the urban environs of Monrovia or smaller regional hubs (Paes, 2005, p. 258).

From the start of Liberian DDR(R), issues of eligibility and size plagued the program. According to early estimates provided by leaders from two of the three largest rebel groups, and adopted by the UN, the number of former combatants participating in the program was between 38 000 and 54 000 (UNDP, 2006, p. 28). These original figures almost doubled as 103 019 men, women, boys and girls were ultimately admitted entry into official DDR(R) (UNDP, 2006, p. 6). The rise in the number of participants has been attributed to the change in the entry requirements into the program itself. The initial entry requirement of 'one-man-one-gun' was scaled back to those presenting 150 rounds of ammunition. In the case of women, who may have been stripped of weapons and ammunition, the requirement was simply to identify as a member of either armed group, to be recognized as such by gatekeepers such as generals, or sufficiently answering questions posed by military observers about their time in and involvement with the armed groups (Basini, 2013, p. 544).

The ultimate gendered breakdown of participants in DDR(R) programs – 78 052 boys and men versus 24 967 girls and women (Sanz, 2009, p. 87) – makes it obvious that women and girls cannot be put forward as the sole 'benefactors' of lax entry requirements and the subsequent challenges in the later stages of the DDR(R) implementation. The rapid increase in the number of participants in the program fueled a crisis in funding for later demobilization and reintegration, which had damaging effects for many involved, not least for women and girls (Jennings, 2008; Paes, 2005, p. 260).

Prior to discharge from cantonment sites, the first of two $US 150 Transitional Safety Allowance (TSA) payments were made (Nichols, 2005, p. 118), and is largely where most view the rapid exploitation of a relaxed entry to official DDR(R) to have occurred. Gatekeepers such as former generals and other leading figures within the rebel forces provided arms (often taken from women who may have previously possessed them) or ammunition and provided them to friends and family members, and thus took a percentage of the lucrative $US 300 available from the TSAs (Paes, 2005, p. 255).

Due in large part to the explosion of numbers and subsequent lack of funding (Söderström, 2011, p. 31), demobilization, initially planned as a one month phase – whereby individuals could receive counseling and trauma-healing services, access to medical attention and make informed choices regarding reintegration training – was quickly shortened to five days (UNDP, 2006, p. 28). Some have even noted this phase was further shortened and lasted as little as three days (Sanz, 2009, p. 88). As one faction commander was quoted in the UNDP's mid-term report (2006, p. 28) as saying, 'it is impossible to demobilise in five days someone who has fought for fourteen years'. Indeed, the task of breaking up existing control structures and systems of command within many of the forces within a short timeframe was doomed to fail (Nichols, 2005, p. 127). Another consequence of the limited timeframe of demobilization was that information regarding the reintegration phase was not widely disseminated. As a result, both men and women were deprived of knowledge and services designed to help them make informed choices for their future (UNDP, 2006, p. 45).

During the demobilization phase, women and girls benefited, if only briefly, from their separation from adult men, in particular from former commanders (Nichols, 2005, p. 127). Women and men were transported to sites separately, screened in different medical centers and babies were tended to (Douglas and Hill, 2004, p. 16). The layout of many of the cantonment sites was done in a gender-responsive manner, keeping men and boys separate from women and girls. Such separation and planning of canton sites was lauded, as was the inclusion of Interim Care Centres (ICCs) within proximity to cantonment sites that involved assistance – albeit also brief – pertaining to reproductive health and trauma counseling for boys and girls (Amnesty International, 2009; Nichols, 2005, p. 127). ICCs were set up for girls and boys who had taken part in the conflict and who had been separated from their parents and family members. Many of these children were struggling with addiction problems relating to substances such as marijuana and cigarettes and several had no memory of their parents at all (Douglas and Hill, 2004, p. 16). Unlike usual cantonment sites, ICCs were designed without razor wire, and UNMIL personnel were present and located closer to communities, so as to facilitate a smoother reintegration into a normal environment for children (Douglas and Hill, 2004, p. 17).

Liberia's disarmament and demobilization phases were officially closed on 31 October 2004. In total 103 019 individuals passed through, with UNMIL collecting 27 804 weapons and 7 129 198 rounds of small arms ammunition (Nichols, 2005, p. 114). Numbers, however, impressive as they are, do not tell the whole story. The subsequent reintegration of such a large number of individuals would prove a difficult task.

LIBERIAN DDR(R) – REINTEGRATION AND REHABILITATION

A meaningful and well-funded attempt at the RR phases in Liberia was placed on the back foot from the start, due in major part to the large number of participants that proved to be a challenge during the DD phases as well. The RR phases of Liberian DDR(R) were ultimately whittled down to just the one: reintegration. The second 'R', rehabilitation, according to the UNDP (2006, p. 42) itself was 'undefined and for which no specific component was developed'.[4] The lack of attention to rehabilitation impacted heavily upon women in particular. Indeed, as Basini argued, the failure to prioritize women's particular psychosocial needs 'was one of the greatest deficiencies of the DDR gender mainstreaming process in Liberia' (2013, p. 551). Ultimately, the lack of focus on psychosocial rehabilitation as well as community-based reconciliation efforts was considered a major shortfall of the process (Candan, 2012, p. 6).

After release from cantonment sites, women were largely subsumed within a reintegration process that operated from a 'default male' perspective (Jennings, 2009). Unlike the DD phases, RR in Liberia was not implemented by a body that took into consideration gender mainstreaming. Instead of adopting a holistic and sustainable reintegration process that took into account the social and political reintegration of all involved in the process, the focus was on the immediate economic reintegration of a specific group of ex-combatants, viewed as 'idle men' (UNDP, 2006, p. 37; Söderström, 2011).

Reintegration occurred in two major caseloads. The first, running from December 2003 to June 2008, was reflective of the so-called 'first generation' approach to DDR (McMullin, 2013, p. 197). It targeted individuals primarily, providing them with educational or training opportunities often with no market analysis or with nuanced gender considerations (Hills, 2015). The second caseload ran from July 2008 to April 2009, and with some improvements, yet still with many deficiencies in terms of women's and girls' experiences. Some 38 percent of the individuals involved in the residual caseload were women (and girls) who had not received reintegration assistance in the initial caseload due primarily to UNMIL's obsession with 'idle men'. Gender-specific training opportunities such as sewing, pastry-making, tie-dying and hairdressing were put forward as appropriate roles for women after war – no matter their particular position within the armed forces, ignoring any new skills they may have gained in the conflict. Due to the gendered division of power and labor in society, such occupations generated limited income, reinforcing women's dependency on a male figure after the conflict (Hills, 2015, p. 79). Ultimately the residual caseload was one that held more positives for women and girls in that its market analysis was a marked improvement on the first, but it was still deficient in its inability to address women's particular psychosocial needs as a result of the violence they suffered at the hands of – primarily – men (Basini, 2013, p. 551).

Though women were not excluded from such training opportunities as carpentry or masonry, which are stereotypically associated with men, most women selected courses designed for them such as pastry production, tie-dying and hairdressing, which were very gender specific (Basini, 2013, p. 548). Programs were fixed and inflexible (Basini, 2013, p. 548). The lack of micro-credit or business training opportunities made it almost impossible for women to gain some form of socio-economic independence. Similar shortcomings were evident in the training opportunities available to men, including the lack of market analysis. While women were trained as tie-dyers and dress-makers, saturating a market with little demand, men were trained as mechanics, often in towns and cities with few working vehicles (Utas, 2003, p. 239). Moreover, poor lines of communication resulted in frustration on the part of DDR(R) participants, both men and women, when their expectations weren't met regarding reintegration training opportunities (Candan, 2012; Jennings, 2007).

In addition to skills training, formal education made up a large percentage of reintegration choices made by ex-combatants. Those choosing education received three years of free formal education and a monthly stipend of $US 30 the first year, $US 15 the second year and no stipend the third (UNDP, 2006, p. 31). With over 38 000 individuals choosing education as a means to reintegrate, it was the largest formal education component of any DDR program (UNDP, 2006, p. 31). Schooling was considered a positive step towards reintegration as it was a community-based approach that did not require relocation.

Priority in official reintegration was given to those schooling between years 7 and 12, as UNICEF's Community Education Investment Program (CEIP) took responsibility with the earlier grades from 1 to 6. The difference was that the CEIP's focus was the entire school, rather than an individual focus from year 7. Put simply, those enrolled in the 7th grade received official DDR(R) benefits, whilst those in the 4th grade received nothing (UNDP, 2006, p. 31). This made it difficult for younger ex-combatants, as some benefited from targeted assistance while others received nothing. Yet, on the whole, schooling was thought to be a successful measure to integrate young ex-combatants with the general population. However, for many girls who wished to continue or begin their education, a lack of income-generating prospects in the wake of war meant that many had to forgo this route to reintegration (Specht, 2006, p. 100).

Throughout both caseloads, 'hotspots' assessments took place where UNMIL deemed emergency reintegration provisions needed to be put in place. The first provisions, initiated in 2005, in anticipation of the elections later that year, were linked closely to communities and were cognizant of including both ex-combatants (XCs) and non-combatant community members (McMullin, 2013, pp. 209–10). Seven hotspots programs were introduced in October 2005, November 2005, April 2006, April 2007, August 2008, January 2009 and May 2009 and were deemed beneficial during the initial election period and indeed in the years following. Throughout this period, the fetishization with this concept of 'idle' men remained at the fore (Jennings, 2009), even against interesting research taking place that seemingly refuted such claims (Bøås and Hatløy, 2008). For example, in a study for the United States Institute for Peace, Hill et al. (2008, p. 5) asked men and women ex-combatants if they could ever envisage fighting again to find relief from poverty. Men replied affirmatively 11 percent of the time, whereas for women 20 percent replied that they could. War in Liberia, it seemed, had shaped and changed many women's ideas around systems of labor and routes to independence (Fuest, 2008).

As McMullin succinctly iterates, 'deeply embedded – and problematic – ideas about DDR and ex-combatants ultimately allowed the conceptualization of reintegration into poverty to prevail' (2013, p. 199). Rather than an *integration* into societies that little resembled pre-war times, the international community seemed transfixed with *re*-integrating individuals back into a time prior to conflict that neither acknowledged their strengths in conflict, skills gained, or desire to be able to transform towards a different kind of life. The unwillingness of the international community to solicit input from local women's NGOs and to consult with women within the various armed groups resulted in grossly inaccurate representation of gender roles, given a non-existent formal neoliberal capitalist economy post-war.

Formally ending in 2009, Liberia's DDR(R) program has brought about a slew of studies focusing on all aspects of the process, from entry requirements to programmatic improvement and adherence to recommendations present within UNSCR 1325. A broader focus on gender in Liberian history, however, uncovers problems with how the process was eventually evaluated.

GENDER MAINSTREAMING AND DDR(R)

There are three seminally important issues pertaining to gender and DDR(R) in the Liberian sense: official rhetoric from gender mainstreaming; ideas about culture and tradition; and notions of 'success'. Looking back at these three aspects remains vital to the particular context of the case of Liberian DDR(R).

At its time of inception, Liberia's foray into official DDR(R) held much promise for addressing the genuine needs of men, boys, women and girls. Following the seminal resolution of October 2000, Liberia's DDR(R) program became a world first for explicitly mainstreaming all recommendations of UNSCR 1325. With regard to DDR specifically, in Article 13 UNSCR 1325 calls for 'considering the different needs of female and male ex-combatants and to take into account the needs of their dependents in the planning of DDR' (UNSCR, 2000). The UN has been clear since 1325 that addressing the needs of women and girls during DDR is centrally important. Table 25.1 highlights the explicit gender provisions put forward within UN resolutions for DDR programs.

The 777-page long UN Integrated DDR Standards (IDDRS) framework similarly implores the need for a gender-responsive approach to all aspects of the process. At the rhetorical level, it is clear from the above that mainstreaming gender in DDR remains important, yet the Liberian instance points to the difficulties in putting theory into practice.

At the same time, a comparison between women and girls in official DDR in Sierra Leone and those in Liberia highlights some key differences between programs that take seriously the gender mainstreaming recommendation of UNSCR 1325 and those with no explicit attention to gender. In Sierra Leone, where gender did not play a key role in DDR, a total of 4751 women and girls were present amongst a total beneficiary population of approximately 72 500, representing just 6.5 percent of the total caseload. In comparison, the numbers in Liberia were significantly higher, with 24 967 included, representing around five times greater than those of neighboring Sierra Leone (Jennings, 2009, p. 482). Though seemingly impressive on numbers alone, a deeper analysis is needed to explore how effective gender mainstreaming was past the first 'D' phase. For instance, Jennings (2009, p. 482) highlights that though these numbers appear impressive, women were often not considered as 'ex-combatants' and often were lumped into the homogeneous category of 'women associated with fighting forces' (WAFFs), no matter their role.

Where the Office of the Gender Advisor-UNMIL assisted with providing gender advisors for the DD phases and subsequently numbers of women included increased (Aisha, 2005, p. 156), problems arose with a

Table 25.1 Gender and DDR in UNSCRs

Resolutions	SCR 1325 (2000)	SCR 1820 (2008)	SCR 1888 (2009)	SCR 1889 (2010)	SCR 1960 (2010)	SCR 2122 (2013)
DDR Specific Provisions	'Calls for considering the different needs of female and male ex-combatants and to take into account the needs of their dependents in the planning of DDR.'	'Effective protection from violence against women in DDR processes.'	'Sexual violence issues to be specifically addressed in DDR processes.'	'Takes into account the particular needs of women and girls in the planning of DDR programmes and ensures their full access to these programmes.'	'States, with support from the international community, to increase healthcare, psychosocial support, legal assistance and socio-economic reintegration services for victims of sexual violence.'	'Further expresses its intention to include provisions to facilitate women's full participation and protection in … disarmament, demobilization and reintegration programmes.'

Note: Adapted from UNDDR website, with an addition of UNSCR 2122.

lack of expertise during the RR phases. For example, there was minimal understanding of what UNSCR 1325 and gender mainstreaming meant during RR, and there were also several problems pertaining to data collection, implementation and monitoring and evaluation (Njoki Wamai, 2011, p. 57). Further, UNMIL largely failed to recognize the impressive work already being done by women's organizations at the community level at the time (Njoki Wamai 2011, p. 60).

UNDP officials reflected critically on the challenges throughout, admitting that 'women were largely treated as adult men during the process' (2006, p. 48) and the rigid, inflexible nature of first-generation DDR planning was often evident in Liberia. In a country with a history of women in leadership positions and women's organizations prominent throughout war and in its aftermath, cooperation with these important gender activists and experts within the country, whose knowledge and insight into the local context should have proved pivotal, was minimal at best (Nduka-Agwu, 2009, p. 197).

The inability of DDR to adequately challenge gendered stereotypes in wartime and to address the prevalence of sexual and gender-based violence experienced predominantly by women in conflict and post-conflict Liberia is indicative of the overall limitations of resolutions such as UNSCR 1325. Basini argues that a narrow focus on sanctions and prosecutions failed to address the real needs of SGBV victims in this setting (2013, p. 553).

Initially, minimal attention was devoted to analyzing SGBV with a focus on the shifting gender roles and relations during and in the aftermath of conflict. As a result, women soon became the targets of frustrated and hyper-militarized men returning home with often useless training opportunities provided to them. CARE's work in Uganda has been an exception as they allowed local men to be 'change agents' and to act as 'role model men' who exhibit 'positive masculinity' and actively profess zero tolerance for gender violence (El-Bushra et al., 2013, p. 34). Similar programs with a health focus have been implemented in other such post-conflict states as Rwanda and Angola as well as Sudan and South Africa (Porter, 2013, pp. 497–501). In Liberia, on the other hand, the absence of such a program explicitly focusing on transforming violent masculinities to 'positive' ones was evident. In an environment which rhetorically espoused the importance of 'economic empowerment' programs for women, often these same women had to bear the brunt of men's violence even after the guns had been put down.

In Liberia a whole generation of fighting left many men and boys 'unable to articulate their identities and gender roles in peacetime, and without weapons' (Douglas and Hill, 2004, p. 19). Alternatives to such

militarized masculinities have remained an elusive focus for the transformative – and poorly designed – reintegration component. And though
a serious conversation on masculinities and men involved in Liberia's
DDR(R) program was not a constant, perhaps as interesting is the lack of
focus on those men who *did not fight*. Moran (2010, p. 268) points to
how important it is to understand these masculine identities as alternatives to the consistent discourse on militarized masculinities put forward
during war. A nuanced gender analysis therefore acknowledges the
injustices faced by women, routes for their socio-economic independence, but also the role that a transformation of masculinities could play in
the post-conflict setting.

DECONSTRUCTING 'TRADITIONAL' GENDER ROLES

Harassment and rape of women was never socially accepted in Liberia before
the war.[5]

War causes serious disruptions to gender systems of labor, and for those
women who have taken up arms, many find it extremely difficult to
reintegrate into societies where gendered norms – be they imposed from
outside, or put forward from within – constrain alternatives for many of
them (Veale, 2003; Coulter et al., 2008). Women may be stigmatized for
their roles in the war and shunned or rejected if they do not adopt
'traditional' gender roles on their return home (Tonheim, 2010, pp. 22–3).

Looking back at the implementation of DDR programs in Africa,
however, with a special focus on reintegration, scholars differ as to the
extent to which gender relations should be transformed, or even if that
should be a tactic of the post-conflict moment (Baare, 2006, p. 31; Fuest,
2008; Smet, 2009, pp. 153–4; Tonheim, 2010, pp. 13–38). DDR is
indicative of a problematique in peacebuilding and state-building more
generally, regarding the role the international community should play in
rebuilding states in the Global South, with those involved often having
very little knowledge of what 'traditional cultures' and 'traditional'
notions of gender roles and gendered systems of labor have been or how
they are continuing to evolve.

The term 'traditional gender roles' often conjures up an ahistorical and
stereotypical idea of gender roles and relations. Often, in the aftermath of
war, the international community has sought to 'do no harm' and not to
interfere with what is perceived as the traditional way of life or a return
to supposed normalcy. Yet the phrases 'do no harm' and 'return to

normal' have not been examined carefully and critically with attention to what is considered 'harm' or 'normal' and by whom? This 'retradition-alization' or reassertion of pre-war patriarchy (Turshen, 2001) remains entirely problematic for women after war. When looking at DDR, it becomes clear that the international community has been unable or unwilling to put in place the necessary mechanisms needed for women's safety, security and particularly routes to socio-economic independence post-conflict.

Gender in Liberian history has been impacted upon greatly by outside influences, 'black colonizers', monotheistic religions and the overall capitalist world economy. To speak of 'traditional' gender roles in the Liberian context remains a 'thought-stopper' (Cohn and Enloe, 2003, p. 1192), as it does in reality in most societies throughout the world. In Liberia, women's political clout, ability to protest, and ability to hold perpetrators of SGBV accountable remained a constant throughout docu-mented history within the south-east of the country (Moran, 1990; 2006; 2012; Hills, 2015). Especially noteworthy was women's ability to main-tain socio-economic independence from men. Within the northern and north-western parts of the country, where a more 'patriarchal' system of governance existed, it was not uncommon for women to hold the position of chief. Additionally, the fact that women held prominent positions in a secret society, the *Sande*, made obvious their standing within society (Bledsoe, 1980).

Liberia's unique experience of colonization seriously altered its gen-dered landscape. Free men and women from America, arriving in 1822, brought with them ideals of gender roles often transfixed with life in the South of the States at that time. Unlike indigenous constructions of gender, which reflected a general trend of dual-sex systems of labor prominent throughout West Africa, Liberia's 'black colonizers' had firm and fast ideas about male breadwinners, female dependency and 'civi-lized' behavior for men and women (Tonkin, 1980; Moran, 1990, 2006; Hills, 2015). The 'civilized' and powerful settler population encouraged women to maintain ideal domesticity and put forward males as the – almost – entire population of wage-earning 'breadwinners'. Liberia's unique experience of colonialism brought about different – but similarly impactful – relationships to gender roles as had occurred in European settled African states.

Even though pre-war Liberian society was characterized by a range of households headed by both men and women (Fuest, 2008), the inter-national community with its DDR programming was unwilling to chal-lenge the gendered division of power and labor, especially the idea that it was culturally 'normal' for men to be the sole breadwinners. This example of reintegration into 'normalcy' is problematic because the idea of so-called normalcy is based in a pre-conflict setting that acknowledges neither Liberia's settler-colonial history of the past nor the fact that women and girls should enjoy the same basic human rights as their counterparts elsewhere in the world (Hills, 2015), Because the IDDRS stipulates that DDR must provide a balanced and contextual approach to gendered systems of labor after conflict, querying who such post-conflict systems of labor benefit must be central to all analyses (United Nations, 2006, Section 5.10, p. 21).

Along these lines, a critical examination of history can explain many of the problems that DDR and other post-conflict peacebuilding initiatives encountered in dealing with SGBV after war. Historically in Liberia, rape and sexual crimes were neither 'tolerated nor ignored' and women had many avenues to seek reparations and sanctions for such behavior (Abramowitz and Moran, 2012, p. 124). After the conflict, however, sexual violence was portrayed as a normal part of Liberian 'culture' (Moran, 2010, p. 268), with many NGOs putting forward the misconceived idea that Liberia is irreversibly patriarchal, dominant and always oppressive towards women (Abramowitz, 2009, p. 195). A prominent anthropologist with years of experience in the country prior to war noted upon return to the country from which she had been absent for 14 years that the discourse that claims that in Liberia 'women were considered property' was inconsistent with her prior research in the country (Moran, 2010, 2012). Furthermore, a lack of historical knowledge or reflection, both on the part of foreign aid workers, but also of Liberians working in the context themselves, has relegated supposedly 'traditional' responses to the issue of SGBV in post-conflict Liberia to the rear in favor of 'expert' views on gender equality imported from the North (Moran, 2012).

DDR's inability to address key concerns of SGBV could have been greatly enhanced as a result of consultation with local experts on women's rights and gender issues. Indeed, the efforts to address issues surrounding SGBV should have begun during cantonment as there was essentially a 'captive audience', including in particular men, who were the perpetrators of most of these crimes (Basini, 2013, p. 553). As rape was used as a weapon of war, disarming such a mindset was vital and could have prevented post-conflict incidences of rape and sexual violence, which have become prevalent crimes in urban environs (Basini, 2013, p. 553). Clearly, local and international expertise on the complex and sensitive issues surrounding SGBV was not taken into account during the implementation of the program. A critical examination of Liberian history is important not only in order to avoid repeating the settler and colonial impositions of the past, but also in order to secure a better chance at a successful DDR program overall.

(EN)GENDERING DDR – WHITHER 'SUCCESS'?

The duplicative nature of post-conflict programs remains consistent to this day. The same could also be said for the general applications of the terms 'success' and 'failure' to studies focusing on them. Methodological approaches differ, from large *N* studies seeking to answer the questions of 'success' at a macro-level (Humphreys and Weinstein, 2007; Pugel, 2007), to those from a feminist perspective which are more qualitatively inclined (Fuest, 2008; Jennings, 2009; Basini, 2013), meaning that both success and failure are loaded terms. Practitioners and scholars have long debated issues of monitoring and evaluation parameters, baseline data (which is often infrequently available), methodological approaches and timing of studies. All of these factors, and more, impact upon how reintegration is understood in the particular context and thus, by extension, the purpose of the process.

Reintegration was not clearly defined in Liberia. As a result, various entities and groups involved in the program had different interpretations of what 'success' meant and looked like (UNDP, 2006, p. 42). Consequently, according to the UNDP, it was difficult to obtain coherent results of the programs (outcomes) and the focus shifted instead to actual activities (outputs) (UNDP, 2006, p. 42).

Parameters for measuring progress and indicators of success in DDR are laid out in the UN's Integrated DDR Standards (IDDRS) manual 2006 (Module 3.50). Additionally, Module 5.10 of the IDDRS, titled 'Women, Gender and DDR' provides extensive guidance on gender-appropriate responses for all facets of the process, including monitoring and evaluation. Module 5.10 remains comprehensive, from its focus on the assessment phase, to demobilization and the social and economic reintegration of women and girls.

Though Module 5.10 (pp. 12–14) places important emphasis on the transitional phase that is demobilization, often, for DD phases, quantitative indicators normally suffice for monitoring and evaluation purposes, while for reintegration, gauging success is not so easy (Jennings, 2007, p. 334). For example, within the DD phases, proxies for success may include the number of individuals permitted entrance, gender disaggregation of these numbers, the number of weapons collected and destroyed and access to health and medical facilities within canton sites.

Yet, when it comes to the often poorly defined reintegration programs, in states with minimal to no formal economy and with ex-combatants who may often have undergone almost no schooling, gauging what is a 'success' for the reintegration phase remains hard to do. Parameters must, of course, relate back to the original remit of the particular DDR program in question; however, in the Liberian case that sought to adhere to the principles espoused with UNSCR 1325, critical questions must be posed.

In the Liberian case, there is a rift between those considering the program overall a 'success' and those remaining more critical. A large UN-commissioned and funded study completed by Pugel in 2007 is often used in contrast to much critical feminist scholarship on the process (Basini, 2013; Fuest, 2008; Hills, 2015; Jennings, 2007, 2009; Specht, 2006). Pugel finds that there was an overall improvement in women's socio-economic situation; noting that women self-reported an improvement as a result of their reintegration training as opposed to men (2007, p. 68). Others, conversely, have argued that socio-economic conditions did not improve for most women and girls, many of whom faced further barriers than their male counterparts in reintegrating into society (Jennings, 2009; Specht, 2006). This is complicated as security and development issues are conflated within different stages of DDR and, as Jennings states, 'the increasing reliance on reintegration to fulfil both security and socioeconomic goals complicates attempts to assess its value' (2007, p. 334). DDR's position at the nexus of security and development remains obvious and developmental issues pertaining to reintegration are often relegated to the background.

A critical examination of Liberian DDR(R), based on both official UN policy documents and the broader gender-specific provisions, calls into question attempts to label the program a 'success' overall. At the same time, it is important not to overlook successful interventions along the way. A case in point was the impressive inclusion of women and girls as well as their segregation from men in canton sites during the DD phases. Yet the reintegration process was managed without an official gender advisor and designed from a default male perspective (Jennings, 2009), thus relegating women to the rear. Indeed one study concluded that for women and girl soldiers, DDR seemed to have ended following the two Ds (Nilsson and Thapar-Björkert, 2013, p. 6). Generally speaking, since women and girls made up almost 25 percent of the entire caseload, the program cannot be considered a success if it overlooked the needs and experiences of such a large constituency. The disparate nature of the phases, the lack of a gender advisor at all stages of the process, and a lack of consensus over such key definitions as 'success' amongst implementing partners exposed different expectations and intentions and eventually compromised both the coherence and the overall success of the program (UNDP, 2006, p. 42).

There exists a consensus in the literature concerning Liberia's DDR(R) that it successfully met the initial goal of contributing to the consolidation of national security (UNDP, 2006, p. 47); beyond this, however, gauging the success of DDR(R) remains almost impossible. Conflating issues of whether or not a state formally returns to war, with how 'successful' those women and girls having passed through official DDR(R) judged the process, remains problematic. Many expectations of the process, both from men and women, were not met (Jennings, 2009) and should have provided a clearer indication of whether or not a 'successful' program was indeed implemented.

CONCLUSION

To look forward, we must look back. As many post-conflict programs over the past more than two decades have produced a string of 'lessons learned' type documents, learning from gendered shortcomings in past programs is vital. Towards this end, it is crucial to unpack the broader gendered history of the particular state or region one is focusing on or working in. Such a process often involves examining critically the prevailing terminology of 'traditional gender roles' to question when and where these roles existed, who and how have they been impacted upon by history and conflict, and how the notion of traditional gender roles may have negatively affected the overall guidance of post-conflict reintegration parameters of 'success'. It is not enough to simply take times of crisis, such as war and post-war moments, as the time to take women seriously; a critical examination of women's social and political involvement throughout history problematizes simplistic notions of gender roles often put forward under the banner of a nuclear family and return to 'normalcy'.

In a similar manner, notions of 'failure' and 'success' and the unwillingness of scholars and practitioners alike to label the program as one or the other were put forward. Knowing that many of the 24 967 women and girls who have passed through official DDR(R) in Liberia – in the immediate timeframe at least – live a life of dependency and stigma means that the program overall cannot be fully considered a success story. Thus, Liberia's example must not be another exemplifier in the cookie-cutter chain.

DDR is all about context. When programs are replicated from other states – even if such a state is a neighboring one – little relevance holds sway within the particular context of that new post-conflict state. In Liberia, a lack of consultation with local people, gender experts and women themselves resulted in many of the 'failures' that had occurred in earlier DDR programs across the continent – even though Liberia had officially adopted the world's first mainstreaming of UNSCR 1325. Notwithstanding the important work that was done on the ground by practitioners, UN officials and NGO workers, one must be critical of an approach that often is transposed to a local population with minimal prior research and consultation.

In order to improve DDR programs in the future, scholars must proceed with caution when seeking to generalize and instead pay careful attention to particular contexts. As the case of Liberia illustrates, despite being praised as the first such program in the world to incorporate gender mainstreaming policies, its implementation was fraught with short-comings and contradictions. Instead of a narrow focus on UN resolutions, this chapter concludes that a 'best practice' would be to use a context-ualized and nuanced historical emic approach to the topic of gender in each and every state that utilizes DDR as a post-conflict peacebuilding mechanism. Looking back to look forward here is not only a reasonable thing to do, but also will safeguard against repeating the mistakes of the past.

NOTES

1. Some label the conflict as the Civil War(s), due to a lull in hostilities between 1997 and 2000. The majority consensus is, however, that the period between 1989 and 2003 was one long time of intermittent conflict, thus the singular term is considered appropriate.
2. Ellis (2007, pp. 312–16) goes into depth regarding the complexity of attempting to accurately count deaths related to the conflict. As such, figures must remain necessarily broad.
3. It must be acknowledged that an early attempt at DDR occurred following the Cotonou Agreement of 1993 and the Abuja Accords of 1996; however, these were rather piecemeal measures with the major factions never seriously considering fully disarming. The focus of this chapter is on the major DDR(R) program following the official end of conflict in 2003.
4. Though some work has been done on the limited amount of rehabilitation assistance, this statement from the organizing body of official RR is enough to limit analysis of this component for the chapter.
5. Specht (2006, p. 45).

REFERENCES

Aboagye, Festus and Alhaji Bah (2005), *A Tortuous Road to Peace: The Dynamics of Regional, UN and International Humanitarian Intervention in Liberia*, Institute for Security Studies.

Abramowitz, Sharon (2009), *Psychosocial Liberia: Managing Suffering in Post-Conflict Life*, PhD Dissertation for Harvard University, Cambridge.

Abramowitz, Sharon and Mary Moran (2012), 'International human rights, gender-based violence, and local discourses of abuse in postconflict Liberia: a problem of "culture"?', *African Studies Review*, **55** (2): 119–46.

African Women and Peace Support Group (2004), *Liberian Women Peacemakers: Fighting for the Right to Be Seen, Heard and Counted*, Africa World Press.

Aisha, F. (2005), 'Mainstreaming gender in peace support operations: the United Nations Mission in Liberia', in Festus Aboagye and Alhaji M.S. Bah (eds), *A Tortuous Road to Peace: The Dynamics of International Humanitarian Intervention in Liberia*, Institute of Security Studies.

Amnesty International (2009), *Lessons from Liberia: Reintegration Women in Post-Conflict Liberia*, Amnesty.

Baare, Anton (2006), *An Analysis of Transitional Economic Reintegration*, Working Paper for Swedish Initiative for Disarmament, Demobilization and Reintegration, SIDDR, Sweden.

Barth, Elise (2002), *Peace as Disappointment: The Reintegration of Female Soldiers in Post-Conflict Societies – A Comparative Study from Africa*, PRIO.

Basini, Helen (2013), 'Gender mainstreaming unraveled: The case of DDRR in Liberia', *International Interactions: Empirical and Theoretical Research in International Relations*, **39** (4): 535–57.

Bledsoe, Caroline (1980), *Women and Marriage in Kpelle Society*, Stanford University Press.

Bøås, Morten and Anne Hatløy (2008), '"Getting in, getting out": militia membership and prospects for re-integration in post-conflict Liberia', *Journal of Modern African Studies*, **46** (1): 33–55.

Candan, Zuleika (2012), *Enhancing Socio-Economic Opportunities for Ex-Combatants in Liberia*, Strengthening the Economic Dimensions of Peacebuilding: Case Study Series, International Alert.

Cohn, Carol and Cynthia Enloe (2003), 'A conversation with Cynthia Enloe: feminists look at masculinity and the men who wage war', *Signs*, **28** (4): 1187–107.

Coulter, Chris, Mariam Persson and Mats Utas (2008), *Young Female Fighters in African Wars: Conflict and its Consequences*, Policy Dialogue No. 3, Nordic Africa Institute.

Douglas, Sarah and Felicity Hill (2004), *Getting it Right, Doing it Right: Gender and Disarmament, Demobilization and Reintegration*, UNIFEM.

Ellis, Stephen (2007), *The Mask of Anarchy: The Destruction of Liberia and the Religious Dimension of an African Civil War*, 2nd edn, Hurst.

El-Bushra, Judy, Henri Myrttinen and Jana Naujoks (2013), *Renegotiating the 'Ideal' Society: Gender in Peacebuilding in Uganda*, International Alert.

Escola Cultura de Pau (ECP) (2008), *DDR 2008: Analysis of Disarmament, Demobilization and Reintegration (DDR) Programmes in the World during 2007*, ECP.

Fuest, Veronika (2008), '"This is the time get in front": changing roles and opportunities for women in Liberia', *African Affairs*, **107** (427): 201–24.

Gbowee, Leymah with Carol Mithers (2011), *Mighty be our Powers: How Sisterhood, Prayer and Sex Changed a Nation at War*, HarperCollins.

Hill, Richard, Gwendolyn Taylor and Jonathan Temin (2008), *Would You Fight Again? Understanding Liberian Ex-Combatant Reintegration*, Special Report 211, United States Institute of Peace, Washington.

Hills, Christopher (2015), 'Gendered reintegration in Liberia: a civilised *'(Kwi)'*, failure?', *Australasian Review of African Studies*, **36** (1): 68–83.

Humphreys, Macartan and Jeremy M. Weinstein (2007), 'Demobilization and reintegration', *Journal of Conflict Resolution*, **51** (4): 531–67.

Jennings, Kathleen (2007), 'The struggle to satisfy: DDR through the eyes of ex-combatants in Liberia', *International Peacekeeping*, **14** (2): 204–18.

Jennings, Kathleen (2008), *Seeing DDR From Below: Challenges and Dilemmas Raised by the Experiences of Ex-Combatants in Liberia*, FAFO.

Jennings, Kathleen (2009), 'The political economy of DDR in Liberia: a gendered critique', *Conflict, Security & Development*, **9** (4): 475–94.

Liebling-Kalifani, Helen and Bruce Baker (2010), 'Women war survivors of sexual violence in Liberia: inequalities in health, resistance and justice', *Journal of International and Social Research*, **3** (13): 188–99.

MacKenzie, M. (2012), *Female Soldiers in Sierra Leone: Sex, Security and Post-Conflict Development*, New York University Press.

McMullin, Jaremey (2013), *Ex-Combatants and the Post-Conflict States: Challenges of Reintegration*, Palgrave Macmillan.

Moran, Mary (1990), *Civilized Women: Gender and Prestige in Southeastern Liberia*, Cornell University Press.

Moran, Mary (2006), *Liberia: The Violence of Democracy*, University of Pennsylvania Press.

Moran, Mary (2010), 'Gender, militarism and peace-building: projects of the postconflict moment', *Annual Review of Anthropology*, **39** (1): 261–74.

Moran, Mary (2012), 'Our mothers have spoken: synthesizing old and new forms of women's political authority in Liberia', *Journal of International Women's Studies*, **13** (4): 51–66.

Nduka-Agwu, Adibeli (2009), '"Doing gender" after the war: dealing with gender mainstreaming and sexual exploitation and abuse in UN peace support operations in Liberia and Sierra Leone', *Civil Wars*, **11** (2): 179–99.

Nichols, Ryan (2005), 'Disarming Liberia: progress and pitfalls', in Nicolas Florquin and Eric G. Berman (eds), *Armed and Aimless: Armed Groups, Guns and Human Security in the ECOWAS Region*, Small Arms Survey, pp. 108–43.

Nilsson, Johanna and Suruchi Thapar-Björkert (2013), '"People constantly remind me of my past … and make me look like a monster"', *International Feminist Journal of Politics*, **15** (1): 110–18.

Njoki Wamai, Emma (2011), 'UNSCR 1325 implementation in Liberia', in Funmi Olonisakin, Karen Barnes and Eka Ikpe (eds), *Women, Peace and Security*, Routledge.

Paes, Wolf-Christian (2005), 'The challenges of disarmament, demobilization and re-integration in Liberia', *International Peacekeeping*, **12** (2): 253–61.

Porter, Antonia (2013), '"What is constructed can be transformed": masculinities in post-conflict societies in Africa', *International Peacekeeping*, **20** (4): 486–506.

Pugel, James (2007), *What the Fighters Say: A Survey of Ex-Combatants in Liberia*, United Nations Development Programme.

Sanz, Eneko (2009), 'Liberia (DDRR 2003–2008)', in Albert Caramés and Eneko Sanz (eds), *DDR 2009. Analysis of Disarmament, Demobilization and Reintegration (DDR) Programmes in the World During 2008*, ECP, pp. 85–92.

Sherif, Abu (2008), 'Reintegration of female war-affected and ex-combatants in Liberia', *Conflict Trends*, **3**: 26–33.

Smet, Stijn (2009), 'A window of opportunity – improving gender relations in post-conflict societies: The Sierra Leonean experience', *Journal of Gender Studies*, **18** (2): 147–63.

Söderström, Johanna (2011), *Politics of Affection: Ex-Combatants, Political Engagement and Reintegration Programmes in Liberia*, PhD Dissertation for Uppsala University.

Specht, Irma (2006), *Red Shoes: The Experiences of Girl-Combatants in Liberia*, ILO.

Tonheim, Milfred (2010), 'Where are the research gaps? Reviewing literature in former girl soldiers' reintegration in the African context', in Bard Mæland (ed.), *Culture, Reintegration, and the Reintegration of Female Child Soldiers in Northern Uganda*, Peter Lang.

Tonkin, Elizabeth (1980), 'Jealousy names, civilised names: anthropology of the Jlao Kru of Liberia', *Man*, **15** (4): 653–64.

Turshen, Meredeth (2001), 'Engendering relations of state to society in the aftermath', in Sheila Meintjes, Anu Pillay and Meredeth Turshen (eds), *The Aftermath: Women in Post-Conflict Transformation*, Zed Books.

United Nations (2006), *Integrated Disarmament, Demobilization and Reintegration Standards (IDDRS) Framework*, December 2006.

United Nations Development Fund for Women (UNIFEM) (2005), 'Women building peace through Disarmament, Demobilization and Reintegration', Beijing +10 Review Conference, 9 March.

United Nations Development Programme (2006), *External Mid-Term Evaluation Report of the Disarmament, Demobilisation and Rehabilitation and Reintegration Programme in Liberia*, UNDP.

United Nations Mission in Liberia (UNMIL) Office of the Gender Advisor (2010), *Gender Mainstreaming in Peacekeeping Operations in Liberia 2003–2009, Best Practices Report*, Accra, Kofi Annan Peacekeeping Training Institute (KAIPTC)/UNMIL, OGA.

United Nations Security Council (2000), *Resolution 1325*, UN.

United Nations Security Council (2003), *Resolution 1503*, UN.

Utas, Mats (2003), *Sweet Battlefields: Youth and the Liberian Civil War*, PhD Dissertation for Uppsala University.

Utas, Mats (2005), 'Victimcy, girlfriending, soldiering: tactic agency in a young woman's social navigation of the Liberian war zone', *Anthropological Quarterly*, **78** (2): 403–30.

Veale, Angela (2003), *From Child Solider to Ex-Fighter: Female Fighters and Demobilisation and Reintegration in Ethiopia*, ISS Monograph Series No. 85, ISS.

26. Girl soldiers and the complexities of demobilization and reintegration

Myriam Denov, Alexandra Ricard-Guay and Amber Green

INTRODUCTION

The presence of women and girls in armed conflict, whether as victims or participants, has long been overlooked and marginalized. It is only over the last two decades that the realities of war and gender have garnered greater consideration (Elshtain, 1987; Enloe, 2014, 2000; Moser and Clark, 2001; Jacobs et al., 2000; Meertens, 2001). While the phenomenon of child soldiers has gained increased academic and popular attention in recent years, girls have been profoundly invisible or marginalized within the scholarship on children's involvement in armed conflict. Literature dedicated to the experiences of girls within armed groups has led to an increasingly complex understanding of their roles, contributions, and wartime and post-war realities. The realities of girls affected by armed conflict are highly contextual and girl soldiers are in no way a homogeneous group. The historical, socio-cultural, political and economic context of the armed conflict, as well as individual trajectories, shape and inform the experiences of girls, which preclude any universalized assertions. And yet, while generalizations are inappropriate, it is notable that there are similarities in many of their wartime and post-war life circumstances and realities.

This chapter provides an overview of the state of knowledge on girl soldiers and their gendered experiences, with a particular emphasis on the post-conflict periods of demobilization and reintegration. After clarifying the terms and definitions used to represent children involved in armed conflict, we provide a global context and a historical overview of the problem. Against this backdrop, we examine the many issues former girl soldiers face in the post-conflict period, especially in the context of post-war demobilization[1] and reintegration[2]. To substantiate our analysis, we highlight the experiences of nine former girl soldiers from Colombia, and eight former girl soldiers from Sierra Leone. These participants, interviewed in 2010 and 2011 by Denov, were part of a larger study[3] exploring the long-term reintegration of former girl soldiers (Denov, 2010; Denov and Marchand, 2014a; Jones and Denov, 2015). Our chapter highlights the importance of taking a gendered approach in the study of war and child soldiery, as well as its contribution to this field of study. A gendered approach facilitates an understanding of girls' experiences that go beyond the traditional dichotomies of 'victim versus perpetrator of violence' or 'victimization versus agency', and 'war versus peace'. Violence perpetrated against girls, their marginalization and status within power structures are not bound by times of war and peace. Instead, girls' options, roles, power relations, both during conflict and following demobilization, are deeply embedded within broader gendered power structures and identities.

CHILD SOLDIERS: TERMS AND DEFINITIONS

The terms 'child soldiers' and 'children associated with fighting forces' have been used to represent the realities of children actively implicated and engaged in armed conflict. Neither of these terms, however, adequately captures the realities of children implicated in war, and are inherently problematic. While the term 'child soldier' encapsulates the paradox of children's involvement in wartime violence, particularly the blurring of constructed notions of childhood 'innocence' with the brutality and violence of war, defining what is considered a 'child' is invariably problematic. The United Nations (UN) Convention on the Rights of the Child defines a child as 'every human being below eighteen years' (Article 1). At the same time, critics argue that defining a childhood based solely upon age not only reflects a bias towards Western notions of childhood which are rooted in biomedical theory (Kemper, 2005), but also may overlook other salient cultural, social, economic, gendered and other status determinants that extend well beyond the notion of age. 'Childhood' is indeed a contested concept and its meanings are socially constructed and vary in form and content across cultures and social groups, and are defined by localized understandings and values (Denov, 2010).

Age is certainly not the only difficulty when considering the concept of 'child soldier'. The term 'soldier' tends to conjure up archetypal symbols of uniformed men with extensive military training in active combat. These images are at odds with the realities of most of the inadequately trained and outfitted child soldiers who fill the ranks of rebel groups in postcolonial wars. Moreover, the stereotypical portrayals of 'soldier' conceal the realities of women's and girls' participation in war, as well as the many supporting roles that children take on during conflict as messengers, bodyguards, cooks, spies, porters or in the realm of sexual exploitation and labor (Denov, 2010).

Recognizing the varied roles that children take on in war, which extend far beyond combat, the term 'children associated with fighting forces' has been introduced into the vernacular. This term is also problematic because it fails to adequately connote children's active contributions to contemporary war, implying that they remain at the periphery. Additionally, the use of such a term may deny children who have served in wartime supporting roles access to programs and privileges provided to those labeled as 'combatants' in the period of Disarmament, Demobilization and Reintegration (DDR).

While acknowledging their obvious imperfections and contradictions, this chapter will employ the terms 'child soldier' and 'girl soldier' and rely upon the definition provided in the *Paris Principles*,[4] a set of guidelines on children in armed conflict established in 2007 at an international conference in Paris. The conference, organized by the French government and supported by UNICEF, introduced the following designation, which represents the most current internationally recognized definition of the child soldier phenomenon:

> Any person below 18 years of age who is or who has been recruited or used by an armed force or armed group in any capacity, including but not limited to children, boys and girls, used as fighters, cooks, porters, messengers, spies or for sexual purposes. It does not only refer to a child who is taking or has taken a direct part in hostilities. (UNICEF, 2007, p. 7)

THE GLOBAL REALITIES OF CHILD SOLDIERY

The Coalition to Stop the Use of Child Soldiers (recently renamed as Child Soldiers International) has produced numerous reports outlining estimates of child soldiers around the world. In their Global Report published in 2004, it was estimated that 250 000 soldiers under the age of 18 were part of fighting forces in conflicts in 41 countries around the globe. In 2008 they reported that the number of child soldiers was fewer than in 2004 as tens of thousands of child soldiers had been released from armed groups and forces following peace agreements and demobilization programs. This includes Afghanistan, Burundi, Côte d'Ivoire, DRC, Liberia and Southern Sudan. However, at the same time conflicts in other countries had broken out, were reignited or intensified and thus child soldier recruitment had, in some regions, increased. Examples include Central African Republic, Chad, Iraq, Somalia and Sudan (Darfur). More recently, Child Soldier International estimated that between January 2010 and June 2012, child soldiers were used in 20 states, including nine countries where they were recruited and used by national state armies. The US State Department noted a 30 percent increase in the number of countries recruiting and using child soldiers in 2012 (cited in United States Department of State, 2013). Child soldiers are said to exist in all regions of the world and, inevitably, wherever there is conflict (Coalition to Stop the Use of Child Soldiers, 2008). Because the majority of reports and international initiatives continue to regard the notion of 'child soldiers' as either male or gender-neutral, the effects of armed conflict on young girls and the gendered implications of children in combat are often rendered peripheral or invisible.

GIRL SOLDIERS: A HISTORICAL PERSPECTIVE

The initial scholarly and policy literature on child soldiers failed to include gender perspectives on armed conflict. Informed largely by traditional perceptions of armed conflict as a phenomenon involving males, as noted above, girls have been frequently deemed peripheral and rendered invisible within armed forces or armed groups (McKay, 2004a, 2006a, 2006b).

Mazurana et al. (2002) suggest that girls have long been involved in militarized conflicts but they have been largely overlooked and under-studied. Among the few historically documented cases of girls' mobiliz-ation are the examples of Joan of Arc, the female combat unit of the Dahomey Kingdom in West Africa, and German girls within the Nazi regime. Using religious fervor to motivate soldiers, sixteen-year-old Joan of Arc led an army of 4000 against the English, successfully expelling them from Orleans in 1429 (Mazurana et al., 2002). The Dahomey Kingdom of West Africa (present-day Benin) had a large-scale girls' combat unit, known as the 'Amazon Corps'. The unit originated in 1727 when Dahomey faced a grave military situation and functioned over a long period as a part of a standing army. Girls who trained to be warriors followed a strict code of celibacy to free them of emotional ties and the possibility of pregnancy. To maintain the girls' unit, fathers were to report every three years with daughters between the ages of 9 and 15; the fittest girls were selected for military duty (Mazurana et al., 2002). The king organized the Amazon Corps to guard the palace and eventually the corps grew in size from about 800 females in the early nineteenth century to over 5000 at mid-century, several thousand being combat forces (Goldstein, 2001). During World War II, within the Nazi regime, German girls were officially 'spared' from shouldering industrial and agricultural responsibilities and it was declared that girls would never have to bear arms. Nonetheless, in 1930, the Hitler Youth instituted a female section called the *Bund Deutscher Mädel* (League of German Girls), which emphasized girls' secondary status, but propagated Nazi ideals and 'was based on physical training, discipline, rationality and efficiency' (Reese, cited in Brocklehurst, 2006, p. 79). Moreover, largely hidden from the German public, in 1944 girls were employed as anti-aircraft gunners, and were instructed how to fire cannons, machine guns, grenades and firearms. Kater (2004) notes that there was a 'death squad' of young girls commanded by the Waffen-SS who 'had painted red lips and fought with abandon' (p. 238). Importantly, when girls have been implicated in armed conflict, or within resistance or revolutionary movements, their contributions have often been denied, forgotten and silenced in the aftermath of war and in the subsequent writing of history. Frequently returning to traditional roles within families and communities in the post-war period, women and girls' participation is often regarded as a 'momentary' or an 'unorthodox' disruption of the accepted social order (Enloe, 2000; Meintjes et al., 2001).

Girls have remained largely invisible within more recent accounts of armed conflict. Writing in 1997, Nordstrom noted that girls' experiences of war have accounted for 'the smallest percentage of scholarly and popular work on social and political violence' (p. 5). Indeed, officials, governments, national and international bodies have frequently concealed, overlooked or refused to recognize girls' presence, needs and rights during and following armed conflict (McKay and Mazurana, 2004). During conflict, the roles girls occupied have been deemed peripheral and insignificant. As will be addressed further below, in the aftermath of war, girls have continued to be marginalized within the realms of education and employment, and have been discriminated against within formal Disarmament, Demobilization and Reintegration (DDR) processes, as well as within the context of their families and communities (Denov, 2010; Coulter, 2008, 2009; McKay et al., 2010).

CURRENT KNOWLEDGE AND UNDERSTANDING OF GIRL SOLDIERS: WHAT HAVE WE LEARNED?

Despite their overall marginalization and invisibility in academic and policy discussions of armed conflict, girls are currently embroiled in armed conflict far more widely than is reported. Between 1990 and 2003, girls were associated with fighting forces in 55 countries and were active participants in conflict in 38 countries around the globe[5] (McKay and Mazurana, 2004). Girls appear to be most often present in armed opposition groups, paramilitaries and militias, yet they are also present in government forces. Girls continue to be involved in fighting forces in Central African Republic, Chad, Colombia, Côte d'Ivoire, Democratic Republic of Congo, Nepal, Philippines and Uganda (Coalition to Stop the Use of Child Soldiers, 2008). While the proportion of girls in armed groups and forces varies according to geographic region, it generally ranges from 10 percent to 30 percent of all combatants (Bouta, 2005). In Africa, girls are said to comprise 30 percent to 40 percent of all child combatants (Mazurana et al., 2002, p. 105).

Our knowledge of girl soldiers has undergone various stages of awareness and understanding. Initially, scholarly discussions of girls focused primarily on their vulnerability and their experiences as victims. Indeed, girls are subjected to grave violations of their human rights through forced recruitment, killing, maiming, sexual violence, sexual exploitation, abduction, forced marriage and increased exposure to HIV/AIDS. The direct effects of armed conflict on girls include victimization through acts of murder, terrorism, torture and rape, while the indirect effects include displacement, loss of home or property, family separation and disintegration, poverty and illness. For girls in fighting forces, the chronic quest for safety and security, regardless of the nature of their roles, is particularly challenging due to the vulnerability exacerbated by their gender, age and physical disadvantage (Denov, 2006). That girls within the context of armed conflict are frequently victims of harsh violence, often under the threat of a gun, is evident.

While highlighting girls' victimization is critical to advancing our understanding of girls' experiences of war and the profound insecurities, human rights abuses, as well as the challenges they face both during and following armed conflict, girls are not merely voiceless victims, devoid of agency (Denov, 2007). New research on girl soldiers has provided a richer portrait of girls' experiences, shedding light on their multifaceted and sometimes contradictory roles within armed groups (Wessells, 2006). More recent literature has also focused on the post-war realities of girls, particularly their complex reintegration process (Boothby et al., 2006; McKay, 2006b; Mazurana and Carlson, 2004; Veale and Stavrou, 2007; Brett and Specht, 2004; Burman and McKay, 2007).

LIFE IN THE AFTERMATH OF WAR

Girl soldiers face the difficult transition from their militarized environments to a civilian life in the aftermath of their participation in fighting forces, whether or not the conflict has officially ended (Coulter, 2009). When leaving fighting forces, girls must readjust to norms and institutions from which they have been disconnected and isolated, often for many years. While demobilization can occur abruptly and within a short period of time, the social reintegration process is a long-term and complex process.

The post-demobilization experiences of girl soldiers are diverse, and this diversity should be acknowledged in the understanding of their post-conflict lives (Coulter 2009; Denov and Ricard-Guay, 2013). At the same time, there are key factors that influence the experiences of girl soldiers in the post-conflict period including gender, ethnicity, socio-economic status, position within the community prior to and following the conflict, and access to social support. Other such war-related impacts as displacement, living in camps and family separation may also influence girls' post-war lives.

Some girl soldiers may be injured and left disabled, while others suffer sexual violence with severe health and psycho-social outcomes. In some cases, girls end up married to a commander, more often than not through coercion or as a way to survive (Denov and Gervais, 2008). Some girl soldiers bear children.

Despite the highly diverse paths of girl soldiers and the critical roles they played during the conflict period, girls are frequently rendered invisible and marginalized in the aftermath of the conflict. Additionally, the dual roles of the girls within armed groups – as both victims and perpetrators of violence – often complicate their reintegration process (Denov, 2010).

KEY ISSUES GIRLS FACE IN THE POST-CONFLICT PERIOD

Some of the key issues that former girl soldiers face in the aftermath of armed conflict include their exclusion from the programs aimed at former child soldiers, as well as the specific features of their gendered experiences related to social stigma, their economic realities, the psycho-social impacts and outcomes of wartime experiences on their sense of self and identity, with a particular attention to motherhood.

Exclusion From Post-War Programming

As noted by the UN, Disarmament, Demobilization and Reintegration (DDR) programming are crucial to increasing security, public safety and protection in the aftermath of conflict, as well as promoting peace (United Nations, 2006). Yet despite the growing recognition of girls in armed groups, they continue to be marginalized within DDR programming (McKay et al., 2010). In many contexts, girls may avoid DDR programmes, as a result of gender-based violence and insecurity in DDR camps, fear of stigmatization as former soldiers, and the lack of medical or hygienic facilities (McKay and Mazurana, 2004). Girl soldiers who become mothers have been identified as being the most underserved population within DDR programmes. The overall lack of attention to the needs of girl soldiers who became mothers, by national governments and the international community, has been regarded as systemic and discriminatory by both researchers and girl soldiers' advocates (Worthen et al., 2010). As a result of the exclusionary nature of many DDR programmes, many girls formerly associated with fighting forces opt for 'spontaneous reintegration' (Denov, 2010). Instead of participating in formal reintegration programs, girls return directly to their communities, join new communities, or drift to camps for the internally displaced in search of alternative forms of support (McKay and Mazurana, 2004). Without formal mechanisms of assistance, many girls are often left to fend for themselves and their children under challenging circumstances. Ultimately, in contexts where programming has downplayed the integral roles of females in armed groups, gender-based insecurity and power differentiation are likely to extend into the post-conflict era. Indeed, not only are the specific needs of former girl soldiers not addressed, such as those related to mothering and consequences of sexual violence, but also being excluded from DDR programming means that they cannot access economic support (program subsidies) as well as housing programs or other assistance aimed at facilitating their reintegration.

Social Stigma

Family and/or community acceptance and support are undeniably critical to the long-term well-being and overall successful reintegration of all soldiers, let alone children (Betancourt et al., 2010). A trusting relationship with a caring adult and living with key family members can be critical factors in children's recovery from the scourge of war. As a result, those children who have family and community support often fare much better compared to those who experience rejection and/or social exclusion following demobilization. Girls formerly associated with armed groups, particularly those that return with children, appear to have higher rates of rejection by community members than their male counterparts (McKay et al., 2010). The issue of social exclusion and stigmatization can have wide-reaching effects for former girl soldiers, making the reintegration process extremely challenging. These Colombian girls note the powerful consequences of post-demobilization stigma and exclusion:

> My son goes to school and I go pick him up at six when the bus comes. My neighbour, a lady who was supposedly my friend, would call me 'guerrilla' in front of my son. My son would say: 'Mom, is it true that you are a guerrilla who has killed people?' (Interview, Colombia, February 2011)

> [A neighbor] would say I was a 'guerrillera' and the guys in the neighborhood would send me threatening letters. One day they broke my window, and I was forced to move. (Interview, Colombia, February 2011)

> My family does not forgive me for what I did [joining the armed group] ... I talk a bit with my mom because we understand each other. With my sisters, I tried but it is hard because we are like strangers to each other. We were not raised together because I left my house when I was young. So it is hard to build a relationship after so many years, more than ten years. So it is very difficult ... (Interview, Colombia, February 2011)

The realities of stigma and marginalization may push many young women to live 'underground', concealing their former status as an ex-combatant. The fear of being discovered and found out may prevent many women from opening up and forming new relationships:

> I am someone who doesn't share her problems with just anyone. I keep my problems to myself and resolve them alone. I hardly talk to anyone about my problems and I think that being alone is better for me because I don't like

telling people my problems. Personally, I like to be alone … more isolated (Interview, Colombia, February 2011).

Because of the circumstances of what happened to me, I have a hard time building relationships … I am always on the defensive … I do not relate to others easily (Interview, Colombia, February 2011).

Frequently relocated to new communities following demobilization for security reasons, these women often begin their lives anew with no friends and relatively few contacts. The issue of social exclusion and stigmatization has wide-reaching effects for former girl soldiers, making meaningful reintegration extremely challenging. Frequently without the support of family, they are forced to build a new social support network, and they must do so within a hostile context.

Economic Realities

As girls leave armed groups, a key challenge to successful reintegration is financial stability and security. Some girls and young women may receive a subsidy through their participation in a DDR program, which may assist them with basic living expenses. However, most must find additional sources of income to be able to provide fully for themselves and their children. According to respondents in the context of Colombia, these subsidies are intended for an individual, and rarely take into account their children (Jones and Denov, 2015).

Among the young women interviewed in Colombia, some shared creative strategies that they had used to find a way to provide for their children. One woman made paintings and sold them for money. Another woman opened a café with her husband using start-up funds from the government. Other women shared that they were studying to fulfill their goals of becoming a nurse, doctor or lawyer. However, childcare was commonly cited as a barrier to advancing in an educational or professional capacity. With the government's assistance, there was scarcely enough money to cover basic expenses, leaving nothing over for childcare expenses. Given the absence of family members and friends for many young mothers, staying at home with the children was often their only choice.

The level of isolation appeared to be a strong predictor of how well a former girl soldier was able to cope financially. Those who were more isolated from family members and who did not have a trustworthy partner struggled to support themselves and their children. These young women were forced to make difficult choices in order to provide for their children in the best way possible, at times relying on a male companion to ensure financial security. For some, this meant staying in high risk and abusive situations to ensure that there was enough to eat:

> I found out through the woman who takes care of my child that he touches my daughter. It was very hard because I cannot count on my family. ... I continue to live with him because I don't have anyone else here. I am alone. And if I leave, I cannot manage economically (Interview, Colombia, February 2011).

A lack of resources and opportunities for this group of girls and young women forces impossible choices to be made, which can have detrimental consequences for the well-being of the child and mother. This young woman was appalled at the knowledge of her daughter's abuse, and disclosed the situation to social workers in the DDR program, yet she continued to stay with the man, believing that there was no other way for her and her daughter to survive financially. She explained: 'My goal is to finish my studies and have a financial base to leave and leave him because that is what I could not do economically. If I leave, I will have to leave my daughter with someone I don't know and that could be a bigger risk.' (Interview, Colombia, February 2011).

This example also points to the risk to the health and safety of the child in situations where ex-combatant mothers are left with no support. Despite educational and vocational opportunities through DDR programming, and subsidies that are distributed, many girls and young women continue to struggle in the aftermath of their experience with an armed group.

Psycho-Social Impacts

Experiences of violence – militarized, organized and extreme forms of violence – impact girls in multiple ways, both physically and psychologically (Derluyn et al., 2004; Betancourt et al., 2008; Schomerus and Allen, 2006). In addition, displacement, family separation, war-related losses and disruptions in child development can have crucial long-term impacts on former child soldiers (Wessells, 2006; Denov and Marchand, 2014a).

A significant amount of research has focused on mental health outcomes for former child soldiers and the process of reintegration to civilian life. Betancourt et al. (2010) suggest that among the various forms of violence to which children are exposed, the wounding or killing of others, as well as surviving rape, had the greatest impact on long-term psycho-social adjustment and were key risk factors with regard to hostility and anxiety (p. 1089). Research has also highlighted that following demobilization former child soldiers may continue to experience disturbing wartime memories and nightmares (Betancourt et al., 2010; Denov, 2010) and may hold feelings of severe guilt and shame for their participation in violence (Boothby et al., 2006; Betancourt and Khan, 2008). These Colombian girls explained:

> There are very horrible things that happened and that I had to do ... like take the life away of one or another person. Now that the war is over it is like a little box, a little box full of explosives. All together [the explosives] form a team. But if one explodes, they all explode ... So I try not to tap the box ... (Interview, Colombia, February 2011).

> The psychologists are of a great help but you cannot forget so easily. So there are nightmares ... it happens to me constantly that if I am sleeping while it rains and there is lightening, it is horrible for me (Interview, Colombia, February 2011).

The after-effects of sexual violence pose serious challenges for former girl soldiers in the post-conflict period. In addition to the physical and emotional scars of sexual violence, girls are often stigmatized by family or community members as being 'impure' or even unmarriageable as a result of sexual violence (Betancourt et al., 2008; Burman and McKay, 2007; Human Rights Watch, 2003; Mazurana and Carlson, 2006). Given that community and family acceptance are often protective factors and can enhance psycho-social adjustment and long-term reintegration, such rejection holds significant psycho-social implications.

Identity

Girls and boys within armed groups are often subjected to harsh and violent indoctrination that attempts to break down their civilian identities and aims to disconnect them from their families and sense of belonging to their communities. Socialized into a violent, militarized and hostile environment, their participation in the practices of the armed group may, over time, become part of their identity (Veale and Stavrou, 2007). Upon demobilization, they must readjust. The reintegration process involves the reshaping of identities from a 'militarized' identity to a 'civilian' one (Denov, 2010). Former child soldiers, both boys and girls, face social readjustment, which is strongly linked with their changing sense of self (Veale and Stavrou, 2003). Transition to civilian life means a shift in relationships, behavioral patterns and expectations. This shift has been referred to as the 'unmaking' of child soldiers (Denov, 2010).

Girls' involvement in military activities as combatants and perpetrators of violence has challenged conventional notions of femininity. In Colombia, many girls within armed groups reported being treated as 'equals' with their male counterparts. Being equal within a context of hyper-masculinity sometimes meant an abandonment of traditionally feminine qualities and roles. This girl from Colombia explained the process of losing her sense of being a woman:

> When one goes over there [to war], one does men things and does not have women's intimacy. It gets lost. You do men things and you are with men. ... The punishments are equal. We have to open trenches, go through the same training and wear the same camouflage. Everything, everything. ... One acts the same and gets used to it, and loses the feeling of being a woman (Interview, Colombia, February 2011).

Some girl soldiers may experience a sense of power, and attain leadership positions within armed groups as they adapt to masculine ideals and behaviors. Their status within the armed group, however, largely remains secondary to that of male combatants (Denov and Gervais, 2008). According to a former girl soldier from Colombia, the experience in the fighting forces required that she give up her femininity, which she reported rediscovering following demobilization:

> When one goes [into an armed group], one does 'men things' ... One acts the same [as men] and you get used to it. You lose the feeling of being a woman ... Before, I did not value myself, I felt like I was not a woman but a man ... I would dress like a man, I would act as a man, everything I would do, I would do it as a man ... You have no space to be a woman ... That has changed ... the difference is huge because now I can wear a skirt, I can fix my hair, I can dye it, I can wear makeup. I can decide if I want to cut my hair, which shoes to wear ... I can be more like myself without them telling me what I have to wear ... . It was three years ago when I entered to the [reintegration] program. There was a teacher who used to tell me that I was too beautiful to dress like a man and act like a man ... So I began very slowly, it was a strong process ... the adaptation was very difficult (Interview, Colombia, February 2011).

The changing identities of girl soldiers in the post-conflict period must be addressed in relation to the community (Veale and Stavrou, 2007) as identity is shaped and renegotiated within social rules, norms and power structures. For girls, social reintegration entails a transition of replacing the militarized identity to being accepted, respected and building a sense of belonging in their communities. The complex negotiation of identity and its implications for successful reintegration remains an area deserving further research and study.

Motherhood

As noted earlier, many girls return from armed groups pregnant or with children. Pregnancy and maternity, a unique and highly gendered experience, can have a serious impact on girls' lives. Girl soldiers' experiences with pregnancy and maternity within armed groups vary significantly, depending on the context. For some, being pregnant or giving birth may mean greater protection, while for others these experiences may involve considerable risks and danger to both the mother and child (Wessells, 2007). One such risk involves giving birth as a soldier among armed groups because of the precarious conditions that may be detrimental to the health of both the mother and the child.

In the aftermath of their wartime experiences, motherhood often complicates the reintegration of girl soldiers (McKay et al., 2006, 2006; Worthern et al., 2010). In particular, former girl soldiers who care for young children face challenges in the area of access to education and employment opportunities. These challenges limit the options available to these girls to earn money and often impede their reunification with their families and communities. Former girl soldiers who are mothers may be the targets of the social stigma that already affects former girl soldiers disproportionally. In some contexts, children conceived during armed conflict whether as a result of rape or a forced marriage with a male combatant (sometimes called 'bush marriage') are considered a violation of accepted social and cultural norms. As a result, both girl mothers and their children can face ostracism and social exclusion (McKay et al., 2010). Additionally, the experiences of pregnancy and motherhood at a relatively young age and under difficult circumstances may trigger strong feelings of shame and guilt. Some girl mothers choose to reintegrate into another community because of the fear of stigma and rejection from their families, or as a result of it (Denov and Marchand, 2014b). By doing so, young mothers may further disrupt and alter traditional kinship arrangements, and find themselves without support (McKay et al., 2006). Without family support and in absence of other forms of assistance for childcare, young mothers may have to bring their child along to their workplace, which may interfere with their plan to earn money and care for themselves and their child. As a result, some young mothers may have no other choice but to give their child to a foster family, given their lack of resources to feed them properly. This 16-year-old girl from Sierra Leone explained: 'I have many plans [for my baby]. Now I want to give him to someone to take care of him because I don't have [enough] to take care of him properly. I have not found the person yet, but I hope to find one.' (Interview, Sierra Leone, January 2010).

The experience of becoming a mother can have varied consequences for the emotional and psychological states of the young mother. While few girl soldiers chose to become mothers, some reported not being ready to experience motherhood, both physically and psychologically. Moreover, for girl soldiers who got pregnant as a result of sexual violence, motherhood can be accompanied by mixed emotions, compounded by the lingering effects of their traumatic experiences. Regardless of how motherhood is experienced by former girl soldiers, it marks their transition from girlhood to womanhood (McKay et al., 2006).

At the same time, motherhood does not only carry negative implications. Some young mothers associate successful social reintegration with 'good mothering', and 'self-care skills' (McKay et al., 2010). Pregnancy and motherhood can become a source of motivation and hope for a better future. This former girl soldier from Colombia shared her experience of pregnancy and the hope and security that it provided her:

> Pregnancy [is a] unique experience – an experience that emanates a lot of tenderness. [It brings] a lot of hope. One feels that one has someone to fight for, someone who will accompany you, that part of you will start living … It gave me more security, I would walk on the streets and feel safer, safer about what I could say or affirm as a woman. (Interview, Colombia, February 2011).

Some former girl soldiers view motherhood as an opportunity to give to their children what was stolen from them: their childhood – as expressed by this former girl soldier in Colombia:

> Even though I am not well, I try to give to them what I could not have in my childhood because I had no childhood. I never had a childhood because they destroyed it so I always try to, what I have is that I am affectionate, affectionate. I treat them well, like affectionate I don't know why, but I never hit them. (Interview, Colombia, February 2011).

MOVING FORWARD: INTEGRATING THE REALITIES OF GIRL SOLDIERS

Following decades of scholarship on war and child soldiers that neglected gendered realities, there has been a recent surge in research on the wartime experiences of girls and women. Through a gendered analysis of war and its aftermath, the distinct realities of girls within armed groups during and post-war are slowly emerging. Although both girls and boys are often subjected to similar violence and trauma during war, current literature reveals myriad ways in which their experiences differ, both during conflict and following demobilization. These gendered differences span from the roles and powers of boy and girl soldiers during conflict and the type of violence they endure or perpetrate – with special attention to sexual violence. In the post-war period, these gendered differences impact the struggles that former girl soldiers have with their sense of identity as well as the level and types of social stigma and isolation they encounter after demobilization.

A gendered analysis of wartime experiences attempts to go beyond a mere description of differences in experiences between boys and girls. Scholarship on girl soldiers has evolved quickly from early research focused primarily on their vulnerabilities and victimization, to a more complex analysis of their roles and experiences, including an in-depth examination of girls' lives in the aftermath of violence. The emergent body of literature on girl soldiers highlights how the experiences of girl soldiers are deeply embedded within social structures and power dynamics. Most notably, although girl soldiers are defying traditional gender assumptions of war by engaging in combat, their experiences are invariably shaped by their status as girls, and any sense of authority they might have gained within armed groups is often stripped away upon demobilization. Not only do girl soldiers' statuses remain consistently secondary to those of men and boys during combat, but they must also navigate elevated social stigma and rejection from communities and families due to the fact that they have transgressed gendered norms by taking arms (Denov and Maclure, 2006, p. 78; Coulter, 2009, p. 88).

A key contribution of taking a gendered approach to studying war and child soldiers is the dismantling of simple dichotomies based on 'victim versus perpetrator', and 'war versus peace'. Narratives of girl soldiers shed light on how victimization is intertwined with agency, and how their marginalization and status within power structures are not bound by times of war and peace (Moser and Clark, 2001). For girls and women, violence is not merely perpetrated against them during armed conflict, but is an integral component of their lived realities before, during and after conflict.

Recent scholarship and research has reached a turning point in the study of girl soldiers. With the growing body of literature on gendered experiences of war and conflict, we now have a more nuanced and complex understanding of the strengths of girl soldiers as well as the challenges facing them, including their continued marginalization throughout wartime and following demobilization. Yet, an important gap still exists in our knowledge of how to develop and implement appropriate post-conflict reintegration programs that meet the unique needs of girls.

In order to sustainably support girls in the aftermath of violence, current demobilization and reintegration programs must better meet the distinct challenges faced by former girl soldiers. To do so, it is essential for girls to be actively engaged in the process and build on their knowledge and agency. In addition to economic support, greater attention should be given to other important issues such as long-term education and also social stigma and acceptance by local communities. The gendered impacts of war extend far beyond the literal or metaphorical act of 'putting down the gun'. A careful development and implementation of gender-appropriate programs designed for the aftermath of conflict would not only benefit former girl soldiers but also broader communities.

NOTES

1. Demobilization is the formal and controlled discharge of active combatants from armed forces or other armed groups (United Nations, 2006, p. 6).
2. Reintegration is the process by which ex-combatants acquire civilian status and gain sustainable employment and income. Reintegration is essentially a social and economic process with an open timeframe, primarily taking place in communities at the local level (United Nations, 2006, p. 19).
3. This study, funded by the Social Science and Humanities Research Council of Canada, examined the long-term reintegration of former child soldiers, both male and female, in Sierra Leone and Colombia.
4. These Principles were developed by 'States, human rights actors, humanitarian actors, development actors, military and security actors (state and non-state) associated organisations including UN organisations, other inter-governmental actors, national and international organisations and community-based organisations ... [The Principles] were designed to guide interventions for the protection and well-being of ... children and to assist in making policy and programming decisions ... the principles aim to prevent unlawful recruitment or use of children ... facilitate the release of children associated with armed forces and armed groups ... facilitate the reintegration of all children associated with armed forces and armed groups [and to ensure the most protective environment for all children' (UNICEF, 2007, p. 6).
5. These international and civil conflicts include Angola, Burundi, Colombia, DRC, El Salvador, Ethiopia, Eritrea, Guatemala, Lebanon, Liberia, Macedonia, Nepal, Peru, Philippines, Sierra Leone, Sri Lanka, Sudan, Zimbabwe and others (Mazurana et al., 2002).

BIBLIOGRAPHY

Betancourt, Theresa Stichick and Kashif Tanveer Kahn (2008), 'The mental health of children affected by armed conflict: protective processes and pathways to resilience', *International Review of Psychiatry*, **20** (3): 317–28.

Betancourt, Theresa S., Ivelina Borisova, Julia Rubin-Smith, Tara Gingerich, Timothy Williams and Jessica Agnew-Blais (2008), *Psychosocial Adjustment and Social Reintegration of Children Associated with Armed Groups: The State of the Field and Future Directions*, Psychology Beyond Borders.

Betancourt, Theresa S., Ivelina Borisova, Timothy Philip Williams, Robert T. Brennan, T. Hatch Whitfield, Marie de la Soudière, John Williamson and Stephanie E. Gilman (2010), 'Sierra Leone's former child soldiers: a follow-up study of psychosocial adjustment and community reintegration', *Child Development*, **81** (4): 1077–95.

Betancourt, Theresa S., Ivelina Borisova, Timothy P. Williams, Sarah E. Meyers-Ohki, Julia E. Rubin Smith, Jeannie Annan and Brandon A. Kohrt (2013), 'Research review: psychosocial adjustment and mental health in former child soldiers – a systematic review of the literature and recommendations for future research', *JCPP Journal of Child Psychology and Psychiatry*, **54** (1): 17–36.

Boothby, Neil, Jennifer Crawford and Jason Halperin (2006), 'Mozambique child soldier life outcome study: lessons learned in rehabilitation and reintegration efforts', *Global Public Health*, **1** (1): 87–107.

Bouta, Tsjeard (2005), *Gender and Disarmament, Demobilization and Reintegration: Building Blocks for Dutch Policy*, Clingendael Conflict Research Unit.

Brett, Rachel and Irma Specht (2004), *Young Soldiers: Why They Choose to Fight*, Lynne Rienner.

Brocklehurst, Helen (2006), *Who's Afraid of Children: Children, Conflict and International Relations*, Ashgate.

Burman, Mary and Susan McKay (2007), 'Marginalization of girl mothers during reintegration from armed groups in Sierra Leone', *International Nursing Review*, **54** (4): 316–23.

Cátedra Ciro Angarita pour la Infancia (2002), *Niñez y Conflicto Armado: Desde la Desmovilización Hacia la Garantía Integral de Derechos de Infancia*, Memoria Annual 2002, Universidad de los Andes.

Coalition to Stop the Use of Child Soldiers (2004), 'Child soldiers: Global Report 2004', London.

Coalition to Stop the Use of Child Soldiers (2008), 'Child soldiers: Global Report 2008', London.

Cockburn, Cynthia (2004), 'The continuum of violence: a gender perspective on war and peace', in Wenona Giles and Jennifer Hyndman (eds), *Sites of Violence: Gender and Conflict Zones*, University of California Press, pp. 24–44.

Comisión Nacional de Reparación y Reconciliación (CNRR) (2010), 'La reintegración. Logros en medio de rearmes y dificultades no resueltas', August, II Informe de la Comisión Nacional de Reparación y Reconciliación.

Coulter, Chris (2008), 'Female fighters in Sierra Leone war: challenging the assumptions?', *Feminist Review*, **88**: 54–73.

Coulter, Chris (2009), *Bush Wives and Girl Soldiers: Women's Lives Through War and Peace in Sierra Leone*, Cornell University Press.

Denov, Myriam (2006), *Girls in Fighting Forces: Moving Beyond Victimhood*, CIDA's Child Protection Research Fund, Canadian International Development Agency.

Denov, Myriam (2007), 'Is the culture always right? The dangers of reproducing gender stereotypes and inequalities in psycho-social interventions for war-affected children', Coalition to Stop the Use of Child Soldiers.

Denov, Myriam (2008), 'Girl soldiers and human rights: lessons from Angola, Mozambique, Northern Uganda and Sierra Leone', *International Journal of Human Rights*, **12** (5): 811–33.

Denov, Myriam (2010), *Child Soldiers: Sierra Leone's Revolutionary United Front*, Cambridge University Press.

Denov, Myriam and Christine Gervais (2008), 'Negotiating (in)security: agency, resistance and resourcefulness among girls formerly associated with Sierra Leone's Revolutionary United Front', in Karen Alexander and Mary Hawkesworth (eds), *War & Terror: Feminist Perspectives*, University of Chicago Press, pp. 35–60.

Denov, Myriam and Richard Maclure (2006), 'Engaging the voices of girls in the aftermath of Sierra Leone's conflict: experiences and perspectives in a culture of violence', *Anthropologica*, **48** (1): 73–85.

Denov, Myriam and Richard Maclure (2007), 'Turnings and epiphanies: militarization, life histories and the making and unmaking of two child soldiers in Sierra Leone', *Journal of Youth Studies*, **10** (2): 243–61.

Denov, Myriam and Ines Marchand (2014a), '"One cannot take away the stain": rejection and stigma among former child soldiers in Colombia', *Peace and Conflict: Journal of Peace Psychology*, **20** (3): 227–40.

Denov, Myriam and Ines Marchand (2014b), '"I can't go home". Forced migration and displacement following demobilisation: the complexity of reintegrating former child soldiers in Colombia', *Intervention*, **12** (3): 331–43.

Denov, Myriam and Alexandra Ricard-Guay (2013), 'Girl soldiers: towards a gendered understanding of wartime recruitment, participation and demobilization', *Gender and Development*, **21** (3): 473–88.

Derluyn, Ilse, Eric Broekaert, Gilberte Schuyten and Els de Temmerman (2004), 'Post-traumatic stress in former Uganda child soldiers', *Lancet*, **363** (9412): 861–3.

Elshtain, C. (1987), *Women and War*, Basic.

Enloe, Cynthia (2000), *Maneuvers: The International Politics of Militarizing Women's Lives*, University of California Press.

Enloe, Cynthia (2014), *Bananas, Beaches and Bases: Making Feminist Sense of International Politics*, University of California Press.

Fithen, Casper and Paul Richards (2005), 'Making war, crafting peace: militia solidarities and demobilization in Sierra Leone', in Paul Richards (ed.), *No Peace, No War: An Anthropology of Contemporary Armed Conflicts*, James Currey, pp. 117–36.

Fox, Mary-Jane (2004), 'Girl soldiers: human security and gendered insecurity', *Security Dialogue*, **35**: 465–79.

Giles, Wenona Mary and Jennifer Hyndman (eds) (2004), *Sites of Violence: Gender and Conflict Zones*, University of California Press.

Goldstein, Joshua S. (2001), *War and Gender: How Gender Shapes the War System and vice versa*, Cambridge University Press.

Human Rights Watch (2003), '"You'll learn not to cry", child combatants in Colombia', HRW.

Indra, Doreen Marie (ed.) (1999), *Engendering Forced Migration: Theory and Practice*, Berghahn.

Jacobs, Susie, Ruth Jacobson and Jennifer Marchbank (eds) (2000), *States of Conflict: Gender, Violence and Resistance*, Zed Books.

Jones, Lindsay and Myriam Denov (2015), 'Mothering in the context of isolation and insecurity: young women formerly associated with armed groups in Colombia', in Tatjana Takseva and Arlene Sgoutas (eds), *Mothers Under Fire*, Fernwood.

Kater, Michael (2004), *Hitler Youth*, Harvard University Press.

Keairns, Yvonne (2003), *The Voice of Girl Children Soldiers*, Quaker United Nations Office.

Kelly, Liz (2000), 'Wars against women: sexual violence, sexual politics and the militarized state', in Susie Jacobs, Ruth Jacobson and Jennifer Marchbank (eds), *States of Conflict: Gender, Violence and Resistance*, Zed Books, pp. 45–65.

Kemper, Yvonne (2005), *Youth in War to Peace Transitions*, Berghof Research Center for Constructive Management.

Klasen, Fionna, Gabriele Oettingen, Judith Daniels, Manuela Post, Catrin Hoyer and Hubertus Adam (2010), 'Posttraumatic resilience in former Ugandan child soldiers', *Child Development*, **81** (4): 1096–113.

Lolloy, D. (2004), *The DDR Process in Sierra Leone: An Overview and Lessons Learned*, United Nations Development Programme/Government of Sierra Leone.

Maclure, Richard and Myriam Denov (2006), '"I didn't want to die so I joined them": structuration and the process of becoming boy soldiers in Sierra Leone', *Terrorism and Political Violence*, **18** (1): 119–35.

Maclure, Richard and Myriam Denov (2009), 'Reconstruction versus transformation: post-war education and the struggle for gender parity in Sierra Leone', *International Journal of Educational Development*, **29**: 612–20.

Macmillan, Lorraine (2009), 'The child soldier in North–South relations', *International Political Sociology*, **3** (1): 36–52.

Martin, Susan and John Tirman (eds) (2009), *Women, Migration and Conflict: Breaking the Deadly Cycle*, Springer.

Mazurana, Dyan and Khristopher Carlson (2004), *From Combat to Community: Women and Girls of Sierra Leone*, Women's Policy Commission, Women Waging Peace.

Mazurana, Dyan and Khristopher Carlson (2006), 'The girl child and armed conflict: recognizing and addressing grave violations of girls' human rights', in United Nations Division for the Advancement of Women (DAW), in collaboration with UNICEF Expert Group Meeting, Elimination of all Forms of Discrimination and Violence Against the Girl Child, Florence, pp. 25–8.

Mazurana, Dyan E., Angela Raven-Roberts and Jane L. Parpart (2005), *Gender, Conflict, and Peacekeeping*, Rowman & Littlefield.

Mazurana, Dyan, Susan McKay, Khristopher Carlson and Janet Kasper (2002), 'Girls in fighting forces and groups: their recruitment, participation, demobilization, and reintegration', *Peace and Conflict: Journal of Peace Psychology*, **8** (2): 97–123.

McKay, Susan (1998), 'The effects of armed conflict on girls and women', *Peace and Conflict: Journal of Peace Psychology*, **4** (4): 381–92.

McKay, Susan (2004a), 'Reconstructing fragile lives: girls' social reintegration in northern Uganda and Sierra Leone', *Gender and Development*, **12** (30): 19–30.

McKay, Susan (2006a), 'Girlhoods stolen: the plight of girl soldiers during and after armed conflict', in Neil Boothby, Michael Wessells and Alison Strang (eds), *A World Turned Upside Down: The Social Ecologies of Children in Armed Conflict*, Kumarian, pp. 89–109.

McKay, Susan (2006b), 'Reconstructing fragile lives: girl soldiers' social reintegration in Northern Uganda and Sierra Leone', in Ahmad Sikainga and Ousseina Alidou (eds), *Post-Conflict Reconstruction in Africa*, Africa World, pp. 149–66.

McKay, Susan (2006c), 'How do you mend broken hearts? Gender, war and impacts on girls in fighting forces', in Gilbert Reyes and Gerard Jacobs (eds), *The Handbook of International Disaster Psychology*, **4**, Praeger, pp. 45–60.

McKay, Susan and Dyan Mazurana (2004), *Where are the Girls? Girls in Fighting Forces in Northern Uganda, Sierra Leone, and Mozambique: Their Lives During and After War*, International Centre for Human Rights and Democratic Development.

McKay, Susan, Malia Robinson, Maria Gonsalves and Miranda Worthen (2006), 'Girls formerly associated with fighting forces and their children: returned and neglected', Coalition to Stop the Use of Child Soldiers, available at: www.child-soldiers.org/resources/psychosocial.

McKay, Susan, Angela Veale, Miranda Worthen and Michael Wessells (2010), *Community-based Reintegration of War-Affected Young Mothers: Participation Action Research (PAR) in Liberia, Sierra Leone & Northern Uganda*, ParGirlProject, available at: www.pargirlmothers.com.

Meertens, Donny (2001), 'The nostalgic future: terror, displacement, and gender in Colombia', in Caroline Moser and Fiona Clark (eds), *Victims, Perpetrators or Actors? Gender, Armed Conflict and Political Violence*, Zed Books, pp. 133–48.

Meintjes, Sheila, Anu Pillay and Meredith Turshen (2001), *The Aftermath: Women in Post-Conflict Transformation*, Zed Books.

Mesa de Trabajo Mujer y Conflicto Armado (2003), 'Informe sobre violencia sociopolítica contre mujeres, jóvenes y niñas en Colombia', third report –2002, Bogotà.

Moreno Martín, Florentino, Carmona Parra, Jaime Alberto and Felipe Tobón Hoyos (2010), 'Por qué se vinculan las niñas a los grupos guerrilleros y paramilitares en Colombia?', *Revista Latinoamericana de Psicología*, **42** (3): 453–67.

Moser, Caroline and Fiona Clark (eds) (2001), *Victims, Perpetrators or Actors? Gender, Armed Conflict, and Political Violence*, Zed Books.

Nordstrom, Carolyn (1997), *Girls and Warzones: Troubling Questions*, Life and Peace Institute.

Nordstrom, Carolyn (2004), *Shadows of War: Violence, Power and International Profiteering in the Twenty-First Century*, University of California Press.

Nordstrom, Carolyn and Antonius G.M. Robben (eds) (1995), *Fieldwork under Fire: Contemporary Studies of Violence and Survival*, University of California Press.

Observatorio de Procesos de Desarme, Desmovilización y Reintegración (2009), 'Normatividad, políticas, programas nacionales y voces académicas sobre niños, niñas, adolescentes y jóvenes menores de edad desvinculados de las organizaciones armadas ilegales', Universidad Nacional de Colombia.

Save the Children UK (2005), *Forgotten Casualties of War: Girls in Armed Conflict*, Save the Children UK.

Schmidt, Rachel Anne (2007), *No Girls Allowed? Recruitment and Gender in Colombian Armed Groups*, unpublished Master's thesis, Carleton University.

Schomerus, Mareike and Tim Allen (2006), 'A hard homecoming: lessons learned from the reception center process in northern Uganda: an independent study', United States Agency for International Development / United Nations Children's Fund.

Schroven, Anita (2008), *Women after War: Gender Mainstreaming and the Social Construction of Identity in Contemporary Sierra Leone*, Spektrum, vol. 94, Lit Verlag.

Shanmugaratnam, Nadarajah, Ragnhild Lund and Kristi Anne Stölen (2003), *In the Maze of Displacement: Conflict, Migration and Change*, Norwegian Academic Press.

Shepherd, Laura (2007), 'Victims, perpetrators and actors' revisited', *British Journal of Politics & International Relations*, **9**: 239–57.

Specht, Irma and Larry Attree (2006), 'The reintegration of teenage girls and young women', *Intervention*, **4** (3): 219–28.

Stavrou, Aki (2004), *Breaking the Silence: Girls Abducted During Armed Conflict in Angola*, Report for the Canadian International Development Agency.

Thompson, Martha (2006), 'Women, gender, and conflict: making the connections', *Development in Practice*, **16** (03–04): 342–53.

UNICEF (2005), *The Disarmament, Demobilisation and Reintegration of Children Associated with the Fighting Force: Lessons Learned in Sierra Leone 1998–2002*, UNICEF.

UNICEF (2007), 'The Paris Principles. Principles and guidelines on children associated with armed forces or armed groups', UNICEF.

UNICEF (2009), *Machel Study 10-Year Strategic Review: Children and Conflict in a Changing World*, UNICEF.

United Nations (2006), 'Integrated Disarmament, Demobilization and Reintegration Standards', accessed 15 October 2008 at: http://www.unddr.org/iddrs/framework.php.

United States Department of State (2013), *2013 Trafficking in Persons Report*, 19 June.

Utas, Mats (2005), 'Victimcy, girlfriending, soldiering: tactic agency in a young woman's social navigation of the Liberian war zone', *Anthropological Quarterly*, **78** (2): 403–30.

Veale, Angela (2003), *From Child Soldier to Ex-fighter. Female Fighters: Demobilization and Reintegration in Ethiopia*, Institute for Security Studies.

Veale, Angela and Aki Stavrou (2003), 'Violence, reconciliation and identity. The reintegration of Lord's Resistance Army child abductees in Northern Uganda', *Institute for Security Studies Monographs*, (92).

Veale, Angela and Aki Stavrou (2007), 'Former Lord's Resistance Army child soldier abductees: explorations of identity in reintegration and reconciliation', *Peace and Conflict: Journal of Peace Psychology*, **13** (3): 273–92.

Verhey, Beth (2004), *Reaching the Girls*, Save the Children UK.

Wessells, Michael (2006), *Child Soldiers: From Violence to Protection*, Harvard University Press.

Wessells, Michael (2007), 'The recruitment and use of girls in armed forces and groups in Angola: implications for ethical research and reintegration', Ford Institute for Human Security Working Papers No. 3.

Wessells, Michael (2009), 'Supporting the mental health and psychosocial well-being of former child soldiers', *Journal of the American Academy of Child and Adolescent Psychiatry*, **48** (6).

West, Harry G. (2000), 'Girls with guns: narrating the experience of war of Frelimo's 'Female Detachment', *Anthropological Quarterly*, **73** (4): 180–94.

Williamson, John (2006), 'The disarmament, demobilization and reintegration of child soldiers: social and psychological transformation in Sierra Leone', *Intervention*, **4** (3): 185–205.

Wilson, Richard (2001), 'Children and war in Sierra Leone: a West African diary', *Anthropology Today*, **17** (5): 20–23.

Worthen, Miranda, Angela Veal, Susan McKay and Michael Wessells (2010), '"I stand like a woman": empowerment and human rights in the context of community-based reintegration of girl mothers formerly associated with fighting forces and armed groups', *Journal of Human Rights Practice*, **2** (1): 49–70.

27. The United Nations' Women, Peace and Security agenda

Soumita Basu

INTRODUCTION

Dictated by great power concerns and the need for collective security, the United Nations (UN) was set up, in the aftermath of World War II, with the primary aim 'to save succeeding generations from the scourge of war' (UN, 1945). The establishment of the UN was welcomed by women's organizations. Although women had a marginal impact on the constitution of this intergovernmental organization (and the League of Nations before that), a group of women delegates was successful in ensuring the inclusion of women's rights in the UN charter. They continued to push for further recognition of women in the international sphere after this initial success. In particular, at the end of the first session of the UN General Assembly in 1946, they called on the governments to recognize the role of women in World War II and encourage their participation in 'national and international affairs and in building peace' (Galey, 1995b, p. 12). It was only decades later, however, that the links between gender (initially articulated primarily in terms of women's issues) and matters of war and peace – made increasingly evident over time in feminist advocacy and scholarship on international security – were recognized at the UN. With the passage of the seven UN Security Council Resolutions (SCRs) on Women and Peace and Security during the period 2000–2013 the relationship between gender and war received serious attention in the international policymaking arena.

Security Council Resolution 1325, adopted in 2000, was the first in the series of these resolutions. It is often associated with 3Ps – Participation, Protection and Prevention – relating to protection of women and girls in situations of armed conflict, and recognition and promotion of women's role in conflict prevention and post-conflict reconstruction. In this chapter, these 3Ps are referred to as the Women, Peace and Security (WPS) agenda. The chapter provides a critical overview of gender-related security policies at the UN. The focus is primarily on the SCRs on

Women and Peace and Security, and their implementation by the UN, especially resolution 1325.

The first section presents key highlights in the evolution of the WPS agenda – during the International Women's Decade (1976–85) and at the four UN World Conferences on Women. Additionally, the section examines the rapid policy developments related to women, peace and security during the 1990s. The second section focuses closely on the SCRs, beginning with the passage of resolution 1325 in 2000, an event widely recognized to be historic in policymaking on issues relating to gender and the war at the UN. It includes a critical evaluation of 1325, and a brief examination of the six follow-up resolutions –1820 (UNSC, 2008a), 1888 (UNSC, 2009a), 1889 (UNSC, 2009b), 1960 (UNSC, 2010), 2106 (UNSC, 2013a) and 2122 (UNSC, 2013b). The third section provides an overview of the implementation of the resolutions by the UN. Finally, the fourth section of this chapter evaluates the relative significance of UN policy mechanisms with respect to gender issues in wartime and in post-war societies.

ORIGINS OF THE WPS AGENDA

In 1915, during the early stages of World War I, women from 13 nations – both combatant and neutral – met at The Hague and drafted a peace plan. This manifesto, which included a 'proposal for a permanent institution of arbitration', was rejected by the national delegations engaged in or preparing for war (Brock-Utne, 1994, pp. 207-208; Galey, 1995a, p. 3). The women who met at The Hague subsequently formed the Women's International League for Peace and Freedom (WILPF) under the leadership of Jane Addams. WILPF became an active supporter and defender of the League of Nations (set up in 1919), in contrast to most national governments at that time (Meyer, 1999, p. 110; Charnovitz, 1996, pp. 213–14). Following the failure of the League and the ensuing devastation caused by World War II, the victorious nations came together to establish the UN.

As with feminist politics at the UN in general, the enthusiasm of the first wave of women's peace activism in the 1940s waned over the next two decades, though women continued to mobilize regionally over anti-nuclear issues, national liberation movements and decolonization (Prügl and Meyer, 1999, p. 10). The resurgence was marked by the announcement of the year 1975 as the International Women's Year (IWY), which was followed by the UN Decade for Women (1976–85) and the four World Conferences on Women. Of the three IWY themes –

equality, peace and development – peace received the least emphasis at the IWY Conference in Mexico City but began to gain prominence at the second conference in Copenhagen in 1980 (Stephenson, 1982, p. 295).

It was at the closing conference held in Nairobi in 1985 that women and international peace were substantively discussed. Cockburn writes that, 'the issue of women in relation to war and peace was addressed with particular energy' at this conference (2007, p. 139). The idea of peace, as defined in the outcome document entitled *The Forward Looking Strategies* (FLS), resonated with basic feminist concerns regarding armed conflict, and structural violence more broadly. The paragraphs on peace included such statements as: 'universal and durable peace cannot be attained without the full and equal participation of women in international relations' [para. 235]; and 'full equality between women and men is severely hampered by the threats to international peace and security ...' [para. 236] (UN, 1985; also see Pietilä and Vickers, 1994,' pp. 64–70). The FLS had been preceded by the Declaration of the General Assembly on 'Participation of Women in Promoting International Peace and Co-operation' in 1982. Linking gender relations explicitly with international peace and security, albeit with a focus on equality, the Nairobi Outcome Document emerged as much more progressive. As the first intergovernmental document of its kind, the FLS marked a turning point in the UN's policy on gender and war.

In the 1990s due to the end of Cold War, with changes in international security dynamics, the UN and more specifically the Security Council began to re-evaluate their institutional interests and capacities. The shift in UN policymaking from focusing solely on states to addressing human populations across borders facilitated the growth of the WPS agenda (Basu, 2010, p. 292). The gains in the women's rights agenda at the UN Global Conference for Human Rights in Vienna in 1993 – with the formal recognition of violence against women as a human rights issue – lent support to the growing prominence of issues relating to women and armed conflict among feminist advocates outside and inside the UN (Hall and Shepherd, 2013, p. 60). The increased attention to the gendered dimensions of war and political violence coupled with growing concerns about sexual and gender violence perpetrated against women in the Balkans and Rwanda influenced the outcome document of the Fourth World Conference on Women (1995) held in Beijing. Indeed, the Platform for Action (PFA) identified 'women and armed conflict' as one of the twelve critical areas of concern (UN, 1995).

There was a steep upward curve in the development of the WPS agenda during the period 1995–2000 (see Gardam and Jarvis, 2000; Hill et al., 2003). Women and armed conflict was the theme of the 1998 annual meeting of the Commission on the Status of Women (CSW) at the UN Headquarters in New York. In the same year, the Rome Statute of the International Criminal Court (ICC), which codified sexual and gender violence (among others) as war crimes and crimes against humanity, was adopted (UN, 1998).

A key development around this time was also the growing significance of 'gender mainstreaming' at the UN. According to the UN Economic and Social Council, 'mainstreaming a gender perspective is the process of assessing the implications for women and men of any planned action, including legislation, policies or programmes, in any area and at all levels' (UN ECOSOC, 1997). From the perspective of women's concerns, therefore, gender mainstreaming should be cognizant of gendered experiences of women and men, and the relations between them.[1] The first steps towards 'gender mainstreaming' in policies relating to peace and security were taken by the UN Department of Peacekeeping Operations (DPKO) in the 1990s. This created space for the consideration of WPS issues even though the policy impact was rather limited (see Shepherd and Hamilton, Chapter 22 in this volume).

SECURITY COUNCIL RESOLUTIONS ON WOMEN AND PEACE AND SECURITY

The passage of SCR 1325 by the Security Council in 2000 is widely considered to be a pivotal point on the international WPS trajectory. The resolution recognized the gendered nature of war and peace processes as well as the roles, needs and interests of women and girls at these times. The need to address violence against women, especially sexual and gender-based violence, was given particular attention. Additionally, SCR 1325 places an unprecedented emphasis on the role played by women in the prevention and resolution of armed conflicts, with proposals to increase the number of women in decision-making positions both during and after conflict resolution and to consult with 'women's peace initiatives and indigenous processes' at the local level. The resolution also touched upon women's participation in armed conflict as perpetrators of violence.

As evident in the opening paragraphs of the resolution, 'the ideas and language in the resolution were built on documents and treaties passed through the UN system since its inception in 1945' (Hill et al., 2003, 1295). In addition to references to the Beijing Declaration and PFA (UN, 1995) and relevant provisions of the Rome Statute (UN, 1998), SCR 1325 took note of the Geneva Convention (UN, 1949), the Convention on the Elimination of All Forms of Discrimination against Women (CEDAW) (UN GA, 1979) as well as the more recently adopted SCRs on children and armed conflict (UNSC, 1999a, 2000) and protection of civilians (UNSC, 1999b), among other UN documents. Together, the thematic SCRs adopted in 1999 and 2000 gave precedence to human experiences of war, thereby reinterpreting to some extent the mandate of the state-centric Security Council. With respect to the provisions of SCR 1325, particularly noteworthy are the resolution's emphasis on agency of women, recognition of the gendered experiences of armed conflict and references to conflict prevention (Basu, 2010).

SCR 1325 is the most important and well-publicized UN document that goes beyond identifying women as victims of armed conflict, in need of protection from 'benign' member states and UN agencies (Jacobson, 2008, p. 91; Carpenter, 2006, p. 123). It represents a significant departure from, for instance, the Geneva Conventions and Protocols, which have 43 provisions dealing with women and armed conflict but none that recognize women's agency[2] (Gardam and Charlesworth, 2000, p. 159). The resolution makes a reference to the Geneva Conventions and Protocols but, following in the footsteps of the Rome Statute of the ICC, it suggests a different protection mandate, altering the understanding of women's victimhood. Rape is recognized as a war crime and SCR 1325 '*stresses the need to exclude these crimes, where feasible from amnesty provisions*' (UNSC, 2000, emphasis in the original).

The overall representation of women in the resolution is multi-dimensional, seeing them as political actors, peacemakers and combatants as well as victims. The resolution, along with the Beijing PFA, is a key policy instrument 'which offer[s] backing for work on women's rights in violent, armed conflict and in humanitarian emergencies' (El-Bushra, 2008, p. 30). Further, conflict prevention appears to be a foundational aspect of SCR 1325. In this context, the role of women is recognized and UN member states are urged to increase the participation of women in, for example, mechanisms for conflict prevention.

Notably, however, the resolution was adopted by the Security Council under the mandate to maintain international peace and security, as set out in the UN Charter. As such, the interest of the Council on this matter is limited to the extent that it impacts upon this mandate (Klot, 2002, pp. 18–19); the potential for SCR 1325 to provide greater insights into the interactions between international security and gender are constrained by the resolution's understanding of both 'international security' and 'gender'. The resolution approaches international security in ways that stay true to the 1945 formulation of that concept in the UN Charter. It is consistent with the preference of the Security Council to manage conflicts rather than delve into structural causes for them, for instance, ignoring the links between women's security and disarmament (Otto, 2006–2007, p. 159). The resolution also fails to explore the transformative capacity of gender, based on dynamics of social relations. The resolution, therefore, sits uncomfortably between demands of the 'business-as-usual' politics at the Security Council and the feminist aspirations that it may be seen to espouse. Specifically, the resolution has been criticized for: the lack of conceptual clarity in its references to gender; the focus on women with no references to men, as if gender is only relevant to women; and, inherited remnants of the 'womenandchildren' syndrome that equates women with children, thereby infantilizing them (see, for instance, Shepherd, 2006, pp. 394–5).

Along similar lines, Whitworth argues that gender, as used in matters of peace and security, has become a 'safe idea' at the UN because it is not used to 'challenge prevailing practices in responses to armed conflict, peace and security' (2004, p. 139). Some feminist scholars have contended that talking about security for women within the militarized context of UN operations – as in the case of SCR 1325 – lends 'gender legitimacy' to militarized peace (Otto, 2004; Whitworth, 2004). Feminists who criticized the resolution note that the use of the language of gender gives the impression that the peace operations are responsive to societal concerns and deeper political issues whereas, instead, the concept is used as an appendage to the largely state-centric, militaristic approach to the maintenance of international peace and security. This view is borne out in the trajectory of the WPS agenda at the UN, as discussed below.

It took more than seven years after the passage of SCR 1325 for the Security Council to adopt the second WPS resolution – SCR 1820, which primarily calls for the 'immediate and complete cessation by all parties to armed conflict of all acts of sexual violence against civilians' (UNSC, 2008a). At the time of its drafting and subsequent adoption, gender justice advocates expressed concerns that SCR 1820 narrowed the focus of the WPS agenda (Barnes, 2011, p. 28; Basu, 2010, p. 304). Supporters of the resolution, however, pointed to the need to strengthen the protection provisions of SCR 1325 because of the prevalence of sexual and gender-based violence during armed conflicts, as infamously illustrated in the case of the Democratic Republic of Congo at that time (Cook, 2008a, 2008b). These provisions were later strengthened with the passage of SCRs 1888, 1960 and 2106 (adopted during the period 2009–13), all of which also focused on the protection theme of the WPS agenda.

Resolution 1889, which was adopted by the Security Council days after the passage of SCR 1888, focused on the provisions of SCR 1325 that concern women's participation in conflict resolution. It calls for 'measures to improve women's participation during all stages of peace processes, particularly in conflict resolution, post-conflict planning and peacebuilding ...' (UNSC, 2009b), thus strengthening another important dimension of SCR 1325. Following the efforts of WPS advocates, SCR 1889 also called upon the Secretary General to submit 'a set of indicators for use at the global level to track implementation of its resolution 1325 (2000)' (UNSC, 2009b). With inputs from a working group that included UN and other international entities (including the NGO Working Group, representing civil society), the Secretary General's 2010 report to the Security Council included 26 indicators that were organized under the four thematic pillars of prevention, participation, protection and relief and recovery (Barnes, 2011, pp. 28–9); these indicators were identified in the 2008–2009 UN System-wide Action Plan for the implementation of resolution 1325.

The conflict prevention dimension of SCR 1325 has received much less attention from the Security Council than those of protection and participation. The few occasions on which direct references to this aspect were made include the October 2011 Security Council Open Debate on WPS on the theme of 'Women's Participation and Role in Conflict Prevention and Mediation', and the passage of SCR 2122 in 2013 that called for 'more attention on women's leadership and participation in conflict resolution and peacebuilding' (UNSC, 2013b).

Ultimately, SCR 1325 provided a framework and created a momentum for addressing a range of issues relating to gender, war and peace. Follow-up resolutions can – and must be directed to – improve the efficacy of UN policy mechanisms in this respect but the litmus test lies in the implementation of the existing resolutions.

IMPLEMENTATION OF SCRs ON WOMEN AND PEACE AND SECURITY

The passage of SCR 1325 is considered to be historic not only because the areas of security – gendered experiences of war and peace – that it touches upon are novel (particularly in light of feminist activism and scholarship that had discussed these issues for decades), but also because these had not been previously recognized by the Security Council. Considering the preeminent position of the Council in global security governance, WPS advocates hoped that provisions of the Resolution would be taken seriously and implemented by relevant actors (see Otto, 2009, pp. 1–2). Certainly, as Christy Fujio notes, 'its [SCR 1325] drafters have [had] gone to great lengths explicitly to assign responsibilities to the various players, and in doing so, created a fairly comprehensive framework for accountability, at least on paper' (2008, p. 219). The same would appear to apply to the follow-up resolutions. Fujio's reference to accountability, however, is debatable considering that the resolutions were not adopted under a Chapter VII mandate (which is the mechanism through which the Security Council can sanction enforcement mechanisms) and are therefore not legally binding under international law (Otto, 2009, p. 1). Further, with the possible exception of SCR 1960 and SCR 2106, which have some concrete mechanisms, the provisions of the resolutions are not set out in specific terms. However, there is considerable clarity about the range of actors responsible for implementation, including the UN and its agencies, UN member states, civil society actors and indeed all 'parties to the armed conflict'.

SCR 1325 invited the Secretary General to 'carry out [and submit] a study on the impact of armed conflict on women and girls, the role of women in peace-building and the gender dimensions of peace processes and conflict resolution' (UNSC, 2000). As Felicity Hill (2004–2005) points out, the report of the Secretary General is crucial for subsequent action by the Security Council on thematic resolutions. Supporters of SCR 1325 hoped, as Jennifer Klot writes, that the agenda for the implementation of the resolution would be set by an independent expert assessment because the UN system was so closely linked to the issues in the resolution (2002, p. 19).[3] The independent experts' assessment was subsequently commissioned by UNIFEM, and conducted by Elisabeth Rehn and Ellen John Sirleaf (2002). Klot, a senior member of the UNIFEM team at that time notes that – in the end – both the reports involved external and internal consultations (Klot, 2002, pp. 19–20).

Though there is no report schedule specified in the resolution, the Secretary General has submitted reports to the Council every year since its adoption, except for the years 2001 and 2003. The Inter-Agency Network on Women and Gender Equality (IANWGE) set up a Taskforce on Women, Peace and Security in 2001, which has formulated documents on inter-agency coordination for the implementation of SCR 1325. Both the Office for the Coordination of Humanitarian Affairs (OCHA) and the Department of Disarmament Affairs (DDA) have adopted Action Plans. UNIFEM developed an Internet repository www.womenwarpeace.org on the resolutions, which is now maintained by UN Women. There is a wealth of literature produced by the UN to facilitate the understanding and implementation of the WPS resolutions, and the website maintained by UN Women contains records of these, as do a number of civil society organizations.

The main challenge for the Security Council and UN agencies has been, however, to transform its peace operations into gender-sensitive programs and respond to the recommendations set out in the resolutions and the reports of the Secretary General. Unlike the development of a framework for implementing the recommendations of the Brahimi Report (UN GA SC, 2000), the Council did not put in place adequate mechanisms to implement SCR 1325, failing also to galvanize the necessary resources and UN institutions in this regard (Klot, 2002, p. 20). As a result, the 'infusion' of gender into existing mechanisms has been ad hoc at best (Barnes, 2006; Porter, 2003).

A number of independent studies have analyzed the Security Council's employment of gender in its policies in an attempt to evaluate the institution's commitment to its WPS resolutions (see Basu, 2010; Black, 2009; Butler et al, 2010; True-Frost, 2007). Considering the differences in scope and period of study, the research findings are not the same; however, they are similar enough to merit attention. Clearly, the Security Council has taken note of the gendered nature of armed conflicts more frequently since the adoption of the resolution, but these references demonstrate certain patterns. For instance, the Council notes the relevance of gender in its resolutions but does not make concrete recommendations. Further, the same gender-related terms appear in relation to issues such as human rights, the demobilization, disarmament and reintegration (DDR) process and in the context of diverse UN peace missions in different parts of the world. Such references to gender are reminiscent of the comment made by Angela Raven-Roberts about the practice of staff members at OCHA combing through documents and adding the words 'women', 'girls' and 'gender' in as many places as possible, to make them appear gender-sensitive (2005, p. 50). It is significant that, concurrent to the trajectory of the thematic focus of the WPS resolutions, the Security Council refers to women and gender primarily in context of protection issues, and to some extent in relation to the participation of women. The third 'p' – conflict prevention – has been systematically marginalized (Basu and Confortini, 2011; Saferworld, 2015). Thus, the WPS resolutions are invoked in relation to the humanitarian agenda of the Security Council but do not challenge deeper issues such as the prevalence of armed conflicts and gendered dimensions of militarism.

The deployment of UN personnel is an important area for the implementation of the WPS agenda. Prior to the adoption of SCR 1325, only two UN missions – in Kosovo and Timor-Leste – had specific offices committed to gender issues. As of January 2010, nine out of sixteen peacekeeping and political missions of the UN had dedicated full-time gender advisors. Statistical information provided on the DPKO website suggests that the number of female UN personnel as well as gender officers in peace operations has been increasing (see UN DPKO, 2013). When looking at the big picture, however, these developments are modest. In 2010, women accounted for 4.14 percent of UN Military Experts on Mission, 2.42 percent of troops (including staff officers), and 8.7 percent of police; the total percentage of female military and police personnel in UN Peacekeeping Operations stood at 3.3 percent (UN DPKO/OMA, n.d.). Further, a UNIFEM study on women's participation in peace processes notes that 'the United Nations has never officially appointed a woman to be the chief mediator of a peace process ... however ... a number of women have played a lead mediation role in recent decades' (UNIFEM, 2010, p. 5).

The protection of women and girls during periods of armed conflict has clearly emerged as the most important theme among those identified by the WPS resolutions. Yet, it has also been one of the biggest challenges that the Security Council and the UN have faced in relation to implementing the resolutions. The UN's commitment to the protection of women and girls has invoked a wider public outcry due to its limitations in addressing sexual and gender-based violence against women and girls by parties to armed conflict as well as sexual exploitation and abuse by UN peacekeepers (see Aroussi, 2011). The Secretary General and the Security Council have called for the protection of women and girls from such violence on various occasions, most substantively with the adoption of SCRs 1820, 1888 and 1960. The creation of the post of the Secretary General's Special Representative on Sexual Violence in Conflict in 2010 represents an important step in further institutionalizing the commitments of the UN to the protection-related provisions of the WPS resolutions.

In the contemporary UN system, it may no longer be possible to publicly proclaim in response to charges of sexual exploitation and abuse that 'boys will be boys', as Yasushi Akashi of Japan, the Head of a UN mission in Namibia, did in 1999 (Stiehm, 1999, pp. 53–4). Furthermore, the inadequacy of the UN's responses to its 'in-house' problems has been widely criticized (see, for instance, Prügl and Thompson, 2013). Even though a number of UN peace operations have been tarnished by allegations of sexual exploitation and abuse by mission staff, there is little evidence that the condemnation of the Secretary General and the Council has resulted in effective action. As Joanne Sandler writes, the 'harshest evidence of weak implementation [of SCR 1325] has been regarding SEA [sexual exploitation and abuse] by peacekeepers' (2008, p. 2).

Some of the shortcomings identified in the implementation of SCR 1325 by the Security Council, and the UN in general, can be attributed to the lack of political will and sustained commitment from UN member states. For instance, taking action against peacekeepers found guilty of sexual abuse is ultimately the responsibility of their respective countries and the UN is able to take only limited action in this regard (Fleshman, 2005). Further, the UN is reliant on the international community, particularly donor countries, for the resources to put particular plans into action (Barnes, 2006). Another obstacle for the implementation of such resolutions as SCR 1325 lies in the fact that such resolutions were articulated in the Council, and are generally the least common denominators arising out of negotiations between members of the Security Council, who have the power to legislate.

It is within these challenging political spaces that feminist actors, both inside and outside the UN, have identified opportunities for transformation. UNIFEM (now UN Women) has used its position within the UN, both to increase the participation of women in UN missions and to facilitate the access of local women's groups to formal policymaking. For instance, 'it facilitated women's access to the institutions brokering peace talks on Darfur, and in northern Uganda, where it partnered with the Department of Political Affairs to install a gender adviser with the United Nations envoy to the Juba talks' (UN DPI, 2008; on UN Women's work, also see Hudson and Goetz, 2014).

When considering the implementation of WPS resolutions, UN member states have an important role to play. While some key developments have taken place, the record has been rather uneven. Canada hosted an informal grouping of states committed to the implementation of SCR 1325 in 2001, immediately after the passage of the resolution. Known as the Friends of 1325, this governmental group has not been mobilized in any substantive way and appears to be largely defunct.

Some countries and regional intergovernmental organizations have adopted national policies, and also supported the work of the UN and civil society actors towards implementation of the resolutions. The adoption of National Action Plans (NAPs) on SCR 1325 and, in some cases, follow-up WPS resolutions is particularly relevant. As of June 2015, 49 countries had adopted NAPs, which are intended to provide guidelines to UN member states in relation to their roles as contributors of troops to UN peace operations, as donors for UN and civil society projects as well as for resource mobilization at the country level (see PeaceWomen, 2015). A number of regional organizations, including the Organization for Security and Cooperation in Europe, the European Union, the Economic Community of West African States and the

Organization of American States have all adopted resolutions endorsing SCR 1325. Overall, however, the lukewarm response of UN member states to the resolutions has stalled its effective implementation, including at the UN level.

SCR 1325 notes the relevance of civil society organizations in matters of peace and security. Indeed, civil society actors played an important role in advocating the implementation of the WPS resolutions at the UN, and at national and local levels. In fact, the role played by NGOs and other civil society actors has far exceeded the narrow scope envisioned for them in the Resolution. In his report on Women and Peace and Security to the Security Council in 2008, the Secretary General noted: 'the women's movement has made major contributions to building partnerships for peace utilizing resolution 1325 (2000)' (UNSC, 2008b, p. 3).

The most obvious contribution of civil society actors has been in disseminating information on the resolutions and actively monitoring their implementation by governments and the UN. The work of the NGO Working Group has been particularly important. Their reports – along with those of members of this coalition – have included recommendations on more effective employment of SCR 1325, including measures to enhance the accountability of relevant UN agencies and member states. Indeed, the Working Group has often been called upon by governmental and intergovernmental institutions to provide expert knowledge on the WPS resolutions. Thus, the implementation of the WPS resolutions by the UN has taken place on a canvas that drew together multiple institutions and actors – and their varying interests and commitments – within and outside the UN.

CONCLUSION: THE RELEVANCE OF UN POLICIES

Gender-related policies and international mechanisms relating to women's issues are generally part of the larger intervention by the UN and other international humanitarian organizations in any conflict region. Conventional approaches to post-conflict reconstruction, however, do not always correspond to the local realities; at times, they merely succeed in transposing another set of exploitative power relations by, for instance, giving formal legitimacy to erstwhile warlords who may be responsible for human rights violations or war crimes during the conflict (Peake et al., 2004).

Local dynamics may also be affected by vagaries of donor institutions as donor governments often choose to support short-term crisis management rather than invest in long-term post-conflict reconstruction. As a result, issues such as gender-based violence are pushed down the priority list (El Jack, 2003, p. 27). There are concerns about access to resources as well. In the context of Sri Lanka, for instance, larger NGOs based in the capital city of Colombo have become 'gatekeepers', forcing smaller community-based groups that do not have direct access to the donors to become sub-contractors of such Colombo-based NGOs (Abeysekera, 2008, p. 10). Inconsistent funding policies and limited comprehension of local power dynamics may affect the implementation of international policies, including the ones devised by the UN.

The bureaucratic language used in UN policies can also be an impediment, particularly if it cannot be adapted suitably to the local vocabulary. For instance, there may be no local language equivalents for gender and its relational connotation (Charlesworth, 2005, p. 12). There is also confusion on the part of the staff of international organizations about the meaning of gender and its policy implications. Gender is still viewed by many as being synonymous with women; moreover, those who consider gender equality a threat to their position resist exploring its meaning for their own work. This resistance is reflected in the formulation of policy mandates. Thus, income-generation training programs during post-conflict reconstruction may ascribe traditional roles to women and men, with women ex-combatants expected to return to 'womanly' vocations such as sewing and secretarial work without considering any changes brought about due to their previous role as combatants (Anderlini and Conaway, 2004, p. 35; also see El Jack, 2003, p. 28). Further, as the language becomes more bureaucratic, it is less accessible to those who are expected to implement the policies (Anderlini, 2007, p. 221).

The lack of clarity about concepts such as gender mainstreaming and resistance to these ideas at the policymaking stage generally leads to incoherent gender policies in the mandates of UN missions as well as those of humanitarian agencies. The success of the implementation then depends on the interests and inclination of field staffers and local partners. Couched in bureaucratic language and put together with buzz-words such as 'democratization', 'gender' is perceived by some to be the imposition of 'Western agenda'. Commenting on practices in field offices of humanitarian organizations, Julie Mertus writes, 'when staff wish to work on gender issues, they do; when they do not, they find some reason to steer clear of gender' (2001, p. 10). This mindset lends an ad hoc character to the practice of policies such as gender mainstreaming.

Ultimately, however, no international policy, even if clear or strongly worded, can be implemented consistently and with the same outcomes across diverse local contexts; it is reproduced, resisted, subverted and even transformed by the actors involved and within the structural contingencies in a given local context. Thus, new legislation may encourage the participation of women in parliaments, as in the case of Somalia, but this may not stamp out societal discrimination and marginalization against women (Nakaya, 2004, p. 145).

At the same time, international policies can facilitate the development of progressive gender dynamics in at least two ways. These policy instruments such as the Convention on Elimination of Discrimination Against Women (UN GA, 1979) and resolutions such as SCR 1325 set out minimal standards for ensuring women's rights and security.

Given the limited resources available for conflict alleviation in the international policymaking arena, global gender policies help ensure that at least some of these efforts address the experiences and concerns of women and girls. Thus, while the creation of a Ministry of Women's Affairs in a post-conflict nation can risk ghettoizing women, it can also ensure a dedicated budget for women's concerns (Anderlini and El-Bushra, 2004, p. 63). Commenting on the speedy emergence of gender mainstreaming in state bureaucracies across more than 100 countries in the 1990s, Jacqui True and Michael Mintrom write that these 'represent a powerful challenge to business-as-usual politics and policymaking' (2001, p. 51). In post-conflict societies, policies such as these help ensure that gender advocates have some leverage, and possibly resources, in addressing concerns relating to the gendered aspects of armed conflict. Aware of existing critiques of 'mainstreaming gender in global public policy', True poses this dilemma: 'can [we] afford *not to* engage with such institutions, when the application of gender analysis in their policymaking is clearly having political effects beyond academic and feminist communities' (2003, p. 368, emphasis in the original).

Since the founding of the UN, there has been an exponential growth in policymaking on women and issues of gender and war. It is evident that these can be both carriers of hegemonic interests and tools for transformation. The fragmentation in the global realm and the presence of various actors with multiple interests ensure that there are continuous contestations and negotiations about the premises – including in relation to gender and war – on which these policies are founded. With the passage of the Security Council resolutions, a new equilibrium on matters of gender and security has been reached. While the resolutions are limited both in terms of scope and their implementation in conflict situations, they also provide some of the strongest articulations of gender-sensitive policies in the international security sphere. The 'women, peace and security' agenda at the UN – manifest in the resolutions and related policy mechanisms of the UN such as CEDAW, the Rome Statute of the ICC, and the Vienna Human Rights Declaration – therefore remains a work in progress.

NOTES

1. Within this limited understanding at the UN, there has been little or no space for individuals that do not fall into categories of women and men.
2. The emphasis in these documents is on honor, based on sexual attributes such as chastity and modesty of women, which determine their value from the perspective of men; in contrast, offences against men take into account their mind and bodily attributes (Gardam and Charlesworth, 2000, p. 159; Reilly, 2007, p. 160).
3. This was modeled on Maçhel (1996).

REFERENCES

Abeysekera, Sunila (2008), 'Organizing and mobilizing women for peace', in Dubravka Zarkov (ed.), *Gender, Violent Conflict and Development*, Zubaan, pp. 96–112.
Anderlini, Sanam Naraghi (2007), *Women Building Peace: What They Do, Why it Matters*, Lynne Rienner.
Anderlini, Sanam Naraghi and Camille Pampell Conaway (2004), 'Security sector reform', in International Alert and Women Waging Peace, *Inclusive Security, Sustainable Peace: A Toolkit for Advocacy and Action*, pp. 31–40, accessed 17 September 2013 at: http://www.international-alert.org/sites/default/files/library/TKSecuritySectorReform.pdf.
Anderlini, Sanam Naraghi and Judy El-Bushra (2004), 'Post conflict reconstruction', in International Alert and Women Waging Peace, *Inclusive Security, Sustainable Peace: A Toolkit for Advocacy and Action*, pp. 51–68, accessed 17 August 2012 at: http://www. huntalternatives.org/download/39_post_conflict.pdf .
Aroussi, Sahla (2011), '"Women, Peace and Security": addressing accountability for wartime sexual violence', *International Feminist Journal of Politics*, **13** (1): 576–93.
Barnes, Karen (2006), 'Reform or more of the same? Gender mainstreaming and the changing nature of UN peace operations', *YCISS Occasional Paper No. 41*, York Centre for International and Security Studies.
Barnes, Karen (2011), 'The evolution and implementation of UNSCR 1325: an overview', in 'Funmi Olonisakin, Karen Barnes and Eka Ikpe (eds), *Women, Peace and Security: Translating Policy into Practice*, Routledge, pp. 15–31.
Basu, Soumita (2010), 'Security Council Resolution 1325: toward gender equality in peace and security policy making', in Betty A. Reardon and Asha Hans (eds), *The Gender Imperative: Human Security vs State Security*, Routledge, pp. 287–316.
Basu, Soumita and Catia C. Confortini (2011), 'Weakest "P" in the 1325 Pod?: realizing conflict prevention through Security Council Resolution 1325', unpublished paper presented at the Annual Convention of the International Studies Association, Montreal, 19 March.
Black, Renee (2009), 'Mainstreaming Resolution 1325? Evaluating the impact on Security Council Resolution 1325 on Country-Specific UN Resolutions', *Journal of Military and Strategic Studies*, **11** (4).

Brock-Utne, Birgit (1994), 'Listen to women, for a change', in Robert Elias and Jennifer Turpin (eds), *Rethinking Peace*, Lynne Rienner, pp. 205–209.

Butler, Maria, Kristina Mader and Rachel Kean (2010), *Women, Peace and Security Handbook: Compilation and Analysis of United Nations Security Council Resolution Language 2000–2010*, PeaceWomen, accessed 7 July 2015 at: http://www.peacewomen.org/assets/file/PWPublications/handbook.peacewomen.2010.pdf.

Carpenter, R. Charli (2006), *'Innocent Women and Children': Gender, Norms and Protection of Civilians*, Ashgate.

Charlesworth, Hilary (2005), 'Not waving but drowning: gender mainstreaming and human rights in the United Nations', *Harvard Human Rights Journal*, **18**: 1–18.

Charnovitz, Steve (1996), 'Two centuries of participation: NGOs and international governance', *Michigan Journal of International Law*, **18**: 183–286.

Cockburn, Cynthia (2007), *From Where We Stand: War, Women's Activism and Feminist Analysis*, Zed Books.

Cook, Sam (2008a), 'Editorial', *Women's International League for Peace and Freedom 1325 PeaceWomen E-News* 102, accessed on 8 January 2012 at: http://www.peacewomen.org/publications_enews_issue.php?id=32.

Cook, Sam (2008b), 'Security Council Resolution 1820: a move to end sexual violence in conflict', *Women's International League for Peace and Freedom 1325 PeaceWomen E-News* 102, accessed on 8 January 2012 at: http://www.peacewomen.org/publications_enews_issue.php?id=32.

El-Bushra, Judy (2008), 'The culture of peace or the culture of the sound-bite?', in Dubravka Zarkov (ed.), *Gender, Violent Conflict and Development*, Zubaan, pp. 23–40.

El Jack, Amani (2003), *Gender and Armed Conflict: Overview Report*, BRIDGE.

Fleshman, Michael (2005), 'Tough UN Line on Peacekeeper Abuses', *Africa Renewal*, **19** (1), accessed 13 August 2012 at: http://www.un.org/ecosocdev/geninfo/afrec/vol19no1/191peacekeep.htm.

Fujio, Christy (2008), 'From soft to hard law: moving Resolution 1325 on Women, Peace, and Security across the spectrum', *The Georgetown Journal of Gender and the Law*, **9**: 215–35.

Galey, Margaret E. (1995a), 'Forerunners in women's quest for partnership', in Anne Winslow (ed.), *Women, Politics and the United Nations*, Greenwood, pp. 1–10.

Galey, Margaret E. (1995b), 'Women find a place', in Anne Winslow (ed.), *Women, Politics and the United Nations*, Greenwood, pp. 11–28.

Gardam, Judith and Hilary Charlesworth (2000), 'Protection of women in armed conflict', *Human Rights Quarterly*, **22** (1): 148–66.

Gardam, Judith and Michelle J. Jarvis (2000), 'Women and armed conflict: the international responses to the beijing platform for action', *Columbia Human Rights Law Review*, **32**: 1–65.

Hall, Lucy and Laura J. Shepherd (2013), 'R2P and WPS: theorizing responsibility and protection', in Sara E. Davies, Zim Nwokora, Eli Stamnes and Sarah Teit (eds), *Responsibility to Protect and Women, Peace and Security: Aligning the Agendas*, Martinus Nijhoff, pp. 53–72.

Hill, Felicity (2004–2005), 'How *and* When *has Security Council 1325 (2000) on Women, Peace and Security Impacted Negotiations Outside the Security Council*', Master's thesis submitted to Uppsala University Programme of International Studies.

Hill, Felicity, Mikele Aboitiz and Sara Poehlman-Doumbouya (2003), 'Nongovernmental Organizations' role in the buildup and implementation of Security Council Resolution 1325', *Signs: Journal of Women in Culture and Society*, **28** (4): 1255–69.

Hudson, Natalie Florea and Anne Marie Goetz (2014), 'Too much that can't be said', *International Feminist Journal of Politics*, **16** (2): 336–46.

Jacobson, Ruth (2008), 'Gender, development and conflict in Mozambique', in Dubravka Zarkov (ed.), *Gender, Violent Conflict and Development*, Zubaan, pp. 75–95.

Klot, Jennifer (2002), 'Women and peace processes – an impossible match?', in Louise Olsson (ed.), *Gender Processes – an Impossible Match?*, Collegium of Development Studies, pp. 17–23.

Maçhel, Graca (1996), *Impact of Armed Conflicts on Children*, United Nations.

Mertus, Julie (2001), 'Grounds for cautious optimism', *International Feminist Journal of Politics*, **3** (1): 99–103.

Meyer, Mary K. (1999), 'The Women's International League for peace and freedom: organizing women for peace in the war system', in Mary K. Meyer and Elisabeth Prügl (eds), *Gender Politics in Global Governance*, Rowman & Littlefield, pp. 107–21.

Nakaya, Sumie (2004), 'Women and gender equality in peacebuilding: Somalia and Mozambique', in Thomas F. Keating and W. Andy Knight (eds), *Building Sustainable Peace*, United Nations University Press.

Otto, Diane (2004), 'Securing the "gender legitimacy" of the UN Security Council: prising gender from its historical moorings', accessed 9 September 2013 at: http://papers.ssrn.com/sol3/papers.cfm?abstract_id=585923.

Otto, Diane (2006–2007), 'A sign of "weakness"? Disrupting gender certainties in the implementation of Security Council Resolution 1325', *Michigan Journal of Gender and Law*, **13**: 113–76.

Otto, Diane (2009), 'The exile of inclusion: reflections on gender issues in international law over the last decade', *Melbourne Journal of International Law*, **10** (1): 1–16.

PeaceWomen (2015), 'Member states', accessed 7 July 2015 at: http://www.peacewomen.org/member-states.

Peake, Gordon, Cathy Gormley-Heenan and Mari Fitzduff (2004), *From Warlords to Peacelords: Local Leadership Capacity in Peace Processes*, INCORE.

Pietilä, Hilkka and Jeanne Vickers (1994), *Making Women Matter: The Role of the UN*, Zed Books.

Porter, Elisabeth (2003), 'Women, political decision-making, and peace-building', *Global Change, Peace & Security*, **15** (3): 245–62.

Prügl, Elisabeth and Mary K. Meyer (1999), 'Gender politics in global governance', in Mary K. Meyer and Elisabeth Prügl (eds), *Gender Politics in Global Governance*, Rowman & Littlefield, pp. 3–16.

Prügl, Elisabeth and Hayley Thompson (2013), 'The whistleblower: an interview with Kathryn Bolkovac and Madeleine Rees', *International Feminist Journal of Politics*, **15** (1): 102–109.

Raven-Roberts, Angela (2005), 'Gender mainstreaming in the United Nations peace-keeping operations: talking the talk, tripping over the walk', in Dyan E. Mazurana, Angela Raven-Roberts and Jane Parpart (eds), *Gender, Conflict and Peacekeeping*, Rowman & Littlefield, pp. 43–63.

Rehn, Elizabeth and Ellen Johnson Sirleaf (2002), *Women, War and Peace: The Independent Experts' Assessment on the Impact of Armed Conflict on Women and Women's Role in Peacebuilding*, UNIFEM.

Reilly, Niamh (2007), 'Seeking gender justice in post-conflict transitions: towards a transformative women's human rights approach', *International Journal of Law in Context*, **3** (2): 155–72.

Saferworld (2015), 'Reviving Conflict Prevention in 1325', submission to the Global Study on Women, Peace and Security', accessed 16 July 2015 at: http://www.saferworld.org.uk/resources/view-resource/890-reviving-conflict-prevention-in-1325.

Sandler, Joanne (2008), 'Implementing Security Council Resolution 1325', *Disarmament Times*, **31** (1): 2–3.

Shepherd, Laura J. (2006), 'Loud voices behind the wall: gender violence and the violent reproduction of the international', *Millennium: Journal of International Studies*, **34** (2): 377–401.

Stephenson, Carolyn M. (1982), 'Feminism, pacifism, nationalism, and the United Nations decade for women', *Women's Studies International Forum*, **5** (3): 287–300.

Stiehm, Judith Hicks (1999), 'United Nations peacekeeping: men's and women's work', in Mary K. Meyer and Elisabeth Prügl (eds), *Gender Politics in Global Governance*, Rowman & Littlefield, pp. 41–57.

True, Jacqui (2003), 'Mainstreaming gender in global public policy', *International Feminist Journal of Politics*, **5** (3): 368–96.

True, Jacqui and Michael Mintrom (2001), 'Transnational networks and policy diffusion: the case of gender mainstreaming', *International Studies Quarterly*, **45** (1): 27–57.

True-Frost, Cora (2007), 'The Security Council and norm consumption', *NYU Journal of International Law and Politics*, **40**: 115–217.

United Nations (UN) (1945), *Charter of the United Nations*.

United Nations (UN) (1949), *Geneva Conventions*.

United Nations (UN) (1985), *Nairobi Forward-looking Strategies for the Advancement of Women*, UN Doc No. A/CONF.116/28/Rev.

United Nations (UN) (1995), *Beijing Declaration and Platform for Action*, UN Doc No. A/52/231.

United Nations (UN) (1998), *Rome Statute of the International Criminal Court*, UN Doc No. A/CONF.183/9.

UN Department of Public Information (UN DPI) (2008), 'Women's full participation in conflict prevention, peacebuilding needed to end use of sexual violence as weapon, ensure legal rights, say commission speakers', accessed 27 September 2013 at: http://www.un.org/News/Press/docs/2008/wom1670.doc.htm.

UN Department of Peacekeeping Operations (UN DPKO) (2013), 'Gender statistics', accessed 19 September 2013 at: http://www.un.org/en/peacekeeping/resources/statistics/gender.shtml.

UN DPKO/Office of Military Affairs (OMA) (n.d.), 'DPKO/statistical report on female military and police personnel in un peacekeeping operations prepared for the 10th anniversary of SCR 1325', accessed 17 August 2012 at: http://www.un.org/en/peacekeeping/documents/gender_scres1325_chart.pdf.

United Nations Economic and Social Council (UN ECOSOC) (1997), *Draft Agreed Conclusions. Coordination of Policies and Activities of the Specialized Agencies and Other Bodies of the UN System Related the Following Theme: Mainstreaming a Gender Perspective into All Policies and Programmes in the United Nations System*, UN Doc No. E/1997/1.30.

United Nations Fund for Women (UNIFEM) (2010), 'Women's participation in peace negotiation', accessed 17 August 2013 at: http://www.unifem.org/attachments/products/0302_WomensParticipationInPeaceNegotiations_en.pdf.

United Nations General Assembly (UN GA) (1979), *Convention on the Elimination of All Forms of Discrimination Against Women*, UN Doc No. A/Res/34/180.

United Nations General Assembly (UN GA) (1982), *Declaration on the Participation of Women in Promoting International Peace and Cooperation*, UN Doc No. A/RES/37/63.

United Nations General Assembly [and] Security Council (UN GA SC) (2000), *Report of the Panel on United Nations Peace Operations*, UN Doc No. A/55/305-S/2000/809.

United Nations Security Council (UNSC) (1999a), *SCR 1261 on the Children and Armed Conflict*, UN Doc No. S/Res/1261.

United Nations Security Council (UNSC) (1999b), *SCR 1265 on Protection of Civilians in Armed Conflict*, UN Doc No. S/Res/1265.

United Nations Security Council (UNSC) (2000), *SCR 1325 on Women and Peace and Security*, UN Doc No. S/Res/1325.

United Nations Security Council (UNSC) (2008a), *SCR 1820 on Women and Peace and Security*, UN Doc No. S/Res/1820.

United Nations Security Council (UNSC) (2008b), *Women and Peace and Security: Report of the Secretary General*, UN Doc No. S/2008/622.

United Nations Security Council (UNSC) (2009a), *SCR 1888 on Women and Peace and Security*, UN Doc No. S/Res/1888.

United Nations Security Council (UNSC) (2009b), *SCR 1889 on Women and Peace and Security*, UN Doc No. S/Res/1889.

United Nations Security Council (UNSC) (2010), *SCR 1960 on Women and Peace and Security*, UN Doc No. S/Res/1960.

United Nations Security Council (UNSC) (2013a), *SCR 2106 on Women Peace and Security*, UN Doc No. S/Res/2106.

United Nations Security Council (UNSC) (2013b), *SCR 2122 on Women Peace and Security*, UN Doc No. S/Res/2122.

Whitworth, Sandra (2004), *Men, Militarism and UN Peacekeeping: A Gendered Analysis*, Lynne Rienner.

Index

abortion 220–21
Abu Ghraib prison, Iraq 282, 351–2
    prisoner abuse 274, 344, 351–2
    sexual positioning 277–8
Act Now to Stop War and End Racism
        (ANSWER) 354
Afghanistan 127
    femininity in 137
    homosexualization of Afghan men
        134–5
    'Long War', 2001–14, 127–43
    soldiers deployed in 27
Afghan National Army (ANA), training
        of 134–6
Afghan women 154–5
Africa, forced migration 194–5
African-American women 147
    black women reporters 321
Agency 4, 48–9, 51, 55, 61–2, 105–23,
        156–7, 187, 189–90, 298, 368–9,
        385, 470, 529, 565, 576
Al-Aqsa Intifada 390, 391–2
Al Qaeda 63, 120
Al Shabab, Islamic militant group 223
American antiwar movement 362
American Colonization Society (ACS)
        527
American Psychological Association
        task force 260
Amnesty International 533
Anarchists against the Wall (AATW)
        397
Anglo-Boer War (1899–1902) 68
Angolan peace processes 469–70
anti-nuclear movement, Japan 439–40
Anti-Vietnam War Alliance 441
anti-war activism 338
    feminist anti-base activism in
        Okinawa 452
    see also Okinawa
    gender archetypes 292–4
        anti-war protest in Japan 438–55

opposition to US military bases on
        Japanese soil 339
Women for Genuine Security (US
        affiliate of INWAM) 355
Army of Sierra Leone 120
Association of Female Lawyers of
        Liberia (AFELL) 409
asylum law, gendered aspects 195–6

Bangladesh
    mass rape, forced impregnation,
        1970s 499
Blackwater, now *Academi* 86
Boko Haram 223–5
    Nigerian girls, kidnap 169
Boycott, Divestment and Sanctions
        (BDS) 381, 394–5, 397
Britain 68
    British espionage in First World War
        73–4
        during Second World War 80–83
        significant contributions from
            women 83
    British intelligence, inter-war period
        75–6
    British military, resistance to
        homosexuality 37
    gentleman spy 25, 69
    British Union of Fascists 76
Bush administration 154, 370

Campaign for Nuclear Disarmament
        (CND) 338, 419–35
    challenges to traditional gender
        norms 424, 435
Chechnya, 'Palestinization of' 155–6
child abuse, parental deployment 254
child brides 215–6
child soldiers 123, 551–3
    demilitarization and reintegration of
        463
    former combatants, girls as 224–6
Child Soldiers International 224

China
    equality of men and women 244
    social reorganization, farm
        collectivization 245
CIA 24, 50, 62
civilians in armed conflicts 128, 132,
    213–4
civil society organizations (CSOs) 477
civil war(s) 181, 215–6, 233–5, 237–9,
    316, 318, 321–2, 324, 337–8,
    341–3, 352, 362, 400–402, 411,
    467, 496, 499, 527, 530
Coalition of Women for Peace (CWP)
    392–3, 397
    Israeli attacks on Gaza 392–3
Coalition to Stop the Use of Child
    Soldiers 552–3
    see also Child Soldiers International
CODEPINK 338, 340–41, 348, 350,
    355–7, 368
    CODEPINK US 355
colonialism 127, 446, 490, 497
    genocidal colonialism 490
combat exposure 250–51
combat roles ban removal 366
'comfort women' 443, 446–8, 450, 454
    Asian Women's Fund for 'comfort
        women' 449
    Korean 449
Commission on the Status of Women
    (CSW) 574
concentration camps 81
Conflict-Related Sexual Violence
    (CSRV) 472
conflicts, and political processes 6
    and education 217
    and sexual abuse 218–22
Convention on the Elimination of All
    Forms of Discrimination against
    Women (CEDAW) 446, 575–6,
    585
Copenhagen School 488
counterinsurgency 127–8, 136–7
Counterinsurgency Operations (COIN)
    127–43, 256
Cuba, legislation on gender equality
    245

post–1959 equality of men and
    women 244
Cuban Missile Crisis 422–3
cyber defense measures 118

Defence of the Realm Act, 1914, 71
Defense Science Board Task Force 117
demilitarization 347, 461–3, 520, 526–7
Democratic Accountability for Armed
    Forces (DCAF) 89
Democratic Front for the Liberation of
    Palestine (DFLP) 387
Democratic Republic of Congo (DRC)
    girl child soldiers 224–6
    sexual violence 220, 499
Department of Defense (DoD), US 253
    Task Force on Suicide Prevention 256
desertion rate 251
development/security nexus 483
Direct Action Committee Against
    Nuclear Weapons Tests (DAC) 429
Directorate of Military Intelligence 68
Directorate of Military Operations 68
Disarmament, Demobilization and
    Reintegration (DDR) 11, 472–5,
    188–9, 463, 473, 494, 497–9, 530
Disarmament, Demobilization,
    Reintegration and Rehabilitation
    DDR(R) 526–7, 530–37, 540,
    544–5
disarmament programs, 410, 498
domestic and sexual slavery, Sierra
    Leone DRC 512
domestic violence 155, 170, 177, 179,
    182, 198, 203, 206–7, 240, 242,
    446, 506
    in military families 179, 253–4, 493,
        496
Don't Ask Don't Tell (DADT) 36–7,
    344, 373–4
drones 106–7, 112
drug and alcohol abuse by soldiers
    112–13, 119, 120, 172, 253
    Abu Ghraib 351–2

Enigma, encryption machine 78–9
ethnic cleansing 215

mass rape, forced impregnation, Bangladesh 221
European Court of Human Rights 37
European Union (EU) 57

female Communist spies, media's reporting of 67
'Female Engagement Teams' (FETs) 26, 129, 137–42
female espionage 66–7
female genital mutilation 199
female inclusion, in peace 347
female targeting for sexual favors 171
female terrorists 159
feminine
    attributes, compassion, concern 26, 129
    values, passivity, virtue 24
femininity in Campaign for Nuclear Disarmament 431–2
feminism
    antiwar 352–3, 454
    intersectional 8–9, 349, 438, 447, 520
    and pacifism 320, 420
    and peace 346
    postcolonial 14, 521
    transnational 349, 353
feminist and antiwar organizations, 355
feminist antimilitarism 341, 348–52, 353–7
'human security', 'global security' 5
feminist intersectional analysis 8–9
feminist perspectives on reparations 516–17
Feminist Security Studies 489
feminist solidarity 393–6
'feminization' of US military 272–4
First World War 70–74, 231, 316
forced migration 194, 196–7, 199
Four Mothers 390–93
Fourth World Conference on Women in Beijing 12–3

gay and lesbian soldiers 38, 352
gender mainstreaming 12–14, 575, 585
gender-based crimes 11–12
gender-based violence 156, 175–90, 499

gendered resistance to political violence
    Israel 6–7, 34, 155, 296, 318, 324, 329, 338, 357, 380, 382, 386, 388–97
    Japan, approach through women's activism 445–7
    justice 7, 351
    refugees 210
gender hierarchy 149, 160
gender-neutral studies 158
gender-oriented transformation 464
gender-responsive peacebuilding 474
gender-sensitive designs for refugees 227
    planning in schools 218
    projects in post-conflict societies 464
gender-specific myths 25, 36, 47, 67, 83, 139, 290–91, 292–4, 305–7, 366–7
gender-specific training
    Liberia 534–5
Geneva Convention 188
genocidal colonialism 490
genocide
    criminal trials for Rwanda and former Yugoslavia, 1990s 512
    rape as weapon, Bosnian conflict 182–3
German agents in Britain 69, 70, 76, 77
Germany, woman in reconstruction work 244
    Nazi regime, Germany 553–4
    psycho-social impacts 560–61
    after Second Word War 244
    social stigma 558–9
    subject to sexual abuse 171
Ghana
    Peace Talks in Accra 407
girls
    in armed conflict 557
    armed conflict, becoming mothers 557
    difficulty of readjusting in aftermath of war 556
    no formal schooling 223
    as human shields, suicide bombers 223

killed en masse for refusing captor's
    orders 223
peacebuilding, exclusion of 469
sexual sale 221
soldiers as human shields 171
tradable commodities 221
undervalued due to son-preference
    215
weapons of war 213–28
girl soldiers
    demobilization and reintegration
        550–66
    economic realities 559–60
    identity 'militarized' 561–3
    Joan of Arc 553–4
    in West Africa 553–4
Global North hegemonic masculinity 10
global peace goal for Japan 443–5
Global South and Global North tensions
    16
    armed struggle 34
    international instability 487
    international security and
        development 486
    sources of insecurity for Global
        North 483–4
Golders Green Committee for the
    Abolition of Nuclear Weapons 425
governance of insecurity and danger,
    construction of 98
Government Code and Cypher School
    75
    decoding of messages 79
    Government Communications
        Headquarters (GCHQ) 1942
    Ultra, intelligence 79
Greenham Common 430
    Greenham Common Women's Peace
        Camp 368, 430
Gulf War 1991–92
    women's deployment 137

health care access in wartime,
    difficulties for women 180
*Health Promotion, Risk Reduction and
    Suicide Prevention* report 261
hegemonic masculinity 9–10, 31,
    105–23, 423

heroes and heroism, 47, 70, 107–10,
    116, 118, 362, 367–8, 376
    risk-taking 107, 108, 109
heroic warrior in twenty-first century
    heroine of war 50–56, 74, 293
    'post-heroic' 25–6, 107–10
heterosexuality
    in the military 36–40, 41, 135
Hirohito, Emperor
    death in 1989, 443
    responsible for crimes against
        humanity 450
    supreme Commander in Chief, Japan,
        war crimes 443
Hitler Youth
    Bund Deutscher Mädel (League of
        German Girls) 554
Hitotsubo Antiwar Landlords
    Association 442
HIV/AIDS 220, 233, 555
homicide and violent crime 251–3
homoeroticism/homosocial practices
    32–3, 38–9
homosexuality
    Afghanistan 134–6
homosexuality declaration 373–4
    in the military 37–9
homosexual men 37, 132, 423
honor killings, protection from 217, 227
household roles of women 170
    vulnerability to wars 176–7
human intelligence and signal
    decryption 73
human interdependence and relational
    autonomy
    re-visioning 189
human-interest approaches to covering
    war 328
humanitarian aid 246
humanitarian soldier-scholar 130–31
human-machine interfaces 111
Human Performance Initiative program
    113
Human Rights Watch 120, 156, 220
    child soldiers 123, 551–3
human rights violations 213, 389, 392,
    505–9, 513–15, 517–18, 583
Human Terrain Systems Project 135

human trafficking 180, 224, 226, 239–40, 496

Improvised Explosive Device (IED) 93
infanticide 293
Innocent Child 297–300, 305
Interim Care Centres (ICCs) 533
Internally Displaced People (IDP) 194
International Center for Transitional Justice (ICTJ)
Gender Justice Program 507
recognition of gendered harms 517
International Code of Conduct (ICoC) 88
International Committee of the Red Cross
Treatment by Coalition Forces 352
International Criminal Court's Rome Statute 512, 575
International Criminal Tribunals 182, 187, 514
International Tribunal for the Far East
rape as war crime 219, 511
International Law 8
international criminal law 511
International Criminal Tribunal for Rwanda
rape and genocide 182–3
International Criminal Tribunal, former Yugoslavia (ICTY)
women indicted for genocide 187
international human rights laws 506, 511
international law, gender, transitional justice 509–10
International Network for Women Against Militarism (INWAM) 355
international peace conferences 382
International Relations (IR) 88, 147–8, 156–7, 483, 487–90
and men 9
International Rescue Committee (IRC) 215
International Women's Day 415
International Women's Year (IWY) 573–4
intersectionality 147, 154, 157, 339, 438, 447, 469, 520–21

intersectional analysis 8–9, 383, 520
intifada, first 380, 381–3, 385, 387, 388
Iraq 88
invasion of 251
Iraq Veterans Against the War (IVAW) 338–40, 361–77
Islamic militants 134, 222
Islamic State 224
rape as combat strategy 169, 221
recruiting young girls, strategies for 224, 299
Islamism/radical Islam 150, 153, 155–6, 290
Israeli-Palestinian conflict 155, 339, 380, 382, 386, 390, 395
see also Palestinian-Israeli conflict
Israeli Women Against the Occupation (SHANI) 382
Israeli Women's Peace Net (RESHET) 382

Japan 438–55
aggression during Second World War 438
anti-base activism 450–51
anti-US-Japan Security Treaty protests, 1950, 1959, 440
antiwar movements 443
anti-war protest 438–55
Basic Law on Gender Equality, 1999, 446
Communist Party
popular protest against Japan-US Security Treaty 440
feminist anti-base activism, Okinawa 452
Japanese Constitution, 1947
renunciation of war 439, 444
Japanese feminist activism, racial bias 446
Japanese militarism, challenges to 445
land seizure for US military bases 451
pacifism 438–55
public apology for 'wartime comfort women' 448–9
–US Special Action Committee on Okinawa (SACO)

recommendations 451–2
treaty with US
    on US military involvement with
        Vietnam 439
Jerusalem Link 388–9
Joint Intelligence Committee (JIC) 75

Khmer Rouge regime 234
Korean 438
Korean comfort women 449
    see also comfort women

land mines 218
Lesbian, Gay, Bisexual, Transgender,
    Queer and Intersex (LGBTQI) 8,
    16, 344, 394
Liberation Tigers of Tamil Eelam, 2011,
    216
Liberia
    addiction problems of children in
        Liberian conflict 533
    'black colonizers' 541
    child soldiers, sexual violence,
        violent conflict 400
    Christian and Muslim women
        together 402
    peacebuilding work 403
    Comprehensive Peace Agreement
        (CPA) 409, 410–11, 528, 530
    DDR(R)
        disarmament and demobilization
            530–33
        reintegration and rehabilitation
            533–7
    demilitarization 533
    Liberian history, gender in 541
    Liberian warzone, roles of women
        529
    pregnancy danger, diseases 500
    women activism 492, 404–6, 408
    women fighters 400
    women and girls in Liberia 529
    'Woman's Mass Action for Peace'
        403
    women-only peace movement 339
Liberians United for Reconciliation and
    Democracy (LURD) 406–7

Lord's Resistance Army Northern
    Uganda 200, 225
Ugandan and Sudanese women
    abductions 205
Lysistrata 354

Machsom Watch 392
Madres of the Plaza de Mayo 509
Malayan Emergency
    counterinsurgency 127
male pacifists 423
male privilege 31
man-machine interface 117
masculinity
    hegemonic masculinity, 26, 31–3, 38,
        105–7, 139, 149, 185
    hyper-masculine enhanced warriors
        106
    hyper-masculinity 35
    hypermasculinization of Muslim men
        150
    masculine attributes 24
    men, masculinities and militarism
        9–11
    militarised masculinities 89, 99,
        181–2
    subordinate masculinity 185
masculinism and war 346
masculinist power 345
masculinity, caring forms 32, 409–10
'Mau Mau', Kenya 127
men
    and masculinities 504, 519
    and violence 159–60, 347
    post-conflict 485
mental health, 252, 260–61
    care for invisible mental health
        problems 260–61
    children of service members 254–5
    child soldiers 560–61
        see also child soldiers
    diagnoses of members of armed
        forces 260
    suicide risk 257
    women's depression 264
militarism 129–30, 490
    and masculinism 9–10, 24, 30, 40,
        346–8, 353, 493, 539

masculinist racist militarism 341
militarization 246–7
militarization of femininity 272–4, 283
military and antiwar dissent, gendered
363–9
military deployment, toll of war,
249–66
military families 250, 263
military masculinity 29–41, 421
military response to 9/11 249–50, 423
domestic violence 253
see also domestic violence
policy on military violence 454
military training 31–2, 139
Millennium Development Goals 214
mixed gender teams 58–9
Muslim women 172–3
motherhood 50–54, 563–4
Mothers and Others Day Action 354–5
see also Nevada Test Site
Movement of Democratic Women in
Israel (TANDI) 393

Namibia Plan of Action 471
National Action Plans (NAPs) 471
National Council for the Abolition of
Nuclear Weapons Tests
(NCANWT) 425–6
National Gender Policy, equality
promotion 414
National Patriotic Front of Liberia
(NPFL) 527
'Nazi death machine' 120
Nevada Test Site 354–5
NGO Working Group 55, 578, 583
Nobel Peace Prize
women recipients 400, 415
North Atlantic Treaty Organization
(NATO) 41, 132–5, 161, 324
Operational Mentor and Liaison
Teams (OMLTs) 134
training local security forces 134–5
non-governmental organizations
(NGOs) 101, 171, 200, 211, 440,
453, 464, 507, 531, 536, 542,
583–4
Nuclear Non-Proliferation Treaty
(NPT) 440

nuclear weapons 419, 425, 433
Nuremberg trials 511, 521

Okinawa 439–42, 446–7, 451–4
Battle of Okinawa 452
feminist anti-base activism 452
Operation Fortitude 78
Organisation for Economic
Co-operation and Development
(OECD) 13, 215
Organization of African Unity 211
Orientalism 132–3, 136, 149
Military orientalism 133–4
Neo-orientalism 143, 147–50, 154,
158, 160
Oslo Accords of 1993, 385, 387–8, 391

pacifism 420
Palestine 6–7, 155, 322, 338, 357,
380–81, 384–5, 387–9, 391,
394–5, 397
Palestinian–Israeli conflict 383, 394,
397
Palestinian Liberation Organization
(PLO) 382, 387
Palestinian National Authority (PNA)
387
Palestinian Queers for BDS (PQBDS)
394
Palestinian uprising, first intifada 380,
382–3
Paris Principles 552
PATRIOT Act 154
peace agreements 207–8, 491–2,
512–20
in Sudan 207–8
peacebuilding 462, 467, 468–70
'peacebuilding masculinity' 141
peacekeepers 222
peacekeeping missions, women's
involvement 13
Peace Outreach Project 402
PeaceWomen 355–7
Persian Gulf War 249, 346
Pinkwatching Israel 395
Popular Front for Liberation of
Palestine (PFLP) 158, 387

population-centric counterinsurgency
    (COIN) 128–30, 133
pornography 508
post-conflict security 501
Post Traumatic Stress Disorder (PTSD)
    122, 233, 251–2, 257, 260–61, 323
prisoners, abuse 277–8
Private Military Security Companies
    (PMSC) 86–102
prostitution 35, 179–80, 225, 236
process theory 156–60
protection myth 91, 184–5
    protector/protected 93

Rational Actor Model 152–3
racism, racial bias 150, 278, 343, 441
rape in war 11, 152, 175, 181, 183,
    218–9, 220, 227, 346, 372–3, 451,
    453, 511
    see also wartime rape
refugees 179, 195–7, 204–8, 209–11,
    582–3
    Refugee Convention, definition of a
        refugee 198
    resettlement places for Syrian
        refugees 196
    Sudanese as refugees 209
    women refugees 33–4, 170, 202, 204,
        208–9
reparations, feminist perspectives
    516–17
Rome Statute of ICC 586
'Rosie the Riveter' 240
Russia and the Caucasus 156
Russia, human rights records 156
Russian Revolution 316

San Francisco Peace Treaty 442
second intifada 391
    see also Al-Aqsa intifada
Second World War 76–83, 178, 188,
    237–8, 240, 243, 316–19, 321, 423
Security Council Resolution 1325, 572,
    575–6, 578–9
Security Sector Reform (SSR) 473–5
security studies 7, 485–7
Serbian genocidal rape strategy 187
sex-trafficking 89

sexual abuse
    coercion to commit violence 225
Sexual and Gender-Based Violence
    (SGBV)
    gender-based violence 181–2
    Liberia 528
sexual assault 345
Sexual Assault Prevention and
    Response Office (SAPRO) 345
sexual benefits to service personnel
    271–2
sexual harassment 343, 372
    in US army 279–80
    of women by servicemen 35
sexualization of war 270
sexual offences by US soldiers 172
sexual slavery 12, 448
sexual victimization of men 512
sexual violence 170, 213, 215, 219–20,
    496–500, 510, 537, 542
    see also Sexual and Gender-Based
        Violence (SGBV)
South African anti-apartheid movement
    394
South African Truth and Reconciliation
    Commission 515–16
Sri Lanka 160–61
    Liberation Tigers of Tamil Eelam
        (ILTTE) 158
Sudanese camps in Uganda 200, 204
Sudanese People's Liberation Army
    (SPLA) 205
suicide bombers 120, 152–3, 255–8,
    290, 295, 296–7
    girls 225
Syrian civil war 215

Taliban 222–3, 242, 247
Tamil Tigers 160–61
technology 105–23
terrorism 27, 146–61, 187, 290–92, 294,
    301–2, 305, 307, 323, 445, 487,
    555
Terrorism Studies 146, 152, 156–7
trangender soldiers 339
    veterans 374–5
transitional justice, 7, 11, 462, 476,
    505–6, 507, 508–12, 512–20

Truth and Reconciliation Commissions (TRCs) 495–6, 516
Truth Commissions (TCs)
Chile, El Salvador 515
Sierra Leone 496–7

Uganda
Christianity for men and women 202
men refugees, advantages for younger 209
women refugees, improvement in standing 208
UNIFEM (UN Women) 408, 515, 582
Uniform Code of Military Justice (UCMJ) 119, 252–3, 365
United Nations (UN)
charter 572, 576
Convention on the Rights of the Child (CRC) 453, 551
Decade for Women 573
policies, relevance of 583–6
peacekeepers 12, 47, 171, 222, 412, 581
Population Fund 223
Security Council Resolution (SCR) 188, 219, 464, 509, 572, 575, 587
United Nations Development Programme (UNDP) 413, 530, 533–4, 539, 543
United Nations High Commissioner for Refugees (UNHCR), 198, 200, 211
children
after-war impacts on, violence and neglect 254–5
separation from parents 217
United Nations Mission in Liberia (UNMIL) 410–11, 530–31
United Nations Peacebuilding Committee (UNPBC) 474
United States
9/11 attacks 151–2
gender hierarchy in US military 361
Government Accountability Office 253
Marines, women 137–8

US declaration of war against Germany, 1917, 71
UNSCR 1325, 219–20, 464, 476, 572

Veterans for Peace 369–75
Vienna Declaration and Platform for Action 449–50
Vienna Human Rights Declaration 585
Vietnamese National Liberation Front 431
Vietnam War 249, 319–23, 439
black women reporters in 'mainstream' media 321
violence
gender-based violence 181–2
Violence against Women in War Network, Japan 450

war of independence in Eritrea 239
War on Terror 150, 160, 342–3, 361–2, 370
Bush Administration 357
wartime rape 182–4, 188–9, 219, 236, 499–500
war trauma 257, 259
West Africa Network for Peacebuilding (WANEP) 401
Westphalia 146–7, 150–53, 156, 161
WikiLeaks 374–5
Windhoek Declaration 471
Winter Soldier 371–3
woman war reporters, 313–21, 323–4
woman warrior 2, 172, 293, 295–7, 305–6
women
in armed forces 33–4, 158, 270–84, 366
in military service 11, 272, 282–3
US armed forces 172, 272
and health risks in war 173, 179
and militaries 33–6, 40, 56–61, 137–9
see also Female Engagement Teams; UK woman combat ban
and pacifism 421
as perpetrators of violence 48, 50–51, 54–6, 60–61, 186–8

gender-based violence 186–7
and political protest 381–3
and political violence 51, 62–3, 156
refugees 33–4, 170, 202, 204, 208–9
    see also refugees
rights as human rights 510–11
suicide bombers 153, 172, 290, 295,
    297, 306
terrorists 158, 290–94, 302–6
UK woman combat ban 27, 34, 56–62
in warfare 47–8
as war victims 2, 485, 494–5
women's liberation 8
    Women's Liberation movement,
        Britain 425
Women and Mothers for Peace 390
Women in Black (WIB) 338, 348, 355,
    382, 356–7
Women in Peace and Security Network
    (WIPSEN-Africa) 415
Women in Peacebuilding Network
    (WIPNET) 338, 400, 401–2, 529,
    531
Women, Peace and Security 13–14,
    347, 504
Women, Peace and Security (WPS)
    agenda 573–4, 413, 580, 583, 402

Women PeaceMakers Program 478
Women Strike for Peace 368
Women's Auxiliary Air Force (WAAF)
    79
Women's Initiative for Gender Justice
    507
Women's International League for
    Peace and Freedom (WILPF), 338,
    348, 392, 420, 573
Women's International League for
    Peace and Freedom (international)
    355
'Women's Mass Action for Peace'
    403–4
Women's Network Against Militarism
    348
Women's Organization for Women
    Political Prisoners (OPFPP) 382
Women's Refugee Commission 214
Women's Royal Naval Service (WRNS)
    78
World Conference on Women 573
World Food Programme 202
World Peace Now (WPN) 445
Wounded Knee Massacre 313

Zionism 385